Tb L
2

NOMICS

september 2017.

MAX WEBER

Weber's methodological writings form the bedrock of key ideas across the social sciences. His discussions of value freedom and value commitment, causality, understanding and explanation, theory building and ideal types have been of fundamental importance, and their impact remains undiminished today. These ideas influence the current research practice of sociologists, historians, economists and political scientists and are central to debates in the philosophy of social science. But, until now, Weber's extensive writings on methodology have lacked a comprehensive publication.

Edited by two of the world's leading Weber scholars, *Max Weber: Collected methodological writings* will provide a completely new, accurate and reliable translation of Weber's extensive output, including previously untranslated letters. Accompanying editorial commentary explains the context of, and interconnections between, all these writings, and additional useful features include a glossary of German terms and an English key, endnotes, a bibliography, and person and subject indexes.

Hans Henrik Bruun is Adjunct Professor at the Department of Sociology, University of Copenhagen. He collaborated on the first comprehensive Danish translation of Weber's selected writings. His *Science, Values and Politics in Max Weber's Methodology* (Ashgate, 2007, 1st edn 1972) has remained a standard reference work on values in Weber's methodology for over three decades.

Sam Whimster is Professor at the Global Policy Institute, London, and Fellow at the Centre for Advanced Study ("Recht als Kultur"), University of Bonn. His publications include *Reforming the City: Responses to the global financial crisis* (2009), *Understanding Weber* (2007), *Essential Weber* (2004), *Max Weber and the Culture of Anarchy* (1999) and, with Scott Lash, *Max Weber, Rationality and Modernity* (1987). He is the editor of the journal *Max Weber Studies*.

MAX WEBER

Collected methodological writings

Edited by Hans Henrik Bruun and Sam Whimster
Translated by Hans Henrik Bruun

Routledge
Taylor & Francis Group

LONDON AND NEW YORK

First published 2012
by Routledge
2 Park Square, Milton Park, Abingdon, Oxon, OX14 4RN

Simultaneously published in the USA and Canada
by Routledge
711 Third Avenue, New York, NY 10017

Routledge is an imprint of the Taylor & Francis Group, an informa business

British Library Cataloguing in Publication Data
A catalogue record for this book is available from the British Library

Library of Congress Cataloging in Publication Data
Max Weber: complete methodological writings/edited by
Hans Henrik Bruun and Sam Whimster.
p. cm.
Includes bibliographical references and index.
1. Social sciences – Methodology.   2. Weber, Max, 1864–1920.
I. Bruun, Hans Henrik.   II. Whimster, Sam, 1947–.
H61.M4293 2011
300.92 – dc22   2011008991

ISBN: 978–0–415–47898–4 hbk
ISBN: 978–0–203–80469–8 ebk

Typeset in Bembo
by Florence Production Ltd, Stoodleigh, Devon

Printed and bound in Great Britain by
CPI Antony Rowe, Chippenham, Wiltshire

CONTENTS

MAX WEBER BIBLIOGRAPHY, WITH ABBREVIATIONS

The Weber Bibliography covers all books, articles and sections of books by Max Weber translated or mentioned in this book. For ease of reference, it has been separated from the general Bibliography (pp. 502ff.) and put at the very beginning of the volume.

Each entry comprises:

- the full relevant bibliographical references (for articles: the text from which the articles have been translated);
- the English translation of the title (except for translations of Weber's work);
- a short abbreviated reference (preceded by "Q:"), in italics, for quotation in the main text.

A few other abbreviations frequently employed in this volume can also be found here.

German titles

Books

Max Weber Gesamtausgabe, Tübingen: J.C.B. Mohr (Paul Siebeck), 1984–
("Max Weber. Complete edition")
Q: *MWG*

Gesammelte Aufsätze zur Wissenschaftslehre (ed. Johannes Winckelmann), 3rd ed., Tübingen: J.C.B.Mohr (Paul Siebeck), 1968
("Collected methodological essays")
Q: *GAW*

Gesammelte Aufsätze zur Soziologie und Sozialpolitik (ed. Marianne Weber), Tübingen: J.C.B.Mohr (Paul Siebeck), 1924
("Collected essays on sociology and social policy")

Gesammelte Aufsätze zur Religionssoziologie (ed. Marianne Weber), Tübingen: J.C.B.Mohr (Paul Siebeck), 1920–1921
("Collected essays on the sociology of religion")

"Die protestantische Ethik und der Geist des Kapitalismus", GARS, pp. 17–206)
("The protestant ethic and the spirit of capitalism")
Q: *Protestant Ethic*

Wirtschaft und Gesellschaft. Grundriß der verstehenden Soziologie (ed. Johannes Winckelmann), 5th ed., Tübingen: J.C.B.Mohr (Paul Siebeck), 1976
("Economy and Society. Outline of interpretive sociology")
Q: *WG*

"Soziologische Grundbegriffe", *WG*, pp. 1–30
("Basic sociological concepts")
Q: *Basic Concepts*

Articles

"Roscher und Knies und die logischen Probleme der historischen Nationalökonomie", GAW, pp. 1–145
("Roscher and Knies and the problems of historical economics")
Q: *Roscher and Knies*

"Roschers 'historische Methode'", GAW, pp. 3–42
("Roscher's 'historical method'")
Q: *Roscher*

"Knies und das Irrationalitätsproblem", GAW, pp. 42–105
("Knies and the problem of irrationality")
Q: *Knies I*

"Knies und das Irrationalitätsproblem (Fortsetzung)", GAW, pp. 105–46
("Knies and the problem of irrationality (continued)")
Q: *Knies II*

"Geleitwort", *Archiv für Sozialwissenschaft und Sozialpolitik* 19 (1904), pp. I*–VII*
("Accompanying remarks")
Q: *Accompanying Remarks*

"Die 'Objektivität' sozialwissenschaftlicher und sozialpolitischer Erkenntnis", GAW, pp. 146–214
("The 'objectivity' of knowledge in social science and social policy")
Q: *Objectivity*

"Kritische Studien auf dem Gebiet der kulturwissenschaftlichen Logik", GAW, pp. 215–90
("Critical studies in the logic of the cultural sciences")
Q: *Critical Studies*

"R. Stammlers 'Überwindung' der materialistischen Geschichtsauffassung", GAW, pp. 291–359
("R. Stammler's 'overcoming' of the materialist conception of history")
Q: *Stammler*

"Nachtrag zu dem Aufsatz über R. Stammlers 'Überwindung' der materialistischen Geschichtsauffassung", GAW, pp. 360–83
("Addendum to the essay on R. Stammler's 'overcoming' of the materialist conception of history")
Q: *Addendum*

"Die Grenznutzlehre und das 'psychophysische Grundgesetz'", *GAW*, pp. 384–99
("The theory of marginal utility and the 'fundamental law of psychophysics'")
Q: *Marginal Utility*

"'Energetische' Kulturtheorien", *GAW*, pp. 400–26
("'Energetical' theories of culture")
Q: *Energetics*

Review of Adolf Weber, *Die Aufgaben der Volkswirtschaftslehre als Wissenschaft* ("The tasks of economic theory as a science"), *Archiv für Sozialwissenschaft und Sozialpolitik* 29 (1909), pp. 615–20. (Excerpts)
Q: *Adolf Weber*

"Über einige Kategorien der verstehenden Soziologie", *GAW*, pp. 427–74
("On some categories of interpretive sociology")
Q: *Categories*

"Die drei reinen Typen der legitimen Herrschaft"
("The three pure types of legitimate rulership")
Q: *Legitimate Rulership*

"Der Sinn der 'Wertfreiheit' der soziologischen und ökonomischen Wissenschaften", *GAW*, pp. 589–40
("The meaning of 'value freedom' in the sociological and economic sciences")
Q: *Value Freedom*

"Wissenschaft als Beruf", *GAW*, pp. 582–613
("Science as a profession and vocation")
Q: *Science*

English translations

The Methodology of the Social Sciences (ed., tr. Edward A. Shils, Henry A. Finch), New York: The Free Press, 1949

Roscher and Knies. The Logical Problems of Historical Economics (tr., intr. Guy Oakes), New York: The Free Press, 1975

Critique of Stammler (tr., intr. Guy Oakes), New York: The Free Press, 1977

Archival references

GStA I   Geheimes Staatsarchiv Preußischer Kulturbesitz, Hauptabteilung I (Berlin)
BSB   Bayerische Staatsbibliothek (Bavarian State Library) (Munich)

Other abbreviations

The present volume as a whole will be referred to in abbreviated form as *Meth. Writings*.

The journal *Archiv für Sozialwissenschaft und Sozialpolitik* ("Archive for social science and social policy") will be referred to in abbreviated form as *Archive*.

INTRODUCTION

Hans Henrik Bruun and Sam Whimster

Methodology is not a hard and fast category. In Max Weber's day, it could perhaps be said to refer, in formal terms, to the constitution, by means of concepts, of scientific knowledge. Methodology in this sense was linked to the discussion of the constitution, by means of categories, of knowledge in general (epistemology), to formal logic, and also to the discussion of theoretical approaches or systems within a particular branch of scientific investigation (scientific theory). This is the general criterion that we have applied in identifying the "methodological" parts of Weber's oeuvre (although it must be said that Weber himself was not always consistent in his use of terms such as "method", "logic" and "methodology").[1] It should be noted that the sense of the term "methodology" adopted for this purpose may differ from the way in which the term is used nowadays, where the emphasis is often on practical methods of survey analysis and the use of qualitative data and related concepts of validity and reliability.

The selection of texts

The editors have sought to reflect the range of Weber's methodological concerns to the widest possible extent by bringing together in this volume, as far as possible, all his methodological writings. It may be an overstatement to say that this collection is *complete*: when one is dealing with the whole, vast corpus of Weber's writings, in which many methodologically relevant passages have to be identified and excerpted from larger units of material, such a claim would necessarily be subjective. But we can confidently claim that what we present is by far the most extensive collection of Weber's methodological writings published to date, in any language. Almost a hundred pages of text included in the present volume have never appeared before in full in English; and most of the notes and drafts, and some of the letters, have never before been published in full, even in German. Moreover, we feel justified in adding that, in terms of textual criticism, the state of the texts translated in the *Methodological Writings* (apart from a few texts and many letters, which have already appeared in the *MWG*) is better than that of any other published version, in any language.[2]

---

1   For a detailed discussion, see Bruun, *Methodology*, pp. 7–11.
2   For a detailed description of the state of the texts included, see pp. xxix–xxx.

The main source of Weber's articles translated in the *Meth.Writings* is the German collective volume, *Gesammelte Aufsätze zur Wissenschaftslehre* ("Collected Essays on the Theory of Science"), originally published shortly after Weber's death by his widow Marianne. Some of these texts, however, turn out to be borderline cases.

Thus, we have it on Weber's own authority that the *Categories* essay is a hybrid between methodology and sociological theory.[1] It would have been unwarranted, however, to include only the "methodological" first part of the essay in the present volume, since Weber himself, in three separate letters to his publisher, says that (the whole of) *Categories* should form part of a planned collective volume of "methodological" essays.[2]

There are shadowy references in *Categories* to a study of what Weber calls "legitimacy consensus". The essay on *Legitimate Rulership*, which was posthumously published in *GAW*, is certainly such a study, and the *Categories* references might be seen as an argument for including it in the *Meth. Writings*. But, in substance, *Legitimate Rulership* deals with sociological theory, not with methodology, and the essay has therefore not been included here.[3]

As far as the important piece on *Basic Concepts* is concerned, it does contain methodological considerations of the same kind as those to be found in the first three sections of *Categories* – indeed, *Categories* can in many respects be seen as an early draft of *Basic Concepts*. However, *Basic Concepts* was written for, and has its natural place within, the framework of *Economy and Society* (*WG*); moreover, in the form in which it is included in *GAW*, it is only an *excerpt* from the first chapter of *WG*, not a fully rounded unit. It has therefore been left out of the present volume and belongs properly to the final version of WG.

All the other essays in *GAW* have been included in the *Meth. Writings*, since each of them indisputably and as a whole falls under the heading of methodology as we understand it.

A careful screening of all other printed Weber texts of a methodological nature has led to the inclusion of three further items: the *Accompanying Remarks*, the *Declaration* and the *Adolf Weber* review. These items raise other problems, however.

In the case of the *Accompanying Remarks* and the *Declaration*, the problem is that of authorship. The major part of the *Accompanying Remarks* was probably drafted, not by Weber, but by Werner Sombart.[4] However, it is highly probable that Weber left his definite mark on it, and the text as a whole, which is signed by all three editors of the *Archive* (of whom Weber was one) is closely linked with Weber's *Objectivity* article, which it was originally meant to precede immediately. The *Declaration* was signed both by Max Weber and by Werner Sombart, but it was a rebuttal of remarks made in an article (by their co-editor Edgar Jaffé!) in which they were both singled out for comment, and the text seems to bear the clear imprint of Weber's style and ideas.

---

1   In a letter to Heinrich Rickert of 5 September 1913 (see below, p. 407), he says that text of *Categories* "starts with some 'method[olog]ical' remarks, although all the purely logical aspects have been 'minimized' as much as at all possible". This undoubtedly refers to Sections I–III of the essay.

2   Letters of 24 May and 1 December 1917 (*MWG II/9*) and 8 November 1919 (BSB, Ana 446). In the 1919 letter, Weber also suggests including his "Survey on the Selection and Adaptation of the Work Force of the Self-Contained Heavy Industry". The fact that Weber proposes this Survey, which almost wholly deals with *method* and not with *methodology*, for inclusion in what he himself calls a "collection of methodological–logical essays" is eloquent proof of the inconsistency of his terminology in this area. (See also the Glossary entry on *Methode*.)

3   It should be noted that *Legitimate Rulership* did not form part of the first or second edition of *GAW*. Its inclusion in the third edition was justified by the editor, Johannes Winckelmann, precisely on the basis of the above-mentioned internal references.

4   For the full discussion, see the Introduction to the *Accompanying Remarks*, p. 99.

The *Adolf Weber* review raises a different problem: Should all texts be translated in full, or should only the (in our judgement) methodologically relevant passages be included? Ideally, of course, everything should be included, so that the selection is left to the discretion of the reader. But a moment's consideration of the texts involved – in particular the interventions and letters – will show that this procedure would increase the bulk of the volume to unacceptable proportions, with little substantive gain. The reader would need to spend much unprofitable time sifting long passages dealing with theoretical or substantive issues of quite a different sort in order to identify the occasional methodological nugget. Others may dispute some of the choices that we have made in selecting the passages that seemed relevant; but we feel reasonably confident that everything of general methodological importance has been included. Any deletion has, of course, been carefully indicated in the text.

Weber's active involvement in the contested field of methodology meant that he was not content just to write critical reviews and essays. He attended conferences, debating and arguing with colleagues and insisting on proper methodological approaches. Marianne Weber collected these interventions in the debates of the German Sociological Society and the Association for Social Policy in her edition of Weber's *Gesammelte Aufsätze zur Soziologie und Sozialpolitik* (1924). In these interventions, Weber is often at his most fluent and polemical. All the passages that deal with methodology have been selected for inclusion in this volume.

The Letters section comprises a large number of excerpts of methodological importance taken from Weber's correspondence. Here, too, the style is direct, and no punches are pulled. An emblematic example of Weber's delight in polemics is his brutally friendly demand that his correspondent (Friedrich Gottl) should "polemicize *as sharply as possible*" when discussing points where he disagreed with Weber (*MWG* II/5, p. 50). The exchanges of views reflected in the letters provide some of the freshest and most illuminating insights into Weber's own thinking.

We are presented with similar rewarding insights in the Notes and Drafts, where Weber notes his first, unvarnished reactions when confronted with new books (for instance, by his friend and mentor Heinrich Rickert), or launches himself (as in the draft on Simmel) into rough-and-ready discussions of the ideas of others. Here, the selection of texts has been based on the same principles as elsewhere, but, occasionally, a text has had to be deselected in spite of the interest that it might present because it seemed, even as a whole, to be too fragmentary or delphic to be of wider interest.

Existing English translations

All of the essays of *GAW* have already been translated into English. Some of the interventions and one or two of the letters included here have also been translated. The problems that these translations present the anglophone reader with, however, are multiple. To begin with, almost all of the translations are more than thirty years old. The historic translation by Edward Shils and Henry Finch of three of the main essays (*Objectivity, Critical Studies* and *Value Freedom*) was even published well over half a century ago, in 1949. This is not just a question of age, but also one of context: in Weber's day, these essays were authoritative, but occasional interventions: setting the new direction of a leading social science and policy journal, correcting an esteemed classical historian, or establishing the protocol of handling values in the debates of the Association for Social Policy. Post 1945, however, they were taken as the systematic bedrock for those social sciences that demanded the assurance of objectivity and empirical science when dealing with the meanings and intentions of volitional social actors.

Moreover, the translations are widely scattered: in book form, apart from the Shils/Finch edition, we have the translation by C. Wright Mills and Hans Gerth of *Science* (1947), as well as the two major separate translations by Guy Oakes of *Roscher and Knies* (1975) and *Stammler* (1978). The rest of the translations of articles (*Accompanying Remarks, Marginal Utility, Energetics* and *Categories*), as well as the translated interventions and letters, were published in a wide range of not always very accessible journals.

All these translations were pioneering, but they were of widely varying quality. Each solved translation problems in its own way, so that the anglophone reader with a more general interest in Max Weber's methodology has hitherto lacked an integration of the translation terms employed. In the same way, the indispensable editorial apparatus of introductions, explanatory endnotes, glossary, bibliography and indexes has obviously been fragmented (if indeed it was present at all, which was by no means always the case). All the editorial apparatus of this kind is provided in integrated form in the present volume.[1]

Max Weber as a methodologist

Max Weber only started to write on methodological issues, properly speaking, after his recovery from a serious and lengthy nervous breakdown around the turn of the century. Before then, he had pursued a successful and productive research career in fields as different as legal and socio-economic history and contemporary survey research. The methods that he employed as a legal scholar, as an agrarian historian and in his survey analyses were, by the standards of the day, extremely sophisticated (on important points, they may even be seen as foreshadowing his post-1900 methodological positions). But method, as a body of skills and expertise, was something that was taught and discussed in the professorial seminar. It must be explicated in scholarly publications, but that was all.

There was therefore no intrinsic reason why Weber, on the road to recovery, should turn to writing dedicated articles in the difficult field of methodology. He certainly did not regard such studies as an end in themselves, as he wrote in an article in 1906:

> Methodology can never be more than a self-reflection on the means that have *proved useful* in [scientific] practice; and one does not need to be made explicitly aware of those means in order to produce useful work, just as one does not need to have knowledge of anatomy in order to walk "correctly".
>
> (p. 140)

This severely instrumental view of methodology remained unchanged until the end of his life. According to a report by a student who took part in his seminar on sociological categories in the summer of 1919, Weber had, only half jokingly, said that he had almost wanted to throw the notes for this seminar out of the train window (he had just arrived in Munich from Heidelberg); and, towards the end of the semester, he delivered himself of the following clipped judgement: "Method is the most sterile thing that exists [. . .] Method *alone* has never yet created anything".[2]

It seems probable that, in fact, the determining factor behind at least Weber's first properly methodological work (*Roscher and Knies*) was simply one of academic courtesy: he had felt unable to evade a request by his colleagues for an article, for a quasi-official *festschrift*, about his immediate predecessor as professor of economics at the University of Heidelberg, Karl Knies[3]

1   See p. xxx.
2   GStA Berlin I, Rep. 92, Nl. Max Weber, no. 30/5.
3   See the Technical Introduction to *Roscher and Knies* below, p. 94.

– a piece of work which then quite outgrew its original proportions (and outran its deadline), ending up in the unwieldy shape of three lengthy methodological articles discussing a number of authors besides Knies. However, the 400 or so pages of this volume are weighty testimony to the fact that, once engaged, willy-nilly, in the field of methodology, Weber was driven to involve himself deeply in a variety of methodological issues that he found too important to be left unresolved or, worse, were being treated in damagingly erroneous formulations. His methodological writings thus became a running commentary on developments and new approaches during a period of rapid expansion of academic knowledge. The complexity of these developments is reflected in the range of topics and subject materials Weber was prepared to tackle: philosophy (in particular epistemology), history, politics, ethics, religion, economics, psychology, psychiatry, law, philology, statistics and sociology, as well as the natural sciences (where the range of his knowledge is impressive).

Weber never wrote a book on methodology (indeed, he did not write a single new book from 1891 to the end of his life). All his methodological work is in article or pamphlet form and has an occasional background (reviews, editorial introductions or contributions to debates, lectures, and the like), and this variety of forms is matched by a variety of styles. Weber himself ruefully described *Roscher and Knies* as a "wretched patchwork, in which [I] in fact work almost exclusively with other people's ideas" (p. 374). At least, *Roscher* has a single subject – the methodological naïvety of one "old master" of German economics – but the two *Knies* essays are a disjointed succession of shapeless and often awkwardly formulated critiques of authors whose writings and theories were important in their day, but have now largely been forgotten. At the same time, however, Weber's presentation and discussion of problems already demonstrate considerable philosophical sophistication; his comments are often both acute and profound; and his growing enjoyment of this kind of intellectual task is evident. *Objectivity* has quite a different, and much more accessible, character. It provides a clear exposition of the methodological principles on which a social science journal mainly devoted to social economics should proceed. This leads Weber to a painstaking examination and relativization of the contentious concept of "objectivity", and to a lengthy presentation and discussion of the logic and possibilities of the ideal type concept, which is one of Weber's main contributions to the methodology of the social sciences (see pp. 190–204). Here, we see Weber at his most pedagogic and constructive. *Critical Studies* is an elegantly polite argument with the methodological views of a distinguished historian, Eduard Meyer. "The intention is to take M[eyer]'s treatise as a starting point, to go on by illustrating, one by one, a number of separate logical problems, and then to give a critique, from the standpoint thus arrived at, of a number of other recent works dealing with the logic of the cultural sciences" (p. 140). On the basis of his specific criticism of Meyer for equating the voluntarism of action with the privilege of the irrational, Weber presents his own solution to this central problem of social theory. In his subsequent methodological essay on Stammler, and the posthumous *Addendum*, Weber launches a massive attack on this influential thinker who, by claiming that he could, on a Kantian conceptual basis, "overcome" the materialist conception of history and furnish the historical sciences with a secure methodological basis, in many respects seemed to occupy the same intellectual territory as Weber himself. Weber was quite aware of this dangerous proximity, and he is correspondingly vehement in his treatment of Stammler's – in his view – deliberate conceptual confusion and unclear presentation, employing rhetorical devices of sarcasm and ridicule to considerable (albeit often clumsy) effect. *Marginal Utility* is another extended review essay that provides Weber with the opportunity to criticize the use of psychology in underpinning economic theories of marginalism. Because of his respect for the author in question (Lujo Brentano), Weber's critique in this essay is much more constructive and deferential. But, in the next one (*Energetics*), there is little sign of such respect.

The Nobel Prize-winning chemist Wilhelm Ostwald had imprudently tried to extend the significance of his "energeticist" approach into the wider fields of social life, and this provides Weber with an occasion for hauling him, with great energy and occasional flashes of grim humour, over some very uncomfortable methodological coals.

This marks the end of the six-year period (1903–1909) of Weber's concentrated involvement with methodology. What follows are some more incidental pieces, albeit of major significance. In *Categories*, the polemical aspect is entirely absent. The author is here at his most innovative and constructive, as he combines fundamental methodological discussions with an attempt to fashion a systematic conceptual language of interpretive sociology. *Value Freedom* spells out, clearly and in great – occasionally somewhat tedious – detail, the implications of Weber's central concept of "value freedom" for academic teaching, for the logical analysis of value positions in a number of different fields, and for empirical investigations. Finally, in *Science* – the reworked text of a lecture – we can hear Weber's distinct speaking voice as he presents the over-expectant students with a cool and dispassionate analysis of the current situation of the universities, followed by an intensely moving personal statement of the preconditions and consequences of embracing science as a vocation.

The occasional and often polemical character of Weber's published methodological work is compounded by his frequent and deliberate neglect of literary form,[1] and by his impatience to move on to ever new fields of investigation.[2] Necessary details, for example, are often found and secured in footnotes or within rampaging critiques, rather than developed through sober exposition. Nor was Weber consistent in his definition and use of terms such as methodology, theory, interpretation, and even ideal types.

Against this background, it is understandable that there have been prolonged and heated debates among Weber scholars as to whether Weber's writings on methodology should be read as a unified theory of knowledge of the social sciences, or whether they are simply to be taken as a collection of occasional pieces, each with its own agenda. Some bold commentators, such as Wilhelm Hennis, have searched out central questions that in their view govern the whole of Weber's oeuvre. Others (Alexander v. Schelting, Dieter Henrich, Thomas Burger, to name but a few) have claimed to find an underlying unity at least in Weber's methodological thought, often tied to the systematic ideas of neo-Kantian thought; the opposing camp, with Friedrich Tenbruck as its most radical protagonist, reject the notion that Weber's methodological writings constitute a systematic whole.

In looking for an answer to this question, we lack the aid of a major synthetizing introduction by Weber himself to a collection of his methodological writings (such as the one written, for

---

1   Weber's adoring widow Marianne is a reliable witness in this respect: "Once the material is in flow, so much streams out of the storehouse of his mind that it often cannot be forced into a transparent sentence structure. And after all, he wants to finish the work quickly and, if possible, to be brief, since reality presents him with ever new problems [. . .] Much has to be formulated quickly in sentences that pile up one after the other, and what cannot find room there must be accommodated in footnotes. The reader will 'kindly' have to take as much trouble with [the result] as he himself had taken!" (Weber, *Biography*, p. 322). This is not just an ex post justification: In a revealing early postcard from Marianne Weber to her husband, who is sending her bits of manuscript for *Roscher and Knies* to transcribe, she says. "It is a pity that you put so many wise comments into the footnotes: they should be in the main text, that is much nicer" (30 December 1902; Düsseldorf Max Weber Centre). If Max Weber actually took this suggestion to heart, we can only quake at the thought of what we might otherwise have been faced with: already as it is, major parts of his early methodological work abound in often page-long footnotes.

2   A telling circumstance testifying to this is the constantly recurring footnote at the end of Weber's articles: "A further article was planned".

example, for his studies on the economic ethic of world religions). As mentioned above (p. xii), he had made plans, together with his publisher, for such a collected edition to appear after the war. Because of his untimely death in 1920, the title under which the methodological essays were brought out by his widow Marianne in 1922 (*Gesammelte Aufsätze zur Wissenschaftslehre* ("Collected essays on the theory of science")) was certainly not that envisaged by Weber himself.[1]

As editors, we do not wish to venture into pronouncements on such large and intractable differences of interpretation. What we have done in this volume is to lay the evidence, in its totality, before the reader. In addition to this abundant material, we only wish to offer some brief observations by way of initial guidance:

In spite of the fragmented and unsystematic appearance of Weber's methodological writings, his thinking about methodology does tend to keep to defined, if not always precise, tracks. The outlines of his own methodological stance can often be traced through the condemnation and refutation of his enemy's position.

This collection of his voluminous and disparate writings in this field, with their many overlaps, repetitions, reworkings and different applications, therefore makes it possible to accumulate a number of his key ideas under certain headings. We may think of these headings as silos, and, as we proceed through his methodological writings, these silos fill up. The contents are not always well structured, but one can at least impose a certain basic order on the material in this fashion. This facilitates the attainment of a more coherent understanding of Weber's methodology, or at least a more precise identification of the gaps and unresolved issues that it contains.

The historical background

Weber's engagement with methodological problems took place against a background of fundamental disagreements about how science and academic knowledge should be conceived, and about their relationship to practical policy. These controversies had already lasted for decades. Following the era of liberal economic policy in Prussia and the North German Confederation in the 1860s, the Association for Social Policy was founded under the leadership of Gustav Schmoller, who argued that the policies of the state should override the *laissez aller* of liberalism. Schmoller and his leadership of academics within the Association for Social Policy were known as "academic socialists". Max Weber belonged to a younger academic and political generation of such "academic socialists" who, while accepting the basic orientation of their elders, were opposed to their belief that academic research could and should in itself provide ethically based social and economic policies.[2] Weber vigorously led the opposition to this attitude, arguing that policy was a matter of practical judgement and could not be directly derived from scientific research.[3] But, at the same time, another, more general debate was in full swing between the methodological claims of the natural sciences, on one side, and the claims of the humanities and social sciences to pursue their own distinctive methods, on the other. By the end of the nineteenth century, enormous advances had been made by the natural sciences, whose objectivity seemed beyond doubt, and this led their disciples to claim a methodological monopoly in all

---

1   For an overview, see Bruun, *Methodology*, p. 3.
2   For a general history of the Association for Social Policy, see Lindenlaub, *Conflicts*.
3   His inaugural lecture as professor of economics in Freiburg astounded its academic audience by the brutality with which this was expressed, and Weber himself, in a letter to his brother (GStA I, Nl. Max Weber, No. 4, letter of 17 May 1895), expressed satisfaction at having given the "ethical culture" a "firm kick".

scientific disciplines. The cultural and historical sciences were constantly on the defensive against this self-confident positivism (see Ringer, *Mandarins*). In this debate, Weber was squarely on the side of the historians and the humanities in rejecting the sociological positivism of Comte and Spencer and other naturalistic methodologies. Within the science of economics (where the debate was known as the "quarrel about methods"), Weber opposed the extreme idea that economics could or should simply be reduced to quantifiable laws. But we know from his lectures of the 1890s, and from remarks in the methodological essays, that his sympathies were really on the "Austrian" side of the quarrel, and he approved of what he saw as the balanced theoretical stance of its chief spokesman, Carl Menger (see below, p. 249).

Weber's position in this debate, which owed much to the views of the neo-Kantian philosopher Heinrich Rickert (see pp. xix–xxi), was above all set out in *Objectivity*: "The social science that *we* want to pursue is a *science of reality*. We want to understand *the distinctive character* of the reality of the life in which we are placed and which surrounds us . . ." (p. 114). Weber was pleading for an independent methodology unimpeded by claims that lay outside the proper sphere of social science.

Philosophy of history

In the three essays on Roscher and Knies, Weber conducts a critique of a wide range of philosophies of history: the Hegelian philosophy of the movement of reason in history, the materialist philosophy of history in its naturalistic, evolutionist, monist and Marxist guises, and neo-Hegelian philosophy as represented by Roscher and Knies and by the Italian philosophers, Croce and Lipps. In *Energetics*, Comte's philosophy of history of evolutionary stages is attacked, and Comte himself is dismissed as a "grandiose pedant" (p. 260). Weber sums up his account as follows: "The fracture in both Knies' and Roscher's basic epistemological [position] must be explained by the withered remainders (which have [moreover] been warped in an anthropological–biological direction) of Hegel's great ideas; these remainders were still very characteristic of the philosophies of history, language and culture of various influential currents of thought in the middle decades of the last century" (p. 93). What these philosophies of history had in common was the assumption that history proceeded on the basis of hidden yet ineluctable forces. Development or evolution, as he noted in a fragment, "is not some hidden agent behind the course of history, so that our foremost task would then be to ferret it out everywhere and without exception and to extract its essence from the material" (p. 416). At the level of research methods, adherents to a philosophy of history were often involved in the close scrutiny and analysis of facts and phenomena. This might look like academic science, but, in Weber's eyes, that appearance was deceptive. These scholars were simply looking for material that would underpin their preconceptions. For Weber, this was a totally unacceptable starting point for scientific and empirical research, the more so when it was pretended that the facts could "speak for themselves" (p. 346).

Neo-Kantianism

While Roscher, Knies and others represented the remaindered part of Hegelian panlogism, the new and formidable enemy was what Weber termed "naturalistic monism" (p. 122). As was described above, the rapidly growing prestige of the natural sciences had led many to believe that by "uncovering law-like regularities, [it was possible] to arrive at a monistic knowledge of total reality" (p. 122). In particular, when it seemed to become possible to encompass within a "generally valid evolutionary principle" everything of importance in the field of *biology* – the science of life itself – "then it looked as if the twilight of the gods for all valuational viewpoints in all sciences was drawing near" (p. 122). In other words, the battle against what is now termed "positivism" was about to be lost.

One possible defence against the positivist onslaught would be to demonstrate that the objects of the "humanities" (as we would call them) were intrinsically different from those with which the natural sciences dealt. This was the view put forward by Wilhelm Dilthey, who argued that knowledge of the object of the "sciences of the human spirit" ("Geisteswissenschaften") – the "spirit" – required intuition and empathy, which did not form part of the methods of natural science. This solution had a natural appeal, as it corresponded to what actually went on in many branches of the humanities. But it suffered from a central weakness, since the very science dealing with the "spirit" – psychology – seemed increasingly accessible to a treatment along the lines of the natural sciences. (Weber's strong aversion to any "psychologistic" interpretation of economic concepts such as "value" (as discussed in *Marginal Utility*) or of basic logical truths was no doubt in part due to his desire to avoid being identified with Dilthey's line of thought.)

Instead, it was the neo-Kantian school of philosophy, in particular its so-called "South-Western" branch (Windelband, Rickert and Lask), that opened what seemed to be the right path out of the humanist predicament, through a return to Kant's epistemology. Kant's basic idea was that we can only attain knowledge of the world around us indirectly, by means of categories and concepts: as Weber himself put it towards the end of *Objectivity*, "the basic idea of modern epistemology, which goes back to Kant, is that concepts are, and can only be, theoretical means for the purpose of intellectual mastery of the empirically given" (p. 123). Therefore, the important thing was to show that the methods and concepts on which knowledge in the humanities was necessarily based were essentially different from those which the natural sciences, with equal necessity, had to employ.

It was Wilhelm Windelband who first, in a lecture in 1894 (*History and Natural Science*), established the argument for separating the natural sciences from the "historical sciences" on the basis of differences of approach rather than of subject matter. The approach of the natural sciences, he said, was "nomothetic" ("law-seeking"), but the historical sciences are "idiographic" ("describe what is distinctive"): they want to know about the individual or concrete reality, whose particularity is unique and unrepeatable.

Windelband's distinction was central. But he did not elaborate the argument underlying it, nor did he face up to the challenge of producing a convincing argument that established the idiographic method as having a methodological status as firm and unquestioned as that of the generalizing natural sciences.

This was left to the great systematizer of the movement, Heinrich Rickert, to accomplish in his book *The Limits of Concept Formation in the Natural Sciences*, whose second part was published in 1902. His epistemological point of departure was that the historian – like any scientist – confronts a reality (usually in the past) that presents an infinite multiplicity of phenomena, both intensively and extensively: the horizon of the past can be infinitely extended, and at any one point there exists a reality that can be subdivided into ever more particular components (Rickert, *Limits of Concept Formation*[5], pp. 35–38). How, then, would the historian select those elements of infinite reality that he wanted to deal with? Here, Rickert argued that the concepts of the historical sciences (corresponding to Windelband's "idiographic" disciplines) are formed by being linked to theoretical values, by a "value relation" ("Wertbeziehung"). These values, in their turn, in order to have general validity, must be valid for a community: they must be "cultural values". Thus, designating a period of history under a concept, as for example when Jacob Burckhardt named a period in fifteenth- and sixteenth-century Italian history "the Renaissance", not only created an analytic concept, but also established a value relation between what happened in the past and the present value interests of the historian.[1] This, in brief, is Rickert's central thesis, his central concept, and the central prop underpinning the status that he wishes to ascribe to the historical (or "cultural", as he also calls them) sciences.

There is no doubt that Weber was much impressed with Rickert's book, which he read immediately after its publication. A series of postcards to his wife (p. 374) chart his progress through the work, which, he concluded, was "*very* good". His early methodological essays are full of references to Rickert and to the logic of his concept of "value relation". This was precisely the instrument that he needed to cut down the various pernicious methodological errors of the day, as he identified them. In particular, *Objectivity* applied the neo-Kantian standpoint towards knowledge to the practical sphere of social economics, which at its most extensive was concerned with the determination of cultural life by economic factors and, conversely, how economic life is influenced by culture.

But, at the same time, one senses that Weber's adherence to the Rickertian doctrine is not quite wholehearted. He has "doubts about the terminology", he writes to his wife (and to Rickert himself), and his own methodological essays are designed, he says, to "test" the usefulness of Rickert's very abstract philosophical constructions within more down-to-earth scientific disciplines. In any event, as we shall see, there were limits beyond which he could not follow Rickert's construction. Ever since the earliest systematic exposition of Weber's methodology (Schelting, *Theory of Science*), and particularly since the early 1970s, a constant debate has therefore been going on as to the precise extent to which Weber's methodology is dependent on Rickert's thought.[2] In the section on "Values" below, we shall return to some of the premises of this debate, which remains inconclusive, although one may perhaps see a growing tendency to stress Weber's independence of his philosophical mentor (and close personal friend). Certainly, some of the drafts reproduced below (pp. 413–14) seem to point in that direction. At any rate, the debate has given added point to the cruel jest by the German philosopher Karl Jaspers, who, in a heated argument with Rickert a short time after Weber's death, when Rickert denied Weber the rank of philosopher, retorted that Rickert's own philosophy would only be remembered through Max Weber's writings.[3]

The third member of the South-West German school, Emil Lask, although still quite young at the time (born in 1875, he was Rickert's pupil), made his independent contributions to Weber's conceptual universe. He coined the term "emanationism", which Weber took over, for Hegelian and neo-Hegelian theories where reality was seen as an emanation of abstract concepts; and he figuratively burnt any vestigial bridgehead from concrete reality to scientific deductions and inferences by arguing in his doctoral thesis of 1901 (*Fichte's Idealism*) that a *hiatus irrationalis* – an irrational chasm – separated the bruteness of reality from the way that scientists and academics construed and manipulated that reality by their methods. As Guy Oakes explains this extreme version of scepticism: "There is a hiatus because reality cannot be derived from concepts. And it is irrational because reality can be rationalized only by conceptualizing it, which according to analytic theory is impossible" (Rickert (Oakes), *Limits of Concept Formation*, p. xvi).

1 The example is illustrative, and is not Weber's own.
2 For a recent overview and discussion, see Bruun, *Methodology*, pp. 7–11, 115–64.
3 See Adair-Toteff, *Confrontation*. In fact, Weber never claimed to be a philosopher, though he had followed philosophical lectures at university and was quite capable of arguing on equal terms with Rickert on philosophical matters.

Values

The "values" silo overflows with methodological contributions from Weber's hand, of many different kinds. The concept of "value relation" had allowed the neo-Kantians to define a method that seemed to match the generalizing method of the natural sciences. But the question was whether the results obtained by this method of value relation could claim the same kind of objectivity that the generalizing sciences so confidently boasted of. Rickert tried to solve this problem by way of an intricate philosophical argument intended to demonstrate that the values in question were not just generally valid empirically (for a particular "culture"), but that they had a necessary connection with values that were in their turn (metaphysically) objective. Philosophically, this argument made (neo-Kantian) sense. But there is general agreement that Weber did not accept it. Nowhere in his writings do we find him embracing it, and, in the note usually referred to as the "Nervi fragment" from 1903, he definitely distances himself from such metaphysical constructions (pp. 413–14). More than that, he regularly, and with great rhetorical vehemence, advances the exactly opposite view: that the ultimate values are in necessary conflict, and therefore can in no way be said to be objective.

In fact, this conception of a fundamental "value conflict" is the necessary corollary of the principle of the "value freedom" of science, which is a major Weberian contribution to the methodology of the social sciences. Value freedom as a principle was also part of Rickert's argument. The values to which reality was related in order to guide the selection of material for the "cultural" or "historical" sciences were theoretical, not practical. A political history of Germany, for example, would rest on the conviction that politics as such was a cultural value, but it would not imply the taking of any particular political side. Rickert even went so far as to opine (after Weber's death) that Weber owed the idea of the value freedom of science to him.[1] But that was going too far. Weber accepted the logic of value freedom in its methodological form, but there is often a characteristic fuzziness about his pronouncements in this context. His memorable statement that "the transcendental precondition of every *cultural science* is *not* that we find a particular, or indeed any, 'culture' *valuable*, but that we *are* cultural *beings*, endowed with the capacity and the will to adopt a deliberate *position* with respect to the world, and to bestow *meaning* upon it" (p. 119; Scaff, *Iron Cage*, pp. 83–87) certainly does not make a strong case for "theoretical" values. And when Weber argues that social scientists are forced to make a choice as to what aspect of that infinite reality they will study, he says that this choice is governed by the "value ideas" of the social scientist, which determine what is "worth knowing": "only a finite *part* of [that infinite reality] should be the object of scientific comprehension, – should be 'important' (in the sense of 'worth knowing about')" (p. 114). Again, these, "value ideas" may well be practical rather than theoretical.

But, if Weber sometimes seems a little unwilling to reproduce Rickert's rather bloodless philosophical version of the argument concerning value freedom (the more so, perhaps, as it was ultimately tied to a system of metaphysically objective values), he is on the other hand entirely clear and consistent in his demand for value freedom in practice, as far as both scientific concepts and – not least – scientific results are concerned: science cannot, and therefore should not pretend to be able to, prove the validity of any practical value whatsoever, he says, over and over again. As is to be expected, this argument in its manifold ramifications forms the main substance of Weber's essay of *Value Freedom*. But it is noteworthy that it is already present, fully fledged, in his early (1904) essay on the "objectivity" of the social sciences. (In fact, this essay – *Objectivity* – mainly deals with the *subjective* preconditions of science, that is to say: with its

1   Rickert, *Limits of Concept Formation*[5], p. 758.

"value relations". Generally speaking, a putative methodological "silo" with the heading "objectivity" would remain embarrassingly empty in Weber's case.)

However, alongside his repeated insistence on the fundamental demand for the value freedom of science, Weber expends much time in explaining what this principle does *not* imply, and what science *can* do with values. Social action is constantly motivated by people's valuations or value judgements concerning the world that surrounds them. But this in no way debars social scientists from dealing with that action, nor does it detract from the scientific status of their conclusions: "When the normatively valid becomes the object of an *empirical* inquiry, it loses, as an object, its normative character: it is treated as 'existent', not as [normatively] 'valid'" (p. 328).

The reverse also holds. What is scientifically shown to be valid cannot transfer that validity to the realm of value choices and beliefs. The latter may be informed by science, but they belong to an autonomous sphere of values. Medical science, to take an example that Weber uses in *Science*, cannot tell a physician how long the life of a terminally ill patient *should* be prolonged, even though it can tell him how to prolong that life (p. 345). And, writing to Rickert in July 1911, he rages: "I find it *unacceptable* when the highest problems concerning *values* are mixed up with the question *why* the price of pork in Berlin today is *x* pfennig; – when it is claimed that the ultimate standpoints that have the power to move the human soul can be read into woolly concepts of 'productivity' (or something similar); – and when [those ultimate standpoints] are inseparably welded together with purely *empirical* questions. Only when we have rendered to *our* king – the realm of the empirical – the things that are his can we render unto 'God' – the philosophy of value – the things that are his" (p. 403).

Weber is also quite willing to accept the possibility of a scientific study of "value ideas" as such. In *Objectivity* and *Value Freedom*, he gives pedagogic examples of how one may, with (in his view) scientific validity, analyse the implications of a particular practical value position. And in *Critical Studies*, he discusses in detail the possibility of what he calls "value interpretation" – that is to say: the systematic study of the different value positions under which a particular object of the cultural sciences may be "worth studying".

Finally, Weber is at pains to emphasize that "value freedom" within the sphere of science in no way prescribes or implies that the academic should remain passive in the affairs of the world: "*Lack of conviction* has no inherent affinity whatsoever to *scientific* 'objectivity'" (p. 106).

Values, then, constitute an important thread in Weber's methodological thought. The academic and social scientist belongs to a world of culture within which value ideas are generated. These operate as criteria for the selection of a finite aspect of cultural reality, which is composed of the ideas, ideals and cultural meanings of human beings. This aspect can become an object of knowledge for scientific study. Furthermore, it is open to citizens as well as academics in their public persona (outside the lecture hall) to form value judgements, perhaps in the light of social-scientific research, but never with the presumption that these value judgements are covered by scientific proof, or that they can claim objective validity.

The disparate senses of the word "value" have created difficulties (some of which are discussed in the Glossary) for translators. Shils and Finch's translation can be singled out as illustrative of the problem. They translated the title of Weber's 1917 *Value Freedom* essay as "The Meaning of 'Ethical Neutrality' in Sociology and Economics", whereas the literal translation adopted in this volume is "The Meaning of 'Value Freedom' in the Sociological and Economic Sciences". Weber, who did not subscribe to formal Kantian ethics, saw the world of value judgements as one of unavoidable clashes. The stress in his methodology is not on neutrality – an idea he strongly disliked – but on an existential realm of value choice, though one informed by the clarity and technical knowledge that scientific analysis can supply. And the necessary value freedom of science was in no way restricted to the ethical sphere.

The values that determine what is worth knowing, and the influences acting on value choices are all, Weber stresses, time dependent. All historical disciplines, said Weber, "are constantly confronted with new questions by the ever advancing flow of culture" (p. 133). This is an exigency that includes the social sciences, and demands the constant "reshaping" of immediate reality and its ordering through concepts that correspond "to the state of knowledge and the focus of interest at that time". Advances in the cultural sciences occur through "struggle". "The history of the sciences of social life therefore is and remains in constant flux between the attempt to order facts intellectually . . . and the new formation of concepts . . ." (p. 134).

Flux and contingency, and what Weber called "the irrational reality of life" (p. 137), have an unsettling effect, not only on value formation, but also on our rational orientation in this world. This means that an "ethic of responsibility" has a central place in Weber's philosophy of values (Schluchter, *Value Neutrality*). But, in the face of flux and contingency, a person's outlook on the world also needs to be anchored to ultimate values, come what may. Hence, Weber is also identified with a value-affirming "ethic of conviction" in a world of agonistic value conflicts. Weber's, what may be termed, "will to values", the idea that each person is forced to choose an ultimate value position in the face of the "polytheism of values" has parallels to Nietzsche's "will to power" and the "re-evaluation of values" (see Baier, *Society*; Scaff, *Iron Cage*, p. 206; Bruun, *Methodology*, pp. 39–41).

Logic

"Logic" is a recurring term in Weber's methodological writings, to such an extent that it may be useful to devote some paragraphs to its implications.

Traditionally, logic was the study of the True, just as aesthetics was the study of the Beautiful and ethics the study of the Good. For the neo-Kantians, it was therefore natural to apply the term "logic" to their theory of knowledge. In its turn, the discipline of "logic", thus conceived, could be subdivided into epistemology, methodology and formal logic.[1]

Weber valued the use of logic as an obligation by scientists to clear thinking, stressing (in a letter to Bortkievicz) "I must very strongly emphasize that logic has the duty strictly to distinguish between contradictory positions which may sometimes get blurred in practice in science" (p. 385). But he did not use the term "logic" in the precise sense of the neo-Kantians. When we find him talking about "the terminology of modern logicians", he mentions not only Windelband, Rickert and Lask, but also Gottl and Edmund Husserl, who do not qualify as neo-Kantians. In fact, Weber was not at all consistent in the way that he employed the term "logic". As we have seen (p. xii n2), he wrote to his publisher about his "logical–methodological writings", as if "logic" was somehow for him co-terminous with "methodology". In other places, though, the two terms stand side by side (p. 324), and sometimes they are jumbled up with "epistemology" (p. 153). At the same time, it is obvious that not every philosopher would, in Weber's parlance, qualify as a "logician". He seems to have reserved that designation for thinkers who did not just pursue formal Aristotelian logic, nor work along the lines of propositional logic pursued by Frege and Russell, but who nevertheless, like the neo-Kantians, thought deeply, carefully and accurately about the definition, the interrelation and the proper and improper use of concepts.

However, when it came to according the accolade of being "scientific" to philosophers of this kind, Weber was apparently more restrictive. This can be seen in the telling admission by Rickert in the introduction to *Limits of Concept Formation*[5]: "[Weber] had formed a somewhat

---

1   For the more detailed definition of the first two concepts, see pp. xiv–xvi.

one-sided view of the possibilities of scientific philosophy; in fact, he only believed in 'logic'". We have no exhaustive definition from Weber's own hand of the "logic" that he saw as "scientific". We can only observe that, in certain concrete instances, he includes under it the conceptual analysis of values in terms of their intrinsic meaning (letter to Tönnies, p. 398), and also the "value interpretation" mentioned above (p. xxii), but excludes from it, for instance, neo-Kantian value philosophy.[1]

We must content ourselves with the conclusion that, for Weber, "logic" was, apart from its formal, Aristotelian sense, a – fairly vague – designation of the basis on which he could formulate *binding* critiques of improper methodological thought and practices. It was also the basis for certain distinctions – chief among them that between "Is" and "Ought" – which in his eyes were beyond doubt.[2]

Ideal types

The ideal type requires little by way of introduction. It is the one concept in Weber's methodology that has been seared into the mind of modern social science; moreover, his own explication of it in the last third of *Objectivity* is a model of clarity, and we possess letters where Weber enlarges interestingly on certain aspects of the concept.

This is not to say that the ideal type does not present problems. The first of these is its name. There is no doubt that it was extremely important for Weber to stress that the ideal type was *not* an ideal in the normative sense. But, in view of this, why did he not choose a different name – the more so since he himself writes to Rickert that "how it is termed is of course a minor consideration"?[3] He borrowed the term from Jellinek (letter to Rickert, p. 375), thinking (wrongly) that Jellinek did not use it normatively. However, that does not help the unwary reader with no endnotes to consult.[4] In relation to causal procedure, ideal types – such as the "ideal general" discussed below, in the section on Causality – are indispensable as framing devices; in this sense, ideal types are simply heuristic instruments or models[5] and could easily have been given a corresponding name. We can only offer the explanation that Weber has a disconcerting habit of coining terms that somehow go against the grain of the substance that they are meant to cover ("value freedom" being another example).

In the letter to Rickert mentioned immediately above, Weber says that he feels "that a category of this kind is indeed necessary to distinguish between 'valuation' and 'value relation'". This is also puzzling. A "valuation" is a practical value judgement, and Rickert has spent scores of pages in his *Limits of Concept Formation* making sure that the reader understands that the values that go into a value relation are *not* practical, but theoretical. So why create a wholly new category for the seemingly redundant purpose of distinguishing between the two? And where

---

1   This is obvious, since Rickert, in the quoted passage, goes on to say that he could never persuade Weber that his [Rickert's] own value philosophy qualified as "scientific".
2   It is interesting to note that Weber never explicitly refers to the "logical" justification for this distinction, but simply takes it as given.
3   Rickert (letter from Weber, p. 375) seems to have asked the same question, but Weber evades it.
4   These considerations are also germane to the question of whether the term "ideal type" should (as sometimes happens in English translations) be given a hyphen ("ideal-type"). In our opinion, a hyphen would only strengthen the misconception that the ideal type was somehow a (normative) ideal.
5   Right from the beginning, Weber was careful to take a severely instrumental view of the ideal type: "The construction of abstract ideal types can only be considered a *tool*, never an end [in itself]" (p. 126).

is the "necessity"?[1] Interestingly, in another letter (to v. Below, p. 376), Weber says that the section of the *Objectivity* essay dealing with the ideal type is *not* based on Rickert's neo-Kantian ideas. So the ideal type is in fact a massive intervention from outside into Rickert's careful construction, with potentially uncertain consequences for the latter.

It has frequently been debated whether ideal types must cover general phenomena or can also cover specific and individual ones. The prime examples of the "early" ideal types – the "Protestant Ethic" and the "Spirit of Capitalism" – can perhaps be said to be syntheses of many individual phenomena; the same goes for the example in a letter from Weber to Rickert (p. 381) in which he discusses Bismarck as the ideal type of a German (with, among other things, the typical characteristic of being thirsty!). But there are places where Weber himself describes such ideal types as being "individual", although they are constructed according to general principles. The question need not be further pursued – let alone answered – here.

Another and more interesting circumstance is the following: in *The Protestant Ethic and the Spirit of Capitalism* (in 1904–5), the ideal type is directly linked to the concept of the "historical individual" and has correspondingly clear connotations of cultural density and weightiness. But in 1913, when the *Categories* essay is written, Weber introduces for the first time a systematic sociological terminology by which regularities of social behaviour can be typified. This shifts the ideal type from being a construction of a historical individual, like the Protestant Ethic, to serving as the concept of choice for a sociology with a definite role to play in the division of labour between historians, who ascertain causal linkages, and theory and model constructors. This shift becomes ever more noticeable. The terminology "ideal type" gradually disappears, being replaced by "pure type" or just "type", and the definitions of such types become "thinner" and more generalized. In a late letter to Robert Liefmann (9 March 1920, p. 410), ideal types are linked indissolubly with theory: "Theory creates ideal types and this contribution is, precisely in my eyes, the most indispensable." The highly structured theoretical first chapters of *Economy and Society* consequently abound in such "types": high-level concepts functioning as orientating devices for the empirical verification of causal links. Against this background, it still remains open to debate whether the ideal type of 1904–6 was the same conceptual instrument as that of *WG* in 1920.[2] We are also left slightly bewildered by the gradual thinning down and instrumentalization of the ideal type concept, in the light of his creative and imaginative constructions of 1904–1905 and the extensive theoretical investment of his later typologies.

Causality

Weber's extensive remarks on causality, when accumulated, fill our metaphorical silo in a coherent way, even though the reader is not afforded a complete exposition at any one point. His account of causality is one of his most original and enduring contributions to the philosophy of social science. It was a subject in which he, as a practising social scientist, was heavily invested. In his study of the farm workers of western Prussia, Weber wanted to explain why they were leaving the land and moving into the cities. In his study of the productivity of factory workers, he wanted to show the influence of the differing social and cultural backgrounds to labour

---

1 In another letter to Rickert (p. 401), Weber says that the ideal type is necessary for the distinction between the normative ideal and the generic concept. That makes much better sense; but there is nothing "generic" about value relations, and this revised formulation sits oddly with Weber's affirmation in *Objectivity* (p. 126) that "the aim of ideal-typical concept formation is always to bring out clearly what is *distinctive*, and *not* what is generic, in cultural phenomena".

2 See Bruun, *Methodology*, pp. 207–37 and Gerhardt, *Ideal type*.

productivity in the manufacturing process.[1] As co-editor of the *Archive*, which was in large part a policy journal, he saw the need for social scientists to have reliable methods of determining what changes would result from a particular policy initiative. And in his comparative study of the religions of the world, he wanted to isolate the factor that marked out the development of capitalism in the West as being qualitatively different from the variants of capitalism and forms of economic activity of other major civilizations.

From a more general viewpoint, however, this was also the heart of any social-scientific undertaking. Academics are free to study whatever subject they wish, and in ways of their devising. But if they want to call themselves cultural, historical or social *scientists*, then they should possess the required methodological expertise of demonstrating in the appropriate manner why and how defined phenomena have been caused. Weber was therefore led to criticize various misguided accounts of causality, especially among historians. The field was wide. Leaving aside the class of neo-Hegelians who mistook historical events as an emanation from some essentialist property such as the spirit of the nation, even very good professional historians, like Eduard Meyer and Georg v. Below, made basic methodological errors.

Weber did more than just criticize others. He actually made suggestions for a more structured, systematic and innovative approach in this field, both in his discussion of the ideal type (see pp. xxiv–xxv) and in the discussion (in *Critical Studies*, pp. 167–84) of objective possibility and adequate causation.

Neo-Kantianism provided Weber with the necessary philosophical grounding. On this basis alone, Weber would have been able to reject the inductive empiricism of J.S. Mill. In fact, he went much further and defined a new logic of causation on the basis of the ideas of the statistician von Kries, as well those of a number of other writers.

Weber's solution was based on the neo-Kantian premise that the object of knowledge for research in the social sciences was chosen through value ideas and the scholar's selection of what seemed worth studying. A delimited slice of reality was carved out of the multiplicity of the world. The next step in Weber's arguments was for social scientists to work backwards from an effect (given in phenomenal reality) by ascribing or imputing possible causes to its appearance. The research design had to be able mentally to remove one factor (the possible cause) and ask whether the outcome of the empirical situation would thereby be different. "The most important aspect of historical work, i.e., the causal regression, . . . only acquires that validity if, in cases of dispute, it has passed the test of isolating and generalizing the individual causal components, utilizing the category of objective possibility and [performing] the synthesis of casual imputation which then becomes possible" (p. 177). Gustav Radbruch supplied Weber with the useful analogy of the ascription of causal responsibility in a court of law. With the crime as the known effect, could the behaviour of an accused person be imputed as an "adequate cause" of the crime?[2]

Weber discusses causality and teleology at length in a number of other passages as well. This occurs in critical form when he argues against the determinist view of society as being caused by an unfolding movement within history. But teleological thinking also has a more neutral, and very important, function in his work, as he is essentially concerned with the purposive behaviour of individual people. Weber would not have dissented from Immanuel Kant's statement: "The will is a kind of causality belonging to living beings insofar as they are rational".[3] However, he objected strongly to the misuse of Kant's "causality through freedom" as a justification of the right of the personality to act irrationally, which German historians such as

---

1   For a discussion of Weber as an empirical social scientist, see Eliaeson, *Methodologies*, pp. 84–96.
2   The classical explication of Weber's work on these questions is Turner/Factor, *Objective Possibility*.
3   Quoted in Caygill, *Dictionary*, p. 208.

Treitschke saw as the defining characteristic of the "great man of history" but which, for Weber, was a romanticization of destiny (p. 85). Weber stresses repeatedly that acting rationally is acting (towards known or assumed goals) in accordance with knowledge of the situation. This is the starting point in the process of causal imputation. Weber gives the example of a general in a battle whose decisions can be empirically analysed as diverging from what is modelled (in what is, in essence, some sort of ideal type) as ideally rational. Only by establishing mentally what *should have* occurred can alternative hypotheses be pursued – for example, that a general made sub-optimal decisions because of insufficient knowledge, or under the influence of non-rational factors such as indecisiveness, over-confidence or stress (p. 330).

Interpretation and understanding

This is a silo that, perhaps unexpectedly, appears to be only half full. It has not gone unremarked that Weber is sparing in his explication of how historians and cultural and social scientists practise expert methods. This contrasts markedly with the situation today where the nature of qualitative research and its methods receive intensive scrutiny. Interpretation and understanding would seem to be at the heart of Weber's methodology, yet little practical guidance or analysis of problem areas is offered.

We can make an initial observation. Prior to around 1910, Weber tends to use the terms "interpretation" and "to interpret", whereas he thereafter prefers to use "understanding" and "to understand". To a large extent, these terms are interchangeable in the way Weber uses them. This merits attention (see the relevant entries in the Glossary), since these are two different words, albeit with some overlap in what they denote. Therefore, when one tries to gain a more structured view of Weber's scattered expositions on the method and role of "understanding" – more often known in its German form: *Verstehen* – it is advisable also to look at his comments on interpretation (particularly in *Roscher and Knies*, where it is discussed in detail, often in long dense footnotes).

The *Knies* essays carry critiques of two approaches to understanding and interpretation. One concerns the reduction of subjective states of mind to a scientific psychology, as argued for by Wilhelm Wundt and Hugo Münsterberg. The other is an attack, never fully developed by Weber, against the major proponent of the method of "understanding" in the human sciences, Wilhelm Dilthey. In both cases, the problem is highlighted by Rickert's statement that "the life of other minds is fundamentally inaccessible" (quoted by Weber, p. 10n1).

Psychologists such as Wundt and Münsterberg – as well as later positivist movements within the philosophy of social science – wanted to exclude direct access to subjective consciousness, which includes values, beliefs, attitudes and what Weber later referred to as the "meant meanings" of social actors. Wundt and Münsterberg construed subjective consciousness as an essential 'I' or a creative synthesis that could never be captured by scientific method. Rickert's epistemological objection also seemed hard to rebut.

Dilthey, for his part, made what was then termed a "transcendental presupposition": as living sentient human beings, we act from feelings, wants and beliefs, and this capacity is common to humankind. Therefore, he argued, we can understand other people's volitional states of mind. For Dilthey, this involved a mental process of empathizing with the actions of ordinary people, as well as with historical personalities, and reproducing that experience. Simmel, in his *Philosophy of Money*, succinctly formulated the presumption that this was feasible: "One does not have to be Caesar to understand Caesar" (quoted by Weber, pp. 65, 274).[1]

1 This is discussed in Whimster *Understanding Weber*, pp. 76–83, 97–101.

The essays in the *Meth.Writings* allow us to follow how Weber developed his thinking on these issues – but not with ease. At the outset, Weber was trapped between two battle lines. On one side were the scientific psychologists who wanted to develop the laws of the development of the mind. Weber's critique of this finished by observing that these so-called scientific theories ended in a philosophy of history, i.e. evolutionism. On the other side, Weber was faced with the acute problem that the method of *Verstehen* – which he had in his own way brilliantly executed in *The Protestant Ethic and the "Spirit" of Capitalism* – had been explicated by Dilthey, but on unacceptable, epistemological grounds. In *Roscher and Knies*, Weber does not confront this issue head on. However, he does come to terms with many of the issues in the intricate footnotes of those essays, and he pursues and encourages a debate with Friedrich Gottl, who accepted the Diltheyan ontological position. (In many ways, the difficult writings of Gottl present Weber with an opportunity for making some of his objections to Dilthey known.)

As late as 1917, in *Value Freedom*, Weber wrote: "Every science dealing with interrelations in the [human] mind or in society is a science of *human* behaviour (a term which, in this case, includes every act of thought in the mind and every psychical disposition). It has the aim of 'understanding' this behaviour and, by that means, to give an 'explanatory interpretation' of it. Now, the difficult concept of 'understanding' cannot be dealt with in detail here" (p. 329). The most detailed examination of that concept to be found in the essays contained in this volume was the introduction to the *Categories* article. However, Weber did not explore it further until he gave it breathtakingly full attention in the first chapter of *Economy and Society*, written at the end of his life. His famous introductory definition there of sociology as "a science that seeks to understand social action interpretatively, and thereby to explain it causally in its course and its consequences" encapsulates the central problem of sociology, as it was then and as it remains today, more precisely than even a whole volume of his Collected Methodological Writings can hope to do.

EDITORIAL PREFACE

The state of the text

Obviously, the quality of a translation depends on the quality of the text on which it is based. In this respect, the German *Max Weber Gesamtausgabe* – the essential critical and scholarly edition of all Weber's works, with every textual variant and a full substantive commentary on every relevant point – represents the highest standard of quality. Unfortunately, the major part of the essays, interventions and notes included in the *Methodological Writings* have not yet been published in the *Gesamtausgabe*. The only methodological texts published there so far are *Science as a Profession and Vocation* (in *MWG I/17*), the Kantorowicz intervention (in *MWG I/8*) and the letters written between 1906 and 1917. The translation of these pieces is of course based on the *MWG* texts, but, for the translation of all the other essays, interventions, letters and notes, we have had to base ourselves on other versions. For the essays, the source has been the third edition (the fourth edition is an unchanged reprint) of the *Gesammelte Aufsätze zur Wissenschaftslehre*, edited by Johannes Winckelmann.

In spite of the great care and dedication with which Winckelmann edited these texts over many years, we have established in the course of our work that they were still beset with a number of inaccuracies and errors. Whenever the translator has come across such errors, they have been silently corrected, in many cases with the invaluable help of the editors and collaborators of the *Gesamtausgabe*. A special problem in this respect is the fact that Weber is often somewhat careless in his direct quotations of others and in his accounts of their views. An attempt to rectify all these unevennesses would go beyond the scope of this volume; that task must await the appearance of the relevant parts of the *MWG*, with its full apparatus of textual criticism. However, when we have found material errors in Weber's references, they have have been silently corrected. On the whole, though, whenever Weber quotes other authors or summarizes their views, the reader will be well advised to treat his account with a certain amount of caution. In particular, italics in quotations will often be found to be Weber's rather than the author's.

The translation of most of Weber's interventions and contributions is based on the texts in the *Gesammelte Aufsätze zur Soziologie und Sozialpolitik* (edited in 1924 by Marianne Weber); these texts have been checked against the proceedings in the relevant fora, as originally published. A few minor printed pieces (*Accompanying Remarks*, *Declaration* and *Adolf Weber*) have not been included in any critical edition, and the translation is therefore based on the original printed texts in the *Archive*. The translations of letters not yet published in the *MWG* are based on transcripts from the originals, made either by the translator or (in a few cases) by the Düsseldorf Max Weber Centre. As far as the notes and drafts are concerned, the translations are all based on the translator's own transcripts from the (mostly handwritten) originals.

The editorial apparatus

The usefulness of any translation of this kind is greatly enhanced by a well-thought-out and comprehensive editorial apparatus, and we have endeavoured to provide a maximum of help in this respect.

First of all, the text has been provided with copious *Endnotes*, indicated by a number in chevrons ‹1 to 479› in the Weber text. These Endnotes have been prepared with the general reader in mind who may find it difficult to identify and elucidate all Weber's references. These references are indeed extraordinarily varied. They range across the fields of physics, chemistry, philosophy, theology, history, architecture, music and the fine arts, from non-Euclidean geometry to obscure German nineteenth-century novelists. We have done our best to track them down and put them in a wider context. The annotations to texts already published in the *MWG* have been an invaluable help in this respect.

The endnotes are followed by an equally extensive *Glossary*, which not only gives the English translations of a large number of German terms, but also discusses in detail many of the choices made by the translator. The *Glossary* is organized on the basis of the German terms, but is supplemented by a comprehensive English–German *Key*, which allows the reader to identify the German word underlying a particular term in the English translation and thus to find the relevant entry in the Glossary.

The full *Bibliography* has been structured so as to provide the basis for a more consistent and more readable version of Max Weber's original text. Weber makes a considerable number of references to works by other authors in his methodological writings. Unfortunately, these references are inconsistent. Occasionally, they conform to ordinary bibliographical standards, but usually they are incomplete, giving only author and title; sometimes, they are even more lapidary (or plainly erroneous); and, at one point, Weber even displays a touching, but unhelpful, hesitancy: "if my memory does not fail me – Breysig (in a passage which I cannot for the moment locate) believes that . . .". In every single case, the reference in question has been identified and completed (mostly on the basis of the invaluable bibliography established and kindly put at our disposal by the Max Weber Centre in Munich, working on indications by Professor Horst Baier). The reference is given in its full standard form in the bibliography itself, but, at the same time, we have defined a system of short, simplified titles, so that it has become possible to render the references in Weber's text in clear and standardized form. In doing this, we have of course, technically speaking, in places altered the original text. But we have done so with a clear conscience, for what has been done usually supplements, and never detracts from, Weber's own bibliographical indications, and the simplified rearrangement offers the reader an accessible and unambiguous identification of the work to which Weber is referring. Rather than carry a second bibliography for references in the Introduction, Endnotes and Glossary, these have been entered into the single Bibliography on the same basis of short titles in the text.

A full *Index of persons* gives dates and elementary information about every person referred to in Weber's text or the Endnotes, coupled with complete page references. This is followed by a comprehensive *Subject index*.

A note on the translation

This translation of Weber's collected methodological writings aims at the greatest possible faithfulness towards the source text. This is true, first of all, in a literal sense: we have wished to ensure that the impact of the English text on an English-language reader should approximate as closely as possible that made by the original German version on a native German. Great care has therefore been taken to carry over into the English version, if at all possible, the sense of every word in the original text. These words, however small or awkward, usually have an identifiable function of calibrating or adjusting the thrust of the sentence. On the basis of the same principle, all Weber's – very numerous – quotation marks have been respected. Their implications are not always clear, but there is no reason to suppose that they were much clearer to the ordinary German reader at the beginning of the twentieth century. Weber's paragraph arrangements and occasional (not always transparent) dashes separating sentences have also been carried over into the translated text. In the same way, Weber's – equally numerous – italicizations have been retained throughout. They do not, broadly speaking, have a systematic function, but they serve as useful indicators of the points that Weber wishes to stress.

The principle of maximum faithfulness towards the original has also been our guideline in a wider sense. These texts date back a whole century. Many of the arguments that they contain are complicated, not to say convoluted, and they contain a large number of passages that lend themselves to interpretation. It might therefore seem natural to try to update and clarify them, so that the reader is presented with more accessible discussions conducted by means of more familiar and contemporary terms and concepts. Such a procedure might well be presented as an act of reader-friendliness. Our conception of "reader-friendliness" is a different one. As we see it, the translator should not make more choices than strictly necessary: instead, readers should be put in a position where they can, as far as possible, make these choices for themselves. The translator should try not to interpose himself unduly between the text and the reader. This imposes on him an obligation of great self-restraint. He should avoid transmitting a version that already takes sides in the possible discussion of the correct interpretation of the German text. If the original version leaves room for interpretation, he should try to keep open that space. If the German text is obscure, he should try to transmit that same obscurity. Ideally, the reader of the English text should, on the basis of the translation, be able to follow arguments based on the original German version.

Nevertheless, these translated texts of course read quite differently from the original German ones. This is unavoidable. German is and remains very different from English. Its grammar permits – indeed, invites – a condensation of formulations which are usually impossible to reproduce in English. Nouns, particularly the substantivized verbal forms beloved by Weber, play a far greater role in German, and they can carry loads of adjectives which, in English, may demand whole, separate, relative sentences. Experience shows that the systematical endeavour to retain these German linguistic peculiarities in the English translation has the disadvantage of leading to knotty and impenetrable constructions. In such cases, the dense German text needs to be "rolled out" into longer sentences, which must at the same time remain manageable and understandable. In order to achieve this, we have made liberal use of the whole available range of punctuation marks – commas, dashes, colons and semicolons. These marks may often have no counterparts in the original text, but they help to preserve the structure and flow of the original argument. It has also been necessary to insert a number of extra words to explicate the frequent pronominal German references, and to make the text clear whenever Weber's text suffers from ellipses so that a literal translation would not transmit the obvious sense. All such clarifying additions have been marked by square brackets. This may seem tedious and pedantic, but it is meant to ensure that the reader will always know when and how the translator has intervened actively.

The fact that the translator's mother tongue is Danish – a language which combines many direct counterparts to the German vocabulary with an informality of construction akin to that which characterizes English syntax – has actually in some cases been useful for the transition from the concentrated German version to a "rolled-out" English equivalent, by permitting a kind of linguistic triangulation between German, Danish and English.

Admittedly, Weber is not an easy writer to understand, in any language, and, as was described above, his literary form and style are usually of little help in this respect (although it must be said, in all fairness, that, once his thoughts have been unpacked from the dense, yet protracted, sentence constructions in which they are embedded, they are as a general rule quite clear). Some of his essays – in particular *Roscher and Knies* – make very awkward reading. Other ones (*Stammler* being a prime example) overflow with polemical gusto. On the other hand, *Science*, as well as the interventions, letters and notes, has a refreshing clearness and directness. We hope that some of these distinctive stylistic variations have been carried over into the translation. We have not gone so far as to preserve Weber's ungainliness for its own sake, but it is no bad thing if the reader senses the difference of style between, say, the *Knies* essays, *Stammler* and *Science*. Ideally, the text should transmit not only Weber's argument but also his living personality.

The translator's fidelity to the original German text, and his consequent deliberate attempt to restrict himself to a minimum of interpretation in the translation itself, have in places resulted in a slightly austere style. However, this should be compensated to a considerable extent by the extensiveness of the Glossary. Here, the reader can not only gain an overview of the translation of a particular term, but also, in many cases, go beneath the surface of the English text and obtain a direct insight into the deliberations underlying the choices made by the translator.

The Weber Methodology Website

Translation is always, properly understood, a cumulative endeavour. We have tried to take this into account by collating the finished translation with previous ones, both the older "standard" English translations (by Shils and Finch, Oakes, Edith Graber and others) and some excellent French versions by Grossein and Feuerhahn. This has allowed us to avoid a number of errors and pitfalls and has, at the same time, considerably enriched our field of choice; for this, we are grateful to our predecessors.

However, any translation of texts such as these is also, by its very nature, a work in progress. We hope and trust that the public will find the text that we now lay before it reasonably authoritative and useful, but we are fully conscious of the fact that it may still have its imperfections. In order to ensure that this becomes a source not of frustration but of constructive improvement, we have taken the innovative step of establishing the Weber Methodology Website (http://maxweberstudies/wordpress.com) to which readers can send their suggestions for the improvement of the translation or the editorial texts of the *Meth. Writings*. Thus, the suggestions can be registered and discussed by the entire scholarly community and may eventually constitute accessible virtual corrections to the printed edition. We cherish the hope that this step will mark the beginning of a new and positive phase in the field of scholarly translation and intellectual engagement.

ACKNOWLEDGEMENTS

The whole of this volume is the result of a truly collaborative effort, involving swarms of emails and thousands of comments, both on the translations and on the editorial texts, crossing and recrossing the North Sea in cyberspace between the two editors. The book has, however, also benefited greatly from the invaluable and unstinting help of other members of the scholarly community:

First and foremost, we wish to express our warmest thanks to the editors and staff of the *Max Weber Gesamtausgabe*, with whom we have collaborated closely in the preparation of this volume.

Above all, our thanks are due to Professor Horst Baier (Konstanz) who, with exemplary generosity and in the finest tradition of academic openness, put his commentaries on Weber's methodological essays, which he had worked on for decades, at our free disposal, thus lightening our work and underpinning its quality to a degree that we could only have dreamed of.

Professor M. Rainer Lepsius (Heidelberg) kindly opened the *Gesamtausgabe* store of letters to us. Professor Johannes Weiss (Kassel) has been a constant and constructive interlocutor, expending much time and no doubt dreary effort in elucidating murky points in the Weber text for us. The same is true of Dr Edith Hanke (Max Weber Arbeitsstelle, Munich), who also extended to us boundless hospitality, help, support and encouragement, helped by her able and cheerful colleagues Anne Munding and Ursula Bube.

We would particularly like to thank Gerhard Boomgaarden for his enthusiastic support and encouragement over the long haul of this undertaking. Our thanks are also due to the Routledge production team, and in particular to Rosie Stewart at Florence Production, who battled through in the face of a complex and difficult task.

Many others who deserve our special thanks should be mentioned here, all too briefly (in alphabetical order): Rita Aldenhoff-Hübinger, Karl-Ludwig Ay, Knut Borchardt, Sven Eliaeson, Michael Fend, Wolfgang Feuerhahn, Morten Frederiksen, Werner Gephart, Inge Gorm Hansen, Mogens Herman Hansen, Ida Holmegaard, Minna Højland, Gangolf Hübinger, Martin Høigaard, Jon Mark Mikkelsen, Tom Neuhaus, Albrecht Götz v. Olenhusen, Michael Raunkjær, Constans Seyfarth, Henrik Selsøe Sørensen, Keith Tribe, David Woodruff, Per Øhrgaard.

An ESRC Fellowship supported Sam Whimster in the editorial work, and the Department of Sociology, University of Copenhagen, has continued to extend its generous hospitality to Hans Henrik Bruun as Adjunct Professor.

The willingness of our wives to live not only with us, but also with Max Weber and his methodological problems, year after year, is beyond praise. Indeed, they occasionally say, beyond belief.

ARTICLES

ROSCHER AND KNIES AND THE LOGICAL PROBLEMS OF HISTORICAL ECONOMICS

Preliminary remarks

The following fragment[1] is not intended as a literary portrait of our great masters. Instead, it limits itself to an attempt to show how certain elementary problems of logic and method, which during the last generation have been discussed in the science of history and in our own specialized discipline, manifested themselves in the early stages of historical economics,[2] and how the first great achievements of the historical method have tried to come to terms with those problems. It is only natural that this discussion will in many instances to a large degree also demonstrate the *weaknesses* inherent in those achievements. Weaknesses of just this sort can lead us to constant reflections on the general presuppositions with which we approach our scientific work; and that is the only meaningful purpose of such investigations which must, quite deliberately, abstain from presenting an "artistic" overall picture, in favour of an extensive analysis of subjects which are, or seem to be, self-evident.

Nowadays it is usual to name Karl Knies and Bruno Hildebrand together with Wilhelm Roscher as founders of the "historical school". Without wishing in any way to disparage Hildebrand's great importance, he can be disregarded for our purposes, even though it was precisely Hildebrand − and, in a certain sense, only Hildebrand − who really employed the method which is nowadays called "historical". On the points which we are concerned with here, the relativism embodied in his *Economics* is merely an application of ideas which had already been developed, partly by Roscher, partly by others. On the other hand, in [giving] an account of *Knies'* methodological views, it is indispensable [for us] first to set out Roscher's method[olog]ical position. Knies' principal methodological work ‹2› − which was dedicated to Roscher − discusses those of Roscher's works which had already been published just as much as [it deals with the works of] the representatives of [the school of] classical economics which,

---

1   It was originally intended to be a contribution to the Heidelberg *Festschrift* ‹1› published this year, but it was not finished in time; in any event, in its present form it would not have been very suitable for [the *Festschrift*].

2   In so doing, however, we shall only be concerned with elementary forms of these problems. Only this circumstance allows me to discuss them here, as I naturally do not have a *professional* command of the rapidly growing body of literature in the field of logic. But even scholars in specialized disciplines ought not to ignore those problems; and above all: although they are quite elementary, even their very existence is not widely recognized − as will also become apparent in the context of this study.

apart from Roscher, dominated our universities and whose acknowledged leader at that time was Rau, Knies' predecessor at Heidelberg.

Consequently, we shall begin with an exposition of Roscher's basic method[olog]ical views, as they can be found in his book *Thucydides* (1842), his programmatic *Outline* (1843) and his essays from the 1840s; ⟨3⟩ we shall also consider the first editions of the first volume of his *System* (1st ed. 1854, 2nd ed. 1857), which were only published *after* Knies' book, as well as Roscher's later works, inasmuch as they merely contain a consistent elaboration of that standpoint which Knies intended to subject to critical discussion.[1]

I Roscher's "historical method"

Roscher's taxonomy of the sciences

Roscher[2] distinguishes between two kinds of scientific treatment of reality, which he calls the "philosophical" and the "historical": the first is *conceptual* comprehension, by way of generalizing abstraction, where the "contingent" elements of reality are eliminated; the second is *descriptive* representation of reality in its full actuality. One is immediately reminded of the distinction made nowadays between *sciences of laws* and *sciences of reality*, a distinction which manifests itself most clearly in the method[olog]ical contrast between the exact natural sciences on the one hand, and political history on the other.[3]

---

1   On the main points that are important *to us*, it is hardly possible to find changes of substantive importance even in the last volumes and editions of Roscher's massive work. A certain rigidity sets in. Although he was acquainted with authors such as Comte and Spencer, the significance of their basic ideas eluded him, and he did not subject them to thorough treatment. His *History of Economics* (1874) in particular turns out to be unexpectedly meagre for our purposes, since R[oscher] is throughout mainly interested in the *practical purposes* of the writer under discussion.

2   For obvious reasons, the following analysis will, in accordance with its purpose, be the opposite of a *complete* portrait of Roscher's significance. For an appreciation of that significance, see the essay by Schmoller (most recently published in Schmoller, *Literature*) and Bücher's memorial address (Bücher, *Roscher*). Both authors, in these articles which were published, respectively, in Roscher's lifetime and immediately after his death, leave aside a point of importance for Roscher's scientific personality, namely his fundamentally *religious* outlook; but this is only natural, considering the subjectivistic sensibilities of our generation in these matters. A more thoroughgoing analysis of Roscher's method would – as we shall see – have to deal with this factor; and Roscher himself was also, as the posthumous publication of his *Religious Reflections* makes clear, thoroughly "old-fashioned", insofar as it did not occur to him to feel in any way embarrassed by publicly professing his strictly traditional beliefs. The analysis below will be marked by Roscher's manifold repetitions and exhibit a comprehensiveness that will often seem unnecessary; this is owing to the inconclusive and often inconsistent character of his views, whose individual ramifications must again and again be measured against the standard of the same logical position. In logical investigations, there is simply nothing which is "self-evident". Here we shall analyse the *logical* character of views held by Roscher, but long since obsolete, although no one in our discipline would probably now waste a single word commenting on their *substance*. *Nevertheless, it would be erroneous to suppose that for this reason, the logical weaknesses which [Roscher's] views contain are clearer to us today than they were to him.*

3   In the further course of our discussion, we shall frequently refer to this distinction, whose significance for the methodology of economics was to a certain extent already (as will be noted later) recognized by Menger, although his conclusions were in part incorrect. After early attempts, to be found in Dilthey (*Sciences of the Human Spirit*) and Simmel (*Philosophy of History*), the precise logical formulation [of this distinction] was first, on important points, briefly sketched out in Windelband's Inaugural Rectoral Address (*History and Natural Science*), and then comprehensively elaborated in Heinrich

On the *one* hand, [therefore, we have those] sciences which strive to order the extensively and intensively infinite multiplicity [of phenomena] by means of a system of concepts and laws which, as far as possible, have unconditionally general validity. The logical ideal [of these sciences] – which is most perfectly realized in pure mechanics – compels them to strip away progressively the individually "contingent" elements of perceived [reality] from "things" and events as they are ideationally given for us, in order that the content of their concepts can attain the precision which the[se sciences] must by necessity strive for. They are unceasingly compelled by logic to [attempt a] systematic subordination of the general concepts formed in this way, under other, even more general ones; and this, combined with their striving for strict precision, impels [these sciences] to reduce, as far as possible, the qualitative differentiation of reality to quantities which can be measured exactly. If they want, finally and fundamentally, to go beyond the mere classification of phenomena, then their concepts must comprehend potential judgements with general validity; and for these judgements to be absolutely *strict* and mathematically evident, it must be possible to express them in *causal equations*.

The result of all this is an increasing remoteness from the empirical reality, which is, everywhere and at all times, only given and *perceivable* as concrete, individual and qualitatively differentiated. The ultimate consequence is the creation of entities which are conceived as being absolutely nonqualitative, and therefore absolutely unreal, and which are subject to purely quantitatively differentiated processes of change, [processes] whose laws can be expressed in causal equations. The specific logical *instrument* [of these sciences] is the use of concepts with ever wider *scope* and, consequently, with an ever increasing lack of *content*. The specific logical *products* [of these sciences] are *relational* concepts with *general validity* (laws). Their *field of inquiry* is to be found wherever those features of a phenomenon which, in our eyes, are *essential* (worth knowing about) coincide with its *generic* features; in other words, wherever our scientific interest in an empirically given individual case lapses as soon as we are able to subsume it under a generic concept as a specimen.

And on the *other* hand, [we have] sciences which set themselves the task which the sciences of laws described above are necessarily prevented from fulfilling, owing to the logical nature of their approach: [the task of] attaining knowledge of *reality*, with its constant and universal character of qualitative differentiation and uniqueness. However, since it is in principle impossible to reproduce *exhaustively* even the most limited part of reality with its (at least always intensively) infinite differentiation from all the other [parts of reality], [the object of this second group of sciences must be] knowledge of those constituent parts of reality which, with their individual *distinctive character* and because of that character, are in our eyes the *essential* ones.

Rickert's fundamental work (*Limits of Concept Formation*). Gottl (*Dominance of Words*) – influenced by Wundt, Dilthey, Münsterberg and Mach, occasionally also by Rickert ([*Limits of Concept Formation*], vol. I), but in essence quite independently – approaches the problems of concept formation in economics in a completely different manner; in its *methodological* aspects, however, his book has now in many respects – but certainly not the most important ones – been superseded by the second half of Rickert's work that appeared in the meantime. Apparently, Rickert was not familiar with [Gottl's] work, nor was Eduard Meyer, whose account (*Theory and Method*) is in many places close to Gottl's. The reason is probably to be found in Gottl's language, which is refined almost to the point of unintelligibility: as a consequence of his psychologistic epistemological standpoint, he is positively anxious to avoid traditional terminology, which is tied to concepts and therefore in his eyes "denatured"; [instead], he resorts to (so to speak) ideograms in his attempts to reproduce the contents of immediate "experience". Admittedly, much of what he puts forward, including some of the fundamental theses of his work, is controversial; and he does not arrive at a genuine conclusion. Nevertheless, the distinctive way in which he illuminates the problem, with sensitivity and acuteness, merits attention, and, in the present study, we shall a number of times have occasion to return to it.

The logical ideal of those sciences is to separate the *essential* features of the individual phenomenon which is being analysed from the "contingent" (which in this context means: unimportant) ones and to bring them out in a clearly perceivable form. This ideal, together with the need to place the individual [elements] in a universal *context* of concrete "causes" and "effects" which are immediately and clearly evident, compels these sciences to a continual refinement of concepts, [and] these concepts will constantly *approximate* the invariably individual, actual reality [because they are elaborated] by means of a selection and synthesis of those features which we judge to be "*characteristic*".

The specific[1] logical instrument [of these sciences] is therefore the formation of relational concepts[2] with ever greater *content*[3] and, consequently, with ever narrower *scope*.[4] The specific[5] products [of these sciences] are (to the extent that they have the character of concepts at all) individual *object concepts*[6] with universal (or, as we usually say, "historical") *significance and importance*. Their *field of inquiry* is to be found wherever what is essential about the phenomena – that is to say, what we regard as worth knowing [about them] – is not limited to their [being placed] [as a specimen] in a generic concept; [in other words], where it is concrete reality *as such* which interests us.

It is certain that, apart from pure mechanics on the one hand and certain parts of historical science on the other, none of the empirically existing "sciences" – whose division of labour is of course based on quite different and often "accidental" factors – can form its concepts solely from one or solely from the other of the two [above-mentioned] points of view [concerning the aims of science]; we shall return to this point later. But it is equally certain that the difference [between the two kinds of concept formation] is in itself a fundamental one, and that any taxonomy of sciences from a method[olog]ical point of view must take it into account.[7]

1   It should be well understood that this is not their sole or even *main* instrument, but that which distinguishes them from the exact natural sciences.
2   [That is,] concepts that place the concrete historical phenomenon in a *context* which is concrete and individual, but as far as possible [also] universal.
3   Since the knowledge of the *characteristic* features of the context in which the phenomena are placed will increase as knowledge progresses.
4   Since the *individual* character of knowledge of a phenomenon will necessarily increase together with the knowledge of the *characteristic* features of the phenomenon.
5   See n1.
6   This sense of the word (which is unusual from the point of view of everyday language) indicates a contrast with naturalistic *relational* concepts and includes, for instance, the portrait of the "character" of a concrete "personality". – The term "concept", which is nowadays as contentious as ever, is used here, and will be used in what follows, to indicate *any* theoretical construct, however artificial, that is formed by the logical processing of a perceptual multiplicity [of phenomena] with the aim of *acquiring knowledge of what is important*. For instance, the historical concept "Bismarck" contains the (in our eyes) *important* features of the perceptually given personality who bore this name; [these features] are placed in a social and historical context, as having been caused by or having an effect within it. For now, we shall leave aside the question – which is one of principle – whether methodology has an answer ready to hand as to *what* those features are – that is to say, whether there exists a general *method[olog]ical* principle according to which those features are selected from the mass of scientifically unimportant ones (for a *contrary* view, see Ed[uard] Meyer (*Theory and Method*)).
7   In the preceding account, I believe that I have more or less faithfully reflected the main points of view – to the extent that they are relevant for us – in Rickert['s *Limits of Concept Formation*]. It is one of the purposes of this study to test [the possibility of] using [Rickert's] ideas in the methodology of our discipline. I therefore do not refer to him in every single case where I would normally have been required to do so.

Now, since Roscher describes his own method as "historical", his version of economics would apparently have the exclusive task of producing a clearly perceivable reproduction of the total reality of economic life, in the same way and with the same instruments as historical science, – in contradistinction to the ambition of the classical school, [which was] to reveal the law-like, uniform way in which elementary forces were at work in the multiplicity of events.

In Roscher's work, one does indeed occasionally find the general remark that economics "should study the *differences* between things with the same interest as their similarities".

One is therefore astonished to find the statement (*Outline*, p. 150) that, before Roscher, the work of "*historical*" economics was in particular advanced by Adam Smith, Malthus and Rau, and (p. V) to see the last two described as those scholars to whom the author feels especially close. It is no less astonishing when (p. 2) the work of the *natural scientist* is described as being similar to that of the historian, and (p. 4) politics (which includes the "science of political economy") as the science of the evolutionary *laws* of the state; when, furthermore, Roscher – as is well known – again and again deliberately speaks of the "laws of nature" of the economy; and, finally, when (p. IV) knowledge of what is *essential*[1] is even identified with knowledge of what is *law-like* in the mass of phenomena, and [the acquisition of such knowledge] is taken to be the only conceivable task of all science.[2] Now, since genuine "laws of nature" governing events could only be formulated on the basis of conceptual abstractions and by eliminating "historically contingent" elements, then it must follow that the ultimate goal of economic inquiry must be the construction of a system of generic and law-like concepts; and these concepts must be as logically perfect as possible – that is to say: as far as possible stripped of all individual "*incidental features*", and therefore as abstract as possible. This in spite of the fact that Roscher had apparently in principle rejected precisely this goal. But only apparently. In reality, Roscher's critique was not aimed at the logical form of classical theory, but at two quite different points, namely, (1) the deduction of absolutely valid practical *norms* from abstract-conceptual premises (this is what he calls the "philosophical" method) and (2) the hitherto prevailing principle for the *selection of the subject matter* of economics. In principle, Roscher does not doubt that the interrelation of economic phenomena can only and should only be conceived as a system of *laws*.[3] For him, "causality" and "law-like regularity" are identical: the former only exists in the shape of the latter.[4] But – and this is what is important for Roscher – the aim of scientific

---

1   The practical effect that such an identification – if it is taken seriously – has on the nature of the historical account can probably be most easily seen in the first supplementary volume of Lamprecht's *German History*. Here, certain ephemeral specimens of German literature are described as "important from the point of view of historical development", because the allegedly law-like, uniform course taken by the various "impressionisms" etc. in the social psyche could not have been construed as corresponding to the theory without the existence of these authors, an existence that is therefore deemed to be theoretically valuable; on the other hand, personalities such as Klinger, Böcklin and others, who do not fit into the theory, are inserted, so to speak, as mortar in the crevices between the elements of the construction (they are subsumed under the generic concept of "transitional idealists"). We are also told that the life's work of Richard Wagner "stands or falls" not with his *significance* for us, but with the question whether it is in line with a certain theoretically postulated "development".

2   However, at least in the fundamental discussions in his *System*, Roscher has *not* included the remark quoted above, which already goes to show that the purpose of this and similar occasional statements is not to formulate a clear method[olog]ical principle.

3   Completely in line with Rau, he demands that "our theories, laws of nature etc. must always be formulated in such a way that they are *not exploded* by future changes in the discipline of public finance and administration" ⟨4⟩ (See Rau, *Utility*, pp. 3–7, and Roscher, *Ideas*, p. 158).

4   The same view – albeit with certain reservations concerning the psychological motivation – [can be found], for instance, in Schmoller's review of Knies' work (Schmoller, *Knies* , reprinted in Schmoller,

inquiry is to find out how the laws work themselves out not only in simultaneous, but also in successive, phenomena: it should establish not only the law-like interrelation of contemporary phenomena, but also, and above all, the evolutionary laws governing the *historical* course of phenomena.

This position of Roscher's prompts the question: What is his conception, in principle, of the relationship between law and reality in the course of history? Is it certain that that part of reality which Roscher wants to catch in his net of laws can be integrated into the envisaged conceptual system in such a way that the system really contains those elements of the phenomena which are *essential* for our knowledge? And *if* we have to be certain that this is the case, what would then be the logical nature of those concepts? Has Roscher recognized these logical problems for what they are? –

In method[olog]ical matters, Roscher followed the example of the approach of the German historical school of jurisprudence, ‹5› whose method he expressly referred to as being analogous to his own. In fact, however – and this was already in essence clear to Menger – [Roscher performed] a characteristic *reinterpretation* of that method. What mattered to Savigny and his school in their struggle against the legislative rationalism of the Enlightenment was to demonstrate that law which originated in and obtained for a national community had a fundamentally irrational character which could not be derived from general principles. They emphasized the inseparable connection between law and all other aspects of national life; and in order to make clear that any truly national legal system must *necessarily* have an individual character, they hypostatized the concept of the – *necessarily* irrational and individual – "genius of the nation" as being the creator of law, language and the other cultural assets of nations. In this connection,[1] the concept of the "genius of the nation" is treated not as a temporary receptacle – an auxiliary concept used to designate provisionally a multitude of perceivable individual phenomena which had not yet been subjected to logical treatment – but as a unitary real entity with metaphysical character; it is viewed not as the *resultant* of innumerable cultural influences, but, on the contrary, as the *real cause* of all individual cultural manifestations of the nation, which *emanate* from it.

Roscher stood squarely within this intellectual set of ideas, which in its origins goes back to certain lines of thought of Fichte's. As we shall see, he, too, believed in the metaphysical unitary nature of the "national character"[2] and saw the "nation" as an *individual*[3] which in itself

---

Literature, pp. 203ff, see esp. p. 209) and in the Preamble to the first edition of Bücher's *Origins*: "All the lectures are governed by a uniform conception of the *law-like* course of the historical development of economics". Since it would be odd to use the term "law" to refer to a *unique* development, the meaning can only be either: that the law-like course of the development will – as Roscher assumes – recur with respect to the scientifically *important* points discussed by B[ücher] wherever a development occurs at all, or (more probably): "law-like" and "causal" conditionality are identified with each other because we currently use the term "law of causality".

1   While this was by no means universal or true of *all* representatives of the historical school of law, it did apply to their successors in the domain of economics.

2   See [his] comments on the relationship between national character and geographical circumstances in §37 of the *System*, in which he almost naïvely attempts to maintain [that] the status of the "genius of the nation" as a primary "original element" [constitutes an argument against] the possibility of a "materialist" interpretation.

3   Here, the way of reasoning in Herbart's psychology ‹6› about the relationship between the individual and the totality has no doubt played a role, the precise extent of which is, however, difficult to estimate and uninteresting in the present context. Roscher occasionally (§§16, 22) quotes or refers to Herbart. On the other hand, the "national psychology" of Lazarus and Steinthal ‹7› is of course of more recent date.

experiences the gradual development of economy, like that of the political constitution or of law, as part of its vital processes – which [Roscher] conceived as analogous to the development of the life of human beings. "The national economy comes into being together with the nation. It is a natural product of the predispositions and instincts which make human beings human."[1] The concept of "nation" in itself is not discussed further in this connection. But the fact that Roscher occasionally ([*System*,] §12, note 2) applauds Fichte and Adam Müller for their opposition to the "atomistic" conception of the nation as a "mass of individuals" in itself seems to indicate that [the "nation"] should not[, in his opinion,] be seen as an abstract generic concept with little substantive content. He is (§13) too cautious to unreservedly regard the concept of the "organism" as an *explanation* of the essence of the "nation" or the "national economy"; instead, he emphasizes that he only wishes to employ the concept [of "organism"] as "the shortest common expression of a large number of problems". But one point at least emerges clearly from these remarks: he is not satisfied with the purely rationalistic view of the "nation" as being the totality of politically associated citizens at some given time. In place of this generic concept, formed by means of abstraction, he saw [the "nation"] as the *intuitable* totality of a complete entity which was *significant* as a bearer of culture.

Now, in order to be able to construct concepts that are *historical* and not emptied of [substantive] content as a result of abstraction, the logical processing of these infinitely manifold totalities would have to bring into relief those of their constituent elements which are *significant* in the *concrete* context which is being discussed. Roscher was quite aware of the principles defining the nature of this task: he is in no way a stranger to the logical nature of historical concept formation. He knows that it presupposes a *selection* from the multiplicity of the perceptually given, [a selection] oriented not towards the *generic* features, but towards the "historically" *essential* ones.[2] But here, the "organic" theory of society[3] intervenes, with its unavoidable biological analogies, and gives him the idea – which he has in common with so many modern "sociologists" – that [the generic] is identical with [the significant] and that, consequently, the recurrent elements of history must, as such, be its only significant parts.[4] Therefore, Roscher believes that he can treat the perceivable multiplicity of "nations", without further elucidation of the concept of "nation", in the same way as biologists treat the perceivable multiplicity of, say, "elephants" of a particular type.[5] In his view, "nations" are in reality as different from each other as individual human beings; but just as the differences between human beings do not prevent those engaged in anatomical and physiological inquiry from abstracting from those differences, so the individual distinctive character of nations does not prevent the historical theorist from treating them as specimens of their genus, nor from comparing them with each other as they develop, in order to find *parallelisms* in this development; and Roscher believes that by steadily perfecting these observations, those parallelisms can eventually be elevated to the status of "laws of nature" which hold for the "nation" as a genus. – In a given case, a complex of regularities discovered in this way may have considerable provisional *heuristic*

---

1   *System*, Vol. 1, §14.

2   See the discussion of the concept "Denmark" on p. 19 of his *Thucydides*.

3   As already mentioned, Roscher refers to Adam Müller in particular as the author who has the merit of [defining] the state and the economy as an entity alongside and "above the individual and even above generations" (*System*, vol. I, 12, note 2). But see, on the other hand, his reservations in *System*, vol. I, §28, note 1.

4   This is already his view in *Thucydides,* p. 21, in spite of all the reservations [in the same work], pp. XI and XII of the Preamble and pp. 20 and 188.

5   As we shall see, Knies was also of the opinion that what is understood by "nation" is directly intuitable and evident and does not need *conceptual* analysis.

value. Nevertheless, it is obvious that it could never be considered the final cognitive *goal* of any science – a "natural" [science] or [a science of the] "human spirit", a science of "laws" or a science of "history".[1] Let us assume that [such a "science"] had succeeded in discovering vast numbers of "empirical" laws covering the course of historical events. Even in that case, it would, above all, still lack any kind of *causal* transparency; the parallelisms [that Roscher hoped could be found] would just constitute the material which this science could only then start processing; and in so doing, it would above all have to decide what *kind* of knowledge it was aiming at. Either, [(1) such a "science"] would be looking for knowledge that was exact in the same sense as in the natural sciences. Then, the aim of the logical processing of the material would be the progressive elimination of the remaining individual elements, and the progressive subordination of those "laws" that had been discovered, as special cases occurring under relatively individual conditions, under even more general ["laws"]; but this would also mean that the general concepts to be formed would to an increasing degree be emptied of [substantive] content, and that the[ir] distance from empirical and intelligible reality would increase. The logical ideal [of such a science] would be a system of *formulas* that would have absolutely general validity and that would, in abstract form, represent what was common to all historical occurrences. It is obvious that historical reality, including those events and cultural phenomena to which we ascribe the greatest possible "epochal" significance and importance, could never be deduced

---

1   As is well known, Dilthey employs the first, and Windelband and Rickert the second, distinction in their attempt to elucidate the distinctive logical character of history. It is one of Rickert's basic theses that the way in which psychical objects are "given" to us *cannot* furnish the basis for a specific distinction between history and the natural sciences that would be of fundamental importance for the way in which the concepts [of these sciences] are formed. The point of departure of Gottl, (in *Dominance of Words*), who builds on Dilthey, is that there is not just a "logical", but an "ontological" difference between inner "experiences" and "external" phenomena. The standpoint on which this study will be based is close to that of Rickert inasmuch as he – in my opinion quite correctly – takes as his point of departure the assumption that "psychical" or "mental" phenomena (however one defines those ambiguous terms) can in principle be subsumed under generic concepts and laws just as much as "inanimate" natur[al phenomena]. It is in no way specific to the concepts and laws covering "psychical" or "mental" objects to have a low degree of precision and to lack quantifiability. Instead, the question is simply whether those generally valid formulas which might be discovered [concerning such objects] have any major *cognitive* value for the *understanding* of those elements of cultural reality that are important to us. – Moreover, the following point should also be kept in mind: Gottl claims that the "primal complete interconnectedness", intuited as an inner experience, excludes the use of naturalistic causal reasoning and naturalistic abstraction (it would be truer to say that it means that this reasoning and abstraction are often useless for gaining knowledge of what is important for us); however, we would also be faced with this "primal universal interconnectedness" in the field of inanimate nature (and not only with regard to biological objects, for which Gottl makes an exception) *as soon as* we attempted to grasp the total concrete reality of a process of nature. That we do not attempt to do this in the natural sciences is owing not to the substantive character of its material, but to the distinctive logical character of its cognitive goal.

  On the other hand, even if one accepts Rickert's standpoint in principle, it is beyond doubt (and Rickert himself would of course not dispute this) that the method[olog]ical distinction which his account aims at establishing is not the only possible, and in many sciences not even the most important, one. In particular, even if one accepts Rickert's thesis that the objects of "external" and "inner" experience are "given" to us in basically the same way, it still remains true – contrary to his strongly emphasized view that "the life of other minds is fundamentally inaccessible" – that the course of human action and every sort of human expression are susceptible to *meaningful interpretation*; in the case of other objects, an analogous interpretation would only be possible in the sphere of metaphysics. It is owing to [the possibility of] this meaningful interpretation that, for instance, the logical character of certain kinds of economic knowledge has a peculiar affinity to mathematics which many, including Roscher, have emphasized, and which has profound consequences, although these are often exaggerated,

from those formulas.[1] Causal "explanation" would simply consist in the formation of *more general* relational concepts, with the aim of reducing, as far as possible, all cultural phenomena to purely quantitative categories of some kind, as for instance relations of "intensity" between as few and as simple psychical "factors" as possible. Methodologically speaking, the question whether this would give the course of [events in] the reality which surrounds us, in its concrete causal context, greater empirical "intelligibility" would necessarily be unimportant.

If, on the contrary, [(2)] the aim [of such a science] were that of acquiring an intellectual *understanding* of the reality which surrounds us, as it has developed [as a result of] its necessarily individual conditions and in its necessarily individual context, then the necessary treatment of the parallelisms [mentioned above] must have the single aim of creating an awareness of the characteristic *significance* of single, concrete cultural elements, with their concrete causes and effects which are *intelligible* to our "inner experience".[2] The parallelisms themselves would then be nothing more than tools for the comparison of several historical phenomena, in their full individuality, with the purpose of bringing out what is characteristic about each one of them. The [parallelisms] would be an indirect way of going from the individual multiplicity of what is perceptually given to us – a multiplicity which is boundless, and therefore insufficiently intelligible – to an image of that multiplicity, an image which is no less individual, but not boundless because those elements which are significant to us have been brought out, and which is therefore *intelligible*. In other words: the parallelisms would be one of many possible tools for constructing *individual* concepts. However, the question whether the parallelisms could be a useful tool for this purpose – and, if so, in what instances – is quite problematical, and must be decided in each individual case. The reason for this is that, a priori, there is of course not the slightest probability that the generic features comprehended in the parallelisms would contain precisely that which was *significant* and essential in the concrete context. If this point is not kept in mind, the parallelisms might lead research into completely blind alleys, as has in fact all too often been the case. And one thing is completely certain: the idea that the ultimate *goal* of concept formation would be to subordinate concepts and laws, established with the aid of the parallelisms, under concepts and laws with ever greater general scope (and therefore with ever more abstract content) would then, self-evidently, be impossible.

[Thus, we have described] two possible approaches: either the *generic* features are selected as being those worth knowing about and subordinated under generally valid abstract *formulas*; or

---

for instance by Gottl. The [meaningful] interpretation opens the possibility of taking this step beyond what is "given"; and, in spite of Rickert's objections, it is this possibility that provides the specific justification for classifying as a special group ([viz.] the sciences of the human spirit) those sciences which employ such interpretations for method[olog]ical purposes. In accepting this, one need not fall into the error of thinking that those sciences must be grounded in an (as yet undeveloped) systematic science of social psychology that would have a role similar to that of mathematics (this point will be discussed later).

1   This would be impossible not only in practice, but also in principle, because of the logical nature of "law-like" knowledge: the formulation of "laws" – relational concepts with general validity – is identical with the progressive depletion of conceptual content by means of abstraction. Even conceived as an infinitely remote ideal, the demand that the substantive content of reality should be "deduced" from general concepts would be absurd (as will be shown below with the aid of a concrete example). When Schmoller, in his rejoinder to Menger (Schmoller, *Methodology*, p. 979), writes that: "All perfect science is deductive: when one has complete mastery of the elements, even the most complex [phenomenon] can only be a combination of [those] elements", he – in my view – makes concessions that are not even valid in those areas to which exact law concepts can most specifically be applied. We shall return to this point later.

2   If, at this point, we accept that expression without [subjecting it to] closer analysis.

the individually *significant* features are selected and ordered in universal – but individual – *interconnections*.[1] With respect to the phenomena of historical development of culture, a third approach would obviously be possible: to attempt, basing oneself on the Hegelian theory of concepts, to surmount the "hiatus irrationalis" ‹8› between concept and reality by forming "general" concepts – metaphysical realities in which individual things and events are comprehended and can be deduced as instances of *realization* [of these concepts]. The adoption of this "emanationist" view ‹9› of the nature and validity of the "ultimate" concepts makes it logically permissible, on the one hand, to conceive the relationship of the concepts to reality as being strictly *rational* (that is to say, reality can be deduced as descending from the general concept) and, on the other hand, to comprehend this relationship as having at the same time a completely intuitable character (that is to say, reality, in *ascending* towards the concepts, loses none of its intuitable content). In this case, the content and the scope of the concepts are not, quantitatively speaking, inversely proportional; on the contrary, they are congruent, as the "single case" is not only a specimen of the genus but also a part of the whole represented by the concept. The most "general" concept, from which everything could be deduced, would then at the same time be the richest in content. However, we are constantly kept away from conceptual knowledge of this kind by our analytical–discursive cognition, ‹10› which by means of abstraction divests reality of its full actuality; and such conceptual knowledge could only be accessible to a [form of] cognition analogous (but not similar) to that [by which we acquire] knowledge in the field of mathematics.[2,3] And the metaphysical precondition of the substantive *truth* of such knowledge would be that the contents of the concepts would, as metaphysical realities, stand behind [empirical] reality, which could with necessity be deduced from these conceptual contents, in a way similar to that in which mathematical propositions "follow" from each other. – As for Roscher, he was by no means unfamiliar with the problem implicit in this way of thinking.

His relation to Hegel[4] was determined by the influence of his teachers: Ranke, Gervinus and Ritter.[5] In *Thucydides*,[6] he formulates his objection to the method of the "philosophers"

---

1   A fundamental discussion of the different meanings of the term "general" – differences which, although they are so elementary, are so often misunderstood – is found in Rickert's article *The Universal* (1901).

2   On this point, and these problems in general, see the excellent work *Fichte's Idealism* by a very gifted student of Rickert, E[mil] Lask.

3   For the moment, we shall here deliberately leave aside the logical problems raised by the special sort of clearly intuitable evidentness that the interpretation of human motivation can achieve; these problems, which are of central importance for the science of economics, have most recently been treated by Gottl (*Dominance of Words*). We can [ignore them here], as Roscher has in no way adopted this perspective. According to him, when we attempt to attain knowledge of the interrelations of human behaviour, we do so discursively and from the outside, just as when we seek knowledge of interrelations in nature. Concerning "self-observation" as a source of knowledge, see the brief remark in his *History of Economics*, p. 1036. Here [we also find] the oft-quoted passage on the relatively limited significance of the distinction between "induction" and "deduction"; the latter is identified with self-observation, but Roscher does not, here or elsewhere, pursue the logical problems which this gives rise to.

4   Roscher's detailed comments on Hegel (*History of Economics*, pp. 925ff.) are irrelevant to us, as he almost exclusively criticizes Hegel's position concerning concrete, practical questions. The only noteworthy point is the respect with which he treats the "three-stage development from the abstractly general through the particular to the concretely general", a development that, [in his words,] "is connected with one of the most profound laws of historical evolution" – without further explanation.

5   He also includes among them B.G. Niebuhr, to whom he has written a fine memorial (*History of Economics*, pp. 916f.).

6   *Thucydides*, p. 19. Here, he does not *mention* Hegel by name; later in the work (pp. 24, 31, 34, 69), he occasionally quotes him or refers to him.

in the following manner: "there is a great difference between the idea of a concept and the idea of its content"; if the "higher" concept of the philosopher is the "cause" of the lower one – in the sense that the idea of the lower concept as being part of the *conceptual* system is caused by the higher one – the historian cannot transfer this [relationship] to the real world, since every "philosophical" explanation is [a matter of] definition, while every *historical* one is [a matter of] *description*.[1] Philosophical truth and necessity are on the same level as *poetic* [truth and necessity]; they are valid "in a vacuum".[2] They necessarily lose out if they descend to the level of the historical, just as history will necessarily lose out if it wishes to assimilate the conceptual constructions of philosophy: concrete historical institutions and events cannot in any way be part of a conceptual system.[3] What gives coherence to the work of historians – and of poets – is not an ultimate *concept*, but a "comprehensive intuition".[4] This "comprehensive idea" cannot, however, be adequately grasped in a formula or a conceptual definition. Like poetry, history wishes to comprehend the fullness of life;[5] to look for analogies is a means to this end; but it is a tool "with which the inept may easily injure themselves" and which will "never be of great service even to the skilful".[6] However one may judge the details of these formulations, they do at first glance seem to indicate that Roscher had an adequate conception of the nature of historical irrationality. But many statements even in the same work show that Roscher is nevertheless unaware of its significance.

[This is demonstrated by the fact that] the sole purpose of all these passages is to reject Hegel's dialectics[7] and to put history on the basis of *empirical* knowledge, *in common with the natural sciences*. Roscher is *unaware* of any difference of principle between the concept formation of the exact natural sciences and that of history. According to him, the relationship between the two is the same as that which Lessing in his *Laokoon*[8] ‹11› defines between sculpture and poetry: the differences between them are due to the *material* with which they work, not to the logical nature of the *knowledge* which they strive to attain. And history, like "philosophy" – in Roscher's sense of the term – has the "blissful task" of "ordering an apparent disorder" according to general principles".[9]

As the purpose of history[10] is to elucidate the way in which cultural phenomena (in the widest sense of the term) are causally conditioned, the "principles" referred to can only be those governing causal relations. And, here, Roscher makes the peculiar statement[11] that, when several objects are connected causally, it is the normal practice of science – in fact of *every* science – "to *designate* what seems *more important* as the *cause* of the less important". This statement, whose emanationist origins are plain for all to see, is only intelligible if we assume that, by "more important", Roscher means what Hegel understands by "general", and that, on the other hand, Roscher does not distinguish that which is "general" in a *generic* sense from [the Hegelian

1 *Thucydides*, p. 28.
2 *Thucydides*, pp. 24f., especially p. 27.
3 *Thucydides*, p. 29.
4 *Thucydides*, p. 22. The distinction between *artistic* and *scientific* truth is elaborated on pp. 27 and 35.
5 *Thucydides*, p. 35.
6 Preamble [to *Thucydides*], p. XII.
7 Roscher never undertook a more thorough critique of the form of Hegelian dialectic represented by Marx's *Das Kapital* . His critical comments on Marx in his *History of Economics*, pp. 1221 and 1222 (one single page!) are dreadfully thin, and demonstrate that, at that point (1874), he no longer had any awareness of Hegel's importance.
8 See *Thucydides*, p. 10.
9 *Thucydides*, p. 35.
10 *Thucydides*, p. 58.
11 *Thucydides*, p. 188.

sense of "general"]. During the further examination of Roscher's method, we shall again and again see that this assumption is in fact warranted. Roscher identified the concepts "general in a generic sense" and "comprehensive in content" with each other. Moreover, he did not distinguish between the general *validity* of the concepts (which he saw as identical with the universal interconnectedness) and the universal *significance* of their content: as we have seen, the "law-like" features of a phenomenon are[, according to Roscher,] the "essential" ones.[1] And, finally, he (like so many others, even today) finds it self-evident that, as general concepts are formed by ascending from reality by means of abstraction, it must in turn be possible to deduce reality by *descending from* these general concepts, provided they have been constructed correctly. In his *System*, he occasionally[2] refers explicitly to the analogy with mathematics and the possibility of expressing certain theorems of economics as mathematical formulas; his only fear is that the abundant character of reality might render such formulas too "complicated" to be of practical use. Roscher is unaware of any difference of principle between conceptual and perceptual knowledge: he regards mathematical formulas as abstractions formed in the same way as generic concepts. In his view, all concepts are ideational reproductions of reality,[3] while "laws" are objective norms to which "nature" stands in a relationship similar to that of the "nation" to the laws of the state. While Roscher's position is in principle distinct from Hegel's, the general character of his concept formation shows that he nevertheless makes use of metaphysical ideas which, to be consistent, could only fit into Hegelian emanationism. He does see the method of constructing parallelisms as the specific form in which causal–historical knowledge advances;[4] but it *never reaches its goal*, and, *therefore*, the whole of reality can never *actually* be deduced from the concepts constructed in this way. This [deduction] would, in his view, be possible if we ascended to the ultimate and highest "laws" of all events; [but] historical events, as we identify them, lack *necessity*:[5] we are always left with an "inexplicable background", and in fact, it is precisely and only this background which establishes the *unity* of the whole – apparently because reality emanates from it. But we are incapable of grasping and formulating it intellectually – the very task that Hegel wanted to accomplish. In Roscher's opinion, it is of no consequence whether one calls this background "*vital force* or generic type or *God's ideas*" (note the peculiar mixture of modern biological terminology with Platonic and scholastic formulations!). The task of scientific research is to "push it ever further back". That is to say: the Hegelian general concepts are present as metaphysical realities, but, precisely because they have this character, we are not capable of grasping them intellectually.

What was the obstacle which, in principle, prevented Roscher from accepting Hegel's way of transcending the limitations inherent in discursive cognition, in spite of the fact that his view of the relationship between concept and reality was fundamentally similar [to Hegel's]? The answer to this question is probably above all to be found by reference to [Roscher's] religious

---

1   This extends even to *artistic* creation: the "main feature" (what the artist tries to, and ought to, grasp in the phenomenon) is that which "*recurs* in every age, among all peoples and in every heart", and this is all that interests Roscher (*Thucydides*, p. 21, with [Goethe's] *Hermann and Dorothea* ‹12› and the speeches in [the *Peloponnesian War* of] Thucydides ‹13› as illustrative examples).

2   *System*, Vol. I, §22.

3   Among other discussions of this point, see Rickert (*Limits of Concept Formation*, pp. 245f.).

4   "Every historical judgement is based on innumerable *analogies*", as he puts it in *Thucydides*, p. 20 – a statement which, formulated *thus*, is akin to the erroneous belief that the study of (an as yet inexistent!) *psychology* is the precondition of exact historical investigation; it is also most surprising, considering [Roscher's] vigorous denunciation of the misuse of historical analogies (Preamble [to *Thucydides*], p. XI).

5   See *Thucydides*, p. 195

standpoint. As he sees it, the ultimate and highest – in a Hegelian sense: the "most general" – laws governing the course of events *are* indeed simply "God's ideas", and the laws of nature [His] decrees;[1] and [Roscher's] agnosticism concerning the rationality of reality is based on the religious idea that, in spite of their qualitative affinity, the nature of the finite, human spirit is limited, in contrast to the infinite, divine spirit. Quite characteristically, he expresses the opinion (*Thucydides*, p. 37) that philosophical speculations are a product of their age; their "ideas" are created *by us*; but on the other hand, as Jacobi says, we need "a truth whose creatures *we* are".‹14› All the driving forces which are active in history, he says (*Thucydides*, p. 188), can be assigned to one of three categories: ["]human acts, material conditions and *supra-human decrees*". The historian could only really speak of *necessity* if he were able to understand [these decrees], since the (concept of) free will permits the use of the category [of necessity] in empirical research only in cases of compulsion by the "real superiority of another will". But Roscher, like Thucydides and Ranke, holds that history analyses everything in terms of human, this-worldly, intelligible motives which are a consequence of the character of the acting person: it is in no way the purpose of histor[ical research] to *find* "God in history"; and if we ask what is then left to the τύχη of Thucydides‹15› (and Roscher's divine providence), Roscher replies (*Thucydides*, p. 195) by referring to God's preordained creation of *personalities*. The metaphysical *unity* of the "personality" (which we shall encounter again when dealing with Knies, and whose emanation is its action) is in Roscher's work based on his belief in providence. Consequently, he regarded the limitations of discursive knowledge as natural, because they followed from the conceptual essence of finiteness and were ordained by God. One might say that what immunized Roscher against Hegel's need for panlogism‹16› – which was problematical for him because it dissolved the [idea of a] personal God in the traditional sense – was not only his sober attitude as a conscientious scholar but also his religious faith (which had a similar effect on his teacher, Ranke).[2] In the scholarly work of Ranke and Roscher, the role played by the belief in God may be illustrated (if the comparison is permissible) by an analogy to the role of the monarch in a strictly parliamentary state: Here, the fact that the highest position in the state is [already] occupied – even though the incumbent is completely without personal influence on the concrete affairs of state – leads to an enormous economy of political power because it (at least relatively) diverts the existing power-holders *away from* the pure power struggle for dominance in the state and *towards* positive work in the service of the state. The same sort of gain is achieved [in Ranke's and Roscher's scholarly work] where metaphysical problems, which cannot be solved in the domain of empirical history, are from the outset excluded and left to religious belief, so that the historical work remains *untainted* by speculation. Roscher did not to the same extent as Ranke cut the umbilical cord connecting his conception of history with the "doctrine of ideas" (in the metaphysical sense). This was due to the overwhelming power of the Hegelian intellectual universe, from which even its opponents – Gervinus, for instance – were only able

1   Roscher's position concerning miracles is reserved and moderate (see *Religious Reflections*, pp. 10, 15 and elsewhere). Like Ranke, he attempted to explain concrete events solely by [reference to] natural motives. Roscher, too, would be of the opinion that, whenever God might project himself into history, our *knowledge* would come to an end.
2   On the whole, therefore, Roscher stays within the confines of Kantian analytical logic, although he did not use it correctly and probably was not completely familiar with it. On the whole, his only references to Kant are to his *Anthropology* (§11n6 of the *System*, vol. I) and to the metaphysical first principles of the theory of law and of virtue. The section on Kant in [Roscher's] *History of Economics* (p. 635f.), where he is simply, and quite superficially, disposed of as a representative of "subjectivism", is evidence of the deep dislike that Roscher, both as a historian and as a religious person, felt for all purely *formal* truth.

to free themselves slowly and in the form of Humboldt's gradually fading doctrine of ideas.[1]⟨17⟩ Evidently, Roscher was dominated by the concern that, if he abandoned every *objective* principle for structuring the enormous historical material with which he was flooded, he would either become immersed in the material or be forced to have recourse to subjective and arbitrary "views".[2] And finally, as has already been noted, he was influenced by the seductive model of the historical school of jurisprudence.

Roscher's concept of development and the irrationality of reality

Let us now consider how Roscher's epistemological standpoint – to the extent that he can be said to have had one – manifests itself in his treatment of the problem of "laws of historical development" – since, as we have seen, he saw the establishment of such laws as the purpose of history.

Naturally, the precondition of treating "nations" as *generic beings* is that the development of each nation can be seen as a typical, closed cycle of the same kind as the development of individual living creatures. In Roscher's opinion, this precondition holds, at least for all those nations where a *cultural development* has taken place,[3] as evidenced by the fact that culturally developed nations rise, mature and decline. This, as Roscher sees it, is a process which, in spite of the apparent variety of the forms [that it takes], affects all nations, as surely as [it affects] all physical individuals. As part of this vital process of nations, economic phenomena must be conceived "physiologically". In Roscher's view, nations are – as Hintze[4] very aptly puts it – "biological generic beings". Therefore – and Roscher states this explicitly – before the bar of science, the development of the life of nations is in principle *always the same*, and, in spite of appearances to the contrary, the truth of the matter is that "nothing new" happens under the sun,[5] but always the same as before, garnished only with accessory trimmings which

1 In his *Thucydides*, p. 44, Roscher quotes Humboldt's study (*Historian's Task*), which has recently again been the subject of much discussion; here, and frequently elsewhere, he also quotes Gervinus' *Theory of History*. (On the gradual disappearance of the metaphysical character of the "idea" in Gervinus' work, see (inter alia) Dippe's Jena dissertation (*Investigations*) from 1892).

2 See his polemic – in which we probably also hear the voice of his teacher, Ranke – against Droysen's standpoint concerning the question of "impartiality", ⟨18⟩ *Thucydides*, pp. 230–31. The formal character of Roscher's historical epochs (which will be discussed shortly) can no doubt also in part be explained by his striving for "objectivity". He could find no other (in his view) incontestable basis than the simple fact that nations "grow old". –

3 This is the reason why Roscher, as is well known, believed that the study of the cultural development of the nations of classical Antiquity, whose completed life cycles lie before us, would to a particularly high degree yield insights into the course of our own development. Certain early statements by Eduard Meyer still betray the influence (to a certain extent) of these lines of thought of Roscher's. However, Meyer has now – probably as a reaction to the course that Lamprecht has steered – adopted the position that, as we shall see, was already taken by Knies.

4 Hintze, *Roscher*.

5 Modern historians (v. Below, *Method*, p. 245) speak of the "crippling idea of law-like development" and invest history with the task of liberating us from the "oppressing and stupefying feeling induced by the doctrine, propounded by the natural sciences, according to which we are dependent on general laws". Roscher saw no such need. On the basis of the *religious* idea of the Last Judgement, he regarded the development of mankind as limited in time; and the fact that God had drawn up in advance the particular paths and stages of the life of nations could [in Roscher's view] no more detract from the statesman's duty to work and the pleasure that he derived from it, than an individual is paralysed by his consciousness of the fact that he will necessarily grow old and die.

Moreover, experience does *not* bear out the truth of v. Below's remark. He is otherwise an acute and extremely successful critic of a priori constructions; but, in this particular case, it is his own

are "incidental", and therefore scientifically unimportant – an approach which is evidently specific to the natural sciences.[1]

This typical course of life of all culturally developed nations must of course manifest itself in typical cultural stages. In fact, Roscher already draws this conclusion in *Thucydides* (Chapter IV). In accordance with the "main principle of all historical craft: that in every work one must rediscover humanity as a whole", the task of the historian – in this passage, Roscher is mainly thinking of the literary historian – is to compare the complete literature of Antiquity with those of the Romance and Germanic nations in order to uncover the evolutionary laws of *all* literatures. But when this comparison is then extended to the development of the arts and sciences, of world views and of social life, it establishes a succession of essentially similar stages in *all* cultural domains. Occasionally, Roscher reminds us that people have even claimed that they could taste the character of the different nations in their wines. The metaphysical soul of the nation, which finds expression in [this character], is on the one hand conceived as something constant which stays identical to itself, and from which all the "characteristic qualities" of the concrete nation emanate,[2] because the soul of the nation, exactly like the soul of the individual, is directly created by God. On the other hand, the soul of the nation is deemed to be subject to a process of development which is in all essentials the same for all nations and in every single area, analogously to the ages of man. In poetry, philosophy and historiography – indeed, in art and science in general – typical, conventional and individualistic eras succeed each other in a rigorously determined cycle that always ends in the inevitable "decline". Roscher carries out this [analysis], using examples taken from ancient, medieval and modern literature, and well into the eighteenth century;[3] and, in characteristic fashion, Roscher interprets the well-known remarks by Thucydides on the aim of his work ([*Peloponnesian War*] I, 22)‹22› as being in agreement with his own theory, according to which we can learn from history because the future "tends, like human beings, to repeat the past". Roscher's own view concerning the value of historical knowledge[4] – that it liberates us from idolization of human beings and from misanthropy by [giving us] insight into what is *"durable"* in the flux of the ephemeral – has a slightly Spinozist tinge,‹23› and, now and then, his statements sound almost fatalistic.[5]

In *Antiquity* (1849), Roscher applied this theory[6] to the area which is of interest to us here.

---

approach that is probably too "constructive". The most radical innovators have been motivated and influenced by the Calvinist doctrine of predestination, ‹19› the [doctrine of] "l'homme machine" ‹20› and the Marxist belief in [a coming] catastrophe. ‹21› We shall several times revert to this point.

1   Here and later, the term "natural science" should be understood as meaning "science of laws", that is to say, employing the *exact* method of the natural sciences.

2   See the characteristic passage in §37 of the *System*, vol. I, and the passages from *Thucydides* referred to below.

3   *Thucydides*, pp. 58, 59, 62, 63.

4   *Thucydides*, p. 43.

5   For instance the conclusion of the whole work (p. 502): "Thus, from the earliest times, the most cherished plans of declining eras have brought not the freedom and bliss which they promised, but only greater servitude and hardship."

6   Among present-day historians, it is especially Lamprecht who makes use of this kind of biological analogies and concepts. In his work, too, the nation is hypostatized as a "social–psychical" entity; and this entity is subject to an evolution that – as Lamprecht (*Herder and Kant*, p. 199) explicitly states – has a "biological character", that is to say, an evolution that proceeds in "typical", "regular" evolutionary stages and according to definite *laws*. The evolution takes the form of "constant growth of the psychical energy" of the nation (Lamprecht, *Cultural History*, pp. 109f.): it is the task of science, taking as its object nations with "completed development" (another Roscherian idea), to observe and to "explain causally (?)" how those typical cultural epochs, which occur in every "normally developed" nation,

The economy is obviously no exception to the general phenomenon of the typical succession of stages. Roscher distinguishes between three typical stages of the economy, according to which of the three typical factors of goods production – "nature", or "work", or "capital" – is the predominant one; and he believes that it must be possible to demonstrate three corresponding periods "in every fully developed nation".

From our contemporary point of view with its Marxist orientation, it would be quite obvious to regard the development of a nation's life as being *determined* by those typical stages of the economy; and, if we assume the correctness of Roscher's thesis according to which the development of culture leads to the demise of nations, it might be equally obvious for us to try to demonstrate that this stemmed from certain inevitable consequences of the domination of "capital" for the life of the state and of individual persons. Roscher was so little concerned with this possibility that, in the discussion of basic principles in his *System*, he merely refers to the theory of the typical stages of the economy[1] as a possible criterion of *classification* (§28), and does not base his further discussion on it. Instead, he believes that the problem of the underlying vital process as such – that is to say, the question *why* nations grow old and perish – is impossible to answer, just as we cannot find a law of nature explaining the fact that human beings must, with inescapable necessity, die – a fact which is nevertheless unquestioned. For Roscher, death is implicit in the "essence" of finiteness,[2] and the fact that, empirically, it occurs without exception can perhaps be interpreted metaphysically, but is not amenable to any exact causal explanation;[3] in du Bois-Reymond's words: it is a "world riddle". ‹25›

necessarily grow out of each other. The passages from Roscher's *Thucydides*, chapter 4, quoted in [Lamprecht's] text, anticipate both Lamprecht's "diapasons" (!) ‹24› and his – very amateurish – constructions of art history; and the same can be said of the categories (with the exception of "animism" and "symbolism" on one hand and "subjectivism" on the other) according to which the epochs are differentiated. The logical device employed by L[amprecht] – hypostatization of the "nation" as the collective bearer of those psychical processes, which should, in his view, be discussed by "social psychology" – is the same as in every "organic" theory. The reliance on the "law of large numbers" for substantiation of the claim that the changes in comprehensive social phenomena are "law-like", although the "individual" is empirically "free", also reappears in Lamprecht's work, albeit in veiled form.

The difference between Roscher and Lamprecht derives exclusively from Roscher's sober and scrupulous approach: he has never believed that it was possible to *formulate* the *essence* of the unitary cosmos in one or a few abstract concepts; and while he in *practice* employed his [conceptual] scheme, within certain limits, for purposes of organization and illustration, he would never have prejudiced his scientific work by giving it the *aim* of substantiating [that scheme]. See the discussion (referred to above, pp. 12–13) in Roscher's *Thucydides*.

1 Contained in Roscher's *Views*, vol. I, in the essay on *Antiquity*, which, as already indicated, [originally] appeared in 1849.

2 See the highly characteristic remarks at the end of §264 [of the *System*], with footnotes. The argument has a pronounced religious tinge; its logical character is clearly emanationist, but [notice] how careful Roscher is in avoiding a direct appeal to a divine order in his formulation!

3 Consequently, when dealing ([*System*], §264) with the "demise" of nations, Roscher contents himself with some fairly vague remarks in which the "inevitable erosion of all ideals" and the "enervation through pleasure" play a role. In his *History of Economics* (p. 922), [Roscher], basing himself on remarks by Niebuhr, describes the disappearance of the middle classes at certain stages of culture as "the principal form of ageing of highly cultured nations". R[oscher]'s standpoint, with its optimism conditioned by religion, has no inner affinity with the modern historico-philosophical cultural pessimism found in, for instance, the scholarly work of Vierkandt. – In later editions of his *System* (§16n7), Roscher's view that every "organism", and *consequently* also the "life of the nation", must "necessarily" be subject to "decay" is explicitly reaffirmed as a point on which he must differ from Schmoller. – Basing himself on Aristotle's *Politics*, V, 7, 16, ‹26› Roscher goes so far (*Thucydides*, p. 469) as to call

Even if Roscher's position concerning the philosophy of history had been different, he would naturally have found it difficult to solve the *logical* problem of establishing a firm connection between[, on the one hand,] this basic biological scheme of development and[, on the other,] empirical research which took individual facts as its point of departure and proceeded by way of the construction of parallelisms. The proposition that nations by necessity grow old and die simply has a different logical character from that of a law of motion based on abstraction, or from a mathematical axiom which is intuitively evident. Understood as an *abstract* proposition – to the extent that this would be at all possible[1] – it would of course be completely *empty of content*, and therefore could not render the services to Roscher that he expects from it: When he [explains economic developments by] referring to the ages of nations, his intention is clearly not to subsume economic processes under a general concept as *specimens*, but to incorporate the course of those processes causally into a *universal interconnectedness* of events of which they are *component parts*.[2] Consequently and self-evidently, the concepts of national "ageing" and "dying" must be understood as being more comprehensive in content; the process of "ageing" and "dying" should be regarded as infinitely complex, and the knowledge not only of its empirical regularity but also of its *law-like necessity* (this is Roscher's assumption) could only, in its axiomatic form, be revealed intuitively. From the point of view of science, there would be two possible [ways of looking at] the relationship between the total process and the economic partial processes: Either the goal is seen as being that of explaining the (in Roscher's view) constantly recurring complex process as a result of constantly recurring individual processes – a goal that one can attempt to approach by demonstrating the law-like necessity of the succession and the interconnections of the partial processes. In that case, the total process designated by the more comprehensive concept [mentioned above] will become the resultant of the individual partial processes. Roscher did not make this attempt, since he viewed the matter differently and saw the total process (ageing and dying) as the cause.[3] We shall see later on that, in line with his position regarding discursive knowledge,[4] he maintained that, in economics as well, the view [according to which the total process is a resultant] was impossible not only in practice but also in principle. Or one can adopt the position of emanationism and construe empirical reality as the emanation of "ideas" from which the individual processes must necessarily be conceptually derivable; the highest of these ideas must manifest itself as intuitively perceivable

it one of the "most profound laws of evolution" that *the same* "forces" which raise a nation to the pinnacle of its cultural development will, as they continue to act, cast it down again from [that eminent position]. This brings him to formulate (§264n7 in his *System*) the following phrase: "Great rulers who are famed for having conquered the world by their determination would, fifty years later, quite certainly (!) have lost the world again by that same determination." These constructions are half Platonic, half Hegelian in form, but with a religious turn: the "idea" of *finitude* implicit in the necessity of that course of events is firmly ordained by God.

1   As far as the "death" of nations is concerned, this would only be possible if the concept of "nation" were to be identified with the political organization of the state, conceived generically – that is to say, if the concept of a "nation" were to be *depleted* in a rationalist manner. [The same procedure applied to the concept of] "ageing" would merely yield the idea of a considerable lapse of time – an idea that is empty of content.

2   Admittedly, Roscher himself is completely unaware of the fundamental logical difference [between the two procedures]. Characteristically, he identifies ([*System*,]§22n3) conceptual abstraction with analysing an *interconnectedness* into its component parts. The dissection of muscles and bones by the anatomist is, in Roscher's eyes, analogous to abstraction.

3   Here, we may recall what Roscher said in *Thucydides* about the principle of causality: what is "more important" must be regarded as the real cause, from which the individual phenomena emanate. See pp. 13–14.

4   See p. 14.

in the complex total process. But, as we have seen, Roscher did not take this position, either, for two reasons: first, because he regarded the content of such an "idea" – which would from his standpoint necessarily have been a *divine* one – as lying beyond the limits of our cognition; and, second, because his conscientiousness as a historical scholar preserved him from believing that reality could be deduced from concepts.

However, this meant that his *method[olog]ical* standpoint remained inconsistent with his fundamental idea of the laws of historical development.[1] It is true that Roscher's comprehensive historical scholarship manifests itself in his collection and inspired interpretation of enormous quantities of historical facts; but (as already strongly emphasized by Knies) one cannot say that [Roscher had] a consistently applied *method*, not even when investigating the historical *succession* of economic institutions, to which he attributes so much importance.

Roscher adopts just the same attitude in his writings on the development of the forms of *political* organization.[2] By means of historical parallelisms, he tries to work out a (supposed) regularity in the succession of state forms; according to him, this succession has the character of a development which is to be found in all culturally developed nations: one may find exceptions to it, but they can be completely explained in such a way that they do not invalidate the rule but instead confirm its validity. No attempt is made to place the (allegedly) typical stages of political development in the context of the general culture of the individual nations, nor to explain them empirically. They are simply stages in the process of maturation, which the "nation", as a generic being, experiences in the course of its life;[3] but although [Roscher] provides a huge amount of factual material, [he makes] no attempt to explain *how* this process of "experiencing" actually comes about – because, as we know, he believes that it cannot be explained. –

One finds the same reasoning, in even more striking form, in Roscher's analysis of *concurrent* economic processes and their mutual "static" interconnection – the task to which [economic] theory had hitherto essentially limited itself. Here, too, the consequences of Roscher's "organic" conception manifest themselves at once in the discussion of the concept of "national economy". Understandably, he regards the "national economy" as something more than a simple aggregate of individual economies, just as its analogue, the human body, is not merely "a welter of chemical effects". – Before and after Roscher's time, the fundamental problem of economics, both substantively and methodologically, has been the following: How can we explain the formation and the continued existence of institutions of economic life which, although they were *not* created collectively for a particular purpose, seem to us to function purposively? – In exactly the same way, the problem of how to explain the "purposiveness" of organisms dominates [the science of] biology. When we consider concurrent economic phenomena, the question is therefore: in what conceptual form can we scientifically construe the relationship between the individual economies and the context in which they are enmeshed? In Roscher's opinion – which he shares with his predecessors and most of his successors – this question can only be answered on the basis of certain assumptions concerning the psychological roots of the *action of individuals*.[4] Here, Roscher's method[olog]ical position again exhibits those contradictions

1   In his memorial address (*Roscher*), Bücher voices his regret that Roscher "did not rely on the conceptual apparatus of his own science" for his formulation of the principle of periodization. But Roscher (like Knies, as will be shown below) simply was not convinced that this was at all possible, and, if so, to what extent it would be valuable from a method[olog]ical point of view (and, indeed, this is certainly not in itself self-evident).
2   Collected as *Politics*.
3   See the apt remarks by Hintze [in his] *Roscher*.
4   Here we shall leave aside the question whether this view is method[olog]ically correct.

which, as we have seen above, came to the fore in his philosophy of history. Since Roscher announces that he wishes to observe the processes of life historically, that is to say: in their full reality, one would assume that he would focus his attention on the constant influence that *non-economic* factors also exert on the economic action of human beings: the *causal heteronomy of the human economy*.⟨27⟩ This has, since the work of Knies, been the approach taken by the historical school of economics in contrast to the classical economists.

However, Roscher continues to maintain that the fundamental task of [economic] science is to formulate economic *laws*. Therefore, here again the following problem then ought to arise: how is it possible, on the one hand, to abandon [the method of isolating abstraction] in favour of the reality of life and, on the other, still to retain the possibility of acquiring knowledge in the form of law-like concepts? As far as Roscher is concerned, he did not recognize this difficulty at all; what helped him to surmount it was the extremely simple psychology on which he based his analysis, following Enlightenment psychology⟨28⟩ with its concept of the "instinct".

Roscher's psychology and its relationship to classical theory

For Roscher, human beings are in all respects, and [therefore] also in the domain of economic life, dominated, on the one hand, by the striving for worldly goods: self-interest; and on the other hand, by a second, comprehensive, basic driving force: the "love of God", which comprises the "ideas of equity, justice, benevolence, perfection and inner freedom" and which nobody lacks completely (*System*, Vol. I, §11).

As regards the relation between the two driving forces, Roscher's work contains the rudiments of a purely "utilitarian" derivation of the driving forces directly from enlightened self-interest.[1]

But this line of thought is not pursued further; instead, Roscher, in accordance with his religious views, [believes that] it is the higher, divine instinct which restrains the worldly self-interest to which it is and must be opposed,[2] permeating it in the most varied proportions and thereby creating those different gradations of the *sense of common good* which underpin the life of the family, the community, the nation and humankind. The narrower the social spheres with which the sense of common good is concerned, the closer that spirit is to self-interest; the wider the spheres, the more the public spirit approximates a striving after the Kingdom of God. Thus, the different social driving forces of human beings are conceived as the forms in which a basic religious impulse manifests itself in combination with self-interest.

One would expect that this conception would lead Roscher to attempt to offer a purely empirical explanation of the origins of the individual processes and institutions as consequences

---

1   §11: "Even a purely calculating intellect must admit that countless institutions . . . are necessary . . . for every individual, but that they are impossible [to achieve] without the sense of common good, because no single individual would be able to make the necessary sacrifices." – For quite a similar view, see Roscher, *History of Economics*, p. 1034, where the following remark, which is quite typical of the pseudo-ethics that historicism risks falling prey to, has slipped in: "The wider the circle of those who benefit and the further into the future they try to look, the more closely the demands of reasonable self-interest coincide with those of *conscience*."

2   In this connection, Roscher ([*System,*] §11n6) refers to the remarks in Kant's *Anthropology* on virtue limiting the propensity to a life of luxury. Later on, Roscher comes to regard the "sense of common good" as the emanation of an objective social *force*: in the later editions, he underlines that, by "sense of common good", he means essentially the same as that which Schmoller calls "proper behaviour" ⟨29⟩. As we shall see, Knies disagrees with this in the second edition of his main work [*Economy²* (1883)].

of the operation of those two driving forces, in proportions which would have to be determined in each case.[1]

But Roscher proceeded in a different way. He, too, had to acknowledge that in the specific domains of modern economic life – in the transactions of stock exchanges and banks, in the modern wholesale business, and in those areas of goods production which had been subject to capitalist development – there were in reality no indications that "economic" self-interest was in any way modified by other "instincts".

Accordingly, Roscher took over, unconditionally, the whole conceptual apparatus and system of laws of classical economics, which were constructed on the basis of self-interest. Hitherto, German theorists – in particular Hermann, but also Rau – had posited not only the complete predominance of self-interest in *private* economic life[2] but, equally, the predominance of the sense of common good in *public* life.[3] In this context, we find, as characteristic elements of the "classical" conception, on the one hand, [the position] that the whole sphere of human activity was divided into private economy and public functions,[4] and, on the other, that "Is" and "Ought" were seen as identical.[5] Roscher, however, rejects this view, because, as he says (suddenly abandoning his psychology), self-interest and the sense of common good "are neither coordinated nor even exhaustive opposites".

Instead, Roscher, for his part, puts forward a third conception of the relationship of self-interest to social life in common, with the remark: "It [self-interest] is transfigured into an instrument accessible to temporal reason, but working towards the realization of an eternally ideal purpose."[6]

This immediately gives one the impression of being back on the ground of the optimistic eighteenth-century theories of "self-interest".[7]⟨30⟩

Mandeville, in his fable of the bees,⟨31⟩ in his own way both posed and solved the problem of the relationship between private and public interests by means of the formula "private vices,

---

1 Classical theory did not have this problem, as it proceeded from the assumption that, in the domain of economic life, only *one* constant and simple motive *should be taken into account by science*: [this motive was] "self-interest", which in the market economy manifests itself in the endeavour to maximize private economic profit. From the perspective of classical theory, the exclusive interest in this driving force in no way implied an *abstraction*.

2 As is well known, this principle was not implemented consistently, even by Rau. He contented himself with the basic assumption that the predominant influence of the "compelling natural driving force" of self-interest was the *normal* [state of affairs]; as for other, contrary motives of an "unworldly" and "lofty" nature, they could not, at any rate, be considered a relevant basis for the formulation of "laws" – because they are irrational. (It went without saying that the formulation of *laws* was the only possible goal of science.)

3 In "pre-historical" economic theory, man was *not*, as assumed by contemporary theory, abstract *economic* man, but, even in the economic field, the abstract *citizen* of the rationalist theory of the state. This view manifests itself in characteristic fashion in Rau's work (*Economics*, §4): "The state consists . . . of a number of men who live together under the rule of law. They are called citizens to the extent that they . . . enjoy certain rights; their totality is the people – the nation, as it is termed in political science." Rau considers this to be different from the concept of the nation "in the historical–genealogical sense, with reference to descent and individuation" (See Knies, *Economy*, p. 28).

4 A more thorough examination would demonstrate that this distinction is rooted in certain, quite definite, *Puritan* ideas which have been of very great importance for the "genesis of the capitalist spirit".

5 It will be recalled that A[dam] Smith (unlike Mandeville and Helvetius), did *not* posit this identity as far as the predominance of self-interest in private life was concerned.

6 *System*[2], p. 17 (Vol. I, §11).

7 Peculiar echoes of these theories may perhaps already be found in Mammon's speech to the fallen angels in Milton's "Paradise Lost"; ⟨32⟩ indeed, [Roscher's] whole idea constitutes a sort of inversion of puritan modes of thought.

public benefits"; and many later writers leaned, consciously or unconsciously, to the opinion that it was decreed by *providence* that economic self-interest was the force "which would do evil constantly and constantly does good".‹33› But [all these writers] believed that self-interest, directly and without any break, just as it was, served (in their words) the "divine" or "natural" cultural goals of mankind.

The limits of discursive knowledge and the metaphysical causality of organisms in Roscher's work

Roscher, on the other hand (*System*, Vol. I, §11, note 6), explicitly rejects this view of Mandeville's and the [writers of the] Enlightenment. The reasons for his rejection are to be found partly in the religious domain,[1] partly – and this again brings us to the ultimate cause of all these contradictions – in the epistemological consequences of his "organic" conception. When dealing with phenomena that – like ground rent, interest and wages – manifest themselves as vast numbers of recurrent *individual* events and direct relations between private economies, Roscher saw no problem in explaining them as being derived from interlocking private economic acts guided by self-interest. But he refused to extend this explanation to those social institutions which cannot exhaustively be viewed in the same way as the phenomena mentioned above, and which manifest themselves as "organic" structures – "purposive systems", in Dilthey's terminology.‹35› As Roscher sees it, it is not only those forms of human communal life which, like the state or law, are based on the *sense of common good*, which cannot be conceived in this manner. In his view, the sphere of purely economic relationships as a *whole* is not susceptible, either, to that sort of explanation, or indeed to any purely causal one, because "cause and effect cannot be identified independently". Roscher adds by way of explanation that this statement should be understood to mean that, in the domain of social life, every effect will, or at least may, conversely be a cause, and that all individual phenomena "are reciprocally conditioned by each other". Therefore, Roscher says, every causal explanation is circular,[2] and the only means of escaping from this circle is the assumption that *the sphere in its totality possesses an organic*

---

1   *Religious Reflections*, p. 33, Roscher, with a simple clarity that many modern evolutionists would profit from, rejects both the presumption that one must see something akin to a theodicy in history and the external course of human life, and Schiller's formula according to which "the history of the world" is "the court of final judgement of the world". ‹34› Roscher's religious faith led him to dispense altogether with the leitmotif of "*progress*": the idea of "progress" only presents itself as a necessity when the course of human fate no longer has religious significance, and one feels a need to endow it with a this-worldly, but nevertheless objective, "meaning". (As is well known, *Ranke*, both as a sober scholar and as a religious person, also had a cool inner attitude with regard to the concept of "progress".)

2   *System*, vol. I, §13. – Roscher had already made similar statements in his *Thucydides* (p. 201), where he claims, quite generally, that every *successful* historical explanation is *circular*; he derives this peculiarity of discursive knowledge from the *co-ordination* of the real objects which the sciences of empirical experience deal with, in contrast to the subordination of concepts in (Hegelian) philosophy. ‹36› But [Roscher's *Thucydides*] does not yet contain the fundamental distinction between history and (inanimate) *nature*, and his discussion of it [in the *System*] is still unclear. In the *System*, §13 (*System2*, p. 21), he argues that, for example, it is possible to regard the wind purely as the cause of the rotation of the sails of the windmill, while there is no simultaneous *reciprocal* causal connection (the sails as the cause of the wind?). An example that is so imprecisely formulated is patently useless. The underlying, unclear idea is akin to the view, originally advanced by Dilthey (*Ideas*, p. 1313 (bottom) and many other passages) and others, and now also by Gottl (*Dominance of Words*), [according to whom] there is a fundamental, "not only logical, but ontological" difference between the *intuited* "complete interconnectedness" of all (human) psychical objects of knowledge, and inanimate nature that can be explained "analytically". But, while Gottl concedes that the necessity of employing anthropomorphic

life, of which the individual phenomena are manifestations. In our analysis, we are again confronted with the "inexplicable background" – which we have encountered previously – of the individual phenomena; and, as we have seen, the scientific task of the analysis can only be to make [this background] recede ever further.

Here, too, it is evident that what leads Roscher to postulate a fundamental obstacle to acquiring knowledge in the field of economics is not, or at least not directly, the "hiatus irrationalis" between reality, which is always and only given concretely and individually, and those general concepts and laws which are formed by means of abstraction from the Individual. He has not the slightest doubt that, *in principle*, the concrete reality of economic life can be grasped conceptually in the form of laws. Admittedly, to do so exhaustively would require "innumerable" laws of nature – but precisely: *laws*. The object which, in his view, is not only more difficult than natural organisms[1] to analyse and explain causally, but which *must*, in principle, remain unexplained is not the irrationality of reality, which defies subsumption under "laws", but the "organic" *unitary character* of the historical–social *interconnections*. In Roscher's

concepts when we are dealing with objects of biology is a peculiarity due to the inherent nature of the[se] object[s], Roscher, on the other hand, believes that he is applying biological concepts to social life. It would go too far to provide a thorough critique of this view, and it is not for me to do so. The following should be noted, however: we can find "interaction" and "complete interconnectedness" in exactly the same sense and to exactly the same degree in the domain of inanimate nature as in that of inner experience (if we accept the fundamental difference between these two [domains]), *as soon as* we attempt to acquire knowledge of an *individual* phenomenon in its *full*, concrete, intensive infinity; moreover, closer reflection shows us that there are "anthropomorphic" elements in *all* areas of investigation of nature.

1   This is the characteristic feature of the epistemological standpoint of that "organic" view of society which *rejects* Hegel's point of view. In fact, the opposite is true: in the domain of the sciences of society, we are in the fortunate position of [being able to] observe the internal structure of "smallest elements" of which society is composed and which must permeate the whole web of its relations. Menger was the first, followed by many others, to make this point.

It is significant that the epistemological standpoint of Gierke, who in his Inaugural Rectoral Address at Berlin University in 1902 (Gierke, *Groupings*) has once again broken a lance for the "organic theory of the state", is the same as Roscher's. He considers the *essence* of [a] "total personality" to be a "mystery", which science apparently, in his view, *cannot* "unveil". This impossibility is not just provisional, but definitive and *necessary* (p. 23); that is to say: [this essence] can only be *interpreted metaphysically* (by means of "imagination" and "belief", as Gierke puts it). It is understandable that Gierke – whose argument is probably mainly directed against Jellinek's (in my opinion) conclusive critique ‹37› – continues to argue that communities have a "supra-individual unity of life". After all, this idea has been of the greatest heuristic value to him (and hence to science). But it is rather odd that Gierke, in order to believe in the power and significance of a moral idea or even (p. 22) of patriotic sentiment, needs to picture to himself the content of those sentiments as an entity (pardon the expression!); and, when he, conversely, *deduces* the real existence of his communal personality from the moral significance of those sentiments – that is to say: hypostatizes their content – the objections which Hegel raised against Schleiermacher ‹38› could be directed, with far greater justification, at Gierke. Neither (1) the cosmos of *norms* that govern a community, nor (2) the totality (viewed as a given state) of the *relations* – governed by these norms – between the individuals in the community, nor (3) the *influence* of those norms and relations on the *conduct* of individuals (viewed as a complex of processes) represent a total entity in Gierke's sense [of the term], nor do they in any way have a metaphysical character; nevertheless, all three of them are something else than a mere "summation of individual forces". Anyway, even the legally ordered *relation* between buyer and seller, together with its consequences, are something *different* from the mere *sum* of the *interests* of the two persons involved; nevertheless, there is nothing mysterious about it. In the same way, what lies behind the cosmos of norms and relations is not some mysterious living being, but a *moral idea* which governs the willing and feeling of human beings; and it is hard to believe that an idealist such as Gierke could in earnest regard the fight for ideas as a fight for "empty words".

view, what limits the acquisition of rational knowledge is not that the individual phenomena are not covered by the general concepts – and by necessity the fewer, the more general the concept – but that the universal interconnections and the existing structures, because of their dignified status as "organisms", cannot be explained [as being derived] *causally* from individual phenomena. And, in Roscher's eyes, the impossibility – not only in practice, but in principle – of explaining the totalities as being causally derived from the individual phenomena is a *dogma*, whose correctness he does not even attempt to prove. However, he in no way regards those existing structures and interconnections as standing outside all causal dependence. But they are part of a (metaphysical)[1] causal complex of a higher order, and, while we can occasionally grasp the expressions of this complex, we are unable to penetrate it in its essence – again, as Roscher sees it, by analogy with the natural processes of life. Even though Roscher ([*System*,] § 13) does not believe that the economy is "bound to nature" to the same extent as a natural organism, he finds the (metaphysical) lawfulness of even those "higher" phenomena of economic life expressed in the so-called "law of large numbers" of statistics, which demonstrates how the apparent arbitrariness of concrete, individual cases levels out into "wonderful harmonies", as soon as the interconnections are viewed as a whole.[2]

What does Roscher conclude from the difference between the social cosmos and the individual events which can in principle be analysed? Not that there is a method[ologic]al and logical limit to the extent to which reality can be covered by generic concepts and abstract laws; but that forces which transcend our knowledge project into reality. Here again, as above, we find ourselves on the threshold of emanationism. Roscher's sense of reality prevents him from claiming the status of an explanation for the view that the "organic" elements of that cosmos are emanations of "ideas". But he does not reject the view as such.

Roscher and the problem of practical norms and ideals

Finally, Roscher's position of principle[3] concerning the scientific treatment of economic *policy*[4] is explained by his cyclical theory, on the one hand, and the category of the "sense of common good" which he employs, on the other hand. First of all, the necessary consequence of the inseparable connection between the economy and the totality of cultural life must be the *heteronomy* of the striving for goals [in the domain] of economic policy. The "promotion of national wealth" – a concept which Roscher has not brought himself to reject – cannot be

1   One is reminded of the "dominants" in the biological theories recently put forward by Reinke. ‹39› It is true that Reinke has in the end divested [these dominants] of the metaphysical character that they must conceptually possess in order to serve as a valid real cause of the purposiveness of organisms, and has reinterpreted them from being a *forma formans* to being a *forma formata*. But, in so doing, he has also sacrificed whatever [these dominants] could contribute to a *speculative* view of the universe, without gaining anything from the point of view of specialized empirical research. See the controversy between Reinke and Drews ‹40› in the most recent volume of the *Preussische Jahrbücher*.
2   It hardly needs saying that this quite improper way of using the "law of large numbers" is quite far removed from Quetelet's "homme moyen". ‹41› Still, Roscher does not really reject Quetelet's method in principle (§18n2 in *System*, Vol. I). He says that statistics can only properly "regard as truly belonging to it those facts" which can be deduced from "established laws of development". The collection of *other* (unexplained) rows of figures should be interpreted as "an unfinished experiment" (§18). Here, the belief in the dominance of "laws" is combined with the common sense of the empirical researcher, who wants to *understand* reality, not to cause it to evaporate in formulas.
3   We are only concerned with the question of principle. Here, we do not have the remotest intention of attempting a systematic analysis of Roscher's views on economic policy.
4   Roscher himself underlines the fact that, in his main work, he incorporates the questions of economic policy into the relevant sections on theory.

the self-evident and only goal of economic policy, and political economy cannot simply "be chrematistics".[1] ‹42› Moreover, the knowledge that economic phenomena change over time makes it impossible for science to formulate norms which are more than relative – relative, that is, to the stage of development of the nation concerned.[2] But here, Roscher's relativism reaches its limits: he never goes so far as to attribute only *subjective* importance to the value judgements which are at the basis of the maxims of economic policy[3] – which would entail a rejection of the view that it is possible to establish norms in general with scientific precision. Roscher summarizes his method[olog]ical position as follows: He refrains in principle from elaborating general *ideals* ([*System*,] §26), and wishes to show the way "not as a guide, but as a map"; but this does *not* mean that his answer to those who turn to science to find "ideals to show the way" is: "Become what you already are".‹44› Instead, he is, at least in theory, convinced that there are *objective* foundations for the formulation of norms – norms not only for every concrete situation but, beyond that, for each of the individual, typical stages of development of the economy.[4] Economic policy is oriented towards a therapy of economic life.[5] Naturally, such a therapy is only possible when one can define a normal state of health (which will vary according to the individual state of development, but can always be ascertained objectively); and the self-evident goal of the practical economist will then be to establish this state of health and make sure that it is not disturbed, just as the doctor will do with regard to the physical organism.

The question whether it would be at all possible, without deluding oneself, to make such an assumption from the point of view of a purely this-worldly view of life will be left aside for the moment. For Roscher, the correctness of that assumption was given in principle, because of his conception (based on his philosophy of history) of the typical course of the fate of nations, coupled with his religious faith, which, for him, excluded the – otherwise unavoidable – fatalistic consequences of his theory. Admittedly, as Roscher sees it, we do not know what stage human development in general – which he conceives as a finite process in the Christian sense – has reached, nor do we know at what stage of the development of our national culture – which is

1   However, Roscher did not remain consistent with himself on this point, either. Even the strictly theoretical parts of Roscher's *System* are filled with purely material economic value judgements of the most various kinds. This begins with the "ideal" formulated in §1, which strikes one as thoroughly socialist: "That all human beings should only have completely praiseworthy needs, but that these praiseworthy needs would be absolute; and that they should be entirely clear about all the means by which [the needs] could be satisfied, and be in free possession of those means." And [so] it goes on until the discussion of the concept of productivity (§§63ff.) and the formulation of the "population ideal" in §253: "The economic development attains its summit where the greatest number of human beings simultaneously achieve the fullest satisfaction of their needs."
2   §25: "The leading-strings of the child and the crutches of the old man would be heavy chains to the [grown] man." There are "as many ideals . . . as there are national peculiarities"; moreover, "any change that affects the nations themselves and their needs will also mean that the economic ideal suitable to them will become a different one" (ibid.).
3   Nor does Roscher recognize any subjective limits to the moral imperatives in the domain of the ethics of everyday life. See [his] protest against "home-made" morals, with special reference to Goethe (*Religious Reflections*, p. 82). ‹43› In the same book, p. 76, he makes some extremely narrow-minded remarks concerning Faust.
4   See the comparison between the necessarily *individual* economic ideals of nations with the, just as necessarily *individual* (albeit objectively determinable), *measurements for the clothes* of individual persons (§25), and above all the discussion in §27, where Roscher comes to the completely utopian conclusion that all partisan conflicts can be traced back to insufficient *insight* into the true state of development.
5   *System*, vol. I, §§15, 264. – Ranke had exactly the same conception of the task of the "state economy" (*Collected Works*, vol. 24, pp. 290f.).

of course also destined to die away – we find ourselves. But Roscher argues that it is of benefit to us (which in this case means: of benefit to the politician) not to know this, just as it is an advantage for physical individuals not to know the hour of their death. And it does not prevent Roscher from believing that conscience and common sense *may* be able to reveal to the collective individual the tasks that God has given it in a particular situation, just as they may reveal those tasks to the individual human being. In any event, it stands to reason that this general position will naturally only leave economic policy with a narrowly restricted field of activity: as Roscher sees it, the "real needs of a nation" will in actual life again and again prevail unaided,[1] by virtue of the fact that the evolution of the economy has the character of a *law of nature*; the contrary assumption would contradict the belief in divine providence. Since the finite character of our discursive knowledge prevents us from grasping the *totality* of "evolutionary laws", it is perhaps in principle impossible to conceive of a *system* of imperatives of economic policy which would – even if it were only relative – be in some sense closed. But [if] in fact [it could be] developed, it would certainly not be exhaustive, any more than in the domain of political activity; and Roscher occasionally states this explicitly.

Thus, Roscher's numerous pronouncements on economic policy certainly reflect his mild, moderate and mediating personality, but certainly not any clear and consistently developed ideas. Serious and lasting conflicts are simply impossible between the march of historical destiny and the tasks which God has assigned to both individuals and nations; and the individual in no way has to face the problem of establishing his ultimate ideals on his own. Consequently, Roscher could stick to his relativist position without becoming an ethical evolutionist. He also explicitly rejected evolutionism in its *naturalistic* form,[2] but he was unable to see that the idea of *historical* evolution might imply that moral precepts could in a completely similar way lose their *normative* character – since his *own* position was secure in this [latter] respect.

---

1   *System*, Vol. I, §24. – On this point, as one can see, Roscher completely agrees with the classical economists.

2   In a critique of Kautz' *Theory and History*, Roscher says the following (§29n2) in the later editions of his work: "Kautz states that economics is based not only on history but also on the 'practical and moral human faculty of reason', together with its ideals, so that the science [of economics] becomes not only a reflection of, but also a model for the economic life of nations. However, I cannot consider th[ese two factors] as standing in real opposition to each other. Leaving aside the fact *that only the practical moral human faculty of reason is able to understand history*, the ideals of any given period are among the most important elements of its history. *In particular, it is usually in [those ideals] that the needs of a given age are reflected with the greatest clarity.* The historical[ly oriented] economist certainly lacks neither the inclination nor the ability to make plans for reforms. But he will hardly recommend them on the grounds that they are absolutely better than the present state of affairs; instead, he will demonstrate *the existence of a need* which can probably be most effectively met by [those reforms]."

The first of the passages in italics is in its way a classical answer to the question of the "lack of presuppositions" of historical research – a question which is still the subject of much dispute nowadays, and which we shall return to later. The second [of the italicized passages] contains, albeit covertly, that mixture of what will happen, what ought to happen and what is morally correct which is peculiar to evolutionary history and which we shall also discuss later. Here, the idea of historical evolution is transformed from a *method* into a world view by means of which norms can be found; and this [procedure] gives rise to the same fundamental objections as the analogous process that we can still witness today with respect to the ideas of evolution in the natural sciences. This includes, for instance, the naïve advice of many evolutionists to the effect that religion should "enter into new relationships" – as if [religion] were able to give herself away like a woman who had been unhappily married. Even when Darwinism, which he abhorred on religious grounds, was not involved, Roscher rejected ethical evolutionism in favour of his psychology, which was idealistic in a religious sense. See *Religious Reflections*, p. 75: "He who only looks downwards, at the rise [of humankind] out of [base] matter, will also regard sin, particularly cultivated sin, with great tranquillity of mind, and consider it as

To summarize: we see that, from a purely logical point of view, Roscher's "historical method" is a thoroughly inconsistent construction. [His] attempts to embrace the total reality of historically given phenomena stand in contrast to his endeavour to reduce those phenomena to "laws of nature". In trying to identify the general character of concepts with the universality of the context, Roscher, moving along the lines of an "organic" conception, comes close to an emanationism of the Hegelian kind, [although] his religious standpoint prevents him from embracing it. When he considers individual phenomena, [however], he chooses to ignore that organic conception to a certain extent, in favour of a scheme of juxtaposed conceptual systematizations, like those elaborated by the classical economists, and he explains empirically and statistically why the propositions developed within that scheme are valid in reality (or have only relative significance, as the case may be). It is only when he describes systems of economic policy that the organic–constructive ordering of phenomena according to the stages of ageing of nations remains predominant. When it comes to establishing *value* judgements for economic policy, his historically oriented relativism mostly produces negative results, insofar as the objective norms whose existence he constantly assumes are not coherently developed, or even formulated.

In relation to Hegel, Roscher['s standpoint] is not so much one of opposition, but rather represents a *regression*: In Roscher's work, the Hegelian metaphysics and the supremacy of speculation over history have disappeared, and, instead of their brilliant metaphysical constructions, we find a fairly primitive form of simple, unquestioning religious faith. But, at the same time, we do observe that this goes hand in hand with a process of recovery – one might almost say: an *advance* in the direction of unbiased or, in the clumsy modern terminology, "presuppositionless" scientific work. If Roscher did not succeed in distancing himself fully from Hegel, the main reason for this was that he did not to the same extent as Hegel recognize the methodological implications of the *logical* problem of the relationship between a concept and what it conceptualized.

II Knies and the problem of irrationality

The irrationality of action ‹46›

The character of Knies' work

The first edition of Knies' main work on methodology, *Political Economy from the Standpoint of Historical Method*, was published in 1853, before the publication of the first volume of Roscher's *System*, which Knies discussed in the "Göttinger gelehrte Anzeigen" in 1855 [Knies, *Roscher*]. Knies' work received relatively little attention outside a narrow circle of specialists. In his own view, he had occasion to complain that Roscher had not referred to him more often and discussed him more thoroughly,[1] and he got into a fierce dispute with Bruno Hildebrand. –

[a sign of] still unattained perfection; but the truth is that [sin is] the absolute evil, which is antagonistic – indeed fatal – to the innermost core of our nature."

Roscher was equally wedded to the idea of the theodicy, ‹45› which it was possible for him to maintain from a religious point of view because of his belief (which admittedly was hardly orthodox) in the continued development of the individual after death (*Religious Reflections*, p. 33, together with the almost childishly naïve passage, pp. 7–8).

1 Incidentally, [this complaint was] hardly justified: in his *System*, Roscher quotes Knies abundantly, and, in his *History of Economics*, he treats him with approval. However, it is remarkable that Roscher did not come up with any detailed reply to Knies' attacks – some of which were quite intensive – and did not modify his own position to take account of them.

Subsequently, as the Free Trade school registered one success after the other in the 1860s, the book was almost forgotten. It was only when the movement of "academic socialists" ‹47› took hold among younger [scholars] that the book again increasingly found a readership. Consequently, in 1883 – thirty years [after its first publication] – Knies was looking at a second edition of the work [*Economy²*]. (The other main work by Knies, *Money and Credit*, which was written in the 1870s, had nothing to do with the "historical" method). This second edition appeared immediately before the "quarrel about methods" ‹48› in [the discipline of] economics reached its highest temperature with [the publication of] Menger's *Investigations*, Schmoller's review of Menger's book [Schmoller, *Methodology*] and Menger's vehement rejoinder [Menger, *Errors*]. Dilthey's *Sciences of the Human Spirit*, which contained the first large-scale attempt [to establish] a logic of cognition of the *non*-natural sciences, also appeared at this time.

The analysis of Knies' work presents considerable difficulties. For one thing, its style is awkward to the point of unintelligibility. This is owing to the approach of its learned author, who writes a sentence and then, as a result of his continued ruminations, piles one subordinate clause on top of the other inside it, not caring whether the syntax of the resulting phrase comes completely unstuck.[1] The abundance of the ideas that came flooding to him sometimes led Knies to overlook even the most patent contradictions between almost adjacent sentences; consequently, his book resembles a mosaic whose component stones, of quite varied hues, are only matched broadly, but not always in detail. The additions to the second edition have on the whole not been integrated into the (almost unchanged) original text; some of them represent a clarification and further development of the ideas [presented] in the first edition, while others also represent a deliberate modification [which changes those ideas] into quite different viewpoints. If at all possible, the only way to render to the full the profoundness of the whole content of this work, which is so exceptionally rich in ideas, would be, first, to sort out the threads [of thought] which have their origin in (so to speak) different tangles of ideas and run alongside and across each other, and then to systematize separately each set of ideas.[2]

It is only in the second edition that Knies specifies his definitive view of the position of economics among the [other] sciences;[3] but he does so in a way that is wholly consistent with his lines of thought in the first edition. As he puts it, economics discusses those phenomena which stem from the fact that man is dependent on the "external world" in order to satisfy the needs "of human personal life" – a demarcation which is obviously in some respects too wide and in others too narrow when compared with the set of tasks that have historically become

---

1 For a completely impossible sentence of this sort, see *Economy¹*, p. 203.
2 Here, our only concern is to develop certain logical problems, and we therefore do not intend to provide [the reader with] such an exhaustive account. For our purposes, the *first* edition, and Knies' essays from the 1850s, ‹49› will form the basis [of our discussion]. Wherever the exposition in the second edition and in the later works, particularly *Money and Credit*, is simply an amplification of the earlier ones, it will also, as a matter of course, be taken into account; to the extent that the divergent viewpoints from the later period contain *new* logical and method[olog]ical ideas – which is only infrequently the case – they will be treated briefly, together with those rudiments that can already be found in the early works. As in [our treatment of] Roscher, this means that we are doing the exact opposite of what we would have to do if we were to give a "historical" appreciation of Knies' achievements. His formulations are viewed in their relation to scientific problems which still exist today; and the intention is not to provide a picture of Knies, but to depict the problems which must necessarily arise in our field of activity, and to show how he dealt with them – and [in fact] had to deal with them, since he based himself on certain ideas, which even nowadays have wide currency. Of course, this in no way provides an adequate picture of Knies' scientific importance; indeed, the account given in this first section must at first glance give the impression that Knies is only the "pretext" for what is being said.
3 *Economy²*, pp. 1ff., 215.

those with which our science deals. Knies wishes to derive the method of economics from its tasks [as he defines them]. Alongside the [two] groups already defined by Helmholtz according to their *object*: the "natural sciences" and the "sciences of the human spirit", ‹50› Knies therefore establishes a *third* group [of sciences], the "historical sciences"; [these are defined by him] as being the disciplines dealing with phenomena [of the] "external" [world] which are, however, *partly* determined by motives from within the "human spirit".

"Freedom of the will" and "conditioning by nature" in Knies' work, compared to modern theories

Knies takes for granted that the scientific "division of labour" consists in apportioning the objectively given factual material, and, moreover, that it is this material, assigned on objective grounds to each science, which dictates the method of that science. He approaches his discussion of the methodological problems of economics on the basis of these assumptions. Since [the science of economics] deals with human action under conditions that are partly given by nature and partly historically determined, he concludes that the following determinants "enter into" the material investigated by economists: in one respect (that of human action), the *"freedom of the will"* of human beings; and, in contrast to this, on the other hand, "elements of *necessity*": first, the blind necessitation of natural events [as it manifests itself] in the *natural* conditions, and, second, the force of collective relationships [as it manifests itself] in the historically given conditions.[1]

For Knies, as for Roscher, causality is identical to law-like regularity,[2] and he therefore, as a matter of course, regards the influence of natural and "general" relationships as being *law-like*. For Knies, the distinction between, on the one hand, purposeful human action and, on the other hand, the conditions of this action as given by nature and by the historical constellation, is therefore replaced by *an entirely different* distinction: on the one hand, "free" *and therefore irrational-individual* human action; on the other hand, the *law-like* determination of the conditions of action, as [they are] given by nature.[3] In Knies' opinion, the influence of "nature" on economic phenomena would, taken by itself, necessarily cause these phenomena to follow a law-like course. Actually, however, while the laws of nature *affect* the human economy, they are not laws *of* the human economy,[4] since, according to Knies, the human economy is affected by the freedom of the human *will* as it manifests itself in "personal" action.

As we shall see later, this explanation "in principle" of the irrationality of economic events almost flies in the face of what Knies says about the influence of natural conditions on the economy in other passages, where the element that appears to *make it impossible* to formulate general laws of rational economic action is precisely the geographically and historically "individual" configuration of the conditions of the economy.

It is worthwhile, however, already at this point to consider rather more closely the whole question that Knies has touched upon here.[5] To identify, on the one hand, what is determined with what is law-like and, on the other hand, "free" action with "individual" (that

---

1   See *Economy*, p. 119 (in what follows, all [references to Knies] are to this first edition of *Economy*, unless something else is specially indicated).
2   He explicitly says so on p. 344.
3   The collective relationships disappear as a separate category. Since they include "action", they, too, are seen as irrational by Knies.
4   See pp. 237, 333–34, 352, 345.
5   In his review of Knies' work, Schmoller already rejects his formulation[s], on the grounds that even nature does not repeat itself exactly (Schmoller, *Literature*, p. 205).

is to say, non-generic) action is a truly elementary error; nevertheless, Knies is by no means the only one to commit it. On the contrary: we occasionally meet with it, even today, in the methodology of history; and this is particularly true of the manner in which the "question" of the freedom of the will enters into the methodological discussions of the specialized sciences. Although they have no need of it at all, historians still introduce this problem, understood in quite the same sense as Knies does, into their discussions of the importance of "individual" factors in history. In this context, one constantly encounters the view that the specific *dignity* of humankind, and hence of history, resides in the "unpredictability" of personal action. The references to this "unpredictability" – which is rooted in "freedom" – may be quite direct;[1] but they can also be veiled, as when the "creative" importance of the personality of the acting individual is contrasted with the "mechanical" causality of natural events.

In view of this, it does not seem wholly unjustified to push the examination a little further here and to throw some more light on this problem, which has been "settled" hundreds of times, but continues to reappear in new guises. [The analysis] can yield nothing but "self-evident truths", sometimes of the most trivial kind; but, as we shall see, precisely such "self-evident truths" always run the risk of escaping notice or even falling into oblivion.[2] – In this connection, we shall for the time being accept without discussion Knies' position according to which there is an inner affinity between those sciences where human "*action*" is the sole, or the preferred, *object* of study. And, as history indisputably belongs in this group, we shall here speak of "history and the sciences related to it", while leaving open at present the question of *which* sciences belong to that group. Whenever we speak simply of "history", this should always be understood in the widest sense (including political, cultural and social history). – By the "importance of the personality" for history – [an idea] which is still so highly controversial – one may mean either of two things: (1) the specific *interest* in knowing as much as possible about the "substance" of the "life of the mind" of historically "great" and "unique" individuals – a life which is seen as having "intrinsic value"; or (2) the importance to be attributed to the action, under concrete conditions, of certain individual persons (irrespective of whether we *evaluate* these persons as "intrinsically" "significant" or "insignificant") as a *causal* factor in a concrete historical context. These two conceptual relationships are obviously totally heterogeneous from a logical point of view. Naturally, if someone in principle denies [the

1   This is the case with Hinneberg (*Foundations*, p. 29), who claims that the problem of freedom is "the fundamental question of all the sciences of the human spirit". Just like Knies, Stieve, to take one example, also maintains that [in the sciences of the human spirit], we cannot assume the existence of law-like regularities [of the kind] met with in the natural sciences, because "the freedom of the human will is a[n established] fact" (Stieve, *Maximilian*, p. 41). Meinecke (*Rejoinder*, p. 264) believes that "if one knows that within mass movements in history, the achievements of many thousands of freely acting Xs are concealed, then, surely, one looks at [those movements] with quite different eyes than if we consider them simply as the interplay of forces working in a law-like way". – In the same article, p. 266, the same author calls this "X" – the irrational "residue" of the personality – its "inner sanctum", just as Treitschke, with a certain reverence, speaks of the "enigma" of personality. The *method[olog]ically* legitimate core of all these statements is of course the appeal to the "art of ignorance"; but they also proceed from the strange assumption that the dignity of a science, or of its object, stems from those features of the object that we, in the concrete case and generally, *must remain ignorant about*. Thus, the specific significance of human action would reside in the fact that it is *inexplicable* and consequently *incomprehensible*.

2   It should be emphasized that the question whether the *practical* methodology of economics will "gain" anything from this [analysis] will be *ignored* from the very outset. What we are seeking is knowledge of certain logical relationships *for its own sake*; and we have the right to do so, just as the science of economics wishes not to be evaluated exclusively by whether its work leads to the formulation of "prescriptions" for "practical purposes".

existence of] the interest mentioned under (1), or dismisses it as "unfounded", [that] cannot be refuted [on the basis afforded] by a science of empirical experience; and the same is equally true of someone who holds the contrary view: that the only worthy task for human beings, and the only worthwhile result of inquiries into cultural relationships, is the analysis of "great" individuals in their "uniqueness" by means of understanding and "re-experiencing". Certainly, these "standpoints" can in their turn be made the object of critical analysis. In that case, however, the problem under discussion will not concern the methodology of history, nor will it purely be [a matter of] epistemological critique; [it will ask about] the "sense" of looking for scientific knowledge of historical events, and [come under the heading of] the philosophy of history.[1] On the other hand, the only basis on which it is possible to dispute, in general, the *causal* importance (mentioned under (2)) either of concrete single acts or of that complex of "constant motives" which we – in a formal sense – call "personality", is an a priori decision to disregard those elements of a historical interconnection that have been causally determined [by those "personality" factors], on the grounds that precisely that [causal determination by "personality" factors] makes them *unworthy* of [meeting] our need for causal explanations. [Such an a priori decision] also lies outside the empirical domain and cannot be justified on empirical grounds, because it contains a value judgement. In the absence of such [an a priori] decision, each individual case must of course be considered on its own merits – that is to say: [the question to be answered is] what elements of the given historical reality, in a [given] individual case, *are to be* causally explained and what is the source material at our disposal. On this will depend: (1) whether, in following the chain of causation backwards, we arrive at a concrete act (or omission) by a *single* individual, which constitutes a cause whose *distinctive* character is important – say, the Trianon decree; ‹51› furthermore, (2) whether it will in such cases be sufficient for the causal interpretation of that act to make clear [that] the constellation of incentives to action that lie "outside the acting person" constitute a cause which, according to general experience, provides him with sufficient motivation; or (3) whether we are furthermore obliged to establish, and justified in establishing, his "constant motives", with their distinctive character, but also obliged to go, and justified in going, no further; or, finally, (4) whether the [further] need arises to provide a characterogenetic ‹52› causal explanation of [these constant motives], for instance by explaining them, to the extent possible, as a result of "inherited dispositions" and the influence of education, the concrete circumstances of life and the individual characteristics of the "milieu". – When we consider the question of irrationality, there is of course, in principle, no difference at all in this context between acts by *a single* individual and acts by *many* individuals. Naturalistic dilettantes would have us believe that when "mass phenomena" are considered as *historical* causes or effects in a given context, they are "objectively" *less* "individual" than the acts of "heroes". It is to be hoped that this laughable old prejudice will not continue to assert itself much longer, even in the minds of "sociologists".[2] In the context described above, Knies, too, speaks of

---

1   This is because the epistemology of history demonstrates and analyses the significance for historical knowledge of [its] relation to values, but does not *establish* the validity of the values.

2   Simmel's remarks (*Philosophy of History*[2], p. 63, bottom) obviously do not affect the individual character of the "mass phenomenon", considered as an element of *historical* interrelations, as Simmel himself would undoubtedly agree. The fact that the "mass phenomenon" is constituted by what the multitude of *individuals* participating in it generally have in *common* is no obstacle to [the fact that] its *historical* importance resides in the *individual* content, the individual cause, the individual effects of what these many [individuals] have in common (for instance a concrete religious idea or a concrete constellation of economic interests). Only real – that is to say: concrete – objects are, in their individual manifestations, *real* causes; and these are what history is looking for. Concerning the relation of the categories "real cause" and "cause of knowledge" to the methodological problems of history, see my critique of Eduard Meyer and others (pp. 150f.).

human action in general and not of the acts of "great personalities". Consequently, [it should be stated] once and for all that, in what follows, whenever expressions such as "human action", "motivation" or "decision" are used, they refer not only to the conduct of single individuals, but in exactly the same way to "mass movements" – unless the context makes it clear beyond any doubt that the opposite is the case, or this is expressly stated.

Wundt's category of "creative synthesis"

We shall begin with some remarks concerning the concept of "the creative", which Wundt, in particular, has incorporated as a fundamental element into his methodology of the "sciences of the human spirit". ‹53› Irrespective of the sense in which one uses this concept in relation to "personalities", one must be very careful not to try to interpret it as containing anything besides the manifestation of a *valuation* that we apply to the causal factors, on the one hand, and, on the other hand, to the end effect that we impute to those factors. In particular, it is completely erroneous to believe that the "creative" character (in the sense in which this concept may be understood) of human actions is connected with "objective" differences in the character of causal relations – that is to say: differences which, *independently* of our valuations, are given in empirical reality *or* can be deduced from it. The distinctive character and the concrete acts of a concrete "historical" personality do not "objectively" – that is to say, as soon as we abstract from our specific interest – affect the course of events more "creatively" (in any understandable sense [of that term]) as *causal* factors, than *may* equally be the case with "impersonal" causal factors – geographical or social circumstances, or individual processes of nature. This is because the concept of "creativity" – unless we just generally equate it with the concept of "novelty" in cases of qualitative change, so that it becomes quite colourless – is not a purely empirical concept: it is connected with value ideas in the light of which we observe qualitative changes in reality. For instance, the physical and chemical processes leading to the formation of a coal seam or a diamond are, from a formal point of view, "creative syntheses" in exactly the same sense as, say, the concatenations of motives connecting the intuitions of a prophet with the formation of a new religion; [the two examples of "synthesis"] only differ with respect to the content of the valuational points of view governing them. From a logical point of view, the series of qualitative changes has in both cases taken on the same distinctive colouring. The reason is simple: this series of changes – like any change as such in the individually separate reality, when viewed solely under its qualitative aspect – can be represented as a causal *inequation*; ‹54› and because of the *value* relations of *one* of its parts, this causal inequation is perceived as a *value* inequation. Consequently, the reflection on this [value] relation becomes the determining *reason* for our historical interest. If the proposition "causa aequat effectum" ‹55› does not hold for human action, this is not because the course of psychophysical processes possesses some sort of "objective" superiority over the "realm of laws of nature" in general, or over special axioms such as (for instance) that concerning the "conservation of energy" ‹56› (or others of that kind). Instead, the reason is a purely logical one: precisely those points of view under which "action" becomes the object of our scientific investigation a priori exclude causal equations as the goal of that investigation. The same holds, to a degree which is even one step higher, for that "action" – by individuals or by a multitude of persons that is conceptually categorized as a group – which we [call] "historical", and which we single out from the mass of behaviour that does not engage our historical interest. What is "creative" about this ["historical"] action is simply the following: in our "conception" of historical reality, the *significance* of the causal sequence of events can *vary*, both qualitatively and quantitatively. In other words: when [we] apply those valuations in which our historical *interest* is rooted, to the infinity of causal components that are in themselves historically meaningless and trivial, this sometimes yields trivial results; but, at other times, this produces a constellation that is significant – that is to say: certain of its elements engage that historic interest and are coloured by it. In the latter case, new value relations, which were hitherto lacking, have been added to our "conception". And if we then [pursue an] anthropocentric [line of reasoning and] causally *impute* this result to the "action" of human beings, then we consider this [action] to be "creative". However, as mentioned above, purely "natural processes" *can*, from a strictly logical point of view, lay claim to the same ["creative"] dignified status: this [becomes possible] as soon as one abstracts from the anthropocentric [causal] imputation, which "objectively" is by no means self-evident. Moreover, the "creative" element can of course also – depending on one's "standpoint" – be viewed as negative and herostratic, ‹57› or simply indicate a qualitative *change* in value, without an explicit indication [as to whether this change is positive or negative]. But above all: for all these reasons, there is obviously no necessary relationship between the significance and scale of the "intrinsic value" of the human being who acts "creatively" and of his actions[, on the one hand,] and of the results [causally] imputed to him and to his actions[, on the other hand]. Action that – measured in terms of its "intrinsic value" – seems to us absolutely worthless and even meaningless may have results which, through the concatenation of historical destinies, render it eminently "creative". And, on the other hand, human deeds that, "conceived" in isolation, are painted by our "feelings of value" in the most splendid colours may engender results which disappear into the grey, infinite reaches of the historically trivial and therefore become causally unimportant for history; or – something that regularly recurs in history – they may see their "meaning" altered, qualitatively and quantitatively, perhaps beyond recognition, by the concatenation of historical destinies.

Our historical interest is usually particularly strongly attracted by cases of the latter sort, in which the historical *significance* is *changed*. In this respect as well, the specifically historical work of the cultural sciences may therefore be seen as the most complete antithesis of all those [scientific] disciplines that try to establish causal equations: [in the historical cultural sciences,] the crucial category is that of the causal *in*equation as an inequation of *value*; consequently, it is only in this sense that one can talk of the "creative synthesis" as a phenomenon that is peculiar to processes in the individual psyche, to cultural interconnections, or to both of these. On the other hand, I am inclined to believe that the way in which *Wundt* utilizes this concept in the most diverse contexts[1] is untenable and directly misleading (although no one would of course blame this eminent scholar for the use that historians such as Lamprecht have occasionally attempted to make of it). – At this point, we may set out a compressed analytical sketch of Wundt's allegedly "psychological" theory.

According to Wundt,[2] certain causal relations do exist between the "psychical structures" and the "elements" of which the[se structures] are composed; this must evidently be taken to mean that the [structures] are unambiguously *determined*. *But*, in addition, they possess *new* characteristics, which those individual elements "do not contain". – However, it seems beyond doubt that this also holds, in quite the same sense and to quite the same extent, for *all* natural processes, whenever we view them as *qualitative* changes. For instance, water, considered with respect to its distinctive qualities, possesses characteristics that are certainly not "contained" in its elements. Indeed, as soon as a value relation is performed, *no* natural phenomenon will fail to contain specifically "new" characteristics when compared to its "elements". Even the purely quantitative relationships in the solar system do not in any sense form an exception to this,

1   Including, for instance, in his *National Psychology*.
2   *Logic²*, II, 2, pp. 267ff.

compared to the individual planets considered in isolation as its "elements", or compared to the mechanical forces that may have caused [the solar system] to develop from a hypothetical primeval nebula; and this in spite of the fact that we are here faced with a concatenation of individual processes that are of interest [to us] purely as physical phenomena – that is to say: each of which could be expressed in a causal equation. – But let us again hear what Wundt has to say. According to him, a crystal can for the natural scientist be "nothing else" than "the sum of its molecules together with the external interactions specific to them". The same holds for an organic form, which for the natural scientist is simply "the product of certain elements, which is completely formed in advance in those elements", even when the scientist is as yet unable to "derive the whole causally". The crucial concession which has slipped into Wundt's account here is implicit in the words "for the natural scientist" – since the natural scientist, for his purposes, precisely has to abstract from the given relationships in immediately experienced reality. If we leave aside the subtleties of intermediate cases and go straight to the economist, the situation is evidently different for him. The "interrelation" of the chemical elements may be such that they constitute blades of corn fit for human consumption, or perhaps a diamond; or the compound formed by elements that are chemically identical [to those just mentioned] may be one that has no relevance for satisfying human needs for nourishment or adornment. From the perspective of the economist, these two cases are fundamentally different since, in the first one, the natural process has produced an object to which economic *value* can be assigned. One might object that, precisely for this reason, we are here dealing with the involvement of "psychological" factors – "feelings of value" and "value judgements" that have to be interpreted by means of "psychical causality". Put like that, the objection would be wrongly formulated; but the point that it intends to convey is of course entirely correct. However, *exactly the same* is true of "psychical" events as a whole. Considered "objectively" – which in this case means: [if we] abstract from all value relations – ["psychical" events] also constitute nothing more than a sequence of qualitative changes, which we become aware of either directly, through our own "inner experience", or indirectly by interpreting the expressive movements of "others" by means of analogy. There seems to be no reason at all why it should not be possible to subject these sequential changes, absolutely and without any exception, to an examination that would be *free* from "valuations" in exactly the same sense as [the examination of] any sequence of qualitative changes in "inanimate" nature.[1] But, as for Wundt, he contrasts the crystal and the organic structure with the "idea", which is something that "never simply" represents "the sum total of the sensations into which it can be broken down"; furthermore, he describes "intellectual processes" – a judgement or a conclusion, for instance – as structures that can never be "conceived as mere aggregates of single sensations and ideas". The reason for this, he adds, is that "what makes these processes *significant* arises *from* [their] component elements" (here, too, we can undoubtedly interpret Wundt as believing that this happens in a [process of] strictly causal determination), "but is not contained *in* the[se elements]". [This is] no doubt [true]. But is the situation different with respect to the formation of those "natural products"? Was the "significance" of the diamond or of the blades of corn for certain human "feelings of value" "formed in advance" in the physical and chemical conditions of their development to a higher degree or in a different sense than is the case – if we assume a strict application of the category of causality to the psychical domain – with the "elements" from which ideas and judgements are formed? Or, to bring "historical" events "into the picture": was the significance of the Black

1 Incidentally, no one has emphasized this more clearly than Rickert – it is actually the basic theme of his *Limits of Concept Formation*, which is, in this respect, in essence also an attack against Dilthey. It is astonishing that many "sociologists", with a kind of blind zeal, continually overlook this point.

Death ‹58› for social history, or the significance that the invading waters of the Dollart ‹59› had for the history of the colonization movement etc., "formed in advance" in the bacteria and the other causes of infection which determined the first of these events, or the geological and meteorological causes which determined the second one? Both events are in absolutely no respect different from the invasion of Germany by Gustavus Adolphus ‹60› or the invasion of Europe by Genghis Khan. ‹61› All those events have had effects that are historically *significant* – that is to say: that we regard as being anchored in "cultural values". All of them were also causally determined – provided that one takes the universal applicability of the causal principle seriously, as Wundt does. All of them were the causes of "psychical" events as well as "physical" ones. But in none of these cases did the way in which the event was causally determined indicate that we would ascribe historical "significance" to it. And, in particular, this [ascription of "significance"] could not in any way be deduced from the fact that they contain "psychical elements". Instead, in all these cases, the fundamentally heterogeneous and disparate factor that cuts across the procedure of "derivation" from the "elements" is the *meaning* which we ascribe to the phenomena, that is to say: the relations to "values" which we perform. When "we" relate "psychical" events to values – whether in the form of an undifferentiated "feeling of value" or as a rational "value judgement" – the "creative synthesis" is accomplished. Astonishingly, Wundt conceives the matter precisely the other way round: according to him, the principle of "creative synthesis", which is "objectively" founded in the distinctive character of psychical causality, finds its "characteristic *expression*" in ascriptions of value and value judgements. It would be quite unobjectionable if, in saying so, Wundt simply meant that it is a legitimate aim of psychological research to try, for instance, to find the psychical or psychophysical "conditions" under which feelings of value and value judgements arise, and to uncover psychical or psychophysical "elementary" processes as causal components of them. But one only has to read a few more pages to realize what the real implications of Wundt's allegedly "psychological" approach are intended to be: Wundt believes that "in the course of every individual or general development" – which naturally includes the development of the born drunkard or sex murderer, as well as that of the religious genius – spiritual (which he interprets as logical, ethical and aesthetic) values are *engendered*; "originally, these [values] did not at all possess their specific qualities" *because*, so he says, when we are dealing with the phenomena of life, the principle of conservation of physical energy is complemented by the law of "*increasing psychical energy*" (that is to say: increase in actual and potential values). Admittedly, the general "tendency" towards the formation of "increasing magnitudes of value" may, it is true, be "partly or completely thwarted" by "disturbances". But even "one of the most important of these interruptions of psychical development: the cessation of individual mental activity" (apparently, this refers to what is generally, in simpler terms, called "death") "is usually . . . more than compensated by the increase in spiritual energy within the community to which the individual belongs" – a circumstance which, in Wundt's words, is "after all worth noting". The same holds for the relationship of the individual nation to the human community [in general]. However, a discipline that aspires to being empirical would also need to possess the ability to *demonstrate* this with some approximation of "precision", however remote. And, as it is obvious that not only the professor, but also the statesman, indeed *every* individual, experiences a "psychical development", the following question arises: *who* is to be the beneficiary of this comforting circumstance of "being compensated"? Put more concretely: who will be "*psychologically*" compensated for the death of Caesar or of some ordinary street cleaner: (1) the deceased or dying person himself; or (2) his bereaved family; or (3) the person for whom his death created a vacant "position" or a fresh field of "activity"; or (4) the tax collector's office; [or] (5) the call-up authority; or (6) certain party-political tendencies etc.; or perhaps (7) God's providential direction of the world;

or, finally, the psychologistic *metaphysician*? Only this last assumption seems to be warranted, since it appears that here we are not dealing with psychology, but with a construction of the a priori postulated "progress" of humanity – a construction that, [although] it appears in the garb of "objective" psychological observation, [in fact] belongs to [the realm of] the philosophy of history. Furthermore, from the "creative synthesis", [Wundt] also derives the "law of historical resultants", which, together with the law of historical "relations" and that of historical "contrasts", constitutes the psychologistic trinity of historical categories. Moreover, the "creative synthesis" is also called into service to interpret the formation and "essence" of "society", and of totalities in general, in a way that is supposedly based on "psychology". And, finally, the ["creative synthesis"] is supposed to make clear why we are (allegedly) capable of explaining cultural phenomena only by means of causal regression (from the effect to the cause) – while in fact *exactly* the same is the case with every concrete "natural process" to be interpreted with the means offered by physics, *as soon as* one *focuses*, for whatever reason, on the individual complications [of that process] and the details of its consequences for concrete reality. This question will be taken up later, however. At this point, we only wanted to give an account of the most elementary features of [Wundt's] theory. – The wide-ranging intellectual activity of this eminent scholar merits our extraordinary and grateful esteem; but this should not prevent us from pointing out that, when dealing with these particular problems, this variety of so-called "psychology" is almost fatal to the scientific impartiality of the historian: by employing so-called psychological categories, he is led to conceal from himself the fact that he is relating history to values that he has derived from the *philosophy* of history, and therefore to delude himself and others with a false appearance of exactitude. Lamprecht's work is an exemplary warning in this respect.

As Wundt's views are so extraordinarily influential in the domain of psychological work, let us pursue a little further [our discussion of] the relationship to "norms" and "values" of a psychology that employs causal explanations. Above all, it should be stressed that, when [we] reject Wundt's so-called psychological "laws" and point out that certain allegedly "psychological" concepts have the character of *value* judgements, this is not because we somehow wish to belittle the importance or reduce the scope of psychology and of the "psychophysical" disciplines linked with it; even less do we wish to demonstrate that there are "gaps" in the validity of the causal principle for the empirical sciences. The exact opposite is the case. Psychology as an empirical discipline only becomes possible when it eliminates value *judgements* (such as those that can be found in Wundt's "laws"). Psychology may hope to identify, some day, those constellations of psychical "elements" that are unequivocally the causal conditions of our "feeling" that we "are formulating" or "have formulated" an "objectively" *valid* judgement with a certain content. The [discipline dealing with the] anatomy of the brain may at some future time wish to determine what physical processes are indispensable for [the existence of such a "feeling"] and constitute the unequivocal conditions for it. In our context, the question is not whether this is in fact possible; at any rate, it is not *logically* absurd to assume [that] such a task [could be defined]. As for the substance [of the assumption], we can take the example of the law of [conservation of] energy. This law is dependent on the introduction of the concept of "potential energy"; and some of the elements of this latter concept are just as "incomprehensible" (which in this context means that they cannot be *pictured*) as any of the conditions in the anatomy of the brain – however complicated they may be – which are necessary for the psychophysical explanation of the "explosive" character of certain "release" processes. It is highly unlikely that such findings can be made. But, in spite of this, the assumption that it is possible to make them is, as an ideal goal of psychophysical research, positively meaningful and fruitful, at least for the purpose of problem definition. Let us consider yet another aspect. Biology may "understand" the "psychical" development of our logical categories – for instance, the deliberate application of the principle of causality – as being, in some sense, the product of "adaptation": it is well known that the attempt has been made to explain in principle the "limits" of our knowledge by assuming that "consciousness" only came into being as a means of preserving the species, ‹62› and that the sphere of consciousness could therefore not extend beyond what was required for that purpose (since knowledge "just" for its own sake was held to be a product of a "play instinct"). One may try to replace this interpretation, which is admittedly essentially "teleological", with a more causal one, where the gradual realization of the importance of [the category of causality] is interpreted as the result of innumerable specific "reactions" to certain "stimuli" – which must somehow be more closely determined – in the course of a long phylogenetic ‹63› evolution (for which the necessary millions of years are available at no extra cost). Furthermore, one may go beyond the use of summary and rough categories such as "adaptation", "release" and so on, as general formulas, and try, by means of a strictly historical analysis, to find the origins of the special "processes of release", which liberated modern science, in certain "practical" – in the broadest sense of this word – problems that our intellect was faced with as a result of concrete constellations of social circumstances. One may continue by demonstrating that the use of certain ways of "conceiving" reality would at the same time, in practice, produce the greatest degree of satisfaction of the decisive interests of particular social strata. In that way, one may – albeit in a strongly modified sense – carry the proposition of historical "materialism", according to which the ideal "superstructure" is a function of the total state of society, to its conclusion in the intellectual domain as well: the proposition that, in the last resort, it is *usually* only that which is "useful" to us which is accepted as "valid" truth, would in that way, so to speak, be historically confirmed. We may be very sceptical as to the substance of those constructions; but the [last] proposition would at any rate only constitute a *logical* absurdity if the "cognitive value" were mixed up with the "practical value" and the category of the "norm" were missing. In that case, the proposition would be that what is useful *is* also true *because* it is useful; and that, if mathematical propositions have the status of truths that are not only *recognized* in practice but that *possess* normative validity, it is only *by virtue* either of the "practical importance" of those propositions, or of the processes of "release" and adaptation mentioned above. *That* proposition would indeed be "nonsense". Otherwise, as far as their *epistemological* status is concerned, all those considerations are in principle only limited by the immanent *meaning* of their cognitive goal; and the limit to their *substantive* usefulness is found only at the point where it cannot "explain" the empirically given facts consistently in such a manner that the explanation is borne out by "all experience". But even if all those problems that the future might present, with respect to giving a physiological, psychological, biogenetical, sociological and historical "explanation" of the phenomenon of thought and of particular intellectual "standpoints", had found their most ideal solution, this would of course still not in any way affect the question of the *validity* – the "cognitive value" – of our "intellectual processes". Strictly *logically* speaking, one might in the future, by means of "exact" research of some kind, hope to discover the anatomical processes that correspond to the knowledge of the "validity" of the multiplication table, and to establish how these anatomical constellations had developed phylogenetically. The *only* question to which neither the microscope nor any biological, psychological or historical observation can ever, for *logical* reasons, furnish the answer is that of the "correctness" of the judgement that $2 \times 2 = 4$. From the viewpoint of any *empirical* psychological observation and causal analysis, the claim that the multiplication table is "valid" is simply transcendental, and meaningless as an object of investigation: *from the point of view of empirical psychology*, it is one of the quite unverifiable logical preconditions of its own psychometric ‹64› observations. It is a fact that the bankers of Florence in the Middle Ages, because of their ignorance of the Arabic numerals, quite regularly, and even when dividing their own estates, made "miscalculations" – as we, from a "*normative*" standpoint, would call it – and that, if we look at the larger entries in many account books of those days, it is almost the exception to find completely "correct" calculations. These facts are causally determined to quite the same extent as the fact that, *today*, "correctness" is the rule, and that we would tend to put a very negative "interpretation" on the presence of ["miscalculations" like those of the Florentines] in the accounts of modern bankers. To explain [why we find those "miscalculations"] in, say, the Peruzzi account books, ‹65› we can put forward all sorts of reason – except one: that the multiplication table was not yet "correct" at that time. In the same way, the "correctness" of the multiplication table would not, for instance, today be called into question if the statistics of the yearly number of cases where calculations had in fact been "incorrect" showed an "unfavourable" result: Such a result would not constitute an "unfavourable" judgement as to the validity of the multiplication table; it would be an "unfavourable" criticism – which would build on and presuppose that validity – of our ability to do mental arithmetic "in accordance with the norms". All these observations are somewhat on the simple side, and Wundt would of course be the last to dispute them, although he does not take them into account in substance. If we continue to consider the example of intellectual development, the comment of [someone whose] approach was oriented according to Wundt's concepts might be that the principle of "creative synthesis" or "increasing psychical energy" precisely means, among other things, that, in the course of "cultural development", we become increasingly "capable" of intellectually grasping and "accepting" such timelessly valid "norms". But *that* [answer] would simply demonstrate that [Wundt's] allegedly empirico-"psychological" approach does not constitute an empirical analysis that is "presuppositionless" (in the sense of being free from valuations): the so-called "law" of "development" would *only* be seen as coming into play *in those instances* where a change occurred in the direction of accepting those "norms", and [Wundt's approach] would therefore imply an evaluation of the "cultural development" from the point of view of a "value" whose validity was already presupposed, i.e. the value of "correct" knowledge.[1] However, this value – in which the sense of all our scientific endeavours is rooted – is not "empirically" self-evident. If we *decide* – for whatever reason – to acknowledge the purpose of scientific analysis of the empirically given reality as being valuable, then the "norms" of our thought *force* us to respect them in our scientific work (to the extent that we remain conscious of them, and, at the same time, as long as the purpose [of the analysis] remains the same). But the "value" of that purpose in itself is something that can in no way be established *by* science as such. The pursuit of science may serve clinical, technical, economic, political or other "practical" interests; if we want to judge the value of science in those cases, this value is based on the assumption of the value of the interests that science serves, and this latter value is then an a priori. What is, however, completely problematical from an empirical point of view is the "value" of "pure science": from the standpoint of empirical psychology, the value of science pursued "for its own sake" has in fact not only been contested in practice – from certain standpoints of a religious nature and, for instance, from that of the "reason of state" – but also been denied in principle, by persons who base themselves on a radical affirmation of purely "vitalistic" values or, conversely, on a radical negation of life. Such contestations and denials by no means involve a *logical* inconsistency – or at least only in cases where [those persons] do not realize that their position simply implies that *other* values are ranked more highly than that of scientific truth.

1 Psychologistic theoreticians of development would probably put this into the form of the following thesis: "wherever development" occurs, it moves in the direction of those "values". Actually, the fact of the matter is that we *only* refer to change as "cultural development" *when it is related to* values: when it is "relevant" from a perspective that is oriented towards values; that is to say: when the change is either in itself a "change of value" or is causally related to such a change.

It would go too far if we were now also, after this laborious account of "self-evident [truths]", to discuss the fact that precisely the same is true for other values than that of striving for scientific knowledge. There is absolutely no bridge that leads from a *purely* "empirical" analysis of given reality with the tools of causal explanation to establishing or contesting the "validity" of *any* value judgement; and Wundt's concepts of "creative synthesis", of the "law" of constant "intensification of psychical energy" etc. contain value judgements of the first water. Let us, very briefly, elucidate the rationale behind these constructions. It is quite obvious that their source must be that we simply *assign to* the development of those nations that we call "culturally developed nations" the *quality of an intensification* of value; this value judgement leads us to regard the processes of qualitative change that we register in those nations as a sequence of value inequations and therefore, in a specific way, directs our "historical interest" towards these [developments]. Or, to be more precise: [this] constitutes the reason why we conceive those developments as being "history". The value inequations that are the product of our evaluative judgement, [together with] the manifestations of historical changes of value and significance, [and with] the fact that those elements of the temporal course of events which, in our *judgement*, constitute "cultural development", and which we therefore single out from the meaninglessness of the unending flight of infinite multiplicities – are, in our value judgement, a manifestation of "progress", particularly when measured by the standard of the scope of "knowledge". All these elements give rise to the metaphysical belief that, *even if we abstract* from our valuational position, a fountain of youth exists which, mediated by the "personality" of genius or by the "socio-psychical development", bubbles over from the realm of timeless values into the realm of historical events and which "objectively", over and over again, perpetuates the "progress" of human culture into the limitless future.

Wundt's "psychology" offers itself as an apologist for this belief in "progress". Knies, too, clearly held this belief, which, from the standpoint of an *empirical* psychology, belongs to the domain of metaphysics; and he certainly had no reason to be ashamed of his belief, since someone greater than himself had already given it a formulation that was (in its own way) classic. Kant's "causality through freedom", ‹66› together with the multiple ramifications arising out of this concept in the subsequent development of philosophical thought, is the philosophical archetype of all metaphysical theories of "culture" and "personality" of this sort. [Implicit in Kant's concept was the idea that] the intelligible character affects the empirical causal concatenation through action in conformity with *ethical* norms. [This idea] can with greatest ease be transposed and given a more general form, resulting in the view that everything that is in conformity with a norm must in the same way, from the world of "things in themselves", be interwoven with empirical reality; or, going even further, that all changes of value in the real world are brought about by "creative" forces governed by a causality specifically different from that governing other sequences of qualitative changes which are indifferent to our "value judgement". In this latter formulation, that train of thought is apparent in Wundt's concepts of "creative synthesis" and of the law of "increasing psychical energy"; but, admittedly, it is a sadly degenerate version compared to the grandeur and, above all, the ruthlessly candid logical character of Kant's idea (irrespective of all the inconsistencies to which – as any closer examination will demonstrate – that idea leads).

We shall not at all concern ourselves with the question whether such constructions might be meaningful in the domain of *metaphysical* reflection, and what significance they might have; nor will the *substantive* difficulties raised by [the concept of] "causality through freedom" and all related constructions – difficulties that would perhaps precisely first manifest themselves in the metaphysical domain – be treated here.[1] At any rate, "psychologism" – which we shall

---

1   On this point, see, for instance, Windelband's discussion in *Freedom of the Will*, pp. 161ff.

in this context understand to mean: the claim by psychology to be, or to create, a "world view" – is just as meaningless, and just as dangerous for the impartiality of empirical science, as "naturalism" based either on mechanics or biology, or "historicism" based on "cultural history".[1]

Münsterberg[2] has already clearly demonstrated that this so-called "principle" of psychical events is of absolutely no use whatsoever to any psychology. The only concept relevant to "psychical" events that are "objectivized" (that is to say: free from the relation to value ideas) is that of qualitative change, and the only [concept relevant to] the objectivized causal observation of this change is that of the causal inequation. The concept of "the creative" can only have a function when we begin to relate individual elements of those sequential changes – which are "intrinsically" completely neutral – to *values*. But, if we do this, then the development of the solar system from some primeval nebula, or – if one wants to emphasize that the suddenness of the event [is important for] the applicability of the concept – the sudden flood of the Dollart, *may* (as was said above) be subsumed under the concept of "the creative" in quite the same way as the creation of the Sistine Madonna ‹68› or the inspiration leading to Kant's *Critique of Pure Reason*. It is not possible to deduce a *specific* "creative importance" of "personalities" or of "human action" from some characteristic feature – which is free from value judgements [and] "objective" – of their causal mode of operation. Although this is self-evident, it must be stated explicitly in this context.

The irrationality of concrete action and the irrationality of concrete natural events

We shall not discuss here in what other sense[s] the historian utilizes the concept of "the creative" and is "subjectively" justified in doing so. Instead, we shall again approach the point of departure of these discussions – Knies' views – by offering a few remarks concerning the belief that human action or the human "personality" is characterized by a specific *irrationality*. Here, we shall to begin with simply use the concept of "irrationality" in the vulgar sense of "incalculability". This "incalculability" is, in the opinion of Knies – and of so many others, even today – supposed to be the symptom of human "freedom of will"; and [they] attempt to make this the basis of some sort of specific dignity of the "sciences of the human spirit", since [these sciences] deal with those creatures [– human beings –] who are specifically worthy of esteem *because of this incalculability*. However, to begin with, it is certainly not possible to find traces in "experienced" reality of a *specific* "incalculability" of human conduct. Every military command, every criminal law, indeed every utterance that we make in our intercourse with others, "calculates" with producing certain effects in the "psyche" of those to whom it is addressed. [This calculation] does not assume [that the effects] will be absolutely unambiguous in every respect, nor [that they will be found in the "psyche" of] everybody; but it does assume an unambiguousness that is sufficient *for the purposes* which the command, the law or, generally, the concrete utterance

---

1   The use of real or ostensible research methods or research results of empirical disciplines for the construction of "world views" has become an almost trivial occurrence. In its classical purity this can once again be observed in the fairly "terrible" results that certain remarks by Mach (*Analysis of Sensations*, p. 18n12) have engendered in the last chapter of L.M. Hartmann's *Historical Development*. I shall reserve for another place the discussion of this work, ‹67› which is a manifestation of strange aberrations on the part of a scholar with a deservedly high reputation. Methodologically, the book is quite instructive, although this was not the author's intention. (Concerning this work, see the review by F. Eulenburg (Eulenburg, *Hartmann*).)

2   *Outline of Psychology*, I. We shall soon come back to this work [and discuss it] in detail.

is meant to serve. From a logical point of view, this calculation in no respect differs from the "static" calculations of a bridge-builder, the calculations of farmers with respect to chemicals for agricultural use, and the physiological reflections of stock breeders; and these, in their turn, are "calculations" in the same sense as the economic deliberations of a dealer in arbitrage and futures: as far as their degree of "exactitude" is concerned, each of these "calculations" aims no higher than is necessary for it, and contents itself with what can, in the concrete case, be attained for its specific purposes on the basis of the [available] source material. [This is], *in principle*, no different from [when we deal with] "natural events". In the area of "weather prophecies", for example, the "calculability" of "natural events" is far from being as "certain" as the "calculation" of the actions of a person whom we know; indeed, [the "calculability" of "weather prophecies"] would simply not be able to attain that level of certainty, however perfect our nomological ⟨69⟩ knowledge were to become. And this is the case wherever we are concerned, not with certain abstracted relationships, but with a *future* "natural event" in its full individuality.[1] Moreover, as even the most trivial reflection will show, in the domain of causal *regression*, the situation is in a certain sense exactly the opposite of what the "thesis of incalculability" assumes; in any case, one certainly cannot say that human action is "*objectively*" – in the sense of what remains valid even *when we abstract from* our valuational points of view – characterized by more irrationality (as that term was defined above) [than natural events].

Let us consider the case of a boulder that has been flung down from a rockface by a storm and has thereby been shattered into numerous scattered fragments. What can then, on the basis of well-known laws of mechanics, be causally "explained" (that is to say: be "calculated after the fact") is the following: the fact [that it has fallen down]; the general direction of its fall (but already with rather less precision); the fact that it has been shattered and, perhaps (but here again, with rather less precision), the general degree of its fragmentation; and, in addition, in the most favourable case and after intensive prior observation, the approximate direction in which one or other of the fragments has flown. But, *if*, for some reason, what was important for us was [to find out], for example: how many fragments the boulder had been shattered into, the shape of those fragments, the pattern in which they were scattered, [or] a quite infinite number of similar "aspects" of the event, then we would – in spite of the fact that all those questions concerned purely quantitative relationships – be satisfied, as far as the[ir] causal explanation was concerned, with the conclusion that there was at least nothing "inexplicable" (that is to say: nothing *which contradicted* our "nomological" knowledge) in the facts as we found them. Not only would we regard it as wholly impossible to construct a proper causal "regression", since those aspects of the event were absolutely impossible to "calculate" (because their concrete determinants had disappeared without trace); that apart, we would also find it completely "pointless" [to construct such a "regression"]. Our need for a causal explanation would reassert itself only if the result of the fall of the boulder included some individual phenomenon that, at first glance, seemed to us to contradict the "laws of nature" as we knew them. – The substance of these considerations may be elementary, but it is still useful to be as clear as possible in one's own mind about the following: the form of causal explanation described above, which is quite imprecise and *excludes* any judgement of *necessity* formulated on the basis of the material – and in relation to which the universal validity of "determinism" simply remains an a priori – is entirely typical of the process of "causal" explanation of concrete, individual events. – When we approach sciences like, not only meteorology, but also geography and biology, with a demand for an explanation of concrete *individual* phenomena, [those sciences] are very often

---

1 This is why the question of "calculability in advance" should certainly not be treated as the focal point of methodology in the way in which Bernheim (*Historical Method*[3], p. 97) does so.

obliged to try to satisfy our need for a causal [explanation] with answers formulated in a way that is, in principle, completely similar to that employed in the trivial example [which we have just discussed]. And nowadays, it should hardly still be necessary to emphasize how infinitely far removed the concept of "adaptation", for example, is from "exact" [causal] imputation of established (or presumed) phylogenetic processes, and, in particular, how little it has to do with judgements of causal *necessity*.[1] In such cases, we simply content ourselves with [the fact] that the concrete, individual phenomenon is generally *interpreted* as "comprehensible" – that is to say: that it does not contain anything that runs directly counter to our nomological knowledge of empirical [reality]. And if we do not demand more than this, it is either (as in the case of the phylogenetic phenomena) mainly because there is nothing more to be known now, and perhaps never will be, or (as in the case of the falling boulder) because we, over and above this, do not feel the need to know any more.

When [we are] dealing with the "explanation" of concrete events, the possibility of formulating judgements of causal *necessity* is by no means the rule, but [rather] the exception, and such judgements always concern individual elements of the event: these elements are the only ones considered [by us], while [we] abstract from an infinite number of others which have to be, and can be, left aside as being "unimportant". In the domain of historically relevant human action, the chances of [establishing] a causal regression are usually subject to complexities and individual differentiations that are no less great than in the example of the pattern formed by the boulder fragments. This is true whether we are dealing with concrete, historically relevant acts by a single person, or with a process of change within social groups that has been brought about by the complex interrelations of many individuals. In the example of the pattern of rock fragments, one could, by entering further into the details of the event and [its] effects, make the number of causal elements that might have to be taken into account "larger than any given number, however large"; in other words, this event, like *every* individual event, no matter how simple it may appear, [comprises] an intensive *infinity* of multiplicity, as soon as one *chooses* to comprehend it in that way. Therefore, no sequence, however complex, of human "acts" can, in principle, "objectively" contain *more* "elements" than can be found in that simple event in physical nature.

The category of "interpretation"

However, we can find differences between [human "action"] and that "natural event" in the following respects:

(1) Our need [for] causal [explanation] *may* be satisfied in a *qualitatively* different sense when we are analysing human behaviour, and this circumstance carries with it a qualitatively different colouring of the concept of irrationality. When we wish to interpret [human behaviour], we can, at least in principle, set ourselves the goal not only to make it "comprehensible" [in the sense of] being "possible" (that is to say: consistent with our nomological knowledge), but also to "*understand*" it; that is to say, to uncover a concrete "motive" that we can "re-experience" "within ourselves", or a complex of such "motives", to which we can impute [that behaviour] (with a degree of precision which will vary according to the nature of the source material). In other words: because, and to the extent that, it can be meaningfully *interpreted*, individual action is in principle in a specific sense less "irrational" than the individual natural event. But only to the extent that it can be interpreted: beyond that limit, human action is no different from the

---

1   However, the views expressed by L.M. Hartmann (in *Historical Development*) show that the nature of the concept [of adaptation] still continues to be misunderstood. I shall deal with this question elsewhere.

fall of that boulder: "incalculability", in the sense of inaccessibility to interpretation, is, in other words, the principle [governing the actions] of the "*madman*". Whenever our search for historical knowledge leads us to focus on behaviour that is "irrational" in the sense of being *inaccessible to interpretation*, our need for causal [explanation] will indeed, as a rule, have to be content with having a "conception" of [that behaviour] on the basis of the nomological knowledge of, say, psychopathology or similar sciences, just like [having a "conception" of] the pattern of those rock fragments – but, on the other hand, [it will] *not* [have to be content] with *less* than that. It is easy to illustrate in what sense events that are "accessible to interpretation" are qualitatively rational. Unless the die is "loaded", [it is] completely impossible [to provide] a causal explanation of the fact that the die shows a six after a particular throw. We regard [that outcome] as "possible" (that is to say: it does not contradict our nomological knowledge); but the conviction that this "necessarily" *had to be* the outcome, remains *purely a priori*. We find it "plausible" that – provided the die is not "loaded" – the outcome of a very large number of throws will be that the numbers on the six faces of the die have come up with a more or less equal frequency; we find this, empirically verifiable, validity of the "law of large numbers" ⟨70⟩ "comprehensible", in the sense that the opposite outcome – that certain of the numbers would continue to come up more frequently, however long one continued to throw the die – would force us to ask ourselves what might be the cause to which this difference [in frequency] could be imputed. But evidently, the characteristic feature [of this example] is that our need for a causal [explanation] must content itself with an answer of an essentially "negative" kind. On the other hand, we can "interpret" statistical figures that, for instance, convey the influence of certain changes in the economy on, say, the number of marriages and, by means of our imagination – which is schooled by our everyday experiences – arrive at a truly positive *causal* interpretation based on "motives". In the domain of "non-interpretable" phenomena, the *individual* event, taken in isolation (the single throw of the die, the fragmentation of the falling boulder), remained completely irrational, in the following sense: we had to content ourselves with the confirmation of the nomological possibility [of the event] – [that is to say]: it did not contradict the rules of [our] experience; and it was only [on the basis of] a *multitude* of individual cases that we could, under certain conditions, go further [and formulate] "judgements of probability". On the other hand, the conduct of [King] Frederick II [of Prussia] in 1756 ⟨71⟩, that is to say, in an individual situation, considered completely on its own terms, seems to us to be not only nomologically "possible", like the [pattern of] fragmentation of the boulder, but also "teleologically" *rational*. This latter expression should not be understood as implying that we would be able, by way of causal imputation, to formulate a judgement of *necessity*, but in the sense that we judge the [actions in question] as having an "adequate cause" – that is to say, as being "sufficiently" motivated, assuming that the king had certain intentions and was under certain (correct or incorrect) impressions, and that he acted rationally on that basis. In this case, the "possibility of interpretation" makes [the process] more "calculable" than in the case of the non-"interpretable" natural events. Viewed simply under the aspect of how our need for causal [explanation] is satisfied, [the "possibility of interpretation"] can be compared to "the law of large numbers". And even when we cannot interpret [an event] "rationally" on the basis of intentions and impressions (for instance, if "irrational" affects play a part), there is at least a possibility that the situation remains more or less the same – provided we know the "character" [of the king] – as we will then also be able to include those emotions, as factors with an "understandable" effect, in the [causal] explanation. Only when we are faced with reactions that are so senseless and immoderate as to be downright pathological, and that [consequently] cannot be interpreted – as is sometimes the case with [King] Frederick William IV [of Prussia] – do we arrive at a degree of irrationality similar to that which characterizes the natural events [described above].

But if there is a decrease in the "interpretability" (and, consequently, an increase in the "incalculability") [of action], we usually assume that the acting person has, to that extent, *less* "freedom of the will", in the sense of "freedom of action".[1] (This is where the [preceding] discussion is linked to our [general] problem.) In other words: already at this point it appears that, if there is any general relationship at all between *"freedom"* of *"action"* (however that concept may be defined) and the irrationality of historical *events*, this relationship is at any rate *not* one in which their reciprocal influence is such that when one is present or increases, this means that the other one will also increase; in fact (as will become ever clearer [in what follows]), exactly the opposite is the case.

(2) However, our need for a causal [explanation] also *requires* that, in cases where an "interpretation" is in principle possible, it should be carried out. That is to say: when we interpret human "action", we are not content with relating it to what, according to purely empirical observation, happens as a *rule*, however strict that rule may be. We require that the action should be interpreted in terms of its "meaning". If it is, in an individual case, possible to establish this "meaning" – we will defer the examination of the problems raised by this concept – as being immediately evident, then it is of no importance to us whether it is possible to *formulate* a "rule" of events that covers the concrete, individual case.[2] And, on the other hand, the formulation of such a rule, even if its character were strictly law-like, can never result in the task of "meaningful" interpretation being *replaced* by a simple reference to [such a law-like rule]. More than that: "laws" of that kind have no *intrinsic "significance"* at all for us with respect to the interpretation of "action". Let us suppose that we would somehow succeed in establishing the strictest possible empirical–statistical demonstration that every human being who had ever been exposed to a particular situation had always and everywhere reacted to it in exactly the same manner and to exactly the same degree, and that the reaction would be the same whenever we created the situation experimentally [in the future] – which would amount to saying that the reaction in question could, in the most literal sense of the word, be "calculated". In itself, however, that [demonstration] would not move [our] "interpretation" one single step forward: Taken by itself, such a demonstration would still not in the very least enable us to "understand" "why" that reaction had ever occurred, – and certainly not ["why"] it always occurred in that way. We would lack that understanding as long as we were not also able to *reproduce*[3] the motivation "within" ourselves, in our imagination. And *without* that ability, even the most comprehensive empirical–statistical proof imaginable of the law-like occurrence of a reaction would therefore be *in*sufficient, as far as the *quality* of knowledge was concerned, to meet the demands that we make on history and on the "sciences of the human spirit", which are in this respect akin to it. (As already noted, we shall for the moment leave completely aside the question of what disciplines constitute the "sciences of the human spirit".)

---

1   For a more detailed discussion of this point, see Windelband, *Freedom of the Will*, pp. 19ff.

2   This does not mean that relating [events] to "rules" becomes *irrelevant* from a logical or a substantive point of view. We shall very soon have to emphasize this strongly. Here, the aim is simply to stress that the "interpretation" does not phenomenologically fall into the category of subsuming [cases] under rules. From an epistemological point of view, "interpretation" has a complex nature, as we shall see later on.

3   As we shall see later, it is only justified to speak of "reproduction" in a quite figurative sense. But, in the present context, where the focus is on the contrast, in phenomenological terms, to what is "uninterpretable", the expression cannot be misunderstood.

Epistemological discussions of the "category" [of interpretation]

1 Münsterberg's concept of the "subjectivizing" sciences

As a consequence of this incongruity between the formal cognitive goals of "interpretive" investigations and the conceptual constructions of [scientific] work that aims at formulating laws, the claim has been made that history, as well as other, related, "subjectivizing" sciences – including, for instance, economics – has as its object a kind of *being* which is in principle different from the object of all those sciences that – like physics, chemistry, biology and psychology – seek to construct general concepts by means of "objectivizing experience", which proceeds by way of "induction", "hypothesis formation" and verification of hypotheses by [confrontation with the] "facts". This [claim] is not [a restatement of] the absolute disparity between all "physical" and all "psychical" being – a disparity that no reasonable person would deny. Instead, what it means is that any "being" – whether "physical" or "psychical" – which is at all capable of becoming the "object" of analytical treatment, has an "existence" in a sense quite different in principle from that of immediately "experienced" reality (where the concept of the "psychical", as it is utilized by "psychology", cannot be applied at all). This view would also provide a foundation of principle for the concept of "interpretation" (which we have not yet analysed in any detail), since that way of attaining knowledge would evidently be the distinctive mode of expression of the "subjectivizing" method. But clearly, the [view that a] gulf separates the two kinds of science would make the validity of all the categories of "objectivizing" cognition – "causality", "law" and "concept" – problematical. Probably the most consistent development of the fundamental theses of a theory of science along these lines is to be found in Münsterberg's *Outline of Psychology*, and those theses immediately began to influence the theory of the "cultural sciences". This is not the place for an exhaustive critique of that profound[1] work; nevertheless, as it ascribes a completely different meaning, both to the concept of the irrationality of the "personal", and to the concept of "personality" in itself, it is necessary to comment on at least those of [Münsterberg's] constructions that touch on the problem of causality in the domain of human action and that have in that respect been utilized in the field of epistemology of history and related sciences by certain authors – in particular F[riedrich] Gottl. Münsterberg's line of thought with regard to the points that are important to us[2] in the

---

1 When one has no right to judge a work, even to praise it is presumptuous. It should therefore be noted that I shall in the present context only comment on those parts of the work which deal with the epistemological problems of the historical disciplines and which I believe that I am able to evaluate, even though I am not a specialist [in that field]. As far as [Münsterberg's] extremely interesting discussions of the methodology of psychology are concerned, I do not in any way allow myself to pass judgement on them. Nor shall I make any real attempt to obtain information from professional psychologists as to the value or lack of value of those discussions: At present, those scholars tend to behave like the two lions in the [well-known] song: they devour each other so [completely] that no trace remains visible to outsiders. ‹72› However, in my opinion even non-psychologists may register dissent with respect to a few passages of Münsterberg's, in particular when he gives an "epistemological" explanation of the introjection ‹73› of the psychical [element] into the brain. At that point, one feels the need for a discussion of the "limits of epistemology": the increasing interest in epistemology is in itself a welcome phenomenon; but it does carry with it the danger[ous temptation] to solve *substantive* problems on the basis of *logical* principles; which would result in a revival of scholasticism.

2 Those are the only points that will be discussed. Consequently, a large number of precisely those theses that are no doubt of decisive importance to Münsterberg, will not be gone into at all. Not only the way in which the psychical is made the object of experimental psychology, but also the concept of "immediately experienced reality", of the "subject taking a stand" etc. will be left unconsidered. From Münsterberg's point of view, the essential element is the dispute over the boundary between

present context may perhaps be summarized as follows: The "I" of actual life, which we "immediately experience" at every moment, cannot be the object of analytical investigation that makes use of concepts, laws and causal "explanation"; this is because it is never "found" in the same way as, for instance, our "surroundings": it has an "indescribable" character. The same holds for the world which [this "I"] actually "lives in", since the "I" never simply perceives, but always and at every moment "takes a stand, evaluates, passes judgement". Consequently, from the point of view of this "I" – of every one of us, as long as we are "in activity" – the world is not at all relevant as something that "can be described", but only as something that "can be evaluated". It is only when I, for the purpose of information and explanation, *conceive* the world as being detached from the dependence on the "I" that it becomes a complex of facts that is "simply perceived". Already at this point, it should be remarked that the rational consideration of the means serving the purpose of a concrete "activity", and of the possible effects of a contemplated action, could of course within this theory (if we wanted to take it literally) have no place as part of the still unobjectivized "immediate experience", since, in any such reflection, the "world" as a "perceived complex of facts" *becomes* an "object" governed by the category of causality. Without "empirical" experience of how events occur *as a rule*, there can be no "rational" action;[1] and that ["experience"] can only be gained by objectivizing pure "perception". To this, however, Münsterberg would give the following reply: Admittedly, the objectivization of the "world" for the purpose of gaining knowledge is ultimately grounded in that rational action, which for its purposes underpins the world of the "immediately experienced" with a cosmos of the "empirically experienced", with the aim of providing a basis for our "expectation" of the future in order to allow us to take a stand; this is indeed the source of all science[s] that employ concepts and laws. But the "experience" created by the objectivizing science necessarily presupposes the detachment of reality from the actuality of genuinely immediate experience. [This empirical "experience"] is a product of unreal abstraction, created for certain purposes that were originally of a practical, later of a logical, nature. In particular, the actual "*volition*" will never be "experienced" in the same sense in which one becomes "aware" of the *objects* of volition – which later become the subject matter of the "objectivizing" sciences. ["Volition"] is therefore in principle different from all the substance of empirical experience, which is "found". One's first inclination would be to object that this represents nothing more than the "difference" between the "existent" as such and the "existential *judgement*", and that we can, and in fact do, apply the latter to a concrete volition (including our own), just as we can apply it to any "object". The fact that the volition *is* existent – that is to say: *is* "immediately experienced" – is of course, from a logical point of view, something different from our "knowing" about this immediate experience, but the same is true of "perceived" objects. Against this, Münsterberg would argue that what he means to say is simply that the "will" can only become an object of "*description and explanation*" once the "introjection" of the psychical [element] into a body has been accomplished, and that this introjection in its turn only becomes possible once the separation of the "psychical" from the "physical" has been accomplished (a separation that is quite unknown to immediate "experience"), that is to say: *after* the "objectivization" of the world has been accomplished. But then, that will is no longer the "real" will of the "actual subject", but an "object", which has been created by means of abstraction and is now subjected to analysis. But, in his view, we also *have knowledge* of the *real*

the "subjectivizing" and the "objectivizing" sciences, a dispute which, in particular, includes [the question] of the place of history. Rickert gives a brief but very lucid analysis of Münsterberg's book in Rickert, *Münsterberg*.

1   We shall also revert more than once to this point.

will as immediately experienced actuality. But this "knowledge" – both of one's own "actuality", which ceaselessly "takes a stand" and valuates, and of the actuality of another subject (a human being *or, as he now and then explicitly points out, an animal*), which takes a stand (that is to say: strives and valuates) – [this knowledge] moves in the sphere of immediately lived reality, in the "world of values". It therefore also implies an immediate "understanding" – which means that one shares in or reproduces the immediate experience of "actualities", re-feels, appreciates and evaluates them. This stands in contrast to the object of the *"value-free"* analytical acquisition of knowledge, which can only be created by "objectivization" – that is to say: by artificial detachment from the original, "understanding and evaluating" subject. And the aim of that [analytical acquisition of knowledge] is precisely *not* to gain an inner "understanding" of a world of actuality, but to "describe" a world of "found" objects and to "explain" it by reducing it to its elements. However, already for [the purpose of] mere "description", and even more definitely for [the purpose of] "explanation", this "objectivizing" knowledge needs not only "concepts" but also "laws"; they are, on the other hand, neither valuable nor even meaningful for acquiring knowledge in the domain of the "understanding" by the "actual" "I". This is because the actuality of the "I", from which a "science of reality" cannot abstract, is the "world of freedom", and, as such, it is manifest to us, when we *search for knowledge*, as the world of that which can be interpreted and *understood* – "reproduced in immediate experience". The knowledge that we have of that world is precisely that "immediately experienced" knowledge which cannot in any way be extended by employing the instruments of "objectivizing acquisition of knowledge": concepts and laws. – However, in Münsterberg's view, the "objectivizing" psychology also takes the immediately experienced substance of reality *as its point of departure*, in order to proceed to analyse it by way of "description" and "explanation". Therefore, the only remaining difference between the objectivizing and the subjectivizing disciplines is the "dependence on the 'I'": the [subjectivizing disciplines] *cannot* (nor should they) give up this dependence, while all that is retained of it in the [objectivizing disciplines] is the purely theoretical, value-free [status of] its objects [as] "being experienced", so that the unity of the "I" "taking a stand" simply cannot be grasped by the constructions of the [objectivizing] disciplines, as this "I" simply cannot be "described", but only "immediately experienced". History gives an account of "acts" of "personalities" and seeks to create a "context of will" within which human valuation and volition are "re-experienced" in their full, "immediately experienced" actuality; therefore, history is a subjectivizing discipline.

What is substantively important for *us* in Münsterberg's conception, [as set out above,] of the specific character of history and of the "sciences of the human spirit" related to it, is (if we remove a number of obvious errors of logic)[1] based on the following theses: "Empathy" and

---

1   In my opinion, these logical defects include the following:
    (1) [Münsterberg] fails to realize that *all* empirically given multiplicities are intensively infinite (p. 38), although this [fact] is the ("negative") precondition of the selection of material that takes place in every empirical science. As Rickert has already noted, this failure is only possible because [Münsterberg retains] the pre-critical viewpoint according to which the totality of what is given at any moment is identified with those of its aspects and elements that "matter" to us – and that are precisely the product of that selection. This viewpoint, in combination with another error, leads [Münsterberg] to:
    (2) a flawed conception of the relationship between "law" and "individual" (in the logical sense), and in particular to the opinion (p. 39) that the individual, "objectivized" reality is included in the laws. Th[is] error is most manifestly evident when Münsterberg (p. 114) emits the view that "if the ideas that Nero experienced had been different, the ideal system of *psychology* would have to be altered", a view that rests on [the presupposition that], if the "conditions" are formulated with sufficient specificity, the law will cover even the most individual concrete case – indeed, that it is possible to

have a law *for* the concrete case. In this argument, [Münsterberg] fails to realize that, if we assume that the ideas that passed through Nero's mind were different, this will primarily lead us to suppose that the constellation of *conditions* was different. These "given conditions", in their turn, first of all comprise, as [possible] causes, the whole individual course of ancient history, no less than Nero's whole family tree etc. etc., and therefore more than the objects of any *psychology*, however "multifaceted". Moreover, second, there is an *infinite* number of such conditions – even if we simply take them as just "given" – *unless*, and to the extent that, we have from the beginning considered only certain general clinical–psychological qualities of Nero's ideas as being that which we want to explain, and have therefore taken only them into account; *no matter how* "specific" those qualities are assumed to be, this [explanandum] is therefore an object that has been produced by means of selection, and [does] not [amount to] the individual passage [of ideas through Nero's mind] in its totality. What is "historical" about the phenomenon – that is to say, the object that can only be explained historically – is the *fact* that precisely *those* conditions were actually *given* in *this* context; and this fact can certainly never be deduced from a *law* – or even from [a constellation of] laws, however large. (Admittedly, it may equally well give rise to misunderstanding when Simmel (*History of Philosophy*[2], p. 95) states that, if our nomological knowledge were absolutely complete, "*one* single historical fact" would suffice to "perfect our knowledge altogether". In that case, this "one" fact would still need to have an infinitely great content. It has been said that, if we imagined that the position of *one* grain of sand were different from its actual position, the total course of events in the world would by necessity have been different; however, this would not justify the belief that – if we remain within this example – if we had absolutely perfect nomological knowledge, the knowledge of the position of *this* grain of sand at a certain time would be sufficient for construing the position of *all* grains of sand. For that purpose, we should still need to know the position of *all* grains of sand (and of all other objects) at a *different* time.)

(3) Another [problem] – which Rickert has already indicated (in Rickert, *Münsterberg*) – is that, in [Münsterberg's] repeated discussions of the fact that history deals with something "general", the quite different meaning of the concept of "generality" (in this case: universal *significance*, as opposed to general *validity*) remains unclear. (Rickert has since then given a transparent account of [this] meaning of "generality". ‹74›) This problem is connected with the erroneous viewpoint discussed under point (1) [above].

(4) Münsterberg develops the distinction between his two categories of sciences, and [demonstrates their] parallelism, with perspicacity and elegance; but, in spite of this, the subject–object relationship – which can have so many different meanings from a logical point of view – is not completely elucidated, and [he] does not always adhere to the definitions that he has provided. (In two places – in the middle of p. 35 and at the top of p. 45 – the "*epistemological*" subject is even, no doubt inadvertently, conflated with the "subject taking a stand".) Consequently, the category of "objectiv-ization", which is [of] crucial [importance] to Münsterberg, is gravely unsettled, since the decisive question is precisely *where* it applies: whether *history* and the disciplines related to it are to count as "objectivizing". It is a misleading formulation when Münsterberg says (p. 57) that the "experiencing" subject (that is to say: the subject who faces the objectivized world) is the real subject, when we "abstract" from its actuality. Either the "experiencing" subject *exists* in reality as an actual subject, and the *only relevant* actuality of this subject for the successful progress of knowledge is oriented towards the realization of the values of empirical knowledge. Or else we are dealing with the theoretical *concept* of a purely imagined "epistemological subject", whose limiting case is the much-disparaged concept of the "consciousness in general". Münsterberg then immediately proceeds to enlarge the concept of "empirical experience" to include that of reduction to component "elements" and, further, that of going back to the "*ultimate*" elements – although biology, for instance, which is (in his view) undoubtedly "objectivizing", is (as he himself occasionally mentions) far from [doing] that. At least on the basis of Münsterberg's view of the relationship between law and (logical) individuality, it is not at all apparent why that which is said (at the bottom of p. 336) about the natural sciences should not also be valid for history, economics, etc. If so, they would in no way become "applied psychology", since they in fact concern themselves not only with the course [of] psychical [events] – [an element] that many historians (Ed[uard] Meyer) are almost indifferent to – but also and *in particular* with the external *conditions* of action. – If history is "a system of intentions and purposes", the sole decisive [question] is whether there is a kind of "understanding" that is "objective" in the sense that it does

"understanding" – which are only possible in the domain of "mental" processes – are the category peculiar to the "subjectivizing" acquisition of knowledge; no bridge leads from that [category] to the instruments of the objectivizing search for knowledge; [and] we are therefore not justified in, so to speak, jumping at will from one (for instance psychophysical) interpretation to another, "noëtic" one ([based on] understanding);[1] nor may we use [the means of] one kind of search for knowledge to fill the gaps left by the other one. It was Schopenhauer who first said that "causality is not a cab which one can stop at will". ⟨75⟩ But, as Münsterberg believes that the gulf separating the "subjectivizing" from the "objectivizing" approach would make it unavoidable to stop in that way at the boundary of what was "noëtically" accessible, he *denies* that the category of causality can be applied at all to the "subjectivizing" acquisition of knowledge. For, so he argues, once we have begun a causal explanation, we "simply cannot stop the [process of] explanation" "if we happen to encounter an act of will which, apart from its constitution, which can be empirically experienced, also has an internal tendency, which can be understood" (p. 130). Instead, we must at that point attempt also to reduce this act of will to a series of (psychophysical) elementary processes. If we are unable to do that, then "a dark place would remain" that we would not "elucidate" (which surely should only be taken to mean: "elucidate" in a psychophysical sense) by means of "empathy" (p. 131). And conversely, we can acquire no extra knowledge (which surely should only be taken to mean: no additional understanding by means of "reproduction of immediate experience") of subjective configurations "by categorizing non-understood elements as objective configurations" (p. 131). Let us begin with the more peripheral arguments reproduced immediately above. At any rate, they are not compelling. Let us take the example of a cultural–historical analysis of, say, the interconnections between religious and social upheavals at the time of the Reformation. As far as the "internal aspect" of the acting persons is concerned, the "subjectivizing" interpretations that would be applied in such an analysis would, to begin with, deal with conceptions which, from the point of view of experimental psychology, have an incredibly *complex* character. So complex[, indeed,] that, at the present time, the first beginnings have hardly been made towards a "reduction" of [these conceptions] to simple "sensations" or other "elements" that, even provisionally, cannot be further reduced. To this quite trivial fact can be added a further, even more trivial one: It is difficult to see how one would ever be able to obtain the material for such a "reduction", which would obviously only be possible by way of "exact" observation (in the laboratory). But apart from all this, the crucial point remains that, of course, history does not confine itself to the "internal aspect", but "conceives" the whole historical constellation of the "external" world, on the one hand as a motive for, and on the other hand as the result of, the "internal processes" of the bearers of historical action. Those matters, in their concrete multiplicity, really cannot be accommodated within a psychological laboratory, nor can they be part of purely "psychological" considerations, however limited a concept of "psychology" one might wish to define. And by itself, the fact that the act of will is "irreducible" and a "teleological unity" – or rather: the circumstance that a science *treats* "acts" and their "motives", or perhaps "personalities", as irreducible *for its purposes*, because a reduction would not have any cognitive value with respect to the problems which *that science*

---

not "take a stand" – in the sense of "*evaluating*" its subject matter (i.e. those intentions and purposes) – but simply aims [to formulate] "valid" judgements concerning the actual course and interconnection of "factual [events]". In Münsterberg's work, the crucial concept of the theoretical *relation* to values is *lacking*; instead, he conflates it with the concept of "evaluation". For another objection to the theory of the distinction between objectivizing and non-objectivizing empirical disciplines (in Natorp's version), see also Husserl, *Logical Investigations II*, pp. 340f.

1 On the other hand, Münsterberg allows (p. 92) for the possibility of interpolating psychological findings where knowledge of the anatomy of the brain is incomplete.

wishes to solve – is certainly not sufficient to remove that discipline from the group of "objectivizing" sciences. The concept of the "cell", as it is used by biologists, manifests exactly the same features in its relation to physical and chemical concepts. Moreover, it is not at all obvious why, for instance, the exact psychological analysis of, say, religious hysteria *might* not at some future time produce results that could, and must, be utilized by historians as conceptual tools for the purpose of causal imputation of certain individual events, just as [historians], whenever it suits their purposes, freely utilize concepts [belonging to] any other scientific discipline that can be of use to them. *If* this happens – if, to take an example, the historian were to accept a view formed by pathologists that certain "acts" of Frederick William IV ‹76› were in conformity with certain "regularities" of psychopathic reactions which had been established by pathology – then what happens is precisely that which Münsterberg claims to be impossible: by means of "objectivization", we explain what "cannot be understood".[1] And Münsterberg himself shows that the "subjectivizing" sciences proceed in the same manner whenever the results of "objectivizing" disciplines become relevant for them: he emphasizes that the results of experimental psychology can be of use to *pedagogy*,[2] and only adds the reservation – which is certainly correct, but which is irrelevant for history and for all theoretical disciplines – that the *practical* pedagogue *in* his practical activity – that is to say, in his active contacts with his pupils – cannot simply become an experimental psychologist, and that he should not do so. Münsterberg gives two reasons for this: (1) Because the teacher in this context – where (to use Münsterberg's terminology) he is a "subject taking a stand" and, for that very reason, *not* a man of science, not even of a "subjectivizing" one – has the task of realizing ideals of what *ought to* be. The results of an analytical science of empirical experience cannot determine the value or lack of value of those ideals. – (2) Because "common sense" and "practical experience" are far more important for the purposes of education than the (in that respect) extremely meagre results of experimental psychology. Let us dwell for a moment on this example, which is quite instructive. Münsterberg does not offer any reason for the claim [made under (2)], in spite of the fact that it is really the only interesting point. How can the phenomenon [which he describes] be explained? Apparently in the following way: For the purposes of practical education, the concrete pupil, or the multitude of concrete pupils, are considered as *individuals*; and those of their qualities that are relevant for the task of exerting pedagogical influence have, in important respects, been conditioned by an immense number of quite concrete influences emanating from their "disposition" and their individual "milieu" (in the widest sense of the term). In their turn, these influences can from every possible point of view be made the object of scientific investigation, including "objectivizing" investigation; but they certainly cannot be produced experimentally in the laboratory of

---

1   A little later on, we shall see to what extent Münsterberg may nevertheless be right as far as *history* is concerned. But, in other disciplines, the distinction between the "noëtic" and the "law-like" does not apply in the same way at all. Münsterberg's description of the tasks of "social psychology" as [the] "psychophysics of society" is completely arbitrary. For investigations in the field of social psychology, the psychophysical parallelism is just as irrelevant as, say, "energistical" hypotheses. ‹77› Moreover, we shall see that "interpretation" is by no means restricted to being *only* the interpretation of individual occurrences. To the extent that investigations in the field of "social psychology" have already been carried out, they have without exception worked with the instruments and the goal of interpretation, but have [nevertheless] been *generalizing*, "nomothetic" efforts. They note how they can make use of the results of experimental psychology, psychopathology and other disciplines of the natural sciences; but, in themselves, they do not in the least feel compelled to define the general goal of their concept formation as being that of going back to "psychical elements" in a strict sense. Similarly, they are content with that degree of "precision" of their concepts which is sufficient for the purpose of their inquiries.

2   *Outline of Psychology*, p. 193 (bottom).

a *psychologist*. From the point of view of the "sciences of laws", each individual pupil represents an individual constellation of an infinite number of individual causal chains. However many "laws" there may be, and even if we have attained a maximum of nomological knowledge, the pupil can only be subsumed [under those laws] as an "example" if we assume that their operation presupposes an infinite number of conditions that are "simply" given. And, in this respect, there is absolutely no difference between the "immediately experienced" reality of "*physical*" occurrences and the "immediately experienced" reality of "psychical" occurrences. This will certainly not be denied by Münsterberg himself, who has strongly emphasized that the division of the world into "physical" and "psychical" [elements] has a secondary character and only occurs in the wake of "objectivization". Here, as elsewhere, even the most comprehensive nomological knowledge – that is to say: knowledge of "laws", i.e. of abstractions – is not equivalent to knowledge of the "ontological" infinity of reality. It is quite undeniable that scientific–psychological knowledge, acquired for quite heterogeneous purposes, *may* in some individual case indicate the "means" for attaining a pedagogical "end"; but it is equally certain that this cannot be guaranteed a priori: the question whether *general*, "exact" psychological observations of that kind – as for instance concerning the conditions of fatigue, and concerning attention and memory – can also lead to the formulation of pedagogical rules with *general* and "exact" validity is naturally also dependent on the substance of the concrete end of the pedagogical activity. The fundamental quality of "empathetic understanding" is that it is able to synthetize *individual* "spiritual" realities, in their context, into a mental image, in a way that allows the creation of a "community of minds" between the pedagogue and his pupil or pupils, so that a spiritual influence can be exerted [on the latter] in a particular, desired direction. The endless stream of ever individual "immediate experiences" that flow through our lives "schools" the "imagination" of the pedagogue – and of the pupil – and makes possible that "interpretive understanding" of the life of the mind which the pedagogue needs. But to what extent the pedagogue – over and above that, and through his reflection on abstract "laws" – has reason to transfer his "insight into human nature" from the realm of the "perceptual" to that of the "conceptual"; and, in particular, to what extent the subsequent logical processing, oriented towards the formation of law concepts possessing the greatest possible "precision" and general validity, is of positive value for the interests of pedagogy – the answer to those questions solely depends on whether the "exact" *precision* of a conceptual formula carries with it some kind of "new" knowledge that *cannot* be attained by means of "popular psychology" and that has some sort of practical value for the pedagogue.[1] Since the conditions which the pedagogue has to consider are of an eminently "historical" nature, [those

---

1   In my opinion, Münsterberg, like so many others, has an inadequate grasp of the significance of the contrast – which is so often met with – between "scientific" psychology and the "psychology" of "insight into human nature"; and he is not justified in pressing that distinction into the service of his dualism. When he says (p. 181, bottom) that "a person who has insight into human nature either knows the whole man, or does not know him at all", the answer is: what he knows of the man is that which is *relevant* for certain concrete *purposes*, and nothing else. For *logical* reasons alone, a purely psychological theory which tries to formulate laws is unable to encompass those [aspects of] man that become significant under certain, concretely given points of view. In *practice*, however, this depends on the, infinitely varied, constellations of life that are relevant in the concrete case, and that of course do *not* only contain "psychical" [elements]: no theory in the world can comprehensively include [all] those constellations of life among its "preconditions". – As an illustration of the [fact that a] gulf separates the "psyche" of psychology, obtained by means of objectivization, from the "subject" of practical life, Münsterberg contrasts the *un*importance of psychological knowledge for politics with the importance of physical knowledge for bridge-building. But this comparison is not an apt one: Let us leave aside the difference between, on the one hand, the technical situation, which is stable and patiently remains the same in the face of long and complicated calculations, and, on the other hand,

instances where "precision" gives "new" knowledge] will constitute relatively small enclaves within a wide domain of "insights into life"; the conceptual precision of those insights is only, and can only be, relative (in fact: quite small), nor *need* it be any greater to be useful for the purposes in question.

The same holds for the historical disciplines. Everything that Münsterberg says about the situation of those disciplines is correct, as far as the purely negative importance for history of everything that cannot be "interpreted" is concerned. The empirically founded conclusions of psychopathology and the laws of psychophysics are only relevant for history in exactly the same sense as physical, meteorological and biological knowledge. That is to say: it entirely depends on the individual case whether history, or economics, has any reason to pay attention to the established *results* of a psychophysical science of laws. It is occasionally asserted that "psychology" in general – or some, as yet undeveloped, special kind of psychology – *must* be the indispensable "fundamental science" for history or economics in general, because all historical and economic occurrences traverse a "psychical" stage and must "go through" it. Of course, this view is untenable. Otherwise, we should also have to consider acoustics and the theory of guttiform fluids ‹78› as indispensable, fundamental sciences of history, since the "actions" of statesmen of our time "go through" the form of the spoken or written *word*, that is to say: through sound waves and drops of ink etc. It is very popular nowadays to believe that the demonstration of the "importance" of certain real "factors" for the causal interconnections of cultural life is a sufficient reason for establishing, as speedily as possible, a special science of those "factors". But [those who hold that belief] overlook that the first question must surely always be whether there is something *problematical* about those "factors", viewed in *general*, that can only be solved by the application of a specific method. If it were the rule at least to raise this question, we would have been spared many "—ologies". – Already, for these reasons, it is even impossible to maintain that history must a priori have a "closer" relationship to some sort of "psychology" than to other disciplines. This is because history does not deal with the *internal* processes – triggered by certain "stimuli" – of human beings for their own sake; instead, it is concerned with the "external" conditions and effects of the way in which human beings relate to the "world". Admittedly, in this respect the "standpoint" [of history] is always in a specific sense "anthropocentric". In the history of England, the causes of the Black Death are not sought, for instance, among [factors within] the domain of bacteriological knowledge; instead, it is treated as an occurrence whose origins lie in a world that is, so to say, "outside history" – as [a] contingent [element]. In the first place, this is simply owing to the "principles of composition" to which every scientific account is also subject; and to that extent, the reason [for this treatment] is not *epistemo*logical, as it is quite possible [to write] a "History of the Black Death" that, on the basis of medical knowledge, provides a careful analysis of the concrete conditions and the

the volatility of political opportunities. [That apart], from the point of view of the bridge-building technician, the bridge must possess qualities that can in the main be *generally* determined; consequently, means which can be generally determined play a role for the bridge-builder that is absolutely different from [that which they play] for the politician. If you look at, say, a brilliant billiards player instead of the bridge-builder, it becomes quite obvious that, even in the domain of physics, knowledge of abstract laws is insufficient for the "practitioner". Münsterberg also makes the following point, which is intended to counter the view that some [kind of] "objectivization" of what is "only" psychical can have an importance for practical life: The "content of the psyche" of another person can have "no practical importance at all" for us; instead, [he says,] "our practical anticipation of our neighbour and his *actions*" is only based on "his body and its movements" (p. 185). This formulation is misleading. In innumerable cases, we – the mother, the friend, the "gentleman" in general – cannot be indifferent to the "feelings" of another person, even when we do not expect [those "feelings"] to result in any sort of action, least of all in a "bodily movement".

course of the epidemic. That [work] is "history" in the proper sense of the word *if* it is governed by those cultural values by which we are governed when we consider the history of England during the same period – that is to say: if the goal of the analysis is not to find bacteriological laws (to take one example), but to provide a causal explanation of "facts" of cultural history. And because of the nature of the concept of "culture", this *invariably* means that [the historical analysis] will as its culmination lead to knowledge of a context which *understandable* human action (or, more generally, "behaviour") is conceived as being fitted into and influenced by – because that is what "historical" *interest* is concerned with.

[If] psychology were to form concepts that, in the interest of "precision", were to go below the limits of the "noëtic" [in order to] grasp elements that could not be re-experienced by "understanding" in the empirically given psyche, then the situation of those concepts vis-à-vis history would become exactly the same as that of nomological knowledge [provided by] any other natural science, or – at the opposite limit – as that of any sequence of statistical regularities which could not be interpreted in an understandable manner. To the extent that psychological concepts and rules, or statistical figures, are *not* susceptible to "interpretation", they represent true [facts] which are taken by history as "given", but which do not contribute anything to the satisfaction of the specifically "historical interest".

Consequently, the link between the *historical interest* and the "possibility of interpretation" constantly remains as the only point that really has to be analysed.

In his discussion of the significance of this fact, Münsterberg muddies the waters considerably. In particular, in order to widen the gulf between the "objectivizing" and the "subjectivizing" approach as much as possible, he mixes up with each other, terminologically or in substance, quite heterogeneous epistemological categories and concepts, with the result that his line of reasoning becomes quite alarmingly confused. In his various constructions concerning [the subjectivizing] epistemological category, it is at first unclear to what extent the terminological pair "understanding and evaluating" (the term used by Münsterberg to designate "the natural [way of] considering the 'life of the mind'")[1] is meant to describe a unitary form of "subjectivizing" treatment of the "life of the mind", or [to describe] two forms, which are intrinsically different, although they will, within the "subjectivizing" approach, constantly occur in association with each other. What is certain – and Münsterberg does not dispute this – is that the "subject taking a stand" also "evaluates" things that are *not* "mental" and therefore cannot be "understood". The [converse] question therefore remains: Is it possible to have a "subjectivizing" "understanding" – of "mental" life – without "evaluating"[?]. It might seem to be beyond doubt that the answer would be affirmative, since Münsterberg distinguishes between "normative" and "historical" subjectivizing sciences. But everything again becomes doubtful in view of the fact that, in the table of the taxonomy of the sciences that Münsterberg has later published as an addition to his book,[2] *philology*, the mother of all "exact" sciences, is in its totality categorized as an "objectivizing" science. This in spite of the fact that philology without any doubt (not *only*, but also, and to a very high degree) proceeds by way of *interpretation* and must *also*[3] appeal to "understanding by means of re-experiencing". This is true not only of [philological conjectures] (which Münsterberg might perhaps describe as "part" of the work

1   *Outline of Psychology*, top of p. 14.
2   In Münsterberg, *Position of Psychology*. In *Outline of Psychology*, p. 17, we still find the opposite [standpoint]. Münsterberg's views are in a state of flux. In itself, the title of a book by one of his pupils, Mary Whiton Calkins: *The Double Standpoint in Psychology*, shows what has become of the "subjectivizing" approach.
3   On this point, see Karl Voßler's work *Positivism and Idealism*, which is mainly directed against Wechssler's contribution to the Suchier festschrift (Wechssler, *Phonetic Laws*), but more generally against the

of the *history* of literature (that is: of culture) but also, exclusively, within the field of grammar (unless the work is of a purely classificatory kind), and even (although this is the "limiting case") within the theory of phonetic changes. Consequently, it would seem that some scientific work may be "*interpretive*" but must nevertheless be [categorized as belonging to the] "objectivizing" disciplines, *because* it does *not* involve "evaluation". But generally speaking, in Münsterberg's work, [completely] heterogeneous standpoints are brought to bear on th[is] problem. This becomes completely manifest when he identifies the "understanding", the "entering into the spirit", "appreciation" and "empathy" of the "subjectivizing sciences", with "teleological *thinking*".[1]

However, "teleological thinking" can of course mean *very* different things. Let us start by assuming that what it means is: the interpretation of occurrences on the basis of their *goal*. In that case, it is certain – we shall discuss this in more detail – that "teleological thinking" has a *narrower* range than that of our ability to "subjectivize and enter into the spirit", and to "understand". On the other hand, teleological "thinking" in this sense is in no way limited to "mental life" or human action, but can be encountered, at least as a most important "transitional stage", in all sciences dealing with "organisms" (plants, for instance). And finally: as soon as the categories of "ends" and "means" – without which teleological "thinking" would be entirely impossible – are used as instruments of science, they include intellectually formed nomological *knowledge*, that is to say: concepts and rules, developed with the aid of the category of *causality*. For while there may be causal connections without teleology, there can be no teleological *concepts* without causal rules.[2] – [Another possibility is to] assume that "teleological thinking" simply means the structuring of the material by means of *value* relations – "teleological concept formation" or the principle of "teleological dependence", in the sense in which Rickert and, following him, others use these concepts.[3] In that case, it would of course neither have anything to do with "replacing" causality by some sort of "teleology", nor would it in any way be opposed to the "objectivizing" method: we would simply be dealing with a principle of selection, by means of value relation, of that which is *important* for the concept formation, and the "objectivization" and analysis of reality would in that case even be a precondition. –

---

exclusively psychophysical treatment of this central methodological problem of linguistics; see also Wundt's rejoinder [to Wechssler] in his *Psychology*, Vol. I, in which Wundt, however, mistakenly identifies "law-like character" with "causality".

1 *Outline of Psychology*, pp. 14, 17 (bottom). – It is even more confusing when [he] formulates the thesis (pp. 14–15) that "whoever sets goals is free", and then mixes up the setting of goals – which is a rational function – with the "intuitable multiplicity" of what is "immediately experienced". In the same way (p. 106), "taking a stand" is identified with an "act of will", and "immediately experienced" reality with what is "valid".

2 We shall revert in more detail to the subject of "teleological" concept formation in this sense. The following remark by Bernheim (*Historical Method*[3], pp. 118–19) is extremely unclear: "Our knowledge can only grasp the historical activities of human beings teleologically, that is to say, essentially as acts of will that are determined by purposes; and the conceptual knowledge [of these activities] is for this reason essentially different from that of the natural sciences, where the cohesion and unity of concepts is not determined by the psychological factor of purposes which have been or should be realized." He makes no attempt at all to define the difference more precisely, since a concept formation surely cannot qualify as "teleological" [simply] because the events which it is to comprehend are subject to "psychical *causality*", [a category] to which, as we are told in the following sentence, "purposes belong".

3 With respect to the "teleological concept formation" in *this* sense, Conrad Schmidt, too, is in error when (in his review (Schmidt, *Adler/Hilferding*) of Adler's book (Adler/Hilferding, *Marx Studies*), p. 397) he groups Rickert with the "teleologists" of Stammler's kind, and quotes me *against* him. – Obviously, "teleological concept formation" in [Rickert's] sense has nothing to do with replacing causality by some sort of teleology.

[A third possibility] would be to identify [the use of] "teleological thinking" in the historical disciplines with the fact that they take over and utilize concepts from "normative" disciplines, for instance [concepts] originating in jurisprudence. – Now, of course, juridical concept formation is not "causal". To the extent that it consists in conceptual abstraction, it is governed by the following question: We want to define the concept X. How can this concept be construed intellectually so that all positive norms which utilize that concept, or for which it is a precondition, can be maintained, consistently and meaningfully, alongside and in conjunction with each other? There is no reason why the term "teleological" should not be used to describe this kind of concept formation, which constitutes the peculiar "subjective world" of juridical dogmatics.[1] Obviously, the significance of the juridical conceptual constructions which have been arrived at in that way is completely independent of the concept formations of all the disciplines that seek causal explanations: [those juridical constructions] have nothing to do with a causal interpretation of reality. But, on the other hand, there is no doubt at all that *history* and all the varieties of the *non*-normative "sciences of society" make use of those concept formations in quite a different sense than the dogmatic juridical [disciplines do]. The question to be solved by [the dogmatic juridical disciplines] is that of the conceptual sphere of validity of certain legal norms; the question that every empirical–historical approach [has to tackle] is that of the causes and effects of the *actual* "existence" of a "legal order", a concrete "legal instrument" or a "legal relationship". When [disciplines working with an empirical–historical approach] establish this "actual existence" in historical reality, the "legal norms" (including the products of dogmatic juridical concept formation) are only found in the form of *ideas* that are present in people's minds; [these ideas] are *one* factor *among others* determining [people's] striving and actions; and the [empirical–historical disciplines] subject these elements of objective reality to the same treatment as all other [such elements]: that of causal imputation. For instance, from the point of view of abstract economic theory, the substance of the "validity" of a certain "legal rule" can, conceptually, sometimes be reduced to the fact that certain economic future expectations *in fact* have a chance of realization that is close to certainty. And when political history and social history make use of juridical concepts – as they continually do – then they do not discuss the ideal *claim* to validity [implicit in] the legal rule; as far as the situation makes this possible, the juridical norms are only [used] as *terminological* substitutes for [the fact that] human beings *actually* carry out certain external acts among themselves – which is the only relevant [thing] from the point of view of history. The word is the same – what is *meant* [by it] is, *logically* speaking, something totally different. The juridical term either is used here to designate one or several *actual* relationships, or it has become an "ideal-typical" collective concept. The reason why this is easily overlooked is that legal terms are [so] important in our daily practical life. Moreover, this defective view does not occur more frequently, nor is it more serious, than the opposite one: that of identifying juridical intellectual constructions with natural objects. What actually happens is that, as was said above, the juridical *term* is used to designate an *actual* state of affairs that is susceptible to a purely causal analysis; and it can normally be used in that way because we immediately attribute the [qualities of] the social collective entity, which in fact exists, to the juridical conceptual constructions with their *claim* to validity.[2]

---

1   On the fundamental logical difference between the theoretical constructs of jurisprudence and those of the purely empirical–causal disciplines, see Jellinek's lucid formulations in *System*[2], pp. 23ff.

2   If one speaks of "Germany's interests in the field of commercial policy", the concept "Germany" used in that connection is quite obviously different from the juridical concept of the "German Reich", which, as a legal person, concludes [a] trade agreement. Admittedly, one may ask whether the use of collective [concepts] precisely in *those* cases may not be a source of serious ambiguities; but this is a separate question. Such [collective concepts] cannot be entirely avoided.

[There is a] final [possibility] – which in all probability represents Münsterberg's real view, although that is obscured by his own discussions: "subjectivizing", and *therefore* "teleological", thinking may mean one that does not trouble itself with the abstractions of psychological theory, but takes "volition" as an empirical and unbroken given, and tries to comprehend its course, its conflicts and connections both with the volition of others *and* (something which is constantly overlooked because of Münsterberg's way of expressing himself) with the resistance and "conditions" of "nature". But if [this is what is meant], then the fact that other disciplines, for their purposes, treat "volition" as a "complex of sensations" would not be a reason for asserting [that there is] a fundamental – as Münsterberg terms it: an "ontological" – gulf between the two approaches. And, in view of the foregoing arguments, it is quite obvious that the fact [that such other disciplines exist] would not exclude the formulation of causal rules by a discipline for which "volition" is once and for all the ultimate "unit", which cannot be further reduced.

Again and again, the aim of "empathy", "re-experiencing" – in short, of "interpretive understanding" – therefore remains the specific characteristic of the "subjectivizing" sciences, insofar as they are *historical* sciences and not normative disciplines. But in the disciplines that aim at this [kind of] understanding, the concrete psychical phenomenon – for instance, the "immediately" understandable "volition", as well as the "I" as an "immediately" understandable "unity" – will never escape objectivization [in any instance] where [the aim is to give] a *scientific* account of facts; an account that, as an essential feature, claims to be supra-individually *valid* as "objective truth". In cases where we draw on our capacity of "interpretive" *understanding*, this objectivization will, in part – especially with respect to the kind of precision possessed by its concepts – employ means of demonstration that are different in character from those cases where the goal [of the scientific endeavour] *should* be, and only *can* be, to trace [a phenomenon] back to "not-understood" but clearly defined "formulas"; but it still remains "objectivization". In Münsterberg's view,[1] historians make use of subjectivizing "re-feeling" (as distinct from psychology, which also takes the "recognition" of other subjects as its point of departure, but then, in the interests of description, explanation and communication, chooses to follow the path of "introjection"); and, as he sees it, this ["re-feeling"] is related to the "timeless" element of "immediate experience" and is therefore in its essence equivalent to the "understanding" of the "subject taking a stand". Consequently, the less the historian's account is characterized by "conceptual" precision, the greater will be his chance of achieving his purpose. We shall revert to this point in more detail. Here, we shall only make the following comment: The category of "*interpretation*" has two faces. It can (1) aim at providing a stimulus for taking a particular emotional *stand* – as in the case of the "suggestive" [interpretation] of a work of art or of "natural beauty"; in that case, it represents the presumption that a *valuation* of a certain kind should be made. Or, it can (2) be the presumption of [the existence of] a judgement in the sense of an affirmation that an *actual* relationship has been validly "understood"; in that case, it is "interpretation" that leads to *causal* knowledge,[2] – which is the only [kind of interpretation] that we are discussing here. In the absence of metaphysical constructions, it is impossible as far as "natural beauty" is concerned; and, where works of art are concerned, it is limited to the historical "interpretation" of the "intentions" and the "distinctive characteristics" of the artist, as they are conditioned by the innumerable relevant determinants of his artistic work. [The two

1   *Outline of Psychology*, p. 126.
2   We shall leave out for the present a discussion of the fact that a *third* category lies between the two others: that of an "interpretation" which is neither "causal" nor evaluating, but prepares a valuation by analysing the possible value relations of an object (say, [Goethe's] *Faust*). ‹79›

kinds of interpretation ((1) and (2))] tend to enter jointly into the "enjoyment" of a work of art and, all too often, they are not kept apart in the expositions of art historians; moreover, it is unusually difficult to separate the two, and one has to work hard to acquire the ability; and, finally and most importantly, the evaluating interpretation is to a certain extent indispensable for paving the way for the causal one. [In spite of all this,] the fundamental distinction between the two must of course be unconditionally upheld from a *logical* point of view. Otherwise, the "cognitive goal" becomes conflated with the "practical goal", in the same way as so often happens with "causes of knowledge" and "real causes". Everyone is free, even in the form of a historical account, to assert himself as a "subject taking a stand", to propagate political or cultural ideals or other "value judgements", and to make use of the whole material of history to illustrate the practical importance of those ideals, or of those that he fights against. In the same way, biologists or anthropologists introduce certain very subjective ideals of "progress", or philosophical convictions, into their investigations; in so doing, they are of course acting no differently from someone who perhaps employs the whole panoply of knowledge furnished by the natural sciences as an edifying illustration of the "grace of God". But in every such case, it is not the scholar, but the evaluating human being who speaks, and his exposition is aimed, not only at subjects who seek theoretical knowledge, but [also] at those who make value judgements. For precisely that reason, those elements may, in that marketplace of life where [people] strive passionately and pass ethical or aesthetic judgement, be regarded as the really "valuable" part of a "historical achievement". Logic is totally unable to prevent that, but what logic can at least do – and must do, if it is to remain true to itself – is to state that, in those cases, the standard applied is not that of gaining *knowledge*, but other goals and emotional values of lived reality. Münsterberg states[1] that, in the early stages of its concept formation, psychology deals with "objectivized positions of selves". So does history. The difference is that history *employs* general concepts and "laws", when they are useful for the causal imputation of individual [phenomena], but does not itself seek to formulate such laws; therefore, for its purposes, history has no reason for moving away from reality along the path taken by *psychology*.

It is quite correct that, in the "interpretive" synthesis of an individual historical event or a historical "personality", we make use of *value* concepts, and that we ourselves in our actions and feelings, as subjects taking a stand, constantly have an "immediate experience" of the "meaning" of [those concepts]. This occurs most comprehensively in the domain of the "cultural sciences" because of the distinctive character of their object, which is constituted and defined by [their] cognitive goal; however, it is by no means peculiar to [those sciences]. In "animal psychology", for instance, "interpretations" are also an unavoidable transitional stage;[2] and when we look at the original content of the "teleological" elements of biological concepts, they, too, include "interpretations". In that case, instead of a "meaning" that is metaphysically read into [the biological concepts], we simply have the actual existence of functions that are "suitable" for sustaining life; and, similarly, [in the discipline of history,] the theoretical value *relation* replaces the "valuation", and instead of "immediately experiencing" subjects "taking a stand", we have causal "understanding" by the interpreting historian. In all these cases, categories of "immediately experienced" and "re-experienced" reality are made to *serve* "objectivizing" knowledge. This has method[olog]ically important and interesting consequences, but not those

---

1   *Outline of Psychology*, pp. 95–96.
2   Münsterberg himself occasionally says that we also "recognize" animals as subjects taking a stand. In view of this, one looks in vain for *logical* reasons why the "subjectivizing" disciplines should be limited to human beings.

assumed by Münsterberg. Only a *theory of interpretation*, which has apparently still to make its way, could tell us what those consequences are.[1] Here, we can only, in continuation of what has already been said, make some comments to situate this problem and estimate its significance for *us*.

By far the most elaborate attempt, from the point of view of logic, to formulate a *theory* of "understanding" is found in the second edition of Simmel's *Philosophy of History* (pp. 27–62).[2] The most comprehensive *methodological* application of the category [of "understanding"] to history and economics has been attempted by Gottl, to a certain extent under the influence of Münsterberg's writings;[3] as for aesthetics, it is well known that Lipps and B. Croce have dealt in depth with [the category of understanding].

---

1   The works by Schleiermacher and Boeckh on "hermeneutics" ⟨80⟩ are not relevant in this context, since their aim is not epistemological. The discussion by Dilthey (*Ideas*), which was vigorously rejected by the psychologists (Ebbinghaus[, *Psychology*]), suffers from his presupposition that there must be particular systematic *sciences* that correspond to certain of our formal cognitive categories. (On this point, see Rickert, *Limits of Concept Formation*, p. 188 (footnote).) It is preferable not to enter into a special discussion of [Dilthey's] ideas in *this* context, as we should then also have to refer to Mach and Avenarius in order to understand Münsterberg's views (as well as Gottl's, which will be treated later), and the discussion would become endless. However, on many of the points which will be treated in the following, reference should be made to Dilthey's contribution to the *Festschrift* to Sigwart (*Hermeneutics*), his *Individuality* and his *Foundations*; with respect to Dilthey's attitude to sociology, see Othmar Spann, *Dilthey*. – The lecture by Elsenhans (Elsenhans, *Psychology of Interpretation*) only deals with the psychological aspect of the problem, but not with the epistemological one, which is at present more important. We shall revert briefly later to the psychological aspect.

2   On the epistemological points that are of decisive importance in the present context, Simmel is now on the whole in complete agreement with Rickert's point of view (in *Limits of Concept Formation*), whereas formerly he differed [from Rickert] in many important respects. I am unable to see that [Simmel's] polemical remarks ([*Philosophy of History²*,] p. 43, bottom) concern a matter of any consequence: Simmel, too, cannot fail to acknowledge that the infinitude and absolute irrationality of every concrete multiplicity – [a conception] that he himself accepts – constitute the only truly *compelling* epistemological proof of the absolute absurdity of the idea that any kind of science can "reproduce" reality. On the other hand, Rickert would not wish to dispute that [those qualities] cannot – as a "negative" instance – be considered the historical cause or, generally speaking, the *real* cause determining the way in which our empirically given scientific practice is logically constituted, and that this logical constitution must be derived from the positive configuration of our cognitive *goals* and of our *instruments* of cognition. – [Simmel] is of course completely correct in saying (p. 121) that, by using [the term] "values" to designate those sources of historical interest which shape the historical concept formation, one only solves the problem in [the sense of] referring to a generic concept. Undoubtedly, this only defines, but does not accomplish, the task of a *psychological* analysis of the historical interest, and the problems concerning the *substance* of the values remain [unsolved]. But for the purposes of determining the *logical* basis of the *specifically* historical concept formation, that formulation [of Rickert's] – which is not intended to solve psychological and metaphysical problems – is quite sufficient. – Moreover, in my opinion, many of Simmel's formulations (pp. 124, 126, 133n1) may not be unobjectionable from a logical point of view. Let me only mention one point, where Simmel['s views] coincide with Münsterberg's. [As an argument] against Rickert's theory of the importance of the value relation for knowledge of the Individual, both authors emphasize that value feelings by no means always attach themselves only to "uniqueness", but may also attach themselves to repetition as such. However, this psychological observation is not relevant to the logical problem [that Rickert tries to solve], because Rickert's thesis does not, in any case, depend on a claim that *only* the unique has a relation to values. [For his purposes,] it is sufficient that, in any event, historical knowledge of individual interconnections cannot meaningfully be acquired *in the absence of* a value relation, whatever the role of values *outside* history might be.

3   Concerning [Gottl], see the first part of this article [p. 4n3 and p. 10n1], as well as Eulenburg (*Gottl*). We now also have the published version of Gottl's lecture at the 1903 Annual Meeting of Historians (Gottl, *Limits of History*). While Gottl went his own way (only somewhat influenced by Dilthey and

2 "Understanding" and "interpreting" in Simmel's work

First of all, Simmel[1] has the merit of having made a clear distinction, within the widest possible field that can be covered by the concept of "understanding" (as opposed to that of having a "conception"[2] of that reality which is inaccessible to "inner" experience), between the objective "understanding" of the *meaning* of a statement and the subjective "interpretation" of the *motives* of a person who is speaking or acting.[3] In the first case, we "understand" what is said; in the second one, [we "understand"] the speaking (or acting) person. Simmel is of the opinion that the first form of "understanding" *only* occurs when we are dealing with theoretical *knowledge*, with the presentation of substantive content in logical form, which can – *because* it is knowledge – simply, in a cognitive process, be apprehended and reproduced with a completely identical meaning. This is not correct. When, for instance, a command is heard and obeyed, we are also dealing with an understanding simply of *what is said*; and the same is the case with [similar reactions to] an appeal to conscience, [or] generally to the listener's value feelings and value judgements, where the purpose is not to bring about a theoretical interpretation, but to engender feelings and actions that immediately become "practical". And precisely Münsterberg's subject of real life who "takes a stand" – that is to say: who is striving and evaluating – will normally be content with understanding what is said (or, to put it more correctly, what is "expressed"); and [that subject] has neither the inclination nor – in most cases – the ability to perform an "interpretation", in the sense in which this is the allotted task of Münsterberg's "subjectivizing" sciences: "Interpretation" is a completely secondary category belonging to the artificial world of science, while the "understanding of what is said", in the sense given to it by Simmel, is also to be found in real life, where [one] "takes a stand". To "understand" [in this sense] is to take a stand concerning the "objective" *meaning* of a *judgement*. The expression which is "understood" can have every possible logical form, including, of course, that of a *question*. [But,] in every case, we are dealing with the relation of this expression to the *validity* of *judgements* – which might even be elementary, existential judgements – with respect to which the "understanding" person takes a "stand" [in the form of an] affirmative, negative, questioning [or other] judgement. Simmel, in his psychologizing way, expresses this by saying that "what goes on in the mind of the speaker . . . is also produced in that of the listener by means of the spoken word", and that[, in this process,] the speaker is "eliminated", and only the content of what is spoken remains in the mind of the listener, as in that of the speaker. I doubt whether this psychological description makes the *logical*

Mach, as well as by Wundt) to arrive at his fundamental views, [this lecture] clearly shows a stronger influence by Münsterberg. The only point in Gottl's writings in which we are interested is the way in which he looks at "interpretation". It should only be noted in passing that Gottl had already worked out all that is correct, or even worth discussing, in the confused discussion that is at present in full swing concerning the importance of the "telos", as *opposed* to causality.

1   In this context, we shall leave entirely aside Simmel's scattered remarks in various of his publications about the concept of society and the tasks of sociology. On this point, see Othmar Spann, *Concept of Society*, pp. 311ff.
2   Gottl uses those two terms in exactly the reverse sense. Considering the way in which they are used both in everyday and in scholarly language (Dilthey, Münsterberg and others), this is in my opinion just as inappropriate as when he uses the term "formulas" to designate concepts that are meant to cover *understandable* action (p. 80).
3   [*Philosophy of History²*], p. 28. Dilthey (*Hermeneutics*, p. 109), limits the process of "understanding", which is dealt with by "hermeneutics", to the "interpretation on the basis of external signs". This does not always hold true even for the "understanding of what is spoken" (in Simmel's sense). On the other hand, [Dilthey] (*Hermeneutics*, p. 187) sees "raising the intelligibility of the singular to [a level of] general validity" as a specific problem of the sciences of the human spirit as opposed to the natural sciences. That is going too far.

character of *this* kind of "understanding" sufficiently evident. At any rate – as was already demonstrated above – it would in my opinion be a mistake [to assert] that this kind of "understanding" could only take place with respect to "objective" knowledge. The crucial point is that, in those cases of "understanding" – [be it] of a command, a question, an affirmation, an appeal to sympathy, to patriotism or the like – we are dealing with a process situated within the sphere of "the actuality of taking a stand" – to use Münsterberg's terminology, which is quite appropriate here. This "actual" understanding has nothing to do with our [category of] "interpretation". In such cases, "interpretation" would only intervene if, for instance, the "meaning" of an utterance – whatever its substance – were *not* immediately "understood", [if] an actual "understanding" with its author about [this "meaning"] were not possible, and [if, moreover,] it were absolutely necessary to "understand" it. To take an example from "actual", real life: An ambiguously formulated written order compels the recipient (the officer leading a patrol, say) to "interpret" it by considering the "purposes" of the order, i.e. its *motives*, in order to be able to act in accordance with them.[1] That is to say: in this case, the *causal* question (how did the order "psychologically" *come into being* [?]) is raised for the purpose of answering the "noëtic question" of the "meaning" [of the order]. Here, the *theoretical* "interpretation" of personal actions and perhaps of the "personality" (of the person giving the order) serves an actual, practical purpose.

It is when ["interpretation"] serves empirical *science* that it has the form in which it interests us here: it is (as the preceding discussion has again shown), in contradistinction to [its place in] Münsterberg's constructions, a way of gaining *causal* knowledge. *So far*, we have not found that it differs, in any respect that Münsterberg would consider fundamental, from the forms of "objectivizing" knowledge, since the fact that the "interpreted" material is "introjected" into a "subject" – which in the present context means: a psychophysical individual – as the idea, feeling, [or] striving of this "subject" does not, in Münsterberg's own view, constitute such a difference.[2]

3 Gottl's theory of science

In our further discussion of the nature of "interpretation", we may usefully take Gottl's views as our point of departure, as his account provides us with a convenient basis for making clear what the epistemological significance of "interpretability" does *not* consist in.[3] This will also enable us to state our position concerning certain important propositions of Münsterberg's on which Gottl (in his second work) bases himself, and which have not yet been discussed; at the same

---

1 Simmel ([*Philosophy of History²*,] p. 28) uses the example of statements provoked by "prejudice, annoyance and the wish to scorn". But the crucial point is whether [the listener] for some reason *reflects*, in a cognitive process, on the origins of these *motives* for the utterances – even if this reason might be in the nature of a practical purpose. Only *then* does that which we have *here* called "interpretation" come into operation.

2 That this category *may* nevertheless contain other elements is something that we shall concern ourselves with later.

3 Here, we cannot furnish a critique of Gottl that is in any way exhaustive. His main accomplishment so far, the extremely profound [book] *Dominance of Words*, went quite unremarked because of the form that he chose to give it. Nevertheless, a renewed reading of it has allowed me to satisfy myself again as to the large number of excellent passages that it contains. Among other things, I see that the criticism that I have voiced elsewhere concerning the idea of the "systematic" character of economics is already to be found in rudimentary form in Gottl's account, pp. 147 and 149. Unfortunately, the present context offers no room for a "positive" critique, which I shall have to reserve for another occasion. Let me instead briefly outline the points where Gottl seems to me to be in error from a *logical* point of view:

(1) Gottl interprets the gulf between knowledge of nature and knowledge of action – this seems to be the way to formulate his distinction between objects – as an "ontological" one. In order to do this, he has to oppose the world of natural science, which has already been *subjected to* scientific *treatment* (this is brought out particularly clearly in *Dominance of Words*, p. 149, bottom), to the inner "immediate experience", which has *not* yet been *subjected to* logical *treatment*. [This is necessary,] because the actual "external" world that is given in "immediately experienced" reality does not at all manifest itself as the "rattle of pure succession and juxtaposition " that Gottl speaks of. It is well known that precisely Mach, who has influenced Gottl strongly, has a different position of principle on this point. Mach has even occasionally gone so far as to voice the following opinion: If we had full intuitive knowledge of the Lisbon earthquake ‹81› as it manifested itself to the senses [of those who lived through it], and if we had, in addition, the same degree of intuitive knowledge of the subterranean processes that could potentially be accessible to the senses, and that would have to be ascertained by science, then it would be neither necessary nor in principle possible to know anything *more* [about that earthquake]. Within the "pure", and always individual, reality, this is in fact the case. It is only when [this reality] is subjected to generalizing treatment that the abstract system of laws, and of objects governed by those laws, is created that no longer has anything intuitive about it, and that is therefore naturally *logically* inferior to action that is intuited. But it is a logical error when Gottl believes that we are capable of *thinking* [of] "immediately experienced" events – in contradistinction to "nature" – in the same way that they are "immediately experienced". This is only true, in a certain sense, of objectivized, strictly teleological, rational considerations viewed in isolation – considerations that are precisely, in themselves, "thought". Apart from this, a "concept", *even* in the domain of the personal, is in any event something different from the "immediate experience" to which it relates: [it is] a theoretical construct, produced either by generalizing abstraction or by isolation and synthesis. This is true not only, as Gottl assumes, of "existing structures" but quite as much of the individual "inner" process. His error is linked to the fact that

(2) Gottl's conception of the principles of the scientific selection of material is, in my opinion, unclear. He believes (*Dominance of Words*, pp. 128, 131) that, in the world of real events, there are interconnections that are *objectively* more "dense" and that are "immediately experienced" as such; consequently, the "conception" of the material is taken from the (shared or reproduced immediate experience of the) material itself. But, in fact, we are everywhere dealing with a *theoretical* selection of what is significant in relation to "values"; and that is also the criterion of, for instance, *what* is a "big event" and *who* is an "uncrowned king".

(3) The same judgement must be passed on the idea of Gottl's which corresponds to this, and according to which the object of the "descriptive science" of action (which, in his work, constitutes the generalizing counterpart of the historical knowledge of action) can simply be identified as the "non-history", as "everyday occurrences", *without* a selection of material (pp. 133ff., 139–40, 171ff.); [as Gottl sees it], the distinction of certain "aspects" within this general concept [cannot rest on] a principle of logic, or even of method, but is at most [to be regarded as] acceptable for pedagogical purposes, and otherwise as "arbitrary" or simply as "convenient". But it is not true – and Gottl would easily come to this conclusion if he made the (hopeless) attempt to register accurately *all* the elements of *all* his everyday experiences during just one single day of his own life – that scientific treatment, however comprehensive a form it may take, can cover simply *every action*, of whatever kind. An account, however comprehensive, of the "cultural content" of an epoch, always throws a light on how it was "experienced" under several qualitatively different *points of view*, which in their turn are value-oriented; and those "*everyday*" experiences which come under consideration at all as objects of the "cultural sciences" will also, as objects of scientific examination, be fitted into intellectually structured concrete contexts, and will then, under a large variety of partly disparate "points of view", become the objects of "historical" or "nomothetic" concept formation.

(4) As I see it, the core of Gottl's erroneous views centres on the confusion – which every sort of psychologism is so prone to – between the psychological process that takes place when substantive knowledge is acquired and the logical nature of the concepts in which this knowledge finds its *form*. Let us assume that the paths that we take in order to acquire knowledge of the interconnections of "action" to a large extent exhibit *psych*ological peculiarities; even so, *that* would in no way permit [us to draw] the conclusion that the logical character of the concepts that we use both for heuristic purposes and as means of exposition differs in principle from that of the concepts of other sciences.

time, this will allow us either to make use of Simmel's formulations or to reject them, while giving our reasons for this rejection.[1] Moreover, we shall try to provide a short discussion of the views of Lipps and Croce, to the extent that they belong in the present context.

Gottl claims that the acquisition of "historical" knowledge is essentially different from the "experience" of the natural sciences in the following way:

(1) [It] *infers* that which is to be known. That is to say: it begins with an act of (as we would put it) interpretive insight into the *meaning* of human action and, as it proceeds further, it interpretively grasps ever new elements of the context of historical reality and incorporates them; it uncovers ever new, "interpretable" "sources" [of understanding] of the *meaning* of that action of which they are the traces; and, thus, an ever more comprehensive complex of meaningful action is constructed, whose individual elements support each other because the total context remains transparent for us "from within". This [process of] "inferring" is, in Gottl's view, peculiar to the acquisition of knowledge of human action and distinguishes it from all natural science[s]. The latter can only strive, by means of conclusions by analogy, towards the highest possible degree of probability, as [the validity of] the hypothetical "laws" is *demonstrated* again and again. For a start, [however, in Gottl's conception] the psychological *process* of acquiring knowledge is identified with its epistemological *meaning*, the goal of the acquisition of knowledge identified with its method, and forms of description identified with instruments of research; moreover, it is claimed that a distinction must be made which in fact does not exist in that respect, even as far as the actual process of acquiring knowledge is concerned. To begin with, as a matter of fact, it is not generally true that the acquisition of historical knowledge *begins* with the "interpretation". Furthermore, the role played by our "historical" – or, more generally speaking: our interpretive – imagination in "inferring" historical processes is, for instance, in the domain of physical knowledge allotted to the "mathematical imagination"; and the testing of the hypotheses – since that is what we are dealing with in both cases – formulated on this basis is in principle, from a logical point of view, quite the same [in both cases]. Just as Ranke "divined" the historical interconnections, ‹82› what is usually admired as being the specific basis of Bunsen's success is his *artistic* [way of] experimenting. If there is a distinction [between the two cases], it cannot, at any rate, be characterized by the function of "inferring", which Gottl constantly comes back to. – Now, Gottl more specifically claims that:

(2) He claims that this [process of] "inferring" the course of history is made on the basis of *laws of thought*, and that therefore the *only* relevant elements of the course of events to be

---

Gottl says that you cannot define "elephant" and "friend" in the same way. Of course not: one is an object concept, the other contains a relational concept. For the same reason, one cannot, for instance, define "elephant" and "communicating ducts" in the same way. On the other hand, the logical *form* of the definition of some relational concept specific to "social psychology" is not different from that of some relational concept [in the field of] chemistry, irrespective of the fact that the content is totally disparate. We shall have to deal in the main text with certain consequences of Gottl's logic, which is (in my view) based on wrong assumptions: [When he writes that], in the world of action, the concept is present before its content, this formulation is just as misleading as [his] claim that economics has absolutely no need for anything else than "general experience" and "nous". The first claim is not *only* true of the "world of action"; as for the second one, it can only mean that the *goal* of economics is to give a [generally] understandable *interpretation* of economic phenomena. In economics, "general experience" is also subjected to logical processing, by means that are in fact quite analogous to those utilized in the natural sciences.

1   Here, it is not the intention to provide a systematic critique of Simmel's position. I shall probably revert shortly in the *Archive* to many of his theses that are, as usual, subtle in substance and artfully expressed. For a recent logical critique of the second chapter (On the Laws of History) of his [*Philosophy of History*], see Othmar Spann (*Concept of Society*).

described by history are those that can be "grasped by means of logical laws of thought"; everything else – as for instance historically relevant natural occurrences, such as the flood of the Zuider See or of the Dollart etc. – is only [to be considered as] a "shift" in the "conditions" of human action – and human action is all that history is interested in.

Here, one must object to the ambiguous distinction between "cause" and "effect" (we shall not here go into the details of what it means) being used in this context. Let us take the example of someone who writes a "history" of syphilis. That is to say, he traces the cultural–historical changes that have had a causal influence on the incidence and the spread [of the disease]; and he then, on the other hand, explains the cultural–historical phenomena that have been called into existence, or have at least in part been determined[, by the disease,] as having been caused by it. [That writer] will generally have to treat the agents of the disease as the "cause", and the cultural–historical situations as either changeable "conditions" or as "effects". But *insofar as* his work is intended as a contribution to *cultural* history, and not as a preliminary study for a clinical theory, one element still remains as the justified core of Gottl's exposition with its erroneous formulations: The scientific *interest* is in the last resort rooted in those elements of the course of history that contain human behaviour which can be understood by means of *interpretation*; [it is oriented towards] the role that this behaviour – which we find "meaningful" – has played in its interchanges with the action of "meaningless" forces of nature, as well as towards the influences that those forces have exerted on the behaviour. Therefore, insofar as history always relates "natural events" to human cultural values, and, consequently, [insofar as] the points of view of [scholarly] research that has the ambition of being historical are determined by the influence of those ["natural events"] on human action, Gottl is justified in his view. But only to that extent. Here again, what Gottl is thinking of is simply the specific direction of our interest (determined by *values*), which is to be found in connection with meaningful interpretability – a point that has already been discussed. – [Gottl] is of course decidedly mistaken, though, in saying that the course of history can be inferred on the basis of "logical laws of thought", as what he means is simply that the course of history is accessible to our understanding, by way of re-experiencing – a reference precisely to its "interpretability". This terminology is certainly not substantively irrelevant: it leads Gottl, in another passage, where he ought to have said: "understandable action", to speak of a course of events "*in accordance with reason*" – which obviously means something entirely different that is qualified by a *value* judgement. Moreover, Gottl's terminology, which is in this respect decidedly shimmering, also implies that what we are able to understand by way of "interpretation" can be identified with behaviour that can be *logically* inferred; and this identification even today sometimes plays a role in the practice of the cultural sciences, including the science of history, and may in those cases provide the foundation for a rational construction of historical processes that does violence to reality.[1] When we "infer" some meaning of an act from the given situation, and on the assumption that its motivation had a *rational* character, this is always simply a hypothesis that we formulate for the purpose of "interpretation"; in principle, this hypothesis always needs to be verified empirically, however certain it may seem in thousands of cases, and it is susceptible to such verification. In fact, we "understand" the irrational workings of the most extreme "affects" no less well than the process of rational "deliberations"; and, in principle, we are able to *re*-experience the actions

1 See Meinecke's extremely sensitive criticism of the attempt to explain the behaviour of Friedrich Wilhelm IV in all-important respects from *rational* viewpoints (*Frederick William IV*). (Whether Meinecke's adversary – Rachfahl – was perhaps *substantively* correct in his interpretation in that case [see Rachfahl, *Germany*] is something that I cannot judge and that is of no consequence in this context. We are only interested in the criticism of the *principle* of explanation, not in that concerning the substantive result [of the explanation], which may perhaps in that case nevertheless have been correct.)

and feelings of the criminal and the genius – although we are fully conscious of the fact that we *ourselves* would never have been able to experience them – as well as the activities of the "normal human being", provided we are furnished with an adequate "interpretation" of them.[1] Only this [should be added]: The "interpretability" of human action as a precondition of the emergence of a specifically "historical" *interest* is also implied by the "axiom of all historical knowledge": that human nature is "in principle [always] *the same*" – an axiom strongly stressed both by Ranke and by more recent writers on methodology:[2] The "normal" human being and the "normal" action are of course ideal-typical theoretical constructs [elaborated] for particular purposes, in quite the same way as – in the reverse sense – the well-known "sick horse"

---

1   Simmel ([*Philosophy of History*[2]], p. 57) has a special discussion of this point (that one "does not have to be Caesar to understand Caesar"). ‹83› Curiously, he sees the question whether it is possible for our interpretive understanding to reach beyond the area of our own experience as being a *psychogenetic* problem, rather than one that concerns the genesis of individual concrete *knowledge*; and, in order to solve the [psychogenetic] problem, he believes that he must resort to a kind of biological version of the Platonic idea of anamnesis. ‹84› This would only be acceptable, even as a hypothesis, if every human being in fact counted among its ancestors a Caesar, with his individual "experiences", which would then in some fashion have been handed down. But, *if* there is a difficulty here which can only be solved by such means, then every increase in one's own experiences, [and] of every peculiar or unique feature of *every* single individual inner process within every individual, presents exactly the same problem [with respect to the possibility of interpretive understanding]. Consider a constellation of psychical "elements" (whatever we understand by that expression) that vary widely in quality and intensity, that occur in innumerable complications and relationships – both among themselves and with respect to the sphere of their activity in its always individual configuration – and that, as far as their *meaning* is concerned, enter into quite innumerable combinations. It does not in itself seem particularly difficult to explain that this constellation appears to us to be something unique, which we value as "genius" by virtue of this uniqueness, but that it nevertheless does not seem to us to contain any completely unknown "elements" – no more difficult, at any rate, than that every one of us is constantly able to have an inner "experience" of something qualitatively "new". Simmel makes the acute observation (ibid., p. 61) that "sharply delineated", highly "individual" personalities are usually "understood" more deeply and unambiguously – or at least, that we believe this to be so in the concrete case. This is owing to the way in which our acquisition of knowledge is structured: here, it is the "uniqueness" which creates the relation to the *value* and which attracts the specific *interest* in "understanding" [something] that is significant by virtue of its distinctive character – an interest which necessarily decreases with every approximation to the "average". The establishment of the "unity" of the historical individual, which Simmel falls back on, is of course also carried out by means of value relation. The same is true of that part of Simmel's discussion (pp. 51–52) of the importance of a pronounced individuality of the *historian* for the success of his "interpretations", where it must be granted that he is absolutely correct. (We shall not here go into the question of how great that part is. The concept of "pronounced individuality" is fairly vague. If, as would be natural, one started by looking at the example of Ranke, [that concept] would get one into an awkward predicament.) The fact that the entire meaning of our knowledge of individual [phenomena] is anchored in value ideas also manifests itself in the "creative" influence that the historian's own strong value judgements can exert towards the successful attainment of historical knowledge. In the same way, the teleological "interpretation" served the cause of [acquiring] biological knowledge – as well as the cause of acquiring knowledge of nature in general, while the development of modern natural science was still in its first stages – in spite of the fact that the [whole] meaning of acquiring knowledge of nature is to eliminate [that kind of interpretation] as completely as possible. [In the example of the historian,] value judgements serve the cause of interpretation in the same way. (Simmel himself, in the last chapter of [*Philosophy of History*[2]], makes some excellent remarks of a similar nature concerning speculations as to the "*meaning*" of history.)

2   Bernheim's formulations on this point (*Method*[3], p. 170) give rise to serious misgivings: The "analogous ways of feeling, conception and volition in human beings"; the "identity of human nature"; the "identity of the general psychical processes" and of the "laws of thought", the "invariably identical dispositions of mind and spirit" etc. are[, so he says,] the "fundamental axioms" of all historical

in Hoffmann's *The Stalwart Cavalry Captain*; ‹85› and we "understand" the "nature" of the affect of an animal in quite the same *sense* as that of a human being. This in itself shows that, contrary to Gottl's assumption, we should not of course think of "interpretation" as something that can only come about by way of intuition – *free* from "objectivization" – and simple reproduction. Not only is it sometimes necessary to have recourse to knowledge of clinical pathology in order to "infer" a concrete thought by means of interpretation,[1] but [such an "inference"] also self-evidently, contrary to Gottl's assumption, constantly and generally makes use of "control" through "empirical experience", in a sense that is *logically* identical to that [which applies to] the hypotheses of natural science.

To support [the contention] that "interpretations" possess a specific "*certainty*" lacking in other kinds of knowledge, it has, however, been asserted – and Gottl in essence argues along the same lines – that what we know with the greatest certainty is "our own immediate experience".[2] That is correct – in a certain sense, which will be discussed presently – provided that the opposite [of our own immediate experience] is the "immediate experience" of *others*; provided, moreover, that the concept of "immediate experience" is extended to include the psychical *and physical* world immediately given to us at a certain moment; and provided that what is meant by the content of the "immediate experience" is not the reality that is to be formed by *scientific* observation, but the totality of "perceptions", combined with the "feelings" and "volitions" to which they are inseparably joined – that is to say: the "stands taken" by us at every moment, which we at the time only become "conscious" of to a highly variable degree and in very different senses. If this is what is meant by "immediate experience", then it is not made the object of *judgements* such as explanations of empirical facts, and therefore remains in a state of indifference to any empirical knowledge. If, on the other hand, that which we have "immediate experience" of is to be understood as the "psychical" occurrences "within" us, in contradistinction to the *totality* of occurrences "outside" us – irrespective of how the boundary between the two is drawn – and if these "psychical" occurrences are to be understood as objects of a valid knowledge of facts – then the situation, even according to Münsterberg's conception, which Gottl accepts, is really quite different.

But let us suppose that we – in accordance with Gottl's intentions – remain in the area where the "separation of immediate experience" into "physical" and "psychical" parts of the objectivized reality – a "separation that leads to introjection" – has not been performed, and we therefore only "conceive" the "physical" world as the occasion of [the] stand [that we take]. Even in that case, any knowledge of concrete interconnections that can be the subject of immediate experience – if [this knowledge] wishes to lay claim to validity – presupposes

---

knowledge. What is meant, however, is simply this: that history with its distinctive character is possible because, and insofar as, we are able to "understand" human beings and to "interpret" their behaviour. It would then *have to be investigated* to what extent this presupposes [that human beings are] "identical". Nor is it, on the other hand, acceptable when Bernheim (p. 104) gives "the qualitative *difference* between individuals, this fundamental fact of all *organic* life", as being the reason why laws of history are impossible. That difference characterizes all "individuals", including the non-organic ones.

1 Psychopathology, too, for instance in cases of hysteria, adopts an approach that is – if not *exclusively*, then at least *partly* – "interpretive". We shall later provide further examples of the relationship of "empathy" to "empirical experience" in this area.

2 Münsterberg, too ([*Outline of Psychology*], p. 55) is, like so many others, of this opinion. The "a-mechanical significance" of the "subjective act" of another person is "immediately given"[, he says]. That can only mean: understood – or *mis*understood. Or, finally: *not* understood. In the *first* two cases, this [significance] is formally "evident"; but whether it is empirically "valid" is a question of "empirical experience". – See also Husserl (*Logical Investigations II*, Appendix, p. 703), who argues *against* [the idea] that inner experience possesses a specific "*certainty*" and a higher "[degree of] reality".

"empirical experience" that has the same logical structure as that which pertains to any processing of the "objectivized" world. For a start, the conduct of human beings that is made the object of interpretation will everywhere contain elements that have to be accepted as ultimate "empirical experiences" in just the same way as any "object". Let us take the simplest possible [example]: the process of acquisition of mental skills by "practice" – a concept in general use in cultural history – is certainly immediately "understandable", both in itself and in its consequences. *How* it takes place can, as far as certain measurable elements are concerned, be investigated by exact "psychometrics"; apart from that, we know its *effects* through our own vast experience, in particular of how we learn foreign languages. But, in the last resort, the fact that this process takes place and is possible can only be simply "registered", in a sense that is in no way different from [the sense in which we] register the fact that, say, bodies are "heavy". But, moreover, our own "moods" (in the sense which this word carries in "popular psychology", and in which it is used countless times in the cultural sciences), which partly determine our evaluation and action, are certainly *not* immediately "interpretable" for us as far as their meaning, their "together-, apart- and becauseness" (to use Gottl's terminology), is concerned. But, it is the rule, not the exception, that we *can* in all these respects "interpret" [these "moods"] by *analogy*; this comes out most clearly with respect to aesthetic enjoyment, but also, to the same extent, in relation to inner attitudes conditioned by class [positions]. This [process of "analogy"] implies drawing on the "immediate experiences" of *others*, which we *choose* intellectually for the purpose of comparison, something that necessarily presupposes that they have to a certain degree been isolated and analysed. Not only [can we do so], but we virtually *must* control and analyse [the "moods"] in this fashion, if they are to have that clear and unambiguous character which Gottl a priori [ascribes to them]. The indistinct vagueness of "having an immediate experience" must – and this is no doubt also Gottl's opinion – be broken, in order that even the first beginnings of a real "understanding" of *ourselves* can be made. When it is said that every "immediate experience" is the most certain of all certainty, this of course applies to the fact *that* we have that immediate experience. But the actual *content* of our immediate experience can only be grasped, even by an "interpreting" procedure of whatever kind, when the stage of "having an immediate experience" as such has been left behind, and the content of the "immediate experience" is made the "object" of judgements that, for their part, are no longer "immediately experienced" with indistinct vagueness, but can be acknowledged as "valid". This "acknowledgement", however, which is seen as part of "taking a stand", does not – as Münsterberg, oddly enough, assumes – apply to the other "subject", but to the *validity* of one's own *judgements* and those of others. The maximum of "certainty", in the sense of validity (which is the only relevant sense for any kind of science), belongs to propositions such as $2 \times 2 = 4$, once they have been "acknowledged", but not to the immediate, but indistinct, experience that we "have" – or, which comes to the same thing, simply "*are*" – at a given moment. And the category of "validity" starts to function formatively as soon as we put the questions of the "what?" and "how?" of the object of immediate experience even to ourselves and need a *valid* answer to it.[1] – How that happens is the only question that is relevant for formulating a judgement concerning the logical nature of knowledge that has been acquired by "interpretation", and that is all that we shall occupy ourselves with in what follows.

1 Münsterberg, too, states (p. 31) that the "immediately experienced unity" is not even an "interconnection of processes that can be described". To the extent that it is "immediately experienced", this is certainly correct; but to the extent that it is "thought", it is undoubtedly [such a describable process]. If the circumstance that the "state" of something can be "determined" is sufficient, even at the pre-scientific stage, to make it an "object" – and from the standpoint chosen here, this terminology

III Knies and the problem of irrationality (continued)

4 *"Empathy" in the work of Lipps and "intuition" in the work of Croce*

In order to discuss the logical position of "interpreting" (in the sense that we have chosen here), it is indispensable to start by looking at certain modern theories about the psychological process that is involved.

Lipps[1] has evolved an original theory of "interpretation", although his point of view is that of inquiring into the basis of aesthetic values. According to him, "understanding" the "expressive movement" of another – for instance an affective sound – is "more" than a purely "intellectual understanding" (p. 106). It contains "empathy", and this category, which is of fundamental importance to Lipps, is in its turn (as he sees it) an aspect of the driving force of "imitation", namely the exclusively "inner" imitation of an event (p. 120) – for example, an acrobat's tightrope walking – as if it "happened to oneself". And this is not a reflective observation of the activity of another, but one's own "immediate experience" – which, however, remains completely internal, and besides which the "judgement" that (in the example) not I, but the acrobat is standing on the tightrope remains an "unconscious" one (p. 122).[2] This "complete" empathy means that the "I", inwardly, completely enters into the object that one "empathizes" with. It is therefore one's own (inner) *actual*, fantastical activity, not just an *imagined* activity, that is made the object of a "representation".[3] Lipps elevates this "complete" empathy, in the form of aesthetic "empathy", to [the status of] the constitutive category of aesthetic enjoyment, and he believes that "intellectual understanding" is developed from [the "complete" empathy] in the following way (we stay with the example used above): First, the "unconscious" judgement – "not I, but the acrobat is (or was) standing on the tightrope" – is raised to the conscious level; this means that the "I" is split into a "represented" one ([being] on the tightrope)

---

is not in itself objectionable – then there is no doubt that history as a science deals with "objects". The distinctive characteristic of the *poetic* "rendering" of reality – although it, too, of course does not constitute an "image" of reality, but gives [that reality] a spiritual form – is to treat it in such a way that "everyone *feels* what he carries in his heart". ‹86› Simple and clear records of "immediate experiences" are not yet "history", although they, too, represent an intellectual processing of the immediate experience; just as, say, a description by Zola still does not represent *scientific* knowledge, however faithfully it reproduces an occurrence at the Stock Exchange or in a department store that has precisely been an actual "immediate experience" of that kind. If one finds the *logical* nature of history in the fact that the words of historians, as Münsterberg puts it, "laugh and cry", one might just as well find it in the illustrations that may accompany the account, or – to carry the idea to its conclusion – look for it in the "ornamentation" with which, in the modern fashion, books are occasionally provided in order to create an atmosphere. – We shall later see that at least the "immediacy" of "understanding", which has been so much emphasized, belongs to the theory of psychological origins, but not to that of the logical meaning of historical judgements. The confused notions that history is "not" or "not really" a science are usually based on erroneous conceptions concerning precisely this point.

1   *Foundations of Aesthetics* (1903). Only those few points that are important for our considerations will be singled out here.
2   Consequently, Lipps underlines (pp. 126–27) that the designation "inner imitation" is only provisional, as what we are actually dealing with is not imitation but one's own immediate experiencing.
3   Lipps (p. 129) strongly emphasizes this distinction. In his view, there are three kinds of *actual* activity, which must be distinguished from one another: (1) "fantastical" inner activity; (2) "intellectual" activity (reflection and judgement); (3) that kind of activity which can only "be fulfilled in actual existence, that is to say: in sensations, and in the consciousness of the reality of something" – which one would take to mean: actual *external* activity. Here, we cannot furnish a critique of the psychological value of this distinction.

and an "actual" one (which does the representing of the first one to itself) (p. 125). Then, the "objectivization" (as Münsterberg would put it) of the event, and in particular the *causal* interpretation of it, can begin. On the other hand, "empathy" without preceding causal "experience" is impossible: a child does not have an "immediate experience" of the acrobat. But we may add (following Lipps' train of thought) that this [causal] "experience" is not the objectivized product of nomological science, but the subjective everyday causality of which one has, and can have, intuitively "immediate experience", and which is connected to the concepts of "having effect", of "effective force" [and] of "striving". This particularly manifests itself in connection with "empathy" with purely "natural events". For Lipps by no means restricts the category of "empathy" to "psychical" events. We also "empathize" with the external physical world, by "immediately experiencing" its elements with our feelings as the expression of a "force", a "striving", a particular "law" etc. (p. 188); and, in Lipps' view, this anthropomorphic individual causality in nature, which is accessible to fantastical "immediate experience", is the source of "natural beauty". Contrary to nature that is objectivized – that is to say: which is, or will be, reduced to relational concepts – "immediately experienced" nature is constituted by "things", just as one's own, immediately experienced "I" is a thing. The difference between "nature" and "I" is that the "immediately experienced 'I'" is *the only real "thing"*, from which all individuals in "nature" hold their material quality and their "unity" – [both of] which are accessible to intuitive "immediate experience" (p. 196).

However one may appraise the value of these constructions for the foundations of aesthetics, one thing (which is in fact at least intimated in the work of Lipps [himself]) should above all be kept in mind for the purposes of discussions of *logic*: "individual understanding" is *not* an "empathetic immediate experience". Nor does ["individual understanding"] evolve from "empathetic immediate experience" in the way described by Lipps. A person who "empathizes" with Lipps' acrobat will of course neither have "immediate experience" of what the acrobat on the tightrope "immediately experiences", nor of what that person would "immediately experience" if he himself were standing on the tightrope. What he "immediately experiences" is something that has a quite ambiguous, fantastical relation to [those other "immediate experiences"]; and therefore, above all, it does not contain "knowledge", of any sort, nor does it contain the object of "historical" experience at all, as that [object] would in the given case be the immediate experience of the acrobat, not of the person empathizing with [the acrobat]. What happens, therefore, is not that the empathizing "I" is split, but that one's *own* immediate experience is supplanted by the consideration of [the immediate experience] of another person, viewed as an "object", when reflection begins. Only the following is correct: "Intellectual understanding" in fact also entails "inner participation", that is to say: "empathy"; but, if [the intellectual understanding] has the purpose and goal of [acquiring] "knowledge", the "participation" [concerns] elements that have been purposefully selected. Therefore, [those who hold] the view that empathy is "more" than mere "intellectual understanding" cannot claim that [empathy] has more "cognitive value" (in the sense of "being valid"); that view only implies that we are dealing not with objectivized "acquisition of knowledge" but with pure "immediate experiencing". Otherwise, the important point is whether the *real* "material quality" that Lipps ascribes only to the "I" is to have consequences for the way in which events that are "reproducible in inner immediate experience" are analysed *scientifically*. This last question is part of a more universal problem, namely that of the logical nature of concepts of objects. In its most general formulation, this [latter] problem can in its turn be reduced to [the question]: are there really *concepts* of objects? This has constantly been denied; and the consequences which that [denial] must have for the logical assessment of history, in particular, have most recently again been demonstrated in typical fashion by Benedetto Croce, the brilliant Italian opponent of the views of Lipps and of psychologism in general in philology and aesthetics.[1] "Things are intuitions", Croce says, "concepts, on the other hand, relate to relations between things." The concept, which by nature can only be general and consequently abstract, is therefore "no longer" intuition, but, on the other hand, it "nevertheless still is" [intuition], as it is in the last resort substantively nothing more than processed intuition. However, as a consequence of the necessarily abstract character of [the concept], "things", which are always individual, cannot enter into concepts but can only be "intuited": that is, one can only gain knowledge of them by "artistic" means. A "concept" of something individual is therefore a contradiction in terms, and history, which wants to acquire knowledge of the Individual, is for that very reason "art", that is to say: a composition of "intuitions". Whether a fact in our life "was [a] real [fact]" – the only question that history is concerned with – cannot be found out by means of any conceptual analysis, but only by the "reproduction of intuitions" – "history is memory"; and, as the judgements of which it is composed are simply "the vesting of the impression of an experience", they imply no "positing of concepts"; they are simply "expressions" of intuitions. Consequently, history cannot become the object of "logical" evaluation at all, since "logic" only concerns itself with (general) concepts and their definition.[2]

Propositions of this sort are based on the following naturalistic fallacies: (1) Only relational concepts, and – since the relational concepts of immediate everyday experience of course contain just as much "intuition" as any concept of an object[3] – only relational concepts that are absolutely precise, that is to say: which can be expressed in causal equations, can be [said to be] "concepts" at all. However, not even physics exclusively employs such concepts. – (2) The claim (which is connected to [(1)]) that "concepts of objects" are not "concepts" but "intuitions". [This] is a consequence of the conflation of different meanings of the category of "intuitability". The intuitable evidentness of a mathemathical theorem is something else than the "intuitability" of a multiplicity; the latter is directly given for [our] "experience" and is, and can be, "immediately experienced" "within" and "outside" us (in Husserl's terminology:[4] "categorial" intuition, in contrast to "sensuous" intuition). In the same way, Croce's ["]thing["] and, in particular, Lipps' ["]thing["] par excellence – that is: the "I", as it is used in empirical science – are something completely different from the "immediately experienced" complex of conceptions, which has merged into a purely sensuously or emotionally intuitable "unity", and which is psychologically held together as such by "memory" or "I-feeling". Whenever empirical science treats a given multiplicity – for instance the "personality" of a concrete historical figure – as a "thing", and consequently as a "unity", this object is always only "relatively determined", that is to say: a theoretical construct that always and without exception contains something empirically "intuitable". But it is nevertheless a completely *artificial* construct:[5] its "unity" is

---

1   For the sake of convenience, I shall quote from the German translation (by K. Federn) of his *Aesthetics* (1905).
2   B. Croce's *Outline of Logic* (1905), which has appeared in the meantime, has deliberately been left aside. What is intended is not a discussion of Croce [in particular], but [to give] a typical example of views that are widely held, and that are formulated with particular precision [in his work]. I hope to revert to his book on another occasion.
3   Naturally, this is not contradicted by Husserl's remarks (*Logical Investigations II*, p. 607, see also p. 333), which primarily relate to "expressions of judgement": [it] is also [true] of the *concept* of an object that it, on the one hand contains "less", but on the other hand "more", than purely sensuous intuition or pure "immediate experience". On this point, see [my] remarks below.
4   Husserl, *Logical Investigations II*, pp. 607, 637ff.
5   The various erroneous views of Münsterberg, too, have their origin in a lack of awareness of the artificial character of history. For instance, he, too, assumes ([*Outline of Psychology*], pp. 132, 119) that

determined by the selection of what is "important" in relation to certain research purposes; therefore, it is an intellectual product, which only has a "functional" relation to the "given". Consequently, [it is] a "concept" (unless this term is artificially restricted to cover only part of the mental constructs that are created by an intellectual transformation of the empirically given, and can be designated by words). – For this reason alone, it is quite erroneous to believe – as so many laymen do, and Croce accepts – that (3) history is a "reproduction of (empirical) perceptions" or a depiction of previous "immediate experiencing" (on the part of the depicting person, or others). Even one's own "experience", as soon as it becomes an object of *thought*, cannot simply be "depicted" or "replicated": [such a "depiction" or "replication"] would precisely be something else than thinking *about* the "immediate experience"; instead, it would constitute a renewed "immediate experiencing"[1] of the former ["immediate experience"], or rather – as that is impossible – a *new* "immediate experience" that includes the "feeling" (which, when it is subjected to intellectual examination, will always turn out to be only relatively justified) of having once already "immediately experienced" "this" – ["this"] being a part, which remains indeterminate, of what is given as the present "immediate experience". Elsewhere, ‹87› I have, without, of course, saying anything "new", explained that whenever even the simplest "existential judgement" ("Peter takes a walk", to use Croce's example) wishes to be a "judgement" and to consolidate its "validity" as such – and *that* is the only relevant question – this presupposes logical operations that comprise, if not the "positing", at least a constant *use* of general concepts, and consequently isolation and comparison.

In fact, [if we look at] all those theories (unfortunately so very often accepted even by professional historians) according to which the specifically "artistic" and "intuitive" character of historical knowledge, for instance in the "interpretation" of "personalities", is the privilege of history, they all commit the fundamental error – and here we come back to Gottl's account – of confusing the question of the psychological *process* when knowledge is formed with the completely different one of the logical "character" and the empirical "validity" of [that knowledge]. As far as the psychological process [connected with] the acquisition of knowledge is concerned, the role that falls to "intuition" is by its very *nature* – as was already shown above – the same in all areas of knowledge; there is only a variation – depending on the cognitive goal – in the *degree* to which we then, when we process [the material] intellectually, are able to, and wish to, attain precision of the concept in all respects. The *logical* structure of knowledge, however, only manifests itself when its empirical validity in the concrete case is problematical and therefore has to be *demonstrated*. Only this demonstration carries with it the absolute requirement that the concepts used must be (relatively) precise, and it always and without exception presupposes generalizing knowledge; and both [these requirements][in their turn] demand an intellectual processing of the purely "empathetic" sharing in, or re-experiencing of, immediate experience, that is to say: its transformation into "empirical experience".[2] In that connection, it is an utterly superficial impression that the use of "rules of experience"

what shapes the historical [material] is the specific direction of [our] interest, that is, [our] valuation; but, in answering the question of *what* "volitions" will consequently enter into history, he refers to the[ir] "importance", so that there is no place for the "accidental (!) palpitations of the will, which are immediately cancelled out by contrary movements" (p. 127). [This shows] the prevalence of the vague idea – which Gottl, too, is governed by – that the "stuff of immediate experience" in and of itself begets the historical constructs.

1   See also Husserl (*Logical Investigations II*, pp. 333, 607).
2   This also holds for (for instance) areas such as that of psychopathological research. Not only does the "empathetic" "psychoanalysis" of a sick psyche remain the incommunicable private property of the scholar who has a specific gift for [such analysis]; but, moreover, its results also remain completely

for the purpose of verifying the "interpretation" of human action is any different from the same procedure when concrete "natural events" are concerned. This impression is due to the circumstance that, when we "interpret" human action, our imagination – which is conditioned by our everyday knowledge – to a greater extent refrains from [what it sees as the] "uneconomical" explicit *formulation* of the substance of our experience as "rules"; in other words, it uses the generalizations implicitly. For, if one asks the following question: when, from a scientific point of view, does it make any *sense* for "interpretive" disciplines to use their material – immediately understandable human conduct – to construct for their purposes, by way of abstraction, special [empirical] rules and so-called "laws"?, then [the answer] will completely depend on whether the historian (or the economist, as the case may be) can expect by this means to gain new insights that can be of use for his interpretive causal knowledge with respect to a concrete problem. It is not in the least *generally* obvious that this *must* be the case, as the "rules of experience" that can be formulated in this manner are, in the overwhelming majority of cases, not only imprecise but also trivial. If one wants an illustration of the results that would be achieved if the principle of formulating "rules" were realized unconditionally, one only has to read the works of Wilhelm Busch. This great humorist precisely obtains his most comical effects by presenting the innumerable, trivial, everyday experiences, which we constantly, and in countless combinations, use "interpretively", in the garb of scientific maxims. The charming verse from "Plisch und Plum" ‹88› – "If you rejoice when someone else is sad,/ then chances are that people will get mad [at you]" – is a quite flawlessly formulated "law of history", the more so since it, quite correctly, formulates the generic features of the event not as a judgement of necessity but as a rule of "adequate causation". – It contains [a measure of] empirical truth that indisputably makes it a useful instrument (together, of course, with a great many other, perhaps considerably more important, elements) for the "interpretation", for instance, of the political tension between Germany and England after the Boer War. Evidently, an analysis by social psychologists of such changes in the political "atmosphere" might well produce results that would be of great interest from a large variety of perspectives; and these results *may* also become of very considerable value for the historical interpretation of phenomena such as the one referred to [immediately above]. But it is *not* at all certain that [the results] will *necessarily* acquire such a high value; nor [is it certain] that, in the concrete instance, the experience of "popular psychology" will not be completely sufficient. [If this were the case,] then the wish (which has its roots in a kind of naturalistic conceit) to be able to adorn the historical (or economic) account with as many references as possible to psychological "laws" would, in [that] concrete instance, offend against [the principle of] the economy of scientific work. In an investigation into "cultural phenomena" which in principle retains the goal of "understandable interpretation", concept formation may conceivably have quite heterogeneous aims from a *logical* point of view; and among [those aims], one will without doubt necessarily *also* find that of formulating generic concepts, as well as "laws" in the broader sense of "rules of adequate causation". The latter will be of value only in cases where "everyday experience" is not sufficient to ensure that causal imputation has the degree of "relative precision" necessary for making the interpretation of cultural phenomena "unambiguous"; but, in those cases, it will[, on the other

undemonstrable, and their "validity" is therefore absolutely problematical as long as a link has not been successfully established between the empathetically reproduced immediate experience of the mental context, and the *concepts* formulated on the basis of general psychiatric " empirical experience". The [psychoanalytic results] are "intuitions" (of scholars who have that gift) "concerning" the object; but it is in principle impossible to verify the extent to which they are objectively valid; consequently, their scientific value remains quite uncertain. On this point, see W. Hellpach, *Methodology of Psychopathology*.

hand,] always be of value. However, for precisely that reason, the cognitive value of their results will as a rule be the greater, the *less* they conform to the trend of trying to achieve formulations and systems like those of the quantifying natural sciences, to the detriment of engaging in immediately understandable "interpretation" of concrete historical entities – and, consequently, the *less* they assimilate of the general preconditions that the natural sciences apply for their [own] purposes. Concepts such as, for instance, that of "psychophysical parallelism" lie beyond [the domain of] what can be "immediately experienced" and will, for that reason, of course be of no immediate importance at all to such [interpretive] investigations; the cognitive value of the finest results available to us of interpretation in the field of "social psychology" is independent of the validity of such premises, and it would be equally meaningless to [try to] fit [those achievements] into a perfect "system" of "psychological" knowledge. The decisive *logical* reason for this is the following: Although history is not a "science of reality" in the sense that it would be able to "depict" the total content of any reality – that is impossible in principle – it is [a science of reality] in this other sense that it integrates elements of the given reality – [elements] that can, as such, only possess relative conceptual precision – into a concrete causal inter-connection as "real" elements [of that interconnection]. Every single such judgement concerning the existence of a concrete causal connection can in itself be subjected to a virtually infinite process [of subdivision],[1] and only such [an infinite subdivision] could – provided our nomological knowledge were quite ideally perfect – lead to a complete [causal] imputation by means of exact "laws". Historical knowledge will only proceed with the subdivision as far as the concrete purpose of the inquiry demands it; the [causal] imputation will only be relatively complete, and this manifests itself in the fact that the "rules of experience" used to perform [this imputation] will by necessity possess only relative precision – in other words: in the fact that those "rules" which we have formulated and will still try to formulate on the basis of methodical work will always just be an enclave surrounded by the stream of "popular–psychological" everyday experience that historical [causal] imputation makes use of. But even this ["popular–psychological"] experience is, logically speaking, empirical experience.

"Evidentness" and "validity"

"Immediate experiencing" and "empirical experiencing" – [two categories] that Gottl contrasts so sharply with each other[2] – are indeed opposites; but the nature of [this opposition] is the same in the domain of "inner" processes as in that of the "external" ones, in the domain of

---

1   See on this point my discussion in *Critical Studies* (pp. 162ff.).
2   According to Gottl, the difference is that the [method of] inferring the historical is *un*able to point beyond itself to "empirical experience". The reason for this[, he believes,] is that the "logical laws of thought" are in the same position, and that, in the domain of history, "logic is to be found in the events themselves, so to speak". Consequently, those "laws of thought" have the "ultimate decision" with respect to the acquisition of historical knowledge; they determine it in a "compelling" manner, so that valid historical knowledge *always* represents an "approximation to that which is absolutely certain". Gottl contrasts this with what he calls "metahistorics": geological and biogenetic knowledge. Even if ["metahistorics"] fulfils its task in the most ideal way, [he claims,] it is still, from an epistemological point of view, simply a chronological ordering of spatial "phenomena" by means of an "interpolation" of events; therefore, it can never go further than formulating by analogy a proposition according to which things, as they are experienced, have a configuration *as if* a cosmic or biogenetic process of a certain kind had taken place. However, experience shows (and every historian will have to agree with this), that, when we submit "personalities", "actions" and "developments in non-material culture" to causal "interpretation", we have to be satisfied, again and again, with the result that the indisputably established "facts" are configured "as if" the interpreted [causal] interconnection had

"action" as in that of "nature". On the one hand, "understanding" – in the sense of evident "interpretation" – and "empirical experiencing" are not opposites, since all "understanding", psychologically speaking, presupposes "empirical experience" and can only, logically speaking, be demonstrated as valid by reference to "empirical experience". But, on the other hand, the two categories are not identical, insofar as that which is "understood" and "understandable" has a quality of "*evidentness*",[1] in contradistinction to that which is merely "apprehended" (by reference to rules of experience). The play of human "passions" can be "reproduced in immediate experience" and "intuited" in a way that is surely qualitatively different from the way in which "natural" events can possess these qualities. But this "evidentness" possessed by what has been made "understandable" by interpretation must be carefully distinguished from any relation to "validity". The only presuppositions of [this "evidentness"] are (from a *logical* point of view) the *conceivability* and (from a *substantive* point of view) the objective possibility[2] of the interconnections that can be grasped by "interpretation". As for its significance (simply by virtue of its quality of "*evidentness*") for the analysis of reality, it can be either that of a hypothesis – when we are trying to explain a concrete event – or that of an "ideal-typical" theoretical construct – when we are constructing general concepts, either for heuristic purposes or in order to arrive at a precise terminology. However, the same dualism of "evidentness" and empirical "validity" that can be found in [the domain of] the interpretation of human action is also present within those disciplines that are oriented towards mathematics – indeed, precisely with respect to the acquisition of mathematical knowledge as such.[3] But, while the "evidentness" of mathematical knowledge, and of knowledge of *quantitative* relationships in the

existed. This circumstance has even prompted the conclusion that not only all attainable historical knowledge, but even any historical knowledge that one could be looking for, is in a specific sense "uncertain"; and this has in turn led to the further – erroneous – conclusion that [this knowledge] is in a specific sense "subjective". Simmel, in particular (*Philosophy of History*[2], pp. 9ff.) attaches decisive importance to the *hypothetical* character of interpretation, and underpins this view with graphic examples. Against this, however, I must once again insist [on the following point]: even though it is only the actual direction of the decision, once taken, which gives us information as to the "psychical disposition" that has been present, this is not a peculiarity of "psychical" causal explanation. Countless times, as we have seen, exactly the same is the case with "natural" processes; in fact, when one is concerned with the qualitative and individual aspect of concrete "natural events", the only way of determining the actual constellation is, generally speaking, [to look at] the way the event turned out. In the case of events that are "conceived" individually – and this is something that should also be emphasized as an objection to Ed[uard] Meyer['s view] – the causal explanation regularly runs backwards, from the effect to the cause. And (as was previously demonstrated even in the case of purely quantitative relationships) it is quite normal that it can only reach a conclusion according to which the event was "consistent" with our empirical knowledge; it is only with respect to certain abstracted individual elements of the event that it is possible, with reference to "laws", to demonstrate their "necessity", even in the concrete case.

1   This expression is used here, instead of "[having the] inner intuitability of the processes of consciousness", in order to avoid the ambiguousness of the expression "intuitive", which also refers to "immediate experience", which has *not* been subjected to logical treatment. I am quite aware that, when the expression "evident" is otherwise used by writers on logic, it does not have this sense, but that of referring to insight into the reasons on which a judgement is based.

2   Concerning the meaning of the concept of the "objectively possible", particularly in the historical domain, see my remarks in *Critical Studies* [below, pp. 171ff.], in which I completely follow [the lines of] v. Kries' well-known theory.

3   The "pseudo-spherical space" ‹89› can be constructed in a manner that is entirely consistent from a logical point of view and completely "evident". Many mathematicians, including (as is well known) Helmholtz – who thought that this implied a refutation of Kant – have believed that it even possesses categorial intuitability. Its undoubted "lack of empirical validity" is compatible at least with the first of these conceptions.

physical world expressed in mathematical form, has a "categorial" character, the "psychological" evidentness, in the sense in which it is discussed here, belongs to the domain of pure phenomenology. Phenomenologically, it is conditioned (here, Lipps' terminology turns out to be quite appropriate) by the special colouring characterizing the "empathy" with those *qualitative* events that we can become *aware* of as [an] objectively *possible* content of our *own* inner actuality. What gives it an indirect *logical* significance for history is the following circumstance: The content of other people's actuality with which we can "empathize" also includes those "valuations" in which the meaning of "historical interest" is rooted; consequently, a science whose object, in the terminology of the philosophy of history, represents "the realization of values",[1] will always treat "valuating" individuals as the "bearers" of that process.[2]

Between those two extremes – the categorial mathematical evidentness of spatial relationships, and the phenomenologically conditioned evidentness of the life of the mind, which can be the object of "empathy" – lies a world of knowledge that cannot attain either of those two kinds of "evidentness", but that does not of course in the least lose its dignified status or its empirical validity because of this phenomenological "imperfection". For, to repeat, the fundamental error of the epistemology that Gottl accepts is that it confuses a maximum of "intuitable"[3] *evidentness* with a maximum of (empirical) *certainty*. The chequered fate of the so-called "axioms of physics"[4] has provided repeated illustrations of the process whereby a construction that is borne out by experience lays claim to the status of a *necessary* [way of] thinking. In the same way, the identification of "evidentness" with "certainty" – or even (as many of C[arl] Menger's epigones would have it) with [being a] "necessary way of thinking" in the case of "ideal-typical" constructions in the domain of the social sciences – has led to analogous errors, and Gottl, for instance, has also gone down the same path in many of the constructions in his *Dominance of Words*.[5]

The historian's heuristic "feeling" and "suggestive" description

In spite of all that has been said, there are those who will maintain that, at least in one area, the significance of "interpretation which reproduces immediate experience" – a significance that in itself pertains only to the psychology of cognition – will de facto come to acquire the

1   It really should not be necessary to emphasize particularly that this in no sense refers to some cosmic process that "objectively" "strives" to "realize" an "absolute" as an *empirical fact*, or indeed refers to anything metaphysical at all; the statements in the last chapter of Rickert's account (in *Limits of Concept Formation*) have occasionally been read in that way, although they are quite unambiguous.

2   On this point, too, Rickert's concept of the "historical centre" ⟨90⟩ already contains all that is required.

3   ["]Intuitable["] here of course means ["]categorially intuitable["] on the one hand, ["]inwardly understandable["] on the other hand.

4   The "evident" proposition "cessante causa cessat effectus" posed an obstacle for the formulation of the law of [conservation of] energy until the [development into a] "necessary element of thought" of the proposition "nil fit ex nihilo, nil fit ad nihilum" led to the introduction of the concept of "potential energy"; ⟨91⟩ and then, in spite of the "lack of intuitability" of this latter concept, the "law of [conservation of] energy" in its turn began to move towards [the status of] a "necessary element of thought". On these points, Wundt's early essay on the axioms of physics (*Axioms*) is still very much worth reading. ⟨92⟩

5   It is not possible in this context to analyse, on the one hand, the intuitable evidentness, and, on the other hand, the [status as] "necessary elements of thought" and the logical structure of the fundamental categories of economic thought proposed by Gottl (in *Dominance of Words*). The following example must suffice. According to Gottl (*Dominance of Words*, pp. 82–83), the "fundamental condition" no. 1 ("exigency") means that "a striving can never be fulfilled without somehow impairing the success of other strivings"; 2. the fundamental condition of "power" stems from the fact that "we are at all

status of "being valid": namely, in those instances where mere, unarticulated "feelings" are the object of historical knowledge, so that the only possible ideal of knowledge must be suggestively to call forth corresponding "feelings" within ourselves. When a historian, an archaeologist, a philologist, "enters into the spirit of" "personalities", "artistic epochs" [or] "languages", this takes the form of certain "feelings of commonality", "feelings for a language" etc., and it has even been claimed[1] that those feelings are the most reliable "canon" for the historical determination of, for instance, the provenance of a document or a work of art, or for the interpretation of the reasons behind, and the meaning of, a historical act. On the other hand, the aim of the historian is, and must be, to let us "re-experience" the "cultural phenomena" (which of course also include, for instance, certain "climates of opinion" that have historical,

times free, by striving together, to achieve successful results which cannot be achieved by individual striving". For a start, the substance of those conditions does not possess that absolute character which one would require of "fundamental conditions" of "everyday life", since [such "fundamental conditions"] should encompass everything without exception, and not just that which is *important* from the point of view of particular sciences. It is not invariably the case that different *goals* collide, and that, consequently, there is a necessity of *choice* between them. Nor is it true of every conceivable goal that the association of a number of persons is a suitable means of increasing the chance of reaching it. Gottl does anticipate the possibility of being faced with such objections and therefore emphasizes that the "valuation", which is a consequence of the "fundamental condition" no. 1 ("exigency"), does not imply a conscious choice between "goals", but should only be understood to mean that, in any given situation, only one of a number of conflicting *possibilities* will *actually* be realized. But in *that* form, this "state of affairs" is in fact already a naturalistic theoretical construct that has been built up with the aid of the category of "possibility": the various "*possible*" courses of action – which Gottl assumes to be [possibilities] not from the point of view of the "acting person", but only from the point of view of the intellectual analysis of the "action" – are contrasted with the "*fact*" that actually, only *one* concretely determined course of action ensues. But exactly the same is the case with every "natural event", whenever we analyse it with the aid of the category of "possibility". In this context, we shall not discuss *when* that happens; but *that* it happens is something that every theory of probability teaches us (among other things). As far as the "formula" for "householding" is concerned (adjustment of a continual striving in action, in order to guarantee that this action can continue over time – *Dominance of Words*, p. 209), this ["formula"] obviously contains nothing that was not already present in a concept like "adaptation". For if we analyse the formula with respect to the judgements that it contains, it means only this: that there *are* recurrent actions (that is to say: [actions that are] similar in certain respects which, because of their importance, are the only ones regarded as relevant), and that their recurrence is based on their "adaptation" to situations of constraint. The "concept" [of "householding"] – since it is in fact a concept, and indeed an abstract one – does not, and probably is not intended to, contain a *causal* "explanation"; nor does it help us to gain "insight" into anything – as we should, according to Gottl's theory. In that respect, it has completely the same character and the same value as the corresponding biological concepts. – This apart, it is certainly not our intention to portray Gottl's further development of the rational construction provided by the Austrian school ‹93› as worthless, far from it. Instead of supposedly "psychological" abstractions, [his] point of departure is quite clearly a *situation* that is generally given in reality ([is] "objective") – namely the limitations of what we can, compared with what we want. As the ultimate foundation of [the] theses [of the abstract school], this is a [definite] advance, and so is the fact that, as a consequence, the "abstract" theory can no longer be characterized as [furnishing] "psychological" grounds for the theory of value – a characterization that is repeated over and over again, and that is absolutely misguided (although [the "abstract" theory itself] must take part of the blame for it, in view of a number of statements made by Bonar, John and Menger). The "marginal utility theory" has not one jot or tittle to do with any kind of "psychology", be it "individual" or "social".

1   For instance by Elsenhans, *Psychology of Interpretation*, p. 23. The feelings of totality with which we accompany the idea of a particular "historical epoch" might – so the author thinks – "in spite of all their apparent vagueness provide [us] with a reliable canon of knowledge", and in particular, it will be "decided with instinctive certainty" whether a complex of ideas "fits into" this totality of feeling – analogously to the "feeling for a language".

and especially purely political, importance), [and] to convey them "suggestively" to us; therefore, at least in those cases, this suggestive "interpretation" is a process that is autonomous – even epistemologically – from [a] conceptual articulation.

Let us try to distinguish what is correct from what is incorrect in this argument. First of all, [let us look at] the alleged significance of "feelings of commonality" or "feelings of totality" as a "canon" for cultural–historical classification or for the interpretation of "personalities": There is no doubt that a "feel [for something]" is extremely significant – indeed, almost indispensable – for the psychological genesis of a hypothesis in the mind of the historian (provided, it should be noted, that what has given [the historian] this "feeling" is his constant *intellectual* occupation with the "material" – that is to say: practice, and therefore: "empirical experience").[1] One does not "create" any sort of valuable historical knowledge – or any sort of knowledge of any other kind – simply by shuffling around "perceptions" and "concepts". But as for the alleged "certainty", in the sense of scientific "validity", [of "feeling"], every conscientious scholar must categorically deny that references to "feelings of totality" – for instance to the "general character" of an epoch, an artist, etc. – can claim to have any sort of value, unless [those references] can be translated into precisely articulated, demonstrable *judgements* – that is to say: "conceptually" formed "empirical experience", in quite the usual sense of that word – and can therefore be tested. – Actually, in saying this, we have also described the situation with respect to the historical "reproduction" of *emotional* mental states, whenever they are historically (causally) relevant. "Feelings" cannot be "defined" conceptually in the same sense as, say, a right-angled triangle or as the abstract products of the quantifying sciences; but this is something that they share with everything that is qualitative. All qualitative elements as such, whether we "project" them into the external world as qualities of "things" or "introject" them into ourselves as immediate psychical experiences, possess this character of being by necessity relatively "indeterminate". What holds for colours of light, timbres of sound, nuances of scent, etc., holds in quite the same sense for religious, aesthetic or ethical "value feelings": in the final analysis, when giving a descriptive account of them, "each one sees what he carries in his heart". ⟨94⟩ Consequently, as far as only this circumstance is concerned, the interpretation of psychical events utilizes concepts that are in principle not absolutely precisely determined, but does so in absolutely the same sense as every science must necessarily do if it does not completely abstract from qualitative elements.[2]

---

1 Therefore, [his "feeling"] is in essence completely the same as the "feeling" – which is in no way consciously articulated – that guides, say, the captain of a ship in imminent danger of collision, where everything depends on a split-second decision. In both cases, condensed "empirical experience" is of decisive importance; and, in both cases, there is in principle the same possibility of articulation.

2 Naturally, this is in no way altered by the fact that certain [outward] expressions of psychical processes can be "measured" by experimental psychology. It is certainly not correct to say ([as] Münsterberg [does]) that the "psychical" cannot as such be communicated at all (rather, that is one distinctive characteristic of those "immediate experiences" which we, for that very reason, call "mystical"); but, as is the case with everything qualitative, the precision with which [the "psychical"] can be communicated is only relative, and measurement in this area – like computation in [the area of] statistics – can only register that part of the psychical which is expressed externally in *one* particular way – or rather: [it can] only [register] that mode of expression. Psychometric measurement does not ([contrary to what] Münsterberg [says]) establish communicability *in general*; but it increases its degree of *precision* by quantifying, in each given instance, *one* form of expression of a "psychically conditioned" process. But science would be in a bad way if this would prevent the classification of the "psychical" material and its formation as a concept with a relative precision that would be sufficient from the point of view of the concrete goal of the investigation. In fact, [these operations] are constantly carried out and utilized by *all* non-quantifying sciences. It has often been said – and rightly so, provided [the sense] is correctly understood – that the enormous importance of *money* [stems from the fact that] it

If the historian in his account addresses our "feelings" with methods that have a suggestive effect – and therefore, in other words, attempts to evoke within us an "immediate experience" that cannot be articulated conceptually – we are dealing with one of two things: *Either* [this is] a shorthand for the description of partial aspects of his object that can be left conceptually imprecise without prejudicing the concrete goal of the inquiry; this is a consequence of the fact that, as the empirically given multiplicity is in principle inexhaustible, *any* account can only become "valid" as a "relative" conclusion to the process of acquiring historical knowledge. *Or* the evocation of a purely felt "immediate experience" within us is supposed to serve as a specific *heuristic* instrument – as an "illustrative example", for instance, of the "character" of a cultural epoch or of a work of art. In that case, its logical character can be twofold: Either [(1)] it may claim to be a "*re*-experiencing" of the – depending on the terminology – "spiritual" or "psychical" "substance" of the "life" of the epoch or personality in question, or of the concrete work of art. In that case, it contains value feelings belonging to the *writer* [of the account]. In the *reader*, it also calls forth value feelings and helps him to "empathize"; [but] as long as [the process of evocation] remains at the stage of what is "felt", [his value feelings] will always and unavoidably be non-articulated; and there is not the slightest guarantee that those value feelings will in any way correspond to the feelings of those historical human beings that he empathizes with.[1] Therefore, [the evocation] will also lack any controllable standard for distinguishing between the *causally* "important" and "unimportant". The "feeling of totality" which, for instance, a strange town evokes in us, is usually – as long as it [remains] at the stage of pure feeling – determined by things such as the position of the chimneys, the shape of the cornices and similar elements that are absolutely incidental, that is to say: of no *causal* importance for the "lifestyle" of the inhabitants. The same is, according to all experience, true of all non-articulated historical "intuitions" without exception: their value as scientific knowledge mostly decreases in parallel with their aesthetic charm. ‹95› They *may* in certain cases acquire major "heuristic" value; but they may also, in other cases, directly impede the acquisition of substantive knowledge, because they make [the reader] less conscious of the fact that, in substance, the feelings are not those of the "epoch" described (or, respectively, of the creative artist) but those of the observer. In this case, the subjective character of such "knowledge" is identical with [its] lack of "validity", precisely *because* the conceptual articulation is lacking, and it is therefore impossible to demonstrate and verify the substance of the "emotional participation". Moreover, it carries with it the enormous danger of suppressing a causal analysis of the interconnections in favour of a search for a "total character" that matches the "feeling of totality"; and, since the need for empirical analysis is supplanted by the wish to find a *formula* conveying the "synthesis of feeling", the "epoch" will then be labelled with this ["total character"]. In this form, the subjective emotional "interpretation" represents *neither* empirical historical knowledge of actual interconnections

permits the expression of subjective "valuations" in substantive form, and makes it "measurable". But, in this connection, one must not lose sight of the fact that the "price" is certainly *not* a phenomenon [that can be seen as a] parallel to the psychometric experiment, and above all, [that it is] not a standard for a "social–*psychical*" valuation, for a social "utility value"; instead, [it] is the product of a compromise between conflicting interests, which has come into being under quite concrete, historically peculiar conditions. But what [the price] does have in common with the psychometric experiment is the circumstance that *only* those strivings become "measurable" that, in accordance with the given social constitution, have achieved a certain kind of expression (as "purchasing power" etc.).

1   As an illustrative example of the distinctive character of this evocation of interpretations of feelings – as opposed to conceptually articulated, and therefore empirical, analysis – one may, in Carl Neumann's *Rembrandt*, compare the interpretation of "The Nightwatchmen" with that of "Manoah's Sacrifice". Both are unusually fine achievements in the domain of the interpretation of works of art; but only the first, not the second, one has a consistently empirical character.

(causal interpretation) *nor* what it might otherwise have been: [(2)] *value-relating interpretation*. This is the other sense in which one can have "immediate experience" of a historical object within the "category" [of "interpretation"] that we are dealing with here – a "category"] that also covers causal imputation. I have elsewhere[1] dealt with the logical relationship [of this kind of "interpretation"] to history. Here, it must suffice to state the following: In this function, the "interpretation" of an object that can be evaluated aesthetically, ethically, intellectually or from cultural value perspectives of every conceivable kind is not a *component* of a (logically speaking) purely empirical–historical account – that is to say: [an account] that imputes concrete "historical individuals" ‹96› to concrete causes – but rather, from the point of view of history, constitutes the *formation* of the "historical individual". In *this* sense, what the "interpretation" of *Faust* – or, say, of "puritanism" or of certain elements of "Greek culture" – means is this: to determine what "values" "we" *can* find "realized" in those objects, and what the – always and invariably individual – "form" is in which "we" find [those values] "realized" there, and because of which those "individuals" become the objects of historical "explanation". Consequently, this is a task to be accomplished by the *philosophy* of history. *That* task is indeed "subjectivizing", if this term is understood as follows: if we refer to the "validity" of those values, this can never imply that they are "valid" in the sense [in which one refers to] the validity of empirical "facts". In the sense in which it is at issue here, this ["interpretation"] is not understood to mean interpreting what those who historically participated in the creation of the "evaluated" object subjectively "felt" from their point of view. (If the ["interpretation"] has intrinsic value, that kind of knowledge can only serve as a possible aid to improving our "understanding" of the value.[2]) Instead, it is an interpretation of the values that "*we*" "can" find in the object – or maybe even "should" [find in it]. In the latter case, it adopts the goals of a normative discipline – of aesthetics, for instance – and performs its own "evaluation"; in the former one, it is, logically speaking, based on "dialectical" value *analysis*, and has the sole task of establishing "possible" value relations of the object. At the same time, however, this "relation" to "values" has the function – which is of decisive importance in our context – of being the only way in which one can leave behind the complete imprecision of [what has been grasped by] "empathy" and reach that kind of precision that knowledge of individual spiritual and intellectual conceptions is capable of attaining. For, in contrast to the simple "emotional content", we describe something as a "value" precisely if, and only if, it is capable of becoming the content of a stand [that one takes] – that is to say: an articulate and conscious positive or negative "judgement", something that approaches us "demanding validity", and whose "validity" as a "value" "for" us must accordingly be accepted, rejected or, in the most various combinations, be subjected to a value *judgement* "by" us. The "ascription" of an ethical or aesthetic "value" invariably implies the passing of a value *judgement*. A closer analysis of the nature of value judgements cannot be undertaken here,[3] but one point should be stated [which is relevant] for our discussion: It is the *determinacy of the substance* [*of the judgement*] which lifts the object of the value judgement out of the sphere of what is merely "felt". No available means allow us to establish definitely whether anybody [else] sees the "red colour" of the wallpaper "just as" I do, whether it is imbued with the same "emotional tones" for him; the relevant "perception" necessarily remains indeterminate in its communicability. On the other hand, the presumption that an ethical or aesthetic *judgement* concerning [certain] facts can be shared

1   [*Critical Studies*] (pp. 157ff.). Otherwise, in this context as well, reference should generally be made to Rickert's exposition.
2   In this respect, [I can] completely agree with B. Croce.
3   The fact that Croce denies the existence of "value *judgements*" in this sense – although his own construction stands and falls with them – represents a psychological element in Croce's anti-psychologistic account.

[by someone else] would be completely meaningless if the "ascribed" substance of the judgement were not – in spite of the part played by incommunicable elements of "feeling" – "understood" in the same way with respect to the points "that mattered". The relation of something individual to possible "values" always means that what is simply intuitively "felt" is eliminated to a [certain] – [but] always only to a relative – degree. It is precisely for this reason (and here we come back, in order to conclude, to some of the points that were hinted at earlier) that this "interpretation", performed by the philosophy of history, can apparently, in both its possible forms – the directly evaluating (and therefore metaphysical) ["interpretation"] and the purely value analytical one – be of constant service to the historian's "empathetic understanding". In this respect, we can in general refer [the reader] to Simmel's remarks[1] (which are here and there not conclusive in their formulation, and about which one may occasionally have substantive reservations). Only the following supplementary remarks should be added: The "historical individual" – even in the special sense of the "personality" – can in a *logical* sense only be a "unity" produced artificially by means of value relation. *Therefore*, "valuation" is the normal *psychological* transitional stage for "intellectual understanding". Indeed, a complete elucidation of the historically relevant elements of the "inner development" of a "historical personality" (Goethe or Bismarck, say), or simply of the concrete action [of that "personality"] in a concrete, historically relevant context, will usually only be attained by means of a confrontation between *possible "valuations"* of [the] behaviour [of the "personality"] – although one must unconditionally demand that the historian should surmount this psychological transitional stage in the genesis of his search for knowledge. In the earlier example of the leader of a patrol, ‹97› causal interpretation was made to serve the practical "taking of a stand" by permitting a noëtic "understanding" of the order, which in itself was not unambiguous. Conversely, in the situation that we are now discussing, one's own "valuation" is made to serve "understanding" – which in this case means: the causal interpretation – of the actions of others.[2] In *that* sense and for that reason, it is true [to say] that a pronounced

---

1   Here, too, Simmel's formulations ([*Philosophy of History*²], pp. 52, 54, 56) have a psychological–descriptive character; consequently, although they are extremely acute, [these formulations] are not always, in my opinion, completely flawless from a logical point of view. Simmel is right on the following points: (1) Strong "subjectivity" on the part of the historian as a "personality" *may* be uncommonly useful for the causal interpretation of historical action and historical individual entities (often precisely those with which he is *not* in harmony). And (2) not infrequently, our historical understanding of "sharply delineated", highly "subjective" personalities has a particularly "evident" character. *Both* these phenomena are connected with the role played by *value relation* in the cognitive formation of the Individual. Moreover, intensive "valuations" by the "rich" and "idiosyncratic" personality of the historian are heuristic device of the first order for uncovering those value relations concerning historical events and personalities that are not immediately obvious. But what is relevant in this connection is *not* some irrational quality of his personality, but precisely *that* ability of the historian to formulate *valuations* that are clearly articulated in his mind, and [his] consequent ability to identify value relations. Psychologically speaking, "understanding" begins as an undifferentiated combination of valuation and causal interpretation, but, when this is logically processed, valuation is replaced by the purely theoretical "relation" to values by means of which "historical individuals" are formed. – It is also questionable when Simmel (pp. 55 bottom, 56) puts forward the view that the historian is bound by the *material*, but "free" when it comes to giving historical events their *form* as a whole. In my view, the opposite is the case: The historian is "free" in his choice of guiding values, which in their turn determine the selection and forming of the "historical individual", which is to be explained (here, of course – as everywhere else – [the term "historical individual" is used] in its *im*personal, purely logical sense). But as he proceeds, he is completely bound by the principles of causal imputation and only "free", in a certain sense, to arrange the logically "incidental" [elements]: that is to say, to shape the purely aesthetic "illustrative material".

2   In cases where the assumption is that a "teleological" valuation is made, utilizing the categories of "end" and "means" – the usual textbook example being military history – the situation is, logically

"individuality" on the part of the historian – that is to say: precisely defined "valuations" which are peculiar to him – *may* serve as extremely effective midwives of causal knowledge; but, on the other hand, the strong weight of the influence [of these valuations] is also likely to endanger the "validity" of the concrete results as empirically true.[1]

While the manifold theories of the allegedly distinctive character of the "subjectivizing" disciplines, and of the significance of this distinctive character for [the science of] history, shimmer in a variety of colours and forms, the foregoing discussion of the[se theories] has unavoidably been somewhat monotonous. To conclude: the discussion has yielded the following insight, which is in fact quite trivial, but is nevertheless constantly called into question: The *logical* meaning of a certain [piece of] knowledge, and the preconditions of its "validity", are determined neither by the "substantive" qualities of the "material", nor by the "ontological" differences of its "being", nor, finally, by the character of the "*psychological*" process by which it is attained. *Empirical* knowledge, [both] of the "life of the mind" and in the domain of "external" "nature", of processes both "within" and "outside" ourselves, is always bound to the instruments of "concept formation"; and the nature of a "concept" is, from a logical point of view, the same in th[os]e two substantive "domains". The distinctive *logical* character of "historical" knowledge, as opposed to knowledge within the "natural sciences" (in the *logical* sense), has nothing at all to do with the distinction between the "psychical" and the "physical", between "personality" and "action" [on the one hand] and the inanimate "natural object" and the "mechanical process of nature" [on the other].[2] And it is even less justified to regard the "evidentness" of empathy with actual or potential "conscious" inner "immediate experiences" – which is a purely phenomenological quality of "interpretation" – as being identical to a specific empirical "certainty" of "interpretable" phenomena. We give a "reality" comprising psychical or physical elements, or both, the form of a "historical individual" because, and to the extent that, it can have "*significance*" for us; when we look for a "historical" explanation of such a [historical] individual, our *causal* interest is caught in a specific way by "meaningfully" interpretable human behaviour ("action"), because [action] can be determined by "valuations" and "meanings"; and, finally: to the extent that it is oriented towards, or can be confronted with, meaningful "valuations", human behaviour can be "understood" in a way that is specifically "evident". The special role in "history" played by that which can be "interpretively" understood, concerns differences (1) in the [degree of] our causal *interest*, and (2) in the quality of the "evidentness" that we look for [when investigating] individual causal interconnections; but it does *not* concern differences of causality, or differences in the significance and character of the concept formation.

speaking, exactly the same. When we establish, on the basis of strategical "doctrines of good procedure", that a certain measure taken by Moltke was an "error" (that is to say: it did not pick the correct "means" to attain the given "end"), the *only* significance that this can have for the *historical* account is to help us to recognize the *causal importance* of that (teleologically speaking) "erroneous" decision for the course of historically relevant events. Strategic doctrines only give us knowledge of the "objective" possibilities that one can imagine as being realized in case one [or the other] of the various possible decisions is taken. (On this point, too, Bernheim's account [*Method*[3]] is logically quite unclear.)

1   Jacob Burckhardt is an extremely good example of both of these aspects of the phenomenon.
2   On this point, see Rickert (*Limits of Concept Formation*). Nevertheless, since [Rickert] uses the term "natural-scientific concept formation" to designate research that seeks to formulate laws, his opponents have of course in their polemics against him continually confused the "institutional" concept of the "natural sciences" with the logical one.

The "rational" interpretation

It only remains for us to make a few observations concerning a particular kind of "interpretive" knowledge – that of "rational" interpretation making use of the categories of "end[s]" and "means".

There is no doubt that, whenever we "understand" human action as being determined by definite, conscious "ends" that are clearly striven for and by a clear awareness of the "means" [required], our understanding attains a specifically high degree of "evidentness". If we then ask why this is so, we shall quickly find the reason to be that the relationship of the "means" to the "end" is a rational one, which is to a specific degree accessible to a *generalizing causal approach*, in the sense of "[formulating] law-like regularities". There is no rational action without causal rationalization of that section of reality which is considered to be the object of [causal] influence and the means of that influence – that is to say: without fitting [that section of reality] into a complex of *rules* of experience that tell us what results a given behaviour can be *expected* to yield. It must be maintained that it is in every sense totally erroneous to claim that the "teleological"[1] "conception" of a process must for this reason be considered to be an "inversion" of the causal one.[2] But it is true that, without a belief in the reliability of

1   Particularly after the publication of Stammler's works – which are ingenious, but contain a large amount of fallacious reasoning – astonishing confusion reigns in many quarters concerning the relationship between "telos" and "causa". The summit of confusion in this respect has probably for the time being been reached by Dr Biermann (*Wundt, Nature and Society* and, to the fullest extent, *Social Science* (pp. 552–53)). He "explicitly" "protests" that he does not advocate "opposing theory to history", since such an opposition seems to him "to *lack clarity* and to be unjustified in principle". There is certainly a lack of clarity, but only insofar as that relationship [between theory and history] has unfortunately remained completely unclear to the *author*; otherwise, he could not have referred to scholars such as Windelband and Rickert in support of his position. (They would be quite astounded to find themselves enlisted as [Biermann's] sworn allies in this way.) – Nevertheless, if this lack of clarity were the only problem, the situation might still be acceptable: even economists of much greater weight sometimes deliver themselves of palpably erroneous opinions on the complex problems connected with [the] opposition [between theory and history]. What is worse is that the author's "telos", in its unbounded enthusiasm, even swallows up the most elementary dichotomy of all: that between "Is" and "Ought". He then proceeds to weave "freedom of the will", "total causality" and "law-like regularity of development", in gaudy confusion, into the allegedly all-important antithesis between "telos" and "causa"; and, in conclusion, he opines that, in order to surmount "individualism", it is necessary to adhere to a special "principle of research" – in spite of the fact that it is precisely the confusion between the question of "method" and that of "programme" that makes the controversies [of] former [times] look outdated (from a contemporary perspective). Altogether, this makes one wish for the speedy demise of the current fashion according to which every beginner must garnish his work with epistemological investigations. They are really unnecessary for the presentation, in this and other works, of the fairly simple, and certainly not original, ideas of the author concerning the relationship between "state and economy". One must hope that the author, who is no doubt inspired by the most sincere enthusiasm for his ideals, may in the future endow us with works that can be read without constantly stumbling over amateurish logical blunders, [an experience] that taxes one's patience. Only then will it be at all possible to have a fruitful discussion of his practical ideals. As for Stammler himself – who can by no means be held responsible for all Biermann's imperfections – a fundamental discussion of [his views] would add another score or so of pages to this article and is not called for in this context.

2   It is astonishing that Wundt, too, (*Logic*[2], I, p. 642) shares this popular misconception. He says: "If, in apperception, we (a) let the idea of our movement precede the external change, then the movement seems to us to be the cause of the change. If, on the other hand, we (b) let the idea of the external change precede that of the movement by which that change is to be brought about, then the change seems to us to be the goal and the movement [to be] the means by which the goal is reached. – Consequently, in this early [stage of] the development of psychological concepts, goal and causality have their origins in different ways of looking at *one and the same* process" (Wundt's italics). – This

empirical regularities, there could be no action based on the calculation of means [to bring about] an intended result; and, in this connection, [it is also true] that, if the goal is given and clear, then the choice of means, while not necessarily equally clear, will at least be "determined", not as something quite imprecise and ambiguous, but as a selection from a definite number of possibilities – greater or smaller, as the case may be. The rational interpretation can therefore assume the form of a conditional judgement of necessity (of the form: if the intention x is given, then, according to established rules of experience, the acting person "*had to*" choose the means y (or, respectively, one of the means y, y′, y″) to achieve it); and consequently, [this interpretation] at the same time merges with a teleological "valuation" of the *empirically* demonstrable action (of the form: according to established rules of experience, the choice of the means y offered a greater chance than [the means] y′ or y″ of achieving the goal x, or involved the smallest sacrifice in order to achieve it etc.; the means chosen were therefore more "appropriate" [to the given end] than the other ones, or [they were] even the only "appropriate" means). As this valuation has a purely "technical" character – that is to say: simply registers, with the aid of empirical experience, that the "means" was adequate for [achieving] the goal that the acting person actually wanted to achieve – it does not in any way, in spite of its "valuational" character, overstep the bounds of an analysis of the empirically given [material]. And in the same way, within the domain of knowledge of *actual* occurrences, this rational "valuation" *only* has the role of a hypothesis or of an ideal-typical conceptual construct: We confront the actual action with action that – from a "teleological" point of view, according to general causal rules of experience – is rational[, with one of the following two purposes]: *either* to uncover a rational motive that may have guided the acting person, and that we establish by showing that, in fact, his actions were appropriate means for the achievement of a goal which he "could" have pursued; *or* to make it understandable why a motive, which we know that the acting person had, led to a result *different* from that which the acting person subjectively expected, because of [his] choice of means [to achieve that result]. But, in neither of these cases do we carry out a "psychological" analysis of the "personality" with the aid of some special heuristic instrument; instead, we analyse the "objectively" given *situation* with the aid of our nomological knowledge. The "interpretation" therefore fades into the general knowledge that we can act "purposefully" – that is to say: that

calls for the following comment: Clearly, the two sentences above (which I have designated (a) and (b)) do not describe "the same" process at all; instead, each of them describes *a different part* of a process that can roughly, following Wundt, be rendered in schematic form in the following manner: (1) The "idea" of a desired change (v) in the "external" world, together with (2) the idea of a movement (m) [which is] suitable for bringing about this change; then (3) the movement m, and (4) a change (v′) in the external world, brought about by m. Wundt's sentence (a) above obviously only covers the elements (3) and (4): the external movement and the external effect of the movement, while [the elements] (1) and (2): the *idea* of the result and of bringing it about (or, from a consistently materialist point of view, at least the corresponding brain process) are *not* covered [by sentence (a)]. As for Wundt's sentence (b), we must leave open whether it covers only the elements (1) and (2) or, in some undefined combination with them, the elements (3) and (4) as well. In *neither* of those two cases, however, does sentence (b) contain another "conception" of *the same* process than sentence (a), already because, above all, it is of course in no way permissible to assume as self-evident that the change (v′), which was *brought about* by the movement (m) as its cause, is necessarily *identical* to the change (v) that it was the *aim* to achieve by means of the movement (m). As soon as the "intended" result differs, even partly, from the one actually "achieved", Wundt's whole scheme obviously no longer applies. But precisely such a difference between what is intended and what is achieved – the *non*-achievement of the goal – is undoubtedly also constitutive for the psychological genesis of the concept of ["]goal["]. (In his discussion, Wundt completely mixes up the psychological genesis [of this concept] with its logical meaning.) It is impossible to see how we could ever become aware of the "goal" as an independent category if v and v′ were once and for all seen as identical.

we can act on the basis of reflections on the different "possible" courses that events might take in the future if we in fact acted (or refrained from acting) in each of a number of ways that we consider as possible. Action that is, in this sense, "consciously purposive" is extremely important in empirical reality, and, consequently, "teleological" rationalization can be used as an instrument for the creation of theoretical constructs that are extraordinarily valuable, from a heuristic perspective, for the causal analysis of historical interconnections. These theoretical constructs can (1) have a purely individual character: they are interpretive *hypotheses* relating to concrete individual contexts. An example of this has already been mentioned: the construction of the policy of Frederick William IV as being determined, on the one hand, by goals that he supposedly [pursued], and, on the other hand, by the constellation of the "great powers". In that case, it serves as an intellectual instrument for the purpose of measuring his actual policy against it, with respect to its degree of rationality; by this means, we can find out, on the one hand, what the rational elements of his *actual* political actions were, and, on the other hand, what elements of those actions were *not* rational (when measured against the supposed goals imputed to him). This enables us to make a historically valid interpretation of [the king's] actions, to estimate the causal importance [both of the rational and of the non-rational elements of his actions] and, on this basis, to assign, in a valid manner, the "personality" of Frederick William IV to its proper place as a causal factor in the historical context. Or – and this is what interests us here – [the "teleological" concepts] can (2) be ideal-typical constructions of a general nature, like the "laws" of abstract economics, which are intellectual constructions [showing] the consequences of certain economic situations, on the assumption that action is strictly rational. In *all* [of these] cases, however, the relation between such rational, teleological constructions and the reality with which the sciences of empirical experience deal is of course *not* that which exists between a "law of nature" and a "constellation", but simply that of an ideal-typical concept [constructed] to facilitate an empirically valid interpretation, in the sense that the given facts are *compared with* a possible interpretation – an *interpretive model*; therefore, its role is *to that extent* akin to that played by teleological interpretation in biology. Even in the case of rational interpretation, we do not – as Gottl thinks – "infer" "actual action" but "objectively *possible*" interconnections. Nor does the teleological evidentness of these constructions imply [that they have] a specific degree of empirical validity. On the contrary: the "evident" rational construction can, if it is put together "correctly", [help us to] identify precisely those elements of actual economic action that are teleologically *non*-rational and, consequently, to make the actual course of that action understandable. Therefore – contrary to what has been claimed – those interpretive models are not *just* "hypotheses", analogous to the hypothetical "laws" of natural science. They can *function as* hypotheses when the interpretation of concrete processes is employed for heuristic purposes. But just as, for instance, the empirical lack of validity of the pseudo-spherical space [does not affect] the "correctness" of its construction, the cognitive value [of those interpretive models] – unlike the hypotheses of natural science – is not affected when it is established that, in a concrete case, they do *not* contain a valid interpretation. In *that* case, an interpretation with the aid of the rational model was just not possible – because the "goals" presupposed in the model were not present as motives in the concrete case – but this does not exclude the possibility of using that interpretation [as an instrument] in any other case. A hypothetical "law of nature" that in [just] *one* instance definitively fails to work will once and for all have collapsed as a hypothesis. On the other hand, the ideal-typical constructions of economics – properly understood – in no way claim to be generally valid, while a "law of nature" *must* lay that claim; otherwise, it will lose its significance. – Finally, a so-called "empirical" law is an empirically valid rule whose causal *interpretation* is problematical, while a teleological model of rational action is an interpretation whose empirical *validity* is problematical: the two are therefore, logically speaking, polar opposites. – Those [teleological] models are "ideal-typical conceptual constructs",[1] and, if it is possible to construct them, it is *because*, and only because, the categories of "end[s]" and "means", when applied to empirical reality, lead to its rationalization.[2]

The two aspects of the category of causality and the relationship between irrationality and indeterminism

This throws renewed, and definitive, light on the claim that "personality" and "free" action possess a specific empirical irrationality.

The more "freely" the acting person "decides" – that is to say: the more [the "decision"] is based on [that person's] "own" *deliberations*", which have not been blurred by "external" constraint[s] or irresistible "affects", the more completely (other things being equal) will the motivation fit into the categories of "end" and "means"; the more successfully can it therefore be analysed rationally and, in a given instance, be made to fit into a model of rational action; consequently, the greater will be the role played by the nomological knowledge possessed both by the acting person and by the scholar who performs the analysis, and the more "constrained" will the acting person be with respect to the "means" [to be used]. And not only that. The more "freely", in the sense used here, [the person] "acts" – that is to say: the *less* [the action] has the character of a "natural occurrence", the greater the effect will be, in the last resort, of a concept of "personality" whose "essence" is to be found in a constant inner relationship to certain ultimate "values" and "meanings" of life – "values" and "meanings" that in the actions [of the "personality"] are translated into goals, and are thereby converted into teleological–rational action. And, to the same extent, this implies a fading away of the romantic–naturalistic version of the idea of "personality", which seeks the real inner sanctum of the personal in the opposite direction: in the vague, indistinct, vegetative "underground" of personal life, that is to say: in an "irrationality" based on a tangled infinity of psychophysical conditions for the development of temperaments and moods – an "irrationality" that the "person" in actual fact completely *shares with* the animal. This romanticism is at the root of the "enigma of personality", in the sense in which Treitschke occasionally, and many others very often, speak of it; and romanticism may even invent a place for the "freedom of the will" in those regions of nature. The palpable senselessness of this endeavour can already be registered by our immediate experience, as it is precisely those "irrational" elements of our behaviour that make us "feel" that we are (at times) almost "forced", or [that we are] at least partly determined, in a way that is not "immanent" in our volition. For the historian who "interprets", "personality" is not an "enigma". Quite on the contrary: it is the only element that can be made "understandable" by interpretation; nor are human action and [human] behaviour at any point – especially where rational interpretation

---

1   On this concept, see my essay (*Objectivity*) (pp. 190ff.). I hope to continue that sketchy, and therefore perhaps partly misleading, discussion in more detail at an early opportunity.

2   Therefore, it is just about the worst of all possible misunderstandings to believe that the constructions of the abstract theory – for instance, the "law of marginal utility" – embody the products of "psychological" interpretations (or, even worse, interpretations of "individual psychology"), or the attempt to provide "economic value" with a "psychological basis". What gives those constructions their distinctive character and their heuristic value – and what limits their empirical validity – is precisely that they do not contain *one jot or tittle* of "psychology" in any possible sense of that term. Admittedly, many adherents of the school that utilizes these models are partly to blame for that erroneous conception, since they have occasionally used all sorts of analogies with "stimulus thresholds" – something that these purely rational constructions, which are only possible against the intellectual background of the money economy, have nothing at all in common with, apart from certain external forms. See above, p. 77n2.

is no longer possible – more "irrational" (in the sense of "incalculable" or impervious to causal imputation) than *any individual event* as such. On the other hand, wherever rational "interpretation" is possible, [human action] rises far above the irrationality of the purely "natural". The impression that the "personal" [element] is quite specifically irrational is due to the fact that the historian measures the action of his heroes, and the constellations arising out of that action, against the ideal [standard] of teleological–*rational* action, instead of confronting it with the course of individual events in "inanimate nature" – as he ought to do in order to compare like with like. Least of all should the "freedom of the will", however defined, at any time be linked with "irrationality" (in the above sense). [It is] precisely the person who is empirically "free" in his actions – that is to say: who acts on the basis of *deliberations* – who is teleologically bound by the means for reaching his goals, [means] that may not always be equally available and discernible in the objective situation. It is of precious little use to the entrepreneur struggling with the competition, or to the stockbroker, to believe that they have "free will". [They] have the choice between economic extermination and compliance with very precisely defined maxims of economic conduct. If [they] do not, to their obvious detriment, comply with [those maxims], and we want to explain why this was so, we may, among other possible hypotheses, also consider the possibility that [they] precisely *lacked* "free will". As is naturally also the case with every other purely rational interpretation of an individual historical event, the "laws" of theoretical economics proceed from the necessary *assumption* of the existence of "freedom of the will", in every possible sense of that term within the empirical domain.

On the other hand, if the "problem" of the "freedom of the will" is formulated in any other way than with [the above] reference to purposeful rational action, it will, in any form that it may possibly assume, lie completely beyond the domain where history is pursued, and is without any importance for it.

The historian's investigation of motives by means of "interpretation" is *causal* imputation in absolutely the same *logical* sense as the causal interpretation of any individual natural event; this is because [the] goal [of the historian's interpretation] is to establish a cause as being (at least hypothetically) "*sufficient*", exactly as this is the only possible goal of research into complex natural events, when one is concerned with the individual components [of those events]. If [the historian] wants to avoid falling victim to Hegelian emanationism, ‹98› or to some variety of the modern anthropological occultism, ‹99› the purpose of his inquiry cannot be to acquire knowledge of why [the acting person] *necessarily* (in the sense of a law of nature) *had to* act the way he did. This is because a human as well as non-human ("living" or "inanimate") *concrete* entity, viewed as a (somehow limited) section of the totality of cosmic occurrences, can at no point within that totality be completely "defined" in terms of purely "nomological" knowledge, since [that entity] is always (and not only in the domain of the "personal") an intensively infinite multiplicity – and every conceivable individual element [of that multiplicity] (which can only be taken as "given" by science) may, from a logical point of view, come to be considered causally important within a [given] historical causal context.

The fact of the matter is that the category of causality is employed in different forms in the various disciplines; and admittedly this means that, in a certain sense, the content of the category itself also varies, in such a way that sometimes one, sometimes another, of its elements loses its meaning precisely when the principle of causality is carried through in its ultimate consequences.[1] In its full – one might say: its "original" – sense, [the category of causality] has

---

1   On these problems, see O. Ritschl, *Causal Approach*. However, I cannot at all agree with R[itschl] when, basing himself on Münsterberg's *Outline of Psychology*, he claims that whenever there is a striving for an "understanding re-experiencing" of an event, the *scientific* approach, and particularly the idea

two components: on the one hand, the idea of "*having an effect*", as a (so to speak) dynamic link between phenomena that are qualitatively different from one another; on the other, the idea of being bound by "*rules*". The substantive content of the category of causality – [that is to say]: "having an effect" – and therefore also the concept of "cause" [as such], lose their meaning and disappear whenever quantifying abstraction results in a mathematical equation as the expression of purely spatial causal relations. The only sense in which the category of causality can be maintained here is that of a rule according to which movements succeed each other in time; and even so, [this] can only be seen as the expression of the metamorphosis of something that in essence forever remains *the same*. – Conversely, the idea of the "*rule*" disappears from the category of causality whenever one starts to reflect on the absolute qualitative uniqueness of the course of the world through time, and on the *singular* qualitative *character* of any spatial and temporal section of that [world] process. Viewed in relation to an absolutely unique total or partial cosmic evolution, the concept of the causal *rule* loses its meaning, just as the concept of having a causal *effect* does in relation to the causal equation. If one wants the category of causality to retain some meaning in relation to that infinity of concrete occurrences, which can never be comprehensively known, it can *only* be the idea of "being effected", in the following sense: What is completely "new" within any time differential "had to" evolve from the "past" in exactly that, and no other, way – which is actually nothing more than pointing out the fact that [the "new" element] in its "present" state "came into being" purely and simply like that, as something that was absolutely unique, but nevertheless had its place within a *continuum* of occurrences.

Those empirical disciplines that employ the category of causality and deal with the *qualitative* elements of reality – and history, as well as all "cultural sciences" of whatever kind, belong to [that group] – consistently use that category with its full set of meanings: they consider states of reality, and changes within it, as "having been effected" and "having effect"; and they endeavour to uncover "rules" of "causation" within the concrete interconnections, by means of abstraction, as well as to "explain" concrete "causal" interconnections by reference to "rules". But what role the formulation of "rules" has in that respect, what logical form they assume – indeed, whether rules are formulated at all – depends on the specific cognitive goal. However, the goal is not invariably that of formulating [those rules] as judgements of causal *necessity*; and it is by no means only within the sciences of the human spirit that it is impossible to [give them] an apodictic form. For history, in particular, the form of the causal explanation is a consequence of its postulated goal of understandable "interpretation". History, too, certainly has the intention and the obligation to utilize concepts that are sufficiently precise, and it endeavours to make its causal imputations as unambiguous as the state of the source material permits. But the historian's interpretation is not addressed to our ability to categorize "facts" as specimens of general generic concepts and formulas, but to our familiarity with the task, which we are faced with every day, of "understanding" individual human action in terms of its

---

of causality, is no longer applicable. This is only correct [to the extent that] no causal approach, of whatever kind, is ever *equivalent* to "immediate experiencing". We cannot here examine the significance that this circumstance might have for metaphysical constructions. But that lack of equivalence is also true of any articulate "understanding" of concatenations of motives; and there seems to be no reason why the principles of empirical causal investigation should cease to be applicable at the border of "understandable" motivation. The [causal] imputation of "understandable" events is carried out according to principles that are *logically* quite the same as those applied to the [causal] imputation of natural events. In the *empirical* domain, there is only one kink in the application of the principle of causality, and this is when the causal *equation* is no longer possible as a goal – even an ideal goal – of scientific work.

motivation – although we will then utilize our "empirical experience" to verify the hypothetical "interpretations" provided by our empathetic "understanding". However, as we saw in the example with the falling boulder, [if we want] the exclusive goal of any causal imputation concerning the individual multiplicity of the given [reality] to be the formulation of judgements of *necessity*, this goal can only be realized with respect to partial components abstracted from [that multiplicity]. The situation is the same with history, which can only establish that a "causal" interconnection of a certain kind *has* existed and try to make this "understandable" by referring to [known] regularities in the way things happen. Consequently, the demand that history should establish the strictly "necessary" character of concrete historical events is not only an ideal, but one [whose fulfilment] would require an eternity. But, on the other hand, the irrationality of all cosmic individual occurrences, however partial, in no way forms a basis for deriving a concept of indeterministic "freedom" that would be specific and relevant for historical investigation. From the point of view of history, the "freedom of the will", in particular, is something completely transcendent; and [it would be] almost absurd to conceive it as the basis of historical work. Formulated negatively, the situation is the following: *both* ideas [("necessity" and "freedom")] lie beyond the "empirical experience" that history can verify, and neither idea should be allowed actually to influence practical historical work.

It is not rare for methodological discussions to contain a sentence [to the effect] that human beings, "too", "*are*" in their actions (objectively) subject to a "causal nexus" that is "*invariable*" (and consequently has the character of a law).[1] However, this protestation of faith in favour of metaphysical determinism does not affect the domain of scientific practice; its formulation cannot be unreservedly [approved]; and the historian can draw no consequences from it [that are relevant to] his practical work. For the same reason, however, it is totally irrelevant, both in principle and according to [general] experience, when a historian, perhaps on religious grounds, or for other reasons that lie beyond [empirical] experience, rejects the metaphysical belief in "determinism" – whatever meaning that rejection may have – as long as that historian in practice remains true to the principle of interpreting human action on the basis of [its] understandable "motives", which are in principle and invariably subject to verification by reference to *empirical experience*. The belief that deterministic postulates *imply* a *method[olog]-ical* demand that the formulation of generic concepts and "laws" should be the exclusive goal within some area of knowledge is erroneous.[2] But it is no more erroneous than the converse assumption: that a metaphysical belief – of whatever kind – in "freedom of the will" *excludes* the application of generic concepts and "rules" to human behaviour; or, more generally, that the human "freedom of the will" is linked to a specific "incalculability", or to some specific kind of "objective" irrationality, of human action. As we have seen, the opposite is the case. –

---

1 For instance in Schmoller, *Knies*.
2 Let us suppose that the "material" of a concrete historical interconnection would exclusively consist of processes that were rooted in hysterical, hypnotic or paranoid conditions, and that would therefore for us have the character of "nature"; nevertheless, the principle of historical concept formation would remain the same: in that case, too, the exclusive point of departure of the scientific treatment [of that material] would be the "significance" that an individual constellation of such processes, in conjunction with the equally individual "external world", would acquire by means of a value relation; the goal would be [to attain] knowledge of individual interconnections; and the means would be individual causal imputation. Even Taine, who occasionally makes concessions to [that kind of construction], remains a historian throughout.

The concept of the individual in Knies' work: Anthropological emanationism

After this long digression into the domain of modern problems, we have to return to *Knies*. First of all, we have to clarify what is, in principle, the philosophical basis of his concept of "freedom", and what are the consequences of this for the importance of [this concept] in the logic and methodology of economics. – It soon becomes apparent that – and in what sense – Knies, too, was completely under the sway of that historical version of the "organic" theory of natural law which – in Germany, mainly under the influence of the historical school of jurisprudence‹100› – permeated all the areas where human cultural activity was investigated. – We can most usefully begin with the following question: What is the "concept of personality" that is combined with the idea of "freedom" in Knies' work? What emerges is that this "freedom" is not conceived as "lack of a cause", but as the outflow of action from the, necessarily completely individual, *substance* of personality; and [it also becomes apparent that,] because of the substantive character imputed to the personality, the irrational character of the action is soon deflected into a rational one.

First and foremost, Knies sees the essence of "personality" as that of being a "unity". But in his hands, this "unity" is soon transformed into the idea of a naturalistic, organically conceived *unitary* character, and this in its turn is interpreted as ("objective") inner "consistency", and is therefore ultimately [interpreted] *rationally*.[1] Man is an organic being and therefore shares with all organisms the "fundamental instinct" of "self-preservation" and "perfection" – an instinct that, so Knies says, implies "self-love" and is as such completely "normal" *and consequently* "moral". In particular, it is not opposed to "love of one's fellow men" and a "sense of common good": it is only when it "degenerates" into "self-seeking" that it becomes "abnormal", and therefore contrary to those social "instincts" ([*Economy*], p. 161). On the other hand, in the normal human being, those two categories of "instinct" are simply different "aspects" of one and the same "striving towards perfection" (p. 165) and, together with what Knies occasionally (ibid.) calls the "third main economic" (or, as it should properly be called: "economically relevant") "instinct": the "sense of equity and justice", they lie together, undifferentiated, in the unity of the personality. The constructive general character of certain concrete "instincts", in particular that of "self-interest", in the older [school of] economics, and, based on this, the religiously conditioned ethical dualism of the driving forces in Roscher's work, are replaced in Knies' work by the constructive unitary character of the concrete individual as such; and, as "culture progressively develops", [this unitary character] makes the "one-sided develop-ment" of "self-interest" occur less, and not more, frequently – something that, in Knies' opinion, characterizes the nineteenth, as opposed to the eighteenth, century. After a discussion of the marked development of charitable activity in recent times, he continues:

> If this kind of activity can only be seen as donations of [what one has] earned, and is therefore contrary to self-interested consumption, would this not in itself constitute an insoluble psychological contradiction with the idea that the masses, on the other hand, when they earn by engaging in production, are only filled with self-seeking and self-interest, with no concern for the welfare of their neighbour and for the common weal as long as they strive to acquire goods?
>
> ([Economy], pp. 164–65)[2]

1 Knies' theoretical – albeit quite inadequate – formulation of his point of departure is the following: "Personal life in the absence of a unitary focus is a contradiction in terms; wherever [this contradiction] is observed, it is *only* apparent" ([*Economy*], p. 247).
2 Similarly, and showing even more clearly the rational character of this construction: "The self-love of human beings is not conceptually (!) opposed to the love of one's family, of one's neighbour, of

And yet, the experience of all those who know the type of entrepreneur brought forth by the heroic age of capitalism – [a knowledge that they have gained] either from history or from their own observation of the late-comers who even today belong to that group – will be directly contrary [to Knies' view]; and powerful cultural movements, as for instance puritanism, bear that stamp which Knies finds "psychologically" contradictory. But, as the reference in p. 89n2 above to the concept of "self-love" shows, the individual simply is not allowed to be "a human being with its contradictions": it is a "book whose mysteries have been worked out" ‹101› for the simple reason that, otherwise, it would not be in conformity with the fundamental demand of inner consistency.

Knies continues by making the method[olog]ical deduction from his concept of the psychological "unitary character" of the individual that it is scientifically *irreducible*. In his opinion, the fundamental error of the earlier (classical) method is that it tries to "reduce" human beings to discrete "instincts".[1] – One might have thought that, with this last statement, Knies had declared war on the view – shared by Mandeville and Helvetius, as well as by their opponents – according to which the propositions of theoretical economics must be deduced from a constructed instinctual life of human beings. This was a view that – since the instinct which was considered the decisive one, that of "self-interest", does in fact have a certain *ethical* colouring – led to a hopeless confusion of theory with theodicy, ‹102› description with valuation, a confusion whose effects are still felt today. Actually, Knies – at least at one point – comes very close to a correct conception of the basis of economic "laws": In an – admittedly not very clear – phrase directed against Roscher's construction of the "instincts" (*Economy*[2], p. 246), he writes: "From the [very] beginning, when (Rau and Roscher) refer to the 'expressions of self-interest', they do not distinguish between [on the one hand,] the 'principle of proper economy' in an – *objectivized – householding* and [on the other hand,] the psychological instinct of self-interest and self-seeking in the human subject." As will be seen, here [Knies] comes extremely close to realizing that the economic "laws" are models of rational action, deduced not through a psychological analysis of individuals but – by means of an ideal-typical reproduction of the mechanism of price struggle – from the theoretically defined *objective situation*. Whenever it manifests itself in its "pure" form, [this situation] only leaves the individual, entangled in the market, with the choice between the alternatives: "teleological" adjustment to the "market", or economic ruin. However, Knies did not draw any methodological conclusions from this realization, which is only expressed sporadically. As shown in the quotations already given, and as we shall see again and again, Knies' belief is, in the last resort, unshaken: In order to comprehend why factory owners in general intend to buy their raw materials cheap and to sell their products dear, we really need almost a complete overall analysis of the totality of empirical human action and of its psychological driving forces. – Instead, in his work, the rejection of the "reduction" of the "individual" has another meaning:

> The peculiar character of the *individual human being*, like that of a *whole nation*, reveals itself as flowing from a unitary source; and all the phenomena of human activity relate back to a totality, and for that very reason interact with each other. Therefore,

the motherland. Self-seeking does contain this opposition: it has a privative and negative element which is inconsistent with the love of everything that does not coincide with the 'I' of the individual" (pp. 160–61).
1 "The chemist may separate the 'elementary', 'pure' body from the compounds in which it is to be found, and subject it, as a discretely separable body, to all manner of further investigations. This elementary body is also, as such, actually present and efficient in the compound. On the other hand, the human soul is unitary and cannot be reduced to [its] component parts; and it is theoretically

neither the driving forces of economic activity nor the economic facts and phenomena can reveal their real character and their full nature if they are only observed
in isolation.

([*Economy*], p. 244)

First of all, this sentence shows that Knies – whose thought on this point is completely
parallel to that of Roscher – in principle applies his "organic" theory of the nature of the
individual to the "nation" as well. In that connection, he does not find it necessary to define
what [we are] to understand by "nation", in the sense [in which this concept is used] in his
theory. Apparently, he sees it as an object that is unambiguously given in general experience;[1]
occasionally (*Economy*[2], p. 490), he explicitly identifies it with the community organized as a
state. As far as this community is concerned, not only – and self-evidently – does he see it as
something different from the "sum of individuals", but this fact in its turn can in his opinion
be derived from the far more general principle according to which (as he puts it, [*Economy*,]
p. 109) "a similar harmony" (to that which characterizes the manifestations of life of a
"personality") "everywhere and necessarily, also resounds from the manifestations of life of a
whole nation". This is because "the historical existence of a nation comprises, as if from a *unitary
core*, the different circles of life." This "unitary character" must be understood as something
more than the purely juridical one, and [also as] more than the mutual influence of all domains
of life on each other, determined by common historical destinies, traditions and cultural goods
and developed through history; instead, Knies regards the "unitary character" as being the origin
from which the culture of the nation emanates. This is clear not only from the parallel – quoted
above and repeatedly drawn – between the "totality" of the individual and that of the nation,
but also from numerous other statements. In particular, it also holds for the nation that the
"totality" carries the meaning of a *unitary psychological conditionality* of all its cultural manifestations:
for Knies, too, "nations" are the carriers of unitary "driving forces". The historically emergent
and empirically demonstrable individual cultural phenomena are not components of the "total
character". On the contrary; the "total character" is the *real* cause of the individual cultural
phenomena: it is not a composite, but *the* unitary element, which effects itself through everything
that is individual. The only composite is the "body" of the national organism[2] – [which in this
respect differs from] the natural organisms. Science cannot grasp the individual "aspects" of a
national culture separately and independently, but only from [the standpoint of] the unitary
total character of the nation; this is because their amalgamation into a "unity" is not determined
by processes of mutual "adjustment" and "adaptation" (or however else one might term the

---

unacceptable to assume that the soul of 'human beings with a social nature' [can be coupled] with a
discretely separable instinct of pure self-preservation, etc." (*Economy*[2], p. 505).

1   "In the case of some objects, it is irrefutable that [our] general experience of life offers all the elements
necessary for their conceptual establishment, so that they are always to be found when reference is
made to them. In the case of other [objects] the[ir conceptual] establishment will, in certain respects,
be subject to agreement, so that [the concept, as established,] can only become generally valid under
certain conditions. The concept of the nation belongs to the first group, the concept of the economy
to the second one" ([*Economy*], p. 125).

2   On this point, see *Economy*[2], p. 164: "We are not only justified, but actually forced to consider the
national economy, with its structure as a society and its legal ordering as a state, as being an organic
entity. But it is an organism of a higher order, whose particular essence is due to the fact that it is not
a natural, individual organism – like vegetable and animal organisms – but a "composite body", a
collective organism that has come into being as a product of culture, and whose elements are individual
organisms, equipped and destined to live [their] individual lives simultaneously, and [entering into]
the sexual relations necessary for the preservation of the species."

mutual influences that all "individual" [elements] exert on each other because of the interconnectedness of all events); on the contrary, [it is due to the fact that] the "national character", which is in itself unitary and consistent, will constantly and inevitably "strive" to establish a state of *homogeneity* within and between *all* domains of national life.[1] No attempt is made to analyse the nature of this mysterious force, which is conceived along the same lines as the vitalistic "life force": like Roscher's "background", it is simply the ultimate agent that one encounters when analysing historical phenomena. That which constitutes the "personality", the "character" of individuals, has the character of a "substance" (this is, after all, the way in which Knies' theory of the personality must be understood); and in the same way, this substantive character is here, quite in keeping with the spirit of romanticism, transferred to the "soul of the nation" – a pale metaphysical echo of Roscher's pious belief that the "souls" of individuals, as well as of nations, originate directly from the hand of God.

And, finally, above the "organisms" of the individual nations we find the ultimate organic relationship: that of humanity. But, as the evolution of humanity is an "organic" relationship, it cannot manifest itself in the successive and simultaneous [relations] of nations, each of which has, in the historically relevant respects, evolved in a cyclical form. That would be an "unorganic" succession and simultaneous existence of generic beings. Instead, the evolution of humanity is a total one, in which each nation plays its role, which is ordained by history and *therefore individual*. This conception, which belongs to the philosophy of history and on which Knies' book is everywhere tacitly based, marks the decisive break with Roscher's intellectual universe, because that conception implies that, in the last resort, individuals as well as nations will be relevant for science, not as "generic beings" that generally share the same qualities, but as "individuals" with a significance that is "functional" (from the perspective of the "organic" approach). As we shall see, this conception actually manifests itself very forcefully in Knies' methodology.

Knies' presuppositions had a metaphysical – or, in logical parlance: an *emanationist* – character: the "unity" of the individual was conceived as a "force" with actual, so to speak biological,

---

1   The following passages will be a sufficient illustration of this: "Even if, with the passage of time, the evolutionary driving force may initially expand its scope more in certain [individual] areas . . . the movement will always extend to the whole and strive to keep all elements in a *homogeneous* [relationship]" ([*Economy*], p. 114). Quite analogously (p. 115): "In general, one will only have gained insight into the situation of the national economy at a given time when [this situation] has been considered in its relation to the comprehensive phenomena of the historic life of the nation. In the same way, within the domain of economics in particular, we are only able to discern the historical significance of one single evolutionary form by means of the parallelism that manifests itself in the *analogous configuration* of all other [such forms]." "Not only do all the particular areas of the national economy stand in a mutual relationship that points to the position and the character of the total economy *as being the explanation* [*of these areas*]; but this overall [relationship] is in its turn indissolubly linked to the total life of the nation. Whenever one asks about the causes of some economic situation, it is to this linkage that one will constantly be referred; and, conversely, whenever one tries to establish the effects of some economic situation, one will also have to enter into the phenomena of other areas of life [than the economic one]" (p. 111). "Consequently, the general character that manifests itself in the different areas always retains its common nature; all forms of external life manifest themselves as configurations of *unitary* driving forces, which strive to make themselves felt everywhere and whose evolution is conveyed to us through the transformations of those forms: the [driving forces] strive to move [those forms] in one particular direction" (ibid.). And finally: "New configurations, resulting from an advanced development, may possibly at first evolve, in a clearer form and with a strongly marked character, in [only] one single area of the general life of the nation; but this partial existence is only the *manifestation* of a gradual process of coming into being, which takes place in a series of not only simultaneous, but also successive transformations comprising life in its totality" (p. 110).

effect. However, if this conception were not to turn completely into mysticism disguised as anthropology, it necessarily reintroduced into the discussion those rationalist consequences that, as a legacy of Hegel's magnificent constructions, still marked the epigones of Hegelian panlogism. ‹103› Foremost among these [consequences], we find that conflation of the *actual* collective entity and the generic *concept* that is so characteristic of the emanationist logic in its decadent phase. "It must be maintained", Knies says ([*Economy*,] p. 345), "that in all human life and activity, there is something eternal and identical, because no single human being could *belong to the species* if he were not in that way, together with all individuals, *bound to the common whole*; and this eternal and identical [element] also manifests itself in the communities, since they will always be based on the distinctive character of the individuals." Evidently, the "general" interconnection merges with the "general" concept, and the actual membership of a species with the subsumption under a generic concept. Just as Knies conceived the "unitary character" of the actual totality as being a conceptual "consistency", here the actual interconnections of humanity and its evolution in fact turn into a conceptual "identity" of the individuals comprehended by it. To this a further element is added, [in the form of] the identification of "causality" with "law-like character" – another legitimate offspring of the panlogistic dialectic of evolution, and one that can only be consistently maintained on the basis [of that dialectic]:

> Whoever regards economics as a science will in no way doubt that [economics] is concerned with laws governing phenomena. What distinguishes science from mere information is that the latter consists of knowledge of facts and phenomena, while science imparts knowledge of the causal interconnections between these phenomena and the causes by which they were brought forth, and strives to establish those *laws* governing phenomena which manifest themselves within its field of inquiry.

So says Knies ([*Economy*], p. 235). That passage is nothing short of astounding against the background of what we learnt at the beginning of this section concerning Knies' views on the "freedom" of action and the relationship between "personality" and irrationality; and when we come to consider his theory of history, it will become evident that he is in deadly earnest with respect to that irrationality. In order to explain [the passage], we have to take into consideration that what Knies understands by "law-like character" is nothing more than the fact that the actual development of human history is determined throughout by the unitary "driving force" underlying it, [and that] all that is individual emanates from [that "driving force"] as a manifestation of it. The fracture in both Knies' and Roscher's basic epistemological [position] must be explained by the withered remainders (which have [moreover] been warped in an anthropological–biological direction) of Hegel's great ideas; these remainders were still very characteristic of the philosophies of history, language and culture of various influential currents of thought in the middle decades of the last century. In Knies' work, at least, the *concept* of the "Individual" comes into its own and takes over from the naturalism of Roscher's cyclical theory; the preceding account already leads us to assume this, and it will soon be demonstrated in more detail. However, it was partly the fault of Knies' basically emanationist conception of the real substantive character of [the "Individual"] that his theory did not even attempt to determine the relationship between concept and reality; therefore (as will also become apparent) [his theory] could only yield results that were essentially negative and almost destructive.[1]

---

1   A further article was planned.

The three parts of the article: *Roscher, Knies I* and *Knies II*, were first published in separate volumes of the periodical *Jahrbuch für Gesetzgebung, Verwaltung und Volkswirtschaft im Deutschen Reich*: "Roscher's 'Historical Method'" in *Jahrbuch* 27 (1903), pp. 1181–221; "Knies and the Problem of Irrationality" in *Jahrbuch* 29 (1905), pp. 1323–84; and "Knies and the Problem of Irrationality" (continued) in *Jahrbuch* 30 (1906), pp. 81–120. It should be kept in mind that *Knies I-II* actually appeared later than the *Accompanying Remarks* and *Objectivity*, and *Knies II* appeared simultaneously with *Critical Studies*.

Translated from: "Roscher und Knies und die logischen Probleme der historischen Nationalökonomie", in Max Weber, *Gesammelte Aufsätze zur Wissenschaftslehre* (ed. Johannes Winckelmann), 3rd ed., Tübingen: J.C.B.Mohr (Paul Siebeck) 1968, pp. 1–145.

Weber probably started working on the article in the late summer or early autumn of 1902. As can be seen from p. 3n1, it was originally intended as a contribution (on Knies, rather than Roscher) to a *Festschrift* to be published in the summer of 1903, but it quickly outgrew the more modest proportions of such a contribution, and Weber was unable to finish it in time. Instead, it was published as three separate articles in Schmoller's *Jahrbuch*. When *Roscher* came out in the autumn of 1903, only one more article (on Knies) was envisaged. However, the length of that article also increased apace, and work on the two *Knies* essays was only finished late in 1905, retarded by Weber's intensive work in 1904 on other publications (*Objectivity* and *The Protestant Ethic*), by his month-long journey to the USA in the autumn of 1904, and by his studies on the Russian Revolution of 1905.

The subtitles are original.

ACCOMPANYING
REMARKS

When the *Archive* came into being half a generation ago ‹104›, it exercised an extraordinary attraction, particularly on younger persons such as ourselves. The success achieved by the *Archive* showed that this feeling [of attraction] was in fact widely shared. Although it was edited by an "outsider" and had to find its place alongside old and well-established journals within our discipline, [the *Archive*] was able, within a short span of time, to secure a distinguished academic position and to gain quite a considerable influence on practical efforts in the field of social policy. How did that come about? If we were to answer this question by pointing to the editorial talent of the founder of the journal, this would still not constitute a satisfactory explanation, as that talent – which was completely beyond doubt – could only manifest itself by determining the distinctive character of the *Archive*. And we are [therefore] confronted with another question: What was this distinctive character?

If this question is to be answered properly, reference must above all be made to the fact that [the editor's talent] has in a certain sense led to the creation of a new type of periodical literature in social science, or that this was at least the intention. The *Archive* was founded as a "specialized journal": and the "speciality" which it was to cultivate was the "labour question" in the widest sense [of that term].

Now, numerous journals in Germany and abroad had already concerned themselves with the "labour question", but, compared with its predecessors, the *Archive* took the further step of placing the problems designated by the name "labour question" in their most general context; [it] considered the "labour question" in its *cultural significance*, as the most clearly perceivable external expression of a much greater complex of phenomena: the fundamental process of transformation that our economic life, and hence our cultural existence, have experienced through the advance of capitalism. The task of the new journal was to offer the services of science for [the solution of] the practical problems arising from this world-historical fact. In essence, this determined the distinctive character of the *Archive*.

The new journal became a "specialized journal", not by virtue of its subject matter (like, for example, the *Financial Archive* ‹105›), but by virtue of its viewpoint. Consequently, its field of activity encompassed the treatment of all the phenomena of economic life and of social life as a whole, viewed in the perspective of the revolutionary changes wrought by capitalism; and, naturally, what first of all had to be considered in this connection were the effects on the situation of the working classes of the processes of restructuring that were taking place, as well as the reactions [either] of those classes themselves, or [in the form of] legislation.

In view of [the] distinctive problems [with which it was intended to deal], the new journal was fully justified in carrying on its banner the ambiguous and so often misused word "social", provided that the word "social" is used in the strictly defined sense which can alone guarantee its unambiguousness and precision. In that sense, this word, too, does not so much imply a delimitation of a distinct group of phenomena, but rather [refers to] the *perspective* from which the phenomena of economic life and the rest of social life in society are viewed. [This means] that all individual economic phenomena are [seen as being] oriented towards a certain economic system, and that they should therefore be viewed from the perspective of their historical conditionality; and [it also means that] the causal interconnections between economic development and all other social phenomena should be uncovered; in both respects, [the investigation] is deliberately limited to the present, that is to say: to the historical epoch marked by the advance of capitalism.

The distinctive way in which the problems were to be treated in the *Archive* automatically brought with it other distinctive features. Obviously, if the journal wanted to fulfil its task, it had to seek out capitalism wherever it was to be found, quite irrespective of national barriers. Consequently, from the very beginning, all countries [that had experienced] capitalist development were drawn into its field of inquiry. This systematic extension to cover the widest possible geographical area gave the *Archive* an "international" character, to a larger degree than other organs in this discipline. For practical reasons, the internationality of [the journal's] subject matter naturally developed into an internationality of persons. From the first issues onwards, the circle of contributors spanned the entire civilized world – in certain respects, it even testified to a marked preference for [contributions from] abroad.

However, since the *academic* character of the journal was underlined from the very beginning (it may well be that the personality of the founder also had a strong influence), the contributors were from the start recruited not only from all parts of the world but also from all partisan camps. The *Archive* was not only international, it was also the first *truly* "cross-partisan" journal of our discipline. –

Now, the *Archive* had from the beginning set for itself, as one of its most prominent fields of activity in addition to the purely scientific gathering of factual knowledge, the task of *critical* scrutiny of the course of legislation. However, such *practical and critical* work is inevitably affected by value judgements. It includes the pursuit, not only of social science, but also – at least as far as the findings are concerned – of social policy, and this prompts the following question: When the *Archive* engaged in this *practical* critical work, did it also have a particular "tendency"? That is to say: did the leading contributors advocate a distinct social-policy standpoint? Were they united, not only by their shared scientific interests, but also by a certain measure of agreement on ideals, or at least on fundamental points of view from which practical maxims could be derived?

That was in fact the case; and, in a certain sense, the success of the journal was due precisely to this uniform character, since this practical "tendency" was, in the decisive respects, simply the result of particular *insights* concerning the historical situation that had to be taken into account in the field of social policy. In other words, it was rooted in shared theoretical views concerning the actual assumptions on which any attempt to do practical work in the field of social policy *must* be based in the given, simply unalterable historical situation. It was therefore based on convictions that were completely independent of personal wishes. These insights, which defined the "tendency" of the journal, chiefly concerned the following points:

1   Capitalism was a result of historical development: it could no longer be abolished and must therefore simply be accepted; and today, there was no longer any way back from it to the patriarchal foundations of the old society;

2   Consequently, the old forms of social orders, which corresponded to those patriarchal foundations, will, whether we like it or not, yield to new ones that are able to adapt to the altered conditions of economic life. In particular, this meant that the integration of the proletariat as a new, independent element into the cultural community of modern states, now that it had been created as a class by capitalism and had become conscious of its distinctive historical character, had become a problem for all state policy that could not be ignored;

3   To the extent that the process of social restructuring is to take the form of legislative measures, it can only be the product of a gradual, "organic" reshaping of historically obsolete conditions and institutions; and for that purpose, it is indispensable to have the aid of scientific knowledge of the historically given situation.

These fundamental views are also shared by the new editors of the *Archive*. If this is stated explicitly here, that should of course *not* be taken to mean that those views will be beyond or above criticism in the columns of our journal. It only means that, in the *practical* criticism that finds expression in the journal alongside [its] scientific work, *we* are guided by those insights, and that we know that the previous contributors to the *Archive* are in agreement with us on this point. To the extent that social *policy* is discussed in the *Archive* at all, it will continue to be a "policy of *realism*", based on what is simply [and] unalterably given.

However, the new editors are convinced that the situation today requires a change in two respects, in comparison with the way in which the *Archive* tried to cope with its task in the first years of its existence; and they intend to take this altered situation into account when they give the journal its shape.

First of all, the field of activity of the *Archive*, which hitherto had only been extended tentatively and on a case-by-case basis, must now be fundamentally enlarged. Today, our journal has to consider the historical and theoretical investigation into the *general cultural significance of the development of capitalism* as the scientific problem that it is dedicated to [dealing with]. And, precisely *because* it proceeds, and must proceed, from a quite specific point of view: the economically conditioned nature of cultural phenomena, it cannot avoid being in close contact with the neighbouring disciplines: the general theory of the state, legal philosophy, social ethics, with studies in social psychology and with those inquiries usually categorized under the name of sociology. We shall closely follow scientific movements in these areas, particularly in our systematic surveys of literature. We shall have to devote particular attention to those problems that are commonly called social–anthropological – that is to say: the questions concerning, on the one hand, the repercussions of economic conditions on the modalities of racial selection, and, on the other hand, the influence of inherited physical and psychical qualities on the economic struggle for existence and the economic institutions. These questions, lying on the boundary between biology and the social sciences, have hitherto been treated in a dilettante fashion; we, too, wish to make our contribution towards overcoming this [state of affairs].

The second change concerns an adjustment of the *form* in which [our subject matter] is treated.

When the *Archive* was founded, the editor believed that the most important task that it would have to perform was the collection of material. And, behind this [belief] undoubtedly lay an idea which was entirely correct at the time: it was necessary to create an organ for the collection of the scattered data of social statistics, as well as the increasingly accumulating social laws, and their publication in an accessible and orderly form. At that time, this was the primary and most urgent need both for academics and practitioners, as such an organ of collection was lacking. But our age has progressed swiftly. Since the foundation of the *Archive* in 1888, almost a dozen journals have come into being whose sole function is this collection of material. Above all, the governments of nearly every civilized country have created official organs for the publication of social statistics data: England, the *Labour Gazette* (since 1893); France, the *Bulletin de l'Office du Travail* (since 1894); Belgium, the *Revue du Travail* (since 1896); Austria, the *Soziale Rundschau* (since 1900); [and] Germany, the *Reichsarbeitsblatt* (since 1903). In addition, there are private collections [of material] in most countries: [in] Germany, the *Soziale Praxis* (since 1892) and *Der Arbeitsmarkt* (since 1897); [in] France, the *Questions pratiques de législation ouvrière* (since 1900), and so on. And a near comprehensive publication of legislative material is provided by the *Bulletin* of the International Union for the Legislative Protection of Workers (since 1902), the *Annuaire de la Législation du Travail* (published by the Office du Travail de Belgique, since 1897) and others beside them.

This has completely altered the situation. On the one hand, there is no longer a need to devote a scientific journal like the *Archive* to the mere collection of *material*, alongside the [above-mentioned] publications, which are equipped with ample funds and do excellent work. We shall cut down on the reports on social *statistics* (this had in fact already been done to an increasing extent); and we shall in many instances be able to reduce the verbatim reproduction of *texts* of laws – something which hitherto took up a lot of space – in favour of detailed *critical reports* on the meaning and significance of laws, and quite especially of *draft* laws. On the other hand, an important new task has arisen: that of (so to speak) breathing life, by means of scientific synthesis, into the infinitely accumulating material contained in the organs of collection listed above. The hunger for social facts that still filled the best of men half a generation ago has now, concurrently with the general reawakening of philosophical interest, been followed by a hunger for social theories; and the satisfaction of this [hunger], to the best of [our] ability, will constitute one of the main future tasks of the *Archive*. To a considerably greater degree, we shall have to give consideration both to the discussion of social problems from *philosophical* viewpoints and to that form of inquiry in our area of specialization which is called "*theory*" in the narrower sense [of the term]: the formation of clear concepts. We are far removed from the belief that the richness of historical life should be forced to fit formulas; but we are just as strongly convinced that only clear and unambiguous concepts can pave the way for research aimed at a thorough investigation of the specific significance of social phenomena of culture.

However, no organ would today be able to devote itself to social theory in a way that satisfies the demands of strict scientific rigour unless it is also able, by means of epistemological [and] methodological discussions, to achieve *fundamental* clarity concerning the relationship between the theoretical conceptual constructs and reality. Consequently, we shall constantly follow scientific work in the area of epistemological critique and methodology. And by opening the New Series of the *Archive* with an essay by one of the editors that subjects these problems to thorough investigation, we wish to demonstrate our intention of constantly participating, for our own part, in these discussions of principle.

First published as, and translated from, "Geleitwort", *Archiv für Sozialwissenschaft und Sozialpolitik* 19 (1904), pp. I*–VII*.

Written in the early spring of 1904 on the occasion of Werner Sombart, Max Weber and Edgar Jaffé taking over as editors of the *Archive*. Until recently, the generally accepted view among Weber scholars was that the *Accompanying Remarks* were drafted by Max Weber. However, a newly published article (Ghosh, *Authorship*) forcefully argues that the original drafting was in fact done by Werner Sombart, although Weber probably revised Sombart's draft in order to bring the *Accompanying Remarks* more into line with his *Objectivity* article (which he in turn revised on certain points to ensure a sufficient harmony of views with those expressed in the *Accompanying Remarks* – see below, p. 100). In view of these close links between *Accompanying Remarks* and *Objectivity*, and since the *Accompanying Remarks* were signed by "The Editors" (Weber, Sombart and Jaffé), they have been included in this collection.

THE "OBJECTIVITY" OF KNOWLEDGE IN SOCIAL SCIENCE AND SOCIAL POLICY[1]

When a journal dealing with [questions of] social science, and especially with social policy, makes its appearance in this country, or new editors take over, the first question with which it is greeted usually concerns its "tendency". We, too, have to furnish an answer to this question, and in this essay we want to go into it in a more fundamental way, further to what has been said in our *Accompanying Remarks* ‹106›. This gives us the opportunity to shed light in various ways on the distinctive character of what we understand as "social science"; and even though we are dealing with points which usually "go without saying" – indeed: precisely because [they have that character] – [such a discussion] may be useful, if not for the professional, then at least for readers who are less familiar with the actual practice of scientific work. –

As long as it has existed, ‹107› the declared aim of the *Archive* has been *not only* to extend our knowledge of the "social conditions of all countries", that is to say, of the *facts* of social

1   In Section I of the following article, whenever comments are explicitly made on behalf of the editors, or tasks are set for the *Archive*, those comments are of course not the private views of the author, but have been expressly approved by his fellow editors. As far as Section II is concerned, the author bears *sole* responsibility for its form and content.

The fact that not only the contributors to the *Archive* but also its editors have standpoints which are by no means completely identical, even concerning questions of method, ensures that the *Archive* will never fall under the influence of a particular school of thought. On the other hand, the editors have obviously only felt able to assume their joint editorial task because they have a number of basic viewpoints in common. In particular, they agree on the positive value of *theoretical* knowledge gained by [applying] "one-sided" points of view, and on the demand for the *formation of clear concepts* and for a strict *distinction between empirical knowledge and value judgements* – a demand that is voiced in this essay, although we naturally do not claim that we are thereby calling for anything "new".

The extensiveness of the discussion (in Section II) and the frequent repetition of the same idea have the sole aim of making an exposition of this kind as *intelligible to the ordinary reader* as possible. This consideration has led to the sacrifice of much – hopefully not too much – precision of expression; and, for the same reason, no attempt has been made here to provide a *systematic* investigation rather than an enumeration of various methodological points of view. That would have required introducing a large number of epistemological problems, some of which lie even deeper. We do not want to provide an exercise in logic, but rather to make use of well-known findings of modern logic. We do not intend to solve problems, but to demonstrate to the layman in what way they are significant. Anyone familiar with the writings of modern logicians – let me just mention Windelband, Simmel and, especially for our purposes, Heinrich Rickert – will immediately notice that, in all important respects, this essay builds on the[ir work].

100

life, but also to educate our *judgement* of *practical problems* of social life and thereby – to the admittedly quite modest extent to which private scholars can further this goal – to criticize social policy in practice, right up to the legislative level. Nevertheless, the *Archive* has, from the very beginning, maintained its intention to be an exclusively scientific journal, and to employ only the means provided by *scientific* research – which raises the question: how can that aim, in principle, be reconciled with the restriction to those means? What does it mean when legislative and administrative measures or proposals for such measures are *judged* in the columns of the *Archive*? On what *norms* are those judgements based? What sort of *validity* can be ascribed to the value judgements expressed by those who judge [such measures], or on which a writer bases his practical proposals? In what sense can such persons be said to remain in the field of *scientific* discussion, since the distinguishing feature of scientific knowledge must of course be the "objective" validity of its results as *truth*? We shall begin by stating our position on *this* question, and then go on to consider the further question: in what sense do "objectively valid truths" *exist at all* in the domain of the sciences of cultural life? This question must be addressed, in view of the fact that even the seemingly most elementary problems of our discipline, its methods of work, the way in which its concepts are formed and the validity of those concepts, are subject to constant change and give rise to bitter strife. What we want to do here is not to offer solutions, but to point to problems – the kinds of problem to which our journal will have to turn its attention if it is to achieve its present and future purposes. –

I

It is common knowledge that our discipline, like any other scientific discipline dealing with the institutions and processes of human culture (except perhaps political history), had its historic roots in *practical* considerations. Its main – and, at the outset, its sole – purpose was to produce value judgements concerning certain economic policy measures of the state. It was [a] "technical" [discipline] more or less in the same sense as the clinical disciplines of medical science. As is well known, this situation gradually changed, but it was not accompanied by the elaboration of a distinction of *principle* between knowledge of "what is" and [of] "what ought to be". What inhibited [the formulation of] this distinction was initially the idea that economic processes were governed by immutably invariant laws of nature, and, later, the belief that they conformed to an unambiguous evolutionary principle. Consequently, what *ought to be* was seen as coinciding, in the first case, with what immutably *existed*, and, in the second case, with what would inevitably *emerge*. With the awakening of the historical sense, a combination of ethical evolutionism and historical relativism gained the upper hand within our discipline and attempted to divest ethical norms of their formal character, to give *substantive* content to the realm of "morals" by incorporating into it the totality of cultural values, and in this fashion to raise economics to the dignity of an empirically based "ethical science". The result of labelling as "moral" the totality of all possible cultural ideals was that ethical imperatives lost their specific dignity, while nothing was gained with regard to the "objectivity" of the validity of those ideals. Here, we can and must abstain from a fundamental discussion of this development, and simply register the fact that, even today, the confused opinion has not disappeared but is still current, particularly and for obvious reasons among people concerned with practical policy, that the discipline of economics produces, and has the task of producing, *value judgements* derived from a specifically "economic world view". –

We wish to state at the outset that our journal, which represents a specialized empirical discipline, must, *as a matter of principle*, *reject* this view: we are of the opinion that it can never be the task of a science of empirical experience to determine binding norms and ideals from which practical prescriptions may then be deduced.

What follows from this statement? Certainly not that, because value judgements are in the last resort based on certain ideals, and are therefore "subjective" in origin, they simply cannot be the object of scientific discussion. Both the practice and the purpose of this journal would constantly negate such a proposition. Criticism does not stop before value judgements. The question is rather: what can a scientific critique of ideals and value judgements *mean*, and what is its purpose? We need to examine this question in somewhat greater detail.

Any conscious reflection on the most fundamental elements of meaningful human action is from the beginning tied to the categories "ends" and "means". In any concrete case, we want something either "for its own sake" or as a means of obtaining what we are ultimately striving for. First of all, there is no doubt that the question whether certain means are appropriate for the achievement of a given end can be subjected to scientific consideration. Since we are, within the limits of our knowledge at any given time, able to make valid statements as to *what* means are appropriate or inappropriate for the achievement of an imagined goal, we can in this manner estimate the chances of achieving a certain end with certain means at our disposal; and consequently we can, against the background of any given historical situation, indirectly make a critical evaluation of the choice of the goal itself as being practically meaningful, or as being meaningless under the given circumstances. Moreover, *if* it seems possible to attain an imagined goal, we are (obviously within the limits of our knowledge in each case) able to determine what would be the *consequences* – *apart from* the possible attainment of the desired end – of using the means necessary to that end, because of the complete interconnectedness of all events. In so doing, we make it possible for the acting person to weigh those unwanted effects against the desired effects of his action, and thereby to [furnish] an answer to the question: "What is the '*cost*' of the attainment of the desired end, in terms of the foreseeable violation of *other* values?". In the great majority of cases, any end that is striven for will (in this sense) "cost" something, or may at least do so. Therefore, any person who acts responsibly and reflects [on his actions] has to weigh the goal of his action against its consequences; and one of the most important functions of the *technical* critique with which we have been dealing so far is to make this possible. However, the task of deciding what the result of this assessment should be is *not* one that science can perform; that decision must be taken by the striving person who, in accordance with his own conscience and his personal world view, weighs the values in question and chooses between them. Science can help him to be *conscious* of the fact that *any* action – and naturally, under given circumstances, *abstaining from* action – will have consequences that imply *taking sides* in favour of certain values and therefore as a rule (something that is particularly often overlooked nowadays) – *against other ones*. To make the choice is his own affair.

Furthermore, as a help towards making this decision, we can offer him *knowledge* of the *meaning* of what he is striving for. We can teach him how those goals that he is striving to attain, and that he chooses between, are interconnected, and what they mean. For a start, we can do this by pointing out the "ideas" in which the concrete goal is, or could be, rooted, and by setting them out in a logically consistent manner. Indeed, it is obviously one of the most important tasks of any science of human cultural life to make accessible to intellectual understanding those "ideas" for which people, now as in the past, fight (or believe that they fight). That does not overstep the boundaries of a science that aims at an "intellectual ordering of empirical reality", even though this interpretation of spiritual values is in no way carried out by means of "induction" in the usual sense of that word. However, at least some parts of this task do not fall within the area with which the specialized discipline of economics deals according to the customary division of labour: instead, this is a task for *social philosophy*. But, historically, the impact of ideas on the development of social life has been, and still is, so massive that our journal will not leave aside this task, but will on the contrary regard it as one of its most important duties.

But science might want to go further in its treatment of value judgements and, not only let us understand and re-experience the goals that are striven for and the ideals in which they are rooted, but also, and above all, teach us to "judge" them critically. *Such* a critique, however, can only have a dialectical character; that is to say, it can only consist in judging the substance of historically given value judgements and ideas from the point of view of formal logic, i.e. in testing the ideals against the fundamental demand for the internal *consistency* of what we strive for. By setting this goal, [the "critical judgement"] can help the striving person to reflect on the ultimate axioms that form the basis of what he is striving for, on the ultimate value standards that he applies, or that he should apply in order to be consistent. But to make us *aware* of the ultimate value standards that manifest themselves in a concrete value judgement is as far as [the "critical judgement"] can go without entering the realm of speculation. Whether the individual who makes a value judgement *ought to* subscribe to those ultimate value standards is purely his own personal affair; it is a question which concerns his striving and his conscience and which cannot be answered by empirical science.

An empirical science cannot tell someone what he *ought to* do, but only what he *can* do and – possibly – what he *wants to* do. Admittedly, within our disciplines there is an unremitting tendency towards introducing personal world views – even into scientific arguments, where they again and again cause confusion. The result is that, even in inquiries into simple causal relationships between facts, scientific arguments are assessed differently according to whether they improve or reduce the chances [of success] of the ideals of the person in question – that is to say, the possibility of striving to attain a particular goal. In this respect, the editors of this journal and its contributors will certainly "consider nothing human to be foreign to them". ⟨108⟩ But that confession of human weakness is far removed from the belief in an "ethical" science of economics whose task would be to produce ideals from its [own] material, or to produce concrete norms by applying general ethical imperatives to that material. – It is also true that precisely the innermost elements of our "personality" – the highest and most fundamental value judgements that determine our action[s] and endow our life with meaning and significance – are experienced by us as something "*objectively*" valuable: we can only espouse them if we regard them as valid, as stemming from the highest values that guide our life, and if they are further developed in the struggle against the difficulties of daily life. And it is certain that what constitutes the dignity of a "personality" is that it espouses certain values to which it relates its life. This is true even though those values may be exclusively situated *within* the sphere of one's own individuality; in such cases, [the personality] "lives its life to the full" in accordance with *those* interests for which it claims *validity as values*, and considers this "living to the full" as the idea to which it relates [its life]. In any event, in order to be meaningful, an attempt to assert value judgements presupposes a belief in values. *Nevertheless*: to *judge* the *validity* of such values is a matter of *belief*, *possibly* also a task for speculative observations and interpretations of the meaning of life and of the world, but certainly *not* the object of the kind of science of empirical experience that this journal is dedicated to practising. Contrary to a widespread belief, the decisive argument in favour of this distinction is not the empirically demonstrable fact that the ultimate ends [referred to above] have historically been subject to change and controversy: even our knowledge of the most established theoretical propositions – in the exact natural sciences or mathematics, for instance – is a product of culture, in just the same way as our conscience is developed and refined by culture. If we think more especially of the practical problems of economic and social policy (in the ordinary sense of the word), it is true that the discussion of numerous, even countless, practical *individual questions* is conducted on the basis of general unanimity concerning certain goals that are *regarded as self-evident* – one could mention emergency credits, concrete tasks in the field of public health and public assistance, and measures such as factory inspections, industrial tribunals, ‹109› employment centres and large parts of the legislation concerning the protection of workers – so that, at least apparently, only the *means* to be employed in order to reach the goal are at issue. But, even if we took such an appearance of self-evidence to be the truth – something that science could never do with impunity – and even if we (quite often mistakenly) regarded the conflicts that we soon encounter when trying to achieve those goals in practice as being purely technical questions of the suitability [of means to ends], we would nevertheless have to face the fact that regulatory value standards lose even their *appearance* of self-evidence as soon as we move from the concrete problems of *furthering* welfare and the economy by means of charity and public surveillance to questions of economic and social *policy*. The distinctive characteristic of a problem of social *policy* is precisely that it *cannot* be settled on the basis of purely technical considerations applied to given ends: [that] the regulatory value standards themselves can and *must* be the subject of *dispute*, because the problem projects into the region of general *cultural* questions. And the dispute is not only, as we are nowadays so prone to believe, one between [different] "class interests", *but also between* [*different*] *world views*. Of course, it still remains completely true that what is usually – together with many other factors, but no doubt to a remarkably large extent – decisive for the *content* of an individual's world view is its degree of elective affinity with the individual's "class interest" (if we here, for once, agree to use that concept, which is not as unambiguous as it looks). In any event, one thing is certain: the more "general" the problem under consideration – that is to say, in the present context: the greater the scope of its cultural *significance* – the less amenable is it to an unambiguous solution based on material provided by empirical science, and the greater will be the part played by the ultimate, entirely personal axioms of one's belief and value ideas. It is simply naïve when even professionals occasionally still believe that what is important is above all to set up "a principle" for the practical social sciences and to corroborate its validity [by scientific means], so that norms for the solution of individual practical problems can then be unambiguously deduced from it. There is a definite need within the social sciences for "fundamental" discussions of practical problems, that is to say, for uncovering the ideas underlying the value judgements that unreflectingly push themselves forward; and our journal in particular has the firm intention of devoting itself to precisely those kinds of discussion. But it certainly cannot be the task of the journal, or indeed of any science of empirical experience, to establish a practical common denominator for our problems in the shape of generally valid ultimate ideals. Thus defined, that task would not only be impracticable, it would also be inherently absurd. And no matter why and how ethical imperatives are regarded as binding, one certainly cannot, from the[se imperatives] – that is, from norms for concretely determined actions of individuals – unambiguously *deduce* certain normative *elements* of *culture*; and the greater the area encompassed by those cultural elements, the less likely such a deduction is to succeed. Only positive religions – or to be more precise: *sects* bound by dogma – are capable of endowing the content of *cultural values* with the dignity of unconditionally valid *ethical* imperatives. In all other contexts, the dignity of cultural ideals that the individual *wants* to realize is fundamentally different from that of ethical duties which he *ought to* fulfil. The fate of a cultural epoch that has eaten from the tree of knowledge is that it must realize that we cannot read off the *meaning* of events in this world from the results – however complete they may be – of our scrutiny of those events, but that we ourselves must be able to create that meaning. We have to realize that the advance of empirical knowledge can never produce "world views", and that consequently, the most lofty ideals, those that move us most profoundly, will forever only be realized in a struggle against other ideals, [ideals] that are just as holy for others as ours are for us.

Only an optimistic syncretism – which sometimes results from the relativism of developmental history – will be able to ignore the theoretical implications of this immensely serious state of affairs, or to elude its consequences in practice. Of course, a practising politician may in a given situation subjectively be as duty-bound to mediate between opposing views as to side with one of them. But that has nothing at all to do with *scientific* "objectivity". The "middle course" *is not one hair's breadth closer to scientific truth* than the most extreme ideals of parties on the right or the left. Nowhere is science worse off in the long run than in the hands of those who refuse to face uncomfortable facts and the tough realities of life. The *Archive* will unconditionally oppose the grave delusion that it is possible to arrive at *scientifically valid* practical norms by synthesizing a number of partisan viewpoints, or by drawing a median line between them: that point of view is characterized by a fondness for disguising one's own value standards by relativizing them, and therefore poses a far greater danger to the impartiality of [scientific] research than the old, naïve belief of parties that their dogmas could be "demonstrated" scientifically. What we want is to strengthen once more our ability to *distinguish* between knowing [something] and judging [it], and to fulfil both the scientific obligation to see the truth of facts and the practical duty of standing up for one's own ideals.

There is and remains – and *this* is what matters to us – an eternal, unbridgeable difference as to whether an argument is aimed at our feelings and our capacity for embracing with enthusiasm concrete practical goals, or forms and elements of culture; or, if it is a question concerning the validity of ethical norms, [whether it is aimed at] our conscience; *or* finally, [whether it is aimed] at our ability and need to *order* empirical reality *intellectually* in a manner that claims *validity* as empirical truth. And this proposition remains true even though, as we shall see, the ultimate "values" underlying our *practical* interest are, and will remain, of decisive importance for the *direction* that the intellectual activity of ordering within the cultural sciences will take in each particular case. For it is, and continues to be, true that a methodically correct proof in the field of social science must, in order to have reached its goal, also be accepted as correct even by a Chinese – or, to put it more correctly: that goal must at any rate be *striven for*, although it may not be completely attainable because the data are lacking. In the same way, moreover, the *logical* analysis of an ideal with respect to its contents and its ultimate axioms, and the demonstration of the logical and practical consequences of pursuing this ideal, must also, if it is to be deemed successful, be valid for [a Chinese]. Even though he may not be "attuned" to our ethical imperatives, and even though he may, and most probably often will, reject the ideal and the concrete *valuations* flowing from it, this in no way detracts from the scientific value of that intellectual *analysis*. Our journal will certainly not ignore the constant and inevitably recurring attempts to determine with precision the *meaning* of cultural life. On the contrary: those attempts are in themselves among the most important results of that cultural life, and can occasionally be one of the strongest driving forces behind it. Consequently, we shall always include among the discussions that we follow with care those that deal with "social philosophy" (defined in *this* sense). What is more, we here certainly do not share the prejudice that reflections concerning cultural life which go beyond the intellectual ordering of empirical facts and seek to interpret the world metaphysically *could never*, simply because they have that character, make any contribution to our knowledge. What that contribution might be, however, is in the first instance an epistemological question, to which an answer cannot, and indeed need not for our purposes, be provided here, since the kind of work that *we* do rests on the following single, firm premise: to the extent that a journal of social science (as we understand it) works *scientifically*, it must be a place dedicated to seeking [a kind of] truth that can – to stay with our example – even for a Chinese claim to have the validity of an intellectual ordering of empirical reality.

Of course, the editors cannot once and for all forbid themselves, or the contributors [to the journal], to give expression to the ideals that inspire them, even in the form of value judgements. But this imposes two important obligations [on them]. First of all: at all times to make perfectly clear to their readers, and to themselves, *what* are the standards by which they measure reality and from which their value judgement is derived, instead of concocting a vague mixture of the most diverse values (an all too common practice), thus closing their eyes to the conflicts between the ideals and attempting to "have something on offer for everyone". If this obligation is strictly fulfilled, then the practical judgement – the stand taken – may, from a purely scientific point of view, be not only harmless but positively useful and even required: when legislative and other practical measures are subjected to scientific criticism, the full implications of the legislator's motives, and of the ideals of the author who is criticized, can very often only be formulated in a lucid and understandable manner if one *confronts* the value standards on which they are based with *other ones*, and of course ideally: with one's own. Any *valuation* of what others are *striving for* only makes sense if it is a criticism based on one's own "world view": a fight against *another person's* ideal on the basis of *one's own* ideal. Therefore, *if* one wishes, in a given case, not only to identify the ultimate value axiom in which a [particular] practical striving is rooted and to subject it to scientific analysis, but also to demonstrate its relations to *other* value axioms, this can only be done by formulating a "positive" critique by means of a coherent exposition of those other axioms.

Consequently, what will find expression in the columns of our journal is not only social *science* – the intellectual ordering of facts – but, inevitably, also social *policy* – the exposition of ideals; this will especially be the case in comments on legislation. But it would never occur to us to pass off discussions of [social policy] as "*science*", and we shall, to the best of our ability, endeavour to keep them from being mixed up with and confused with [science]. [When social policy is discussed], it is no longer *science* that is speaking. Therefore, the second fundamental commandment of scientific impartiality is [that one should] in such cases at all times make clear to the reader (and, to repeat, above all to oneself) *that* and *where* it is no longer the reasoning scholar who speaks, but the striving human being who takes over – *where* the arguments are aimed at our reason, and *where* they appeal to our feelings. One of the most widespread, but also most harmful, features of work within our discipline is that the scientific discussion of facts is constantly mixed up with evaluative argumentation. What the criticism in the preceding remarks is aimed at is this [practice of] *mixing-up*, but certainly *not* standing up for, one's own ideals. *Lack of conviction* has no inherent affinity whatsoever to *scientific* "objectivity". – The *Archive* has never been – that was at least the original intention – and shall never become a place for polemics against particular political parties or partisans of particular social policies, or for the promotion or denigration of political ideals or ideals of social policy; there are other organs dedicated to those purposes. On the contrary: it has precisely been – and will, as far as this is within the power of the editors, continue to be – a distinctive feature of the journal since its inception that, within its confines, bitter political opponents can work together for scientific purposes. Hitherto, it has not been a "socialist" organ, and it will not in future be a "bourgeois" one. No one who is prepared to place himself within the framework of scientific discussion is excluded from its circle of contributors. It cannot be an arena for "objections", rejoinders and counter-rejoinders; but it protects nobody, not even its contributors, nor its editors, from being exposed in its columns to the sharpest imaginable criticism [based on] substantive, scientific [criteria]. Anyone who finds that intolerable, or who takes the position that he does not, even in the interests of science, want to work with people who serve other ideals than he [himself] does, can stay away from the journal.

However, we are fully aware that, at the present time, this last sentence unfortunately has wider implications in practice than might at first sight be supposed. First of all, as has already been suggested, experience shows that everywhere, and particularly in the German context, there are psychological barriers that limit the possibility of associating in an unconstrained manner with political opponents on neutral – social or professional – ground. This circumstance is a symptom of fanatical and narrow-minded partisanship and of a backward political culture; and, as such, it deserves to be opposed unconditionally. Moreover, it is a factor with particularly strong implications for a journal like ours, since experience shows that, in the field of the social sciences, the analysis of *scientific* problems is regularly motivated by *practical* "questions", so that a personal union [(so to speak)] exists between the simple acknowledgment of the existence of a scientific problem and the striving of active human beings towards certain goals. The contributors to a journal which has come into being under the influence of [the] general interest in a concrete problem will therefore often be individuals whose personal interest in that problem stems from a belief that certain concrete circumstances are incompatible with, and threaten, ideal values that they believe in. What will then hold together this circle of contributors, and [guide] the recruitment of new members, will be the elective affinity of kindred ideals, and this will give the journal a particular "*character*", at least in its treatment of problems concerning practical social *policies*. Such a character is the inevitable concomitant of any collaboration between human beings who feel deeply, and do not always completely suppress, their valuational attitude to problems, even within the purely theoretical sphere; and this attitude – quite legitimately (subject to the conditions discussed above) – manifests itself in criticism of *practical* proposals and measures. Now, the *Archive* came into being during a period when certain practical problems connected with the "labour question" (in the traditional sense of the term) were in the foreground of discussions within the field of social science. For certain persons, the problems that the journal wanted to treat were bound up with the highest and most crucial value ideas, and they therefore became its most regular contributors; at the same time, and for precisely this reason, they stood for a conception of culture imbued by those value ideas with a colouring common, or at least similar, to them all. It is common knowledge that the journal therefore, although it explicitly limited itself to "scientific" discussions and expressly invited "persons from all political camps", and thus firmly rejected the idea that it was pursuing a "tendency", nevertheless certainly had a "character" (in the sense discussed above), which it owed to the circle of its regular contributors. Generally speaking, these persons, while they might otherwise hold very different views, saw it as their goal to protect the physical health of the working masses and to enable them to enjoy, to an increasing extent, their share of the material and spiritual benefits [provided by] our culture; as means towards those ends, they envisaged state intervention in the sphere of material interests, coupled with the further development of the existing political and legal order in the direction of greater freedom. And, whatever their views concerning the shape of the social order in a more distant future might be, for the *present* they accepted capitalist development, not because they regarded [capitalism] as better than older forms of social organization, but because they saw it as inevitable in practice, and because, in their view, the attempt to wage a fundamental combat against it would not further, but would on the contrary inhibit, the rise of the working class towards the light of culture. Under the existing conditions in Germany [at the time] – which it is unnecessary to explain further here

– this was unavoidable and would still be so today. Indeed, it actually led directly to a more comprehensive participation in the scientific discussions, and was on the whole a source of strength for the journal, perhaps even – under the given conditions – one of the elements that justified its existence.

Undoubtedly, however, if a scientific journal develops a "character" in this sense, this *may* bring with it a danger of bias in the scientific work; and that danger *would* certainly arise if the contributors were deliberately selected in a partial manner. In that case, cultivating a "character" would be practically tantamount to having a "tendency". The editors are fully aware of the responsibility that this circumstance imposes on them. They do not intend to alter the character of the journal deliberately, nor is it their aim to preserve it artificially by the deliberate practice of only accepting contributions from scholars who hold particular partisan views. They accept [that character] as [a] given [fact] and await its further "development". *What* it will be in the future, and how it may *change* as a result of the inevitable widening of the [journal's] circle of contributors, will first and foremost depend on the distinctive character of the persons who enter into that circle with the intention of rendering a service to science, and who feel, or come to feel, at home in the columns of the journal. Moreover, this [process of change] will be determined by the widening of the range of *problems* that it is the aim of the journal to further.

With these remarks, we have arrived at the question – which has not been discussed so far – of the *substantive delimitation* of our field of inquiry. However, no answer can be given to this without addressing at this point the general question of the nature of the goal [that we pursue when seeking] knowledge in the field of the social sciences. Hitherto, when making a distinction in principle between "value judgements" and "empirical knowledge", we have assumed the actual existence of an unconditionally valid form of knowledge (i.e. of intellectual ordering of empirical reality) in the field of the social sciences. This assumption now becomes a problem, insofar as we have to discuss what objective "validity" of the truth that we want to obtain *can* mean in our field. That this problem is genuine, and not just the fruit of empty speculations on our part, will be apparent to anyone who observes the conflict about methods, "basic concepts" and presuppositions, the constant shift in "viewpoints", and the continual redefinition of the "concepts" employed – and who recognizes that the theoretical and the historical approaches are still separated from each other by an apparently unbridgeable gulf: "*two* sciences of economics!", as a despairing examinee in Vienna once sorrowfully complained. What does "objectivity" mean in this context? *That* is the only question that will be addressed in the following discussion.

II

From the beginning, this journal has treated its subject matter as belonging to social *economics*; and we need to make clear to ourselves in a summary fashion what that means – even though it would not make much sense in this context to embark upon definitions of concepts and delimitations of scientific disciplines.

Roughly speaking, the basic circumstance that all the phenomena that we describe as belonging to "social economics" (in the widest sense) are bound up with is the following: in our physical existence, as well as when we satisfy our most ideal needs, we everywhere find that the external means necessary for those purposes are limited in quantity and insufficient in quality, and that, in order to satisfy those needs, we must make planned provision, labour, struggle with nature and establish social relations with other human beings. However, the quality of an event as a "social–economic" phenomenon is not something that is "objectively" inherent in it. Instead, it is determined by the direction of our cognitive *interest* resulting from the specific cultural significance that we, in each case, attach to the event in question. The specific *significance* of an occurrence in cultural life may in our view be rooted in certain distinctive characteristics; and whenever those characteristics are, directly or however indirectly, anchored in the circumstance [described above], that occurrence will present – or may at least, to the *extent* that this is the case, present – a *problem* for the social sciences, that is to say, constitute a task for a discipline whose object is to throw light on the implications of that basic cirumstance.

Within the group of social–economic problems, we can make certain distinctions: [First of all, there are] processes (simple and complex), norms, institutions etc., whose cultural significance for us is principally rooted in their economic aspect[s], and which – like, for instance, processes in the stock exchange and banking world – are primarily of interest to us only from *that* point of view. This will as a rule (but not exclusively) be the case when we are dealing with institutions *deliberately* created or used for economic purposes. We can call such objects of our inquiry "economic" (in the narrower sense of the term) processes or institutions, as the case may be. Next, we have other processes, for instance in the *religious* world, which do not (or, at the very least, do not primarily) interest us because of their economic significance and under that aspect, but which may [nevertheless] under certain circumstances acquire an importance in that perspective because they have *effects* which interest us from economic points of view: [they are] "economically relevant" phenomena. And finally there are, among the phenomena which are *not* "economic" (as we define that term), some whose economic effects are of little or no interest to us, as for instance the trend followed by the artistic taste of a certain epoch, but which have on the other hand in concrete cases been more or less strongly *influenced*, as far as certain significant aspects of their distinctive character are concerned, by economic motives (for instance, in the example just mentioned, by the social composition of the public interested in art): economically *conditioned* phenomena. For instance, the complex of human relationships, norms and normatively determined circumstances that we call the "state" is an "economic" phenomenon with respect to its management of public finances; to the extent that it influences economic life by legislation or by other means (even when the conscious motives governing its actions have nothing to do with economics), it is "economically relevant"; and, finally, it is "economically conditioned" to the extent that its actions and its distinctive character, [in areas] apart from its "economic" relations, are (partly) determined by economic motives. From what has been said, it is obvious that the boundaries of the [group of] "economic" phenomena are fluid and cannot be precisely defined; and it is [equally obvious] that, for instance, the "economic" aspects of a phenomenon are in no way *solely* "economically conditioned", nor do they *solely* have "economic effects"; and, generally speaking, it goes without saying that a phenomenon will have an "economic" character only to the extent that, and *only* as long as, our *interest* is exclusively focused on its *importance* for the material struggle for existence.

Now, our journal, like the science of social economics since the times of Marx and Roscher, concerns itself not only with "economic" phenomena, but also with those that are "economically relevant" and "economically conditioned". The boundaries of [the group of] such objects depend on the direction of our interest at any given time and are therefore fluid; but it is obvious that they naturally extend across the totality of cultural life. Specifically economic motives – that is to say, motives that, in [that part of] their distinctive character which is significant to us, are anchored in the [above-mentioned] basic circumstance – will come into play wherever the satisfaction of a need (however immaterial) is tied to the use of *limited* external means. The impact of those motives has therefore everywhere influenced and transformed, not only the form in which even the innermost cultural needs have been satisfied, but also the substance of those needs. The indirect influence of the social relationships, institutions and human groupings affected by the pressure of "material" interests extends (often unconsciously) to all fields of culture without exception, even to the finest nuances of aesthetic and religious sensibility. They influence everyday occurrences no less than the "historical" events of high politics, [and] collective and mass phenomena as well as the "singular" acts of statesmen or individual literary and artistic achievements; [all of these are] "economically conditioned". On the other hand, within a historically given culture, the shaping of material needs and the manner in which they are satisfied; the creation of material interest groups; the nature of their instruments of power; and, consequently, the course of "economic development" – [all] these are influenced by the totality of manifestations and conditions of life in that culture, which therefore become "economically relevant". To the extent that our science traces back and causally imputes *economic* cultural phenomena to individual – economic or non-economic – causes, it seeks "historical" knowledge. To the extent that it traces [the course of] *one* specific element of cultural phenomena – the economic one – as culturally significant or important through the most diverse cultural contexts, it seeks to *interpret* history from a specific point of view, and it provides a partial image – [in other words:] it makes a *preliminary contribution* to the complete historical knowledge of culture.

Even though a social–economic *problem* does not exist in all cases where economic elements are involved as effects or causes – as such problems only arise when the significance or importance of those factors is *problematical* and when it can only be determined with certainty by employing the methods of the science of social economics – it is nevertheless evident [from what has been said above] that the area of application of the social–economic approach is virtually limitless.

Up to now, our journal has already advisedly limited its tasks: on the whole, it has refrained from dealing with a whole range of highly important specialized areas within our discipline, such as descriptive economics, economic history in a narrower sense, and statistics. It has also left it to other publications to discuss questions of financial technique and the technical economic problems of market and price formation in the modern exchange economy. Its field of inquiry has been the present importance and the historical development of certain constellations and conflicts of interests that have arisen because of the dominant role played by capital seeking returns on investment in the economies of the modern civilized nations. In this connection, the journal has not limited itself to the practical and developmental problems known as the "social question" (in the narrowest sense of the term), that is, the relationship of the modern class of wage earners to the existing social order. Nevertheless, one of the main tasks of the journal from its outset had to be the scientific exploration of precisely this particular question, [against the background of] the widening interest that it commanded in Germany in the 1880s. But the more the practical treatment of the conditions of the workers, in our country as well, became a constant object of legislative activity and public debate, the more the focus of scientific investigation had to shift towards the task of determining the more universal context in which these problems belong, and thus, in the last resort, of analysing *all* the cultural problems that stem from the distinctive character of the economic basis of our culture, and that are, to that extent, specifically modern. Consequently, the journal very soon also began to make the extremely varied (partly "economically conditioned", partly "economically relevant") conditions of life of the other large classes in the modern, culturally developed nations, and their reciprocal relations, the subject of historical, statistical and theoretical investigation. We are merely drawing the consequences of this practice when we now designate the scientific investigation of the *general cultural significance and importance of the social–economic structure of human communities*, and of their historical forms of organization, as being the most central field of activity of the journal. This, and only this, is what we mean by calling our journal "*Archive of Social Science*". The term ["social science"] should be understood as indicating the historical and theoretical treatment of those problems whose practical solution is the object of "social *policy*" in the widest sense of the term. In this connection, we avail ourselves of the right to employ the term "social" in the sense that it has acquired because of the concrete problems of the present day. If one wishes to use the term "cultural sciences" to refer to those disciplines that view the events of human life from the perspective of their *cultural significance and importance*, then social science (in our sense) belongs in that category. The theoretical consequences of this will soon become apparent.

Undoubtedly, the emphasis on the *social–economic* aspects of cultural life leads to a severe limitation of the subjects with which we deal. It will be said that the economic or, in the imprecise terminology that has sometimes been used, the "materialist" point of view from which cultural life will be considered here is "one-sided". Indeed so, and that "one-sidedness" is intentional. The belief that scientific work, as it progresses, should assume the task of overcoming the "one-sidedness" of the economic approach by broadening it into a *general* social science is flawed from the outset: [this is because] the "social" viewpoint (i.e. that [which focuses] on relations between human beings) can only be sufficiently precise to allow it to be used to delimit scientific problems if it is provided with some sort of particular predicate of a substantive nature. If one were to take [the "social" element, without such a particularizing predicate] as an object of scientific inquiry, it would comprise, for instance, philology as well as ecclesiastical history, and in particular all disciplines dealing with the most important constitutive element of all cultural life – the state – and with its most important form of normative regulation – the law. The fact that social economics deals with "social" relations is no reason for believing that it is the necessary precursor of a "general social science" – just as the fact that it deals with vital phenomena [does not] compel us to regard it as coming under the heading of biology, and [just as] the circumstance that it deals with occurrences on a celestial body [does not] force us to see it as being part of an enlarged and improved future science of astronomy. The fields of inquiry of scientific disciplines are based not on "*concrete*" relations between "*things*", but on "*theoretical*" relations between "*problems*": when new methods are used to investigate a new problem, and this leads to the uncovering of truths that open up new, significant perspectives, then a new "science" comes into being.

Now, it is no coincidence that, if one investigates more closely how the, seemingly quite general, concept of the "social" is employed in practice, it always turns out to possess some quite particular and specifically coloured, albeit mostly indeterminate, meaning. In fact, the "general" character of the concept is exclusively due to its vagueness: taken in its "general" sense, it does not provide any specific *points of view* under which light could be thrown on the *importance or significance* of particular elements of culture.

While we have abandoned the outworn belief according to which the totality of cultural phenomena can be *deduced* as a product or a function of "material" constellations of interests, we for our part still believe that the *analysis of social phenomena and cultural processes*, from the particular perspective of their *economic* conditionality and implications, has been a creative and fruitful scientific principle, and will continue to be so in the foreseeable future, provided it is applied carefully and without dogmatic prejudice. Conceived as a "*world view*" or as the common denominator of the causal explanation of historical reality, the so-called "materialist conception of history" ‹110› must be categorically rejected; [nevertheless,] it is one of the principal aims of our journal to cultivate the economic *interpretation* of history. This calls for a more detailed explanation.

Today, the so-called "materialist conception of history" in its *old* sense – as expressed crudely, but with genius in the Communist Manifesto, ‹111› for example – probably still holds sway only in the minds of laymen and dilettantes. As far as they are concerned, however, one still observes a widespread, peculiar phenomenon: when they attempt to explain a historical phenomenon, their need for causal explanation is not satisfied until it can be demonstrated that economic causes have (or at least appear to have) played a role in some way and at some point; but, on the other hand, if this [demonstration can be made], they are content with any hypothesis, however threadbare, and with the most general formulations, because they have satisfied their dogmatic need to see the economic "driving forces" as the "essential", the only "true" ones, [and] as those that are "universally decisive in the last resort". This phenomenon is not unique, of course. Almost every science, from philology to biology, has at some time claimed to [be able to] produce not only expert knowledge but also "world views". And under the impression of the profound cultural significance and importance of the *modern* economic upheavals, and in particular the far-reaching implications of the "labour question", the ineradicable monistic trend characteristic of any pursuit of knowledge that lacks self-criticism naturally moved in that direction. Now that the political and commercial struggle between nations for world mastery is growing more intense, anthropology reaps the benefits of this same trend, since it is widely believed that "in the last analysis", the whole course of history results from the interplay of innate "racial qualities". [In anthropology,] the uncritical simple description of "national characters" has been replaced by even more uncritical constructions of home-grown "theories of society" based on "natural science". In our journal, we shall carefully monitor the development of anthropological research, to the extent that it proves to be important from our points of view. We can only hope that it will, in time, on the basis of skilled methodical work, be possible to move beyond the situation where the causal ascription of cultural phenomena to [the factor of] "race" has simply testified to our *lack* of knowledge – much like the reference to "the milieu" or, in earlier times, to the "prevailing circumstances". If anything has been detrimental to anthropological research until now, it is the idea entertained by eager dilettantes that [this research] can make a contribution to our knowledge of *culture* that is specifically different from, and more important than, the increased possibility of ascribing with certainty individual *concrete* cultural phenomena found in historical reality to *concrete, historically* given causes, with the aid of material acquired by *exact* observations [made] from specific points of view. Their results will only be of interest to us to the extent that they are able to offer us *that*; and only to that same extent will they be able to qualify "racial biology" ‹112› as something more than a product of the modern feverish desire to establish new scientific disciplines.

The situation is no different as regards the importance of the economic interpretation of historical material. After a period when it was exceedingly overrated, there is today almost a danger of *under*rating the contribution that it can make to science; this is owing to the unexampled lack of critical sense with which the economic interpretation of reality was employed as a "universal" method, in the sense of a deduction of all cultural phenomena – that is to say, everything in these phenomena that was important to us – as being, in the final analysis, economically determined. Nowadays, [that interpretation] is presented in somewhat varied logical forms. When it turns out to be difficult to provide a purely economic explanation, there are various ways of maintaining its general validity as the decisive causal factor. Either every element of historical reality that *cannot* be deduced from economic motives is, precisely *for that reason*, treated as scientifically *unimportant* and "contingent". Or the concept of the "economic" is extended out of all recognition by being made to include all human interests that are in any way bound up with external means. If it is historically indisputable that, in two situations that were, economically speaking, *alike*, reactions were nevertheless *different* – as a result of differences in the political and religious, climatic and countless other *non*-economic determinants – then, in order to retain the supremacy of the economic [element], all these factors are demoted to [the lowly status of] historically contingent "conditions" under which the economic motives are effective as "causes". However, it is obvious that all those elements that are "contingent" from an economic point of view will, in exactly the same way as the economic ones, follow their own laws; and [if one adopts] an approach where the specific importance of *those* elements is the guiding principle, the *economic* "conditions" will, in each particular case, become "historic-ally contingent" in exactly the same sense as in the reverse case. Faced with this [argument], yet another, popular way of trying to rescue the overriding importance of the "economic" [element] is the following: the constant synergy and interaction between the different elements of cultural life are interpreted as if one element were causally or functionally *dependent* on another, or, rather, as if all other elements were dependent on one, namely the economic one. If some particular *non*-economic institution has historically fulfilled a certain "function" in the service of economic class interests (when, for instance, certain religious institutions let themselves be used, and are in fact used, as "black police" ‹113›), then the whole institution is represented either as having been created for that purpose, or – quite metaphysically – as carrying the imprint of a "developmental tendency" emanating from the economic [element].

Nowadays, any expert in the field will be aware that *this* conception of the aim of the economic analysis of culture was partly due to a particular historical constellation that focused the scientific interest on certain, economically conditioned cultural problems, and partly to fanatical scientific parochialism; and, [as is equally well-known,] that conception is today outworn, to say the least. The reduction *solely* to economic causes is never in any sense exhaustive within *any* sphere of cultural phenomena, not even in the sphere of "economic" processes. In principle, a history of the *banking system* of any nation that would only include economic motives among its causal determinants would of course be quite as impossible as an "explanation" of the Sistine Madonna ‹114› in terms of the social–economic foundations of the cultural life at the time of its creation; and, in principle, [that sort of analysis] is in no way more exhaustive than, for instance, deriving capitalism from certain transformations of religious conceptions that played a part in the genesis of the capitalist spirit, or deriving any political structure from geographical conditions. In *all* those cases, the degree of importance that we must attach to economic conditions depends on what group of causes *those* specific elements of the phenomenon in question that we in each individual case consider *significant* – that is to say: those that matter to us – can be *imputed to*. The *one-sided* analysis of cultural reality from specific "points of view" – in the present case, that of its economic conditionality – is first of all, from a purely methodological point of view, justified by the fact that one reaps all the advantages afforded by a division of labour by [being able to] focus on observing the effects of qualitatively similar causal categories, and by consistently using one single conceptual and method[olog]ical apparatus. [That kind of analysis] is not arbitrary as long as its *results* speak in its favour, that is, as long as it produces knowledge of relationships that prove to be *of value* for the causal imputation of concrete historical events. *However*, the *"one-sidedness"* and unreality of a purely economic interpretation of the historical material is only a special case of a principle that is generally valid for the scientific knowledge of cultural reality. The main purpose of the following discussion is to elucidate the logical foundations of this principle and its general method[olog]ical consequences.

There is no absolutely "objective" scientific analysis of cultural life – or (to use a term which is perhaps somewhat narrower but which, for our purposes, does not have an essentially different meaning) of "social phenomena" – *independent* of special and "one-sided" points of view, according to which [those phenomena] are – explicitly or implicitly, deliberately or unconsciously – selected as an object of inquiry, analysed and presented in an orderly fashion. The reason for this lies in the distinctive character of the cognitive goal of any work in the field of social science that seeks to go beyond a purely *formal* consideration of the – legal or conventional – *norms* of social togetherness.

The social science that *we* want to pursue is a *science of reality*. We want to understand *the distinctive character* of the reality of the life in which we are placed and which surrounds us – on the one hand: the interrelation and the cultural *significance and importance* of its individual elements as they manifest themselves today; and, on the other: the reasons why the[se elements] historically developed as they did and not otherwise. Now, as soon as we seek to reflect upon the way in which we encounter life in its immediate aspect, [we see that] it presents an absolutely infinite multiplicity of events "within" and "outside" ourselves, [events that] emerge and fade away successively and concurrently. And, even if we focus our attention on a single, isolated "object" – a concrete act of exchange, for instance – the absolute infinitude of this multiplicity remains entirely undiminished in intensity; [this becomes apparent to us] as soon as we want to make a serious attempt just to describe this "single [object]" *exhaustively, in all* its individual components, let alone to comprehend it in its causal determination. Any knowledge of infinite reality acquired by the finite human mind is therefore based on the tacit assumption that, in any given instance, only a finite *part* of [that reality] should be the object of scientific comprehension – should be "important" (in the sense of "worth knowing about"). What are the criteria, then, according to which that part is selected? Again and again, it has been believed that, in the cultural sciences, the decisive criterion can also in the last analysis be found in the "law-like" recurrence of certain causal connections. According to this view, the content of the "laws" that we are able to discern in the boundlessly multitudinous stream of phenomena must be the only part [of those phenomena] that is "important" to science: as soon as we have either demonstrated, by means of comprehensive historical induction, that a causal connection has the status of a "law" that is valid without exception, or made [its status as a "law"] immediately intuitable and evident to our inner experience, any number of similar cases, however large, can then be subsumed under any formula that has been established in that manner. Once we have singled out the elements covered by the "law", those parts of individual reality that in each particular case have not been apprehended in that process will either be regarded as a residue that has not yet been subjected to scientific treatment but that must be incorporated into the system of "laws" as that system is progressively perfected; or those [non-apprehended] parts will be left completely aside because they are regarded as "contingent" and *for that reason* as scientifically unimportant, precisely *because* they cannot be "apprehended by means of laws", *consequently* are not "typical" of the event and can therefore only be the object of "idle curiosity". Therefore, the idea constantly crops up – even among representatives of the historical school – that the ideal that everyone [who seeks knowledge], including in the field of culture, strives towards, and can strive [to reach] (if only in a distant future), is a system of propositions from which reality could be "deduced". As is well known, a leading natural scientist ‹115› has felt able to describe the goal (which would in practice be unattainable) of such a treatment of cultural reality as "*astronomical*" knowledge of life's occurrences. Even though these matters have already often been the subject of discussion, we for our part should not shirk the effort of examining this point more closely. To begin with, it is obvious that the "astronomical" knowledge to which [that natural scientist] refers is *not* a knowledge of *laws*; on the contrary: the "laws" with which [such an "astronomy"] works are the *preconditions* of that work and are drawn from other disciplines (for instance mechanics). The "astronomy" itself is interested in the following question: what is the *individual* result of the action of those laws on an *individual constellation*, since those individual constellations are *significant* for us. Naturally, any individual constellation which is "explained" or predicted by [this "astronomy"] can only be causally explained as the result of another, equally individual one that preceded it; and, however far we go back into the grey mists of the most distant past, the reality *for* which the laws are valid retains just the same individual character, and it remains just as impossible to *deduce* it *from* those laws. A "primeval state" of the cosmos, which would lack an individual character, or possess it to a lesser degree than the present cosmic reality, would of course be a meaningless idea – but do we not find a ghostly remnant of similar thinking in the assumption within our own discipline of the existence of economic and social "original states" (as for instance "primitive agrarian communism", ‹116› sexual "promiscuity" ‹117› etc.), free from any historical contingencies and either derived from natural law or verified by the observation of "primitive peoples", from which the individual historical process then emerges in a sort of fall from grace into concreteness?

Now, the interest of social science no doubt initially focuses on the *real* (that is to say, the individual) configuration of the social [and] cultural life that surrounds us, in its *universal* context (which is, however, no less *individual* in character), and as it has evolved from other social [and] cultural circumstances, which of course in their turn had an individual character. Evidently, the same situation that we have just described in relation to astronomy – where it is seen as a limiting case, and often referred to by logicians for that purpose – is also present here, but to a specifically higher degree. From the point of view of astronomy, only the *quantitative* relationships of the celestial bodies, which can be measured with precision, engage our interest; [but] what matters to us in the social sciences is the *qualitative* aspect of events. Moreover, the social sciences are concerned with the influence of processes in the *human mind*; and the re-experiencing "*understanding*" of such processes is of course a task that is specifically different from that which the formulas building on the exact knowledge of the natural world are at all able, or designed, to solve. On the other hand, those distinctions are not in themselves as fundamental as they might look at first glance. Apart from pure mechanics, the exact natural sciences are not able to do without qualitative elements, either; in addition, in our specialized field we may encounter the (admittedly misconceived) idea that at least the transactions in the monetary economy – a fundamental phenomenon of our culture – are quantifiable and can *precisely for that reason* be covered by "laws"; and, finally, whether regularities that are not quantifiable, and therefore cannot be expressed numerically, can still be included under the concept of "laws" depends on how narrowly or widely one defines that concept. In particular, as far as the influence of motives [belonging to] the human mind is concerned, at least it does not exclude the possibility of formulating *rules* of rational action; and, above all, one may still encounter the view that it is precisely to *psychology* that the task falls of playing a role in the individual disciplines of the "sciences of the human spirit" that is comparable to that of mathematics: [thus conceived,] psychology would have to analyse the complex phenomena of social life as to their psychical conditioning and effects, which it would have to trace back as far as possible to elementary psychical factors; it must then classify those factors according to their generic features and investigate them in their functional interrelations. In that way, one would have created, if not a "mechanics", at least a sort of "chemistry" of the psychical foundations of social life. We cannot here set ourselves the task of determining whether such investigations could ever lead to valuable individual results, and whether (which is a different matter) those results could be of use in the *cultural* sciences. But [in any event], that would have no relevance at all for the question whether the *aim* of social–economic inquiry as we understand it – that is to say: knowledge of *reality* with respect to its cultural *significance* and its causal interconnectedness – can be achieved by searching for law-like recurrences. Let us suppose that we would eventually, either by means of psychology or in some other way, have succeeded in analysing how all causal interconnections between elements of human life in common – whether the[se interconnections] had already been observed or were at all imaginable in the future – [could be reduced to] elementary ultimate "factors" of some kind; and then [succeeded] in including [these] interconnections in an immense, exhaustive casuistry of concepts, and of rules that had the strict validity of laws. What significance would the result of this [exercise] have for [our] knowledge of the *historically* given cultural world, or just of any individual phenomenon in that world – for instance of capitalism as it had developed, and of its cultural significance and importance? As a heuristic *instrument*: as much and as little as, for instance, a lexicon of the organic chemical compounds [would have] for the *biogenetic* knowledge of the animal and vegetable kingdoms. In either case, a no doubt important and useful preliminary contribution would have been made. But in neither case would it be possible at any time to *deduce* the reality of life from those "laws" and "factors". Not because the manifestations of life must contain some kind of higher, mysterious "forces" ("dominants", "entelechies" or however else they have been termed) – that is a completely separate question – but already for the simple reason that what matters to us when we want to gain knowledge of reality is the *constellation* in which those (hypothetical!) "factors" are to be found, configured as a cultural phenomenon that we find historically *significant*; and because we always, *if* we then want to give a "causal explanation" of this individual configuration, would have to refer back to other, equally individual configurations, by which we would "explain" it – with the aid, of course, of those (hypothetical!) "law-like concepts". To determine those (hypothetical) "laws" and "factors" would therefore at any rate be only the *first* of several tasks that would lead us to the knowledge which we wanted to obtain. The next task (which would of course have to be performed with the aid of that [first] preliminary piece of work, but which would nevertheless be a completely new and *independent* one) would be to analyse and give an ordered presentation of each historically given, individual configuration of those "factors" and of their consequent concrete and specifically *significant and important* interaction – and above all: to make it *understandable* why and how that interaction was significant and important. To trace back, as far back into the past as possible, those individual, particular characteristics of the configurations that have significance and importance [for us] *today*, in order to establish how they came into being, and to show how they were historically caused by earlier, equally individual constellations, would be a third task. A conceivable fourth one would be the estimation of possible future constellations.

For all these purposes, the availability of clear concepts and the knowledge of those (hypothetical) "laws" would obviously be of great value as a heuristic instrument – but *only* as such; indeed, it would be quite indispensable for that purpose. But it quickly becomes apparent that even with that function, its scope is limited in *one* decisive respect; and with this observation, we have arrived at what is crucially distinctive about the approach adopted by the cultural sciences. We have used the term "cultural sciences" to designate disciplines whose aim is to acquire knowledge about the culturally *significant* aspects of the manifestations of life. However, neither the *significance* of the configuration of cultural phenomena nor the *basis* [of that significance] can be deduced, explained and made comprehensible by any system of law concepts, however perfect, since that significance presupposes the relation of cultural phenomena *to value ideas*. The concept of culture is a *value concept*. Empirical reality *is* "culture" for us because, and to the extent that, we relate it to value ideas; it comprises those, and *only* those, elements of reality that acquire *significance* for us because of that relation. Only a tiny part of the individual reality that we observe at a given time is coloured by our interest, which is conditioned by those value ideas, and that part alone has significance for us; it has significance because certain of its relations are *important* to us by virtue of their connection to value ideas. Only for this reason, and to this extent, is it worth knowing for us in its distinctive individual character. And it is obvious that *what* has significance for us cannot be ascertained by some "presuppositionless" inquiry into the given empirical [reality]; on the contrary: the precondition of something becoming an *object* of inquiry is that we have already determined [that it has significance for us]. Moreover, what is significant obviously does not coincide with any law as such, and the more general the law, the less the coincidence, since the specific *significance* that a component of reality has for us is obviously *not* to be found in those relations[hips] that it has in common with numerous other components. The relation of reality to value ideas which lend it significance, and the selection and ordering, according to their cultural *significance*, of the parts of reality coloured by this [value relation] form an approach that is completely heterogeneous and disparate from [that of] analysing reality with a view to finding *laws*, and ordering it in general concepts. No necessary logical relations exist between those two kinds of intellectual ordering of reality. They may coincide in some particular instance, but if this chance coincidence creates the illusion that they are not *in principle* quite different, the consequences may be disastrous. The cultural *significance* of a phenomenon *may* reside in the fact that it occurs as a mass phenomenon; this is, for instance, the case with exchange in a money economy, which is, [as such,] a fundamental component of modern cultural life. But then it is [the] *historical* fact that it plays this role which must be made comprehensible in its cultural *significance*, and whose coming into being must be causally explained. The study of the *general* nature of exchange and of the *technique* of market transactions is extremely important – indeed, indispensable! – [as a] *preliminary* investigation. But not only does it leave unanswered the question of how [economic] exchange has historically achieved its present fundamental importance, but above all, what cannot be deduced from any of those "laws" is that which after all is our main concern: the *cultural significance* of the money economy – which is the sole reason for our interest in [that] description of transaction techniques, and the sole reason for the existence today of a scientific discipline dealing with those techniques. The *generic features* of exchange, purchase and so on are of interest to the jurists; but we are concerned with the task of analysing the *cultural significance* of the *historical* fact that exchange is today a mass phenomenon. If we are to explain that [fact]: if we want to understand what constitutes the *difference* between our social–economic culture and that of Antiquity, in which the generic qualities of exchange were of course exactly the same as today – in other words, to understand the *significance* of the "money economy" – then logical principles with quite heterogeneous origins enter into the inquiry. *To the extent that* they contain significant elements of our culture, the concepts that can be formed as a result of our investigation into the generic elements of economic mass phenomena can be used as *means* of exposition; but no matter how precise an exposition we are able to give of those concepts and laws, this [still] does not mean that we have achieved the *goal* of our inquiry; and the question of what should be the object comprised by the formation of generic concepts has certainly not been decided "without presuppositions", but rather with reference to the *significance* that certain elements of that immense multiplicity which we call "transactions" possess for culture. What we seek knowledge of is a historical phenomenon, that is, one that is *significant* in its *distinctive character*. And the crucial point in this connection is the following: the idea of acquiring knowledge of *individual* phenomena does not make logical sense at all unless one presupposes that only a *finite* part of the infinite multitude of phenomena is *significant*. Even if we possessed the widest imaginable knowledge of *all* the "laws" governing the course of events, we would be at a loss when faced with the question: "How is it at all *possible* to provide a *causal explanation* of an *individual* fact?" – for it is impossible to conceive of a *description* of even the smallest section of reality that could ever be exhaustive. The causes that have determined any individual event are always *infinite* in number and *infinite*ly varied in character; and the things in themselves possess no inherent criterion according to which some of them can be selected as the only part to be taken into account. A serious attempt to obtain "presuppositionless" knowledge of reality would only yield a chaos of "existential judgements" concerning innumerable single perceptions. And even that result would only be apparent, as any perception will in reality, if scrutinized more closely, exhibit an infinite number of individual elements for which it is impossible to formulate an exhaustive set of perceptual judgements. The *only* reason why order can reign in that chaos is the fact that, in each case, it is only a *part* of individual reality that is of interest and has *significance* for us, because only that part has a relation to the *cultural value ideas* with which we approach reality. Consequently, only certain *aspects* of the, always infinitely manifold, individual phenomena – namely those that in our view possess general *cultural significance* – are worth knowing, and they alone are objects of causal explanation. In its turn, however, this causal explanation exhibits the same traits: it is impossible in practice to trace back *exhaustively* the causes of any individual phenomenon in its *full* reality – indeed, [that notion in itself] is simply an absurdity. We only pick out those causes to which the "*important*" elements of a sequence of events can, in each individual case, be *imputed*. Where the *individuality* of a phenomenon is concerned, the question of causes is not a question of *laws* but of concrete causal *relationships*; not a question of the formula under which the phenomenon can be subsumed as a specimen, but a question of the individual constellation to which it should be imputed as a result: it is a question of *imputation*. Whenever one has to provide a causal explanation of a "cultural phenomenon" – of a "*historical individual*", ‹118› as we shall put it, following a terminology that has already occasionally been used in the methodology of our discipline and that is now, precisely formulated, becoming current in the field of logic – knowledge of the *laws* of causation can never be the *aim*, but only the *means* of the investigation. That knowledge helps us and enables us to impute to their concrete causes those parts of the phenomena that are, in their individuality, culturally significant. Insofar as, and only insofar as, it renders that service, [the knowledge of laws] is valuable for acquiring knowledge about individual interconnections. And the more "general" (that is, the more abstract) those laws are, the less they contribute to the causal imputation of *individual* phenomena and hence, indirectly, to the understanding of the significance of cultural occurrences.

What follows from all this?

Not, of course, that knowledge of what is *general*, the construction of abstract generic concepts, the acquisition of knowledge concerning regularities, and the attempt to formulate "law-like" relationships have no scientific justification in the field of the cultural sciences. Quite the contrary: if the causal knowledge of the historian consists in the *imputation* of concrete effects to concrete causes, then it is simply not *possible* [for him] to perform a *valid* [causal] imputation of some individual effect without making use of "nomological" knowledge – knowledge of the regularities of causal relationships. Whether one should, in a concrete case, regard a particular individual element within a [particular] interconnection in [empirical] reality as being causally important for the effect that one wishes to explain causally can, in case of doubt, *only* be determined by estimating the effects which we usually and *generally* expect that element – and *other* elements within the same context that are relevant for the explanation – to have; in other words: [by estimating] the "*adequate*" effects of the causal elements in question. To what extent the historian (in the widest sense of the term) is able to perform that [causal] imputation reliably by bringing his method[olog]ically schooled imagination, enriched by the experiences of his personal life, to bear, and to what extent he will need help from specialized disciplines, that will depend on the individual case. But everywhere, and hence also in the area of complex economic processes, [it is the case that] the more certain and comprehensive our general knowledge is, the greater is the *certainty* of the [causal] imputation. [The validity of] this proposition is in no way impaired by the fact that we are here always – and this also, without exception, holds for all so-called "economic laws" – dealing not with "laws" in the narrower and precise sense employed by the natural sciences, but with *adequate* causal connections expressed in the form of regularities – that is, with an application (which this is not the place to analyse more closely) of the category of "objective possibility". However, [within the cultural sciences] the formulation of such regularities is not the *aim*, but an *instrument* of inquiry; and whether it makes sense to formulate a regular causal connection, known to us from our daily experience, as a "law", is in each individual case a question of expediency. For the exact natural sciences, "laws" are the more important and valuable, the more *general* their validity; [but] for the purpose of gaining knowledge of historical phenomena in their concrete conditionality, the most *general* laws are as a rule the least valuable, because they are the most devoid of substance: The more comprehensive the validity – the *scope* – of a *generic* concept, the more [that concept] leads us *away from* the richness of reality, since it must be as abstract as possible – that is, contain a *minimum* of substance – *in order to* cover what is common to as many phenomena as possible. Knowledge of what is general is never of value to us in the cultural sciences for its own sake.

The result of what has been said so far is that an "objective" treatment of cultural occurrences, in the sense that the ideal aim of scientific work would be to reduce the empirical [reality] to "laws", is absurd. *Not* because – as it has often been claimed – the course of cultural processes or, say, processes in the human mind would, "objectively" speaking, be less law-like, but for the following two reasons: (1) knowledge of social laws does not constitute knowledge of social reality, but is only one of the various tools that our intellect needs for that [latter] purpose; (2) knowledge of *cultural* occurrences is only conceivable if it takes as its point of departure the *significance* that the reality of life, with its always individual character, has for us in certain *particular* respects. No law can reveal to us in *what* sense and in *what* respects this will be the case, as that is determined by those *value ideas* in the light of which we look at "culture" in each individual case. "Culture" is a finite section of the meaningless infinity of events in the world, endowed with meaning and significance from a *human* perspective. This is true even when a human being is opposed to a *particular* culture as its mortal enemy and demands a "return to nature". For he can only arrive at this position by *relating* that particular culture to his value ideas and finding it "wanting". It is this *purely logical and formal* circumstance that is referred to when it is stated [in this article] that all historical individuals must by logical necessity be anchored in "value ideas". The transcendental precondition of every *cultural science* is *not* that we find a particular, or indeed any, "culture" *valuable*, but that we *are* cultural *beings*, endowed with the capacity and the will to adopt a deliberate *position* with respect to the world, and to bestow *meaning* upon it. Whatever this meaning may be, it will become the basis on which we are, in our life, led to *judge* certain phenomena of human existence in common and to adopt a (positive or negative) position with respect to them because we regard them as *significant*. No matter what this position may be, these phenomena possess cultural *significance* for us, and it is upon this significance alone that their scientific interest rests. When we therefore here, following the terminology of modern logicians, state that the knowledge of culture is determined by *value* ideas, we hope that this will not be subject to crude misunderstandings, such as the idea that cultural significance can only be ascribed to *valuable* phenomena. Prostitution is as much a *cultural* phenomenon as religion or money, and all three of them are [cultural phenomena] because – and *only* because, and *only* to the extent that – their existence, and the form in which they manifest themselves *historically*, directly or indirectly affect our cultural *interests* and awaken our thirst for knowledge from points of view derived from the value ideas that make the part of reality comprehended by those concepts *significant* for us.

Consequently, all knowledge of cultural reality is always knowledge from specific and *particular points of view*. When we demand of historians and social scientists, as an elementary prerequisite, that they must be able to distinguish between what is important and what is unimportant, and that they must possess the "points of view" necessary for making that distinction, this simply means that they must be able – consciously or unconsciously – to relate what happens in [empirical] reality to universal "cultural values", and, on that basis, to select *those* relationships which are significant for us. Again and again, the notion crops up that such perspectives can be "derived from the material itself"; but this is owing to a naïve self-deception on the part of academic specialists who do not realize that they have unconsciously, from the very beginning, approached their material with value ideas on the basis of which they have then selected a tiny part of an absolute infinity, as being *all* that they are *concerned with* observing. This selection of *particular*, specific "aspects" of the occurrences of life goes on all the time and everywhere, consciously or unconsciously; and it also includes that element of cultural science which underlies the common assertion that the "personal" aspect of a scientific work is what is really valuable about it, and that any [such] work must justify its existence by expressing "a personality". Certainly, without the investigator's value ideas, there would be no principle according to which the subject matter could be selected, and no meaningful knowledge of individual reality; and just as any attempt to gain knowledge of *individual* reality is simply meaningless if the investigator does not *believe* that some elements of culture are *significant*, so the direction of his personal belief, the refraction of values in the prism of his soul, will give direction to his work. And the values to which the scientific genius relates the objects of his inquiry may be able to determine – that is: be decisive for – the "conception" of a whole epoch, concerning not only what is considered "valuable", but also what is considered significant or insignificant, "important" or "unimportant" about the phenomena.

The search for knowledge in the field of the cultural sciences (in our sense) is therefore *tied* to "subjective" preconditions insofar as it is only concerned with those parts of reality that are – however indirectly – connected with occurrences to which we attach cultural *significance*. Nevertheless, the knowledge [that we are seeking] is of course purely *causal*, in exactly the same sense as knowledge of significant individual natural occurrences that have a qualitative character. The intrusion of formal juridical thinking into the sphere of the cultural sciences has led to many aberrations, among them the recent attempt to refute in principle the "materialist conception of history" ‹119› by means of a series of brilliant but fallacious arguments. These run as follows: As all economic events must take place in legally or conventionally *regulated forms*, all economic "development" must take the form of endeavours to create new *legal forms*; consequently, such developments are only understandable in terms of ethical maxims, and, *for that reason*, they are essentially different from any "natural" development. Knowledge of economic development therefore, [the argument runs,] has a "teleological" character. We shall not here enter into a discussion of the importance of the ambiguous term "development" for social science, nor [analyse] the equally ambiguous concept of the "teleological", but simply point out that [knowledge of economic development] at least does not have to be "teleological" *in the sense implied* by the argument just referred to. In a situation where the prevailing legal norms remain formally completely identical, the cultural *significance* of the legal *relationships* governed by those norms, and consequently of the norms themselves, may change radically. If we permit ourselves for once to digress into visions of imaginary futures, one might for instance theoretically imagine that a "socialization of the means of production" had been accomplished, even though no "efforts" had been deployed with that end in mind, and even though not one paragraph had disappeared from, or been added to, our legislation. On the other hand, the statistical prevalence of the different legally regulated relationships would have been fundamentally altered, and in many cases reduced to nought; a large part of the legal norms would *in practice* have lost their importance; and their whole cultural significance would have changed beyond recognition. The "materialist" theory of history was therefore justified in leaving aside questions of what the law should be, since its central point of view was precisely that the *significance and importance* of the legal institutions would inevitably change. Those who feel themselves to be above the plain and simple effort to reach a causal understanding of historical reality may keep away from it – but no manner of "teleology" can replace it. A "goal" is, as we see it, the idea of a *result* that becomes the *cause* of an action; and we shall take it into account, as we take into account *any* cause that contributes or may contribute to a *significant* result. And the *specific* significance [of a goal] resides only in the fact that we are able, and want, not only to *ascertain* human action, but also to *understand* it. –

Undoubtedly, the value ideas [referred to above] are "subjective". Between the "historical" interest in a family chronicle and the "historical" interest in the evolution of the greatest conceivable cultural phenomena that over long periods have been, and still are, common to a nation or to mankind, there is an infinite scale of "significance", a scale whose elements will for each of us be ordered differently. And, in the same way, they will naturally be subject to historical change, with changes in the character of the culture and the ideas governing human beings. But obviously, it does *not* follow from this that *research* in the cultural sciences can only have *results* that are "subjective" *in the sense of being valid for* one person but not for another. Rather, what varies is the degree to which such results *interest* one person but not another. In other words: *what* becomes the object of investigation, and how far this investigation extends into the infinity of causal relationships – that is determined by the value ideas that govern the scholar and are dominant in his age. As far as the method of investigation is concerned – *how* it proceeds – the guiding "point of view" (as will become apparent) determines the formation of the conceptual tools employed by the scholar; but, in applying these tools, he is obviously, here as everywhere else, bound to the norms governing our thought: scientific truth is only that which *claims* validity for all who *seek* truth.

One thing, however, follows from this: that it is absurd to entertain the idea, which is occasionally prevalent even among the historians within our discipline, that the aim of the cultural sciences could, even if only in the distant future, be to construct a closed conceptual system, in which reality would be configured and structured in a way that was somehow *definitive*, and from which [reality] could then in its turn be deduced. The immeasurable stream of events flows unendingly towards eternity. The cultural problems that move humankind constantly assume new forms and colourings; within that ever-infinite stream of individual events, the boundaries of the area that acquires meaning and significance for us – which becomes a "historical individual" – therefore remain fluid. The intellectual framework within which it is considered and scientifically comprehended shifts over time; thus, the points of departure of the cultural sciences remain subject to change in the limitless future, unless a Chinese ossification of intellectual life should render humanity incapable of confronting life – which remains as inexhaustible as ever – with new questions. A system of cultural sciences, even if it only took the form of fixing, in a definitive, objectively valid and systematic way, the *questions* and *areas* that it would be suitable for those sciences to deal with, would be inherently absurd: and, if the attempt is made, the result can never be more than a collection of several, specifically separate and in many respects heterogeneous and disparate viewpoints, from which, in any given case, reality has been, or is, "culture" (that is, significant in its distinctive character) for us. –

After these protracted discussions, we can at last turn to the question that is of interest to us from a *method*[*olog*]*ical* point of view when we are dealing with the "objectivity" of cultural knowledge: what is the logical function and structure of the *concepts* that our science, like all others, employs – or, more particularly, with [special] reference to the crucial problem: what is the importance of *theory* and of theoretical concept formation for the knowledge of cultural reality?

As we have already seen, economics – at least the focus of its discussions – was originally "technical"; that is to say: it regarded the phenomena of real life from a fixed and practical valuational viewpoint that was (at least apparently) unambiguous: that of increasing the "wealth" of the state citizens. On the other hand, from the very beginning, it was not *only* "technical", since it was integrated into the world view of the eighteenth century with its formidable combination of natural law and rationalism. But the distinctive character of that world view, with its optimistic belief that reality could be rationalized both in theory and in practice, essentially served to *obstruct* the awareness of the *problematical* character of the ["technical"] point of view, which was [instead] regarded as a self-evident presupposition. In its origins, the rational consideration of social reality was closely allied to the modern development of natural science, and its whole approach continued to be related to that [of the natural sciences]. Now, in the disciplines of the natural sciences, the practical valuational viewpoint, which focused on what was immediately technically useful, was from the very beginning closely connected with the hope – inherited from Antiquity and later developed further – that it would be possible, by means of generalizing abstraction and of an analysis of empirical [reality] aimed at uncovering law-like regularities, to arrive at a monistic knowledge of total reality, in the shape of a *conceptual* system with metaphysical *validity* and in mathematical *form* – knowledge that would be completely "objective" (which, in this connection, would mean: detached from all values) and at the same time completely rational (that is to say: free from all individual "contingent elements"). Those disciplines within the natural sciences that were tied to valuational points of view – such as clinical medicine and (to an even greater degree) what is generally known as "technology" – developed into purely practical "doctrines of good procedure". For each of these disciplines, the values towards which it was oriented – the patient's health, the technical perfection of a concrete production process etc. – were fixed. The means that they employed were – indeed, must be – applications of the law concepts that the theoretical disciplines had arrived at. Every theoretical advance towards the formation of such concepts also constituted, or at least might constitute, an advance for the practical discipline. If the goal was fixed, the progressive reduction of the various practical questions (a case of illness, a technical problem) to special cases covered by generally valid laws – in other words: the extension of theoretical knowledge – was of course directly tied to, and identical with, a widening of technical and practical possibilities. And when modern biology then proceeded to subsume even those parts of reality that interest us *historically* – that is to say: because they developed in the way they did, and not differently – under the concept of a generally valid evolutionary principle, which seemingly (though not in reality) allowed for the integration of everything that was important about those objects into a system of generally valid laws, then it looked as if the twilight of the gods for all valuational viewpoints in all sciences was drawing near: Since even so-called historical occurrences were a part of total reality; since the principle of causality – the presupposition of all scientific work – seemed to require the reduction of all those occurrences to generally valid "laws"; and, last, since the immense success of the natural sciences, which had carried out this idea in practice, was evident – [for all these reasons], it seemed totally impossible to imagine another meaningful way of proceeding scientifically than by looking for [the] *laws* of events. Only that which was "law-like" in the phenomena could be important to science; "individual" events could only be considered as "types" (which in this context meant: as representative, illustrative instances of the laws); and an interest in those individual events for their own sake seemed "unscientific".

In the present context, it is not possible to trace the formidable repercussions that this enthusiastic spirit of naturalistic monism had on the economic disciplines. When the socialist critique and the work of the historians began to transform the original valuational viewpoints into problems, the tremendous development of biological research on the one hand, and the influence of Hegelian panlogism ‹120› on the other, prevented the science of economics from clearly and fully recognizing the relationship between concept and reality. The result – insofar as it concerns us here – is that, in spite of the massive bulwark which German idealist philosophy since Fichte, the achievements of the German historical school of law, ‹121› and the work of the historical school of German economics ⟨122⟩ have erected against the infiltration of naturalistic dogma, nevertheless, and partly *because of* that work, naturalistic points of view have still not, on crucial points, been overcome. This is particularly true as regards the – still problematical – relationship between "theoretical" and "historical" work in our discipline.

Even today, the "abstract"–theoretical method uncompromisingly and with apparently insurmountable intransigence confronts the empirical and historical method of inquiry within our discipline. [The proponents of the "abstract" method] acknowledge, quite correctly, that it is method[olog]ically impossible to replace historical knowledge of reality with the formulation of "laws", or, conversely, to arrive at "laws" (in the strict sense of the word) by the simple juxtaposition of historical observations. In order to arrive at such laws – as [they] are convinced that this is the supreme goal that science ought to pursue – they presuppose as a fact that we ourselves have constant and immediate experience of the actual interrelations of human action; therefore – so it is claimed – we are able, with axiomatic evidentness, to render the course of such action directly understandable, and by this means to uncover the "laws" that govern it. Moreover, [according to the "abstract" theory,] the only exact form of knowledge, i.e. the formulation of laws that are immediately and clearly *evident*, is also the only one that makes it possible to draw conclusions concerning occurrences which have not been directly observed; and, consequently, the only way to gain intellectual mastery of the multiplicity of social life, at least as far as the fundamental phenomena of economic life are concerned, must be to draw up a system of abstract and – therefore – purely formal propositions, analogous to those of the exact natural sciences. Despite the fact that the originator of the theory ⟨123⟩ had been the *first* and *only* one to carry through the method[olog]ical distinction of principle between the formulation of laws and historical knowledge, it is now claimed that the propositions of abstract theory are empirically *valid* in the sense that reality can be *deduced* from the "laws". Admittedly, not in the sense that the abstract economic propositions would be empirically valid by themselves, but in the following manner: when, [at some future time,] similar "exact" theories concerning all *other* factors of possible relevance had been formulated, then the *totality* of these abstract theories would contain the true reality of things – that is to say, all of reality that was worth knowing. The exact economic theory would determine the consequences of *one* psychological motive; it would be the task of other theories to develop all the other [possible] motives in a similar way, in the form of hypothetically valid propositions. Accordingly, the fantastic claim has now and then been made that the results of theoretical work – the abstract theories of price formation, interest, ground rent etc. – could, in (ostensible) analogy to the propositions of physics, be used to *deduce quantitatively defined* results – that is to say: laws in the strictest sense of the term – from given real premises, and that these [laws] would be valid for real life, since the economic activity of human beings was unambiguously "determined", as far as the means were concerned, if the goal was fixed in advance. [Those who made this claim] failed to take into account that, in order to achieve the [claimed] result in any given case, however simple, the *totality* of historical reality, including all its causal relationships, would in each particular case have to be assumed as "given" and presupposed as being *known*; and that, if the finite human intellect *were* in fact able to attain that knowledge, an abstract theory would no longer have any imaginable cognitive value. The naturalistic prejudice according to which one must, by establishing those concepts, create something akin to the exact natural sciences, had simply led to a misconception of the nature of those theoretical constructs. It was believed that one was dealing with the psychological isolation of a specific "instinct" – the acquisitive instinct – in human beings, or with the isolated observation of a specific maxim of human conduct, the so-called economic principle. The abstract theory believed that it was supported by psychological *axioms*; and, consequently, the historians clamoured for an *empirical* psychology so that they could disprove the validity of those axioms and provide a psychological derivation of the economic processes. We shall not in this context go into a detailed critique of the belief that a systematic science of "social psychology" – which has yet to be developed – can become important as the future basis of the cultural sciences, and particularly of social economics. But this much is certain: those (in some cases brilliant) attempts to give a psychological interpretation of economic phenomena that have already been undertaken show that [the analysis] does *not* proceed from the human psychological qualities to the social institutions, but that, on the contrary, a close acquaintance with the institutions, and a scientific analysis of their interconnections, is a *prerequisite* for shedding light on their psychological preconditions and effects. What psychological analysis can then contribute (a contribution that may in the concrete case be most valuable) is simply a deepening of our knowledge of the historical cultural *conditionality* and the cultural *significance* [of the social institutions]. Our interest in the psychological [aspects of] human behaviour in social relationships is in each individual case specifically different, according to the specific cultural significance of the relationship in question. The psychological motives and influences that are involved are quite heterogeneous and occur in very concrete combinations. The research of social psychologists surveys a variety of *individual*, often mutually disparate, kinds of cultural element in order to establish their susceptibility to interpretation by means of our re-experiencing understanding. Through social psychology, and taking individual institutions as our point of departure, we will gain an increasing intellectual *understanding* of how they are determined by culture and what is their cultural significance; but we should not [seek to] deduce those institutions from psychological laws or to *explain* them in terms of elementary psychological phenomena.

Consequently, the wide-ranging controversies over the question of the psychological justification of abstract theoretical propositions, and over the scope of the "acquisitive instinct", the "economic principle" and so on, have not been very profitable. –

The propositions of abstract theory are only seemingly "deductions" from fundamental psychological motives; in actual fact, they are rather a special case of a kind of conceptual construction that is specific, and to a certain extent indispensable, to the sciences of human culture. In the present context, it is worthwhile to characterize it in somewhat greater detail, as this will bring us closer to the fundamental question of the importance of theory for the acquisition of knowledge in social science. In this connection, we shall once and for all leave aside the question whether the *actual* theoretical constructions, which we use as examples or which we allude to, are in their present form adequate for the purposes that they seek to serve – that is to say, whether they are in substance *appropriate* for those ends. After all, to take an example, the question of how much further "abstract theory" in its present form should be elaborated is also a question of the economy of scientific work, which also has to deal with other problems: the "theory of marginal utility" is not exempt from the "law of marginal utility". ‹124›

The abstract economic theory offers us an example of those syntheses that are usually called "*ideas*" of historical phenomena. It presents us with an *ideal* image of what goes on in a market for goods when society is organized as an exchange economy, competition is free, and action is strictly rational. This mental image brings together certain relationships and events of historical life to form an internally consistent cosmos of *imagined* interrelations. The substance of this construct has the character of a *utopia* obtained by the *theoretical* accentuation of certain elements of reality. Its only relation to the empirically given facts of [real] life is the following: if it is *established* or *assumed* that interrelations of the same kind as those represented in abstract form in the construct (that is to say: occurrences that depend on the "market") to some extent operate in reality, then we can pragmatically *clarify* the *distinctive character* of that interrelation and make it understandable, by means of an *ideal type*. This possibility can be important, and even essential, both for heuristic purposes and as an aid to exposition. In *research*, the ideal type seeks to render the scholar's judgement concerning causal imputation more acute: it *is not* a "hypothesis", but it seeks to guide the formulation of hypotheses. It *is not* a *depiction* of reality, but it seeks to provide [the scientific] account with unambiguous means of expression. Thus, we see how the "idea" of the *historically* given modern organisation of society as a market economy is developed according to exactly the same logical principles as those that have, for instance, been used to construct the idea of the medieval "city economy" as a "genetic" concept. This is done not by forming the concept "city economy" as, say, the *average* of the economic principles actually to be found in all the cities that one examines, but rather, again, as an *ideal type*. It is obtained by means of a one-sided *accentuation* of *one* or *a number of* viewpoints and through the synthesis of a great many diffuse and discrete *individual* phenomena (more present in one place, fewer in another, and occasionally completely absent), which are in conformity with those one-sided, accentuated viewpoints, into an internally consistent *mental* image. In its conceptual purity, this mental image cannot be found empirically anywhere in reality. It is a *utopia*, and the task of the *historian* then becomes that of establishing, in each *individual case*, how close reality is to, or how distant it is from, that ideal image – in other words: to what extent the economic aspect of conditions in a particular city can be characterized as a "city economy" in the sense defined by the concept. Provided it is employed with care, the concept [of the ideal type] renders specific services for the purposes of research and exposition. – To analyse a further example: it is possible, in exactly the same way, to depict the "idea" of "craft" in [the form of] a utopia, by one-sidedly accentuating the consequences of certain features that can be found diffusely among craftsmen from quite different epochs and countries, combining them into an internally consistent ideal image, and relating them to an expression of *ideas* that seems to manifest itself in [that ideal image]. One can then further attempt to depict a society in which all branches of economic and even intellectual activity are governed by maxims that appear to us to be an application of the same principle which characterizes "craft", elevated to the status of an ideal type. One can then confront this ideal type of "craft" with its antithesis: the corresponding ideal type of a capitalist ordering of industry and trade, abstracted from certain features of modern large-scale industry; and then go on to try to depict the utopia of a "capitalist" culture, that is to say, a culture dominated solely by the interest in getting a return on [the investment of] private capital. [In this utopian ideal type], the distinctive character of a number of scattered features of modern material and non-material cultural life would have to be accentuated and combined into an ideal image that we would regard as [internally] consistent. This would be an attempt to depict an "*idea*" *of capitalist culture*. (Whether and how that attempt could be successful is a question that we shall leave completely aside in this context.) Now, it is possible (or rather: it must be regarded as certain) that more than one utopia of this kind – in fact, surely a great many – can be drawn up in any given case. *None* of these utopias will resemble any other, and, even more definitely, *none* of them will be observable in empirical reality as an actually prevailing ordering of social conditions; but *each* of them will claim to represent the "idea" of capitalist culture, and *each* of them *can* advance this claim, insofar as each of them in fact [contains] certain features of our culture that are *significant* in their *distinctive character* and that have been selected from reality and combined into a consistent ideal image. [This is a reflection of the fact that,] when we are interested in cultural phenomena, our interest in these phenomena – their cultural *significance* – will as a rule be derived from quite disparate value ideas, to which we can relate them. Just as there are therefore many different "viewpoints" from which we can regard these phenomena as significant for us, so one may rely on entirely different principles for the selection of those relationships that are to be included in an ideal type of a particular culture.

What, then, is the importance of such ideal-typical concepts for a science of *empirical* experience as we want to conduct it? From the outset, it should be stressed that the idea of what *ought to* be, of an "ideal", must be carefully distinguished from the theoretical constructs that we are discussing and that are "ideal" in the strictly *logical* sense of the term. What we are concerned with is the construction of relationships that our *imagination* considers to be sufficiently motivated and therefore "objectively possible", and that seem *adequate* in the light of our nomological knowledge.

Those who take the position that knowledge of historical reality should or can consist of a reproduction "without preconditions" of "objective" facts will deny that [the ideal type] has any value at all. And even those who acknowledge that one cannot, in a logical sense, "be without preconditions" [when dealing with] reality, and that even the most elementary excerpt from, or digest of, [historical] documents can only have any sense from a scientific point of view if it has been related to "significant meanings", that is to say, in the last resort, to value ideas, will feel that the construction of any kind of historical "utopia" as an illustrative tool threatens to prejudice historical research; and [they] will on the whole simply regard it as an idle pastime. And, indeed, it is never possible to determine in advance *whether* [such constructive efforts] are mere fantasies or whether they constitute scientifically fruitful concept formation. Here, too, the only standard is whether [the ideal type] is useful for acquiring knowledge of concrete cultural phenomena – their context, their causal determination and their *significance*. Consequently, the construction of abstract ideal types can only be considered a *tool*, never an end [in itself]. However, any careful examination of the conceptual elements of historical accounts will show that, as soon as the historian attempts to go beyond merely registering the existence of concrete relationships, and to determine the *cultural significance* of an individual event, however simple – to "characterize" it – he works, and *has to* work, with concepts that can only be defined strictly and unambiguously in ideal types. Or, can we define concepts such as "individualism", imperialism", "feudalism" and "mercantilism" in a "conventional" manner? And [if we consider] the innumerable similar concepts that we make use of in our attempt to grasp reality by means of our intellect and our understanding – can we define them in substance by *describing* any *single* concrete phenomenon "without preconditions", or by abstracting and synthesizing what is *common* to *several* concrete phenomena? In the language of the historian, there are hundreds of words containing such indeterminate mental images that satisfy an unreflecting need for suitable expressions; and, ordinarily, the meaning [of those images] has not been thought through but can only be perceived figuratively. In a vast number of cases, particularly in the field of descriptive political history, the lack of substantive precision [of the concepts] is surely not prejudicial to clarity of the [historical] account. One can be content with *feeling*, in each case, what the historian had in mind, or with the notion that he intended the content of the concept to be precise [only] in *particular* respects and to have a significance and importance that was *relative* to the case in hand. But the more we wish to have a clear and unambiguous idea of the significance of a cultural phenomenon, the more imperative is the need to work with clear concepts that are not just partially, but completely, determined. A "definition" of those syntheses of historical thought after the pattern "genus proximum, differentia specifica" ‹125› is of course an absurdity, as any attempt [to carry it through] will show. To establish the meaning of words in that way is only possible within dogmatic disciplines working with syllogisms. And although it might seem possible to "break down" those concepts "descriptively" into their component parts, this is not realistic either, since the question is precisely *which* of those components are the important ones. If one wants to attempt a genetic definition of the substantive content of a concept, one is left with no other choice than to use the format of the ideal type, as defined above. [The ideal type] is a mental image that *is* not historical reality, and certainly not "true" reality; still less is it meant to serve as a schema *into* which it would be possible to fit reality as a *specimen*. It has the status of a purely ideal *limiting* concept against which reality is *measured* – with which it is *compared* – in order to bring out certain significant component parts of the empirical substance of [that reality]. Such concepts are constructions in which we apply the category of "objective possibility" to construct connections that our *imagination*, oriented towards and schooled by the contact with reality, *judges* to be adequate.

In this function, the ideal type is chiefly an attempt to comprehend historical individuals, or their component parts, in *genetic* concepts. Let us take the concepts "church" and "sect". By way of classification, they may be broken down into complexes of characteristics; but, in that case, not only the boundary between the two concepts but also their substantive content will necessarily remain fluid. However, if I want to comprehend the concept of "sect" *genetically*, for instance with regard to certain ways in which the "sectarian spirit" has been particularly important for modern culture, then certain characteristics of both concepts become *essential* because they stand in an adequate causal relationship to those effects. At the same time, however, the concepts become *ideal*-typical – that is to say: [empirically,] they cannot or can only rarely be found in [their] completely *pure* conceptual form. Here, as everywhere, any concept that goes beyond *mere* classification leads away from reality. But the discursive character of our cognition, ‹126› i.e. the fact that we only grasp reality through a sequence of ideational changes, demands such a conceptual shorthand. Our imagination can often dispense with the explicit conceptual formulation [of this logically necessary "shorthand"] as a means of *research* – but, for the purposes of *exposition*, if we want it to be unambiguous, the use of [such explicit formulations] in the domain of cultural analysis is in numerous cases quite indispensable. Those who fundamentally reject this kind of concept formation will have to limit themselves to the formal aspect of cultural phenomena – legal history, to take an example. The universe of *legal* norms can of course both be clearly defined conceptually, *and* be *valid* (in the *legal* sense!) for historical reality. But the work of social science (in our sense) is concerned with the practical *importance* [of these norms]; and very often, this importance can only be brought out by relating the empirical data to an ideal limiting case. If the historian (in the widest sense of the term) dismisses the attempt to formulate such an ideal type as a "theoretical construction" – that is to say, as being unsuitable or inessential for the concrete purpose of his inquiry, the consequence will regularly be either that he, consciously or unconsciously, makes use of similar concepts, but *without* linguistic formulation and logical elaboration, or that he remains stuck in the area of what is vaguely "felt".

However, it must be admitted that nothing is more dangerous than the legacy of naturalistic prejudice, which consists in *mixing up* theory with history. This may take various forms: it may be believed that those conceptual images contain the "real" substance or the "essence" of historical reality; or the concepts may be used as a Procrustean bed ‹127› into which history is to be forced; or the "ideas" may even be hypostatized as a "true" reality that exists beyond the fleeting phenomena, as real "forces" that work themselves out in history.

This last danger is particularly obvious because we also, and even primarily, when speaking of the "ideas" of an epoch, tend to understand by that term thoughts or ideals that have *been dominant* among the masses, or within a historically important part of the population, of that epoch, and that have therefore been significant and important [as] components of their distinctive cultural character. To this must be added two further points: First of all, as a rule, there are certain connections between the "idea" in the sense of a practical or theoretical line of thought and the "idea" in the sense of an ideal *type* of an epoch, constructed as a conceptual tool. It is possible, indeed it is quite often the case, that an ideal type of certain social conditions, which can be abstracted from certain characteristic social phenomena of some particular epoch, may have been present in the minds of the people living at that time as an ideal to which one should aspire in practice, or at least as a guideline for the way in which certain social relationships should be regulated. This is already true of the relationship between the "idea" of the "protection of subsistence", ‹128› as well as many of the theories of the canon-law scholars, in particular those of Saint Thomas Aquinas, and the ideal-typical concept of the medieval "city economy" discussed above, as it is used today. And, to an even greater extent, it is true of the notorious "fundamental concept" of economics: "economic *value*". [As far as that concept is concerned], the idea of something "objectively" valid – that is to say: something which *ought to* be – has, from Scholasticism to Marxist theory, been intertwined with an abstraction derived from the empirical process of price formation. And this idea: that the "value" of commodities *ought* to be regulated according to certain principles of "natural law", has had immense importance for the development not just of medieval culture – an importance that still persists. In particular, it has had a massive influence on empirical price formation. But *what* is *actually* meant by the *theoretical* concept [of economic value] referred to above, and what can be meant by it, can *only* be made unambiguously clear by constructing a precisely defined – that is to say, an ideal-typical – concept. This fact should be kept in mind by those who sneer at the "Robinsonades" of abstract theory, ‹129› at least as long as they are not able to replace them with something better – which here means: something *clearer*.

The causal relationship between the historically demonstrable *idea* that governs human beings and those components of historical reality from which its corresponding ideal type can be abstracted can of course be configured in a large variety of ways. But what must be maintained is that those two things are *in principle* quite different. To this must be added a second point: Whenever the "ideas" that govern (i.e. are diffusely active in) the human beings of a certain epoch are mental constructs of a somewhat more complicated nature, we can only grasp those ideas *themselves* with conceptual precision *in the form of an ideal type*, as they are of course empirically present in the minds of a large, indeterminate and varying number of individuals, and can be found there in a multitude of variants with regard to form and content, clarity and meaning. Let us, for example, take those elements of the spiritual life of individual human beings during a particular period of the Middle Ages that we can refer to as "the Christianity" of those individuals: *If* we were able to give a complete account of those elements, they would be a chaos of infinitely differentiated and highly inconsistent complexes of ideas and feelings of all kinds, even though the medieval church had no doubt been able to impose, to a particularly high degree, a unity both of faith and of morals. If the question is then raised as to what part of this chaos constitutes *the* Christianity of the Middle Ages (as one must still be able to employ that term as a well-defined concept) – that is to say: where *that* which we see as "Christian" in the medieval institutions is located – it will immediately become apparent that here, too, we will in each individual case make use of a purely intellectual construct that we have created. It is a combination of articles of faith, canonical and moral norms, maxims for the conduct of life and innumerable individual interrelations that *we* combine into an "idea": a synthesis which we would be quite unable to arrive at in a consistent manner if we did not make use of ideal-typical concepts.

The logical structure of the conceptual systems in which we express such "ideas", and the relationship of those systems to what is immediately given in empirical reality, may of course be extremely varied. The matter is still relatively simple when we are dealing with cases where one or a few theoretical guiding principles, which can easily be expressed as maxims (as for instance Calvin's doctrine of predestination ‹130›), or moral precepts, which can be clearly formulated, have seized hold of people and produced historical effects; here, the "idea" can be structured as a hierarchy of thoughts that can be logically derived from those guiding principles. But already, in such cases, it is easily overlooked that, although the purely *logically* compelling power of ideas has historically been enormously important – Marxism is an outstanding example of this – the empirical–historical process in people's minds must nevertheless as a rule be understood as being *psycho*logically, not logically, determined. The ideal-typical character of such syntheses of historically effective ideas is even more obvious in cases where individuals are guided by thoughts that can logically be derived from guiding principles and precepts [such as those] referred to above, or that are triggered by [these principles] through an association of ideas, but where the principles themselves are not present, or have not survived, in the minds of those individuals – either because the "idea" that was, historically speaking, at the root [of those guiding thoughts] has died off, or because it has only been widely effective in terms of its consequences. The character of the synthesis as an "idea" created by *us* becomes even more evident when the awareness of those fundamental principles has, from the very beginning, been wholly absent or less than complete, or when [the principles] have at least not assumed the form of clearly structured ideas. When (as very frequently happens, and must happen) we then carry out that procedure, the "idea" [which we arrive at in this way] – of the "liberalism" of a certain period, say, or of "Methodism", ‹131› or of some intellectually undeveloped variant of "socialism" – is a *pure* ideal type of exactly the same character as those syntheses of the "principles" of an economic era that were our point of departure. The more comprehensive the relationships are that have to be described, and the more many-sided their cultural *significance and importance* have been, the *more* their comprehensive and systematic exposition in a conceptual and intellectual system approximates the character of an ideal type, and the *less* is it possible to make do with just *one* such concept – hence, the more natural and necessary are the constantly repeated attempts to create an awareness of ever *new* aspects of the significance and importance [of those relationships], by means of a new construction of ideal-typical concepts. All descriptions of the "*essence*" of Christianity, for instance, are ideal types. If they claim to be a historical representation of what can be found empirically, their validity will always and by necessity [only] be very relative and problematical; but if, on the contrary, they are simply used as conceptual tools with which reality can be *compared* and against which it can be *measured*, they possess great heuristic value for research and high systematic value for exposition. In that function, they are virtually indispensable. However, such ideal-typical representations regularly exhibit a feature that complicates [the question of] their significance and importance even further: they are often, wittingly or unwittingly, ideal types, not only in a *logical*, but also in a *practical* sense; that is to say, they are *exemplary* types that – to revert to the example given above – contain what Christianity, in the opinion of the author [in question], *ought* to be, – what is, *for him*, the *permanently valuable*, and *therefore* "essential", part of Christianity. If this is the case, wittingly or – more often – unwittingly, then these types will contain ideals *to which* the author *relates* Christianity in order to *evaluate* it: tasks and aims towards which he orients his "idea" of Christianity, and which naturally may – indeed, undoubtedly always will – be quite different from the values to which the persons living at the time [which he deals with] (say, the primitive Christians) related Christianity. In this sense, however, the "ideas" are naturally no longer purely *logical* tools: they are no longer concepts with which reality is compared and against which it is *measured*, but ideals against which it is evaluated and *judged*. We are *no longer* dealing with the purely theoretical procedure of *relating* empirical [reality] to values, but with value *judgements* incorporated into the "concept" of Christianity. *Because* the ideal type in these cases claims to have empirical *validity*, it enters into the area where Christianity is subjected to an evaluating *interpretation*: we have *left* the field of the science of empirical experience, and what we are now presented with is a personal confession of faith, *not* an ideal-typical *concept* formation. Even though this distinction is fundamental, these two entirely different, disparate meanings of [the word] "idea" are extremely often *mixed up* in the course of historical work. This will always be an obvious [danger] whenever the historian begins to develop his "conception" of a personality or an epoch in his account. In contradistinction to the constant ethical standards applied by Schlosser ‹132› in the spirit of rationalism, the modern historian, schooled in relativism, who on the one hand wants to "understand on its own terms" the epoch that he describes, but on the other hand also wants to "judge" it, feels the need to derive the standards of his judgement from "the material" itself – that is to say: to let the "idea", in the sense of the *ideal*, grow out of the "idea" in the sense of the "ideal *type*". And the aesthetic allure of such a procedure will constantly tempt [the historian] to blur the dividing line between the two: a half-hearted position, where [he] cannot restrain himself from passing judgement, but nevertheless attempts to decline responsibility for the judgements that he has passed. On the contrary, it is *an elementary duty of scholarly self-control*, and the only way to prevent misrepresentations, to distinguish clearly between, [on the one hand,] relating reality to ideal *types* (in the logical sense of the word) by means of logical *comparison* and, [on the other hand,] *judging* reality evaluatively on the basis of *ideals*. To repeat once more: An "ideal type" in our sense of the term is totally indifferent to *evaluative* judgements; it has nothing to do with any other "perfection" than a purely *logical* one. There are ideal types of brothels as well as of religions; and, in the former category, we find ideal types of [establishments] that would, from the point of view of contemporary police ethics, seem to be technically "appropriate", and of others where the exact opposite is the case.

We must necessarily leave aside here a detailed discussion of the by far most complex and interesting case: the question of the logical structure of the *concept of the state*. Only the following remarks should be made in this respect: When we ask what, in empirical reality, corresponds to the idea [that we have] of the "state", we find an infinite number of diffuse and discrete human actions and acts of acquiescence, and of relationships regulated in practice and legally, of which some are unique, while others recur regularly; and all [this] is held together by an idea, namely, the belief in norms and relations of authority of some human beings over others, which are actually or should be valid. This belief is found in manifold nuances in the mind of each individual, partly intellectually well thought-out, partly vaguely felt, [and] partly passively accepted. (If these individuals themselves actually had a clear conception of this "idea" as such, they would have no need for the "general theory of the state", which sets itself the task of articulating it.) Now, the scientific concept of the state, however formulated, is of course always a synthesis that *we* carry out for particular cognitive purposes. But, on the other hand, it is also an abstraction from the imprecise syntheses found in the minds of human beings [at a certain moment] in history. The concrete [historical] substance of the "state", [as it is present] in those syntheses formed by human beings living in history, can in its turn only be expressed in terms of ideal-typical concepts. Moreover, there is not the slightest doubt that the way in which human beings living at that time construct – in a form that is never logically perfect – those syntheses of the "ideas" that *they* entertain about the state (for instance the German "organic" metaphysics of the state, ‹133› as opposed to the "businesslike" American conception ‹134›), is of eminent practical importance. In other words: here, too, the *practical* idea that, *in people's opinion*, is – or ought to be – valid runs parallel to the theoretical ideal *type* that is constructed for cognitive purposes; and the two show a constant tendency to shade off into one another.

Above, we have deliberately treated the "ideal type" mainly – albeit not exclusively – as a theoretical construction for the measurement and systematic characterization of relationships that (like Christianity, capitalism etc.) are *individual*, that is to say, significant by virtue of their uniqueness. We have done so in order to correct the widespread view that, in the domain of cultural phenomena, what is abstractly *typical* is identical with what is abstractly *generic*. That is not the case. Here, we cannot provide a fundamental analysis of the concept of the "typical" – a concept that has been much discussed and strongly discredited because of its misuse. Nevertheless, one result of our discussion so far is that the formation of concepts of types, in the sense of eliminating what is "contingent", is also – indeed, particularly – relevant when we are dealing with *historical individuals*. However, we constantly encounter *generic* concepts that form part of historical accounts and concrete historical concepts; and those generic concepts may of course also be constructed as ideal types by means of abstracting and accentuating certain of their elements that are conceptually important. Indeed, in practice, this way of using ideal-typical concepts is particularly frequent and important, and every *individual* ideal type is composed of conceptual *elements* that are generic and take the form of ideal types. But in these cases, too, the specific logical function of the ideal-typical concepts is manifest. As an example, let us take the concept of "exchange": As long as we do not concern ourselves with the *meaning* of the component elements of this concept and just analyse [its] everyday usage, it is a simple generic concept, in the sense of a complex of features that are common to a number of phenomena. But, if we relate this concept to, say, that of the "law of marginal utility" and construct the concept of "economic exchange" as being an economically *rational* process, then this latter concept, like *any* logically, fully developed concept, involves a *judgement* concerning the "typical" *conditions* of "exchange". It assumes a *genetic* character, and thereby at the same time becomes ideal-typical in a logical sense, that is to say, it diverges from empirical reality, which can only be *compared* – related – to it. The situation is similar for all the so-called "basic concepts" of economics: in their *genetic* form, they can only be developed as ideal types. Obviously, the difference between ordinary generic concepts, which simply comprise what is common to *empirical* phenomena, and generic *ideal* types – as for instance an ideal-typical concept of the "essence" of craft – may vary from case to case. But *no* generic concept as such has a "typical" character, and there are no purely generic "average" *types*. Whenever we speak of "typical" magnitudes – as for instance in statistics – this involves *more* than a simple average. The more we are dealing with the simple *classification* of events that occur in reality as mass phenomena, the more *generic* are the concepts; on the other hand: the more we are dealing with the conceptual shaping of those elements of complex historical relationships on which the specific *cultural significance* [of those relationships] is based, the more that concept – or system of concepts – will have the character of an *ideal* type. This is because the aim of ideal-typical concept formation is always to bring out clearly what is *distinctive*, and *not* what is generic, in cultural phenomena.

From the point of view of *method*, the fact that ideal types, including generic types, can be employed, and are in fact employed, becomes of interest only in connection with another circumstance.

So far, we have on the whole encountered ideal types in the form of abstract concepts of relationships that are conceived by us as stable points in the stream of events, as historical individuals which are *subject to* developments. At this point, however, a complication arises that may, with the aid of the concept of the "typical", quite easily allow the naturalistic prejudice, according to which the aim of the social sciences must be to reduce reality to "*laws*", to sneak in again. [The reason for this is that] *developments*, too, may be constructed as ideal types, and those constructions may have quite considerable heuristic value. But this carries with it a particularly strong risk of the ideal type being mixed up with reality. For instance, one may come to the theoretical conclusion that ground rent can be the only source of capital accumulation in a society that is organized *strictly* according to "craft-oriented" principles. On this basis, one may possibly construct (we shall not here concern ourselves with the question of whether this construction is correct) an ideal image of the transformation from a craft-oriented to a capitalist form of economy. This ideal image would be completely determined by certain elementary factors: limited amount of land; increasing population; influx of precious metals; rationalization of the conduct of life. With the aid of this construction as a heuristic tool, one would then have to determine, by means of a comparison between ideal type and "facts", whether the empirical–historical process of development was actually identical to the constructed one. If the ideal type was "correctly" constructed, and if the actual course of events did *not* correspond to the ideal-typical one, this would prove that medieval society was, in certain respects, *not* strictly "craft"-oriented. And if the ideal type was "*ideally*" constructed from a heuristic point of view (leaving completely aside the question whether and how that might be the case in our example), *then* it will also guide research in a direction that leads to a more precise understanding of what was distinctive and historically important about the elements of medieval society that were *not* craft-oriented. *If* it leads to this result, [the ideal type] has achieved its logical purpose precisely *by demonstrating* its own *un*real character. In that case, it has tested a hypothesis. This procedure is methodologically quite unobjectionable, *as long as* one constantly keeps in mind that the ideal-typical *construction* of a development is something that must be strictly distinguished from *history*, and that the construction was in this case simply a tool permitting the *valid* imputation, in a *systematic* manner, of a historical event to its real causes, among those that, according to our experience, might have been *possible*.

Experience shows, however, that it is often extremely difficult to maintain this distinction, because of the following circumstance: In order to make the presentation of the ideal type, or of the ideal-typical development, more graphic, we try to *elucidate* it by means of illustrative material drawn from empirical–historical reality. This procedure is in itself wholly legitimate; but what is dangerous about it is that here, for once, historical knowledge appears as the *servant* of theory, and not the other way round. The theoretician is easily tempted either to regard this as the normal state of affairs or, which is worse, to merge theory with history, and even to confuse the two. To an even greater degree, this is the case when the ideal construction of a course of development is integrated with the conceptual classification of ideal types of certain cultural construct (for instance, forms of manufacturing enterprise, with the "closed domestic economy" as the point of departure, or of religious concepts, beginning with the "momentary gods" ‹135›) to form a *genetic* classification. On the basis of the selected conceptual characteristics, one arrives at a series of types that gives the impression of occurring as a historical sequence with the necessity of a law. The logical ordering of concepts, on the one hand, and the empirical ordering of the substance of those concepts [according to] space, time and causal connections, on the other hand, will then look so closely knit together that one is almost irresistibly tempted to do violence to reality in order [to support a claim] that the construction is actually valid in reality.

We have deliberately refrained from referring to what is (in our view) by far the most important case of ideal-typical constructions: th[ose made by] *Marx*. We have done so because we do not want to complicate this account further by introducing interpretations of Marx, nor do we want to anticipate those discussions in our journal that will regularly subject to critical analysis the literature dealing with, or building on, that great thinker. Here, we shall therefore merely point out that *all* specifically Marxist "laws" and evolutionary constructions – provided they are *theoretically* correct – have an ideal-typical character. Anyone who has ever worked with Marxist concepts will be aware not only of the eminent, indeed unique, *heuristic* importance of those ideal types, when they are used for *comparisons* with reality, but also of how dangerous they can be whenever they are presented as empirically valid, or even as *real* (which in fact means: metaphysical) "effective *forces*", "tendencies" etc.

Generic concepts – ideal types – ideal-typical generic concepts – ideas, in the sense of combinations of thoughts that are empirically at work in historical human beings – ideal types of such ideas – ideals governing historical human beings – ideal types of such ideals – ideals to which the historian relates history – *theoretical* constructions in which empirical material is used for *illustrative* purposes – *historical* investigations in which theoretical concepts are used as ideal limiting cases – and, in addition, the various possible complications that we have only been able to hint at here: all these are theoretical constructions whose relationship to the empirical reality of the immediately given is in each individual case problematical: – this sample alone is a sufficient indication of the infinite complexity of the conceptual and method[olog]ical problems that continue to exist in the domain of the cultural sciences. And, in the present context, where we only wanted to *point out* the problems, we had to abstain completely from dealing properly with practical methodological questions, and from a more thorough discussion of the relationship between ideal-typical and "law-like" knowledge, between ideal-typical and collective concepts etc. –

Even after all these discussions, the historian will still insist that the dominance within a discipline of the ideal-typical form of concept formation and construction is a specific indication that the discipline is still in its early youth. And, in a certain sense, he will be right, although the consequences of this fact are different from those that he would draw. Let us take a couple of examples from other disciplines. It is certainly true that both a sorely tried third-form pupil and a primitive philologist will regard language as something "*organic*" – that is to say: as a supra-empirical *whole*, governed by norms – and will see the task of science as that of determining what *ought to be* valid as a rule of language. Normally, the first task that a "philology" will set itself is to subject the "written language" to logical analysis – as did, for instance, the Accademia della Crusca ⟨136⟩ – and to reduce its content to *rules*. And, although a leading philologist now takes the opposite view and proclaims that the object of philology is "the spoken language of *every single individual*", even such a programme can only be drawn up if the written language constitutes a relatively well-defined ideal type with which one can (at least tacitly) operate when dealing with the infinite multiplicity of the *spoken language* – a task that would otherwise be completely without orientation and know no bounds. – And in the same way, the constructions of the organic theories of the state, or of those based on natural law, or – to recall an ideal type in *our* sense of the term – Benjamin Constant's theory of the antique state, ⟨137⟩ all functioned as, so to speak, emergency safe havens until one had learnt to find one's bearings when navigating the immense sea of empirical facts. Consequently, if a science is maturing, this will indeed always imply that it *surmounts* the ideal type, to the extent that [the type] is conceived as empirically *valid* or as a *generic concept*. However, not only is it even nowadays quite legitimate to use, for instance, Constant's brilliant construction to demonstrate certain aspects and distinctive historical features of political life in Antiquity, as long as one takes care to maintain its ideal-typical character, but, above all, some sciences are fated to remain eternally youthful, namely all *historical* disciplines: all those that are constantly confronted with new questions by the ever-advancing flow of culture. The very nature of the task of those disciplines implies that *all* ideal-typical constructions are transitory, but that, at the same time, one inevitably needs ever-*new* ones.

Fresh attempts are constantly made to find the "genuine", "true" meaning of historical concepts, and they never attain their goal. Consequently, the conceptual syntheses which historians continually employ will, as a rule, only be relatively determined; or else – whenever one insists on unambiguous conceptual content – the concept becomes an abstract ideal type and thus reveals itself as being a theoretical – that is, a "one-sided" – point of view. From this viewpoint, light can be thrown on reality, and reality can be related to it; but it will obviously prove to be unsuitable as a schema under which reality can be completely *subsumed*, as none of the theoretical systems that are indispensable to us if we want to grasp the elements of reality which are significant in a given case can of course exhaust the infinite abundance of reality. None [of these systems] is anything more than an attempt, on the basis of the state of our knowledge and by means of the conceptual constructs at our disposal, to bring order to the chaos of those facts that we have in a given case chosen to include within the field of our *interest*. The theoretical apparatus developed in the past by intellectually processing – which in fact means: *reshaping* – the immediately given reality and by ordering it in concepts corresponding to the state of knowledge and the focus of interest at that time is constantly challenged by the new knowledge that we are able and *determined* to obtain from reality. It is in this struggle that the advances of the cultural sciences are accomplished. The outcome is a constant process of reshaping of those concepts by means of which we seek to grasp reality. The history of the sciences of social life therefore is, and remains, in constant flux between the attempt to order facts intellectually by means of concept formation; the breaking down – because of the broadening and displacement of the scientific horizon – of the mental images that have been arrived at in this fashion; and the new formation of concepts on this altered basis. This does not mean that attempts to build conceptual systems are misguided *in principle*: every science, even straightforward descriptive history, makes use of the conceptual stock-in-trade of its time; but what it *does* indicate is that, in the sciences of human culture, the formation of concepts is dependent on how the problems are configured, and in its turn, this configuration changes with the substance of the culture itself. The relationship between concept and conceptual content in the cultural sciences implies that any such synthesis must be transient. In our science, ambitious attempts to produce conceptual constructions have as a rule been of value precisely because they demonstrated the *limited* significance of the point of view on which those constructions were based. The most wide-ranging advances in the domain of the social sciences are, as far as *substance* is concerned, tied up with a shift in the practical cultural problems and assume the *form* of a conceptual critique. It will be one of the foremost tasks of our journal to serve this critical purpose and thereby to contribute to the investigation of the *principles of synthesis* in the domain of the social sciences.

Having drawn those consequences from what has been said so far, we now arrive at a point where our views will perhaps here and there diverge from those of many, even eminent, representatives of the historical school of which we ourselves are the pupils. These representatives often – explicitly or implicitly – persist in believing that the final goal – the purpose – of every science is to organize its material in a system of concepts[, and that] the content of those concepts must be obtained and slowly perfected through the observation of empirical regularities and the formulation and verification of hypotheses until, at some point, a "consummate", and *therefore* deductive, science comes into being as a result of this process. [As they see it,] the historical and inductive work conducted at present is a preliminary task necessitated by the imperfect state of our discipline; and, naturally, from this point of view nothing could be more questionable than forming and employing precisely defined concepts, as such a procedure would imply the premature anticipation of the goal that was fixed for a distant future. – This conception would be fundamentally unassailable [viewed] from the epistemological standpoint of antique scholasticism, a standpoint that is in fact deeply embedded in the minds of the bulk of the specialist scholars belonging to the historical school: here, the assumption is that concepts have the purpose of being ideational *reproductions* of "objective" reality, and, consequently, there are constant references to the *irreality* of all precisely defined concepts. The basic idea of modern epistemology, which goes back to Kant, is [on the contrary] that concepts are, and can only be, theoretical means for the purpose of intellectual mastery of the empirically given; and for anyone who carries this idea to its logical conclusion, the fact that precisely defined genetic concepts are by necessity ideal types will not constitute an argument against the formation of such concepts. For him, the relationship between concepts and historical work will be reversed: the [scholastic] goal [referred to above] will appear to be logically impossible; he will view concepts, not as *goals*, but as *means* towards the purpose of acquiring knowledge of relationships that are significant from individual points of view; and, precisely *because* the content of historical concepts is necessarily changeable, those concepts must necessarily be precisely defined in every given instance. He will simply demand that, when those concepts are *employed*, their character as ideal theoretical constructs should be carefully maintained: that the ideal type should not be confused with history. Since the inevitable change in the leading value ideas means that one cannot envisage truly definitive historical concepts as a general goal, he will believe that, precisely because sharply defined and unambiguous concepts are constructed from the *individual* point of view, which is in each case the leading one, this enables us always to keep the *limits* of their validity firmly in mind.

It will be said – and we ourselves have admitted – that it may in a given individual case be quite possible to describe the evolution of a concrete historical situation without constantly relating it to [well-]defined concepts. Accordingly, the claim will be made that historians within our discipline, just as it has been said of political historians, have the right to speak "the language of *life*". Certainly! But it must be added that, if they proceed in that way, it will necessarily – and often to a *very* high degree – be left to chance whether one [is able to] get a clear idea of the point of view from which the relevant course of events is viewed as significant. In general, we are not in the favourable position of the political historian for whom the cultural material to which he relates his account is normally unambiguous – or seems to be so. What is distinctive about the significance of *artistic* representations is also true of any purely descriptive account: "Each one sees what he carries in his heart" ‹138›: valid *judgements* always presuppose a *logical* processing of phenomena, that is to say, the application of *concepts*; and although it is possible, and often tempting for aesthetic reasons, to hide those concepts from view, this will always expose the reader (and often the author himself) to the risk of uncertainty in his orientation about the substance and the implications of [the author's] judgements.

In discussions of practical, economic and social *policy*, it may have quite extraordinarily dangerous consequences if the concepts are not sharply defined. For example, an outsider would find it almost unbelievable how much confusion has been caused by the use of the term "*value*" – the problem child of our discipline, which can in fact *only* be given a reasonably unambiguous meaning if it is defined ideal-typically; or of words such as "productive", "from an economic point of view", etc., which simply do not stand up to a clear, conceptual analysis. And in this context, most of these calamitous concepts are *collective* ones, taken from the language of [everyday] life. Let us take a textbook example that is as easy as possible to understand for the layman: the concept of "agriculture", as it is used in the expression "the interests of agriculture". Let us start by looking at the "interests of agriculture" in the sense of those more or less clear *subjective* ideas that the individual farmers entertain about their interests and that can be empirically established: [even] if we wholly abstract from the innumerable conflicts of interest between those farmers who breed livestock, who fatten livestock, who grow grain, who use grain for fodder, who distil spirits, etc., all experts (but not all laymen) are well aware of the enormous tangle of closely knit and conflicting value relations that indistinctly come to mind [whenever the concept of "interests of agriculture" is used]. We shall only enumerate a few of them here: the interests of farmers who want to sell their property and are therefore only interested in a rapid increase in the price of land; the opposite interests of those [farmers] who want to round off their property, buy or rent land; the interests of those who, for social advantage, wish to retain a certain property for their descendants and who are therefore interested in a stable [distribution of] landed property; the opposite interests of those who, in their own interest or that of their children, wish to see a redistribution of land in favour of the best farmer or – which is not necessarily the same – of the financially strongest buyer; the purely economic interest in economic freedom of action of those farmers who are, in the business sense, the "most able" ones; conflicting with this, the interest of certain dominant social strata in preserving the traditional social and political position of their own "status group" and consequently of their own descendants; the social interest of the *non*-dominant strata of farmers in the disappearance of those higher strata that exert pressure on their own position; the interest [of the lower strata], which may occasionally collide with the one just mentioned, in having political leaders in the dominant strata for the safeguarding of the economic interests of the lower [strata]. – Even though we have proceeded as summarily and imprecisely as possible, the list could be greatly extended, while still remaining incomplete. We shall leave aside the fact that the more "egoistic" interests of this kind mingle and combine with extremely diverse, purely ideal values, which may inhibit and deflect them. What we should above all remember is that, when we speak of the "interests of agriculture", we are as a rule thinking, *not only* of the material and ideal values to which the farmers in question themselves relate their "interests", but also of the, partly quite heterogeneous, value ideas to which *we* may relate agriculture. For instance, interests in production, derived from the interest in cheap food of good quality (the second interest is not always identical with the first one): in this connection, the interests of town and country may collide in many different ways, and it is by no means certain that the interests of the present generation must be identical with those of future generations; – demographic interests: in particular, the interest in a *large* rural population, derived either from the interest of "the state" (be it connected with power politics or domestic politics) or from other ideal interests of various kinds, as for instance the interest in the expected influence of a large rural population on the distinctive cultural character of a country; – this demographic interest may collide with the most diverse private economic interests of all sections of the rural population and, conceivably, with every interest of the bulk of the present-day rural population. Or [we may think of] the interest in a particular kind of social *composition* of the rural population, because of the nature of the political or cultural influence resulting from it: depending on its direction, this interest may collide with every conceivable, even the most pressing, present or future interest of the individual farmers and of "the state". And – to complicate the matter further – the "state", to whose "interest" we are wont to relate such individual interests (and numerous other, similar ones), is often nothing more than the cover address for an extremely complicated tangle of value ideas, to which we relate "the state" in each individual case: purely military external security; securing the dominant internal position of a dynasty or of particular classes; the interest in preserving and enlarging the formal political unity of the nation, for its own sake or in the interest of preserving certain objective, but again quite divergent, cultural values that we, as a people united in a state, believe that we represent; the transformation of the social character of the state in accordance with certain, and again quite divergent, cultural ideals – it would take us too far to make even brief reference to all that goes under the collective name of "state interests", [and] to which we can relate "agriculture". The example chosen here is crude and simple, and our summary analysis even more so. The layman might subject the concept of, for instance, "the class interest of the workers" to a similar (and more thorough) analysis, in order to uncover the underlying contradictory tangle of interests and ideals of the workers [themselves], and of ideals in relation to which *we* view the workers. Emphasizing that, from a purely empiristic point of view, the slogans of the conflict of interests are "relative" will not suffice to overcome them: the only way of moving beyond vague platitudes is to identify the various *possible* points of view by means of clear and distinct concepts. As a *world view* or as a valid *norm*, the "free trade argument" ‹139› is ridiculous; but quite irrespective of *what* ideals of commercial policy an individual cherishes, it has been highly detrimental to our discussions of commercial policy that we have underestimated the heuristic value of the ancient wisdom of the greatest merchants of the world, encapsulated in such ideal-typical formulas. The distinctive character of the points of view that are relevant in each case can only be clearly brought out by means of concepts formulated as ideal types, and by *confronting* the empirical material with the ideal type. The use of the undifferentiated, collective concepts belonging to everyday language is always a cover for woolly thinking or unclear aims of action; quite often, it is a tool that leads to questionable half-truths; and it invariably serves to inhibit the correct formulation of the problem.

We have come to the end of our exposition, the sole aim of which has been to indicate the (often hair-thin) line that separates science from belief and to show in what *sense* knowledge can be sought in the field of social economics. The *objective* validity of all empirical knowledge rests, and rests exclusively, upon the fact that the given reality is ordered according to categories that are in a specific sense *subjective*, in that they form the *precondition* of our knowledge, and that are based on the presupposition of the *value* of that truth which empirical knowledge alone is able to give us. With the means available to our science, we have nothing to offer a person to whom this truth is of no value – and belief in the value of scientific truth is the product of certain cultures, and is not given to us by nature. He will search in vain, however, for another truth to take the place of science with respect to those features that *it* alone can provide: concepts and judgements that are neither empirical reality, nor reproductions of empirical reality, but that allow empirical reality to be *ordered intellectually* in a valid manner. As we have seen, in the field of the empirical social sciences of culture, the possibility of gaining meaningful knowledge of what is important to us in the infinite multitude of occurrences is tied to the unremitting application of viewpoints that have a specifically particular character and that are all in the last resort oriented towards value ideas. These value ideas may be established and experienced empirically as elements of all meaningful human action, but their validity *cannot* be proved on the basis of the empirical material. The "objectivity" of knowledge in social science depends on something else, [namely] that the empirically given is constantly oriented towards those value ideas that are the only source of its cognitive *value*, and that the significance of that knowledge must be understood in the light of those value ideas, but that, in spite of this, the empirically given is never construed as a basis for the demonstration of their validity – a demonstration that is empirically impossible. We all harbour some form of *belief* in the supra-empirical validity of those fundamental and sublime value ideas in which we anchor the meaning of our existence; but this does not exclude – on the contrary, it includes – the constant change in the concrete points of view from which the empirical reality derives its significance: the irrational reality of life, and its store of *possible* meanings, are inexhaustible; the *concrete* configuration of the value relation therefore remains fluid and subject to change far into the dim future of human culture. The light shed by those sublime value ideas falls on a constantly changing, finite part of the immense, chaotic stream of occurrences churning its way through the ages.

All this should not be misinterpreted as implying that the real task of social science is a ceaseless chase after new points of view and conceptual constructions. *On the contrary*: in this context, nothing should be emphasized more strongly than the following proposition: helping to acquire knowledge of the *cultural significance and importance of concrete historical relationships* is the single, exclusive, ultimate goal, for the attainment of which the formation and critique of concepts is *one of* the tools. – In our field, too, there are – to use F.Th. Vischer's expression ⟨140⟩ – "material-seekers" and "meaning-seekers". The first category are hungrily agape for facts and can only be satisfied with documents, voluminous statistics and surveys: they have no feeling for the refinement of new ideas. The second category are connoisseurs who ruin their taste for facts by feeding on constantly redistilled essences of thought. Genuine artistry – which, for instance, among the historians Ranke possessed to such an eminent degree – precisely consists in relating *known* facts to *known* viewpoints but nevertheless creating something new. In an age of specialization, everyone who works in the field of the cultural sciences, having decided to deal with a certain material in order to throw light on a particular set of problems, and having worked out the methodical principles [that he wants to apply], will regard his work with this material as an end in itself: he will not constantly and deliberately check whether each fact, measured against the ultimate value ideas, is worth knowing, and may even lose his awareness that it is anchored in those value ideas. That is as it should be. But, at some point, the colouring changes: the significance of those points of view that have been applied unreflectingly grows uncertain, the way forward fades away in the twilight. The light shed by the great cultural problems has moved on. Then science, too, prepares to find a new standpoint and a new conceptual apparatus, and to contemplate the stream of events from the summits of thought. It follows those stars that alone can give meaning and direction to its work:

And with fresh energies I hurry on to drink
And quench my thirst in its eternal light,
The day before me, and behind me night,
The heavens above me, under me the waves. ⟨141⟩

First published in *Archiv für Sozialwissenschaft und Sozialpolitik* 19 (1904), pp. 22–87. Translated from: "Die 'Objektivität' sozialwissenschaftlicher und sozialpolitischer Erkenntnis", in Max Weber, *Gesammelte Aufsätze zur Wissenschaftslehre* (ed. Johannes Winckelmann), 3rd ed., Tübingen: J.C.B.Mohr (Paul Siebeck) 1968, pp. 146–214. (The subtitles given in the Table of Contents of that volume are not original and have not been retained here.)
Written late 1903–early 1904 on the occasion of Werner Sombart, Max Weber and Edgar Jaffé taking over as editors of the *Archive*. In late February 1904, the article, already set up in type, was subjected to a "superrevision" by Weber, probably in order to harmonize it with the views expressed in the *Accompanying Remarks*. (See p. 99.) As a result, *Objectivity*, which was originally intended to head the first issue of the *Archive*, immediately after the *Accompanying Remarks* (see p. 98), lost its pride of place there, although it was still published in the first issue.

CRITICAL STUDIES
IN THE LOGIC OF THE
CULTURAL SCIENCES

I A critique of Eduard Meyer

When one of our best historians feels impelled to give an account to himself and his professional colleagues of the aims and methods of his work, this must arouse an interest beyond the limits of his [own] profession already, because he thereby transcends the boundaries of his specialized discipline and enters into the area of epistemological reflections. This does initially have certain negative consequences. At its present stage of development, logic is in fact a specialized discipline like any other; and in order to handle logical categories (just like the categories of any other discipline) really competently, one should be dealing with them in one's mind on a daily basis. Eduard Meyer, however, whose treatise *Theory and Method* we are discussing here, naturally cannot and does not claim such a constant intellectual occupation with logical problems; and the writer of the following pages is equally unable to make that claim. The epistemological critique contained in the above-mentioned work therefore constitutes, so to speak, a medical report [written] not by the doctor, but by the patient himself; and that is how it is intended to be evaluated and understood. A professional logician and epistemologist will therefore take exception to a large number of M[eyer]'s formulations, and he will perhaps not learn anything really new for his purposes from [Meyer's] book. However, this in no way detracts from the importance of this work for the neighbouring *specialized* disciplines.[1] Indeed, in their most significant achievements, skilled epistemologists precisely use "ideal-typically" ‹142› constructed ideas of the cognitive goals and methods of the specialized disciplines, and therefore fly so high over the heads of these disciplines that the latter sometimes find it difficult to recognize themselves with the naked eye in these constructions. Therefore, methodological discussions conducted on the home ground of [the specialized disciplines] may occasionally be more useful for their analysis of their own situation, in spite of – and in a certain sense because of – the fact that the formulation [of such discussions] is epistemologically imperfect. In particular, M[eyer]'s transparently clear account offers the specialists of the neighbouring disciplines a whole range

---

1 It is to be hoped, therefore, that the following critique, which deliberately looks for the weak points in [Meyer's] formulations, will not be attributed to [the author's] need to show off his superior knowledge. The errors made by an eminent writer are more instructive than the correct statements of a scientific nonentity. Here, the intention is not to do justice, in a positive sense, to Ed[uard] Meyer's achievements, but exactly the opposite: to learn from his imperfections by seeing how he has tried, with varying success, to come to terms with certain important problems in the logic of history.

of starting points from which they can find solutions to certain logical problems that they have in common with the "historians" in the narrower sense of the term. This is the aim of the following discussions. The intention is to take M[eyer]'s treatise as the starting point, to go on by illustrating, one by one, a number of separate logical problems, and then to give a critique, from the standpoint thus arrived at, of a number of other recent works dealing with the logic of the cultural sciences. [The present discussion] deliberately begins in the area of purely *historical* problems, and only later moves on to those [of the] disciplines dealing with social life that look for "regularities" and "laws" – while, in the past, attempts have so often been made to define the distinctive character of the social sciences by showing where they differ from the "natural sciences". In those attempts, the tacit assumption was always made that "history" is a discipline that simply gathers material, or that is at least purely "descriptive", and that, at best, it may drag together "facts" to serve as building blocks for the "really" scientific work – which will only begin at that point. What is more, the *way* in which professional historians have tried to establish the specific character of "history" as a *professional* discipline has unfortunately also contributed quite substantially to the strengthening of the false assumption that "historical" work is something qualitatively different from "scientific" work, because history does not concern itself with "concepts" and "regularities". [The work of] our discipline is nowadays, under the lasting influence of the "historical school", ‹143› usually conducted on a "historical" basis; and [its] relationship with "theory" has remained as problematical as it was 25 years ago. Therefore, it seems justified to start by asking *what* [it] actually means [when we speak of] "historical" work, in the logical sense of the word, and to conduct the initial discussion of this question with reference to work that is indubitably and by general agreement "historical"; precisely that [sort of] work is the subject of the treatise to which we shall here devote our main critique.

Eduard Meyer begins with a warning against overestimating the importance of methodological studies for historical *practice*: Even the most comprehensive knowledge of methodology does not make anyone into a historian; and incorrect methodological views do not necessarily lead to erroneous scientific practice, but on the face of it only demonstrate that the historian formulates or interprets his own, correct, procedural maxims incorrectly. On the whole, I can agree with this: methodology can never be more than a self-reflection on the means that have *proved useful* in [scientific] practice; and one does not need to be made explicitly aware of those means in order to produce useful work, just as one does not need to have knowledge of anatomy in order to walk "correctly". In fact, a person who constantly wished to check whether he walked in accordance with anatomical knowledge would run the risk of stumbling; and, in the same way, a scholar from a specialized discipline might have the same experience if he tried to define the aims of his work in a different way on the basis of methodological considerations.[1] If there is one point where methodology can be of direct use to the practising historian (which is of course *one of* its aims), it is by enabling him, once and for all, to avoid being impressed by the sayings of dilettantes posing as philosophers. It is always by the demonstration and solution of problems of *substance* that new sciences have been established and their methods further developed; on the other hand, purely epistemological or methodological considerations have as yet never played a crucial role in those respects. As a rule, such [methodological] considerations only acquire importance for the way in which science is pursued at times when a major shift occurs in the "viewpoints" from which [the] material becomes an object of description, and this [shift] leads to the idea that the new "viewpoints" also require a revision of the logical forms that have hitherto provided the framework for that "pursuit", with the result that one

---

1   As will be demonstrated later, this would also happen to Ed[uard] Meyer if he were to put many of his own constructions too literally into practice.

becomes uncertain about the "nature" of one's work. But this is undeniably the situation in which history finds itself at present; and E[duard] M[eyer]'s view that, in principle, methodology is of no importance for the "practice" [of history] has therefore, quite justifiably, not prevented him from now letting himself become engaged in methodolog[ical reflections].

He starts with an exposition of those theories that have recently, from a methodological viewpoint, tried to reshape the science of history. ‹144› On pp. 5ff., he formulates the position that he particularly wants to subject to critical discussion as follows:

1   The following [elements] should be regarded as having no significance for history and, therefore, as not belonging within a scientific account:
    (a)   the [element] of "chance"
    (b)   the "freely" willed decisions of concrete personalities
    (c)   the influence of "ideas" on human action;
2   on the other hand,
    (a)   "mass phenomena", as opposed to individual action,
    (b)   the "typical", as opposed to the "singular", and
    (c)   the evolution of "communities", especially of social "classes" or of "nations", as opposed to the political actions of individuals should be considered as the proper object[s] of scientific knowledge; and finally:
3   as science can only understand historical development causally, that development should be conceived as a process with a "law-like" course. Consequently, the real aim of historical work is to identify the "stages of development" – which will necessarily succeed each other in a "typical" fashion – of human communities, and to fit the rich variety of history into [that framework].

In what follows, we shall for the time being completely leave aside all those points in E[duard] M[eyer]'s account that deal particularly with his critical discussion of Lamprecht. I shall also take the liberty of rearranging E[duard] M[eyer]'s arguments, and of singling out some of them for separate discussion in the following sections, in accordance with the requirements of the following studies, which are after all not just intended as a critique of E[duard] M[eyer]'s treatise. –

To counter the position that he combats, E[duard] M[eyer] initially refers to the tremendous role that "free will" and "chance" – both of which are in his opinion "perfectly definite and clear concepts" – have played in history and in life in general.

Let us begin with the discussion of "chance" (pp. 17ff.). Of course, E[duard] M[eyer] does not understand by that concept an objective "causelessness" ("absolute" chance in the metaphysical sense); nor does he understand by it the subjective, absolute impossibility of knowing the causal conditions ("absolute" chance in the epistemological sense)[1] – [an impossibility] that necessarily recurs in every individual instance in question (when throwing dice, for instance). Instead, he understands ["chance"] as "relative", in the sense of a logical relationship between causal complexes that are *conceived of* as distinct; this [definition] on the whole – although it is naturally not always formulated quite "correctly" – corresponds to the way in which the concept is accepted by specialists in the theory of logic, who [in that respect], in spite of many detailed

---

1   The so-called games of "chance", for instance, (dice or lotteries) are based on this "chance". The fact that the connection between the concrete outcome and certain parts of the conditions determining it is *absolutely* unknowable is constitutive for the possibility of a calculus of probability, in the strict sense of the term.

advances, still base themselves on Windelband's earliest work. ‹145› [Meyer] also, on the whole correctly, makes the following distinction: [On the one hand] (1) this *causal* concept of "chance" (the so-called "relative chance") – here, the "chance" outcome is opposed to the outcome that was to be "expected" on the basis of those causal components of an event that we have combined into a conceptual whole; the "chance" [element] is that which, according to the general rules governing events, cannot be causally *derived* from those conditions that were the only ones taken into account, but is caused by an additional condition lying "outside" them (pp. 17–19). And, [on the other hand,] (2) the *teleological* concept of "chance", which is different from the first one. [This second concept] is opposed to that of "importance": either a *concept* is formed, for cognitive purposes, from which those elements of reality that are "unimportant" for those purposes ([i.e. which are] "chance", "individual") have been eliminated; or certain real or imagined objects are considered as "means" to an "end", so that only certain properties are in practice relevant as "means", while the others are in practice "unimportant" (pp. 20–21).[1] Admittedly, the formulation[s] (particularly p. 20, bottom, where the contrast is taken to be that between "events" and "objects") are less than perfect, and, when we come to discuss E[duard] M[eyer]'s position concerning the concept of development (below, II) it will become clear that all the implications of the problem have not been fully thought out logically. But, that apart, what [Meyer] says is sufficient for the requirements of historical practice. – What is of interest to us here, however, is the way in which he comes back to the concept of chance in a later passage in the treatise (p. 28). There, E[duard] M[eyer] writes as follows:

> Natural science can . . . assert that when dynamite is ignited, an explosion *must* take place. But to predict [. . .] whether and when this explosion takes place in a particular case, and whether a particular person is wounded, killed or saved in that situation [. . .] is something that natural science cannot do, since that depends on chance and *on free will, which is unknown to natural science, but not to history.*

What immediately strikes the eye is that "chance" is so closely linked with "free will". This becomes even more apparent when E[duard] M[eyer] adduces his second example. Here, he refers to the possibility that astronomy, with the means at its disposal, can "calculate" a constellation "with certainty" – that is to say: assuming that there are no "disturbances" (for instance in the shape of foreign celestial bodies straying into the solar system); on the other hand, he states that it is "not possible" to predict whether that calculated constellation will in fact be "*observed*". First of all, the "straying" of a foreign celestial body would also, according to E[duard] M[eyer]'s assumption, be "impossible to calculate"; consequently, "chance" (in this sense) is known not only to history, but also to astronomy. And, second, it is normally very easy to "calculate" that some astronomer will also try to "observe" the calculated constellation, and that he *will* in fact observe it, unless "chance" disturbances occur. One gets the impression that E[duard] M[eyer], in spite of the fact that he interprets "chance" in a completely deterministic way, nevertheless, without stating it clearly, has the idea [that there is] a particularly close elective affinity between "chance" and the "*freedom of the will*", and that this elective affinity gives rise to a specific irrationality in historical events. Let us examine [this more] closely.

1　These concepts of "chance" can never be eliminated from a historical discipline, even if it is (like, for instance, biology) only historical in a relative sense. [When speaking of "chance"], L.M. Hartmann, too, (*Historical Development*, pp. 15, 25) – obviously following Ed[uard] Meyer – only refers to this variant, as well as to the "pragmatic" concept of "chance" mentioned below (p. 144n1); this means that, although his formulation is wrong, he at any rate does not transform "the causeless into a cause", as Eulenburg (*Hartmann*) supposes.

According to E[duard] M[eyer] (p. 14), what he calls "free will" does not, either, in any way contradict the "axiomatic" "principle of sufficient reason", ‹146› which is also in his opinion absolutely valid, even for human action. [As he sees it,] the distinction between "freedom" and "necessity" instead resolves itself into a simple difference between [two] points of view: In the latter case, we look at what *has come into being*, and consider it to be "necessary", including the decision that was once actually taken; in the former case, we look at the event as "*coming into being*", that is to say: as [we see it], it has not yet occurred and is therefore not "necessary", but is one of an infinite number of "possibilities". From the point of view of a development that is "coming into being", however, we can never assert that some human decision *could* not have turned out differently from what it (later) actually turned out to be. "In the case of human action, we can never transcend the 'I will'."

Now, the first question that arises is the following: is E[duard] M[eyer] of the opinion that the distinction between the [two] points of view (the "development" which is "coming into being" and is therefore conceived as "free", and the "fact" that has "come into being" and therefore has to be conceived as "necessary") can only be applied to the domain of human motivation, and therefore not to that of "inanimate" nature? On p. 15, he says that someone who "knows the personality and the circumstances" will "perhaps with very high probability" be able to predict the outcome – the decision that is "coming into being". It therefore looks as if he does *not* believe that there is such a difference [in applicability], since a really exact predictive "calculation" of an individual event on the basis of given conditions is, also in the domain of "inanimate" nature, tied to two preconditions: (1) that we are in fact only dealing with elements of given [reality] that are "calculable", that is to say: that can be formulated quantitatively; and, (2) that "all" the conditions that are relevant for the course of events are actually known and have been exactly measured. If this is not the case – and that is certainly the general rule whenever what *matters* to us is the concrete individuality of the event (for instance: what the weather will be on a given day in the future) – then we must also there content ourselves with judgements of probability of quite varying degrees of precision. Then, "free" will would not have any special status; and the "I will" [quoted above] would be nothing more than [William] James' formal "fiat" of consciousness, ‹147› which is also, for example, accepted by deterministic criminologists[1] without damage to the consistency of their theories of imputation. In that case, "free will" would only mean that causal importance is attributed to the "decision", whose causes it may in fact never be possible to determine completely but which are in any case "sufficient" – something that will not be seriously contested even by a strict determinist. If this were all, there would certainly seem to be no reason why the concept of the irrationality of historical events – a concept that is occasionally brought up in connection with the discussion of "chance" – should not be sufficient.

However, if one were to interpret E[duard] M[eyer]'s view[s] along those lines, it would immediately strike one as strange that he finds it necessary in this context to underline the "freedom of the will", as a "fact of inner experience", as being indispensable for the [idea of] the *responsibility* of the individual for the "exercise of his will". The only reason [for this clarification] would be that [Meyer] wished to assign to history the task of "sitting in judgement" on its heroes. It is therefore a question whether this is in fact E[duard] M[eyer]'s position. On p. 16, he remarks: "we attempt to . . . uncover the motives that led them" (i.e., for instance, Bismarck in 1866 ‹148›) "to [take] their decisions, and we judge the *correctness* of those decisions and the value (NB!) of their personality accordingly." These formulations might lead one to believe that E[duard] M[eyer] sees it as the most important task of history to arrive at *value*

---

1   For instance by Liepmann (*Criminal Law*).

judgements concerning the personality who "acts historically". However, when we consider not only his views on "biography" – [they are to be found] at the end of his treatise and we shall go into them later – but also his extremely pertinent remarks concerning the lack of congruence between the "intrinsic value" of historical personalities and their *causal* importance (pp. 50–51), they seem to leave no doubt that, by the "value" of a personality, in the sentence quoted above, he means – or at least: would have to mean to be consistent – the *causal* "importance", either of certain acts of those persons, or of certain qualities of theirs that might contribute positively or, as in the case of Frederick William IV, ‹149› negatively to an *evaluative* judgement. Again, "judging" the "correctness" of those decisions can mean different things: either (1) judging the "value" of the underlying purpose of the decision – for instance, the goal of driving Austria out of Germany, judged from the perspective of a German patriot, – or (2) an analysis of that decision in the light of the question whether – or rather (as history has [already] answered that question in the affirmative): *why* – the decision to go to war at precisely that time was the appropriate means for attaining that goal: the unification of Germany. We may leave aside the question whether E[duard] M[eyer] in fact in his own mind made a clear distinction between those two perspectives; [but] in an argument concerning historical causality, only the *second* one would be appropriate. For, in an account that is not intended as a book of recipes for diplomats but as "history", that judgement of the historical situation, "teleological" in form and expressed in terms of the categories of "means and ends", [can] obviously only serve the purpose of making it possible to judge the *causal* historical importance of [certain] facts. Such a judgement asserts that, at that precise moment, the "opportunity" to make that decision was not "missed", because the "bearers" of that decision (as E[duard] M[eyer] puts it) possessed the "strength of mind" [necessary] for upholding it in the face of all obstacles. In this way, it is established how much causal "*importance*" should be ascribed to that decision and to its characterological and other preconditions: in other words, to what extent and in what sense the presence of those "traits of character" was a historically "significant" "factor". However, that sort of problem, which concerns tracing back *causally* a particular historical event to the actions of concrete human beings, should of course be strictly distinguished from the question of the meaning and importance of *ethical* "responsibility".

One might interpret that last expression of E[duard] M[eyer]'s ["responsibility"] as meaning, in a purely "objective" sense, the causal imputation of certain effects to given "characterological" qualities and to the "motives" of acting personalities – "motives" that must be explained by those qualities as well as by numerous features of the "milieu" and of the given situation. But, if this were so, one would find it strange that E[duard] M[eyer], in a later passage in the treatise (pp. 44–45), says that precisely the "investigation of motives" is "secondary" from the point of view of history.[1] The reason that he gives is that [this] usually oversteps the boundaries of

1   He does not clearly state what "investigation of motives" means. At any rate, it seems self-evident that we only treat the "decision" of a concrete "personality" as an absolutely "ultimate" fact in cases where [that decision] seems to us to be incidental in a "pragmatic" sense, that is to say: when it is impossible, or useless, to interpret it meaningfully – as for instance [in the case of] the chaotic decrees of Czar Paul, ‹150› which were inspired by [his] madness. But otherwise, surely *one* of the most undoubted tasks of history has always been that of understanding the empirically given external "acts" and their results, in the light of the historically given "conditions", "ends" and "means" of action. This is also what Ed[uard] Meyer himself does. And the "investigation of motives" – that is to say: the analysis of what is really "striven for" and of the reasons why we strive for it – is, on the one hand, a means of preventing that analysis from degenerating into unhistorical pragmatism and, on the other hand, one of the main points to which "historical interest" attaches itself: (Among other things), we do precisely *want to* see how the "significance" of human "striving" is changed by the concatenation of historical "destinies".

what can be ascertained with certainty, and is often no more than a "genetic formulation" of an act that cannot be satisfactorily explained on the basis of the [available] material, and must therefore simply be regarded as a "fact". But, although this may often be true in individual instances, it can hardly be maintained as a criterion distinguishing [the investigations of motives] *logically* from the "explanations" of concrete "external" events, which are also frequently problematical. However that may be, [Meyer's] view concerning motives, in connection with [his] strong emphasis on the significance for history of the purely formal element constituted by the "willed decision" and with his aforementioned remark concerning "responsibility", leads one to suspect that, in fact, the ethical and the causal approach to human action – "valuation" and "explanation" – here manifest a certain tendency to fuse with one another in E[duard] M[eyer]'s mind. One may or may not find Windelband's formulation, according to which the idea of responsibility implies an *abstraction* from causality, sufficient as a positive basis for the normative status of moral consciousness;[1] but, in any event, this formulation is an apt characterization of the way in which the world of "norms" and "values", as seen from the standpoint of empirical–scientific causal observation, delimits itself from [that standpoint]. Of course, the question of how the discovery of a particular mathematical proposition might have come about "psychologically" and whether, for instance, the highest degree of "mathematical imagination" may only occur as a concomitant of certain anatomical abnormalities of the "mathematical brain" is of no importance at all for the judgement concerning the "correctness" of that particular proposition. In the same way, the consideration that, according to the teachings of empirical science, one's own ethically judged "motive" is simply causally determined is of no importance before the forum of "conscience"; and the conviction that a botched work of art must be regarded as being just as much determined as the Sistine Chapel ‹151› is of no consequence for judging its aesthetic value. Causal analysis provides absolutely no value judgements;[2] and a value judgement is absolutely not a causal explanation. For that very reason, the *evaluation* of an event – the "beauty" of a natural phenomenon, for instance – takes place in a different sphere than the causal explanation of [that event]. Consequently, if history were to consider the "responsibility" of the historical actors before their conscience or before the judgement seat of some god or human being, or would in any other way introduce the philosophical problem of "freedom" into the *methodology* of history, this would invalidate its character as a science of empirical experience, just as much as [would] the insertion of miracles into its sequences. Following Ranke, E[duard] M[eyer] (p. 20) naturally rejects the latter procedure with reference to "the strict dividing line between historical knowledge and religious world view[s]"; and, in my opinion, it would have been better if he had not let himself be misled by arguments of Stammler's (to which he refers (p. 16n1)) into blurring the equally strict dividing line [between history and] ethics. The fatal methodological implications of mixing up different approaches in this way immediately become apparent when E[duard] M[eyer] (again on p. 16) [voices his] belief that "*this*" (i.e. the empirically given idea of freedom and *responsibility*) represents a "purely *individual* element" in the historical development, [an element] that can "never be reduced to a formula" without "losing its essence", and when he then seeks to illustrate this proposition by [pointing to] the eminent historical (causal) importance of the

1   Windelband (*Freedom of the Will*, last chapter) especially chooses this formulation in order to exclude the question of "free will" from criminological discussions. However, it is questionable whether this suffices from the criminological point of view, since the question of the nature of the causal connection is precisely *not* irrelevant for the applicability of the norms of criminal law.

2   However, as we shall see, this certainly does not mean that the causal investigation of the genesis of an object (for instance a work of art) cannot contribute very significantly to the "psychological" possibility of "understanding" the value significance of that object.

individual willed decisions of particular personalities. This old error[1] is so dangerous, precisely from the point of view of preserving the distinctive logical character of history, because it introduces problems from quite different fields of investigation into the domain of history and gives the impression that a certain (anti-deterministic) philosophical condition is the precondition of the validity of historical method.

Surely, it is quite obvious what is wrong about the assumption that a "freedom" of volition (however understood) is identical with, or determines, the "irrationality" of action. Specific "incalculability", which is *as great* as – but not greater than – [the incalculability] of "blind forces of nature", is the privilege of the madman.[2] On the other hand, we associate the greatest empirical "feeling of freedom" with precisely those acts that we are conscious of having accomplished *rationally* – that is to say: in the absence of physical and psychical "coercion", passionate "affects" and "accidental" blurring of our clarity of judgement – and by which we pursue a clearly perceived "goal" with the "means" that are, as far as we know – that is to say: according to *rules* of experience – the most adequate ones. However, if history only had to deal with such action, which is in that sense "free" – i.e. rational – then its task would be immeasurably lightened: The goal, the "motive", the "maxim" of the acting person could be unambiguously inferred from the means employed; and all the irrationalities that constitute the "personal" (in the vegetative sense of that ambiguous term) element of action would be excluded. Since all action conducted along strictly teleological lines consists of the application of rules of experience indicating the appropriate means for [attaining] a given end, history would be nothing more than the application of those rules.[3] But, human action *cannot* be interpreted in such purely rational terms; human "freedom" is impaired not only by irrational "prejudices", faulty reasoning and factual errors, but also by "temperament", "moods" and "affects"; therefore, human action, too – to very different degrees – partakes of the empirical "meaninglessness" of natural events; and[, for all these reasons,] a purely pragmatic science of history is an impossibility. But that kind of "irrationality" is precisely something that [human] action *has in common* with individual natural events; and when the historian speaks of the "irrationality" of human action as an element that disturbs the interpretation of historical interconnections, he is comparing historical–empirical action, not with events in nature, but with the ideal of a purely rational action, that is to say: action that is completely purposeful and completely oriented towards the adequate means.

Not only does Eduard Meyer's exposition of the categories of "chance" and "free will" that are specific to the historical approach show a somewhat unclear tendency to introduce

1   I have criticized it in detail in *Knies I* [pp. 30–33].
2   We treat the acts of Czar Paul during the last stages of his chaotic rule as simple facts, since they cannot be interpreted meaningfully and are therefore "incalculable", just as we treat the storm that destroyed the Spanish Armada ‹152› [as a simple fact]. In the first as well as the second case, we refrain from an "investigation of motives"; this is obviously not because we interpret those events as being "free", nor is it *only* because their concrete causes must necessarily remain hidden from us – in the case of Czar Paul, pathologists might perhaps give us certain clues – but because they *do not interest us sufficiently* from a historical point of view. I shall go into this later in more detail.
3   On this point, see my discussion in *Knies I*. Differently put: strictly rational action would be the smooth and complete "adaptation" to the given "situation". For instance, Menger's theoretical models are built on the assumption of strictly rational "adaptation" to the "market situation", and [they] give an "ideal-typically" pure illustration of the consequences of this [adaptation]. Indeed, *if* history were only the analysis of the emergence and interplay of particular "free" – that is to say: teleologically absolutely rational – acts of single individuals, then it would be nothing more than an [account] of pragmatic "adaptation" – which is what L.M. Hartmann would like to transform it into. If the concept of "adaptation" is divested of these teleological–rational connotations, as Hartmann does, then it becomes absolutely indifferent from the historical point of view – as I shall have occasion to show in more detail later on.

heterogeneous problems into the methodology of history; it must also be noted that his conception of historical causality contains striking contradictions. On p. 40, it is strongly emphasized that the direction in which historical research will always and invariably try to uncover causal sequences proceeds from effect to cause. Even this – as E[duard] M[eyer] formulates it[1] – can be disputed. In itself, it is quite possible that, if we are dealing with an event which is a given fact, or which has just been ascertained, the effects that [this event] might perhaps have produced will be formulated in the form of a hypothesis, which will then be verified by means of an examination of the "facts". As will become clear later, what [Eduard Meyer] means is something else, [namely] what has lately become known as the principle of "teleological dependence", ‹153› governing the causal *interest* of history. – Moreover, it is of course also incorrect to speak of that ascending movement from effect to cause as something that is peculiar to history. In this respect, the causal "explanation" of a concrete "natural event" proceeds in exactly the same manner. As we have seen, the view was expressed (p. 14) that what has come into being is regarded by us as completely "necessary", while only that which is conceived of as "coming into being" is regarded as a mere "possibility"; conversely, however, on pp. 40–41, special emphasis is put on the problematical character of inferring the cause from the effect, to such an extent that E[duard] M[eyer] would even prefer not to see the word "cause" being used in historical studies, and that the "investigation of motives" is (as we have already seen) discredited in his eyes.

One might try to resolve this last contradiction along the lines of E[duard] M[eyer]'s own thinking: the inference [from effect to cause] would only be problematical because our possibilities of acquiring knowledge are in principle limited; [the establishment] of the determinate character would remain an ideal demand. But that [solution] is also categorically rejected by E[duard] M[eyer] (p. 23), and this is followed (pp. 24ff.) by a discussion that once more raises considerable doubts. Eduard Meyer had originally, in the Introduction to his *History of Antiquity*, identified the relationship between "the General" and "the particular" with that between "freedom" and "necessity", and both of these with that between "the Individual" and "the totality"; in this way, he had arrived at the conclusion that "details" were governed by "freedom" and, therefore (as we have just seen), by "the Individual", while "laws" or "rules" governed the "broad outline" of the course of history. Formulated like that, this view, which is also prevalent among many "modern" historians, is totally wrong, and, on p. 25, [Meyer] expressly withdraws it, partly following Rickert, partly v. Below. The latter had taken particular exception to the idea of a "law-like development".[2] E[duard] M[eyer] had chosen the following example: We regard the development of Germany into a unified nation as a "law-like necessity"; on the other hand, the time and form of its unification as a Confederation with twenty-five members depended on the "individuality of the historically operative factors". To this, v. Below had made the following objection: "Could it not have happened differently?". E[duard] M[eyer] agrees unreservedly with this critical remark. However, no matter how one judges that formulation by E[duard] M[eyer] which v. Below objects to, I find it easy to see that, in any case, [v. Below's argument] proves too much and consequently proves nothing at all. For the same objection would also be justified in cases to which all of us, no doubt including v. Below and Eduard Meyer, would without hesitation apply the concept of "development according to laws". To take an example: It actually seems to us to be a "development according to laws" that a human being has developed or will develop from a human foetus – even though it can also here "happen

1   In that passage, he says, with an unfortunate choice of words: "Historical research proceeds by inferring the cause from the effect".
2   *Method*, p. 238.

differently" because of external "accidents" or inherited "pathological" traits. Therefore, the dispute with those scholars who espouse theories of "development" can only concern the correct way of understanding the logical meaning of the concept of "development" and of defining its limits: it is obviously impossible to do away with the concept altogether by means of arguments [such as v. Below's]. E[duard] M[eyer] himself offers the best example of [that impossibility], as he again, only two pages later (p. 27), in a footnote where the concept of the Middle Ages is described as a "definite (?) concept", completely conforms to the scheme set down in the Introduction [to *Antiquity*] (which he had [later] withdrawn); and in the [body of the] text, [Eduard Meyer] says that, in history, the word "necessary" only means that the "probability" (of a historical event occurring as a result of given conditions) "attains a very high degree, so that, more or less, *the whole development so to speak presses on towards an event*". He had hardly intended his remark concerning the unification of Germany to have *greater* implications than this. And, when he in this connection emphasizes that the event might, in spite of everything, *not* occur, we wish to recall that he had [also] emphasized the possibility that even astronomical calculations could be "disturbed" by stray celestial bodies. Indeed, in this respect, things are no different than in the case of *individual* natural events: In the explanation of what happens in nature – whenever we are dealing with concrete events – the judgement of necessity is also by no means the only or even the predominant form in which the category of causality manifests itself (to discuss this in more detail here would take us too far away from our main theme).[1] We are probably not mistaken in assuming that E[duard] M[eyer] has come to distrust the concept of "development" through his dispute with J. Wellhausen, ‹154› which was principally (but not exclusively) concerned with the following distinction: whether to interpret the "development" of Judaism as one mainly coming "from within" ("evolutionary" [interpretation]), or as being determined by certain concrete, fateful historical forces coming from the "outside", in particular the imposition of the "law" for political reasons (that is to say: reasons connected with Persian politics, not with the distinctive character of Judaism) by the Persian kings ("epigenetic" [interpretation]). ‹155› However that may be, the formulation used by Eduard Meyer on p. 46 is no improvement on that used in the Introduction [to *Antiquity*] . [On p. 46,] "the General" is presented as the "precondition" that "mainly" (?) has a "negative, or more precisely, a limiting effect"; [and this precondition] sets the "limits" "within which lie the infinite possibilities of individual historical formations", while the question as to which of these possibilities will become a "reality"[2] depends on the "higher (?), individual factors of historical life". Surely, [Eduard Meyer] here again hypostatizes the "General" – that is to say: *not* the "general milieu" (which is sometimes, by misinterpretation, confused with the "General") but (p. 46, top) "the [*general*] *rule*", i.e. an *abstract concept* – into an *effective force* [working] behind history, and [he] fails to appreciate the elementary fact (which he had clearly and strongly emphasized in other passages) that *only* the concrete, the Individual, can have reality.

Ed[uard] Meyer is by no means the only one to formulate the relationship between "the General" and "the particular" in this questionable way, nor is that formulation only to be found in [the works of] historians of his stamp. On the contrary: it is also, for instance, at the root of the popular idea – which is, however, shared by many "modern" historians (but *not* by E[duard] M[eyer] – that, in order for history, as a "science of individuality", to be pursued rationally, one must first determine the "correspondences" between human developments; what would

1 On this point, see my discussion in *Knies I*.
2 This formulation reminds one of certain lines of thought common within the Russian school of sociologists (Mihailovski, Karejev etc.); they are discussed by Th. Kistiakovski in an article (Kistiakovski, *School*), which we shall deal with later.

then remain as a "residue" would be the "peculiarities and indivisibilities" – the "finest flowers", as Breysig once put it. Compared to the naïve idea that the vocation of history is to become a "systematic science", this conception does of course represent an "advance" that is closer to the *practice* of history. But, on the other hand, it is in itself very naïve. For a beginner, it would be a both instructive and amusing exercise to try to understand the historical significance of "Bismarck" by subtracting everything that he had in common with everybody else and then keeping the "particular" [elements]. Provided, of course, that the material was ideally complete (a proviso that must always be made in discussions of logic), one of the "finest flowers" that one would keep would for instance be Bismarck's "thumbprint": that mark, discovered by the technicians of the criminal police, is the most specific indicator of "individuality", and its loss would therefore be almost irreplaceable for history. The indignant retort to this argument might be that, "naturally", only "spiritual" or "psychical" qualities and events could be taken into consideration as "historical"; but, *if* we had "exhaustive" knowledge of [Bismarck's] everyday existence, it would offer us an infinite number of manifestations of life that would simply *not* have occurred in that combination and constellation in the life of *anybody* else, but that would still be of no more interest than the thumbprint. If the further objection were then made that, "self-evidently", only the historically "*significant*" features of Bismarck's life are relevant for science, the answer of logic would have to be that the crucial logical problem lay in just [that word] ("self-evidently"), since what logic asks about is precisely this: *what* is the distinctive logical characteristic of the historically "significant" features.

If one tried to carry out in practice the above-mentioned procedure of subtraction, *one* insight that it would yield would be the following: [Always] assuming that the material was absolutely complete, that procedure could not be brought to a conclusion, even in the most distant future: after the subtraction of a completely infinite number of "common features", a further infinite number of components would still remain; and, after a complete eternity of assiduous subtraction from those components, one would still not have moved a single step closer to [answering] the question as to *which* of these specific features [contained] the real historical "essence". Another insight [that one would gain] would be the following: In order to carry out that subtraction procedure, an absolutely complete knowledge of the causal concatenation of events would be a *precondition*, in a sense in which no science on earth is able even to *strive for* it as an ideal goal. In actual fact, every "comparison" in the historical domain presupposes that an initial selection *has* already *been* made by relating [the components] to cultural "meanings", a selection that determines the goal and direction of the causal imputation, while eliminating a completely infinite number of both "general" and "individual" components. Then, the comparison of "analogous" events becomes relevant, as *one* of the instruments of that imputation, an instrument that I, too, regard as one of the most important ones, and one that has so far not been employed to anything like a sufficient extent. The logical meaning of that comparison will be treated later.

Eduard Meyer's comment at the bottom of p. 48 (which will be discussed later) shows that he, for his part, does not share the erroneous view that the Individual is *as such* already the object of history; concerning the importance of the General for history, he remarks that "rules" and "concepts" are only "means" for, "preconditions" of, historical work (p. 29, middle), and, as we shall see, this is on the whole correct from a logical point of view. But, as has been said, his formulation [on p. 46], which was criticized above, was logically questionable and has the same tendency as the erroneous view just referred to.

In spite of all these arguments, the professional historian will still be left with the impression that even those of E[duard] M[eyer]'s statements that have been criticized here contain a "kernel of truth" (to use a well-worn expression) . And when we are dealing with a historian of his stature discussing his own working methods, this is indeed almost self-evident. In actual fact, on a number of occasions he comes quite close to a logically correct formulation of whatever is correct in his statements. In particular, this is the case with [the passage at] the top of p. 27, where he says that "stages of development" are "*concepts*" that may "serve as guidelines for establishing and ordering the facts"; and it is especially true of the numerous passages where he makes use of the category of "possibility". However, the logical problem really begins here: [Eduard Meyer] should have taken up the question of *how* the historical material is structured by means of the concept of development, what is the logical meaning of the "category of possibility", and in what way [that category] can be used in the shaping of the historical interconnections. But E[duard] M[eyer] has refrained from doing this; and therefore, although his "feeling" about the role that "rules" governing events play in history has been correct, he has not, as I see it, been able to *formulate* [this view] in an adequate way. We shall attempt to do this in a separate section, II, of these studies. Here we shall, after these remarks – which were by necessity mainly negative in character – concerning E[duard] M[eyer]'s methodological formulations, turn to an examination of his discussion, particularly in the second (pp. 35–54) and third (pp. 54–56) part of his treatise, of the following problem: what is the "*object*" of history? – a question that was already touched on immediately above.

This question can, as E[duard] Meyer does, also be formulated as follows: "Which of the events that we have knowledge of are 'historical'?". His initial answer has a quite unspecific form: "The historical is that *which is or has been effective*". That is to say: the "historical" is that which, in a concrete, individual context, has *causal* importance. Leaving aside all the other questions that this statement gives rise to, we can begin by observing that E[duard] M[eyer], having arrived at this concept on p. 36, gives it up again already on p. 37.

It is clear to him that – as he puts it – "even when we limit ourselves to the effective, the number of individual events still remains infinite". He is therefore rightly asks: What guides the "selection which every historian makes among [these events]?" Answer: "the historical interest". After some remarks that we shall examine later, he adds that there is no "absolute norm" [governing] this interest. And he illustrates this statement in such a way that, as [we have] said, [he] again abandons his own [proposition, which] limited the "historical" to what is "effective". He takes as his point of departure Rickert's exemplification, according to which, "it is a 'historical' event that ... Frederick William IV refused the German Imperial crown; ‹156› but it is completely unimportant what tailors made his coats", and remarks (at the bottom of p. 37):

> From the point of view of political history, the tailor in question will of course probably always remain historically completely unimportant; but we can easily imagine that we could still take a historical interest in him, for instance in a history of fashion, or of tailoring, or of prices and the like.

That is certainly correct; but, on closer reflection, E[duard] M[eyer] could hardly fail to notice that, as far as its logical structure is concerned, the "interest" that we take in the first case differs significantly from that which we take in the other one[s]; [he would] also [realize] that, if one does not bear this difference in mind, one runs the risk of confusing two categories – "real cause" and "cause of knowledge" – whose differences are just as pronounced as the tendency to mix them up with each other. The example of the tailor is not entirely unambiguous; let us therefore make the distinction clear by way of another example, where the confusion [between the categories] is particularly pronounced.

In an article on "The Genesis of the State ... among the Tlinkit and Iroquois",[1] K[urt] Breysig has tried to show that certain processes that take place among those tribes, which he interprets as "the genesis of the state from the kinship constitution", are "important as representative of the species" – in other words: that they represent the "typical" form of state formation – and therefore, as he puts it, acquire "importance", even "world-*historical* importance".

The fact of the matter seems to be, however, that – provided, of course, that Br[eysig]'s constructions are correct – the actual genesis of these [American] Indian "states" and the way in which it occurred have to a quite extraordinary degree remained "unimportant" in the causal context of the development of world history. Not one single "important" fact [relevant to] the way in which the world developed later, politically or culturally, has been influenced by it – that is to say: can be traced back to it as a "cause". The way in which those states originated, and probably even their very existence, were "unimportant" for the shaping of the political and cultural situation of the United States as it is today; that is to say: no causal connection between the two can be demonstrated, while we can, for instance, still register the consequences of certain decisions taken by Themistocles – however much that [difference between the two cases] may annoy us, because it thwarts attempts to write history according to an impressively unitary evolutionary scheme. But, on the other hand, if Br[eysig] is right, the importance of the *results* of his analysis of the formation process of those states would in his own estimation be epoch-making for our *knowledge* of the way in which states *generally* originate. In fact, if Br[eysig] is correct in conceiving that process as "typical", and if this constitutes an "addition" to our knowledge, we would be in a position to construct certain concepts that could at least – and quite apart from their cognitive value for the concept formation of the theory of the state – be utilized as heuristic instruments for the causal interpretation of other historical processes. In other words: that process is of no importance as a historical "*real* cause", but his analysis is – in his opinion – of unusually great importance as a possible "cause of *knowledge*". On the other hand, knowledge of those decisions taken by Themistocles is of no importance for (for example) "psychology" or for any other conceptualizing science: we do not need the assistance of any "science of laws" to understand that a statesman in that situation "could" arrive at those decisions. And, while our *understanding* of that fact is a precondition of our knowledge of the concrete causal relationship, it does not in any way contribute to our *conceptual*–generic knowledge.

Let us take an example from the domain of "nature": Those concrete X-rays that Röntgen saw lighting up his screen ‹157› have left behind certain concrete effects which, according to the law of [conservation of] energy, must still be acting somewhere in the cosmos. But the "significance" of those concrete rays in Röntgen's laboratory is not due to [their] quality as a cosmic real cause. Like every experiment, what happened [in Röntgen's laboratory] is only relevant as a cause of *knowledge* [with respect to] certain "laws" governing the occurrence of events.[2] This is precisely the situation in the cases that Ed[uard] Meyer cites in a footnote to

---

1 Breysig, *Genesis*. Of course, I shall not go into the substantive qualities of this work at all: on the contrary, it is *assumed* here, as in all other similar examples, that *all* of Breysig's constructions are *correct*.

2 This is not to say that those concrete Röntgen rays could not also have a place as "historical" facts; [but that would be] in a history of physics. Among other things, such a history would after all *also* be interested in the "fortuitous" circumstances that, on that particular day, created the constellation which led to that lighting up and consequently – as we will suppose in this context – were the cause of the discovery of the "law" in question. Clearly, this [would] completely change the logical status of those concrete rays. This is possible because [those rays would] then play a role in a context that is rooted in *values* ("scientific progress"). One might think that this *logical* distinction is simply the result of having moved into [a different] *substantive* domain, that of the "sciences of the human spirit", since

the passage criticized here (p. 37n2). He reminds us that "[even] the most insignificant persons, whom we learn of by chance (in inscriptions or documents), become historically interesting *because we, through them, acquire knowledge of conditions in the past*". And the same confusion is even more apparent when – if my memory does not fail me – Breysig (in a passage which I cannot for the moment locate ‹158›) believes that he can get around the fact that the selection of historical material is oriented towards what is "significant" and individually "important", by recalling that many of the most important results of scientific investigations are based on "potsherds" and the like. Similar arguments are quite "popular" nowadays; and the[ir] affinity with the "coats" of Frederick William IV and the "insignificant persons" in the inscriptions referred to by E[duard] M[eyer] is quite evident – but so is the confusion that we are once again dealing with here. As has already been said: Breysig's "potsherds" and E[duard] M[eyer]'s "insignificant persons" are not – any more than the concrete X-rays in Röntgen's laboratory – inserted as *causal links* in the historical context; instead, certain of their distinctive features are *heuristic instruments* for uncovering certain historical facts, which then in their turn may become important either for "*concept* formation" (that is to say: again as heuristic instruments, for instance [as indications of] the generic "character" of certain artistic "periods") or for the causal interpretation of concrete historical interconnections. [There are, therefore,] from the point of view of logic, two different ways in which given facts of cultural reality[can be used][1] (1) in concept formation, the "individual fact" is used as an example, as a "typical" representative of an abstract *concept*, that is to say: as a *heuristic instrument*; (2) the "individual fact" is inserted as a link, and therefore as a "*real* cause", in an actual – that is to say: a concrete – *context*; in this connection, the products of the concept formation, too, are utilized, together with other elements: as heuristic instruments (on the one hand) and for descriptive purposes (on the other hand). This distinction coincides with the distinction between what Windelband calls the "nomothetic", and Rickert calls the "natural science", procedure (cf. (1)) and the logical aim of the "historical sciences of culture" (cf. (2)).It is also the only sense in which one can justifiably call history a science of *reality*. The only [proper] meaning of that expression is that individual, particular components of reality are relevant not only as a *heuristic instrument* but [also] purely and simply as the *object* of that knowledge; and that concrete causal relationships are relevant not as causes of *knowledge* but as *real* causes. Besides, we shall see later on how little truth there is in the naïve popular view of history as being "purely" the description of given realities, or the simple reproduction of "facts".[2]

the *cosmic* effects of those concrete rays have been left out of consideration. However, it is irrelevant whether the nature of the "evaluated" concrete object for which those rays had *causal* " importance" is "physical" or "psychical", as long as it is in itself "significant" for us – that is to say: that it is "evaluated". Once we assume that it is actually *possible* to acquire knowledge of [that object], the concrete (physical, chemical etc.) effects of those concrete rays *might* (theoretically) become a "historical fact", but only (and it seems very difficult to conceive of this whole construction) if the causal path originating in them would in the end lead to a concrete result that constituted a "historical individual", that is to say: which was "evaluated" by us as having *universal* significance by virtue of its *individual* distinctive character. As there seems to be no likelihood of *this* [*last condition*] being fulfilled, it would be absurd to attempt the [causal] demonstration, even if we were able to carry it out.

1   Here the author noted in the margin of the first edition: A step in the argument is lacking here! Add: that when a fact becomes relevant as a specimen of a generic concept, it is a heuristic *instrument*. But not every such instrument is a generic specimen. [Note by Marianne Weber.]

2   In the sense in which it has just been used here, however, the expression "science of reality" does correspond completely to the logical nature of history. Rickert and Simmel have already dealt sufficiently firmly with the mistaken view reflected in the popular interpretation of that expression as indicating a pure "description" without preconceptions.

With respect to Rickert's "tailors", criticized by E[duard] M[eyer], the situation is the same as with the potsherds and with the "unimportant personalities" who have come down to us in those inscriptions. From the point of view of cultural *history*, the fact that certain tailors have supplied certain coats to the king is presumably of very little causal importance, even for the causal connection between the development of "fashion" and the "tailoring trade"; it would only have had such causal importance if that particular concrete supply had had historical *effects* – in other words: if, say, the personality of those tailors or the fortunes of *their* business in particular would, from some perspective, have been of causal "importance" for changes in fashion or in the organization of trade and industry, and if the supply of precisely those coats had contributed causally to that historical state of affairs. – But as an aid to *acquiring knowledge* about fashions etc., the style of Frederick William IV's coats and the fact that they came from certain (for instance Berlin) workshops *can* certainly become just as "significant" as any other source material available to us concerning fashions at that time. But, in that case, the king's coats are relevant as *specimen[s]* of a still to be constructed *generic* concept, as a *heuristic instrument*; on the other hand, the refusal of the Imperial crown – which [the example of the coats] was compared to – is relevant as a concrete *component* of a historical *context*, as a real *effect* and *cause* within certain real series of changes. From the point of view of *logic*, those distinctions are fundamental and will forever remain so. In practice, it may certainly happen to scholars in the field of culture that those two totally differing points of view become intertwined in many different ways – something that is the source of the most interesting method[olog]ical problems; but nobody will be able to understand the logical nature of "history" unless he is able to distinguish carefully between those [two viewpoints].

Now, concerning the relationship between those two logically different categories of "historical importance", Eduard Meyer has put forward two mutually incompatible views. On the one hand (as we have seen), he confuses "historical interest" in what is historically "effective" – that is to say: the real causal links of historical interconnections (refusal of the Imperial crown) – with those facts (coats of Frederick William IV, inscriptions etc.) that may be of importance to the historian as heuristic instruments. But, on the other hand – and this is what we shall now discuss – he stresses the difference between the "historically effective" and all other objects that we have or might acquire knowledge of, to such an extent that he is led to make [certain] claims concerning the limits of the historian's scientific "interest"; [however,] the implementation of [these claims] in his own excellent writings would be viewed as deeply regrettable by all those who admire them. What he says is the following (p. 48, bottom):

> For a long time, I believed that the selection [of material] that the historian has to carry out is governed by the criterion of what is *characteristic* (that is to say: the specifically singular [element] that distinguishes an institution or an individuality from all other analogous ones). That is indeed undeniably true; but it only becomes relevant for history insofar as we can only ascertain the distinctive qualities of a culture through its characteristic features; therefore, [for history] it is *never more than a means* which allows us to understand how [that culture] is historically *effective*.

As all the previous considerations have shown, this is entirely correct, as are the conclusions drawn [by Meyer]: The popular way of formulating the question of the "significance" of the Individual and of personalities for history is misleading; it is by no means "personality" in its totality that "enters into" the historical context, as constructed by [the historian], but only those of its manifestations that are causally relevant; the historical importance of a concrete personality as a causal factor has nothing to do with the general "human" significance that it possesses by virtue of its "intrinsic value"; and it may precisely be the "shortcomings" of a personality occupying a crucial position that turn out to be causally important. All this is completely true. Nevertheless, the question still remains whether – or let us rather say at once: *in what sense* – it is correct that, from the standpoint of history, the analysis of cultural phenomena *only* serves the purpose of rendering the cultural processes in question intelligible *as efficient factors*. The logical implications of this question immediately become apparent when we examine the conclusions that E[duard] M[eyer] draws from his thesis. The first of these (p. 47) is that "existing situations in themselves are never the objects of history; they only become [such objects] insofar as they have historical effects". In a *historical* account (and this includes [accounts] dealing with the *history* of literature or art), it is neither possible nor appropriate to make an "all-round" analysis of a work of art or a literary product, constitutional arrangements, manners and customs etc. The reason for this is[, according to Meyer,] that [such an analysis] would always have to include elements which had not "attained any historical effects" – while, on the other hand, the historian would, because of their causal importance, have to include in his account many "details which seem to have a subordinate status within a system" (of constitutional law, for instance). In particular, he therefore also concludes (p.55) from his aforementioned principle of selection that *biography* is a "philological", not a historical, discipline. Why? "Its object is the relevant personality as such, *in its totality*, not as a factor with historical *effects*; in this connection, the fact that [the personality in question] has had such effects is only a precondition: the reason why it is made the subject of a biography" (p. 56). As long as the biography is just a biography and not a history of the times of its hero, it cannot successfully fulfil the task of history, which is to give an account of a historical event. Faced with this, one [may] ask: Why should "personalities" be given this special status? Do "events", for instance the battle of Marathon or the Persian Wars, ‹159› "belong" at all in a historical account in their "totality", that is to say after the fashion of Homer's descriptions, including all the *specimina fortitudinis* ‹160› ? It is obvious that, in those cases as well, only those events and conditions that are of importance for the historical causal interconnections ["belong" in the account]. Ever since the heroic myths and history parted ways, this has been the situation, at least in logical principle. – And how do matters stand in that respect [when we consider] "biograph[ies]"? It it evidently false (or at least a rhetorical hyperbole) that simply "*every* detail . . . of the external and inner life of its hero" belongs in a biography, however much the Goethe "philology" (which E[duard] M[eyer] is perhaps thinking of) might give that impression. But, in this latter case, we are dealing with collections of material that have the aim of preserving everything that might *possibly* become significant for Goethe's life history, either as a direct link in a causal sequence – that is to say: as a historically relevant "fact" – or as a heuristic instrument for uncovering historically relevant facts – as "source material". But, in a scholarly biography of Goethe, obviously only those facts that are "*significant*" can properly enter into the account.

However, here we are faced with an ambiguity in the logical meaning of the word ["significant"] that needs analysis. As we shall see, this ambiguity constitutes the "kernel of truth" in E[duard] M[eyer]'s view[s]; but, at the same time, it allows us to throw light on the inadequate *formulation* of his theory of the "historically effective" as the object of history.

In order to illustrate the different logical viewpoints from which the "facts" of cultural life can become scientifically relevant, let us take an example: Goethe's letters to Frau v. Stein. ‹161› One aspect of these letters at least – let us clear this up in advance – is not "historically" relevant: the actual perceivable "fact" constituted by the written paper. That is only a heuristic instrument for uncovering another "fact": that Goethe had the sentiments expressed in [those letters], that he wrote them down and sent them to Frau v. Stein, and that he received replies from her whose approximate meaning can be inferred from the correctly interpreted "content" of Goethe's letters. This "fact", which must be established by an "interpretation" – possibly with the aids of "science" – of the "meaning" of the letters, is actually what we have in mind [when we speak of] those "letters". First of all, that "fact" might (1) be inserted directly, as such, into a historical causal context: for instance, [Goethe's] ascetic restraint during those years, which was coupled with an incredibly strong passion, of course left profound traces in his development, traces that were not obliterated even when his personality changed under the Mediterranean skies. ‹162› One of the undoubted tasks of the history of literature is to look into those effects in Goethe's literary "personality", to look for traces of them in his creative work, and to give a causal "interpretation" of them, to the extent possible, by showing how they are related to his experiences during those years. In that connection, the facts of which those letters are evidence are "historical" facts – which (as we have seen) means that they are real links in a chain of causation. Now let us assume (naturally, the question of the probability of this assumption, and of all those that we shall make further on, is completely irrelevant here) that it might somehow be possible to demonstrate positively that those experiences had had *no influence whatsoever* on Goethe's personal and literary development – that is to say: that *not a single one* of those of his manifestations of life that "*interest*" us had been influenced by [those experiences]. In that case, (2) those experiences might nevertheless claim our attention as *heuristic instruments*. To begin with, they might represent something that was – as it is usually termed – "characteristic" of Goethe's distinctive historical qualities. This would mean that those experiences might perhaps (no matter whether this was actually possible) allow us to gain insights into a conduct of life and an outlook on life that were peculiar to Goethe throughout his whole life, or at least for a considerable length of time, and that had a decisive influence on those of his personal or literary manifestations of life which interest us historically. The "historical" *fact* inserted as a real link into the causal context of his "life" would then be [constituted by] precisely that "outlook on life" – a collective–conceptual complex of Goethe's personal "qualities" – either inherited or acquired through [his] education, the milieu and the fortunes of his life, as well as (perhaps) deliberately acquired "maxims", in accordance with which he lived and which partly determined his conduct and his creations. In this case, the experiences with Frau v. Stein would still be actual *component parts* of a historical situation (as the "outlook on life" is a collective concept that is "expressed" in the *individual* events of [that] life); but they would obviously not – under the assumptions made above – to any major extent engage our interest from that point of view, but would instead do so as "symptoms" of that outlook on life, that is to say: as heuristic *instruments*; in other words, their logical relationship to the object of our knowledge has shifted. – Now, let us further assume that [the suppositions under (2)] do not hold either, and that [those experiences] contained nothing that was in any respect characteristic of Goethe in contradistinction to [any of] his contemporaries, but just corresponded completely to a "typical" conduct of life in certain German social circles in those days. In that case, [those experiences] would tell us nothing new that was relevant to the historical knowledge of Goethe. However, they might (3) perhaps engage our interest as a conveniently applicable *paradigm* of that "type", that is to say: as a heuristic *instrument* [for grasping] the "characteristic" distinctive qualities of the habits of mind of those circles. The distinctive character of those (according to our assumptions) "typical" habits of mind of those circles during that period, and the conduct of life that was the form of expression of [those habits of mind] would then, contrasted with the conduct of life in other periods, nations and social strata – be the "historical" fact inserted into a cultural–historical causal context as a real, actual cause and effect. It could then historically be subjected to a causal "interpretation" – with respect to, say, its difference from the Italian Cicisbeo ‹163› or similar institutions – in a "history of German manners and customs" or, to the extent that no such national diversities existed, in a general history of the manners and customs of that age. – Let us now further assume that the content of the letters could not be exploited even for that purpose, but that it could be demonstrated that phenomena which were, in certain "crucial" respects, *similar* would as a rule be present under certain cultural conditions; in other words, that what those experiences [of Goethe's] would reveal in *these* respects would not be any *distinctive trait* of German culture or that of eighteenth-century [Italy], ‹164› but instead phenomena that would – under certain conditions to be defined in precise concepts – be common to all cultures. In that event, (4) it would be the task of some "cultural psychology" or "social psychology" to determine – by means of analysis, isolating abstraction and generalization – the conditions under which *those* elements usually occurred, to "interpret" the reason for the[se] regular occurrence[s] and to formulate the "rule" that can be inferred from this in a genetic, *generic* concept. Those elements of Goethe's experiences, which are in every respect generic, but highly irrelevant for his individual, distinctive character, would then, to that extent, only be of interest because they contribute to the formation of that generic concept. – And finally, (5) the possibility cannot a priori be excluded that those "experiences" did not contain anything that was characteristic of any social stratum or any cultural epoch. But, even in [this] case, where all the [previously discussed] sources of "cultural–scientific" interest are lacking, it is conceivable (again, no matter whether it is actually the case) that, for instance, a psychiatrist interested in the psychology of the erotic would discuss [those experiences] from all sorts of "useful" points of view, as an "ideal-typical" example of certain ascetic "aberrations", just as, for instance, Rousseau's *Confessions* ‹165› are of interest to the specialist in nervous diseases. Naturally, in this connection, we also have to take into account that the letters may probably be relevant for all the purposes of inquiry [discussed above] – which of course by no means exhaust the "possibilities" – but [in such a way that] *different* parts of the contents of those letters [are relevant for different purposes]; conversely, the *same* parts [of the contents of the letters] may be relevant for *different* [purposes of inquiry].[1]

If we survey this discussion, we have so far seen that those letters to Frau v. Stein – that is to say: those observations and experiences of Goethe's that may be found in them – have become "significant" in the following ways (going backwards from the last to the first case): (a) in the two last cases (Nos (4) and (5)), as specimens of a genus and consequently as heuristic *instruments* [for grasping] the *general* nature [of that genus]; (b) as a *characteristic* component of a collective [phenomenon] and consequently as a heuristic *instrument* [for grasping] its *individual* distinctive character (Nos (2) and (3));[2] (c) as a causal component of a historical situation (No. (1)). In the cases (4) and (5) under (a), there is a "significance" for *history* only insofar as the generic concept constructed with the aid of that individual specimen may possibly – as we shall see later – become important for checking historical demonstrations. On the other hand, when E[duard] M[eyer] limits the "historical" to what is "effective" – that is to say: to No. (1), (c), in the list above – surely this cannot possibly be intended to mean that the consideration of the *second* category of "significant" cases, (b), lies beyond the purview of history. In other words,

1 Naturally, this would not in any way prove that it is wrong for *logicians* to make strict distinctions between the different points of view (which may even be found within one and the same scientific account) – [a claim] on which many wrong-headed objections to Rickert are based.
2 In a later section, we shall concern ourselves with *this* special case in more detail. Therefore, at this stage we deliberately abstain from discussing whether it should be regarded as having a distinctive logical character. At this point, it should simply be made clear, in order to leave as little uncertainty as possible, that this case of course does not in any way blur the clear logical distinction between the historical and the nomothetic handling of "facts". This is because, in this case, the *concrete* fact is at least *not* "historical" in the sense in which that term is used here, that is to say: as a link in a concrete causal sequence.

that history – if not (as in case no. (2)) a "history of Goethe", at least (as in case no. (3)) a "history of the manners and customs" of the eighteenth century – should once and for all ignore facts that are not in themselves components of historical chains of causation, but only serve to *disclose* the facts that are to be inserted into such chains of causation – for instance, parts of Goethe's correspondence that "illustrate" (that is to say: bring us to *recognize*) those distinctive qualities of Goethe's that were decisive for his literary production, or those aspects of the social culture of [Italy] in the eighteenth century that were important for the way in which manners and customs developed. Indeed, [Eduard Meyer] must in his own work constantly make use of such heuristic instruments. Consequently, what must be meant is that [these elements] are precisely "heuristic instruments" and not "components of the historical situation"; but even "biographies" or "classical studies" do not use such "characteristic" details in any other way. Evidently, this is not the stumbling block for Eduard Meyer.

But now, a further kind of "significance" rises above *all* of those analysed so far: Those experiences of Goethe's (if we keep to that example) are not only "significant" to us as "cause[s]" and as "heuristic instruments", but – whether or not we discover in them something new and hitherto unknown concerning Goethe's outlook on life, the culture of the eighteenth century, the "typical" course of cultural events etc; and whether or not they have had any *causal* influence on his development – the content of those letters, as it is and regardless of any extraneous "significances" that they do not in themselves contain, is for us, in its distinctive character, an object of *evaluation*, and would be so even if nothing at all were otherwise known about their author. Two things are of special interest to us in this connection: first, the fact that this "evaluation" relates to the distinctive character of the object, to what is incomparable and unique, and irreplaceable from a literary point of view, in it; and, second, that this valuation of the object with its distinctive individual character causes us to *reflect* on the object and to submit it to an intellectual – at this point, we shall deliberately avoid saying: a "scientific" – treatment: to *interpretation*. This "interpretation" can take two different courses, which are in practice almost invariably merged together, but which must, from a logical point of view, be kept strictly separate. To begin with, [the "interpretation"] can and will be a "*value interpretation*". That is to say: it teaches us to "understand" the "spiritual" content of that correspondence – in other words, [it] brings into the open that which we have [only] "felt" dimly and vaguely and raises it to the level of clear and articulate "evaluation". For this purpose, it is in no way compelled to formulate or to "suggest" a *value judgement* of its own. Instead, what it actually "suggests" in the course of its analysis are *possible* value *relations* of the object. Moreover, it is certainly not the case that the "stand" with respect to the evaluated object that it calls forth within us must necessarily be a positive one. If we just look at Goethe's relationship to Frau v. Stein, for instance, both the usual modern sexual philistine and, say, a Catholic moralist would, if they showed "understanding" of it at all, essentially disapprove of it. And if we successively consider Karl Marx's *Das Kapital*, or *Faust*, or the ceiling of the Sistine Chapel, or Rousseau's *Confessions*, or the experiences of Saint Teresa, or Madame Roland, or Tolstoy, or Rabelais, or Marie Bashkirtseff, or the Sermon on the Mount ‹166› as objects of interpretation, then we are confronted with an infinite multitude of "evaluative" positions; and *if* the "interpretation[s]" of those objects, whose values are extremely varied, are deemed to be "worthwhile" and are [therefore] undertaken – something that we will assume for our purposes – they will only have the following *formal* element in common: that they are *meant to* uncover the *possible* "standpoints" and "points of application" of the "valuation". It is only when *norms* have to be taken into consideration that [the value interpretation] is able to impose a particular valuation on us as being the only permissible one from the point of view of "science"; this is, for instance, the case with the ideas contained in Marx's *Das Kapital*, where the norms [to be considered] are those of thought. But even in that case, the purpose of an "interpretation" does not necessarily include an objectively valid "valuation" of the object (here: the logical "correctness" of Marxian forms of reasoning); and [such an "objective" evaluation] would completely go beyond the domain of "interpretation" whenever we are dealing not with "norms" but with "cultural values". It is neither logically nor substantively absurd – and that is all that matters in this connection – for a person to view all the products of the poetic and artistic culture of Antiquity or, say, the religious tone of the Sermon on the Mount, as being "without validity" for him, and therefore to reject them; and this may just as well be the case with our example: the letters to Frau v. Stein, where glowing passion on the one hand and ascetic restraint on the other are mixed with all those flowers of emotional life that we find so superlatively fine. But that in itself does not in any way make the "interpretation" "worthless" for that person: it can nevertheless, and even for that very reason, provide him with "knowledge" in the sense that it – to use a common term – expands his own inner "life" and his "mental horizon", and enables him to appreciate and to reflect on possibilities and nuances of lifestyle in themselves, to develop and diversify his own self both intellectually, aesthetically and ethically (in the widest sense of that term), and (so to say) to make his "psyche" more "value-sensitive". Here, the "interpretation" of spiritual, aesthetic or ethical creation[s] in fact has the same effect as these creations by themselves. *This* is the "kernel of truth" in the assertion that "history" is in a certain sense an "art", no less than in the designation of the "sciences of the human spirit" as being "subjectivizing"; but at the same time, this [interpretation] represents the outermost limit of what can still be termed "intellectual treatment of empirical [material]", and it goes beyond "historical work" in the logical sense of the term.

It seems clear that when E[duard] M[eyer] (p. 54) speaks of the "philological consideration of the past", what he refers to is *this* kind of interpretation, which takes as its point of departure those relations of "historical" objects that are by their very nature *timeless* – in other words: their *valuational* status – and shows us how to understand [those relations]. This is reflected in his definition of this kind of scientific activity (p. 55), which, according to him, "transfers the products of history to the present . . . and therefore treats them as static"; which treats its object "not as coming into being and as historically effective, but as existent" and, therefore, contrary to history, [treats it] "from all sides"; and which aims at an "exhaustive interpretation of the individual creations", first of all in the fields of literature and art, but, as E[duard] M[eyer] explicitly adds, also those of state and religious institutions, of manners and customs, of attitudes "and *ultimately of the whole culture* of an epoch treated as a unity". Naturally, this kind of "interpretation" is not "philological" in the sense of a specialized linguistic discipline. However often the interpretation of the linguistic "meaning" of a literary object may in fact, and with good reason, proceed hand in hand with the "interpretation" of its "spiritual and intellectual content" – its "meaning" (in this value-oriented sense of the term) – they are nevertheless fundamentally different procedures from the logical point of view. The first one, the linguistic "interpretation", is elementary (not from the point of view of the value and intensity of the intellectual effort that it requires, but from the point of view of logic) as a prerequisite for all kinds of scientific treatment and utilization of the "source material"; from the point of view of history, it is a technical instrument for verifying "facts", a tool of history, as well as of numerous other disciplines. [The second one,] the "interpretation" in the sense of "value analysis" – which is how we shall, ad hoc, designate the procedure described immediately above[1] – at any rate

---

1   We do this essentially in order to distinguish *this* kind of "interpretation" from the *purely* linguistic one. The fact that this distinction is regularly not made in *practice* should not prevent it from being made in *logic*.

does not have *that* relationship to history. And since the aim of this kind of "interpretation" is neither to uncover facts that are "causally" relevant in a historical context, nor to abstract "typical" components that can be utilized in the formation of generic concepts; since on the contrary, [this "interpretation"] instead considers its objects – that is to say (if we keep to E[duard] M[eyer]'s example), the "whole culture" of, for instance, Hellenic [civilization] at its apogee, conceived as a unity – "for their own sake" and enables us to appreciate them in their value relations, [for all these reasons, the "value analysis"] cannot be subsumed under any of the other categories of knowledge, whose direct or indirect relations to the "historical" were discussed there. Nor can it really, in particular – [contrary to] what E[duard] M[eyer] thinks (p. 54, bottom) – be considered an "auxiliary science" for history, as its approach to its objects is indeed quite different from that of history. The difference between the two approaches would, of course, be of very little consequence if all that it amounted to was that one (the "value analysis") considered its objects as "static", while the other (history) considered them "developmentally", the one working with cross-sections of what had occurred, the other with longitudinal sections: The historian – for instance Ed[uard] Meyer in his own works – must also, to take up the thread [of his account], begin with certain "given" elements, described as being "in a [certain] state", which he takes as his points of departure; and as his account progresses, he will constantly pause to sum up the "results" of the "development" in [the form of] cross-sectional "states". A monographic account of, say, the social composition of the Athenian Ekklesia ‹167› at a particular time, for the purpose of clarifying, on the one hand, how it had been causally determined and, on the other hand, how it had influenced the political "situation" of Athens, would no doubt be regarded, even by E[duard] M[eyer], as a "historical" piece of work. Instead, for E[duard] M[eyer], the distinction would be the following: "Philological" ("value-analytical") work will possibly – and no doubt normally – take into consideration those facts that are *also* relevant for history, but will perhaps in addition consider *facts quite different* from those considered by history – in other words: [facts that are] (1) *neither* themselves links in a historical chain of causation, (2) *nor* utilized as heuristic instruments for uncovering facts of the first category, so that their relationship to "the historical" is not covered by any of those considered so far. But what other relationship [to "history"] do they have, then? Or does this "value-analytical" approach have no relation at all to any kind of historical knowledge? – In order to get ahead with our discussion, let us go back to our example of the letters to Frau v. Stein, and let us add, as a second example, Karl Marx's *Das Kapital*. Obviously, both objects can be submitted to "interpretation", not only the "linguistic" one – which we have decided to leave aside in this context – but also the "value-analytical" one, which gives us an "appreciation" of the value relations [of those objects]. In other words, it analyses the letters to Frau v. Stein and interprets them "psychologically" in the same way that one interprets, for instance, *Faust*; and it examines Marx's *Das Kapital* with respect to the *ideas* that it contains, and gives an account of it in its *intellectual* – not: historical – relationship to other systems of thought *dealing with the same problems*. To this end, the "value analysis" initially treats its objects as "static" (to use Ed[uard] Meyer's terminology); that is to say, more correctly put: it is based on the quality [of these objects] as "values", independent of every purely historical–*causal* importance, which are therefore in that respect, from our point of view, situated beyond [the limits of] the "historical". – But is that all that [the value analysis] does? Surely not; [and this is true of] the interpretation of those letters of Goethe's, of *Das Kapital*, or of *Faust*, or of the *Oresteia*, ‹168› or of the paintings on the ceiling of the Sistine Chapel. Simply in order to attain its own goal completely, [the value interpretation] has to take into consideration that [its] ideal value object was historically determined; and that a great many nuances and variations of thought and feeling remain "incomprehensible" if the general conditions – for instance, the social "milieu" and the quite concrete events [that occurred] on the days when those letters of Goethe's were written – are not known, or if the historically given "problem situation" at the time when Marx wrote his book and his development as a thinker are not discussed. Therefore, if the "interpretation"[of Goethe's letters] is to be successful, it requires a *historical* investigation into the conditions under which those letters came into existence, an examination of all the most minute, as well as the most comprehensive, relationships, both in Goethe's purely personal and "domestic" life and in the cultural life of the total "environment" (in the widest sense of the term) of those days, [to the extent that they] had *causal* importance – were "effective", in Ed[uard] Meyer's sense – for the distinctive character of [those letters]. The knowledge of all those causal determinants gives us an insight into those constellations of [Goethe's] mind against the background of which they were composed and thus teaches us truly to "understand" the letters themselves.[1] On the other hand, it is of course true that causal "explanation", taken by itself and carried out in Düntzer's fashion, ‹169› here, as always, only holds "the pieces in its hand". ‹170› And of course, that kind of "interpretation", which we have here called "value analysis", functions as a guide for the other, "historical" – that is to say: causal – "interpretation". The [value] analysis pointed to the "evaluated" components of the object, while the problem of the "historical" interpretation is the causal "explanation" of those components; the [value analysis] created the starting points from which the causal regression proceeds and thus provided it with the decisive "viewpoints" without which it would indeed

---

1 Without wishing to, Voßler, too, provides confirmation of this in his analysis of a la Fontaine fable in his essay *Language*, pp. 84–85, which is as brilliantly written as it is intentionally one-sided. Like B[enedetto] Croce, whose position is close to his own, he sees it as the only "legitimate" task of "aesthetic" interpretation to demonstrate that, and to what extent, the literary "creation" is an adequate "expression". However, he himself must also have recourse to references to quite concrete "psychical" characteristics of La Fontaine (p. 93) and, even beyond that, to the "milieu" and to "race" (p. 94); and it is difficult to see why this causal imputation, the investigation of how [the creation] came into being, which *always also* makes use of generalizing concepts (see below) should break off precisely at the point that it does in Voßler's most engaging and instructive sketch, and why its continuation would be worthless for the "interpretation". When Voßler withdraws those concessions [to causality] by saying (p. 95) that only the "material" is conditioned in "time" and "space", but that the "form" – which is all that matters from the aesthetic point of view – is a "free creation of the spirit", it should be borne in mind that he is here employing a terminology similar to that of Croce. Accordingly, "freedom" is here equivalent to "conformity to a norm"; and "form" is *true* expression (in Croce's sense), and as such identical to aesthetic *value*. However, this terminology is problematical in that it leads to a conflation of "being" and "norm". – Voßler's sparkling essay has the great merit of reaffirming the following points, in opposition to the strictly glossological and positivist linguists: (1) In addition to the physiology and psychology of language, to "historical" studies and investigations into "phonetic laws", science has the completely independent task of interpreting the "*values*" and "norms" of literary products; (2) moreover, one's own *understanding* and "immediate experience" of those "values" and norms is also an indispensable prerequisite for the *causal* interpretation of the process and conditioning of spiritual and intellectual creation, as the creator of the literary product or the linguistic expression "experiences" it himself. But it should be noted that, in this last case, where [the "values" and "norms"] are not *standards* of value, but *means* of acquiring *causal* knowledge, they are, from the point of view of *logic*, relevant not as "norms", but rather, purely factually, as the "possible" empirical content of a "psychical" *event* – no different, "*in principle*", from the delusions of a paralytic. In my opinion, [Voßler's] and Croce's terminology, which constantly tends towards a logical conflation of "evaluation" and "explanation" and to negate the independence of the latter, weakens the persuasive force of the argumentation. Those tasks remain, as purely empirical – and indeed as substantively and logically quite independent – work *in addition to* those tasks which Voßler calls "aesthetics". That this causal analysis is nowadays described as " national psychology" or indeed as "psychology" at all is due to a fashionable terminology; but in the last resort, this does not alter the fact that this kind of treatment, too, is justified in substance.

have had to steer its course in boundless [waters] without a compass. One may of course say –
and many will do so – that, for their part, they see no need for putting the whole apparatus of
historical analysis into operation to provide a historical "explanation" of a series of "love letters",
however sublime. Certainly – but, however disrespectful this may seem, the same is true of
Karl Marx's *Das Kapital*, and generally of *all* objects of historical research. One may find it
utterly stale and tedious, or at least a very secondary – and indeed, if it is carried out for its
own sake, completely pointless – task, to find out what were the building blocks out of which
Marx created his work and how the genesis of his ideas was determined historically; and the
same [may be true of] any historical knowledge concerning the political constellation of power
today, or the evolution of the German political system, with its distinctive character. Nevertheless,
[that point of view] could not be "proved wrong", either by logic or by empirical experience
– as E[duard] M[eyer] has admitted expressly, if somewhat briefly.

For our purposes, it is worthwhile to dwell a little longer on the *logical* nature of that "value
analysis". H[einrich] Rickert's very clearly developed thesis according to which the construction
of the "historical individual" is determined by "value relation" has in all seriousness been
interpreted as if this "value relation" were identical with subsuming [the historical individual]
under general *concepts*; and attempts have been made to refute the thesis on those grounds.[1]
After all, [(the argument runs),] the "values" in question are "state", "religion", "art" etc.,
together with similar concepts; and the fact that history "relates" its objects to [these "values"]
and thereby obtains specific "viewpoints" is therefore (it is added) just like the separate treatment
of the "chemical", "physical" etc. "aspect[s]" of phenomena in the natural sciences.[2] This
is a strange misconception of the meaning – the only possible meaning – of "value relation".
Surely, an actual "value judgement" of a concrete object or the theoretical formulation of the
"possible" value relations of that object does not imply that I subsume the object under a
particular generic concept such as "love letter", "political structure" [or] "economic
phenomenon": A "value judgement" means that I "take a stand" in a particular concrete way
concerning [an object] in its concrete distinctive character; and as for the subjective sources of
the "stand" that I take – that is to say: *my* "valuational viewpoints" that determine it – surely
they are not a "concept", let alone an "abstract concept", but rather a thoroughly concrete
"feeling" and "willing" that are highly individual in their character and composition, or possibly
the awareness of a definite "Ought", which is also of a concrete nature. And, when I then pass
from the stage of an actual evaluation of the objects to that of a theoretical and interpretive
consideration of the *possible* value relations – in other words: [when I] construct "historical
individuals" from the objects – this means that I make myself and others explicitly aware, by
means of *interpretation*, of the concrete, individual and therefore, in the final analysis, *unique*
form in which (if we start by putting this metaphysically) "ideas" have been "embodied" or
are "realized" in the relevant political structure (for instance, the "State of Frederick the Great"),
the relevant personality (for instance, Goethe or Bismarck) or the relevant literary product
(Marx's *Das Kapital*). Or when formulated without making use of the metaphysical mode of
expression, which is always problematical and can, moreover, be dispensed with: that I elaborate,
in explicit form, the focal points of *possible* "evaluative" stands that the relevant section of reality
exhibits and that constitute the basis for the claim by that section of reality to a more or
less universal "*significance*" (which must be strictly distinguished from a *causal* "significance").

1   For instance by B[ernhard] Schmeidler (*Concept Formation*).
2   I am astonished to see that this is also the view of Franz Eulenburg (*Society* – in our connection
    especially p. 525). In my opinion, his polemic against Rickert "and his camp" (?) is only possible
    because he *leaves out* of consideration that very object – i.e. "history" – whose logical analysis is at
    issue.

Karl Marx's *Das Kapital* shares its status as a "literary product" with all of the combination[s] of printer's ink and paper listed weekly in the Brockhaus Register. ‹171› What makes it into a "historical" individual for us, however, is not the fact that it belongs to that category but, on the contrary, the quite unique "intellectual content" that "we" find "embedded" in it. In the same way, the armchair politics indulged in by ignorant bigots over their sundowners is a "political" event just as much as that complex of printed and written paper, sound waves, bodily movements on drill grounds [and] clever – or foolish – ideas in the minds of princes, diplomats, etc. that "we" synthetize as the individual mental image of the "German Reich", because "we" take a certain "historical interest" in it, which is quite unique for "us" and rooted in countless "values" (and not just "political" ones). It is patently absurd to believe that this "significance" – the possible value relations that the object (*Faust*, for instance) "contains", or, to put it differently, the "*content*" of our interest in the historical individual – can be expressed in a generic concept: What characteristizes the historical individual of the "highest" order is precisely that it "contains" an inexhaustible number of possible focal points for our interest. We classify certain "important" orientations of the historical value relation, and the division of labour of the cultural sciences is then made on the basis of this classification;[1] but this of course in no way alters the fact that identifying a "value" of "general" (= universal) *significance* with a "general" (= comprehensive generic) *concept* is just as strange as the idea that one can express "the truth" in *one single* sentence, or realize "the moral" by *one single* action, or embody "the beautiful" in *one single* work of art. – Let us return to Eduard Meyer and his attempts to deal with the problem of historical "significance". In fact, the preceding discussion left the methodological domain and touched on that of the philosophy of history. From the strictly method[olog]ical point of view, the only possible way of explaining the circumstance that certain *individual* components of reality are selected as objects of historical treatment is by reference to [the] *fact* that a corresponding *interest* exists. Indeed, from that point of view, which is not concerned with the question of the *meaning* of that interest, "value relation" can mean no more than that; consequently, E[duard] M[eyer], too, lets the matter rest there by saying (and justifiably so, viewed under that aspect) that history can content itself with the fact that this interest exists, however slight it might be assumed to be (p. 38). But the lack [in that statement] of the dimension of a philosophy of history does have results that quite clearly manifest themselves in certain vague and contradictory elements in his exposition.

"The" (historical) "selection is based on the historical *interest* [taken by people] *today* in some effect [which is] the result of [a] development, so that they feel the need to trace what has caused [this effect or result] to come about"; so Meyer says (p. 37), and later (p. 45) interprets this in the following fashion: the historian finds "*within himself* the problems with which he approaches the material" and which then "provide him with the guiding principle according to which he orders the events". That is completely consistent with what was said [above]. Moreover, it is the only possible sense in which the previously criticized statement by E[duard] M[eyer] concerning the "ascending movement from effect to cause" is correct. In that connection, what we are dealing with is not – as he assumes – a way of handling the concept of causality that is peculiar to history; instead, the fact of the matter is that the only "historically

1   If I investigate the social–economic *determinants* of a concrete "characteristic form" of Christianity or, say, of the Provencal poetry of chivalry, ‹172› of course that does not mean that I turn [these "determined" objects] into phenomena that are "evaluated" because of their economic *significance*. Naturally, it is of no logical importance in this context, either, how a particular scholar, or a particular "discipline" which is traditionally regarded as separate, delimit their "field": the way in which that is done has its roots in purely technical considerations related to the division of labour.

significant and important" "causes" are those that the causal regression from an "evaluated" cultural element must incorporate as indispensable components: the principle of "teleological dependence", as this has been called (an expression that is admittedly misleading). Then the question arises: must this point of departure of the [causal] regression always be located in the *present*? The first of the quotations from E[duard] M[eyer] given above could give one the impression that this is his view. In fact, E[duard] M[eyer]'s position on this point is somewhat uncertain. As was shown above, he gives no clear indication as to what he really understands by the term "historically effective". If only that which is "effective" should belong in history, then – and this has already been pointed out to him by others – the crucial question regarding any historical account, for instance [Meyer's] *Antiquity*, must be the following: What *final* situation, and which of its components, should be chosen as having been "effected" by the historical development to be described in the account – [a choice] that will also determine whether a fact must be excluded as being historically insignificant because it had no demonstrable causal importance for any component of that final situation? Many of E[duard] M[eyer]'s remarks may give the initial impression that it is indeed the objective "cultural situation" – to put it briefly – of the present that is to be [the] decisive [factor] here: in that case, facts would only belong in a "history of Antiquity" if their effect[s] are *still today* of causal importance, for our contemporary political, economic, social, religious, ethical [or] scientific situation or for any other component of our cultural life, [that is to say:] if we directly perceive their "effect[s]" at present (see p. 37, top). On the other hand, it would be totally irrelevant whether a fact were of even the most fundamental importance for the *distinctive character* of the culture of Antiquity (see p. 48, bottom). If E[duard] M[eyer] were to put this [position] into practice, his work (just think of the volume on Egypt!) would shrink dramatically, and many would find that it lacked precisely that which they expect from a history of *Antiquity*. But [Meyer] leaves another way [out of this difficulty] open (p. 37, top): "we can also perceive it" – that is to say: what has been historically "effective" – "in the past by *pretending* that some instant in the past exists in the present". However, by this means we can "pretend" that any component of culture whatsoever is "effective" from some point of view, however chosen, and thus insert it into a history of Antiquity – and this would remove precisely that limitation which E[duard] M[eyer] is trying to establish. And the question would nevertheless still arise: what "moment in time" will be chosen, for instance in a "history of Antiquity", as the criterion of what is significant for the historian? If we adopt E[duard] M[eyer]'s approach, we would assume [the answer to be]: the "end" of ancient history, that is to say: the caesura which seems to us to be an appropriate "end point". Accordingly, this could be the reign of the Emperor Romulus, or the reign of Justinian, or – perhaps better – the reign of Diocletian. ‹173› In that case, what would at least without doubt, and to its full extent, belong in the [historical] account as [part of the description of] its "end" point would be, first, everything "characteristic" of this *final* epoch, this "era of senescence" of Antiquity, since it was just this characteristic quality that oriented the formation of the object of historical explanation; in addition, and before anything else, the facts that were causally important for ("effective" in) this process of "senescence" [would belong in the account]. On the other hand, everything that at that time (the [reign] of Romulus or Diocletian) no longer exercised any "cultural effects" would have to be excluded from, for instance, the account of Greek culture; and, considering the situation of literature, philosophy and culture in general at that time, this would [exclude] a frighteningly large portion of those very [elements] that make a "history of Antiquity" at all "valuable" for us, and that we luckily do not look for in vain in E[duard] M[eyer]'s own work.

A history of Antiquity containing *only* that which had a *causal* effect on *some* later epoch would – *particularly if one regards political conditions as being the real backbone of the historical* – look quite as empty as a "history" of Goethe which, to use Ranke's expression, "deprives" [its subject] "of its immediate status" in favour of his epigones, that is to say: which is only concerned with those components of his distinctive character and his manifestations of life that have *remained* "effective" in literature. In that respect, a scientific "biography" is in principle no different from historical objects that are delimited in other ways. In the formulation that he himself gives it, E[duard] M[eyer]'s thesis is impracticable. – Or can we here, as well, find a way in which the contradiction between his theory and his own practice can be avoided? We heard E[duard] M[eyer] say that the historian finds his problems "within himself"; and he adds: "The times of *the historian* is a factor that cannot be excluded from any historical account". Could it be the case that a "fact" already gains that "effective quality" that marks it as being "historical" if a modern historian *takes an interest* in it, with its individual distinctive character and as having turned out the way it did and no differently, and knows how to use this to interest his readers? – In fact, in E[duard] M[eyer]'s exposition (p. 36, bottom, on the one hand, and pp. 37 and 45, on the other hand), two different concepts of "historical facts" have apparently been conflated: first, those components of reality that are "evaluated" – one might say: "for their own sake" – with their concrete, distinctive character, as objects of our *interest*; and, second, [the facts] that we encounter in the causal regression [in their quality of] "causes", as being "effective" in E[duard] M[eyer]'s sense, [when we experience] the need to understand those "evaluated" components of reality as being historically caused. We can call the first kind ["]historical individuals["] and the second one ["](real) historical causes["] and, like Rickert, distinguish between them as being, respectively, "primary" and "secondary" historical facts. Of course, we are only able to confine a historical account to the historical "causes" – Rickert's "secondary" facts and E[duard] M[eyer]'s "effective" facts – if the historical individual whose causal explanation is to be our exclusive concern has already been unambiguously determined. However comprehensive that selected primary object may be (let us assume that it is, for instance, the total "modern" "culture" – that is to say: our "culture", characterized by Christianity, capitalism and the rule of law and "radiating" from Europe, in its present stage of development – in other words: an immense tangle of "cultural values" that are, as such, considered from the most diverse "points of view"), nevertheless, when the causal regression by which it is "explained" historically reaches back as far as the Middle Ages, let alone Antiquity, it will have to leave unconsidered, at least in part, an immense amount of objects as being *causally* unimportant. [Those objects] may to a large degree arouse our "evaluating" interest "for their own sake", and they can therefore *for their part* become "historical individuals" from which an "explanatory" causal regression proceeds. It must certainly be admitted that this "historical interest" will be specifically less strong because [these objects] have no causal importance for a universal history of present-day culture. The cultural development of the Incas and Aztecs has [only] to an extremely small degree – comparatively speaking! – left historically relevant traces, so that a universal history of the genesis of *present-day* culture in E[duard] M[eyer]'s sense may perhaps safely be completely silent about them. If that is so – and we will make that assumption here – then what we know of their cultural development will *chiefly* become relevant not as a "historical object", nor as a "historical cause", but essentially as a "heuristic instrument" for the formation of cultural–theoretical concepts. It can be relevant, in a positive sense, for instance, as a distinctive, specified example, for the formation of the concept of feudalism; and in a negative sense, as a means of differentiating certain concepts, which we utilize in the history of European culture, from those heterogeneous elements of [Inca and Aztec] culture. [This differentiation can allow us] to gain a clearer picture, by way of comparison[s], of how the distinctive historical character of the European cultural development was formed. Just the same is of course true with regard to those components of ancient culture that E[duard] M[eyer] [would register] as having become historically "no longer effective" and that he would therefore – if he were consistent – exclude from a history of Antiquity oriented to the present cultural situation. – But in spite of all this, when we look at the Incas and Aztecs, it is apparently not at all impossible, logically or substantively, to make certain elements of their culture, with their distinctive character, into historical "individuals". That is to say: they are first analysed "interpretively" as to their "value" relations and then again made the object of "historical" investigation, so that the causal regression will now try to grasp facts that are part of the cultural development of [those elements] and that become "historical causes" in relation to that [historical individual]. And if someone composes a "history of Antiquity", it is a vain self-delusion to believe that it only contains facts that have a causal "effect" on contemporary culture, simply because it only deals with facts that we find significant *either* "primarily", as evaluated "historical individuals" *or* "secondarily", as causal [elements] (with regard to those or other "individuals"), as "causes". It is our *interest*, which is oriented to "values", and not the substantive causal relationship between our culture and (just) the Hellenic culture, that will circumscribe the group of cultural values governing a history of Hellenic culture. Roughly speaking, we generally, and according to a completely "subjective" evaluation, regard the period between Aeschylus and Aristotle as the epoch of the "apogee" of Hellenic culture. That epoch, with its cultural elements, is taken into consideration, as [having] an "intrinsic value", in every "history of Antiquity", including that by E[duard] M[eyer]; and that would no longer be the case only if, [at] some future [time, one] were unable to establish an immediate "*value relation*" to those cultural creations, just as little as to the "songs" and the "world view" of a Central African people, [elements] that arouse our interest as being representative of their kind – in other words: as instruments of concept formation – or as "causes". – This fact – that we, as contemporary human beings, have *value* relations of some kind to the individual "characteristic form" of the elements of ancient culture – is the only possible meaning that can be given to E[duard] M[eyer]'s conception of the "effective" as the "historical". On the other hand, the way in which E[duard] M[eyer] motivates the specific interest that history shows in the "culturally developed nations" already demonstrates to what degree his own concept of the "effective" is composed of heterogeneous elements. "This", he believes (p. 47), "is due to [the fact that] these nations and cultures have to an infinitely higher extent been *effective*, and are still effective today." This is undoubtedly correct; but [it is] certainly not the only reason for our "interest", which is decisive for the significance [of those nations and cultures] as historical objects. And in particular, one cannot conclude from [E[duard] M[eyer]'s argument] that – as he says (ibid.) – this interest becomes greater, "the more advanced they (the historical culturally developed nations) are". The question of the "intrinsic value" of a culture, which is touched upon [in this last quotation], has nothing to do with that of its historical "effectiveness": here, E[duard] M[eyer] simply confuses "valuable" with "causally important". It is absolutely correct that every "history" is written from the standpoint of the value interests of the *present* and that, consequently, every new age poses – or at least: can pose – new questions to the historical material for the simple reason that its *interest*, guided by value ideas, changes. But it is equally certain that this interest also "evaluates" elements of culture that completely "belong to the past" – that is to say: elements to which an element of contemporary culture can*not* be traced back in a causal *regression* – and makes them into historical "individuals". [This is true] of minor objects, such as the letters to Frau v. Stein, and of major ones, including those components of Hellenic culture whose effects contemporary culture has long ago outgrown. As we have seen, even E[duard] M[eyer] himself has conceded this – but not drawn the consequences – by his assumption that it is possible, as he puts it, to *pretend* that some instant in the *past* exists in the present (p. 37, top) – something that, according to his remarks (on the middle of p. 55) only "philology" is really allowed to do. In fact, this amounts to an admission that cultural elements "belonging to the past" are also historical objects, *regardless* of whether their "effect[s]" can still be felt; consequently, in a "history of Antiquity", for example, the "characteristic" values of Antiquity may also *in themselves* furnish the criterion for the selection of facts and the direction of historical research. – And the implications are even wider:

The only reason given by E[duard] M[eyer] why the *present* does not become an object of history is that one does not yet know, and cannot know, which of its components will show itself "effective" in the future; and this claim – that the present is (subjectively) unhistorical – is true, at least under certain conditions. Only the future finally "decides" about the *causal* importance of the facts of the present. However, this is not the only aspect of the problem, even when we (and this is a matter of course in our context) ignore such external factors as the lack of archival source material etc. The really immediate present has not yet become a historical "cause"; but nor is it yet a historical "individual", just as an "immediate experience" is not an object of empirical "knowledge" at the moment when it happens "within me" and "around me". Every historical "valuation" includes (so to speak) a "contemplative" element: what it comprises is not just, and not primarily, the immediate value *judgement* of the "subject taking a stand"; instead, as we have seen, it essentially consists in a "knowledge" of *possible* "value relations", and it therefore presupposes an ability to change one's "standpoint" in relation to the object, at least theoretically. The usual way of describing this is that we first "have to become objective" in relation to an immediate experience, before it "belongs to history" as an object – which in this context precisely does *not* mean that it is causally "effective". – However, we shall not here spin out further this discussion, which concerns the relationship between "immediate experience" and "knowledge". It suffices that all these long-winded expositions have probably made it clear not only that Ed[uard] Meyer's conception of the "historical" as being the "effective" is inadequate, but also why this is the case. Above all, it lacks the logical distinction between the "primary" historical object – the "evaluated" cultural individual that attracts an interest in the causal "explanation" of its origins – and the "secondary" historical "facts" – the causes to which the "evaluated" distinctive character of that "individual" are imputed in a causal regression. The aim of this imputation is that it should in principle be "objectively" *valid* as empirical truth, as unconditionally as any other piece of empirical knowledge; and the question whether this aim has been attained – a question that is not of a logical, but of a factual nature – is decided solely on the basis of the sufficiency of the data, just as is the case with explanations of concrete natural events. What is "subjective", in a certain sense that need not be discussed again here, is not the determination of the historical "causes" of a given "object" of explanation, but the delimitation of the historical "object", of the "individual" itself, since what are decisive in this latter respect are the *value* relations, the "conception" of which is subject to historical change. Therefore, on the one hand, E[duard] M[eyer] is not correct in asserting (middle of p. 45) that we are "*never*" able to attain "absolute and unconditionally valid" knowledge of something historical: this is not true as far as the "causes" are concerned. It is, however, equally incorrect when it is then asserted that the situation with respect to the validity of knowledge in the natural sciences is "no different" from what it is in the historical disciplines: this is not true for the historical "individuals", that is to say: for the *way* in which "values" play a role in history, nor for the modality of those values. ([This view holds] irrespective of one's opinion concerning the "validity" of those "values" as such: [that "validity"] is in any case different in principle from the validity, as empirical truth, of a causal connection, even if both [kinds of validity] would in the last analysis, from a philosophical point of view, have to be considered as being bound to norms.) This is because those "value"-oriented "points of view" from which we consider cultural objects – from which they become "objects" of historical research for us at all – are changeable; and because, and as long as, they have this [changeable] character, new "facts" will continue, in ever new ways, to become historically "essential". (We are assuming, as we shall once and for all do here when conducting discussions of logic, that the "source material" will remain unchanged.) However, this kind of dependence on "subjective values" is completely alien at least to those natural sciences that take mechanics as their model: in fact, [that dependence] constitutes the specific point on which the historical *differs* from those natural sciences.

To sum up: to the extent that the "interpretation" of an object is "philological" interpretation, in the usual sense of the word (for instance [interpretation] of its linguistic "meaning"), it is a preliminary technical task from the point of view of "history". To the extent that it subjects what is *characteristic* of the distinctive quality of certain "cultural epochs" or certain personalities or certain individual objects (works of art, literary objects) to an "interpretive" analysis, it is an instrument of historical concept formation. From a logical point of view, [it can fulfil this function in two different ways]: either in an auxiliary capacity, by helping to ascertain, as such, *causally* relevant components of a concrete historical context; *or*, on the contrary, as a guide, showing the way by "interpreting" the content of an object – *Faust*, the *Oresteia*, the Christianity of a certain epoch, etc. – with regard to [its] possible value relations; in so doing, it sets "tasks" for the causal work of history and becomes a *precondition* of history. [When] the concept of a "culture" of a concrete nation and age – the concept of "Christianity", of *Faust*, but also for instance (something that is more easily overlooked) the concept [of] "Germany" etc. – [when all these concepts] are formed as objects of *historical* work, they are individual *value* concepts, that is to say: they have been formed through relations to value ideas.

Let us also touch on a further point: If we now take these valuations themselves, with which we approach the facts, as [our] objects of analysis, then we are – depending on the purpose of the inquiry – conducting studies either in the *philosophy* of history or in the psychology of "historical interest". On the other hand, we can subject a concrete object to "value analysis" – that is to say: "interpret" it, with its distinctive character, so that we are "suggestively" presented with the possible valuations that can be applied to it; [in other words], we can aim at a "re-experiencing" (as it is commonly, but quite incorrectly, called) of a cultural creation. That is not *yet* "historical" work (this is the "kernel of truth" in E[duard] M[eyer]'s formulation); but it is, however, the completely necessary "forma formans" ‹174› of historical "interest" in an object, of its primary conceptualization as an "individual", and of the causal work of history, which only then and for this reason becomes meaningfully possible. In many cases habitual, ordinary value judgements have formed the object and paved the way for the historical work (this happens at the beginning of all "history" in political communities, and especially in one's own state); consequently, the historian may believe that he is in his "proper" domain when he is dealing with these solid "objects", which seemingly – but only seemingly, and only for ordinary "household purposes" – do not require any further special value interpretation. Nevertheless, as soon as he wishes to leave the broad highway and also to obtain major new insights into the "distinctive" political "character" of a state or a political genius, he, too, must then, as far as the logical principle is concerned, proceed exactly in the same way as someone who interprets *Faust*. But admittedly, E[duard] M[eyer] is right on this point: where the analysis *remains* at the stage of such an "interpretation" of the "intrinsic value" of the object, where the work of causal imputation is not undertaken and the object is not examined in the light of the question of what causal "importance" it has had for other, more comprehensive and more contemporaneous cultural objects – there, the work of history has not got under way, and the historian can only see the building blocks of historical *problems*. It is only the way in which [Eduard Meyer] argues in support of his position that seems to me untenable. In particular,

E[duard] M[eyer] sees the "static", "systematic" treatment of a [given] material as constituting the difference of principle from the historical [one]; and Rickert, too, for instance, who had formerly seen the "systematical" as that which, in contradistinction to the "historical sciences of culture", was specifically "natural–scientific" – even in the domain of "social", "spiritual" and "intellectual" life – has recently formulated the concept of the "*systematic cultural sciences*". Against this background, we shall have to undertake, in a separate section, ‹175› the task of posing the following question: what are the different meanings of the "systematic", and what are the different relationships of these different meanings to the historical approach and to the "natural sciences"?[1] Of course, that method of treating ancient, especially Hellenic, culture which E[duard] M[eyer] designates by the term "philological method" – [and which takes] the form of "classical studies" – in practice initially came about through the linguistic competence necessary to master the source material. But this was not its only cause. It was also due to the distinctive character of certain eminent scholars and, above all, to the "significance" that the culture of classical Antiquity has until now had for our own intellectual training. Let us try to formulate, in their extreme version and therefore also in a purely theoretical fashion, those positions vis-à-vis the culture of Antiquity that are conceivable in principle: (1) One [position] would be the idea that the value of ancient culture is absolute; its expressions – in humanism; then, for example, in Winckelmann['s thought]; and lastly in all the variants of so-called "classicism" – will not be investigated here. If we carry this position to its extreme conclusion, it means that the components of ancient culture – to the extent that the "Christian character" of our culture or the products of rationalism have not "supplemented" or "reshaped" them – are, at least virtually, components of "culture" as such, not because they *have been* "causally" effective in E[duard] M[eyer]'s sense [of the term], but because they, being absolutely valid as values, *ought to* be causally effective in our education. Consequently, the culture of Antiquity is primarily an object of interpretation *in usum scholarum*, ‹176› for educating one's own nation to become a culturally developed one: "philology", in its most comprehensive sense as "attaining knowledge of what is already known", finds something in Antiquity that is above history and valid for all times. (2) The other, modern [position] would be in radical opposition [to the first one]: [according to it], ancient culture, in its true distinctive character, is so infinitely far removed from us that it is utterly absurd to want to give the "far too many" an insight into its true "nature": it is a sublime object of valuation for the few, who immerse themselves into – and want to "enjoy artistically", as it were – a sublime form of humanity that has vanished for ever and can never be repeated in any of its important points.[2] And, finally, (3) the "classical-studies" approach caters to that orientation of scientific interest for which the store of classical source material is above all a provision of unusually rich ethnographical material, which can be used to formulate general concepts, analogies and rules of development [valid] for the early history, not just of our own, but of "every" culture. One only needs to think of the development of studies in comparative religion: its present upswing would have been impossible if it had not [been able to] exploit the [source material of] Antiquity, aided by a strict philological training. Antiquity is relevant here insofar as the elements of its culture are suitable heuristic instruments for the construction of general "types"; on the other hand, it is neither (as in the first "position") relevant as a permanently valid cultural norm, nor (as in the second one) as an absolutely unique object of individual, contemplative valuation.

1   Only at that point do we enter into a discussion of the various possible principles [underlying] a "classification" of the "sciences".
2   This is probably the "esoteric" theory of U[lrich] v. Wilamowitz, who is of course the primary object of E[duard] M[eyer]'s attack[s].

One immediately sees that all the three positions – which, as was said, were formulated "theoretically" – are, for their [different] purposes, interested in the treatment of the history of Antiquity in the form of "classical studies"; one also [needs] no commentary to see that the interest of the historian is in fact not properly served by any of them, as all three of them have something other than "history" as their primary goal. But if, on the other hand, E[duard] M[eyer] would in earnest exclude from the history of Antiquity everything that was no longer "effective" from the point of view of the present, then he would be regarded by all those who look for *more* in Antiquity than just a historical "cause" as the one who proved the case of his opponents. And every friend of his magnificent work will be pleased to learn that he simply *cannot* carry this idea into practice, and will hope that he does not even make the attempt to do so for the sake of some incorrectly formulated theory.[1]

II Objective possibility and adequate causation in the historical causal approach

"The outbreak of the Second Punic War", Eduard Meyer says (p. 16), "is the consequence of a willed decision by Hannibal; that of the Seven Years' War, by Frederick the Great; that of the war of 1866, ‹177› by Bismarck. All of them could have decided differently, and other personalities would . . . have decided differently; the consequence would have that been the course of history would have been different." In a footnote (p. 16n2), he adds: "This does not amount to claiming, nor to denying, that in [the latter] case, those wars would not have broken out; it is completely impossible to answer that question, which is therefore an idle one." Apart from the lack of consistency between the second sentence and E[duard] M[eyer]'s (previously discussed) formulations concerning the relationship between "freedom" and "necessity" in history, what is above all open to objection is the view that a question which we cannot answer, or cannot answer with certainty, is already for that reason an "idle" one. Empirical science, too, would be in a bad state if those ultimate problems that it cannot solve had never been raised. Here, we are not dealing with such "ultimate" problems, though. To be sure, the question [to be answered] has, on the one hand, been "overtaken" by events; and, on the other hand, it is true that the state of our actual and potential knowledge does not allow us to give a clearly positive answer to it. Moreover, if we look at [this question] from a strictly "deterministic" point of view, it concerns the consequences of something that was "impossible", given the state of the "determinants". But in spite of all this, the question of what *could* have happened if, for instance, Bismarck had not arrived at that decision, is certainly not an "idle" one, since that very question concerns the crucial element in the historical shaping of reality: within the totality of those infinitely numerous "factors", which had to be just like that and no different for just *this* result to come about, what causal *importance* should really be attributed to this individual decision? And consequently, what is its place in the historical account? If history is to rise above the level of merely chronicling remarkable events and personalities, there is no other way for it but to pose such questions. And ever since it was established as a science, [history] has

1 The comprehensiveness of the preceding discussions is obviously quite out of proportion to what "methodology" "gets out of" them in immediate practical terms. If someone, for this reason, finds [those discussions] useless, [we] can only advise him simply to ignore the question of the "meaning" of knowledge, and to content himself with gaining "valuable" knowledge through practical research. The responsibility for posing these questions falls not on the historians but on those who have made the wrongheaded claim – which they continue to put forward in varied forms – that "scientific knowledge" is identical with "uncovering laws". And that *is* undeniably a question that concerns the "meaning" of knowledge.

proceeded in that manner. In a (previously quoted) passage, E[duard] M[eyer] [says that] history observes events from the standpoint of "coming into being", so that its object is not subservient to "necessity", which is [a category] appropriate to "what has come into being". What is correct about this formulation is that the historian who estimates the causal importance of a concrete event is proceeding in the same way as the striving human being who takes a stand and who would never "act" if he regarded his own action as "necessary" and not just as "possible".[1] The only difference is the following: Let us assume here that the human being who acts does so in a strictly "rational" manner. [In that case], he considers the "conditions" of those future developments that interest him (they are "external" to him, and actually given according to the extent of his knowledge); he then inserts into the causal nexus various imagined "possible ways" in which he himself might behave, as well as the results that [these different ways of behaving] can be *expected* to have in combination with those "external" conditions; and, on the basis of the (imagined) "possible" results found in that way, he then decides in favour of one or another kind of behaviour as being appropriate to his "purpose". As for the historian, he at least has the initial advantage over his hero of *knowing*, a posteriori, whether the assessment of the given "external" conditions, in accordance with the knowledge and expectations of the acting person, corresponded to the actual situation at the time. The actual "result" of the action will tell him that. Here, where we are only concerned with the elucidation of *logical* questions, we shall – and may – *theoretically* base ourselves on [the supposition that] the historian possesses an ideal maximum of knowledge of those conditions, even though this maximum may in practice seldom, if at all, be attained. [With that ideal knowledge,] he can retrospectively, in his mind, perform the same weighing up [of possibilities] that his "hero" already more or less clearly performed or "could have performed". Therefore, [the historian] can, with considerably better chances of success than (for instance) Bismarck himself, pose the question: what consequences could have been "expected" if another decision had been taken? Obviously, this consideration is far from being "idle". E[duard] M[eyer] himself (p. 43) follows precisely this procedure [when discussing] those two shots that directly provoked the outbreak of street fighting in Berlin in March [1848]. ‹178› In his opinion, the question of what caused them is "historically irrelevant". But why is it more irrelevant than the discussion of the decisions taken by Hannibal, Frederick the Great or Bismarck? "Things were such that any chance occurrence *must* (!) have made the conflict break out." Here, we see E[duard] M[eyer] himself answering the allegedly "idle" question of what "would have" happened without those shots; and, in this way, the [question of] their historical "importance" (in this case: their irrelevance) is settled. In the case of the decisions taken by Hannibal, Frederick and Bismarck, however, "things" "were" different, at least in E[duard] M[eyer]'s view: and [they were] not such that, if the decision had been different, the conflict would have broken out in any case, or under the concrete political constellations that at that time determined its course and its outcome. If it were otherwise, that decision would of course have been as unimportant as those shots. Thus, it does, after all, seem to be of considerable value for determining the "historical importance" of a single historical fact [if one can make] the following *judgement*: *If* that fact, within a complex of historical determinants, is imagined to be lacking or [as having been] changed, then this *would have* resulted in a course of historical events that was different in certain *historically important* respects. And [such a judgement is of value] even though, in practice, the historian may only in exceptional cases – i.e. if that "historical importance" is in dispute – feel impelled to develop and justify it deliberately and explicitly. It is clear that this circumstance ought to have prompted an investigation into

1   This remains true irrespective of Kistiakovski's critique (*School*, p. 393), which does not at all apply to *this* concept of "possibility".

the logical nature of judgements of this kind, which state what the result "could have been expected to be" if an individual causal component of a complex of conditions had been removed or changed, and into the significance [of such judgements] for history. We shall try to get a somewhat clearer picture of this.

To what extent the logic of history[1] is still in a poor condition is shown, among other things, by [the fact that] the authoritative investigations into this important question have been carried out, not by historians, nor by specialists in the methodology of history, but by representatives of quite unrelated disciplines.

The theory of the so-called "objective possibility", which we are dealing with here, has its origins in the work of the outstanding physiologist v. Kries;[2] and the usual application of this concept is based on treatises – some following v. Kries, some criticizing him – primarily by specialists in criminal law, and otherwise by authors belonging to other legal disciplines, in particular Merkel, Rümelin, Liepmann and, most recently, Radbruch.[3] In the methodology of the social sciences, the line of reasoning of v. Kries has up until now only been adopted by [the discipline of] statistics.[4] It is natural that this problem was precisely treated by jurists,

1 It may be useful to state clearly that the categories to be discussed in the following are applied not only in the domain of what is commonly termed the *specialized* discipline of "history" but in the "historical" imputation of *any* individual event, including those [occurring in] "inanimate nature". In this context, the category of "the historical" is a *logical*, not a specialized, technical concept.

2 *Objective Possibility*. An important part of the basis for these discussions was first formulated by v. Kries in his *Probability Calculus*. It must be said at the outset that, because of the nature of the historical "object", only the most elementary components of v. Kries' theory are of importance for the methodology of history. It is evidently out of the question for causal historical analysis to adopt principles of the so-called "probability calculus" in the strict sense; and even an attempt to utilize the viewpoints [of probability calculus] by analogy demands great caution.

3 So far, the most deeply penetrating critique of the application of v. Kries' theory to juridical problems has been made by Radbruch (*Adequate Causation*); [this work] contains [references to] the most important other literature). It will only be possible to take into account his fundamental analysis of the concept of "adequate causation" later, after the theory has been presented in its simplest possible form (which is therefore, as we shall see, only provisional and not definitive).

4 Among the theoreticians of statistics, [the views of] L[adislaus] v. Bortkievicz (*Epistemological Foundations* (see also *Jahrbücher für Nationalökonomie und Statistik*, Vol. 73) and *Theory of Statistics*) have a very close affinity to v. Kries' statistical theories. ‹179› Another author who bases himself on the theory of v. Kries is A. Tchuprov (whose article on moral statistics in the Brockhaus–Ephron Encyclopaedic Dictionary (*Moral Statistics*) I was unfortunately unable to consult). See his article on the tasks of statistical theory (*Task*). I cannot agree with the critical remarks by Th. Kistiakovski (in his [article] *School*), which admittedly have so far only been sketched out, with the proviso that they may [later] be further elaborated. First of all, he (p. 379) criticizes the theory for employing an erroneous concept of cause, based on the logic of [John Stuart] Mill, and in particular for utilizing the categor[ies] of "compound cause" and "partial cause"; this usage is [in his view] in turn based on an anthropomorphic interpretation of causality (in the sense of "having an effect"). Radbruch also adumbrates a similar objection (*Adequate Causation*, p. 22). However, the idea of "having an effect" – or, as it has also been formulated, less vividly, but with a completely identical meaning: of the "causal bond" – is completely inseparable from any study of causes that considers individual series of qualitative changes. We shall later deal with [the point] that [the idea of having an effect] should not, and need not, be burdened with unnecessary and questionable metaphysical presuppositions. (Concerning plurality of causes and elementary causes, see Tchuprov's account (*Task*, p. 436).) At this point, only the following remark should be made: the "possibility" is a "formative" category, that is to say: it functions by determining the *selection* of the causal links to be included in the historical account. On the other hand, the historically formed material, at least ideally, contains nothing in the way of "possibility": subjectively, the historical account only rarely attains judgements of necessity; but objectively, it is no doubt always governed by the assumption that the "causes" to which the effect is "imputed" must simply be taken to be *the* "sufficient causes" of its occurrence. (Naturally, it should be noted, in combination with

and in particular by criminologists, since the question of penal guilt is purely one of causality, to the extent that it involves the following problem: under what circumstances can it be asserted that somebody has, by his actions, "caused" a certain external effect? The logical structure [of the question of penal guilt] is in fact clearly the same as that of historical causality. Just as in history, the problems of practical social relationships of human beings, and in particular those of the administration of justice, have an "anthropocentric" orientation; that is to say: they pose the question of the causal importance of *human* "acts". And just like the question of the causal determination of a concrete, harmful effect that may have to be punished under criminal law or compensated under civil law, the problem of causality faced by the historian is also invariably oriented towards the imputation of concrete effects to concrete causes: it is not one of determining abstract "law-like regularities". However, jurisprudence – and criminology in particular – again leaves this common path in order to pursue a problem that is specific to it; this results from the introduction of the additional question as to whether, and when, the *objective*, purely causal imputation of the effect to the action of an individual is also sufficient to constitute the *subjective* "guilt" [of that individual]. This [latter] question is no longer a purely causal problem that can be solved by simply establishing facts which can be "objectively" determined by means of perception and causal interpretation; instead, it is a problem of criminal policy, which is oriented towards ethical and other values. It is a priori possible, and in fact often the case (nowadays, it is the [general] rule), that the meaning – explicitly stated or elicited by interpretation – of the legal norms goes in the direction of making the existence of "guilt", for the purposes of the applicable legal rule, primarily dependent on certain *subjective* elements with regard to the acting person ([for instance:] intent, *subjectively* determined "ability to predict" the outcome, and so forth); and this may considerably modify the importance of the categorial distinctions between [different] kinds of causal interconnection.[1] In the first stages of the discussion, however, this difference concerning the purpose of the investigation is of no importance. Precisely as in legal theory, our initial question is the following: How is it at all *possible*, in principle, to impute a concrete "effect" to a single concrete "cause"? And how can this imputation be carried out, considering that the occurrence of the individual "event" was in fact always determined by an *infinity* of causal factors, and that *every single one* of those causal factors was indispensable for the occurrence of the "effect" in its concrete form?

that infinite number of "conditions" which are viewed as being scientifically "uninteresting" and are [therefore] only summarily referred to in the account.) Consequently, the use of this category does not in the least involve the idea – which the theory of causality has long since outgrown – that some elements of real causal connections would, so to speak, have been "up in the air" until they entered into the causal concatenation. V. Kries himself (*Objective Possibility*, p. 107) has – in my opinion quite convincingly – shown how his theory differs from that of J[ohn] St[uart] Mill. For a discussion of this point, see below. The only [similarity between the two] is that Mill, too, discusses the category of objective possibility and that, in so doing, he has occasionally constructed the concept of "adequate causation" (see Mill, *System of Logic*, p. 262).

1 Modern law is directed at the agent, not the act (see Radbruch, *Adequate Causation*, p. 62), and is concerned with subjective "*guilt*", while history, as long as it wishes to remain an empirical science, is concerned with the "objective" *causes* of concrete events and with the consequences of concrete "acts", but does not wish to sit in judgement on the "agent". Radbruch, quite rightly, bases his critique of v. Kries on the above-mentioned fundamental principle of modern – but not of all – law. Consequently, he himself concedes that v. Kries' theory is valid in the following cases: the so-called "offences by causation" (p. 65); ‹180› liability due to an "abstract possibility of influencing [the situation]"; liability for loss of profit; and liability incurred by "persons not accountable for their actions" – that is to say: whenever only "objective" causality is relevant (p. 80). But the *logical* situation of history is precisely the same as in those cases.

First of all, the possibility of selection from the infinity of determinants is conditioned by the nature of our historical *interest*. As we have seen, the statement that history should causally understand the concrete *reality* of an "event" in its individuality obviously does not mean that [history] should "reproduce" and causally explain [the "event"] in its entirety, with the totality of its individual qualities: such a task would not just be impossible in practice, it would also be meaningless in principle. Instead, history is exclusively concerned with furnishing a causal explanation of those "components" and "aspects" of the event in question that, from certain points of view, have "general significance" and are *therefore* historically *interesting*; in just the same way, what is relevant for the deliberations of a judge is not the total individual course taken by an event, but only those of its components that are *important* for the subsumption under [certain] norms. Apart from disregarding the infinity of "absolutely" trivial details, [the judge] is not even interested in all the things that can be of interest from other points of view ([e.g.,] those of natural science, history or art): whether the death "brought about" by the fatal thrust [of the knife] was accompanied by phenomena that may be quite interesting to the physiologist; whether the posture of the dead person or of the murderer could have been an appropriate object of artistic portrayal; whether the death possibly helped an − [otherwise] uninvolved − person who was "next in line" in the civil service hierarchy to "move up", and thus, from his point of view, was causally "valuable"; whether [the death] led to certain measures on the part of the security police; or whether it perhaps even engendered international conflicts and thus proved to be of "historical" importance − [all this does] not [interest the judge]. For him, all that is relevant is this: did the chain of causation linking the thrust [of the knife] to the death have such a character, and was the subjective disposition of the agent, as well as his relation to the act, such that a particular norm of criminal law is applicable? On the other hand, what is of interest to the historian in connection with (for instance) the death of Caesar ⟨181⟩ is neither the criminal–legal nor the medical problems that the "case" may have presented; nor [is he interested in] the details of the event, unless they are relevant either for "characterizing" Caesar or for the situation of the parties in Rome − that is to say: as heuristic instruments − or, lastly, for the "political effect" of his death − that is to say: as "real causes". What [the historian] is first of all concerned with [in connection with Caesar's death] is solely the fact that the death occurred at that particular moment, under a concrete combination of political conditions; and the question arising out of this, which he [then] discusses, is whether that fact may have had certain important "consequences" for the course of "world history".

In history, as in law, this affects the question of [causal] imputation by eliminating an infinite number of components of the actual sequence of events as being "causally irrelevant". This is because (as we have seen) a [given] circumstance, taken by itself, is irrelevant, not only when it was completely unrelated to the event under discussion − so that, if we imagine[d] it to be absent, no modification *at all* in the actual course of events "*would have*" occurred − but also when [that circumstance] does not seem to have in any way affected those components of the sequence of events that, in the concrete case, are important to us and that are the only ones that interest us.

But the real question [that we are faced with] is of course the following: What are the logical operations by means of which we can acquire the insight − and underpin it by demonstration − *that* such a causal relationship exists between those "important" elements of the outcome and certain components among the infinity of determining factors? Obviously, [we can]not [do so] simply by "observing" the sequence of events − at least not if what is meant by [the term "observe"] is a "presuppositionless" mental "photographing" of all the sequences of physical and psychical events that occur during the time and at the place in question (even if that were [in fact] possible). On the contrary: the causal imputation is carried out in the form of an intellectual process that comprises a number of *abstractions*. The first and decisive one is the following: We *imagine* that one or a few of the actual causal components of the sequence [of events] are modified in a certain direction and ask ourselves whether, if the conditions of the sequence of events have been thus modified, the outcome would be the same (as far as the "important" points are concerned) or *what other* outcome "could have been expected". Let us take an example from Eduard Meyer's own work. No one else has so vividly and clearly demonstrated the world-historical "significance" of the Persian Wars ‹182› for the cultural development of the Western world. But how is this done, from a logical point of view? In essence, by [first] setting out two "*possibilities*": on the one hand, the development, under the aegis of the Persian protectorate, of a theocratic-religious culture whose beginnings lay in the mysteries and oracles – [a protectorate] that would, wherever possible (as in the case of the Jews), utilize the national religion as an instrument of domination. [The other "possibility" was] the victory of the secularly oriented, free Hellenic spiritual universe that endowed us with those cultural values from which we still draw sustenance today. [Then, it is shown] that [the struggle] between these two "possibilities" was "decided" in the "battle" of Marathon – a skirmish of tiny proportions. ‹183› This ["battle"] constituted the necessary "precondition" for the creation of the Attic fleet ‹184› and, consequently, for the further course of the struggle for liberty; for the salvation of the independence of Hellenic culture; for providing at the outset a positive stimulus for the specifically Western historiography; [and] for the complete development of the drama, and of all that unique spiritual life for which that theatre of world history – a minuscule one measured in purely quantitative terms – provided the setting.

And it is obvious that the one and only reason why *we* – who are not Athenians – attach historical interest to the battle [of Marathon] is the fact *that* it "decided" between those "possibilities", or at least had a very important influence on [that "decision"]. Without an appraisal of those "possibilities", and of those irreplaceable cultural values that, when we view them in retrospect, [seemed to be] "dependent on" that decision, it would be impossible to establish the "significance" [of that battle]. Indeed, [without that evaluation], there would seem to be no reason why we should not put [the battle of Marathon] on the same level as a brawl between two tribes of Kaffirs or Indians; in so doing, one would really and properly put into practice the obtuse "fundamental ideas" of Helmolt's *World History*, ‹185› as [is in fact] done in that "modern" compilation.[1] Whenever modern historians are compelled by some inquiry, to define the "importance" of a concrete event by an *explicit* consideration and description of "possible" developments, they habitually apologize for employing that seemingly anti-deterministic category; but [in view of what was said above], there is, logically speaking, no reason at all for apologizing. To take an example: in his book on Conradin [of Hohenstaufen] [(*Conradin*)], K[arl] Hampe sets out, in a very informative way, the historical "importance" of the battle of Tagliacozzo; ‹186› he does so by considering the different "possibilities" that the outcome – which was purely contingent, that is to say: determined by completely individual sequences of tactical events – "decided" between. But then he suddenly has second thoughts and adds: "But history knows of no possibilities". This calls for the following rejoinder: [If we] look at the "course of events" as having been "objectivized" on the basis of deterministic axioms, it does not "know of" any [possibilities], simply because it does not "know of" any concepts

1   It goes without saying that this judgement does not apply to the individual essays contained in that work: some of them are distinguished achievements; but, in those cases, the "method" is thoroughly "old-fashioned". However, the notion of a sort of "social–political" justice, according to which the Indian and Kaffir tribes, so disdainfully ignored, should – at last, at long last! – be treated by history as having at least the same importance as the Athenians, and which arranges its material according to geographical criteria in order to make this just treatment quite explicit – [that notion] is simply childish.

at all; but if "*history*" wishes to be a science, it *always* knows of [possibilities]. Every line of every historical account – indeed: every collection of archival material and documents destined for publication – contains "judgements of possibility"; or, more correctly put: it must contain them, if the publication is to have "value as knowledge".

But what does it mean when we talk of several "possibilities" between which those struggles are supposed to have "decided"? In the first place, it means at least that we construct what we may safely call *imaginary pictures*: [we imagine] the absence of one or more of those components of "reality" that actually existed, and we construct in our minds a sequence of events that is modified with respect to one or a few "conditions". This means that even the very first step towards a historical judgement is already – and this is what we want to stress here – a process of *abstraction*; it proceeds by means of analysis and intellectual isolation of the components of what is immediately given (viewed as a complex of *possible* causal relations), and it should lead to a synthesis of the "real" causal interconnection. Consequently, even this first step transforms the given "reality" in order to make it into a historical "fact", a *theoretical* construct. To quote Goethe: there is "theory" in "facts". ‹187›

If one subjects these "judgements of possibility" – that is to say: the statements concerning what the situation "*might*" have been if certain conditions had been absent or modified – to somewhat closer scrutiny, and asks, in the first place, how we really arrive at them, there can be no doubt that it is all a matter of isolations and generalizations. That is to say: we "*break down*" what is "given" into its "components", until each one of these ["components"] can be fitted into a "*rule* of experience", so that it can be determined what effect each single one of them – the other ones being present as "conditions" – "could", according to a rule of experience, have been "*expected*" to have had. Thus, a judgement of "possibility" – in the sense in which that term is utilized here – always implies a reference to rules of experience. The category of "possibility", therefore, is not utilized in its *negative* form – that is to say: as an expression of the fact that we do not, or do not completely, know something (as opposed to the assertorical or apodictical judgement). ‹188› Quite to the contrary, [the judgement of "possibility"] here implies a reference to positive *knowledge* of "rules governing events", to our "nomological knowledge", as it is usually termed.

If the answer to the question whether a certain train has already passed a station is that "it is *possible*", the meaning of this statement is that the person [who answered the question] *subjectively* does not know of any fact ruling out that assumption, but that, on the other hand, he is not in a position to affirm its correctness. Thus, he "*does not* know". But when, in Eduard Meyer's judgement, a theocratic–religious development in Hellas at the time of the battle of Marathon was "possible" (or, under certain eventualities, "probable"), this has the opposite meaning and [amounts to the following] claim: [first,] certain components of the historically given [situation] were *objectively* present – that is to say: their presence can be established with objective validity; and [second], if we *imagine* that the battle of Marathon (and, naturally, a considerable number of other components of the actual course of events) *did not happen*, or *imagine* that they took a different course, those [components that were objectively present] would, according to *general rules of experience*, be positively "appropriate" (we shall provisionally use this phraseology, which is current in criminology) for bringing about such a [theocratic–religious] development. In the light of all that has been said so far, the "knowledge" on which such an assessment in support of the "importance" of the battle of Marathon rests [has two components]: on the one hand, knowledge of certain "facts" of the "historical situation", which can be established on the basis of the source material ("ontological" knowledge); and on the other hand – as we have already seen – knowledge of certain well-known rules of experience, in particular concerning the way in which human beings usually react to given situations ("nomological knowledge"). The way in which these "rules of experience" are "valid" will be considered later. In any case, it is certain that, if E[duard] M[eyer]'s thesis, which is decisive for the "importance" of the battle of Marathon, were disputed, he would, in order to demonstrate it, have to "break up" that [historical] situation into its "components", down to the point where our "imagination" would be able to apply our "nomological", empirical knowledge (derived from our own life experience and our knowledge of the behaviour of others) to that "ontological" knowledge; we could then come to the positive conclusion that the interplay of those facts – under conditions that were, in our imagination, modified in a certain way – "could" bring about the outcome that [Meyer] claimed was "objectively possible". But this would simply mean that, *if* we "imagined" that outcome as having actually come about, we "*would*" accept that those facts – modified in that way – were [its] "sufficient causes".

This formulation of a simple fact – which necessarily had to be somewhat long-winded in order to avoid ambiguity – shows that the formulation of historical causal interconnection[s] makes use of abstraction in both its aspects: isolation and generalization; but, moreover, it demonstrates that, when we make even the simplest historical assessment of the historical "importance" of a "concrete fact", we are far removed from just registering "what is there": that assessment is a categorially formed *intellectual* construct; and, in addition, it only acquires substantive validity by virtue of the fact that we *apply* the whole store of our "nomological", empirical knowledge to the "given" reality.

Now, historians will object to what has been said by claiming[1] that actual historical work proceeds otherwise and that the actual content of historical accounts is different [from what was argued above]. [Their version is the following:] the causal interrelations are uncovered by the "sensitivity" or "intuition" of the historian, not by generalizations and considerations of "rules": history differs from the natural sciences precisely in that the historian is concerned with the explanation of events and personalities, which are "interpreted" and "understood" by direct analogy with the nature of what goes on in our own minds. This is also [(according to them)] completely true with respect to the historian's exposition; here again, it is the "sensitivity", the suggestive vividness of the account that matters and that lets the reader "relive" what is being described, just as the intuition of the historian has re-experienced and beheld it [in his mind's eye], but has not arrived at it by reasoning. Moreover [(they will argue)], a judgement concerning the objective possibility of what, according to general rules of experience, "would have" happened if a single causal component was imagined to be absent or modified, is very often highly uncertain; quite often, it is impossible to form it at all. Hence, this basis for the historical [causal] "imputation" is in fact in permanent danger of collapsing and therefore cannot possibly be constitutive for the logical value of historical knowledge. – In the first place, such chains of argument mix up different things: on the one hand, the psychological process by which [a piece of] scientific knowledge is *constituted*, and the "artistic" form in which this piece of knowledge is *presented*, with the purpose of influencing the reader "psychologically"; and on the other, the *logical structure* of knowledge.

Ranke "divined" the past, and even a historian of lesser standing will find himself badly handicapped in making progress with his investigations if he does not at all possess this gift of "intuition": in that case, he will remain a sort of junior clerk of history. – But the situation is absolutely the same when it comes to the truly great discoveries of mathematics and the natural sciences. They all flash "intuitively" through the imagination as hypotheses and are subsequently "verified" by confrontation with the facts; that is to say: the question of their "validity" is

---

1 For a more comprehensive treatment of what will be said in the following, see my discussion in *Knies II*.

examined in the light of the already existing empirical knowledge, and they are "formulated" in a logically correct way. Quite the same happens in history: when it is claimed here that [the historian] has to make use of the concept of objective possibility in order to know what is "important", this was not meant to assert anything at all about the question – which is psychologically interesting, but does not concern us in this context – of how a historical hypothesis originates in the mind of the scholar. [That claim] is only intended to address the question of the logical category within which the validity of [the hypothesis] must be demonstrated in cases of doubt or dispute, since *that* is what determines its logical structure. And when the historian presents the reader with the logical result of his causal historical judgements in the form of an account where he does not spell out the reasons underlying his findings and "suggests" the course of events instead of "reasoning" pedantically, surely that account would be a historical novel and not a [set of] scientific findings, unless there was a firm framework of causal imputation behind the artistically designed exterior. In the dry perspective of logic, that framework is after all the only thing that matters: The historical account, too, claims to be "valid" as "truth"; and the most important aspect of historical work, i.e. the causal regression – which is the only one that we have considered so far – only acquires that validity if, in cases of dispute, it has passed the test [described above] of isolating and generalizing the individual causal components, utilizing the category of objective possibility and [performing] the synthesis of causal imputation which then becomes possible.

Now, clearly the causal analysis of the actions of persons proceeds in exactly the same way – logically speaking – as the causal uncovering of the "historical importance" of the battle of Marathon, by means of isolation, generalization and the construction of judgements of possibility. Let us right away take a limiting case: the intellectual analysis of *one's own* actions. The logically unschooled view will tend to be that this [analysis] surely presents no "logical" problems at all, since it is immediately given in [our] experience and easily "understandable" – provided we are "of sound mind" – so that it is naturally also possible to "reproduce" it directly in [our] memory. [However,] quite simple considerations show that this is not the case, and that the "valid" answer to the question: "*Why* did I act like that?" represents a categorially formed construct, which can only enter the sphere of demonstrable judgement[s] by using abstractions – in spite of the fact that the "demonstration" is here made in the mind of the "acting person" himself.

Suppose that a temperamental young mother is annoyed by some kind of unruly behaviour on the part of her young child, and that she boxes his ears soundly – since she is a good German who does not subscribe to the theory contained in the fine lines by Wilhelm Busch: "Superficial is the blow; only the power of the mind will penetrate the soul". ‹189› Now, let us further assume that she is sufficiently "sickled o'er with the pale cast of thought" ‹190› to have, for a few moments after the deed is done, "second thoughts" about the "pedagogic effectiveness" or the "fairness" of that box on the ear, or at least about the considerable "display of energy" that it involved. Or, better still, suppose that the howling of the child awakens in the head of the family – who, as a male German, is convinced of his superior grasp of all matters, including the bringing up of children – the desire to remonstrate with "her" on "teleological" grounds. In that case, "she" may, for example, have the reflection, which she may offer as an excuse, that *if*, at that moment, she *had not been* "agitated" (let us suppose: by a quarrel with the cook), that disciplinary measure *would not* have been applied at all, or at least not "in that way"; and she will be inclined to admit to him that "he knows that otherwise, she is not like that". By saying this, she is referring to his "empirical knowledge" of her "constant motives", which would, under the vast majority of all *possible* constellations [of factors], have had another and less irrational effect. In other words, she is claiming that the box on the ear was, on her part, a "fortuitous" reaction to the behaviour of her child, and not one with an "adequate" cause (to anticipate here the terminology to be discussed immediately below).

As we can see, that matrimonial dialogue has already been sufficient to transform the "immediate experience" into a categorially formed "object". If a logician were to tell the young lady that she had performed a "causal imputation" of the kind that historians make; that, for that purpose, she had made "judgements of objective possibility"; and that she had even utilized the category of "adequate causation" (which will be discussed shortly), she would surely be as astonished as Molière's philistine bourgeois, ‹191› who is pleasantly surprised to learn that he has been speaking "prose" all his life. [Nevertheless,] from the point of view of logic there is no other way [of describing it]. Intellectual knowledge, even of one's own immediate experience, is never and under no circumstances truly a "re-experiencing", nor is it a simple "photograph" of the content of that immediate experience: when the "immediate experience" is made into an "object", it always acquires perspectives and contexts that are precisely *not* "known" when it is "immediately experienced". Visualizing some past action of one's own when one reflects on it is, in *this* connection, in no way different from visualizing a past concrete "natural event" that one has "immediately experienced" oneself, or that has been described by others. It is probably unnecessary to give further illustrations of the general validity of this proposition by providing more complicated examples,[1] and to state explicitly that when we analyse a

---

1   Let us briefly examine one more example, which K. Voßler (*Language*, pp. 101f.) analyses in order to illustrate why the formulation of "laws" must fail. [Voßler] refers to certain linguistic peculiarities developed within his family ("an island of Italian language in the sea of German speech") by his children, and imitated by the parents when speaking with the children. The origins of these peculiarities can be traced back to certain, quite concrete occasions that are still remembered quite clearly, and [Voßler] asks the question: "What does national psychology (and, we may add, following his train of thought, any 'science of laws') still wish to explain in those cases?" – Viewed in isolation, the phenomenon is indeed, on the face of it, quite sufficiently [well] explained; nevertheless, this is not to say that it cannot be the object of further treatment, or be of further use. In the first place, the fact that the causal relationship can in this case be determined with certainty may (*theoretically* – which is all that matters here) be utilized as a heuristic means, in order to investigate whether the [existence of the] same causal relation can be established as probable in *other* instances of linguistic development; however, this requires, from a logical point of view, that the concrete case can be subsumed under a general *rule*. In fact, Voßler himself has (p. 102) formulated this rule as follows: "the more frequently used forms attract the less frequent ones". But this is not all. We said that the causal explanation was, "on the face of it", sufficient. But one must not forget that every *individual* causal interconnection, even the apparently most "simple" one can be broken up and divided ad infinitum, and that only the limits of our causal *interest* decide, in the concrete case, at what point we stop. And actually, nothing in the present case tells us that our need for causal explanation has to be content with the "actual" process [which is] described. A close examination would possibly show us that, for instance, the "attraction" that determined the changes in the language of the children, as well as the imitation by the parents of these juvenile linguistic creations, occurred to a quite different extent for different word forms; and one could ask whether something could not be said about why [the "attraction"] or [the imitation] occurred more or less often, or did not occur at all. Our need for causal [explanation] would then only be satisfied when the conditions of those occurrences had been formulated as rules, and when the concrete case had been "explained" as a concrete constellation resulting from the "interplay" of such rules under concrete "conditions". Then, Voßler would have the hunt for laws – which he detests – the isolation and generalization, going on right in the middle of his cosy home. And what is more: it would be his own fault, as his own general statement: "Analogy is a question of psychical power" leads, with absolute necessity, to the question whether it is really the case that nothing at all [of a] general [nature] can be ascertained and stated about the "psychical" determinants of such "psychical power relations". Voßler's statement – as formulated here – straightaway seems to drag his chief enemy, "*psychology*", almost forcibly into [the discussion of] these questions. If we, in the concrete case, content ourselves with the simple description of the concrete phenomenon, this is owing to two

decision by Napoleon or Bismarck, we proceed in exactly the same way, logically speaking, as the German mother in our example. There is a difference, in that the "internal aspect" of the action to be analysed is given to the mother in her own memory, while we must "interpret" the action of a third person from the "outside"; but, contrary to the naïve unsupported belief, this difference is only one of degree, related to the accessibility and completeness of the "material". But, when we find somebody's "personality" "complicated" and difficult to interpret, we always tend to believe that, if only *the person himself* genuinely *wanted to*, he must be in a position to give us decisive information on that score. The fact that this is not the case – and, indeed, that the reverse is often true – and why this is so, is something that will not be discussed further at this point.

Instead, we shall proceed to examine more closely the category of "objective possibility" – which has so far only been described in very general terms, with respect to its function – and in particular the question of the modalities of the "validity" of the "judgements of possibility". Is it not an obvious objection that the introduction of "possibilities" into the "causal approach" implies a renunciation of causal knowledge altogether? In other words: that – in spite of all that was said above concerning the "objective" basis of the judgement of possibility – since the "possible" event must always be established with the aid of the "imagination", the acknowledgement of the importance of that category in fact amounts to an admission that "historiography" is wide open to subjective arbitrariness and that it is, for precisely that reason, not a "science"? Admittedly, [if we pose] the question of what "would have" happened if a certain contributing factor is imagined to have been modified in a certain way, that question often *cannot*, even if the source material is "ideally" complete, be answered positively at all with any significant [degree of] probability on the basis of general rules of experience.[1] This, however, is not absolutely required. – The assessment of the causal importance of a historical fact will begin with the [following] question: If that fact had been removed from the complex of relevant contributory factors, or if it had been modified in a certain way, *could* events then, according to general rules of experience, have taken a course that, in those respects which are *crucial* for our interest, would *somehow* have been different? For we are of course only concerned with how those "aspects" of the phenomenon that interest us are affected by each of the contributory factors. However, if even this essentially negative question does *not* enable us to arrive at a corresponding "judgement of objective possibility" – or, to put the matter [differently but] with the same meaning: if, on the basis of general rules of experience, the course of events could, as far as we can ascertain, "have been expected" to be *exactly the same* in the "historically important" respects (that is to say: those that interest us), even if that fact were removed or modified – *then* that fact is indeed without causal importance and has absolutely no place in that concatenation [of factors] which history wants to, and must, establish [by means of] causal regression.

As E[duard] M[eyer] sees it, those two shots on a March night [of 1848] in Berlin belong more or less in that category; if [they do] not completely [fit into it], this is possibly because

reasons: First, the "rules" that might have been uncovered as a result of further analysis would probably not, in the concrete case, provide science with any new insights – in other words: the concrete phenomenon has no appreciable importance as a "heuristic instrument"; and, second, the occurrence itself has only had effects within a narrow circle and has therefore had no universal importance for linguistic development – in other words: the occurrence was also unimportant as a historical "real cause". [To conclude]: that [linguistic] occurrence in Voßler's family will probably remain exempt from the process of "concept formation", not because [such a process] would have been meaningless from a logical point of view, but because of the limits of our interest.

1   If one makes the attempt to make a positive construction of what "would have" happened, the results can be grotesque.

even Meyer's view does not exclude that [those two shots] did conceivably (together with other factors) determine at least the time of the outbreak [of the March Revolution], and that, if it had broken out later, this could have meant that [events] had taken another course.

However, if we assume that a certain factor, according to our [general] experience, is causally relevant in those respects that are of importance for the concrete investigation, then the judgement of objective possibility that asserts that relevance can have a whole range of degrees of *precision*. E[duard] M[eyer][holds the] view that Bismarck's "decision" "brought about" the war of 1866 in a *different* sense than [what was brought about by] those two shots. This view involves the claim that, if that decision were excluded [from our analysis], then the other determinants that were present must lead us to ascribe a "high degree" of objective possibility to a development that would (in the "crucial" respects!) have been different – for instance the following: expiry of the Prussian–Italian treaty; peaceful cession of the Veneto; and a coalition between Austria and France, ‹192› or at least a shift in the political and military situation, which would in fact have made Napoleon [III] the "master of the situation". To repeat: the nature of the judgement of objective "possibility" admits *differences of degree*; and the logical relationship, which is based on principles applied in the logical analysis of the "calculus of probability", can be conceived as follows: In our mind, we isolate the causal components to whose "possible" effect the judgement refers, and confront them with the totality of all those conditions *that can be at all imagined* as acting in conjunction *with* them; we then take the group of all those conditions in the presence of which the [causal] components that we "isolated" in our minds were appropriate for "bringing about" the "possible" effect, and ask how it compares with the group of all those [conditions] in the presence of which [the isolated components] could *not* have been "expected" to bring about [that effect]. Of course, this operation does not in any possible way establish a proportion between the two "possibilities" that can in any sense be estimated in "quantitative" terms. That is only [possible] in the domain of "absolute chance" (in the logical sense of the term). [This term refers to] cases – for instance, throwing dice or drawing differently coloured balls from an urn that always contains the same mixture of balls – where certain simple and unambiguous conditions will, over a very large number of instances, remain completely unaltered, while all the other [conditions] vary in a way that we are *absolutely* unable to fathom. [In these cases,] the "possibility" of the relevant "aspect" of the outcome – when throwing dice: the number of pips; when drawing from the urn: the colour of the balls – is determined by those constant and unambiguous *conditions* (the character of the die; the distribution of the balls) in such a way that no other conceivable circumstance has any causal relation – which can be expressed in a *general empirical proposition* – to those "possibilities". The way in which I grasp the dice box and shake it before throwing the dice is an absolutely determining factor for the number of pips that I throw in the concrete case; but, in spite of all the superstitions entertained by "expert dicers", there is no possibility whatsoever of even thinking of an empirical proposition that would state that a certain way of grasping and shaking the box would "be appropriate for" throwing a certain number of pips. In other words: this causality is absolutely a "chance" causality; i.e. we are justified in saying that the way in which the dice are physically thrown *has no "general" effect* on the probability of throwing a certain number of pips; we estimate that the "chance" of *each* of the six faces of the die coming out facing upwards is "the same", *no matter how* we [physically] throw the die. On the other hand, there is an empirical proposition which states that, if the point of gravity of the die is eccentric, this will "favour" a particular face of that "loaded" die coming out facing upwards, whatever other concrete determinants are [also] present; and, by a sufficient number of repeated throws of the die, we can even express the extent of this "favourable chance", of the "objective possibility", in quantitative terms. It is fully justified, as is usually done, to place warning signs when the principles of the calculus of probability are applied to other areas; but it is nevertheless clear that this *last* point [that was discussed] has its analogues in the areas of *all* [kinds of] concrete causality, and therefore also in that of history. The only difference is that, here, the possibility of determining [results] in *quantitative* terms is wholly lacking, since that [possibility] presupposes (1) "absolute chance" and (2) that we are only interested in certain outcomes or "aspects" [of outcomes] that are measurable in quantitative terms. But in spite of this lack [of quantifiability], we are quite able to formulate generally valid judgements to the effect that certain situations will, to a greater or lesser degree, "favour" reactions, on the part of persons confronted with them, that are similar in certain features. Moreover, when we formulate a proposition of this kind, we are also able to point to an immense mass of *possibly* attendant circumstances about which it can be stated that they do not alter that general "favourable chance". And finally, although we cannot in any way make a definite estimate of the *degree* to which certain "conditions" favour a certain outcome – let alone estimating it along the lines of the calculation of probabilities – we can make a *comparison* with the way in which other circumstances (which we imagine as having been modified) "would have" "favoured" [that outcome], and by this means estimate the relative "degree" of that general favourable chance. And if we make this comparison in our "imagination" with regard to a sufficiently large number of conceivable modifications of the constellations [of conditions], then it is conceivable, at least in principle – and that is all that we are so far concerned with here – that the judgement about the "degree" of objective possibility can, after all, attain a considerable measure of precision. Now, we constantly make use of such judgements concerning the "degree" of "favourable chance", not only in daily life, but also – and particularly – in history. Indeed, without them it would be impossible to distinguish between what is causally "important" and "unimportant", and E[duard] Meyer, too, has without hesitation used them in the work under discussion here. In E[duard] M[eyer]'s view (which will not be criticized in substance here), those two shots to which reference has repeatedly been made were causally "unimportant" because "*any* chance occurrence *must* have made the conflict break out". Surely that [claim] means that it is possible to isolate intellectually certain "determinants" that belong to the given historical constellation and that would, together with a quite overwhelming majority of [the] conceivable, *possibly* concomitant further determinants, have brought about the described effect; at the same time, it would seem to us that there is only a (relatively speaking) very small group of conceivable causal factors whose concomitant influence would in our view probably have led to a result that (in its "crucial" aspects!) was *different*. (Considering the fact that Eduard Meyer generally underlines the irrationality of historical events, we will assume that, in spite of his use of the word[s] "must have", he does not believe that this latter group simply contained no elements at all.)

When the relationship between certain complexes of "determinants" – combined into a unity by historical reflection and viewed in isolation – [on the one hand,] and a resultant outcome[, on the other hand], corresponds to the logical category described immediately above, we shall call that relationship one of "*adequate* causation" (of those components of the outcome by those determinants), in accordance with the established terminology employed by theoreticians of legal causality since the publication of v. Kries' works; and just like Ed[uard] Meyer – who, however, does not formulate that concept clearly – we shall speak of "*chance*" causation in cases where the historically relevant components of the outcome were affected by facts that brought about a result which was *not* (in that sense) "adequate" in relation to a complex of determinants mentally combined into a unity.

To revert to the examples used previously: Ed[uard] Meyer's view of the "importance" of the battle of Marathon would, logically speaking, mean *not* that a Persian victory *must* have resulted in a certain, quite different development of the Hellenic culture, and thereby of world culture – such a judgement would be simply impossible – but that such a different development "would have been" the *"adequate"* consequence of such an event [as the Persian victory]. And in the same way, E[duard] Meyer's statement – which v. Below objects to – about the unification of Germany, will be rephrased by us in logically correct terms as follows: That unification can be understood, on the basis of general rules of experience, as the *"adequate"* consequence of certain prior events; and, in the same way: the March Revolution in Berlin can be understood[, on the same basis,] as the adequate consequence of certain general social and political "conditions". On the other hand, if one could make [a] plausible [case for the view] that, according to general rules of experience, a revolution "could", with a very strong degree of probability, "have been" avoided, because it could be demonstrated that, in the *absence* of those shots, a revolution would, according to general rules of experience, *not* – or at least not to any considerable extent – have been "favoured" (in the already defined sense of the term) by the combination of the other "conditions", *then* we would speak of "chance" causation; and in that case – which is admittedly hardly conceivable – we would therefore have to causally "impute" the March Revolution to precisely those two shots. In the example of the unification of Germany, the opposite of a "chance" [occurrence] is *not*, as v. Below assumed, a "necessary" [one], but an "adequate" [one] (in the sense of the term that has already been developed along the lines laid down by v. Kries).[1] And it should be strictly maintained that this distinction [between "chance" and "necessity"] is never a matter of differences in the "objective" causality of the course of historical events and their causal relationships; on the contrary: in all cases, what happens is simply that we isolate by abstraction some of the "conditions" present in the "material" [furnished by] events and make them the object of "judgements of possibility", in order to gain, with the help of rules of experience, an insight into the causal "importance" of the individual components of events. In order to grasp the real causal interconnections, *we construct unreal ones.*

The failure to appreciate that [those constructions] are abstractions is particularly often formulated in a quite specific way that finds an analogy in certain theories, based on the views of John Stuart Mill and entertained by a few theoreticians of legal causality; [those theories] have also already been conclusively criticized in the work by v. Kries cited above.[2] Mill believed that the mathematical quotient of probability was the proportion between those *causes* – ("objectively") *existing* at that given moment – that [acted to] "bring about" a [certain] result and those that [acted to] "prevent" it. Reasoning along the same lines, Binding, too, assumes that a proportion *objectively* exists (sometimes in a "state of equilibrium") between those conditions that "work towards a [certain] result" and those that "resist" it – a proportion that can, in a few individual cases, be determined in quantitative terms, or can at least be estimated – and that the process of causation consists in the first [group] outweighing the latter.[3] It should be clear that [Binding's theory] has made the phenomenon of "conflicting motives", which can be an "immediate experience" in the *deliberation* concerning human "actions", into a basis for the theory of causality. Irrespective of the general importance that one might ascribe to that

1 We shall later discuss whether, and to what extent, we have the means of estimating the "degree" of adequacy, and what role, if any, is in that connection played by the so-called "analogies", particularly when complex "total causes" are broken down into their "components" – as we do not, of course, objectively possess a "key" to that analysis. The present formulation is necessarily provisional.
2 I am almost embarrassed by the extent to which v. Kries' ideas are "plundered" here (as they have already been in many of the previous expositions), the more so since the formulations must necessarily often be less precise than those offered by v. Kries. But both [those circumstances] are unavoidable [if] the purposes of the present study [are to be served].
3 Binding, *Norms*, I, pp. 41–42; v. Kries, *Objective Possibility*, p. 107.

phenomenon,[1] it is, however, certain that no rigorous causal approach, not even in history, can accept this anthropomorphism.[2] Not only is the idea of two "forces" working in "opposite directions" a physical and spatial image that can only – if one does not want to delude oneself – be used in cases, particularly of a mechanical and physical nature, where there are two outcomes that are physically "opposed" to each other, and where each of the two [outcomes] would be brought about by the force [behind it]. But above all, it should once and for all be made clear that a concrete outcome cannot be regarded as the result of a struggle between certain causes that work towards it and others that oppose it; instead, the totality of *all* the conditions uncovered by a causal regression from an "outcome" must "act in conjunction" in that way, and no differently, in order to bring about the concrete outcome in that way, and no differently; for every empirical science that works with causality, the realization of the outcome was certain, not just from a certain moment onwards, but "since the beginning of time". If one speaks of conditions that "favour" and "impede" a given outcome, this cannot mean that, in the concrete case, certain conditions *have* tried in vain to hinder the outcome, which finally came about while other ones, in spite of this, *have* finally brought it about. Instead, that phraseology can only, in every case without exception, mean the following: Certain components of the reality that preceded the outcome in time – [components] that we isolate *intellectually* – will *usually*, according to general rules of experience, and *in general* "favour" an outcome of the kind in question; and that, as we know, means: [they] will *usually* bring about that outcome in the majority of those combinations with other conditions that we can conceive of as possible, while (on the other hand) certain other conditions will *in general* bring about not that, but another outcome. When, for instance, we hear E[duard] M[eyer] (p. 27) speak of cases where everything *"presses on"* towards an outcome, this is an isolating and generalizing *abstraction* and not the reproduction of a course of events that has actually taken place. What is meant is, when formulated in a logically correct manner, no more than this: that we can determine and intellectually isolate causal "factors" to which the expected outcome must be *conceived* as standing in a relationship of *adequacy*, because there is only a relatively small number of *conceivable* combinations of those [factors] that we singled out with other causal "factors" from which we would, according to *general rules of experience*, "expect" a different outcome. In cases where the situation is, in our "view", as described in those words of Ed[uard] Meyer's, we usually say that we are in the presence of a *"developmental tendency"* towards the outcome in question.[3]

This [terminology], as well as the use of metaphors such as "driving forces of" – or, conversely, "impediments to" – a development (for instance, the development of capitalism); and equally, the formulation that a certain "rule" of causal interconnection is in a concrete case "annulled" by certain causal concatenations, or (even more imprecisely) that a "law" is "annulled" by another "law" – all such terminologies [can be used without hesitation] provided that one remains conscious of their logical character; that is to say: provided that one bears in mind that they are based [(1)] on the abstraction of certain components of the actual causal concatenation; [(2)] on the intellectual generalization, in the form of judgements of objective possibility, of

---

1   H. Gomperz (*Probability*) has taken that phenomenon [of "conflicting motives"] as the basis of a phenomenological theory of "decision". I will not take it upon myself to pass judgement on the value of his presentation of the process; but even without doing so, it does nevertheless seem to me that Windelband's identification – which, for his purposes, is deliberately the result of purely conceptual analysis – of the "stronger" motive with that in whose favour the decision finally "comes down" (*Freedom of the Will*, pp. 36f), is not the only possible way of treating the problem.
2   To that extent, Kistiakovski (*School*) is completely right.
3   The unattractiveness of the term does not in any way affect the existence of the logical fact.

the rest of [the causal components]; and, [(3),] on the use of these [judgements] to mould the course of events into a causal interconnection with a particular structure.[1] And, in these cases, it is not sufficient to admit and remain conscious of the fact that all our "knowledge" relates to a reality that is categorially formed – so that, for instance, "causality" is a category of "our" thought. For, in this respect, the "adequacy" of causation is in a special position.[2] Although an exhaustive analysis of that category is in no way intended here, it will nevertheless be necessary to give a brief account of it, first of all in order to clarify the nature of the distinction (which is only relative, and determined by the relevant concrete purpose of the inquiry) between "adequate [causation]" and "chance causation"; and moreover to explain how the – in many instances extremely vague – content of the proposition implicit in a "judgement of possibility" accords with the fact that it nevertheless claims "validity" and can nevertheless be used to construct the causal sequences in history.[3]

First published in *Archiv für Sozialwissenschaft und Sozialpolitik* 22 (1906), pp. 143–207. Translated from: "Kritische Studien auf dem Gebiet der kulturwissenschaftlichen Logik" in Max Weber, *Gesammelte Aufsätze zur Wissenschaftslehre* (ed. Johannes Winckelmann), 3rd ed., Tübingen: J.C.B.Mohr (Paul Siebeck) 1968, pp. 215–90. (The subtitles given in the Table of Contents of that volume are not original and have not been retained here.)
There are indications (see below, pp. 417–18) that Weber began reflecting on the subjects treated in this article as early as 1902–1903. This accords well with the fact that Eduard Meyer's book *On the Theory and Method of History*, which is at the centre of the discussions in the article, was published in 1902.
As in the case of *Roscher and Knies*, a further article was planned, but never appeared. This may possibly be owing to the fact that the subscribers to the *Archive* complained that it carried too many methodological articles.

1 It is only when this is forgotten – something that, admittedly, happens only too often – that Kistiakovski's objections (*School*) concerning the "metaphysical" character of this way of looking at causality are justified.
2 Both in Kries' work (*Objective Possibility*) and in Radbruch's (*Adequate Causation*), the conclusive arguments on this point are already either presented explicitly or touched upon.
3 A further article was planned.

R[UDOLF] STAMMLER'S "OVERCOMING" OF THE MATERIALIST CONCEPTION OF HISTORY[1]

1 Preliminary remarks

It is no easy matter to argue that the "second, revised edition" of a book that has quite undeniably had a strong – mostly confusing, but certainly also extremely stimulating – influence on the discussion of fundamental questions of social science has hardly any justifiable claim to scientific status at all. Nevertheless, this is what will be argued here; and, moreover, that argument will be pursued with brutal frankness. This calls for certain reservations, followed by an indication – which can at this stage only be quite general and brief – of the basis for [the argument]. First, it should be acknowledged quite unconditionally that Stammler's work displays a high degree, not only of learning, acuteness and idealistic striving after knowledge, but also of "inspiration". However, what is grotesque about the book is precisely the disparity between the useful results obtained and the enormous ostentation of the means employed. It is *almost* as if a factory owner were to set in motion the full panoply of technology, immense amounts of capital and innumerable workers, in order to produce, in a huge factory of the most up-to-date construction, atmospheric *air* (gaseous, not liquid!). It is "almost" as if this were the case, since the book quite undoubtedly contains *some few* welcome elements of lasting value (this is the second reservation); [when those elements occur in Stammler's book], they will be scrupulously noted and, to the extent possible, emphasized. But however valuable one may find them, [those elements] are, after all, unfortunately only of quite limited importance compared to the utterly extravagant pretensions of the book. Some of them would have their [proper] place in a monograph on, say, the relationship between the concept formations of jurisprudence and economics; others in a monograph on the formal preconditions of social ideals. Both of those [monographs] would no doubt be of lasting value and provide constant inspiration; but they would certainly have created less sensation than this book, which struts around and makes a colossal exhibition of itself. However, in the book [those valuable elements] disappear in a veritable jungle of apparent truths, half-truths, incorrectly formulated truths, and non-truths hidden by unclear formulations, of scholastic fallacies and sophistries, which make the discussion of the book not only a depressing task (already because the result is in essence a negative one), but also an infinitely tedious and extremely lengthy business. Nevertheless, the analysis of a relatively large number of specific

1 Stammler, *Economy*[2].

formulations is quite unavoidable if one is to get an idea of the utter hollowness of precisely those arguments that Stammler advances with the most astonishing assurance. − It is of course quite true that "intra muros peccatur et extra". ‹193› In the work of every writer, without exception, one may find points where the problem under discussion is not fully thought out, [or] where the formulation is careless, unclear or downright wrong. And this is particularly [often] the case when we, who are not logicians by profession, feel compelled to discuss logical problems in the substantive interest of our specialized disciplines. In those cases, and particularly when dealing with issues that were of little or no importance for our solution of the concrete problem at hand, we inevitably tend to lose our mastery of the specific intellectual apparatus of the discipline of logic: of course, we do not use that apparatus every day, and only such everyday use can give us that mastery. But first of all, Stammler in fact *wants to* represent himself as an "epistemologist"; moreover − as we shall see − what we are dealing with here are those links in his chain of argument on which he himself lays particular stress. And then, we should not forget that we are discussing a *second edition*: we are surely justified in expecting it to live up to quite different requirements from those that we would impose on a "first attempt". What clearly calls for the most severe criticism is the fact that Stammler permits himself to present us with a second edition that is in such a [poor] condition. The severity of that criticism is prompted, not by the publication of the book, but by the publication of a second edition of that quality. When [we are] dealing with a "first attempt" − as with the first edition [of Stammler's book] − we are quite willing to keep the adage in mind that it is always easier to criticize the work [of somebody else] than to produce something oneself. But in a second, "revised" edition, published almost a decade later [than the first one], we require the author to engage in self-criticism. And, in particular, we find it inexcusable when his discussions of *logical* problems show that, as is the case with Stammler, he has not in any way profited from the work of professional logicians. And one final point: Stammler claims to be an exponent of "critical idealism": ‹194› he wishes to be recognized as the most authentic disciple of Kant, both in the field of ethics and in that of epistemology. However, those pretensions are based on gross misconceptions of Kant's teaching. Within the framework of the critical analysis that is to follow, it will not be possible to discuss in detail where those misconceptions lie. But, at any rate, the followers of "critical idealism", more than anybody else, have every reason to dissociate themselves completely from [Stammler's] work, since it has a distinctive character that is only too likely to nourish the old naturalistic belief that epistemologists who criticize naturalistic dogmatism ‹195› are reduced to choosing between two kinds of proof: "a blatant non sequitur or a subtle sleight of hand". ‹196›

2 Stammler's account of historical materialism

Stammler claims that the purpose of his book[1] is [to provide a] scientific "refutation" of "the materialist conception of history", ‹197› and this claim is repeatedly emphasized in the book. Consequently, two preliminary questions need to be answered. First: what is [Stammler's] own version of this conception of history? And then, as a further, second question: at *what point* does [Stammler] voice his scientific critique of that conception? It is worth making a small digression in order to make [the answer to] both these questions as illustrative as possible.

1 For the sake of internal consistency, the critique that follows will have a form [which suggests] that the arguments which it contains − some of them quite elementary ones − are presented here for the first time. In many instances, that is of course not the case at all, and this should be noted explicitly, although the informed reader will be aware of it. Occasional reference will be made to the views of earlier critics of Stammler.

Let us assume that, in our time, where the attention paid to the importance of religious factors for cultural history is very much on the increase, an author will before long appear who advances the following claim: "History is nothing but a succession of *religious* attitudes and struggles of mankind. In the last resort, all cultural phenomena without exception (and especially those of political and economic life) are determined by religious interests and attitudes. All events, even in the political and economic domain, are ultimately reflections of certain positions taken by human beings on religious issues. Therefore, they are in the last resort simply modes of expression of religious forces and ideas; and, consequently, they have only been scientifically explained when the causal chain leading back to those [religious] ideas has been established. At the same time, such a [causal] attribution is the only possible way in which the *totality* of 'social' evolution, according to established laws, can be comprehended scientifically as a *unity* ([*Economy*²,] p. 66, bottom, p. 67, top), in the same way that the natural sciences [comprehend] 'natural' evolution." – An "empiricist" might object that there are surely numerous concrete phenomena of political and economic life that exhibit no trace of any religious motivation. Let us further assume that our "spiritualist" would then reply as follows: "It is undoubtedly [true] that not every individual occurrence has only one single cause; consequently, innumerable *individual* events and motivations that have no religious character at all can unquestionably be identified as causes in the chain of causation. However, as is well known, it is possible to continue the causal regression indefinitely, and, in doing so, one will (p. 67, line 11) *invariably* end up by encountering, at some point, the 'decisive' influence of religious motives on the conduct of life of human beings. *Therefore*, every other substantive change in the life of human beings can in the last resort be traced back to changes in attitudes towards religion (p. 31, line 26); and, since they simply reflect these changes, they have no independent, real existence at all (p. 30, line 11 from below). This is owing to the fact that every change in the religious determinants results in a parallel (p. 24, line 5) substantive change in the conduct of life in every domain. In fact, [the religious determinants] are simply, in every instance, the sole driving forces [not only] of social life, [but also] – consciously or unconsciously – of individual human existence; consequently, given *complete* knowledge of the chain of causation in its 'unitary inter-connectedness', one will always find [those religious determinants] (p. 67, line 20). And how could it be otherwise? After all, the external forms of political and economic life do not have an autonomous existence as closed spheres with their own, separate causal chains. They have no independent reality at all (p. 26, line 6 from below); on the contrary, they only have the status of derivative 'individual aspects' that have been abstracted from the totality of the unity of life (p. 68, line 11)."

The "common sense" of our "empiricist" would probably [lead him to] object to this by putting forward the argument that it is a priori impossible to make any general assertion about the nature and extent of the causal interdependence between different categories of "social phenomena". To begin with, the fact that [such a causal] interdependence exists, and, in addition, its nature and extent, can only be established with respect to individual cases. At a later stage, it may then be possible, by comparing cases that are actually (or apparently) similar, to go beyond the simple determination of the extent to which an individual social phenomenon has been determined by religious factors, and to formulate more general "rules". But it should be noted that [these "rules"] would certainly not tell us anything about the causal importance of "the religious [element]" *in general* for "social life" *in general* – that [would be] a completely misguided and vague way of formulating the problem; instead, [they would concern] the causal relationship of certain *classes* of religious cultural elements (which must be quite strictly defined) to [certain] *other classes* of cultural elements (which must be equally strictly defined) under certain constellations (which must also be strictly defined). – And [the empiricist] would add something like [the following]: The individual "points of view" ("political", "religious", "economic" etc.) according to which we classify the cultural phenomena are deliberately one-sided perspectives that are only adopted, whenever this is desirable in [actual] practice, for the sake of the "economy" of the scientific work. Scientific knowledge of cultural development in its "totality" – in the scientific sense of that term, that is to say: "what we find worth knowing" about it – can only be achieved by an integration, by progressing from the "one-sidedness" to the "comprehensiveness" of the "conception". It cannot be attained by [making] a hopeless attempt to present historical formations as being solely determined and qualified by one single component among [those mentioned], which have only been isolated artificially. It seems obvious that, in this respect, it is fruitless [to pursue] the causal "regression": however far back one goes, even to the earliest times, the [act of] singling out the "religious" components among all the phenomena, and of breaking off the regression at the precise point when one arrives at those ["religious" components], will still be no less "one-sided" than at that stage of history where the regression was initiated. In particular case[s], it may be extremely valuable, from a heuristic point of view, to limit oneself to establishing the causal importance of "religious" factors; this [heuristic value] depends exclusively on what it "yields" in the way of new causal knowledge. But the thesis according to which *the totality* of cultural phenomena are "in the last resort" determined *solely* by religious motives is a hypothesis that is not only unfounded in itself, but that, moreover, is incompatible with established "facts".

But those arguments of "sound common sense" would go down badly with our "historical spiritualist". Let us hear what he would reply: "In order to have any force, the doubt whether the causally determining religious factor can also be *identified* everywhere, would have to call into general question the aim of arriving at a fundamental method of [achieving] law-like knowledge from *one single* point of view (p. 66, line 11). However, any individual scientific observation is governed by the principle of the law of causality; *therefore*, it must assume, as a fundamental presupposition, that *all* separate phenomena are universally connected according to *one* general law; otherwise, it would be completely meaningless to assert that knowledge has been attained *according to laws* (pp. 67, line 5 from below, 68 top). The fundamental principle according to which all social phenomena can be traced back to religious driving forces in no way implies a claim that it will in actual fact always, or in the majority of cases, or at least in some instance, be completely possible to trace back social phenomena to those driving forces (p. 69, line 8 from below). [The principle] purports to be a *method*, not just an assertion of facts (p. 68, line 6 from below). Therefore, it is from a *conceptual* point of view quite misguided to reproach it with being nothing more than a generalization, based on individual events in social history, which has been carried too far: the principle is not based on such generalizations, but has been established a priori by asking 'what is the justification for generalizing *at all*?' (p. 69, line 7). Generalization, as a method of attaining causal knowledge, presupposes an ultimate *unitary* point of view that must undertake to represent the ultimate fundamental unity of social life; otherwise, any search for causal knowledge would be an endless pursuit of diffuse ramifications. This means that the thesis is a systematic *method* for determining in what *generally valid* way the concrete processes of social life can *be grasped scientifically at all* (p. 69, lines 12ff.); that is to say: it is a fundamental *formal principle* (p. 69, line 24) of social research. Now, a *method* cannot be attacked or 'refuted' with the aid of historical *facts*, since the question of how such *formal* principles should *in principle* be [correctly formulated] is obviously not in the least affected by [the fact] whether it can be successfully *applied* in some particular case. (After all, the application of even the indisputably most generally valid axioms for arriving at knowledge of law-like [regularities] will often leave people unsatisfied (p. 69, line 10 from below).) Consequently, that fundamental principle is completely independent *of any particular content* of social processes.

It would be valid even if *no* single *individual* fact could actually be explained according to it; [if that were the case], this would be due to the peculiar difficulty – which needs no particular comment (p. 70, top) – arising from the application of the principle of causality to the investigation of the social life of human beings, instead of 'nature'. But, on the other hand, if it is permissible to apply the *formal* principle of *all* causal knowledge to social life as well, then the fundamental principle *must* be respected, and that can *only* be done by reducing *all* social law-like regularities to *one* 'fundamental law-like regularity': the dependence on the religious [element]. Consequently, when we consider the claim that, 'in the last resort', social life is determined by *religious* driving forces, and that the only way to represent it as a *unity*, which can be comprehended scientifically 'according to mechanical laws', is by 'tracing back' *all* phenomena to *those* determinants, then it is *altogether* impossible to refute [that claim] on the basis of 'facts', nor does it stem from a simple generalization of facts (pp. 68 bottom, 69 top). Instead, the proposition is a consequence of the nature of our thought, insofar as this thought is at all oriented towards the acquisition of knowledge of *law*-like [regularities] – [a goal] that every science working with the law of causality must surely have. If someone objects to [the above-mentioned] claim, he is in fact attacking that *cognitive goal* as such. In order to do so, he must therefore enter the field of *epistemology* and ask the following question: [']What constitutes knowledge of the "law-like [regularities]" of social life; and what *does it imply*?['] (p. 69, line 22). The above-mentioned *method* of tracing back all social phenomena to a *unitary* viewpoint can only be attacked by turning the *concept* of 'law-like regularity' *as such* into a problem; and this would be the only possible way of disputing the justification of the claim that religious motives are 'in the last resort' the decisive ones." "But so far" (obviously, the historical spiritualist does not yet know that Stammler has made his appearance), "nobody has made that attempt; instead, there have only been squabbles over isolated facts, and these squabbles do not in any way affect the principle in itself."

What will be the common-sense reaction of our "empiricist" to these statements? If he is a person who is not easily taken in, I think that he will treat them as a – naïve or impudent – [piece of] *scholastic mystification*. [Moreover, I believe] that he will argue that the same "logic" makes it possible to establish a "method[olog]ical principle" according to which "social life" can only, "in the last resort", be derived from craniometric indices ‹198› (or from the influence of sunspots, or possibly from indigestion); and [he will further argue] that this principle would have to be regarded as unimpeachable as long as it had not been established, through *epistemological* investigations, that the "meaning" of the "social law-like regularity" was to be found elsewhere. – Personally, I would agree with that "common sense" [position].

Stammler, however, would obviously see the matter differently. In the preceding exposition of the [views of the] "historical spiritualist" – it was deliberately, and quite in the style of Stammler himself, made as prolix as possible – one only has to replace the word "religious", whenever it occurs, with the word "material" (in the sense of "economic"). As anyone can see by checking the references to Stammler's book given in the parentheses, the result [of that exercise] is in most instances true to the letter, and in every single one to the spirit, of the account of the "materialist conception of history" given by Stammler in that book. And – the only thing that matters to us here – he accepts this account as being quite simply the correct one.[1] His only reservation is that he – Stammler – has now appeared as the man who was able, by entering the field of "epistemology", to "surpass" this Goliath whom no one had ever vanquished before; [he] "surpassed" it, that is to say, not by showing that it was incorrect in

---

1   See pp. 63ff. where it is quite clear that Stammler himself is speaking, and not the "socialist" introduced by him on pp. 51f.

substance, but by demonstrating its unfinished character; and "unfinished" should in its turn be understood as meaning, not "one-sided", but "incomplete". This "completion" and this "surpassing" are then performed in the following manner: By means of a series of intellectual manipulations, it is demonstrated that "social law-likeness", in the sense of the "fundamental unity" of social life and of the knowledge [of social life] (as we shall see, the two are confused with each other) can, as a "formal principle", only be meaningfully conceived within the "world of purposes" as a principle that determines the "form of existence of human beings in society", as a "unitary formal idea which is to serve as the guiding light for all empirical social endeavours".

At this stage, we are not as yet interested in the question whether Stammler's account of the "materialist conception of history" is *correct*. From the *Communist Manifesto* ‹199› up until the modern epigones [of Marx], that theory has passed through a large variety of forms. A priori, we may therefore safely concede that it is possible, and [indeed] probable, that [the theory] may also be found in one of the forms that Stammler has chosen and that are at least similar [to the ones just referred to].[1] And, even if this should turn out not to be the case, a critic [of the theory] might still be justified in attempting to make his own construction of the form that the theory "should have had" in order to be consistent. However, here we are not concerned with [the materialist conception of history], but with Stammler. Consequently, the only question that we formulate here is the following: In what way does *Stammler* develop and underpin the "epistemology" that he – rightly or wrongly – attributes to [the materialist conception of history], and that he regards as unimpeachable, or at least as being open to correction only on the basis of his own position? Perhaps we have done him an injustice; perhaps he does not actually identify himself with it to the extent that we assumed prima facie? In order to provide an answer to that question, let us examine those introductory sections of his book that deal with "epistemology".

3 Stammler's "epistemology"

In order to acquire an insight into the peculiarities of Stammler's mode of argumentation, it is indispensable to quote in full, by way of example, at least some of the chains of inference put forward in th[e] introductory part [of his book]. Let us start with the beginning [of his text] and subdivide it into a series of short propositions, which we will then compare with each other. On the first pages (3–6) of the text we find the following statements: Every "piece of careful individual research" remains valueless and "incidental" (1) unless it has a "dependent *connection with*" a "general law-like regularity"; (2) unless it is guided *by* a "generally valid criterion of *knowledge*"; (3) unless it is "*related to*" a "fundamental law-like regularity"; (4) unless it is related to a "unitary *unconditional point of view*" (p. 3); [and] (5) (p. 4) unless it [is based on] an insight "into a *generally valid* law-like interconnection", since (6) the assumption [that] this law-like regularity [exists] is a "precondition", whenever the aim is to *go beyond* the confirmed individual observation as such. Then, however, the question is (7) (p. 5) whether it is possible "to establish a general *law-like regularity* in the social *life* of human beings, in the same way as the law-like regularity of nature on which the natural sciences are based". But, unfortunately, [an answer to] this question, which concerns (8) "the *law-like character* of all our *knowledge* of social things", is still outstanding. But, "*in practice*", the question (9) concerning the "supreme law which social life can be *known* as being subject to and dependent on (!)" "immediately leads to the *fundamental conception* of the relationship between the individual and the totality" (!). And,

1 For a discussion of the meaning of "materialist" in Marx's work, see Adler, *Causality and Teleology*, pp. 300n1, 303 (with a sound criticism of Stammler), p. 308n1 and in a number of other passages.

in fact, "the endeavour to *configure life* in society [so that it is] *in accordance with laws* does exist
. . . it is called: the social question". (10) "*Therefore*, the possibility of *configuring* human communal
life . . . *in accordance with laws* is dependent on the *scientific* insight into the *laws which are valid*
for the communal life of human beings in general."

Enough for the present. On p. 4, Stammler remarks that anyone who uses the term "*law-
like* processes" should above all know what he *really means to say* by that. Confronted with this
inextricable agglutination of propositions, all of them operating with the concept of "law-like
character", one can only regret that Stammler has shown such an utter lack of respect for his
own injunction. It should be obvious that almost every one of the ten statements quoted above
expresses something different from the rest. Nevertheless, when one reads [Stammler's] book,
it is equally obvious – but certainly astonishing – that he himself is under the illusion that he
is everywhere speaking of one and the same problem, which he simply formulates in different
ways. This [illusion] can be ascribed to the fact that his formulations are nebulous and ambiguous
[to a degree that] must be unparalleled in a work with such pretensions. With this in mind, let
us look again at the statements listed above (which, on the decisive points, were quoted verbatim).
As for (1), its meaning is altogether obscure: it is difficult to see what a "dependent connection
with a law-like regularity" can refer to. The only possible meaning might be, either, that research
[into] individual [phenomena] is only meaningful if it is carried out with the aim of abstracting
general law-like regularities [from the individual results] ([that would be] searching for nomothetic
knowledge) ‹200›; or else, that it is impossible to provide a causal explanation of individual
interconnections without making use of general knowledge – that is to say: knowledge of laws
([that would be] searching for historical knowledge). One might be inclined to see statement
(7) as confirming one or the other of these interpretations (or both of them), as that statement
claims that the "main question" must be whether it is possible to establish laws of "social life"
in the same way in which "laws of nature" can be established with respect to "inanimate"
nature (this seems to be the natural way of interpreting [Stammler's] formulation, which is again
quite nebulous). From statement (3) and statement (6) (the necessity of a relation to a
"fundamental law-like regularity", [a regularity] that is also a "precondition" of all valid
knowledge of individual "facts" as being "*necessary*") one might further conclude that those
propositions are supposed to be motivated (albeit quite insufficiently) by [the] reference to the
universal validity of the category of causality (in the sense of "law-like regularity"). On the
other hand, however, [statements] (2) and (8) suddenly no longer refer to the "law-like regularity"
of the *occurrences* that are the object of knowledge, but to the fact that the *process by which
knowledge is acquired* takes place in accordance with laws. In other words: the reference is no
longer to "laws" that empirically govern *that which is known* or is to be known – i.e. the world
of "objects" ("nature" or "social life") – and that can be established by means of induction
("going beyond the individual observation" ([statement] (6)), in order to "confer on isolated
facts the character of necessity" (p. 4, bottom). Instead, the reference is to *norms* that are valid
for the *process by which we acquire knowledge*. There is no other natural way of interpreting [the
expressions] "generally *valid* criteria of *knowledge*" (2) and the "law-like character" of all our
knowledge of social things" (8). This means that [the distinction between] "norms of thought"
and "laws of nature" is blurred. But there is more to come: In (5), the allegedly indispensable
insight into an *interconnection* of facts (that is: into something concrete) is completely mixed up
with [the insight] into the "*law-like regularity*" (that is: into something abstract). (This in spite
of the fact that, if [the law-like regularity] is to be understood as a law of nature, the two kinds
of insight are direct opposites; and that if, on the other hand, [the law-like regularity is to be
understood] as a cognitive "norm", the two kinds of insight are, as logical relationships,
completely different from each other.) And, on top of that, the "law-like interconnection" (5)

is even given the predicate of being "generally *valid*". That this "validity" is not that [attributable to] a *judgement* of empirical science concerning a purely "factual" interconnection is already indicated by the formulation of [statement] (4). This statement – which is in itself quite unintelligible – refers to the necessity of a "relation" to a *unitary "point of view"*, a point of view that is, moreover, "*unconditional*". It is true that *arranging* facts [so that they constitute] a concrete interconnection, and [establishing] "law-like regularities" by means of abstraction from facts, are both processes that are usually governed by their own separate "viewpoint" (indeed, the division of labour among the various specialized disciplines rests on this foundation). But, for precisely that reason, it surely seems impossible to speak of *one* "unconditional" point of view [governing] all empirical disciplines. [Stammler] might also have been thinking of the principle of quantification and of [giving knowledge a] mathematical form. But that principle is certainly not common to all of the so-called "natural sciences" (in the institutional sense of that term); and, as for [the sciences] usually designated as the "sciences of the human spirit", they are characterized precisely by the fact that they approach reality from *multiple* and varied "points of view". Least of all can a "*unitary point of view*" – in that sense – be identified with a fundamental "*law-like regularity*" and attributed to all sciences. Finally, one might call the category of causality – which is equally constitutive for all [the sciences] – a "point of view". (We shall come back to this). In that case, it might be possible, albeit in a very special sense, to say that the "law-like character" of occurrences was one of the general "preconditions" of the historical disciplines, which explain *individual* objects by tracing them back, in a causal regression, to other individual objects; but, even so, it would certainly not be possible to designate [the "law-like character" of occurrences] as being that *to which* the "individual observation" is *related*. To sum up: While Stammler, with the greatest unconcern, lets "unitary character", "law-like character", "interconnection" and "point of view" whirl haphazardly around each other, they in fact, quite obviously, refer to totally different things. The magnitude of the confusion that [Stammler] has caused becomes completely evident when one realizes, by analysing statement (9), what he actually has in mind [when speaking of] that "point of view". The "supreme *law*" of social life "leads to" – another extremely nebulous expression – the "fundamental *conception* of the relationship between the individual and the totality". If we examine the statement as it stands, formulated in an altogether slovenly manner, the following question obviously arises: Does that "conception" refer to the scientific *explanation* of the "actual" relationship between the "individual" and the "totality"? Or does it represent a daring leap into the "world of values", of what *ought to be*? Statement (10), according to which the "possibility of configuring human communal life according to laws" is conditional on "insight into the laws which are valid for [that communal life]", might still in itself be understood to mean that [the laws referred to] were laws governing *occurrences*. Indeed: if it were possible to uncover "laws" governing social occurrences in the manner of "natural laws" – and [the science of] economics has persistently looked for such ["laws"] – *then* the value of the knowledge [of such laws] for our "purposeful" mastery of social events, and for our influence on the course [of those events] in accordance with our intentions, would no doubt be just as great as the value that the laws of "inanimate" nature have for the techn[olog]ical mastery of the natural world. However, the reference in statement (9) to the "social question" already shows us that, according to the logic of that statement, "configuring social life [so that it is] in conformity with laws" cannot, in any event, be understood as simply referring to measures of social policy taking due account of those "laws" of *occurrences* that are known to be actually valid in the manner of natural laws; it must apparently [refer to] a [process of] "configuration" that is in conformity with laws laying down what *ought to be* – that is to say: [in accordance with] *practical norms*. It is true that Stammler occasionally, with complete composure, uses the same word with two different meanings in the same sentence.

Nevertheless, we must after all assume that the "validity" of the "conformity to laws" must in this case be interpreted as an *imperative*, so that the "insight" into [that lawfulness] represents knowledge of a "commandment" – and indeed of the "highest", "most fundamental" commandment governing all social life. In other words: [Stammler] has actually made his daring leap, and we have arrived at what is – so far – the height of confusion: Laws of nature, categories of thought and imperatives for action, "generality", "unitary character", "interconnection" and "point of view", validity as an empirical necessity, as a method[olog]ical principle, as a logical and practical norm – all this, together with even more [elements], is mixed up here, at the beginning of the book, in a way that certainly does not augur well for a discussion which is intended to defeat the adversary on the terrain of "epistemology".

But perhaps Stammler is only *pretending* to be so confused in these passages! After all, his book is by no means unaffected by the wish to achieve "effects", particularly "suspense" effects. It might be, therefore, that he would deliberately have restricted himself, in the introductory pages, to adapting himself to the vagueness of expression prevalent in his milieu, in order, little by little, to conjure forth logical clarity and intellectual order before the eyes of a reader thirsting for release from that obscure chaos, until that reader was prepared to receive the final, liberating word that lets order reign. – But if one reads on, the confusion does not abate, at least within the confines of the "Introduction" (pp. 3–20). Instead, it increases. We again find (pp. 12, bottom and 13, top) that the ambiguity of expressions such as "social theories" and "unitary fundamental conception" of social life is used (p. 13, next but last paragraph) to present the "insight" into the "law-like character" as being a "criterion" according to which [one] "can consistently conceive, *judge* and *pass sentence on*" all *individual perceptions* (NB!) of social *history* (NB!). In other words: the two first italicized words manifestly represent the goal of "social science" as being that of making value judgements, while the reader gets the impression from the two last italicized[1] words that ["social science"] is concerned with finding theoretical knowledge. And let us take the following sentence (p. 14), which is meant to explain the foundations of social *philosophy* (p. 13, bottom): "If someone speaks of the laws of social life" (ambiguous! – see above), "of social development" (theoretical), "of social damage" (normative) "and [of] the possibility or impossibility" (theoretical)[2] "of repairing it" (normative); "if someone procures (!) the laws of phenomena in the field of social economics" (in that formulation: theoretical), "discusses social conflicts" (*idem*) "and believes in the progress" (normative) "of the existence of human beings in society, or wishes to deny it" (theoretical)[3] – "then [that person] must above all avoid [listening to] irrelevant (?), subjective" (only applies to *value* judgements) "twaddle and get a clear idea of the distinctive features of knowledge within the social *sciences*" (that is to say: not in the domain of social *philosophy*, which until then was the subject [of the discussion]). As one can see, the discussion within each part of this sentence oscillates between the knowledge of facts and the evaluation of facts. Later (at the bottom of p. 15), Stammler claims that "the generally *valid* (NB!) *law-like regularity* of the course of social life within history" (in other words: the "law-like regularity" of the object of knowledge) "implies (!) that *it* (NB!) *is known* in a unitary (?) and (?) generally *valid* (NB!) manner". Here, it is patent that ["]law-like regularity of occurrences["] is conflated with ["]norm of knowledge["],

1 Unless otherwise indicated, the italicizations in the quotations from Stammler are always mine.
2 [and 3] "Theoretical", that is to say, *when* it has been established what state of affairs is to *qualify as* "repairing" and as "progress". Once that has been done, the question whether it is "possible" to bring about this state of affairs, and whether a movement in the direction of it – i.e. "progress" – can be discerned is of course a purely factual one, to which empirical science can (in principle) provide an answer.
3 See n2 immediately above.

just as the discussion of the "cause of knowledge" [is conflated] with that of the "real cause". ⟨201⟩ [Or take] the sentence at the top of p. 16, where the "supreme unity of all social knowledge" is, on the one hand, "to be *valid* as a fundamental *law for* all social life" and, on the other hand (a few lines later), should be the "generally valid basis on which the possibility of law-like *observation* of human life in society can then be realized". Here, Stammler has even succeeded in mixing together laws of nature, practical norms and logical norms. At the same time, the careful reader continually gets the disturbing impression that Stammler by no means remains completely unaware of the ambiguity in his use of expressions such as "accordance with laws", "generally valid" etc. etc.; and even the deletions and additions that have been made in the second edition are often liable to strengthen this impression: in many cases, St[ammler] undoubtedly *knows* that his language is vague and ambiguous. I wish to state explicitly that I am *absolutely not* reproaching St[ammler], on "moral" grounds (even in the most indirect sense of that term) with that ambiguity of expression that he, as I have said, can hardly be completely unaware of, and that meets the eye wherever one looks. No: [what I object to] is that peculiar kind of instinctive "diplomacy" that characterizes a dogmatist obsessed with the "cosmic formula" that is – or allegedly is – his original discovery, and who firmly believes, as an a priori, that his "dogma" *cannot* possibly be in contradiction with "science"; who, therefore, completely secure in his belief and acting with the unerring precision of a sleepwalker, avoids "pinning himself down" by the elimination of ambiguity at points where his argument is problematical, and prefers trustfully to leave in the hands of God the confusion brought about by his hazy and ambiguous language, convinced that [this confusion] can eventually somehow be adapted to the "formula" that he has already discovered and be ordered in conformity with it. However, the unprejudiced observer must find it extremely improbable that someone who sets out so badly equipped, and who – as we have seen St[ammler] doing it already in the introductory pages [of his book] – makes such basic mistakes by mixing up the simplest categories, will be able to arrive at any sort of understanding of what can and ought to be the cognitive goal of an "empirical" discipline such as social *science* in *our* sense of the word. This also makes it easy to understand how the (alleged or actual) arguments of historical materialism parodied above can be reproduced by St[ammler] in the way that he does, and how he can maintain that they are irrefutable (except from *his own* "epistemological" standpoint). [A writer] who cannot distinguish "laws of nature" from logical "norms" is quite simply a scholastic in the strict sense of the term; and, for that same reason, he is also powerless against scholastic arguments. That this is the case [with Stammler] is already quite clearly apparent on p. 19, where [he] for the first time characterizes the general scientific nature of historical materialism. On p. 18 (second paragraph), the *empirical* character of the problem seems to be explicitly acknowledged; and [Stammler] then maintains (in paragraph 3) that historical materialism seeks to discover a fixed "rank order" among the elements of social life – which, on the face of it, amounts to establishing, in a general way, the *causal* importance of those "elements" in their relations with each other. However, a little earlier in that same paragraph, it is said that the materialist historical conception of this point is a "method[olog]ical principle" of "*formal* significance". And, with his usual vagueness, Stammler adds to this the further claim that, according to the "basic idea" (p. 18, last line) of "the materialist conception of history" (p. 19) (he does not say whether this is meant to represent the deliberate position of the representatives [of historical materialism], or whether it is a view imputed to them by Stammler as a "consequence" of their position), it is necessary to *distinguish* between the "individual laws which have been established" and "the general *formal* lawfulness, that is: the fundamental way of producing the correct synthesis between facts and laws". It is well known that nothing is more ambiguous than the word "formal" or the meaning of the distinction between form and content. In *every* single case, it is necessary to define quite precisely what is to be meant by it. Now, Stammler himself claims that the "basic idea" of historical materialism is that the distinctive character and development of "economic phenomena" are invariably decisive for the configuration of all other historical processes – in other words: that ["economic phenomena"] are the unequivocal causes of [those processes]. One may complain about the vagueness of the term "economic phenomena", but one point at least is certain: that claim has a substantive character; [it] concerns the way in which empirical occurrences are causally interconnected. Consequently, it is a thesis that is by virtue of its more *general character*, but *in absolutely no other respect*, different from the claim that in one or several *individual cases*, or in certain *kinds* of cases – defined more or less narrowly – "economic" causes are decisive. It is a hypothesis whose plausibility one can, for instance, attempt to establish "deductively" on the basis of the actual conditions of human life in general, and then to verify "inductively" over and over again [by confronting it with] the "facts"; but it always remains a *substantive* hypothesis. Nor is this state of affairs in any way changed if someone, for instance, declares that he accepts the theory of historical materialism, not as a theorem, but as a "heuristic principle", and in this way tries to set up a specific "method" for the investigation of historical material "from economic points of view". Experience shows that, if one proceeds professionally and soberly, this method may well be extremely fruitful. And once again, it only implies that the general claim with regard to the importance of economic determinants should be treated as a substantive *hypothesis*, and that its scope and the limits of its applicability should be tested [by confrontation with] the facts. There seems to be absolutely no reason why the hypothesis should for that – or for any other – reason change its nature from that of a general substantive claim and acquire a "formal" character that would invest it with a specific *logical* status higher than that possessed by the "individual laws" (i.e. claims or theorems of less comprehensive generality), so that the "validity" and the "scientific justification" of those "special laws" would henceforth be based on [the "formalized" hypothesis]. Of course, from a terminological point of view, one is at liberty to designate the ultimate ("highest") generalizations of a particular discipline – as for instance the principle of the "conservation of energy" ⟨202⟩ – as being "formal" because their validity is as comprehensive as possible, while their substantive content is as limited as possible (but it should be observed that the substantive content is *not* [totally] *lacking*!). In actual fact, this often happens. But, in that case, every "higher" generalization is "formal" compared with all "lower" (i.e. less comprehensive) ones. All the "axioms" of physics, for instance, are "ultimate" generalizations of that kind. That is to say: they are mathematically "evident" hypotheses that have been empirically "confirmed", to an extraordinarily high degree, by confrontation with the facts. Subsequently, these hypotheses are even further "confirmed" whenever they are utilized as "heuristic principles"; but nevertheless – as the debate on radioactivity has shown – the degree of confirmation completely depends on whether [the hypotheses] will again and again "stand up to" [the confrontation with] the facts. But even a student of logic in his first term is bound to know that this [constant empirical "confirmation"] does not mean that [the hypotheses] assume the logical character of "formal" cognitive principles, in the sense of epistemological a priori categories – and [he will also know] that they will never ever be able to attain that status. But *if* someone, like St[ammler], intends to play the role of an "epistemologist" – and even explicitly announces that he wishes to base himself on Kant – then [he] of course [commits] the same inexcusable basic error when he elevates "axioms" (i.e. propositions that "simplify" experience) to the status of a "category", as when he stamps "categories", whose formative power is necessary to make "experience" at all meaningfully "possible", as general empirical statements. (One example of this latter procedure is the following: as we sometimes – quite imprecisely – speak of the *law* of causality, we regard the individual "laws of nature" as instances of the "law" of causality "having effect" under special conditions – that is to say: as "special cases" [of the "law" of causality]; and we accordingly regard the "law of causality" itself as being the most comprehensive generalization of facts.) The second of these two errors represents a retrogression beyond Kant to – at least – Hume; but the first one even goes very much further back, namely to scholasticism. Stammler's entire argument is based on this relapse into massive scholasticism. [For confirmation of this claim], one only needs to reread the parody offered above and, perhaps, to verify once more that it does in fact correspond to what is said in the passages quoted and on pp. 18 and 19 of Stammler's book. As for the second error (that of transforming categories into empirical statements), which is the exact opposite of the first one, Stammler has not committed it "explicitly". On the contrary: he tries to place himself on the basis of Kant's teachings. But we shall soon see that he nevertheless, implicitly, commits that error as well. Moreover, when we later examine [Stammler's] feeble and inconsistent way of treating the "question" of causality more closely, we shall come to realize that, in practice, it does not matter very much whether the "axioms" are raised to the status of "categories" or the "categories" reduced to the status of "axioms". To cap it all, Stammler, in his account of the "materialist conception of history" (which was reproduced in the form of a parody in the introduction to this article), obligingly elevates purely *methodological* "principles" to the rank of "formal principles" rooted in epistemology. This is of course just the same (but in reverse) as transforming the principle of [sufficient] reason into a "heuristic principle" – that is to say: into a hypothesis that must be tested empirically. Those are the sorts of blunder served up by an alleged "disciple" of Kant!

Stammler ends up – at the bottom of p. 12 – by also labelling the "categories" as "viewpoints" "from which" generalizations are made, and in so doing commits a whole tangled series of elementary logical errors, both those mentioned above and others similar to them. In that passage, he claims that it is indispensable constantly to ask oneself "what is the unitary viewpoint according to which" the "generalizations from certain *observations*" (NB!) have been carried out: "Have they been made from the point of view of causality or of the *purposeful idea*? Why the one or the other? And what are the details of the viewpoint under which they have been made?" – Now, first of all, insofar as that alternative exists at all, it is not an exclusive one. To take an example: the general concept of "white objects" has been constituted neither from "causal" points of view nor from the point of view of a "purposeful idea"; it is nothing more than a general idea that has been subjected to logical processing – a simple classificatory concept. But, even if we disregard this imprecision of expression, it still remains completely open what that alternative actually implies. What does "generalization from *observations* according to the point of view of a purposeful idea" mean? We shall briefly review the possibilities, as this may be useful for certain [of our] later discussions. Does [that expression] mean that metaphysical "purposes of nature" are deductively derived from empirical "laws of nature" – more or less in the sense in which E[duard] v. Hartmann occasionally tries to demonstrate the "purpose" of the finite evolution of the cosmos on the basis of the so-called "second law" of thermodynamics? ⟨203⟩ Or does it refer to the use – as for instance in biology – of "teleological" concepts as heuristic principles in order to acquire general insight into the relationships of the phenomena of life? In the first case, the idea is to make empirical propositions support metaphysical belief; in the second one, an "anthropomorphic" metaphysics is used heuristically as an aid to the formulation of empirical propositions. Or, does [Stammler's obscure statement quoted above] refer to empirical propositions concerning the generally "appropriate means" for the attainment of certain, generally defined "purposes"? In that case, we would of course be dealing with ordinary, general causal knowledge, clothed in the form of a piece of practical reasoning. (For instance, the sentence "the measure x in the field of economic policy serves the purpose y" is simply a reformulation of the following empirical proposition asserting [the existence of] a general causal relationship: "*if* x takes place, then y is, in general, the (either invariable or "adequate") *consequence*". The first of the three [possible interpretations of Stammler's statement listed above] could hardly be that intended by Stammler, since he has no wish to engage in metaphysical – least of all naturalistic metaphysical – reasoning; and, as for the two other ones, he would surely have to acknowledge that they are "generalizations from the point of view of causality". Or, does [Stammler] have in mind the logical analysis of general *value* judgements and ethical or political demands? Take the proposition: "The protection of the weak is the duty of the state". If we abstract from the vagueness of the concepts of "protection" and "weak", this is a "general", practical maxim. Its *truth* content – in the sense of whether it *should be* valid – can of course also be a subject of discussion, although [that discussion] would evidently have quite a different character from [the discussion of whether it is] an empirical fact, or a "law of nature". But does that proposition contain a "generalization of observations"? Or should the discussion of its truth content be brought to a conclusion by means of "generalizations of observations"? There is a distinction to be made here. Either the controversy directly concerns the character of the maxim as a valid "imperative"; in that case, the discussion is carried out within the domain of ethical "norms". Or else the controversy concerns the possibility of "carrying out" the maxim in practice; if so, then we are dealing with [an instance of] the third case mentioned above: we are looking for an x which, if it takes place, would have as its general consequence y (in this case: "the protection of the weak"), and we are discussing whether some measure which can be taken by the state can be identified as that x. [In other words,] a purely causal consideration utilizing "rules of experience". Or, finally – and this case is by far the most frequent one – the validity of this putative maxim is not directly challenged; but there will be an attempt to demonstrate that the maxim cannot be an imperative [for action] because action in accordance with it would inevitably have as its consequence that the implementation of *other* maxims which should be recognized as imperatives [for action] would be endangered. To this end, the opponents of the proposition that we have discussed will no doubt endeavour to establish general empirical propositions concerning the *consequences* of implementing that maxim of social policy. And, when they have established – or believe that they have established – such propositions, either by direct induction or by formulating hypotheses that [they] then attempt to demonstrate with the aid of propositions established by other means, they will contest the "validity" of the maxim [by arguing that,] if [the maxim] is implemented, it is to be expected that this will lead to the violation of [some other "maxim" –] for instance, the "maxim" that it is the duty of the state to "defend" the physical health of the nation and the bearers of aesthetic and intellectual "culture" against "degeneration". (Here, too, we are not at all concerned with the question of how this is formulated.) The empirical propositions that will be advanced [as part of that argument] will then in their turn be instances of the "third" case referred to above. They are invariably general judgements concerning causal interrelations, of the form: the consequence of x is – always, or as a "rule" – y. But where, in this connection, have *observations* been generalized "from the point of view of a purposeful idea", *as opposed to* general causal propositions? After all, the two contending maxims as such are *values*, which must in the last resort be "weighed" against each other and which it may possibly be necessary to *choose* between. But the reasons for that choice certainly cannot be found by the "generalization" of "observations", but only by determining the "immanent consequences" [of those maxims] "dialectically" – in other words: by finding the "highest" *practical* axioms to which the maxims can be traced back. And that, as we shall see later, is precisely the method employed by Stammler himself when making the deductions in the last chapter of his book. And that is not the only occasion on which he, too, quite correctly, emphasizes the absolute logical disparity between causal "explanation" and "value judgement", between what is predicted for the future and what ought to [happen]. His exposition of historical materialism already contains a passage (pp. 51–55) in which he, with laudable clarity, illustrates this dichotomy in the form of a "dialogue" between a "bourgeois" and a "socialist". The two antagonists "cavort in separate elements", because one is concerned with what *will* inevitably happen, according to (actually or supposedly) established rules of experience, while the other one [is concerned with] what, out of respect for certain (actual or alleged) cultural values, *ought* on no account to happen. "It is", as Stammler puts it, "a fight between the bear and the shark." All right! But against that background, how does Stammler just a few pages later manage, in the manner that we have already encountered several times, to treat the two kinds of problem – which are, as he well knows, completely heterogeneous – as being *identical*? – Surely this is what happens when he asks the following question (p. 72): What, "then, is the generally valid . . . procedure according to which individual *perceptions* (NB!) in history . . . are generalized (NB!), and identified and determined as being "law-like" phenomena?" – and then, in the same breath and without batting an eyelid, he continues: "If somebody is completely unaware of what it means to *justify* (NB!) a phenomenon of social life, then it is pointless to argue in a given instance about whether or not a certain social opining or striving is *justified* (NB!)"". Here, Stammler "cavorts in separate elements" and actually manages to let "the fight between the bear and the shark" resolve itself into a peaceful, temperate and muddled fraternization between the two [antagonists]. Whoever does not see this, it seems to me, simply does not *want* to see it.

As anybody who reads the book will see, the reader is repeatedly mystified by [Stammler's] constant juggling with two heterogeneous kinds of problem. But that is by no means the worst of those constant equivocations [which Stammler resorts to when he presents] the "epistemological" foundations of his "critique" of historical materialism. We have gradually arrived at the point where we may well ask what Stammler actually *means* by [the term] "social materialism" – the concept that he employs in alternation with [that of the] "materialist conception of history". The "conception" that St[ammler] purports to criticize is – or more correctly: was – called "materialist" for a reason that we may, in spite of all [disputes among its advocates], allow ourselves to formulate in the following manner, as being their "generally accepted view": [The "conception" was "materialist"] because it claimed that "historical" processes are unequivocal consequences of the mode of procurement and use of "material" – that is to say: economic – goods at any given time, and, in particular, that the "historical" action of human beings is unequivocally determined by "material" – that is to say: economic – interests. We may once more, and quite freely, grant Stammler that *every* single concept entering into this definition – which is in this context purely provisional – raises problems, that the substantive content of [all these concepts] is quite indeterminate, that it may not be possible to define them with absolute precision, and that they must [therefore] remain vague; [we may grant him,] moreover, [that] he explicitly states that the distinction between "economic" and non-economic determinants of events always refers to *intellectual* [acts of] isolation (a statement that is quite self-evident for anyone who is aware of the conditionalities of scientific work). All this will not in any way alter the fact that "economic" interests, "economic" phenomena, "material" conditions etc. are at any rate, in that connection, all conceived as being a substantive *part* of the totality of "historical" or "cultural" phenomena and, above all, as also forming a *part* of "life in society" or "social life", as those terms are used by Stammler. He himself had recognized (p. 18) that historical materialism has the ambition of arriving at general statements concerning the "rank order" between *one* "element" of social life and *other* [such elements]. And elsewhere (pp. 64–67), he himself gives examples concerning the mutual causal relationship between "economic" ("material") and *non*-"economic" motives – quite in keeping with the view just quoted (which, in its turn, corresponds to the usual [definitions]) – and discusses them critically.

But three pages later (p. 70, last paragraph but one), we suddenly find the following phrase: "but once the concept of the law-like character of social life has been [recognized as being] identical with [the concept of] the causally explicated process of social change, how is it possible to evade the conclusion that *ultimately*, *all* occurrences in life in society which have been established as having a law-like regularity can be traced back, in [their] dependence (!), to the foundation [provided by] the social economy?"[1]

One asks oneself in vain by what means Stammler intends to make *that* kind of argument plausible – [an argument] whose *conclusion*, as can be seen, gives historical materialism simply everything that it needs (and far more than that). The principle of sufficient reason ‹204› is valid for all historical occurrences and for every phenomenon of social life. But it is really impossible to see how this should entail that it must in the last resort be possible to explain all historical occurrences and every phenomenon of social life *exclusively* by reference to *one* element [of history or social life], and that the contrary case would constitute a violation of the category of causality. But wait! – if we go back a couple of pages, we find (p. 68) a statement according to which it is impossible to accept [the assumption of] a plurality of "fundamental entities" "in which completely separate causal chains run alongside each other". No one with any insight into [the discipline of] history will make any such assumption. On the contrary: everybody knows that any causal regression by which an "individual phenomenon" is traced back will run in all directions forever, and that [the causal regression] may move from "economic" phenomena – that is to say: phenomena that in a given case awaken our interest and our need to find an explanation solely because of their "economic aspects" – to political, religious, ethical, geographical and other conditions, just as well as [it may], conversely, trace political phenomena back to "economic" ones, and to all the other kinds of phenomenon. Therefore, the statement by Stammler [quoted immediately above] does not support his thesis, the less so since he himself immediately afterwards remembers that any examination of a single "aspect" – including, one would suppose, the economic aspect – for the purpose of a separate analysis is simply an intellectual abstraction from the "total context". In other words: the grounds for the sentiments that [Stammler] voices on p. 70 [of his book] have become no clearer to us. However, if we now go back another page (bottom of p. 67), we there find the following claim: "every single observation which is made in accordance with the principle [embodied in] the law of causality must, as a fundamental precondition, accept that all particular phenomena are universally linked according to a (!) general law, and that law then has to be demonstrated (?) in detail." Evidently, this is – at least in Stammler's view – a central epistemological tenet of historical materialism. And he himself also unconditionally subscribes to it, as evidenced by the thesis on p. 70 that we are discussing – and that now immediately becomes understandable as a consequence of that tenet. If we ask how Stammler has arrived at that construction, the answer is probably (as it is impossible to conclude anything with certainty from the chaos in his book) that it is based on logical fallacies from a variety of sources. First of all, there are a number of statements

---

1 An example (top of p. 71): [here, Stammler speaks of] the "crucial" influence, "in the *final analysis*", of economic conditions on the development of architecture (incidentally, this example is in itself less than convincing; moreover, since the attempt is made to support [the claim] on *substantive* grounds, it is in contradiction with the allegedly "formal" character of the principle). – The peculiar diplomatic vagueness that I have already touched on previously also makes itself felt here: "trace back in dependence", "crucial influence" – taken literally, those expressions would still allow Stammler to fall back on the excuse that, after all, he had not (as a strict "materialist" would have done) spoken of a determination that was *exclusively* economic. Nevertheless, "in the final analysis" is an expression that is formulated too much in the style of genuine historical materialism for Stammler to get away with employing it [for that "diplomatic" purpose].

[by Stammler] that suggest that he has been thinking along the following lines: The "exact" natural sciences operate with the idea of "reducing" qualities to quantities – for instance [of "reducing"] phenomena of light, sound, heat, etc. to kinetic processes involving non-qualitative, material "ultimate" elements; as a consequence, the[se sciences] hold the view that only those quantitative, material changes are true "realities", while the "qualitative aspects" are "subjective reflections" in [our] consciousness of those changes, and therefore lack any "true reality". Therefore, he thinks, according to the theory of historical materialism, the only real [elements] of historical life are "matter" (economic conditions and interests) and "changes" in that ["matter"], while everything else is an ideological "superstructure" and "reflection". We know only too well that the minds of many "historical materialists" are still dominated by this fundamentally warped analogy, which is completely worthless from a scientific point of view. Apparently, our author has joined their company. In Stammler's case, this fallacy is complemented by another one, which is also not infrequently met with, and which we have already encountered. Since we speak of a causal "*law*" – [a terminology] that is imprecise and no doubt directly misleading – the "principle of [sufficient] reason" may, at least in its generalizing version, quite easily be regarded simply as the most general statement that [it] is possible [to make] in the domain of empirical phenomena; in other words: as the most abstract "theorem" of empirical science, the "laws of nature" being "instances of its application", each valid under specific "conditions". Now, the "law of causality", interpreted in this way, in itself says simply nothing substantive about any real [world]. However, one may easily think that if [this "law"] is "applied" to the real world, this will yield at least *one primordial* principle with absolutely general validity – a "general law", whose substantive content must simply be the causal "law" that is applied to, and valid for, the *most general* and *simplest* "elements" of reality. This, then, would be the "cosmic formula" ⟨205⟩ that many adepts of naturalism dream of. The individual processes of reality would "in the last resort" be the causal law "having effect" under particular conditions, just as the course of the Earth would be an "instance" of the "effect" of the law of gravity. As we have already noted earlier, Stammler never makes a statement where laws of nature are openly confused with "categories" in this way (that would indeed hardly befit a disciple of Kant); and he would very probably protest if such views were imputed to him. But then I must ask: In what other way is it at all possible to explain the "unadulterated" nonsense that he has written in the two passages which we are discussing here (bottom of p. 67 and next but last paragraph of p. 70), in conjunction [not only] with his idea – which we are already familiar with – that the most general theorem of a science is its "formal" principle, but also with [his] constant confusion of "points of view" and "method[olog]ical principles" with (in a Kantian sense) transcendental, and therefore a priori, "forms", that is to say: with *logical preconditions* of experience?

Be that as it may. In any event, we are soon presented with the bewildering results engendered by the [application of the] proposition concerning the necessity of *one* general law that, as a *unitary* point of view, must be constitutive for the totality of *all* those phenomena of social reality which can be causally explained, in conjunction with the idea that this "ultimate" generality is both the "*form*" of being, and at the same time: [the "form"] of the acquisition of knowledge of social reality, which is the "*matter*" corresponding [to that "form"]. The adjective "materialist" corresponds to the word "matter". Consequently, it is possible to construct a concept of a "materialist" conception of history with a distinctive character whose essence is expressed in the claim that the "form" of historical or "social" life (Stammler, without any explanation, treats the two [adjectives] as synonymous) is determined by its "matter". Of course, that "conception" would – apart from the *name* – have nothing at all in common with what is usually called "historical materialism" (and what Stammler, too – as we have seen – repeatedly calls "historical materialism"). [Why not?] Because [the "constructed" "conception"], formulated like *that*, would mean that *all* the separate "elements" (as Stammler puts it) of "life in society" – in other words: religion, politics, art, science, as well as "economy" – would form part of the "*matter*". While, on the other hand, what has usually – by Stammler, too – been called historical materialism maintains that all the other elements are dependent on the "economy"; [the "usual" historical materialism] therefore makes a claim concerning the dependence of *one* part of the "matter" on *another* part of th[at] matter, but it makes no claim at all with regard to the dependence of the "form" of "social life" – in the new sense which that word has now acquired – on the "matter" [of "social life"]. What is usually called the "materialist" conception of history does also occasionally use the expression that certain conflicts between political or religious ideas etc. are "merely the *form*" in which "material conflicts of interest" *manifest* themselves; and one does speak of the phenomena of light, heat, electricity, magnetism, etc. as being different "forms" of "energy". But it is obvious that [in those cases], the word "form" is used in *exactly the opposite sense* to that in which the word "*formal*" was used by Stammler in the arguments [that we have discussed earlier]. [In those arguments], what was designated as "formal" was the unitary, the General, the "fundamentally universal", as opposed to the multiplicity of the "content". But [in the last-mentioned examples], the "form" is that which is changeable and multifarious about the "phenomenon", and the unity of the only genuine reality is concealed behind [those "formal" features]. Here, the changeable "forms" (in the sense [in which that term is employed by] the materialist conception of history) are exactly what Stammler calls "matter". This illustrates how problematical it is to work with categories such as "form" and "content" without interpreting [them] with complete precision in each given case. But ambiguousness is precisely Stammler's real element: it is by being ambiguous, and only by being ambiguous, that he is able to fish in "murky logical waters" with his scholasticism. It is only by immediately starting to juggle with those two radically different concepts of [what is] "materialist" that Stammler is able to perform the following [conceptual operations]: He gives [a number of] examples that are meant to confirm that the construction[s] of historical materialism are correct: on p. 37, he states that religion and morals, art and science, social ideas, etc. are dependent on *economic life*; and, on pp. 64–65, he refers, on the one hand, to the Crusades ⟨206⟩ and the reception of Roman Law ⟨207⟩ as being *economically* determined, and, on the other hand, to the purchase by large landowners of small peasant holdings ⟨208⟩ as being *politically* determined. But then, on p. 132, "the *co*-operation of human beings for the purpose of satisfying needs" (according to [what is said on] p. 136, this means: "creating pleasure and avoiding pain") is simply described as "matter", and lets the "empirical course of human life go into [that matter] with no remainder" (p. 136, last paragraph but one). At the same time, he most decisively rejects any distinction within that "matter", according to the "*kinds*" of needs that are satisfied (p. 138) and (in cases where there is only co-operation) according to the means employed towards that end (p. 140). *And then* he fondly believes that operating with *this* concept of the "material" (as opposed to the "*formal*") [aspect] of social life can help to "refute" a historical materialism that operates with a totally different concept of the "material" [aspect] (i.e. that which is opposed to the "*ideological*" one). But we have anticipated somewhat:

Well ahead of this, in his remarks on pp. 132–33, which we referred to as an example, Stammler had already introduced a narrower meaning of the pair of opposites ["]content["] – ["]form["]. In his view, this narrower definition is specifically valid for "social life", peculiar to it and constitutive for its concept[ualization]. After [having levelled] so much criticism at Stammler's preliminary discussions, we shall now have to turn to this [definition], and thereby to the positive core of his theory. This is the more incumbent on us as Stammler himself (possibly speaking with the voice of one of his pupils) might argue as follows against all the [critical] conclusions that we have drawn so far: "You have let yourselves be mystified by me because you have taken me seriously! At the beginning, I was forced to employ the conceptual language of historical materialism – but my purpose is precisely to show that this conceptual language leads to absurd conclusions, and I do this by letting it suffocate in the quagmire of its own confusion. Read on, and you will see how that [materialist] conception dissolves from within and how it is replaced by the new, pure theory! I am the prophet of that new theory; and all I have done is to start by – so to speak – howling [in the language of] those wolves, without revealing my true identity."

It must be said that, if this was [only] meant to be an imitation, it was a suspiciously good one. But still, we have to reckon with the possibility that, up to this point, Stammler has simply mystified us. He does not always make quite unambiguously clear at what point historical materialism stops and he starts speaking [with his own voice]. And, at the end of Book One of his work, which is the only one that we have analysed so far – to the extent necessary – he makes a solemn reference to the "as yet unheard songs" ⟨209⟩ that still await us. Well then! Let us look at his offerings. But it may be just as well if we do not completely forget the scepticism aroused by the samples that we have so far been presented with; and we should also keep in mind how radically different cognitive categories were muddled up, in places where Stammler was indubitably speaking for himself and *not* as an agent of historical materialism.

Stammler's explicit purpose is to demonstrate that the "science of social life" is completely different from the "natural sciences", by showing that, as an *object* of investigation, "social life" is quite different from "nature", so that a principle of social science which is different from the "method of natural science" is logically necessary. The distinction is obviously meant as an *exclusive* alternative; and it would therefore evidently be of the utmost importance to have a precise idea of what is to be understood by "nature", "natural sciences" and "method of natural science" [and] what is meant to be the decisive criterion [in this respect]. The logical discussions conducted in recent years – with which Stammler, however, is not familiar, or which he at least has only superficial knowledge of – should have made it sufficiently clear that the answer to this question is not self-evident. At the outset, let us admit that we all only too often use the words "nature" and "natural science" carelessly and imprecisely, in the belief that their meaning is clear in the concrete case. But that practice has its dangers; and, for someone whose whole doctrine is constructed on the basis of the irreconcilable difference between "nature" and "social life", [viewed] as objects, it is at least vitally necessary to reflect on what is to be meant by "nature". Now, even in common parlance, "nature" can mean various things: either (1) "inanimate" nature; or (2) both "inanimate" nature and those vital phenomena that are not specifically human; or (3) – in addition to all objects under (1) and (2) – those vital phenomena of a "vegetative" or "animal" kind that are common to human beings and animals – i.e. excluding the so-called "higher", "spiritual" and "intellectual" phenomena of life that are specific to humankind. Accordingly, the limits of the concept of "nature" would be reached approximately (a large margin of imprecision is unavoidable in this context) where we would begin to find, within the totality of the empirically given [reality], the objects of physiology (both of plants and of animals) (case 1) ; or of the psychology of animals *and* human beings (case 2); or, finally, of the empirical disciplines dealing with "cultural phenomena" (ethnology, "cultural history", in the widest sense of those terms) (case 3). In all the three cases, however, "nature" is always defined as a complex of certain *objects* distinguished from other, heterogeneous ones. Another concept of "nature", which is *logically* different from this conventional one, can be defined by designating as "natural science" the investigation of empirical reality with respect to what is "general" (timelessly valid rules of experience – "laws of nature"), as opposed to the investigation of the same empirical reality with respect to what is "individual", [viewed] in the context of its causal determination. [With regard to this concept of "nature"], the decisive criterion is that of the *approach* [adopted]. Thus, the antithesis of "nature" is "history", and sciences such as "psychology", "social psychology", "sociology", theoretical social economics, "comparative religion" and "comparative jurisprudence" belong to the [group of] "natural sciences"; the dogmatic disciplines are not covered by this distinction at all. Finally,[1] one arrives at a third concept of "natural science" – and thus, indirectly, of "nature" – by [grouping together] all those disciplines whose aim is [to furnish] an empirical–causal "explanation", as opposed to those that pursue normative or dogmatic aims: logic, theoretical ethics and aesthetics, mathematics, legal dogmatics and metaphysical (for instance, theological) dogmatics. The decisive criterion here would be [constituted by] the categories of judgement ("Is" as opposed to "Ought"). Consequently, all the objects of the "historical sciences" (including, for instance, the histories of art and of manners and customs, [as well as] economic history and legal history) would be covered by the concept of "natural science". In this case, [the domain of natural science] would be exactly coterminous with the area within which the category of causality is employed in the investigation.

Later, we shall encounter two more possible concepts of "nature"; [but] let us close this discussion for the time being. Manifestly, the expression "nature" can be understood in many different ways. In view of this fact, we must continue to be attentive to the sense in which Stammler speaks of "nature" whenever he discusses the distinction between "social life" and "nature". But since Stammler's whole argument is based on the concept of "social life", which he has found to be the polar opposite of "nature", we should now examine the constitutive properties of that concept [of "social life"].

4 Analysis of the concept of a "rule"
"Rule" as "regularity" and as "norm": the concept of the "maxim"

According to Stammler, the decisive criterion of "social life", its distinctive "formal" characteristic, is the following: it is *regulated* life in common; it consists of interrelations that are "subject to external rules". Before we follow Stammler['s argument] any further, let us stop here and consider the question of the various ways in which the words "governed by rules" and "rule" can be understood. First of all, [the word] "rules" may be understood as designating (1) general statements concerning *causal* interconnections, [in other words]: "laws of nature". If [the word] "law" is in that connection to be reserved for general causal statements that are strictly unconditional (in the sense of admitting no exceptions), then (a) [the word] "rules" must be restricted to those empirical statements that do not satisfy the criterion [of absolute unconditionality]. Conversely, [the word "rules" can also cover] (b) all those so-called "empirical laws" that, empirically speaking, admit of no exceptions, but where [we] have no knowledge of the causal conditions to which this [empirical] state of affairs should be ascribed, or where that knowledge is at least insufficient from a theoretical point of view. [As an example of] (b), it is a "rule", in the sense of an "empirical law", that human beings "must die"; and [as an example of] (a), [it is a "rule",] in the sense of a general empirical statement, that, if a member of a student fraternity is slapped in the face, then certain reactions of a specific kind on his part are "adequate". – Second, [the word] "rule" can designate (2) a norm by reference to which present, past or future events are "measured" in the sense of a *value* judgement – in other words,

---

1 Here, "finally" is not meant to imply that we have enumerated in a way that is even approximately *exhaustive* the concepts of "nature" that are possible and actually employed. See also later, and pp. 209 and 224.

a general statement of how something *ought* (from a logical, ethical, aesthetic point of view) to be, as opposed to the empirical [statement concerning] "what is", which the "rule" in cases (1a) and (1b) is exclusively concerned with. That the rule "is valid" [means different things in the two cases]. In case (2), it implies, [the existence] of a general[1] imperative, whose content is [identical with] the norm as such. In case (1), it simply asserts the "validity" of the claim that the actual regularities that correspond to the rule are "given" in empirical reality, or can be inferred from [that reality] by means of generalization.

The sense of these two basic meanings of the concept[s] of "rule" and "regulatedness" is quite simple. However, [those concepts have] other meanings that do not on the face of it seem to fit smoothly into either of the two basic ones. [Let us] first [consider] what are usually called "maxims" of conduct. In his isolation, Defoe's Robinson [Crusoe] ‹210› (Stammler occasionally, like theoretical economi[st]s, draws on [the example of] Robinson Crusoe, and we shall therefore also have to do so) leads an *economic* existence that is, according to his conditions of life, a "rational" one; and this means, without any possible doubt, that he subjects his consumption and procurement of goods to certain "rules" – more particularly: [to certain] "economic" rules. Therefore – provided that it is possible to prove anything at all by reference to Robinsonades – it should at any rate be clear that it is wrong to assume[2] that economic "rules" are *conceptually* restricted to "social life" ([because] they presuppose a plurality of agents who are subject to the[se rules] and linked by them). Now, it is true that Robinson is a quite imaginary product of fiction, a purely conceptual entity employed by "scholastics". But Stammler himself is a scholastic; and he will have to accept that, when he himself reasons in a particular way, his readers will respond in the same vein. Moreover, [the following point can be made:] we are discussing strictly "conceptual" definitions; Stammler treats the concept of a "rule" as *logically* constitutive for "social" life; and he claims that "economic phenomena" are only conceivable in the domain of "social regulation"; then even a figure like Robinson, who has been constructed without any "logical" inconsistency and – which is a different matter – without being absolutely inconsistent with what, according to rules of experience, is at all "possible", should not be able to make any dent in the "concept". Stammler himself, in anticipation [of this line of reasoning], offers the counter-argument (p. 84) that, from a *causal* point of view, Robinson, too, can only be constructed as a product of "social life", from which he has been cast away by accident. But this argument is most inappropriate coming from someone who has himself been preaching that the causal origins of the "rule" are completely irrelevant to its conceptual nature: the message is quite correct, but [Stammler] does not appear to have had much success with it, and certainly not as far as his own position is concerned. Stammler also claims (p. 146 and in a number of other passages) that such an imaginary, isolated individual figure must be explained with the means of "natural science", since the object of the discussion is restricted to "nature and the techn[olog]ical (NB!) mastery [of nature]". But we should first of all recall that the concepts of "nature" and "natural science" can have a variety of meanings (something that we have already discussed): *Which* of the different meanings does [Stammler] have in mind here? And then, above all, we should – as we are solely concerned with the concept of "rule" – keep in mind that "technology" precisely refers to a procedure according to "purposefully instituted" "rules". The different parts of a machine, for example, work together according to "rules

1   We shall leave aside for the moment the question whether that imperative is *necessarily* "general".
2   As far as "rules" in the sense of a *moral* norm are concerned, it is self-evident that they cannot *conceptually* be restricted to "social beings". [A] "Robinson", too, *can*, conceptually speaking, conduct himself "in contravention of morals" (see, for instance, the moral norm protected by §175 ([first paragraph,] second case) of the German Criminal Code). ‹211›

instituted purposefully by human beings", in exactly the same sense – "logically" speaking – as draught horses forcibly harnessed together, or slaves, or, finally, as "free" human workers in a factory. In this last case, it may be [a] properly applied, calculated *"psychological* pressure" that keeps the worker captive within the total mechanism. [This "pressure" may be] caused by the worker "imagining" that, if he deviates from the "work regulations", the factory gate will be closed [to him], his purse will be empty, his family will starve, etc.; besides, it may be occasioned by all sorts of other ideas – ethical ones, for instance – and, finally, it may be the effect of simple "habit". On the other hand, the inanimate machine parts [are locked into the total mechanism] by their physical and chemical properties. But obviously, this makes no difference at all with respect to the *meaning* of the concept of "rule" in these two cases. The "worker" has certain ideas in his mind: he knows by experience that, if he is to be fed, clothed and kept warm, this "depends upon" [certain actions on his part]: on the "job", he must utter certain standardized phrases or manifest himself in other ways (which are customary in the context of what is in "legal" language called an "employment contract"); then he must also physically adapt himself to the mechanism – in other words: perform certain movements. Moreover, he knows that, if he does all this, there is a chance that he will periodically receive certain metal discs having a specific shape, or certain slips of paper; that, if he places [those objects] in the hands of other people, they will make it possible for him to provide himself with bread, coal, trousers, etc.; and that this would in fact create a state of affairs where, if someone attempted to take [the things with which he had provided himself] away from him, and if he [thereupon] made an outcry, people with spiked helmets would, with a certain degree of probability, appear and help to put those things back into his hands again. One can expect that, with a certain degree of probability, this whole series of extremely complicated reflections, which have here only been sketched out in the crudest possible outline, will be present in the minds of the worker. The factory owner will take th[ose reflections] into account as causal determinants of the co-operative efforts of human beings [employing their] physical strength in the technical production process, in completely the same way as [he takes into account] both the weight, hardness, elasticity and other physical properties possessed by the materials that the machines are made of, and the physical properties of the substances by means of which the operation [of these machines] is powered. [The reflections] can quite precisely be regarded as causal determinants of a particular "technical" result – as, for instance, the production of x tons of pig iron from y tons of iron ore within the time span z – in the same *logical* sense as the ["physical" determinants]. In any event, the "precondition" of achieving that technical result is in both cases, in a *logical* sense, exactly the same: [namely,] that [the elements of the process] "work together according to *rules*". In one case, but not in the other, "processes in consciousness" are included in the chain of causation; but, in a *"logical"* sense, this makes no difference at all. Therefore, when Stammler contrasts the "technical" approach with that of the "social sciences", the presence of a "rule of joint action", at any rate, cannot be the criterion that in itself constitutes the decisive difference between the two [approaches]. The factory owner knows that certain people are hungry; that [these hungry people] are prevented by those other people with the spiked helmets from just taking, wherever they find it, whatever might be needed to satisfy their hunger; and that those series of reflections [which we sketched out above] must therefore arise in their minds. He takes these facts into account, just as a hunter would [take into account] the qualities of his dogs. And, just as the hunter will expect the dog to react to his whistle in a certain way, or to perform certain tasks when a shot has been fired, the factory owner [will expect] that, if a piece of paper printed in a certain way (the "work regulations") is posted, this will, with greater or lesser certainty, create a certain result. Let us take a further example: Robinson acted "economically" with respect to the available "supplies of goods" and means of production on his island. A lone individual in the world of today will deal in exactly the same way with the small metal discs called "money" that he has in his pocket or that he believes – with more or less justification – that he has a chance of putting in his pocket by performing certain acts (for instance, scribbling on a scrap of paper called a "cheque", or cutting off another scrap of paper called a "coupon" and showing it [to somebody] behind a certain counter): He knows that these metal discs, if used in a certain way, will make it possible for him actually to dispose of certain objects that he sees behind glass windows, on restaurant buffets and in other places, and about which he knows – by personal experience or through instruction by others – that, if he simply appropriated them without further ado, the people with the spiked helmets would appear and put him under lock and key. This modern individual does not need to know how it has actually come about that those little metal discs developed this peculiar capability, just as he need not know how his legs manage to walk. He can content himself with the observation, which he has made ever since he was a child: [money] develops that capability in everybody's hands, as regularly (we are still speaking generally) as everybody's legs manage to walk, and as a stoked oven emits heat and July is warmer than April. According to his knowledge of its "nature", the individual organizes the way in which he uses money, "*regulates*" his use of it, "acts economically" when using it.

How is this regulation actually carried out by a concrete individual? How is it carried out by thousands and millions of other [concrete individuals], as a result of "experiences" (either personal ones or communicated by others) with respect to the "consequences" of the various possible kinds of "regulation"? And: as it is possible to distinguish, within a given population, a number of groups that differ with respect to their [members'] chances of having such little metal discs (or the pieces of paper with a similar "effect") in their safe in the future, and of being able to do with them what they like, how does the way in which the regulation is carried out *differ* between those groups? To consider these questions and to try, as far as the state of the material allows, to give clear answers to them are tasks that must, according to Stammler, fall *not* to the social sciences, but to the "technical" natural sciences. The reason is that, in every case, the aim is to explain the conduct of *single* individuals. In the case [of the "modern individual"], the "rules" that the individuals follow in their conduct are "maxims" – exactly as was the case with Robinson. And, in the ["modern"] case, just as in the case of Robinson, the causal effect [of these "maxims"] on the empirical conduct of the individual is based on rules of experience (which the individual has discovered for himself or learned from others), of the type: If I do x, it is a rule of experience that y will follow. It is on the basis of such "empirical propositions" that Robinson's "rule-governed, purposeful action" is conducted; and the "rule-governed, purposeful action" of the "person who possesses money" is conducted on the same basis. The conditions of existence that [the person who possesses money] must take into account may be immensely more complex than those of Robinson; but *logically* speaking, there is no difference [between them]. The one, like the other, has to calculate, on the basis of experience, how the "world around him" will react to certain kinds of behaviour on his part. In one case, these elements include reactions of human beings, while, in the other, they only include [reactions] of animals, plants and "inanimate" natural objects. But this is of no consequence at all for the "logical" nature of the "maxim". If, as Stammler maintains, Robinson's "economic" behaviour is "merely" technical *and therefore* is not to be treated by social science, then the same must hold for the behaviour of an individual towards a group of human beings – however that group is constituted – to the extent that [this behaviour] is only examined with respect to its "regulation" by "economic" maxims, and the effects [of those "maxims"]. The "private economy" of the single individual – if we now put it in ordinary language – is governed by "maxims". In Stammler's terminology, those maxims would have to be designated as "technical" maxims. Empirically, they (more or less steadily) "regulate" the behaviour of the single individual; but in view of what Stammler has said about Robinson, they cannot be the "rules" that he has in mind. Before we try to take a closer look at [those "rules"], let us ask a last question: What is the relationship between the concept of the "maxim", which we have used so extensively, and the two "types" of concept of a "rule" that we mentioned in the introduction – on the one hand, the "empirical regularity"; on the other hand, the "norm"? That requires an additional, brief general discussion of the sense in which a certain conduct can be described as "rule-governed".

By saying "my digestion is regular", a person is only stating a simple "fact of nature": [the digestion] follows a certain temporal pattern. The "rule" is abstracted from the ["regular"] natural process. But that person can come to feel the need to "regulate" [the digestion] by eliminating "disturbances". He may then say that his digestion "has been regulated". The [physiological] process will be the same as before, but the sense of the "rule" has changed. In the first case, the "rule" embodies an *observation* of [the course of] "nature"; in the second case, it is that which one *desires* "nature" *to conform to*. The observed and the desired "regularity" may in fact coincide – something that is very pleasant for the person in question – but "conceptually", the two ["regularities"] have different meanings: one is an empirical fact, the other one a desired ideal, a "norm" against which facts are "evaluatively" measured. As far as the rule as an "ideal" [regularity] is concerned, it can play a role in two different kinds of investigation. On the one hand, one may ask (1) what *actual* regularity *would* correspond to the "ideal" rule; on the other, (2) what degree of *actual* regularity *is a* causal *consequence* of the endeavour to [conform to] that ["ideal"] rule. To take an example: if a person "measures" [the state of his digestion] against that hygienic norm and [tries to] "conform" to [that norm], that fact is in itself *one* of the causal determinants of the observable, empirical regularity of his bodily functions. In the case in point, the regularity is causally influenced by innumerable conditions, among which we *also* find the medicine taken by that person in order to "realize" the hygienic "norm". As one can see, his empirical "maxim" is the idea of the "norm", which functions as a real motive of his action. The situation is no different when we consider the "regulatedness" of the behaviour of human beings in relation to material goods and to other human beings, and, in particular, of their "economic" behaviour. Robinson and the above-mentioned persons possessing money behave in a certain way with respect to their goods (or, in the latter case, their store of money); and, in fact, their behaviour seems to be "regular". This can prompt us to provide a theoretical formulation of the "rule" that in our eyes (at least partly) governs that behaviour – as a "principle of marginal utility", for example. In that case, this *ideal* "rule" contains a corresponding tenet; and that tenet contains the "norm" that Robinson's actions "should" conform to *if* he wanted to pursue consistently the ideal of acting "purposively". Consequently, [the rule] can, on the one hand, be regarded as a valuational standard – not, of course, as a "moral" standard, but as a "teleological" one that presupposes an "ideal" of acting purposively. But, on the other hand, and in particular, [the rule] is a heuristic principle that can be used to discover the actual causal determinants of Robinson's empirical actions (we shall here, for our concrete purposes, assume that such an individual actually existed). In this respect, it functions as an ideal-typical construct; and we utilize it as a hypothesis whose correctness must be "tested" by confronting it with the "facts"; it would help to establish the *actual* causality of his actions and the degree of approximation to the "ideal type".[1]

In this connection, the "rule" of purposive action would be relevant in two very different ways for the *empirical* knowledge of Robinson's behaviour. On the one hand – possibly – as

---

1   Concerning the logical meaning of the "ideal type", see pp. 124–32.

one of Robinson's "maxims", which constitute the *object* of the investigation; [in other words], as a real "motive" for his empirical action. And, on the other hand, as part of that store of knowledge and concepts with which the *investigator* approaches his task: his knowledge of the ideally possible "meaning" of the action makes it possible for him to acquire empirical knowledge [of that action]. There must be a strict logical distinction between these two aspects [of the "rule"]. In the empirical domain, the "norm" is, from a logical point of view, undoubtedly a determinant of events, but only *one* of those determinants. In just the same [logical] sense, the use of medicine "in accordance with the norm" to "regulate" the digestion – that is to say: the "norm" provided by the doctor – is one, but only one, of the determinants of the actual result. And the degree to which [the acting person] is conscious of the influence of this determinant on his action may vary very considerably. Walking, toilet training and the avoidance of ingesting harmful substances are things that a child "learns". And, generally speaking, [the child] similarly "grows into" the "rules" that it sees other people following in their lives; it learns to "express itself" by means of language; and it learns to conduct itself properly in the outside, "impersonal" world. [A person will do so] *partly* (1) without formulating in his own mind the "rule" that he actually – with extremely varying consistency – follows in his actions; *partly* (2) by deliberately applying "empirical propositions" of the type: if x then y; and *partly* (3) because the "rule", in the form of an idea of a "norm" that *ought* [to be followed] for its own sake, has been implanted in his mind by "education" or by simple imitation, has then been further developed through his own reflections, nourished by his "experience of life", and is now one of the determinants of his action. If, in the last two cases, (2) and (3), we say that the moral, conventional or teleological rule in question is the "*cause*" of a certain action, this is of course an extremely imprecise expression. The action is not based on the "ideal validity" of a norm, but on the empirical idea in the mind of the acting person that the norm "ought to apply" to his conduct. This is true both of "moral" norms and of rules whose "status as [norms that] ought to apply" is based on pure "convention" or on "wordly wisdom". For instance, when I meet an acquaintance, it is obviously not the conventional rule of greeting that, as such, bares my head – that is done by my hand. In its turn, my hand performs this action, either because I am simply "used to" acting in conformity with such a "rule"; or, in addition, because experience tells me that others regard it as unseemly not to [lift one's hat], so that [such a omission] will result in expressions of unfriendliness – in other words, because of a calculation of "pain"; or, finally, I may also act on the belief that it is "not proper" for me to disregard a harmless "conventional rule" that is actually observed by everybody, unless I have some compelling reason for doing so – in other words, on the basis of [my] "idea of a norm".[1]

With these last examples, we have already arrived at the concept of "*social* regulation" – i.e. a rule "valid" "for" people's behaviour towards each other; this is the concept in which Stammler anchors "social life" as an object [of investigation]. We shall leave until later the discussion of whether Stammler is justified in defining the concept in that way; instead, we shall discuss the concept of a "rule" a little longer, regardless of Stammler['s views].

Let us right away consider an elementary example, which Stammler also occasionally uses to illustrate the significance of the "rule" for the concept of "social life". Two persons who otherwise have no "social relationship" at all – two savages from different tribes, or a European and a savage who encounter each other in darkest Africa – "exchange" two objects of whatever kind. It is emphasized – quite correctly – that, in such a case, the mere description of the event

---

1 I hope that the reader will excuse this remark, which – like many that will follow – is almost excessively trivial: it was necessary to make it in order to counter at the outset certain arguments by Stammler that are of a strongly personal nature.

as it can be perceived externally – that is to say: the muscular movements and possibly (if "words" were spoken) the sounds that, so to say, constitute the physical aspect of the event – would in no way capture the "nature" of that event. That "nature" stems from the "meaning" which each of the two participants ascribes to his external behaviour, and, in its turn, this "meaning" of their present behaviour represents a "regulation" of the way in which they will behave in the future. Without that "meaning", it is claimed, there is no possibility at all of performing an "exchange" in reality, nor is it possible to construct it conceptually. Certainly! The fact that "external" signs serve as "symbols" is one of the constitutive presuppositions of all "social" relations. But we must again ask: "[a constitutive presupposition] *only* of 'social' relations?". [And the answer is] obviously: "Not at all". If I put a "bookmark" in a "book", what can then be perceived "externally" as the result of that action is evidently just a "symbol": The fact that, here, a slip of paper, or some other object, is placed between two pages has a "meaning"; if I did not know [that "meaning"], the bookmark would be of no use to me and make no sense to me, and the act in itself would also be "inexplicable" in causal terms. Nevertheless, surely no kind of "social" relation was established in this case. Or let us rather, once again, confine ourselves to the example of Robinson Crusoe: When the stand of trees on his island needs to be protected for "economic" reasons, he takes his axe and "marks" certain trees that he intends to cut down to provide for the coming winter; and when he wants to "husband" his supplies of grain, he rations them and stores one part separately as "seed grain". In all those cases, and in innumerable other similar ones that the reader may construct for himself, the "externally" perceivable event is not [(just as in the case of the "exchange" with the savage)] "the whole of the event". It is only [by having a certain] "meaning" that these measures – which quite definitely do not involve any "social life" – acquire their character and their "significance". Just in the same way (in principle), what bestows significance on small black marks "printed" on pieces of paper bound together in a fascicle is their "meaning as sounds"; in the case of sounds spoken by someone else, [what makes those sounds "significant" is] their "meaning as words"; finally, when we consider the externally perceivable part of the conduct of the two persons involved in an exchange, [its "significance" resides in] the "meaning" that each person attributes to his conduct. If we now make a mental distinction between the "meaning" that we find "expressed" in an object or event and those components [of the object or event] that remain when we abstract from that "meaning", and if we use the term "naturalistic" to designate an investigation that *only* considers those [last-mentioned] components – then we arrive at yet another concept of "nature", which must be carefully distinguished from the ones [that we discussed earlier in this essay]. According to that [concept], nature is that which is "meaningless". Or, more correctly: a phenomenon *becomes* "nature", *if* we do not ask about a "meaning" in connection with it. But obviously, the [conceptual] opposite of "nature", conceived as that which is "meaningless", is not "social life" but that which is "meaningful" – in other words: the "meaning" that *can be* ascribed to an event or an object [or] "found in it". [In this sense, the "meaning" covers the whole span] between the metaphysical "meaning" of the universe [as defined] by some [system of] religious dogmatics and the "meaning" that the barking of Robinson's dog "has" when a wolf approaches. – Having [thus] satisfied ourselves that the quality of being "meaningful", of "signifying" something, is certainly not peculiar to "social" life, we now return to the process of "exchange" discussed above. The "meaning" of the "external" conduct of the two parties to the exchange can be investigated in two – logically speaking – very different ways. On the one hand ["meaning" can be investigated] [(a)] as an *idea*: We can ask what consequences are *logically* implicit in the "meaning" that "*we*" – the observers – ascribe to a concrete event of this kind, or how that "meaning" fits into some "meaningful" system of thought of a more comprehensive nature. From the standpoint that can be arrived at by this method, we can then perform a "valuation" of the empirical course of the event. For instance, we may ask what the "economic behaviour" of Robinson "must" have been if it had been pursued to its ultimate logical "consequences". This is what the theory of marginal utility ⟨212⟩ does. And we could then "measure" [Robinson's] empirical behaviour against the logical standard that we have constructed. In exactly the same way, we can ask the following question: Once the mutual exchange of objects had, in its external aspect, been completed, what would the behaviour of the two "parties to the exchange" "have to be" in order to correspond to the "idea" of the exchange – that is to say: so that it would, in our view, be in conformity with the logical consequences of the meaning that *we* ascribed to their behaviour? In that case, our point of departure is the following empirical fact: certain processes *actually* occur that are ideationally associated with some "meaning" – a "meaning" that is not clearly thought through in its details but only vaguely present in the mind. Then, however, we *leave* the empirical domain and pose the following question: How must the "meaning" of the behaviour of the parties involved be construed *logically* in order for the result to be an internally consistent intellectual construct?[1] [Here,] we are engaging in a "dogmatics" of "meaning". On the other hand we can ask [(b)]: Was the "meaning" that "we" can dogmatically ascribe to such a process also that which each of the actual participants in that process for his part consciously attributed to it? Or, what other ["meaning"] did each of [the participants] attribute to it? Or, finally: Did they attribute any conscious "meaning" to it at all? To begin with, we still have to distinguish between two different "meanings" – *empirical* meanings (which are the only kind that we shall now discuss) – of the concept of "meaning" as such. To revert to our example: What may be meant [by the "meaning" of the process of "exchange"] is that the acting persons consciously *wanted* to assume a "*norm*" that put them under an "obligation"; in other words: that their action, in their (subjective) opinion, had an intrinsic character which put them under an obligation – that a "normative maxim" was created in their minds.[2] On the other hand, [the "meaning" of the process of "exchange"] may simply be that each of the participants wanted the exchange to yield certain "results", and [believed] that his action, according to his "experience", was a "means" to this end – [in other words:] that the exchange had a (subjective), conscious "purpose". In any individual case, it is of course doubtful to what extent each of the two kinds of maxim was actually present (and, as far as the "normative maxim" is concerned, whether it was actually present *at all*). The relevant questions are the following: (1) To what extent were the two parties to the exchange in our example really

---

1 We should not yet in any way be thinking in terms of a "legal" order; moreover, it would obviously be quite possible to construe several versions – perhaps even a large number of different versions – of the *ideal* "meaning" of an act of "exchange".

2 When the "meaning" of the act of exchange – in this first sense of the concept of "meaning": that of a "normative maxim" – is described as a "regulation of the mutual relations" of the participants, and the *relationship* [of the participants] is described] as being "regulated" *by* the "norm" (which is present in their minds) concerning their future *conduct*, it must immediately be made clear that the words "regulated" and "regulation" in no way necessarily imply a subsumption under a general "rule" – or at least only [under the "rule"] that "agreements should be loyally kept", in other words: that "the regulation should be treated as a regulation", and nothing more than that. The two participants do not necessarily have to know anything at all about the general ideal "nature" of the norm of exchange; and, moreover, it is also possible to assume that two individuals perform an act to which they ascribe a "meaning" which is absolutely individual and cannot – like the "act of exchange" – be subsumed under a general type. In other words: from a *logical* point of view, the concept of "regulation" in no way presupposes the idea of *general* "rules" with a specific content. This point should simply be made. [But] for the sake of simplicity, we shall continue to treat the normative regulation as always being a subsumption under "general" rules.

conscious of the "appropriateness" of the action [for a given purpose]? (2) To what extent have they[, moreover,] had the idea that their relationship "*ought*" now to be "regulated" in such a fashion that one [of the exchanged] objects *should* be regarded as "equivalent" to the other one; that each of the participants *should* henceforth "respect" the other participant's "ownership", by virtue of the exchange, of the object that was formerly in his own possession, and so on, and made [that idea] into a conscious "maxim" for themselves – i.e. into a "normative maxim"? In other words: To what extent was the idea of this "meaning" (a) a causal determinant of the decision to enter into that particular "act of exchange"? And (b) to what extent is [the idea of this "meaning"] a reason for their conduct *after* the act of exchange? It is evident that, in [seeking an answer to] these questions, *our* "dogmatic" theoretical idea of the "meaning" of the "exchange" must be very useful for the purpose of formulating hypotheses, [i.e.] as a "heuristic principle"; but, on the other hand, it would certainly not be possible to settle [those questions] by simply claiming that the "objective" "meaning" of what has taken place between the participants can, once and for all, only be a specific one that can be derived dogmatically according to certain logical principles. It would be pure fiction, somewhat along the lines of the hypostatization of the "regulative idea" of the "contract establishing the state", ⟨213⟩ if it were simply decreed that the two [participants] have *wanted to* "regulate" their mutual social relations in a way that corresponds to the ideal "meaning" of [the concept of] "exchange", because we – the observers – on the basis of [our] *dogmatic* classification attribute that "meaning" to [their conduct]. Logically speaking, one might just as well say that, because of the "meaning" that the barking of the dog may have for its *owner*, the dog has "wanted to" realize the "idea" of the protection of private property. From an empirical point of view, the dogmatic "meaning" of the "exchange" is an "ideal type". And, as there are vast numbers of processes in empirical reality that correspond to it with greater or lesser "purity", we utilize [this "ideal type"], partly for "heuristic purposes", partly for "classification". No doubt, "normative" maxims, which treat that "ideal" meaning of the exchange as "constituting an obligation", are *one* of the various possible determinants of the actual behaviour of the "exchange partners", but only one of them. And their actual presence in connection with the concrete act is hypothetical, both from the point of view of the observer and (something that should be kept in mind) from the point of view of each of the participants vis-à-vis the other one. Of course, it is quite common for one of the exchange partners, or both of them, *not* to take the normative "meaning" of the exchange – which they know is usually treated as being ideally "valid", i.e. as something that ought to be valid – as a "normative maxim" for himself. Instead, that partner, or both of them, will gamble on the chance that the *other* partner will do so: in that case, his own maxim is purely "instrumental". Of course, from an empirical point of view, it is quite meaningless to claim that, in those cases, the process *is* actually "regulated" in conformity with the ideal norm – that the acting persons *have* regulated their relations in that way. Nevertheless, we do occasionally express ourselves in that way; but this is an instance of the ambiguity surrounding the word "regulated", which we also noted in the case of the man with the artificially "regulated" digestion, and which we shall repeatedly encounter again. It is harmless as long as one always keeps in mind *what* is understood by it in the concrete case. On the other hand, it would naturally be completely absurd if the "rule" which the two exchange partners have (according to the dogmatic "meaning" of their conduct) supposedly submitted to were then described as the "form" of their "social relationship", that is to say: as a "form" of *events*: That "rule", which has been derived dogmatically, is in itself in every case a "norm" that claims to be ideally "valid" *for* action, but [it is] under no circumstances a "form" of something that empirically "exists".

Of course, if someone wants to discuss "social life" as something that *exists* empirically, he cannot allow himself a logical somersault ⟨214⟩ into the domain of what dogmatically *ought to* be. In the domain of what "Is", the "rule" from our example exists only in the sense of an empirical "maxim" of the two exchange partners that can be causally explained and that has causal effects. In terms of the concept of "nature" developed above,[1] this would be expressed as follows: The "meaning" of an external process will also, in a logical sense, become "nature" when the investigation concerns its *empirical* existence, as this is not a question of the "meaning" that the external process "has" dogmatically, but of the "meaning" that the acting persons in the concrete case either actually associated with it, or – as it seemed from the visible "features" of the process – gave the impression of associating with it. Naturally, this also completely holds for the special case of "legal *rules*".

Rule[s] of the game

But before we move on to the area of "law" in the usual sense of the word, we shall discuss a further example in order to illustrate some aspects of our general problem that we have not yet dealt with. Stammler himself occasionally refers to the analogy with the "rules of the game"; but we must, for our purposes, go much more thoroughly into that analogy. To this end, we have chosen to treat the [game of] skat in this context as being comparable with those fundamental elements of culture that "history" bears witness to and that the "social sciences" deal with.

The three skat players "subject themselves to" the rules of skat, it is said; this means that they adopt a "normative" maxim according to which certain criteria *shall* determine (1) whether someone has played "correctly" – that is: "in conformity with the norms" – and (2) who *shall* be deemed to be the "winner". From a logical point of view, this statement can be examined in very different ways. First of all, the "norm" as such – that is to say: the rules of the game – can be made the object of purely theoretical considerations. These considerations may take two forms. They may lead to practical value judgements, as for instance when a "skat congress" ‹215› (as actually happened some years ago) discusses whether it is not appropriate, in the perspective of the ("pleasure") "values" governing the game of skat, to immediately introduce the rule that, henceforth, any "grand" [contract] shall outrank a "null ouvert" [contract]. This is a question concerning skat *policy*. Or, alternatively, they may be dogmatic and ask whether, for instance, a particular kind of bidding "would" not "have as its natural consequence" a particular rank ordering of those games. This would be a question falling under the general theory of the laws of skat, viewed in the perspective of "natural law". Other matters belong to the domain of the *jurisprudence* of skat, as for instance the question whether a game is deemed "lost" when the player has "played the wrong card", and any question as to whether a player has in a concrete game played "correctly" (i.e. in conformity with the norm) or "incorrectly". On the other hand, the question *why* a player has played "incorrectly" in a concrete game (deliberately? unintentionally? etc.) has a purely *empirical* – and more particularly: a "historical" – character. A question that "involves values" but that can be resolved by purely empirical means is whether a player in a concrete game has played "well" – that is to say: *effectively*. It can be decided on the basis of "rules of experience", which, for instance, indicate whether a particular line of play will in general increase the chance of "forcing out the Ten", or not. These general rules of practical skat wisdom are therefore based on empirical propositions that can be calculated, and – to a varying degree – be given a stringent form, by [reviewing] the "possible" combinations [of cards] and also, possibly, by drawing on one's practical experience of how the other players will probably react. [Such propositions] are "rules of good practice" that can serve as standards for "evaluating" the effectiveness of the player. Finally, the play might

1   p. 209.

be measured against the "ethical norms" of skat: If one plays carelessly, and thereby lets the common opponent win the game, this will usually call forth a solemn reprimand by one's partner; [on the other hand], the empirical ethical norm of skat usually does not judge too harshly the maxim of bringing in as the third player a so-called "sacrificial lamb", so that [the other two] can jointly fleece him – although that maxim is most reprehensible from a "humanitarian" point of view. Corresponding to these different possible varieties of valuations, we can, in the empirical [domain of] skat, distinguish between maxims of "ethics", "lawfulness" and "effectiveness": logically, the principles of valuation in which [these maxims] are rooted are quite different from each other, and the "normative" status [of the principles] varies correspondingly, ranging from the "absolute" down to pure "facticity". But the same was the case in our example concerning ["]exchange["]. In a normative perspective – [that of] skat policy or the laws of skat – the different points towards which the maxims are oriented are treated as being "ideally valid". However, (just as [with the "exchange"]), as soon as we move into the domain of empirical–causal investigation, those points of orientation are resolved into actual complexes of ideas that determine the actual conduct of the player. In doing so, those complexes of ideas may either conflict with each other (for instance, the [player's] interests may be in contradiction with his compliance with the "maxim of lawfulness"); or (as is regularly the case), they will conjointly determine the player's conduct. On the basis of *his* "interpretation" of the "rules of the game", of his general "experience as a skat player" and of his "ontological" assessment of the distribution of the cards, the player will lay his ace on the table because he believes that this is the adequate means of bringing about a state of affairs that, according to the "rules of the game" as he sees them, has the consequence of making him the "winner". For instance, his calculation may be that, as a result of his playing [the ace], the other player will lay down a ten, and that this, together with a series of further plays anticipated by him, will yield precisely that final outcome. On the one hand, he counts on the fact that the others will let their play be guided by the "rules of the game", which are also present in their minds, in the same form as in his own. He counts on this because he believes that their subjective "maxim of lawfulness" is sufficiently constant as a determining factor – as, in general, they are known to him as persons who usually act in conformity with "ethical maxims". But on the other hand, given his knowledge of their qualities as skat players, he also takes into account the probability of their playing more or less "effectively" (i.e. in conformity with their interests) from a teleological point of view – in other words: that they are, in the concrete case, able to realize their "maxim of effectiveness". His considerations, which determine his play, are expressed in propositions of the following form: The other [players] will not deliberately violate some rule A of the game and will play effectively; the distribution [of the cards] is Z; therefore, if I do X, Y is the probable consequence.

There is no doubt that the "rule[s] of the game" can be described as the *"precondition"* of a concrete game. But one must be clear about what this implies for the empirical inquiry that we are now discussing. First of all, the "rule of the game" is a *causal* "factor". The "rule of the game" – [conceived], of course, not as the "ideal" norm of the "laws of skat", but [as] the idea that the players in a concrete game have of its content and its binding force – is one of the motives determining the actual conduct of the players. [Each] *player* will – normally – "assume" that all the other [players] will make the rule of the game their "maxim" of conduct. This assumption is in actual fact normally made (it may subsequently be verified to a greater *or lesser* extent) and, as a rule, it is the *substantive* "precondition" of the decision by each of the players actually to let his own action be determined by the corresponding maxim – or, if he is a cheat, to pretend that it is being so determined. In a causal analysis of the course taken by a concrete game of skat, the assumption by each of the players that the others conform to a "rule" which is in fact usual, and therefore also their "acquired" knowledge of that "rule", would have to be classified, within the causal regression, as a determinant that was – normally – just as constantly effective as all the other causal "preconditions" of the way a player conducted himself. *To that extent*, there is no difference at all between [that determinant] and the "conditions" generally necessary for the life and conscious action of human beings.

However, if we describe the rule[s] of skat as the "precondition" of empirical *knowledge* of skat, the meaning [of this statement] is of course, logically speaking, fundamentally different [from the one discussed in the preceding paragraph]. What it means is the following: Contrary to the other, "general", substantive "preconditions" of events, [the "rules"] are for us the characteristic *distinctive feature* of "skat". To spell it out more elaborately: Phenomena that are considered *relevant* in terms of a *norm* of play that is usually described as the "rules of skat" will, in our eyes, constitute a distinctive complex of performatory acts as being a "game of skat". The intellectual content of the "norm" is therefore the criterion according to which what is "conceptually important" is selected from that multiplicity of cigar smoke, beer drinking, banging on the table and comments of every kind that furnishes the customary context of a good old German game of skat, as well as from the incidental "milieu" of the concrete game. We "classify" a complex of phenomena as "skat" when it contains phenomena that are deemed to be relevant for the application of the norm. Moreover, those are the phenomena whose causal explanation would be the task that a "historical" analysis of the empirical course of a concrete ["game of] skat" would set itself. They constitute the empirical collective entity [that we call] a "game of skat" and the empirical generic concept of "skat". To sum up: What defines the *object* of the investigation is [its] relevance from the point of view of the *norm*. To begin with, it is clear that the sense in which the rules of skat are here the "precondition" of our empirical knowledge of skat – in other words: the specific criterion of a [particular] *concept* – should be strictly *distinguished* from the sense in which they (that is to say: the fact that the players know them and take them into account) are the "precondition" of the empirical *course* of "games of skat". And, furthermore, the function of the normative concept in the classification of [phenomena] and the definition of the object [of investigation] does not in any way alter the logical character of the empirical, causal investigation of the object that has been defined in that way.

The sole – [but] important – function of the norm [in this respect] is that its content constitutes the point of reference from which we [can] identify those facts and processes whose causal explanation a hypothetical "historical *interest*" would focus on. That is to say: [those facts and processes] constitute those points within the given multiplicity from which the causal analysis goes backwards or forwards. Let us assume that someone wanted to perform a causal analysis of a concrete game of skat. In that case, the causal regression, starting at those points, would soon move beyond the processes that were "relevant" from the standpoint of the norm. In order to "explain" the course of the game, [the causal analysis] would have to ascertain, among other things: the abilities and education of the players; the extent to which they were "alert" and could therefore concentrate at a given moment; the amount of beer that each of them had consumed, and to what degree this had influenced his ability to follow the maxim of "effectiveness" consistently; and so on and so forth. In other words: it is only the point of *departure* of the [causal] regression that is determined by the "relevance" from the standpoint of the "norm". This is a case of the so-called "teleological" concept formation, which is not confined to the observation of "social" life and not even to the observation of "human" life. Biology "selects" from the multiplicity of phenomena those which are "important" in a certain "sense" – i.e. from the standpoint of "sustaining life". When we discuss a work of art, we "select" those elements of the multiplicity of the phenomena that are "important" from the standpoint of "aesthetics" (*not* in the sense of being aesthetically "valuable", but in the sense of being "relevant for aesthetic judgement"). The same [happens] even when the aim is not to perform an aesthetic "valuation" of the work of art, but to "explain" its distinctive individual character, or to use it as an example to illustrate general causal propositions concerning the conditions of artistic development – in other words, in both cases, the acquisition of purely empirical knowledge. The relation to aesthetic or biological "values", or – in our [main] example – to the "values" of the laws of skat, "pave the way" for our selection of the object to be explained. And, in those cases, the object itself "is" not artistic norms, nor the vitalistic "purposes" of a god or world spirit, nor the doctrines of the laws of skat. Instead, in the case of the work of art, the object is the brushstrokes of the artist, determined by his state of mind (which can in turn be causally explained by his "milieu", his "ability", by the "fortunes of his life" and by concrete "impulses"). In the case of the "organism", [the object] is certain processes that can be perceived physically. And, in the case of the game of skat, [the object] is the thoughts and the external performatory acts – both of them caused by actual "maxims" – of the players.

There is yet another "sense" in which the "rules of skat" can be described as a "precondition" of the acquisition of empirical *knowledge* of skat. It is connected with the empirical fact that knowledge of, and compliance with, the "rules of skat" is one of the (normal) empirical "maxims" of the skat players – in other words: that it exercises a causal influence on their performatory conduct. The only instrument that we can make use of to ascertain in what way that conduct is influenced (and therefore to identify the empirical causes of the players' conduct) is of course our *own* knowledge of the "rules of skat". We make use of our knowledge of the ideal "norm" as a "heuristic instrument", just as the historian of art, for instance, utilizes *his own* aesthetic (normative) "power of judgement" as a heuristic instrument – which is in fact quite indispensable – in order to determine the actual "intentions" of the artist, and thereby to facilitate the causal explanation of the distinctive character of the work of art. And the situation is quite similar if we wish to formulate *general* propositions concerning the "chances" of a certain course of play, given a certain distribution of cards. In that case, we would formulate the following "presupposition[s]": (1) the ideal rules of the game (the "laws of skat") are actually complied with, and (2) the play is strictly rational – that is to say: teleologically "appropriate". (The same assumptions are made in the "skat problems" – or, in the case of chess, the chess problems – published in the newspapers.)[1] Since experience shows that, in general, a certain "approximation" to the "ideal type" [of those "presuppositions"] is attempted and attained, we would then be able to indicate the (greater or smaller) degree of "probability" with which, given that distribution of cards, games would be played in a way corresponding to that type.

To sum up, we have seen that, in *empirical* investigations, the "rules of skat", playing a role as a "precondition", can have three functions that are logically completely different from each other: in *defining* the object, their function is classificatory and conceptually constitutive; in establishing *knowledge* [of the object], they have a *heuristic* function; and finally, they function as causal *determinants* of the object of knowledge itself. Moreover, we have earlier had a clear demonstration of the fact that the rules of skat can become an object of knowledge in ways that are fundamentally different: in relation to skat policy; in relation to the laws and jurisprudence of skat (in both those cases, as an "ideal" norm); and, finally, in their empirical aspect, where they have an actual effect and are actually caused. From this, we can already draw the conclusion that it is absolutely necessary to establish with the greatest of care, in every case, in *what* sense one is speaking of the "meaning" of a "rule" as a "precondition" of acquiring any sort of knowledge. Above all, we can conclude that, if one does not carefully avoid any ambiguity

---

1   In that respect, [the "presuppositions"] correspond, from a *logical* point of view, to the "laws" of theoretical economics.

of expression, this will increase to its fullest extent the ever-present danger of hopeless confusion between the empirical and the normative.

Legal rules

Let us now move from the domain of the "conventional" norms of skat and the quasi-"jurisprudence" of the "laws of skat" to [the domain] of "genuine" *law*. (The question of the crucial difference between a legal and a conventional rule will be left aside for the moment.) If we therefore now assume that the "exchange" discussed above as an example comes within the scope of a [system of] positive law, which also "regulates" the exchange, then a further complication – in addition to those that have already been discussed – *seems to* arise. In the formation of the *empirical* concept of "skat", the *norm* of skat was a concept-defining precondition, in the sense that it determined the scope of the object. The points of departure of an empirical–historical analysis of skat – if someone wanted to undertake it – would therefore be those performatory acts that [were] *relevant* from the point of view of the *laws* of skat. But the situation with respect to the relation between the legal rule[s] and the empirical course of human "cultural life"[1] is different when a construct normatively regulated by law is the object of an investigation that is not concerned with legal dogmatics, nor just with *legal* history, but that deals with the "history of culture" or the "theory of culture" (we shall use those expressions quite generally to begin with). This means (using again, provisionally, an extremely imprecise terminology) that the aim is either to explain how certain components (which are significant in relation to "cultural values") of a reality that is, ideally, also regulated normatively by law have developed causally (the "historical" approach); or to establish general propositions concerning the causal determinants of the emergence of such components, or concerning their causal effects (the culture–theoretical approach). When we assumed, in the examples quoted above, that the intention was to carry out an empirical–historical investigation of the course of a concrete "game of skat", the formation of the object (the "historical individual" ‹216›) was simply linked to the relevance of the facts from the standpoint of the "norms of skat". But when the approach is that of "cultural" history, not legal history, the role of legal norm[s] is quite different. When we classify economic, political and other phenomena, we do not exclusively do so on the basis of their legal features. Elements of cultural life that are totally irrelevant from a legal point of view may nevertheless be of "historical" interest to us, and this has the following consequence: In a given case, such elements may have features that are *relevant* from the standpoint of an ideally valid legal system and of the legal concepts that can be formulated in accordance with [that system]; nevertheless, it is an open question whether those features are also relevant for concept formation in history or "cultural theory".[2] In principle, the legal norm no longer has the status of a "precondition" of the formation of the collective concept [in these latter cases]. But nevertheless, this does *not* imply that the matter can simply be disposed of by saying that the two kinds of concept formation have nothing at all to do with each other. As we shall see, this is because conceptual constructs (for instance in economics) are quite regularly designated by legal *terms*, [although those constructs] are relevant from points

---

1   The concept of "culture" employed here is that [defined by] Rickert (*Limits of Concept Formation*, Ch. 4, Sections II and VIII). At this point, before criticizing Stammler's views on these issues, I shall deliberately refrain from introducing the concept of "social life". For further discussions of this point, I [can] refer to other essays of mine (*Objectivity* and *Critical Studies*).
2   Exactly the same would of course be true of the norms of skat, *if* we assumed that some phenomenon normatively regulated by the laws of skat were to become part of an object of inquiry that was of interest from the point of view of "world history".

of view [that are] quite different [from the legal one]. And, in turn, there are two reasons why one cannot simply object to this [practice] as constituting an improper use of terminology: first, because the legal concept in question, viewed *empirically*, has very often functioned, and been able to function, as an "archetype" of the corresponding economic concept; and, second, because it goes without saying that the "empirical legal order" – a concept that will be discussed shortly – is usually also of great importance (for the moment, we shall simply formulate this [view] in general terms) for phenomena that are relevant from, say, an economic point of view. But the two [(the "empirical legal order" and the economically relevant phenomena)] quite simply do not coincide. For instance, in an economic investigation, the concept of "exchange" is extended to include phenomena that all possess the [economically] relevant features, but whose legal character will differ very widely. And, on the other hand, as we shall see, the economic investigation very often includes features – and treats them as the [economically] distinctive ones – that are completely irrelevant from a legal point of view. In what follows, we shall again and again come back to the problems arising out of this. Here, we shall for the time being confine ourselves to the following two [tasks]: On the one hand, we shall make clear that those kinds of investigation that in our "skat" example were found to be logically possible are also to be found within the domain of "legal rules". And, on the other hand, we shall indicate the limits of that analogy. (For the time being, this will be done in a purely provisional fashion: we are not yet able to undertake a definitive and correct formulation of the logical [argument on which that indication is based].)[1] We shall only revert to [that logical argument] when we have learned, through further consideration of *Stammler's* way of arguing, how *not* to deal with these problems. –

[If we say that] some particular "paragraph" of the Civil Code can become an object of reflective thought, this statement may mean different things. First of all, [it can become the object of] reflections concerning legal *policy*: On the basis of ethical principles, one may discuss the ethical "justification" [of the paragraph]; furthermore, one may discuss, from the viewpoint of certain "cultural ideals" or of political demands (rooted in "power politics" or in "social policy"), whether [the paragraph] contributes positively or negatively towards the realization of those ideas; or one may discuss, from the standpoint of one's "class" interests or personal interests, whether [the paragraph] "advances" or "is prejudicial to" those interests. At this point, we shall say no more about this kind of directly evaluating discussion – which we have already encountered (mutatis mutandis) in the "skat" [example] – as it does not pose any new problems of logical principle. There are two more ways of analysing the paragraph, however: on the one hand, one can ask: "What is the *conceptual meaning*" of [this paragraph]?"; and, on the other: "What is the *empirical 'effect'* [of this paragraph]?". A fruitful discussion of the ethical or political (or other kind of) value of the paragraph requires an answer to those two questions; but that does not concern us here, since the question of the "value" [of the paragraph] is in any event a completely separate one, which should be strictly distinguished from the two other questions

---

1   See the penetrating comments by G[eorg] Jellinek concerning this problem (*System*[2], Ch. III, pp. 12f. (cf. his *Theory*[2], Ch. VI)). His interest in the problem is based on considerations that are exactly the opposite of [the ones by which we are motivated]. While his task is to prevent naturalistic encroachments on the domain of dogmatic legal theory, ours is to criticize legal–dogmatic distortions of *empirical* thought. So far, Gottl is the only author who has tackled the problem of the principles [underlying] the relationship between empirical and legal thought from an empirical standpoint; in his *Dominance of Words*, one finds suggestions concerning this problem that are quite excellent – but they are only suggestions. As is well known, v. Böhm-Bawerk in his time also offered a consistent, clear and detailed account of legally protected interests ("subjective rights"), in the particular perspective of economic thought. See his *Rights and Relationships*.

formulated above. Let us now examine the logical nature of those two questions. In both cases, the grammatical subject of the interrogative sentence is "the paragraph", but, nevertheless, the expression "the paragraph" covers two completely different things in the two cases. In the first case, "the paragraph" is a complex of ideas that is put into words and is from that time onwards treated as an object of conceptual analysis, [an object] that is purely ideal and defined in its essence by legal analysts. In the second case, "the paragraph" first of all refers to the following empirical fact: someone who opens one of the volumes of the so-called "Civil Code" will regularly find in it, at some particular place, a certain imprint; and if he applies to [this imprint] the principles of "interpretation" with which he has been inculcated, it will – more or less clearly and precisely – awaken in his consciousness certain ideas about the actual consequences that some particular observable behaviour could entail. This circumstance regularly, but not invariably, has the following further empirical consequence: if a person is able, in a particular way, to persuade certain persons usually called "judges" that this observable behaviour has taken place or is taking place in a concrete instance, then [that person] will have at his disposal certain psychological and physical "instruments of coercion". A further consequence is that, even without involving these persons called "judges", every person can, with a large degree of probability, "count on" the fact that other people will behave towards him in a certain way – in other words: there is a certain *chance* that he can, for instance, reckon with actually having a certain object at his undisturbed disposal; and he can organize his life, and does in fact organize it, on the basis of this chance. In this last case, therefore, the empirical "validity" of the "paragraph" in question designates a series of complex causal interconnections in the context of empirical–historical reality: actual conduct of human beings, in relation to each other and to non-human "nature", brought about by the fact that a certain piece of paper has been covered with certain "written characters".[1] On the other hand, the "validity" of a legal rule – in the "ideal" sense that was discussed at the outset – designates a theoretical interrelation between *concepts*, an interrelation that is binding on the scholarly conscience of a person *seeking* "juridical truth": [it implies that] certain lines of thought "*should be* valid" for the jurist. Furthermore, it is a fact that persons who *seek* "juridical truth" in fact *usually* "deduce" from certain concatenations of words that a certain "legal rule" "should", ideally, "be valid". This fact, in its turn, is obviously not without empirical consequences; on the contrary, it is of the highest empirical and historical importance, since the existence of a "jurisprudence", and the actual empirical–historical development of the "intellectual habits" permeating [this "jurisprudence"] at a given time, are also of the highest practical and empirical importance for the way in which people actually conduct themselves. One reason for this is that the "judges" and other "officials", who are in a position to influence this conduct by employing certain physical and psychological means of coercion, are in actual reality precisely brought up to *seek* "juridical truth" and conform to this "maxim" – albeit to an extent that varies very much in practice. The course of our "social life" is empirically "regulated" (which in the present context means: that it exhibits "regularities") in the sense that, for instance, the baker, the butcher and the newspaper boy will day after day turn up – and so on and so forth. And this "empirical" regularity is of course, in part, a fundamental consequence of the fact that a "legal order" exists empirically. ([That it "exists" empirically] means that it "exists" as an idea of something that *should* be, this idea being one of the causal factors determining human action – in other words: that it "exists" as a "maxim".) But, obviously, the juridical idea that "law" "*should*" be valid" is entirely different not only from empirical regularities, but also from the empirical "existence" of "law" (as just discussed): A possible "juridical error" is of course "empirically" valid to exactly the same degree as "juridical truth";

---

1   This is an artificial simplification!

and the question of *what*, in a concrete case, is "juridical truth" – that is to say: what *should* logically *be*, or *have been*, "valid", according to the principles of "[legal] science" – is logically completely different from [the question of] what *has* in fact happened in a concrete case, or in a large number of cases, as a causal "consequence" of [the fact that] a certain "paragraph" "was valid". In the first case, the "legal rule" is an ideal *norm* that can be deduced logically; in the second case, it is a *maxim* for the conduct of concrete human beings – a maxim that can be *established* empirically as being followed more or less consistently and frequently. In the first case, a "legal order" constitutes a system of ideas and concepts; and this system is employed by scholars in the field of legal dogmatics as a standard against which they juridically evaluate the actual conduct of certain people – "judges", "attorneys", "delinquents", "citizens", etc. – and accept or reject [that conduct] as being (or, respectively, not being) in conformity with the ideal norm. In the second case, [the legal order] can be analysed as a complex of maxims in the minds of certain empirical human beings, maxims that causally influence the actual conduct of those human beings and thereby, indirectly, that of others. Up to this point, everything is comparatively simple. What is more complicated, however, is the relationship between "the United States" as a *legal* concept and "the United States" as an empirical–*historical* "construct". From a logical point of view, the two are different already because, in each given case, the following question arises: To what extent will those aspects of the empirical phenomenon that are relevant from the standpoint of the legal rule remain so for an inquiry from the perspective of empirical history, [of] politics and [of] social science? We should not be misled by the fact that the *name* with which [the legal concept and the historical entity] adorn themselves is the same. – Consider the following six sentences: "In relation to [its] individual [member] states, the United States, rather than [its] individual [member] states, is empowered to conclude treaties of commerce." "Accordingly, the United States has concluded a treaty of commerce with Mexico with the content A." "However, the commercial policy interests of the United States would have required the content [of the treaty] to be B." "This is because the United States exports the quantity D of the product C to Mexico." "The state of the balance of payments of the United States is therefore X." "This must have the influence Y on the currency of the United States." The words "United States" have a different meaning in each of these sentences.[1] Therefore, this is a point where the analogy with the game of "skat" breaks down. The empirical concept of a concrete [game of] "skat" is identical with the phenomena that are relevant from the standpoint of the *laws* of skat. There is no reason why we should use concepts of "skat" in a different sense.[2] The situation is different with respect to the concept "United States", and this is obviously connected with the circumstance – which has already been mentioned previously – that juridical *terminology* (for instance, the concept of "exchange") is customarily employed in other domains [as well]. Let us make an attempt in this context as well to clarify more precisely, in its broadest outline, the way in which this [circumstance] influences the logical situation. – First, we shall recapitulate a few points: One conclusion at least can be drawn from what has already been said: it makes no sense to conceive the relationship between legal rules and "social life" as one in which the law could be seen as the – or as a – "*form*" of "social life" – in contrast to something else as its "matter" – and to attempt to draw "logical" inferences from [that conception]. The legal rule, viewed as an "idea", is not an empirical regularity or a "regulatedness". On the contrary, it is a norm that can be *conceived* as something that "should be valid" – in other words: it is certainly not a form of *being*, but rather a standard of value

1   See also Gottl, *Dominance of Words*, p. 192n1 and the pages that follow.
2   This is owing to the purely factual circumstance that the "rules of skat" are of marginal importance for cultural life.

against which actually existing phenomena can be evaluated, *if* we seek "juridical truth". And, viewed *empirically*, the legal rule is even more definitely not a "form" of social being – regardless of how [social being] is defined conceptually – but a substantive component of empirical reality, a *maxim* that is, more or less "strictly", a causal determinant of the empirically observable conduct of some human beings – the number of whom is in any given case indefinite – and that is, in the individual case, followed more or less consciously and more or less consistently. Experience shows that judges follow the "maxim" [that directs them] to "decide" "conflicts of interest" according to a certain legal rule; other people – bailiffs, policemen and so on – then have the "maxim" that they should "carry out" that decision; moreover, generally speaking, most people think "legally" – that is to say: they make compliance with legal rules one of the maxims [governing] their conduct. All these circumstances are elements – extraordinarily important elements – of the empirical reality of life and, more especially, of "social life". We used the term "empirical 'legal order'" to designate the "empirical *existence*" of law as maxim-creating "knowledge" possessed by concrete people. This knowledge – that is to say: this "empirical legal order" – is one of the determinants of the behaviour of the acting human being. And to the extent that his action is purposeful, [the empirical legal order] is, from one point of view, one of the obstacles that he endeavours to surmount – either by violating it while running as few risks as possible, or by "adapting" to it – and, from another point of view, an "instrument" that he tries to make use of for his "purposes", in exactly the same sense [in which he would make use of] his knowledge of any other rule of experience. He may possibly attempt, by influencing other people, to alter the empirical substance [of the legal order] in accordance with his "interests", in exactly the same sense (logically speaking) [in which he would try to alter] some constellation in the natural world by the technological exploitation of the forces of nature. Let us take an example that Stammler occasionally uses: If [somebody] cannot endure the thick smoke coming from a neighbouring chimney, he will consult his own store of experience or that of others (for instance of a "lawyer") on the following point: if certain documents are presented in a particular place (the "court"), is it then to be expected that certain people, called "judges", will go through a series of procedures and then sign a document (called "judgement") whose "adequate" consequence is that certain persons will be subjected to psychological, or possibly physical, coercion in order to prevent them from firing that particular furnace again? When calculating whether this result can be expected with a fair degree of probability, he – or his "lawyer" – will of course above all consider the question of how the judges "ought to" decide the case according to the "conceptual" *meaning* of the legal rule. But this "dogmatic" consideration will not be of much help to him, since its result, however "impartial", will, for his empirical purposes, be only *one* item in the calculation of the probability of the empirical process to be expected. Even though his lawyer has conducted a conscientious investigation and concluded that the "norm" – considered in its ideal aspect – would be in his favour, he is quite well aware that, for innumerable reasons, it may [still] happen that he "loses" in court. (This colloquial way of referring to that outcome is significant and very characteristic.)

In fact, *legal proceedings* are completely analogous to the "game of skat" – [an observation] that should need no further explanation. Here, the empirical legal order is the "precondition" of the empirical course of events – in other words: [it is] a "maxim" for the judges deciding the case, and an "instrument" for the parties to the dispute; and knowledge of the logical "import" [of the empirical legal order] – in other words: its meaning when viewed in the perspective of legal dogmatics – is an indispensable heuristic instrument for the empirical–causal "explanation" of the actual course taken by legal proceedings in a concrete case: [as such,] it plays a role that is just as important as that played by the rules of skat in the "historical" analysis of a game of skat. And, moreover, [the empirical order] is constitutive for the definition of the "historical individual": if we want to arrive at a causal explanation of a concrete judicial process in its judicial aspect, our explanatory interest focuses on the legally *relevant* elements of the process. – In this case, therefore, the analogy with the rules of skat is complete. The empirical concept of the concrete "legal case" is – just like the concrete "skat case" – exhaustively defined by those elements of the given section of reality that are relevant from the standpoint of the "legal rule" (in the "skat case": the rules of skat). But, if we do not wish to establish the "history" of a concrete "*legal* case" (in the sense of explaining its juridical outcome), but instead want to investigate the "history" of some other [kind of] object – even one that is so completely influenced by the legal order as, for example, the history of labour relations in some particular industry (say, the textile industry in Saxony), then the situation is no longer the same. In that case, what "matters" to us is by no means necessarily to be found in those elements of reality that are relevant for some "*legal* rule". It goes without saying that, quite indisputably, legal rules have immense causal importance for "labour relations", irrespective of the "point of view" from which we investigate th[ose relations]. [The legal rules] are one of the general *substantive* "conditions" that are taken into account in th[at] investigation. But the elements of the "historical individual" – that is to say: of those "facts" whose distinctive character and causal explanation "matter" to us – are *no* longer *necessarily* the same as those facts that are the "relevant" ones from the point of view of the *legal* rules – in contradistinction to the relationship between the "rules of skat" and the concrete skat game, and between legal rules and legal proceedings. [This is true] although the distinctive character of the concrete "legal order" [in existence] at [a particular] time and in [a particular] place may be one of the most decisive causal "conditions" of all those facts, and although the *mere existence* of a "legal order" may be a general (*substantive*) "precondition" [of those facts], a precondition that is no less indispensable than is the availability of wool, cotton or flax and the usefulness [of those raw materials for providing] for certain human needs.

One might try – but we shall not make the attempt here – to construct a series of kinds of possible objects of investigation, so that, in the examples [taken successively from each of those groups], the general causal importance of the concrete *distinctive character* of the "empirical legal order" constantly diminishes, [while] the causal importance of other conditions, with their distinctive character, successively increases. In that way, one might try to arrive at general propositions about the extent to which empirical legal orders are of causal importance for cultural phenomena. Here, we shall restrict ourselves to the general statement that, in principle, that importance will vary according to the nature of the object [of investigation]. Even the distinctive artistic character of, say, the Sistine Madonna ‹217› "presupposes" a quite specific empirical "legal order"; and if we imagine that the causes [of the Sistine Madonna] were exhaustively traced back, that [empirical "legal order"] would be encountered as an "element" [of that process of causal regression]. And it would have been empirically improbable – indeed, next to impossible – for [that painting] to have been created in the absence of *any* "legal order" *at all* as a general "precondition". But, in this context, the facts that constitute the Sistine Madonna as a "historical individual" are completely irrelevant from a *legal* point of view.

Of course, the natural inclination of the professional jurist will be to look at cultural human beings as potential litigants, just as shoemakers will tend to see them as potential customers, and skat players [will tend to see them] as potential "third players". But, naturally, they would all be mistaken to the same degree if they were to claim that the cultural sciences may only, or are only able to, discuss cultural human beings to the extent that [these human beings] are [litigants, or customers, or "third players"] – [for instance,] if the jurist only wanted (so to speak) to regard human beings as *potential "players of legal skat"* because he believed that only those elements of the relations between human beings which are *relevant* from the point of view of potential legal proceedings are possible components of a "historical individual". The need for empirical causal explanation may focus on elements of reality – and in particular of the conduct of human beings towards each other and in relation to extra-human nature – that are simply irrelevant from the standpoint of "legal rules"; and, in practice, this is again and again the case in the cultural sciences. On the other hand, we must supplement the previous remarks on this point by pointing out that an important part of the empirical disciplines concerned with cultural life – in particular, [those with] a political or economic approach – employ juridical concepts not only (as has already been noted) for terminological purposes but also to furnish them with, so to speak, a *pre*formation of their own material. If [juridical concepts] are borrowed in this way, with the aim of provisionally ordering the multiplicity of actual relationships within which we move, this is first of all owing to the highly developed state of juridical thought. But precisely for this reason, it is necessary to remain constantly aware of the following point: the juridical preformation is abandoned as soon as the material is furnished with the "viewpoints" of the political or the economic approach, [since] the juridical concepts are thereby reinterpreted as factual elements whose meaning is by necessity a different one. But nothing is more detrimental to the acknowledgement of this fact than the attempt – motivated by those important services rendered by juridical concepts – to elevate the legal regulation to [the status of] a "formal principle" governing [all] knowledge of human communal life. It is easy to fall into this error, because the *actual* importance of the empirical "legal order" is so great. On the one hand, [it is true that] (as was said above) as soon as we leave the area where the events under investigation are *only* deemed to be "interesting" because of their *juridical* relevance, the importance of the "legal rule" as a "precondition" – in the sense of a principle governing the delimitation of the object – diminishes correspondingly. But, on the other hand, the universal *causal* importance of "legal rules" for any investigation into the conduct of human beings towards each other is outstanding (again compared with the example of the game of skat). This is because those rules, as legal rules, are in empirical reality usually backed up by compulsory force; moreover, their area of validity is almost universal. Generally speaking, a person cannot be dragged unwillingly into a game of skat, with the resulting exposure to the consequences of the empirical "validity" of the rules of skat. But, on the other hand, it is a fact that he can by no means – even before coming into this world – avoid encountering situations that are "relevant" from the standpoint of empirical legal orders (in other words: he will again and again, from an empirical point of view, become a potential player of "legal skat"); and he will therefore have to adapt his behaviour to this situation, on the basis of maxims of mere prudence, or of lawful conduct. In this sense, the existence of a "legal order" is quite certainly one of the universal empirical "preconditions" of *that* kind of actual behaviour of human beings – [in relation] to each other and to extra-human objects – which is necessary for the existence of "cultural phenomena". But, in *that* sense, it is an empirical fact, just like, for instance, a minimum of heat from the sun; and, like [this latter "precondition"], it is simply one of the *causal* "conditions" determining that behaviour. And the situation concerning the "objective legal order" in an empirical sense is similar to the situation where, in a particular place and at a particular time, a certain concrete "state of affairs" is "legally ordered". To revert to our example with the smoking chimney: one instance [of such a "legally ordered" "state of affairs"] could be that the effects of the noisome production of smoke have reached a certain level above which the neighbour's efforts to avert them can expect the support of the "legal order", [so that] he possesses a corresponding "subjective right". From an economic point of view, this ["subjective right"] merely represents an *actual probability* for [the neighbour]. This probability [has the following elements]: (1) the "judges" will strictly adhere to the "maxim" that the decision [should be made] "in accordance with the norm" – in other words: they are conscientious, and they cannot be bribed; (2) the judges "interpret" the meaning of the legal norm in the same way as the person who is complaining about the chimney, or his lawyer; (3) [the plaintiff] succeeds in persuading [the judges] as to the actual existence of that state of affairs which, in their view, calls for the application of that "norm"; (4) the implementation of the decision taken in accordance with the norm is actually enforced. This probability can, *logically* speaking, be "calculated" in the same way as some "technical" process or the outcome of a game of skat. If the desired result is attained, then there is no doubt – in spite of Stammler's protest that this is impossible – that the "legal rule" has causally influenced [the fact that], in future, the chimney will no longer belch heavy smoke. Of course, [it has] not [had that causal influence] as a *conceived* ideal "Ought" (a "norm"), but as actually *bringing about* a certain behaviour on the part of the persons involved – for instance, the judges, in whose minds [the "legal rule"] was present as a "maxim" for their "decision", or the neighbour, or the bailiffs.

The "empirical legal order" has the character of a "rule" – that is to say: it is a fact, which can be established as such and which is known to a large number of people, that the "maxim" of "judges" tells them that, if conflicts of interest are accompanied by [the same] *generally* defined states of affairs, the decisions rendered and enforced by [the judges] concerning those conflicts of interest should, generally speaking, be the same. In other words: the "legal norms" have the character of generalized propositions – "legal *rules*" – and they are present in that form as "maxims" in the minds of judges. And the – partly direct, partly indirect – effect of this is to bring about *empirical* regularities in the actual conduct of human beings towards each other and in relation to material objects. Of course, this is certainly not to say that the empirical regularities [exhibited by] "cultural life" generally constitute "projections" of "legal rules". But the fact that law has the character of "rules" *can* be the "adequate" cause of empirical regularities; in that case, it is *one* causal element among others determining that empirical regularity. Naturally, the reason why it is a most important determinant in that direction is that empirical human beings are normally "reasonable" beings – that is to say: from an empirical point of view, they are capable of grasping and following "purposive maxims" and of harbouring "normative ideas". This is the reason why the empirical "regularity" of [human] behaviour brought about by the force of legal "regulation" may be *greater* than the physiological "regularity" brought about by medical "regulation" of the human digestive system. But the "legal rule" that exists empirically (as a "maxim" of certain persons) will – if at all – be effective as a causal determinant of empirical regularities in a way and to a degree that vary from case to case and can certainly not be defined generally. Let us look at the following examples: the empirically "regular" appearance of the clerk in his office; the empirically regular appearance of the butcher [in the butcher's shop]; the empirical regularities exhibited by some person's management of the money and goods at his actual disposal; the periodicity of the phenomena called "crises"[1] and "unemployment" or of "price" movements after the harvest; and the [movement of] birth rates when "wealth" or the intellectual "culture" of certain human groups increases: in each of these cases, [the empirically existing "legal rule"] is the decisive cause; but, in each case, it works in quite a different way and to quite a different degree. [Moreover,] let us consider the situation where a certain new "legal proposition" is "created" empirically. (We define this as the fact that a "symbolic" process takes place in a specific manner that corresponds to what a large number of empirical persons *habitually regard* as the usual and binding way of "establishing" legal rules.) The "effect" that this new "creation" of a "legal proposition" has on the *actual* conduct of these persons, and of *others* whose conduct is susceptible to their influence, can in principle be

---

1   Here, we shall not concern ourselves with the analysis of the *empirical* substance of the states of affairs to which these concepts refer.

"calculated", in accordance with our experience, *in exactly the same manner* as the effect of some "natural phenomenon". Therefore, it is possible to formulate general empirical propositions concerning the "effects" [of legal propositions] in exactly the same sense as other propositions of the form "x is followed by y"; and we are all familiar with such propositions within the domain of everyday political life. From the point of view of logic, these *empirical* "rules", which are statements as to the adequate "effect" of the empirical validity of a legal proposition, are of course the very antithesis of those *dogmatic* "rules" that can be derived as logical "consequences" of precisely the same legal proposition, treated as an object of "jurisprudence". [If these two kinds of rule are polar opposites,] although they *both*, in the same way, take as their point of departure the empirical "fact" that a legal rule with a certain content is regarded as valid, this is because they proceed to perform completely heterogeneous intellectual operations on the basis of that "fact". – One may call a "dogmatic" investigation "formal" because it remains in the world of "concepts"; in that case, it is opposed to the "empirical", in the sense of causal inquiry in general. On the other hand, nothing prevents one from calling the empirical–causal "conception" of "legal rules" "naturalistic" (as opposed to the way in which they are treated in the field of juridical dogmatics). But one must bear clearly in mind that "nature" in this case refers to the totality of empirical being in general; consequently, the "*history* of law", for instance, will also, from a logical viewpoint, be a "naturalistic" discipline, as it, too, has the *factual existence* of legal norms, not their ideal *meaning*, as its object.[1] Stammler's definition of the concept of a "conventional rule" will be discussed shortly; in the present context, we shall refrain from

---

1   It should be mentioned in passing that the intellectual operations underlying the "history of law" are by no means as easily classifiable, from a logical point of view, as it would seem at first glance. For instance, what does it mean from an *empirical* point of view that a certain legal instrument "was valid" during a certain period in the past? The fact that the principle [of the institution] can be found expressed in printed symbols made with printer's ink in a [certain] volume that has come down to us under the designation of "code of law" is of course an extremely important symptom [of the "validity" of that "institution"], but, after all, it is not necessarily in itself the decisive one. Often, even that source of knowledge is entirely absent; and, moreover, it *always* needs to be "interpreted" and "applied" to the concrete case, and the manner in which that "interpretation" and "application" are performed may in its turn present problems. The logical "meaning" of that "past validity", in the sense [considered] by the history of law, might perhaps be expressed in the following hypothetical sentence: *If*, at that time, a "jurist" *had been* asked to decide a conflict of interest according to legal rules of a certain kind, then there would, according to those habits of juridical thought that are known to us – irrespective of the sources of that knowledge – have been a high degree of *probability* that a decision with a certain content *could have been expected*. But we are all too easily inclined not to ask how the judge "would" probably in fact have decided the case, but instead [to ask] how [the judge] *should have* decided that given case – in other words: to introduce a dogmatic construction into the empirical investigation. [We are] all the more [inclined to ask the latter question] for two reasons: (1) In fact, we *cannot* do without such a construction as a "heuristic instrument". Quite regularly, and without thinking about it, we proceed in the following way: first, we ourselves interpret the historical "sources of law" dogmatically; and then, if necessary and possible, we "test" whether our interpretation was historically and empirically valid [at that time] by confronting it with the "facts" (judgements that have been handed down to us etc.). (2) In order to reach any conclusion at all about what "was valid", we must very often – indeed: as a rule – use *our own* interpretation for descriptive purposes: otherwise, it would not be possible at all to convey the historical legal situation in an intelligible and coherent manner, as a well-defined, unambiguous and consistent juridical concept had not [yet] been developed empirically, or had not been generally accepted (one only has to think of the "Gewere" – the "power of ownership" – in certain medieval sources). In this last case, we shall of course carefully try to determine the extent to which the "theory" – or "theories" – developed by *us* as being possible correspond to the empirical "conception of justice" prevalent at the time: our own "theory" merely serves as a provisional scheme for ordering [the material]. But quite definitely, the "conception of justice" prevalent during a historical period is not necessarily an unambiguous given, and still less is

---

analysing it and examining its relation to actual "regularities", as we did [with the "legal rules"]. [In the case of "conventional rules"], as in the case of "legal rules", there is, logically speaking, a world of difference between the "rule" in the sense of an imperative and the empirical "regulatedness". And, from the viewpoint of an investigation whose objects are *empirical* regularities, "conventional rules", in exactly the same sense as "legal rules", are one of the *causal* determinants to be found as part of the object; and – just like the "legal rule" – it is neither a "form" of being nor a "formal principle" of knowledge. –

In any event, the reader will already, a long time ago, have grown tired of this long-winded exposition of completely self-evident points, all the more so since its language is still extremely crude and imprecise – a consequence of the fact (which was noted earlier) that the formulations are purely provisional. But he will have to realize that the sophisms in Stammler's book are responsible for the unfortunate necessity of making these distinctions [developed above], because all the paradoxical effects that Stammler aims at and [actually] achieves are, in part, due to the constant confusion of "regular", "regulated", "legally regulated", "rule", "maxim", "norm" and "legal rule" – "legal rule" as an object of juridical conceptual analysis and "legal rule" as an empirical phenomenon, i.e. as a causal component of human action. [In this confusion], "Is" and "Ought", "concept" and "conceptual content" are constantly whirled around and mixed up with each other, in the manner that we have already noted as being characteristic of [Stammler], to say nothing of [the fact that] he repeatedly – as we shall see – confuses the different senses in which the "rule" is a "precondition". Of course, if Stammler himself were to read this, he would probably be inclined to point out, with great emphasis, that the truth of everything, or almost everything, that has been examined at great length [in this essay] is conceded in many different places in his book, and that he has [even] expressly underlined many of the points made [in the essay]. In particular [– he would say –] he has strongly emphasized that the "legal order" can obviously be investigated from a causal perspective, just as well as from a "teleological" one. Certainly! We shall have to make that same observation ourselves. But, quite apart from the half-truths that, as we shall see, are also to be found [in the passages that Stammler refers to here], the main conclusion that emerges is once again the following: In other passages, and precisely in the *crucial* ones, Stammler himself has completely forgotten those simple truths and their equally simple consequences. Admittedly, the "effect" of his book benefited greatly from his lapse of memory, for the following reason: Let us suppose that he had, for instance, at the outset made the straightforward statement that he was exclusively concerned with what *ought to* be: that he wanted to demonstrate a "formal" principle which could serve as a guide for legislators asking [themselves] what the law should be, and for judges in cases where an appeal was made to their "discretionary judgement". In that case, that attempt[ed demonstration] would no doubt have aroused a certain interest, irrespective of the value that one might attribute to the solution that he proposed; but from the point of view of

---

it a consistent one. In every case, we employ our dogmatic construction as an "ideal type" (in the sense that I have discussed elsewhere – [pp. 124–32 above]). Such a theoretical construct is never the *end* of empirical knowledge, but always a *means*, for heuristic or for descriptive purposes (or both). In its turn, a "legal rule" that has been established as *empirically* "valid" by the history of law – that is to say: within a temporal and spatial section of history – functions, along the lines developed above, as an "ideal type" of the *actual* conduct of those persons who were potentially affected by it: We take as our point of departure the probability that the *actual* conduct of the historical persons in question has, at least to a certain extent, adapted itself to [the "legal rule"]; and then, if necessary and possible, we "test" our hypothesis of the existence of a corresponding "maxim of lawfulness" [in the minds of] the historical persons by confronting it with the "facts". This is precisely the reason why "legal rules" are so often substituted for empirical "regularities", and legal terms [are used to designate] economic phenomena.

empirical "social science", [his enterprise] would then immediately be marked as absolutely irrelevant. And, above all, there would have been no reason at all for Stammler to provide us with that extensive, but at the same time imprecise, discussion of the nature of "social life". We shall now turn to the critique of that discussion, with the parallel aim of analysing more closely the fundamental distinction − which has so far only been sketched out in a quite preliminary fashion − between the empirical and the dogmatic approach.[1]

First published in *Archiv für Sozialwissenschaft und Sozialpolitik* 24 (1907), pp. 94–151. Translated from: "R. Stammlers 'Überwindung' der materialistischen Geschichtsauffassung", in Max Weber, *Gesammelte Aufsätze zur Wissenschaftslehre* (ed. Johannes Winckelmann), 3rd ed., Tübingen: J.C.B.Mohr (Paul Siebeck) 1968, pp. 291–359.

The second edition of Rudolf Stammler's book *Economy and Law According to the Materialist Conception of History* (Stammler, *Economy*[2]) was published in 1906. Originally, Weber had planned to deliver the article on Stammler as one long manuscript. He began work on it in 1906, but other pressing concerns led him to postpone the conclusion of it, the more so as he realized that there would be no room in the *Archive* for its publication before the summer of 1907. The article remained unfinished; the first part was published in the second half of 1907, and it was planned that the rest of it would be published separately when Weber had completed it. This never happened, however. The unfinished draft was published after Weber's death by Marianne Weber as *Addendum* (see pp. 227–41).

1   A further article was planned.

ADDENDUM TO THE ESSAY ON R[UDOLF] STAMMLER'S "OVERCOMING" OF THE MATERIALIST CONCEPTION OF HISTORY

On [*Economy²*,] p. 372, [Stammler] writes: "Whenever . . . we are considering the *causation* of human actions, our approach becomes that of the *natural sciences*", and he continues: "*The nature of 'causes' of action is always physiological*" (*Stammler's* italics!). He then amplifies this [statement] by saying that the "decisive causal determinants of action" "are to be found in the *nervous system*". This claim would hardly be acceptable to any of the different contemporary theories concerning the relationship between somatic and psychical processes. There are two possibilities: Either the claim amounts to saying that, unless "action" can be derived *from* physical processes, it cannot be causally explained *at all*, and moreover that, in fact, the possibility of such a [physical] derivation may always be presupposed in principle; interpreted in that way, the claim is identical with "materialism" in the strict sense of the word. Or the claim [may be interpreted as stating] that whatever cannot be derived "materially" – i.e. *from* physical processes – cannot be subject to causal investigation *at all*; [under that interpretation,] a back door has been left open for indeterminism. An ambiguity that has a similar result can be found on pp. 339 (bottom) to 340 (top). Here, Stammler says that one can look at one's own actions in two different ways: "either as causally determined occurrences in *external* (NB!) nature or as [*acts*] *that I myself have to bring about*". "In the first case, I have" (? the meaning must be: I *try to* get) "firm natural scientific knowledge of certain future acts [viewed] as external (NB!) occurrences . . . In the second case, scientific knowledge (whose?) of the causal necessity of this act in particular is lacking; the act is (NB!) possible, according to experience, but it is *not* intrinsically (?) *necessary*." It is immediately obvious how much ambiguity is caused by the fact that, in the first of the two alternatives, the concept of "acts" is – quite gratuitously – restricted to "external" phenomena. A causal approach will also embrace the "internal" aspect of the process, as well as the idea that an act "has to be brought about", the balancing of the "means" and, finally, the consideration of the "purpose" [of the action]: in a causal investigation, all these phenomena, and not just the "external" ones, will be treated as being strictly determined. In the following paragraph (p. 340, paragraph 1), Stammler himself seems to subscribe to this view when he speaks of looking at "human behaviour as a natural occurrence" and, further on (paragraph 2), of the fact that "someone who is hungry and thirsty craves for food and is *causally driven* to eat". To "crave for" something is obviously something that belongs to the "psyche" – in other words, it is not "external" and cannot be directly "perceived"; it is something that must first be "inferred" from "external" perceptions. And procuring and consuming food are always, in Stammler's own terminology, "actions" which may in their turn – to widely differing degrees – depend on the weighing of "means" and "ends" against each other. The spectrum of cases between an unthinking "grab" for [food] and the most refined composition of a meal from the menu of the "[Grand] Véfour" ⟨218⟩ is at no point broken by a sharp dividing line. But there is no possible doubt that every conceivable [one of these] nuance[s], from totally "instinctive" to completely "reflective" action, is in exactly the same sense an object of *causal* investigation based on the assumption that everything is determined. On pp. 342–43, Stammler himself, in an argument against Jhering, rejects his distinction between "mechanical" causality and causality that is "psychological" (i.e. determined by *purposive* ideas), since there is [in Stammler's view] no precise substantive difference between the two. But why does he then, just two pages earlier, in his own examples make a careful distinction[1] between "rational" and "instinctive" action? It is not [just] a slip of the tongue: on the contrary, at that point Stammler himself completely lapses into Jhering's distinction. On p. 340 (paragraph 3), he writes that (1) the "idea (NB!) of unsatisfied human hunger" will "move along the lines of causal knowledge of nature" in *those* cases where "the consumption of food is regarded (NB!) as causally necessary because [that person] is *instinctively driven*" (example: the infant at its mother's breast). On the other hand, (2) "the idea (NB!) of an exquisite banquet being prepared and finished off (!) . . . is an event that is *in no way* conceived (NB!) to be an inevitable necessity"; "on the contrary, it must first *be brought about* by the acting person himself (or herself)". Here, the "diplomacy of imprecision" that we are already familiar with manifests itself afresh. Sentence no. (1) gives the impression that *only* processes of "instinctive life" can be subjected to *causal* analysis; however, this is not stated directly. In the same way, in sentence no. (2), the "banquet" is treated as belonging to the "realm of freedom"; but [Stammler] takes great care to avoid stating *whose* "idea", "regard" etc. [he is] speaking of: is it the acting person himself who "has an idea" in one case, but not in the other? Or are "*we*" – the investigating subjects – the ones who approach the conduct of the acting person – the *object* [of the investigation] – with different kinds of *question*? It seems as if, in the case of the "idea of unsatisfied hunger" (no. 1), [Stammler] is talking about our idea – the idea of the investigators. On the other hand, in the case of the exquisite banquet, he seems to be speaking of an idea harboured by the person who is greedily looking forward to "finishing it off" (as St[ammler] puts it) – otherwise, the final phrase (*must . . . be brought about*) makes no sense. In other words, we are once more faced with an example of that conflation of objects and subjects of knowledge that Stammler is so fond of using and that allows him to evade precise formulations.

This sort of confusion, however, pervades the whole chapter on "Causality and Telos". ⟨219⟩ The account on pp. 374 (bottom) to 375 (middle paragraph) would have been quite sufficient as a presentation of all that is *correct* in that section of Book Four. The question: "Should an insight furnished by empirical science, or an ethical or aesthetic [opinion], be *approved* in substance, and what are the 'reasons' for that approval?" must be kept completely separate from the question: "what are the *causal origins* [of that insight or opinion] – in other words: what are its 'causes'?". In the passage [just referred to], Stammler himself says, quite rightly, that these two questions are entirely *different* from each other. But, if that is so, what is the meaning of his remark at the middle of p. 375, to the effect that "the latter" (the question of the "systematic importance", i.e. the *validity* of an insight or opinion) "has *substantive priority* and is decisive"? *For whom*? And again: on p. 374, paragraph 1, [Stammler] writes that, if we have "complete" knowledge of the empirical conditions for the existence of an "idea", then it is "*possible*" that

---

1   And this in spite of the fact that Vorländer (*Social Philosophy*) had warned him that those examples could be "misunderstood". What V[orländer] assumes to be a "misunderstanding" is in fact a scrupulous avoidance of clarity on Stammler's part.

"the *empirical* (Stammler's italics!) effect – that is to say: the fact that something happens or does not happen – can be calculated on the basis of the given conditions, with the same certainty as [in the case of] any other natural event". This looks like an acknowledgement of the legitimacy of conducting a strictly empirical investigation of the origins of all contents in life, even "ideal" ones. But already[, if we look at the] language, it seems strangely involved: even when knowledge is "complete", calculation seems to be no more than "possible"; furthermore, instead of stating plainly that the empirical existence of the "idea" is in itself unequivocally determined, [Stammler] introduces the concept of "empirical effect" and explicates it in an ambiguous way. Ambiguous in two respects: [First], the term is suggestive of the restriction (mentioned above) [of that effect] to "external" (physiological) processes; and[, second, Stammler] makes a whole series of remarks in this same chapter and the following ones in which his concession – which he has made more than once – that the strictly empirical approach is just as legitimate in the realm of "ideas" as with respect to in any other section of reality, is *again and again* qualified in the same way [as just described], and occasionally completely *retracted*. Moreover, [when he] discusses in what sense [one can have] empirical–causal knowledge of human action, and what its limitations are, [this discussion] is vitiated throughout by a lack of clarity and consistency that is quite intolerable.

On p. 355, last paragraph, it is claimed that "knowledge of nature" always leads back "from one cause to a *higher* cause, of which the first one is the *effect*" – in other words: laws of nature are hypostatized into "efficient forces". However, five pages previously (p. 350), there is a comprehensive discussion of the proposition that causality is not a connection that is the property of things "as such", but only "an element of thought, a basic, unitary concept within the domain of our knowledge". At the bottom of p. 351, it is stated that "experience" simply "constitutes" the embodiment of "perceptions ordered in accordance with unitary principles ('for instance' – NB! – 'the law of causality')"; and, on p. 371, causality is called an "*example*" of the "certain" empirical "general *concepts*" (!) guiding our knowledge. But, on p. 368, [Stammler] says that the "*only scientific* knowledge of concrete phenomena"[1] is the causal one. This in its turn is completely at variance with the reference (p. 378) to a "*science* of purposes" and (p. 379) to "the *scientific* guidance of human purposes". On p. 378, the "science of purposes" is contrasted with "natural science", which must therefore apparently in this connection be identical with "causal" knowledge. On p. 350, causality is treated as a fundamental category of *all* science of empirical experience; therefore, it seems to follow that the "science of purposes" could *not* be a science of empirical experience. But what, then, is the distinction between the "science of purposes" and the "science of empirical experience"? Here again, we do not get the simple answer that [the two] represent completely different *approaches*, together with an exposition and a logical analysis of those approaches; instead, we are presented with a jumble of misleading constructions that are in every case completely useless.

Page 352 tells us that the "thought of *choices* to be made, of acts to be brought about . . . is included in the content of our ideas". All right. The fact that such *ideas* exist is part of our everyday inner experience, and doubted by no one. What follows from this? "Why should this ideational content be an illusion?", Stammler asks. It should be noted right away that, in a deterministic perspective, this "content" is of course *not* in any way an "illusion". It is an established empirical fact that the ability of human beings to subject their behaviour to conscious deliberation has extremely important consequences for the way in which they actually behave. In order to be *able to* act, the acting person certainly does not need the idea that his behaviour is *not* "determined". Similarly, if [the] behaviour [of the acting person] is regarded as an

---

1   Th[is] totally misleading formulation gives the impression that the essential function of the causal approach is not generalizing, and that value judgements cannot apply to individual phenomena.

unequivocally determined process, this will not transform [his] idea of [making] a "choice" into an "illusion": [indeed,] precisely from a "psychological" point of view, a "struggle" *has* taken place between those purposive ideas that he had become aware of as being "possibilities". And, finally, even [if the person making the choice is a] convinced determinist, the choice that he has made (or is to make) will not lose its character as an act "proper" to him, as being "an act of his" – that is to say: as something that, in an *empirical* sense, can *also* be causally imputed to his personal "distinctive character", his (empirically) "constant motives". Quite the reverse: One would only enter into the domain of "illusion" if the acting person were to start engaging in "indeterministic" metaphysics – in other words: if he claimed that his action was "free", in the sense of being completely or partly "undetermined". But Stammler does engage in that kind of metaphysics: [As we have seen, Stammler refers to the possibility of] the ideational content of the "choice" being an "illusion"; and the argument (pp. 351–52) preceding [this reference] indisputably implies that this would be the case if, in spite of the presence of the idea of a "choice", the "acts to be brought about" were conceived as being *determined*. This, [Stammler] already says on p. 344, would be in contradiction with the concept of "choice", which excludes a "binding causality". However, this unequivocal claim is then (pp. 344–45) qualified and blurred in the following proposition: There is "no doubt" that we "in the vast *majority* of cases" regard the "consequences" of future human actions as something "*which might also not happen*".

The[re are], in Stammler's view (p. 352), [two reasons] why this proposition of his is not in contradiction with the fact that the principle of [sufficient] reason ‹220› is unconditionally valid for all experience: (1) As long as the "choice" between those acts is still open, they are [only] "possibilities", and not *yet* empirical facts. (But this would of course also be true of any "natural event", for instance the fight between two animals, as long as the outcome is still uncertain.) (2) The problem of the "right" choice – in other words: [the problem] of what *should be done* – does not lie within the domain of "natural science". This last thesis is of course completely true; but it would be in a sorry state if its validity depended on the correctness of Stammler's general argument concerning the process by which an acting person "chooses" and the limits of the causal approach – an argument that has nothing at all to do with this "valuational question". However, it goes without saying that this is *not* the case. I can find a sunset "beautiful" and a rainy day "nasty", or take the view that a certain opinion is a "fallacy", even though I am convinced that, in all three cases, the phenomenon is causally determined. I can assess the dietetic "appropriateness" of an "instinctive" ingestion of food and of an exquisite dinner in exactly the same way. Just as with any kind of human "action", I can ask what course any natural process "*must*" have taken (in the past) or "*must*" take (in the future) "in order to" produce a certain result. (Every doctor must (implicitly) ask himself that question several times every day.) A person who acts rationally may regard several different outcomes as "possible", depending on his own behaviour; moreover, he may perhaps also have in mind a possible choice of several different "maxims" as guiding principles for that behaviour; and[, in those cases,] his action will be "constrained" until this inner "struggle" has been settled in one way or another. From the empirical point of view, this is undoubtedly one of the fundamentally important modalities of "psychical processes". But it is naturally out of the question [to suppose] that the domain of causal investigation is abandoned [when one enters into] the analysis of such processes, where the idea of one or more possible "outcomes" is one of the causal determinants (but, it should be noted, invariably only *one* of the determinants) of human conduct. It goes without saying that, if the process of "choosing" between several "ends", which are considered as "possible", is made the object of *empirical* investigation, that process – from beginning to end, and including all the rational deliberations and moral ideas that present themselves in the [mind of the] person making the choice – must be considered to be strictly determined to quite the same extent as any "natural event". Stammler never disputes this in so many words; however, page after page, he avoids taking a clear stand on the issue. At one point (p. 368), he says that "the *accomplishment* is not free"; does this mean that, empirically speaking, freedom can be ascribed to the "volition"? In another passage, "experience" is identified with the epitome of what is "perceived"; and, as mental processes cannot be "perceived", the reader is left in the dark as to whether they are determined – the more so as Stammler (p. 341, top) explicitly states that "the idea of something that must be brought about by human [action]" does not belong within the realm of "perceptions", [a realm] that he (p. 378) identifies with "nature".[1] Or, he argues – for instance in the passage on p. 352 quoted above – that "future" outcomes conceived as "possibilities" have not yet become "empirical facts". And [Stammler] even directly claims (p. 346) that experience is only *possible* with regard to *past* facts, and that it *therefore* in principle remains "unfinished" and "incomplete" – as if [he did not know that], *logically* speaking, the causal chain reaches as far into the future as into the past. Interwoven with this, we find a variety of other statements: experience is not "omniscient"; it does not comprehend "the sum total of human insight" (p. 346 – this represents a categorical leap from object to subject); experience is only valid within [the limits set by] its "laws of form" (?); it *therefore* does not produce "eternal truths" with "immutable validity" and, consequently, it cannot claim to have "absolute *value*". On the other hand, at the top of p. 345, [Stammler] (as we have seen) limits himself to saying that we "*mostly*" regard future acts as something that will not necessarily take place. And so this vague, indecisive talk goes on and on, touching on every possible problem and then completely muddling the[se problems] up. Stammler does (bottom of p. 357, top of p. 358) place the possibility of "*conceiving*" (NB!) an act as one "that must be brought about" – once again, we do not know whose ["conception" Stammler is speaking of]: that of the acting person, or "ours", [i.e. the "conception" of those] for whom his act is an *object* of knowledge – *on the same level as* the possibility of conceiving it as causally determined. But at the same time, he points out that this latter possibility is *limited* by the fact that there is still "not a single established law of nature according to which the causal necessity of future human acts could be predicted in the same way as with, say, the law of gravity"; and if this could be "remedied" (!), that still would not mean that "*all* forthcoming human actions" would "be included" (!) under this law. As if the "totality" of (extra-human) *natural* occurrences could ever, even if we had absolutely complete "nomological" ‹221› knowledge, be deduced and "calculated" on the basis of laws! Stammler has no conception at all – however imperfect – of the relationship between "law" and "[concrete] event", or, more generally, of the epistemological significance of the irrationality of reality. Although Stammler occasionally remembers that *actual* gaps in "experience", no matter how large, have no *logical* relevance at all, he again and again brings [actual incompleteness of experience] into play [in his arguments]. He thereby repeatedly demotes the "kingdom of ends" to [the role of] a mere stopgap; but, on the other hand, he does grant [the "kingdom of ends"] a heterogeneous *epistemological* status. – But let us put Stammler out of his misery: let us state briefly what he *could have* had in mind.

---

1   In this context, it is of course left in that obscurity with which we are only too familiar whether that "idea" is meant to be *our* idea or an empirical *object*. Moreover, it is of course not at all obvious why an "instinct" belongs within that "realm" [of "perceptions"] while an "idea" does not. Surely, an "instinct" is no more "perceivable" than an "idea". And it is of course possible to "enter into" not only the "instinct" (as [Stammler] says at the middle of p. 340), but also, to an even greater extent, [into] the "idea" of somebody else. Incidentally, the remark about entering *into* "instincts" does not prevent Stammler, at the bottom of that very same page, from once more referring only to the causal determination of "external" events.

In order to grasp the distinction, as Stammler sees it, between knowledge in the "natural sciences" and in the "social sciences", we should then have to look for another concept of "nature". Before we proceed with our examination of Stammler's own attempts, let us first try, on the basis of the analyses in the previous section, to get a clear picture in our own minds of the actual possibilities [of defining another concept of nature].

As we have seen, Stammler regards the "external" norms as the "form", the "precondition", the "epistemological condition", etc. of "social life" and knowledge of "social life". We have earlier used the example of "rules of the game" to discuss the various possibilities of making sense out of those repeated constructions, which are presented in ever different forms; let us now draw some conclusions. In so doing, we shall begin by leaving aside the possibility that Stammler might believe that the *only* conceivable way of acquiring "knowledge" of "social life" would be to "evaluate" it – to find an "ideal", which would then serve as a standard against which the empirical findings concerning "social life" would be *measured* with respect to "social policy". Instead, we shall assume that the task is to define the object of an *empirical* science in which the "external" (legal and "conventional") *norms* play the role of a "precondition".

The Second Book of Stammler's work is entitled "The Object of Social Science". As we have already seen, its purpose is to [develop] a concept of "social life" that is to be higher than, and to comprehend, both (Rümelin's) concept of "society" and the concept of the state, ‹222› and to anchor it to the concept of a "rule". But in the passage where this is done for the first time (p. 83, line 15ff.), Stammler already introduces ambiguities. He says that the constitutive factor of "social life as a distinctive object of our knowledge" is "the regulation, due to human beings", (p. 85, this is put even more clearly: a "norm emanating from human beings") "of their mutual dealings and communal life". Does this mean (I) that the "rule" to which the concept of "social life" is anchored must (1) be created by human beings as a norm that "ought to be" followed, or (2) be followed by human beings as a maxim, or (3) be both [a norm and a maxim]? In other words: does ["the rule"] need to be a "maxim" of empirical human beings at all? Or is it sufficient that (II) "*we*" – the observers – "conceive" the mutual conduct of human beings who coexist in space and time as being subject to a "rule", either (1) in the sense that we can "abstract" a "rule" from [that mutual conduct] – in other words: that it follows an empirically regular course; or (2) in the sense (which, as we have discussed at length, is completely different from the first one) that it seems to "us" – the observers – that a "norm" can, or must (NB: "ideally"), apply to it?

At any rate, Stammler would immediately claim that what he means is of course not [what was sketched out above under] case II, (1) (empirical regularity): a "rule" should be understood as an "imperative", not as an empirical regularity. In a comment on a remark by Kistiakovski, he is very much on his high horse and goes so far as to claim that he had never expected that anyone would raise that question, considering how he had dealt with it in [the first edition of] his book.[1] Really? Then what does it mean when he persistently carries on as if the communal existence and mutual influence of human beings would, from a purely empirical–causal perspective, dissolve into "turmoil", "chaos", "disorder" (or some other term in his rich vocabulary)? In Stammler's reply to Kistiakovski, he explicitly states (p. 641) that, if an approach to human relations does *not* employ the concept of a "rule" as an "imperative", it *cannot* be a discussion of "social life" in Stammler's sense of that concept. Against that background, how is it at all possible for Stammler to claim (p. 84) that, "in substance", the opposite of life "in society" is the *isolated* existence of an individual hypothetical primitive human being – one, as he directly say, who lives in complete isolation? Surely, it is obvious that the opposite

---

1   Stammler, *Economy*[2], p. 88n51 (cf. ibid. p. 641).

[of life in "society"] could only (formulated in a provisional and completely imprecise way) be the following: "Those relations of human beings (to nature and) to each other which do *not* fall under "man-made rules" (in the imperative sense of that term). Furthermore, it is peculiar – but typical of Stammler's style, with which we have already become familiar – that, in the passage just referred to, he suddenly refers to "substantive" opposites, and no longer (as on p. 77 and elsewhere) to "conceptual" or "logical" ones. But very soon, at the top of p. 87, the two are again identified with each other: differences concerning the purpose of the investigation are treated as identical to differences with respect to the empirically "given" facts. Actually, it seems that [there are two possibilities:] (1) the "logical" delimitation of a distinctive "object of our knowledge" by demonstrating the specific *purpose* of the investigation; in that case, "*all* relations (to 'nature' and) to other human beings" should be excluded from the domain of "social life" (in Stammler's sense) *insofar as* we are only considering them as facts and not as ideally possible cases of the application of "rules" (in the imperative sense). In other words: only a "dogmatic" science, but not an empirical–causal one, could have "social life" as its object. On the other hand, (2) "substantive" delimitation of components of empirical reality (that is to say: [belonging to] the world of actual, given "objects") on the basis of qualitative differences – whose presence can be empirically established – between the components to be delimited; in that case, what Stammler's concept of "social life" would ("in substance") be opposed to must be formulated as follows: "*all* human behaviour (towards 'nature' and) towards other human beings [for which one of two conditions holds: either] that human beings have *in fact* not "set" a "norm" as obligatory for exhibiting [that behaviour] (*cf.* case I, (1) above); or (*cf.* case I, (2) and (3)) that they actually do not follow such a "norm" as a "maxim". In other words: whether something is a "natural event" or a phenomenon of "social life" would depend on whether an "ordinance" concerning the relevant phenomenon had been agreed upon in the concrete instance (case I, (1));[1] or whether, in addition (case I, (3)), the involved person or persons had, in the concrete instance, acted on the basis of a conscious – positive or negative – attitude towards those "ordinances"; or, finally, whether (case I, (2)), in spite of the absence of an explicit "ordinance", human behaviour had in the concrete instance been subjectively influenced, or at least accompanied, by the idea of obligatory norms for external human conduct.

An appeal to Stammler himself for an unambiguous answer to these questions would be in vain. By employing the peculiar "diplomacy of imprecision" that we have previously commented on, he evades his duty of providing such an answer; and the very simple way in which he does so in the present case is by *personifying* the "rule" and by simply speaking "metaphorically". On pp. 98–99 (top), we are told that the "external" rule – which is in this case opposed to the moral norm, where the "disposition" is what matters – is one "which, according to its meaning (NB!), occupies a position quite independent of the driving force impelling an individual to follow it".[2] Anyone would interpret this metaphor to mean that what Stammler is talking

---

1   The following points should be noted: on p. 92, paragraphs 3 and 4, Stammler introduces "agreement" as a characteristic [of "social life"] which is – quite misleadingly – contrasted with purely "instinctual life"; p. 94 he uses the formulation "human *ordinance*"; and, according to what is said on p. 94, one would have to acknowledge an established "social existence" of *animals* in cases where it could be demonstrated that animals in communities (for instance in a colony of bees) "*had themselves* made such external rules" and now conformed to them.

2   [Stammler's] distinction between "morals" on the one hand and "law" and "convention" on the other corresponds to the usual one. However, it should always be kept in mind that the question of the reasons why external behaviour does *not* conform to a legal norm – and in particular: what is the "disposition" (deliberate intent, lack of due care, good faith, error, etc.) underlying a certain act that violates the legally protected interests of others – is by no means legally irrelevant; therefore, the fundamental sharpness of the distinction should not be overestimated.

about is the ideal "validity" of the norm, [a "validity"] that can be inferred dogmatically. This interpretation seems all the more obvious since Stammler, in the following paragraph (line 8ff.), explicitly states that "the rule" is "not concerned with" "whether the [person] subject [to it] reflects on it at all" (which should include the case where he is not aware of it at all – or perhaps not?) or whether "dull habit" makes him act in conformity with it. (If we base ourselves on a strict distinction between pragmatic, norm-oriented action and all other kinds of action, "dull habit" should of course be indistinguishable from animal "instinct".) Stammler wisely remains silent with respect to the case in which the "rule" is *not* followed in actual practice; but his meaning would only be truly unambiguous if he stated plainly that this case, too, was irrelevant to the ideal (dogmatic) "validity" of the rule. However, that unambiguousness would have made [it] impossible [for him] to perform the following scholastic manipulation: Since the (personified) rule "differs from" (above, the formulation was: "is independent of") "the driving forces (NB!) which are distinctive of . . . the isolated (!) human being", it manifests itself "as a new, independent motive". On pp. 98–99 (top), we are told that the (empirical) motive ("driving force" is the expression employed in that passage) underlying the external behaviour is *irrelevant*; as Stammler puts it: "the rule occupies a position independent [of the motive]". If we strip this statement of its metaphorical elements, it must be taken to mean that, when *we* evaluate normatively, we abstract[1] from the empirical motivation of the acting person and only concern ourselves with the legality of the external behaviour. [That is to say:] the "isolated" human being is suddenly and surreptitiously introduced [in order to function] as the conceptual opposite [of "social life"]. And, moreover, with equal suddenness, the ideal "validity" of a norm as a standard of *evaluation* applied by *us* – the observers – is once more reinterpreted [and transformed into] an empirical motive of human action; and this empirical fact – put more clearly: the possibility that a person (ideally) subject to the norm deliberately conforms to [it] on the basis of his moral or formal–legal disposition, a possibility described at the top of p. 99 as completely irrelevant – is [now] made out to be the specific characteristic of "externally regulated life in common". It is obvious that this sleight of hand[2] is made possible by Stammler's use of the expression "the rule *occupies* an independent position". This does not make it clear to a careless reader that, in the [first] case, where we are reasoning "dogmatically" and therefore treat the "rule" as an ideal *obligation*, the abstraction is performed by *us* – the subjects of the inquiry; and that, in the second case, that of empirical knowledge, the rule is formulated by empirical persons (belonging to the *object* of our inquiry) who, in so doing, intend to bring about a certain "result" and will in fact usually, with varying degrees of certainty, succeed in bringing it about. Indeed, in his attempts to prevent the intrusion of any clarity into his scholastic obscurity, Stammler goes even further and, in the following paragraph (p. 100, line 23), personifies the "law of nature" as a parallel to the "ordinance": he contrasts the latter, which "aims at bringing about" a certain life in common, with the former – the empirical regularity – which is "the *cognizing* (sic!) unity of natural phenomena". A rule that "intends" is a metaphor which is in itself at least tolerable (although it is quite impermissible in the present context); but a rule that "cognizes" is complete nonsense. In view of the extensive discussion in the previous section, it should be unnecessary to proceed further with this critique. Nor

---

1 Stammler carefully avoids the use of this expression.
2 I refer to my previous remarks and repeat that this criticism is at *no* point meant to imply any "deliberate intent" on Stammler's part. But there is no other word in the language to describe the "culpa lata" ‹223› by which such sophistry is not only permitted (in a second edition!), but even *constantly* employed as the *sole* underpinning [of the argument]. By using this and other, similar[ly] harsh expressions, I do at least wish to make one point: *if* the fulfilment of scientific obligations were subjected to "external rules", then Stammler's methods would certainly be classified as "a violation of police regulations".

should we have to draw particular attention to the following: On p. 100, [the rule is] the "independent" (empirical) "motive" of action; at the bottom of p. 101, it again becomes a "formally determining element" of a *concept*; then, at the middle of p. 102, it turns into an "epistemological condition" under which this concept – that of "social life" – becomes "possible"; and then, on p. 105, we are admonished that one must on no account "make the *logical* function (!) of the external regulation into something like a *causal* influence". This admonition obviously comes too late as far as Stammler is concerned, since he himself has done precisely that a few pages earlier. But even in the discussion that immediately follows his own exhortation that logical–conceptual and empirical–substantive relations should not be mixed up – which is the actual meaning, put in more general terms, of the distinction that he makes – Stammler fails to heed it. In the very next paragraph (p. 105), we find the following construction: If we are to believe Stammler, the *concepts* of "social life" and that of (as he puts it) "isolated" life can be represented as forming the strict and mutually exclusive dichotomy that he is aiming at. From this, he draws a similar conclusion with respect to empirical reality: any *actual situation* can be effortlessly subsumed under one or the other of the two concepts; only one of the two [kinds of situation] exists at any given time (NB!): "a third [possibility] is quite inconceivable". Let us now examine this reasoning a little more closely. What are the two situations that are the only "conceivable" ones? On the one hand, "a single (NB!) human being who dwells (NB!) in complete isolation"; and, on the other hand, "human life subject to external rules, in combination with others". Stammler believes that this alternative is so absolutely exhaustive that even a "development" is only possible "within one of the two states", but not from a state of "isolated [life]" to one of "social life". [This is true] "from the standpoint of our inquiry", he casually adds (in the diplomatic manner with which we are familiar); and he illustrates [his point] by referring to . . . Robinson Crusoe.[1] ⟨224⟩ In this case, the sleight of hand takes the following form: Even in this crucial passage, the reader gets the impression that the plurality of human beings held together by "ordinances" (for the sake of precision, we shall use that term, which

---

1 A short comment about the way in which Stammler makes use of that example in this context (pp. 105–06): In the "first stage", he says, there is only the "technical management of [Robinson's] isolated economy" (NB!). "Regulated life in common" begins from the moment when [Robinson] "acquired [Man] Friday ⟨225⟩ as his companion, when (NB!) the young Indian placed the white man's foot on his neck as the visible sign of the fact that "you shall be my master". [Why?] *Because*, henceforth, "for both of them" (NB!), the "technical" questions were complemented by a second "consideration" (NB!): "the social question". In other words: without that symbolic act, whose (empirical "meaning") "was intended to" express submission (or some other act with a corresponding, empirically intended, meaning), "social life" would not exist. [It would not exist], for instance, if Robinson's treatment of the Indian whose life he had saved had been that of a humane dog owner towards a dog that had come into his physical possession: if he had confined and fed him and trained ("taught") him [to be useful] for his [Robinson's] purposes. In this connection, [Robinson] would have had to make himself understood by, i.e. to reach an "understanding" with, [Friday] by means of signs, in order to make him as useful as possible; that also holds, in the same sense, for the relations of human beings to dogs. Furthermore, those signs of Robinson's would have carried the "meaning" of "regulating commands" (on this point, see St[ammler's] remarks at the top of p. 86); that is also true, in quite the same sense, of "commands" given to dogs. But then, [Robinson] would probably also have considered it to be useful (for himself) to teach Friday to speak [his language] (that is, of course, not possible with dogs). If he had done so, then St[ammler]'s remarks at the bottom of p. 96 and the top of p. 97 would lead to the following result: since language is deemed to be a "primitive convention", and since "convention" is "regulated life in common", then "social life" would come into being every time Robinson and Friday exchanged words, and cease when they were not speaking to each other (as everything else would be unchanged). "Commands", "symbolic means of understanding" and so on also have a place in the relationship between man and dog; and when Bräsig ⟨226⟩ says: "For many a man and dog, a whipping is the best way of fraternizing", the slave owners have, as we know, extended this principle

is the one generally employed by Stammler) is solely to be opposed to *one* absolutely isolated individual; but at the same time, in the most varied contexts, Stammler himself refers to *several* individuals who are coexistent, but whose mutual relations are nevertheless not regulated by "ordinances", so that these ordinances cannot be regarded as "motivating" their conduct towards each other.

A state of affairs like this latter one would therefore, from Stammler's own point of view, be conceptually identical to that of "dwelling in isolation". But [Stammler] immediately performs a second sleight of hand by describing such coexistence, which is not regulated by "ordinances" – and which he compares to colonies of animals – as "purely physical" existence in common. This leads the reader to suppose that the only possible antithesis to "social life" is the simultaneous existence in space and time [of elements] between which no relations exist at all; but, in other passages, [Stammler] discusses in detail the predominant [influence] of "instincts", "drives" etc. – which are, after all, "psychical" constituents of such a coexistence. The deliberate emphasis in those passages on the "instinctual" gives the reader the impression of "dull unawareness". But this is yet another sleight of hand: Defoe describes Robinson [Crusoe's] "economy", to which [Stammler] explicitly refers (bottom of p. 105), as being constituted not "instinctively", but instead along the lines of purely teleological "rationality"; nevertheless, Stammler does not include it in the domain of "externally regulated conduct", but categorizes it as "purely technical". And, if Stammler wish[ed] to be at all consistent, Robinson's purposive action "towards" others – in other words: action deliberately intended [by him] to influence the action [of others] in a systematic way – would in that case not belong to [the category of] "social life", unless it [were] governed *normatively* by "ordinances". We have already clarified what the "logical" consequences of this would be; here, we should simply note that Stammler, too, acknowledges them in one passage (bottom of p. 101 to top of p. 102). However, in another passage (bottom of p. 96 to top of p. 97), he makes the reservation that even the use of language implies a "conventional regulation" of human intercourse and therefore constitutes social life. Now, every use of a "linguistic" instrument aims at an "understanding"; but it is not in itself an understanding with respect to ordinances, nor does it depend on "ordinances". Stammler, though, claims that it does [depend on "ordinances"]. His argument is that grammatical propositions are *precepts*, and that "learning" them is meant to "bring about" a certain behaviour. That is indeed the case as regards the relationship of the first-year pupil to his teacher; in fact, in order to make it possible to "learn" a language in *this* way, the "grammarians" had to organize the *empirical* regularities of linguistic practice in a system of *norms*, and compliance with those norms is enforced by pedagogical use of the cane. But Stammler himself, at the bottom of p. 97, says that "completely isolated existence side by side" is only conceivable if one also abstracts from "agreement" in "language and *gestures*" (NB!).

At this point, [Stammler has to] pay the penalty for the sleight of hand implicit in the antithesis between "regulated life in common in accordance with ordinances" and "total isolation". The last remark [in the previous paragraph] is correct. But it has the following consequences: On the one hand, the *fact* that agreement exists will in itself be enough to constitute "social life", no matter how that agreement has causally arisen – whether because of an "ordinance" or as a result of involuntary psychical reactions, "reflexes", "deliberations concerning [the choice of]

to cover the Negroes as well. Perhaps the reader will excuse this ridiculous piece of casuistry when he reads Stammler's triumphant proclamation (p. 106): "It is out of the question [to imagine] something [lying] between the isolated state of Robinson and [his] regulated (NB!) life in common together with his Man Friday; an intermediate stage . . . is *inconceivable*". [Stammler] scoffs at the abstract science of economics because of its predilection for Robinson [Crusoe]; but in actual fact, economics has made rather more sensible use of Defoe's immortal character than Stammler with his scholasticism.

expression", "instinct" or similar [factors]. On the other hand, the same will therefore hold for animals: it is only if they are completely lacking in concordant "gestures" (or, put in more general terms: in "means of achieving an understanding", as this concept covers everything that we are talking about here) that they will – according to Stammler's own conceptual definition and in spite of all the talk that he spouts on pp. 87–95 – be living *non*-"social lives". And [finally], it will certainly be true that, wherever "means of achieving an understanding" can be found to exist – no matter what those means are, and whether they have been created by human "ordinances" or not – people will be living "social lives". However, this cannot really be Stammler's opinion, since it is incompatible with – [indeed,] directly contrary to – the view that he puts forward at the middle of p. 106, according to which "social life" *only* comes into existence where an "ordinance" has been *created*. The somewhat naïve sentence expressing this view runs as follows: "Let us suppose that someone wished . . . to imagine a period of human existence where . . . the urge to associate under external rules *gradually* (NB!) developed in the souls [of men] . . . then everything (NB!) would still depend on the moment at which such ordinances (NB!) first came into being (NB!). From that point onwards, we have social life; before [it], we have not; an intermediate stage . . . is meaningless" (!).[1] It is not surprising that a legally trained scholasticist can only conceive the development of "social life" as possible in the form of a social contract. But the "genuineness" of [Stammler's] scholasticism manifests itself at the top of p. 107, where "development" and "conceptual transition" are identified with each other, so that, in his view, the demonstration of the *logical* impossibility of the latter (the combination of the *words* "conceptual" and "transition" is indeed unthinkable) also implies the *empirical* impossibility of the former.

But, if such a "transition" is deemed to be "unthinkable", the question becomes even more burning: What is the decisive *criterion* of the emergence – or, more generally still, of the existence – of an "ordinance"? As savages normally do not possess written codes of law, the only possible answer to this question would seem to be that the criterion is to be found in human behaviour that (legally speaking) is "conclusive" for the existence of the norm. Is this the case only when [the "norm"] is present in the minds of those persons – in other words: when they live according to subjectively conscious "normative" maxims, or violate [those maxims] while being conscious of the fact that [their behaviour actually constitutes] a "violation" of the norm? But surely, Stammler believes that having a [certain] subjective internal attitude towards the legal norm, and even knowing about it, is irrelevant to the existence of the norm? In his view, "dull habituation" (see above) has the same effect as a conscious "normative maxim". Does this lead us to conclude that an "ordinance" can be recognized by the fact that people are seen to behave *as if* the ordinance existed? The *General State Laws for Prussia* ‹227› legally required mothers to suckle their children, and [in so doing] made the suckling of children part of "social life" in Stammler's sense. But, in general, the Prussian mother who suckled her child probably knew little or nothing about this "norm"; nor does an Australian aboriginal woman, who suckles her child at least as regularly [as the Prussian mother does], know that *no* "external rules" require her to suckle [her baby], and that suckling a child therefore, as Stammler would have it, is apparently *not* a part of "social life" [among the Aborigines] – not even in the sense that a corresponding "conventional" norm exists (unless one simply regards such a norm as being present whenever a certain degree of purely empirical "regularity" in behaviour can be ascertained). It is certainly true that – again, from a subjective point of view – "conventional" normative ideas empirically very often "develop" from purely factual regularities. This may be

---

1   Of course, a sober examination of [the expression] "is meaningless" will show that it simply means "does not fit into my (St[ammler's]) conceptual scheme".

owing to a vague unwillingness to deviate from actual traditional behaviour; or to the fact that other persons show surprise, developing into aversion, when they are faced with such deviation from a [pattern of] behaviour that has actually been adhered to over a longer period of time; or to the concern that gods or men, whose (supposedly quite egoistic) interests might be violated by the behavioural deviation, could possibly revenge themselves. And then, the fear of "unusual" conduct may develop into the idea of a "duty" to conform to what is in fact "customary"; [just as] the purely instinctive or egoistic aversion to "innovation" and "innovators" may develop into "disapproval" of them.

But when would this subjective attitude or behaviour in a concrete instance include the idea of an "ordinance"? That would no doubt quite often remain uncertain, depending on the individual case. To top it all, Stammler is of the opinion that the "subjective" situation, the "disposition", is *irrelevant*; we therefore have no empirical criterion at all [to go by], since the "external" behaviour (the suckling) has remained exactly the same. And, even if [that external behaviour] gradually changes under the influence of emerging "normative" ideas, the question of *when* the empirical existence of an "external" ("conventional" or "legal") norm is to be inferred from [that changed behaviour] is purely a matter of opinion.

Stammler's conception of the emergence of a purposive and goal-oriented "urge" to [live under] "ordinances", in the "souls" of primitive men who "live in" total (NB!) "isolation", is of course completely absurd. Therefore, if we ask – as Stammler himself explicitly does – how the empirical emergence of "social life" from an animal-like herd is in any way at all imaginable, the only remaining answer, conceived in Stammler's own "manner", would be the following: This emergence is simply not to be conceived as a temporal, empirical process; "social life" is so to speak "trans-temporal",[1] because it is [intrinsically] given together with the *concept* of "man" – a piece of information that certainly would not qualify as an answer to an empirical question, but would simply be a mystification. It is, however, the only line of retreat from [the position that Stammler has got himself into by claiming] that the theoretical possibility of constructing a certain "concept" of "social life" implies that an empirical state of affairs corresponding to that concept can in fact only come about in reality if the empirical human beings have regarded precisely the "realization" of that "concept" as the goal of their action. – [On the other hand,] one may [choose to] distance oneself from a naïve pragmatism of that kind. If so, one might instead consider the hypothetical theory of a "gradual" awakening of "normative ideas". In other words, [the theory of] an awakening of the belief that certain acts that have been performed "instinctively" and (in Stammler's own words) "in dull habituation", since time immemorial, with no thought of an "Ought", let alone an "ordinance", [that those acts] are "duties", and that some vaguely feared harm will come to the person who neglects to perform them. There would be no substantive difficulties associated with such a theory: in this sense, dogs, too, have a "sense of duty". However, the idea that such duties would (in Stammler's view) only be based on "human ordinance[s]"; that, contrary to "ethics", they would only lay claim to "external legality" (p. 98); and so on – that [kind of] conceptual bric-a-brac of Stammler's cannot be found, even if we go back to the very beginnings of our "historical" knowledge (in the usual sense [of the word "historical"]). Let us retain the assumption that an "ordinance" is a necessary condition for the existence of some process in the world of human action. In that case, the amount of "social life", thus delimited, has been subject to constant change, concurrently with the – quite gradual – transition from purely factual to "externally regulated" processes;

---

1   There is, in my opinion, hardly any doubt that the related claim made by F[riedrich] Gottl (*Limits of History*) with respect to "historical" life has to a certain extent in one way or another been influenced by Stammler's constructions. St[ammler] himself does not use the term ["trans-temporal"].

and this transition can still be observed, especially if we (like Stammler) include "convention" [under the concept of "external regulation"]. Stammler is careful to leave himself a line of retreat by the evasive statement (bottom of p. 106 to top of p. 107) that this [transition] only constitutes a development in the "content" of social life, [but that] the existence [of social life] is already presupposed. However, this of course does not contribute to proving that a "transition" is *unthinkable*, already because *any* part of what Stammler would nowadays categorize as "social life" may possibly [be due to] a similar development. Moreover, the concept of "*external* norms" as a criterion of "social", as opposed to "moral", life is utterly useless from an empirical point of view. On the one hand, all "primitive" ethics, too, demand legality (particularly "external" legality), and can nowhere be distinguished clearly from "law" and "convention". And, on the other hand, from the standpoint of the primitive "normative ideas", the "norms" do not originate in "human" "ordinances"; whenever the question of the origin of the norm is raised at all, [the answer is] (as a rule) that they originate in divine "decrees". The question of the origins of the individual components of our contemporary concepts of, for instance, "law" and "legal norms" would certainly present ethnographers with an extraordinary number of difficulties; and they may never attain reliable historical knowledge of [the relevant] *facts*. But it is certain that they would never adopt the ludicrous role of the scholastic jurist who, when faced with phenomena from the lives of primitive peoples, would only be able to ask the same naïve question, again and again: Excuse me, should this phenomenon be categorized as behaviour that is regulated externally, i.e. by human ordinance (as defined in Stammler, *Economy*, pp. 77ff.), or as purely instinctual life in common (as defined *Economy*, pp. 87)? It must necessarily be one of the two. Otherwise, I should not be able to fit it into my conceptual scheme, and the result would be perfectly awful: [the phenomenon] would be "unthinkable" for me.

Let us not prolong th[is] critique of a doctrine that constantly confuses the subject and the object of knowledge with each other, because it is based on a false conception of the "meaning" of concept formation. As a final example of this confusion, we may take the following wonderful sentence (p. 91) concerning the concept (NB!) of "social life" that we encounter (!) in experience (NB!): "This empirically given (NB!) social life rests" (presumably, that can only mean: empirically) "on external regulation" (this, as we know, is ambiguous) [a regulation] "which makes it" (this must mean: that *fact*) "conceivable as a separate concept (!) and a distinctive object" (i.e.: a "concept" that becomes "conceivable"!); "this is because we see in it" (the "regulation" – ambiguous) "the possibility . . . of comprehending (NB!) an association of human beings that is intrinsically independent of the mere demonstration (!) of the natural instinctual life of the individual" (that is to say: an empirical *fact* – an "association of human beings" – which is empirically "independent" of our *knowledge* of certain other empirical facts). Again, let us not prolong [our examination of] this chaotic confusion. If we wished to unravel all the threads in this web of sophisms in which Stammler enmeshes his readers – and above all, himself – we should quite literally have to take every sentence of the book and analyse its internal inconsistencies or its contradictions with other sentences in the same book.

Still, we can at least identify the error that is at the root of the absurd contention that the "transition" [from the "unregulated" to the "regulated" state] is "unthinkable". Such a dichotomy, which excludes any "transition", does indeed exist when the "ideal" *obligatory* validity of a "norm" is contrasted with some purely "factual" *situation*, for instance the actual action of empirical persons. That contrast is indeed completely irreconcilable, and a "transition" is conceptually "unthinkable" – but for the very simple reason that we are in that case dealing with quite disparate *approaches* and investigative orientations: on the one hand, the dogmatic inquiry into the ideal "meaning" of an "ordinance", and the evaluative *measuring* of empirical action against [the standard constituted by that "ordinance"]; and, on the other hand, establishing [the existence of] empirical action as a "fact" and "explaining" it causally. What Stammler does is to project this *logical* fact (that we can look for knowledge under two "perspectives", which differ in th[e way described]) on to empirical reality; we are consequently faced with the absurd notion that an empirical "transition" is "conceptually" impossible. And Stammler creates just as much confusion in the domain of logic: here, he commits the reverse error and constantly conflates the two approaches, which are *logically* abolutely heterogeneous. It is precisely this conflation that creates insuperable difficulties for Stammler's accomplishment of the task that he has set himself: to define the domain and the problems of "social science". This is immediately obvious when we now turn our attention to the concluding remarks at the end of the first section of Book Two (pp. 107–08). Here, Stammler discusses the principle [underlying] the manner in which he defines his problem. "Social science", with its "fundamental distinctive character", must be "carried out separately from" – which apparently means: distinguished from – "the (!) science of nature". Stammler is of the opinion (ibid., second paragraph) that the "state" (! – that is to say: the "object", in the sense of "essential nature") of "the natural science" is "philosophically secured". Really? It is common knowledge that, in the logical discussions during the last decade, nothing has really been so controversial as precisely this question. In the earlier sections [of this essay], we have already become acquainted with no less than four possible concepts of "nature";[1] but not a single one of those [concepts] could serve as the antithesis of [what] Stammler [calls] "externally regulated life in common". Those concepts of nature that contrast one part of the empirically given reality with another part – in the last resort: with the so-called "higher" functions of human beings – are unusable already because the whole domain of "merely" ethical norms, which are concerned with "inner" attitudes or conduct, has been excluded by Stammler as lying *outside* his concept [of "externally regulated life in common"]. For the same reason, it is not possible to [use a definition that] contrasts "nature", [defined] as what is "meaningless", with an object considered in terms of its "meaning", as Stammler's concept of the "externally regulated" certainly does not cover everything that is "meaningful", and not even all "meaningful" human action. The logical distinction between general (nomothetic) – "natural scientific" – knowledge and individual (historical) [knowledge] is completely beyond Stammler's horizon. Among the possible meanings of the concept of "nature" discussed so far, the only one left appears to be that defined on the basis of the distinction between "naturalistic" (in the sense of "empirical") and "dogmatic" knowledge. But Stammler's version of "social science" is not meant to be the same as jurisprudence, or a science that – unlike jurisprudence – also discusses "conventional" rules along the lines of dogmatic jurisprudence. Therefore, it is obvious that [this last] distinction is not relevant, either. The term "problems of social policy" (in the widest sense of the term) might be defined as referring to all those *practical* problems that involve the question of how external human conduct *ought to be* governed by "legal" or "conventional" norms. If we then attempted to define an *empirical* science in such a way that it was the precise counterpart of that complex of practical problems; and if we then, out of consideration for Stammler, called [that "empirical science"] "social science" and its object "social life", then the domain of "social life" must probably be defined as follows: "Social life" comprises all those empirical processes whose "external" normative regulation by "human ordinances" is "in principle" – that is to say: without any substantive inconsistency – *conceivable*. In this context, it is quite unimportant whether such a definition of the concept of "social life" would have any scientific "value" at all. It suffices that [the definition] could be applied without any [internal] inconsistency and without compromising the purely empirical nature of its object – "social life". At the same time, it would at least imply the logical

1   See pp. 202–03 and 209.

and substantive possibility of *defining* the object from the standpoint of the "external rule" ([this "rule" being] viewed *not* as an empirical fact but as an "idea") – which is all that Stammler could have wished for, if he had understood his own position "correctly". The conflation of the ideal "validity" of the "rule" with its empirical "existence" would be eliminated [if this definition were applied]; and, by the same token, it would dispose of the misconception that one might, within the field delimited in this way, find a separate "world of purposes" – or, more generally, find anything that would *not* be subject to causal investigation, but would *nevertheless* be empirically existent.

The *Addendum* is a fragment of the planned continuation of *Stammler* (see the editorial note to *Stammler*, p. 226). The manuscript was found among Max Weber's papers after his death and included in the first edition of the *Gesammelte Aufsätze zur Wissenschaftslehre* (1922), edited by Marianne Weber.
Translated from: "Nachtrag zu dem Aufsatz über R. Stammlers 'Überwindung' der materialistischen Geschichtsauffassung", in Max Weber, *Gesammelte Aufsätze zur Wissenschaftslehre* (ed. Johannes Winckelmann), 3rd ed., Tübingen: J.C.B.Mohr (Paul Siebeck) 1968, pp. 360–83.

THE THEORY OF MARGINAL UTILITY AND THE "FUNDAMENTAL LAW OF PSYCHOPHYSICS"

The treatise under review [(Brentano, *Value Theory*)] is partly a summary, partly a critique of the results of [certain] studies into the development of value theory since Aristotle. Those studies, stimulated by Brentano, were initially undertaken by Ludwig Fick (who unfortunately died very young) and subsequently completed – quite independently – by another of Brentano's students, Dr R[udolf] Kaulla.[1] Like every work of Brentano's, this treatise offers a large number of stimulating insights; among these, we shall here only point to the discussion of the relationship between the concepts of "usability" and "utility value" ⟨228⟩ (pp. 42–43), probably the clearest treatment of that subject in such a restricted space.

Here, we shall focus on the only point in Brentano's exposition that invites *contradiction*. It concerns the alleged relations of the "theory of marginal utility" ⟨229⟩ – and more generally, of any "subjective" value theory – to certain general propositions of experimental psychology, and in particular to the so-called Weber–Fechner law. ⟨230⟩ As Brentano himself underlines, this is certainly not the first time that the attempt has been made to interpret economic value theory as an instance of this law. It is quite clearly present in the second edition of F[riedrich] A[lbert] Lange's *Labour Question*; the rudiments of it can even be found in the first edition of Fechner's *Psychophysics*, and, since then, it has recurred with extraordinary frequency. Lange, too, had regarded that famous "law" as a confirmation and generalization of Bernoulli's propositions ⟨231⟩ concerning the relationship between the relative (personal) assessment of the value of a sum of money and the absolute level of wealth of the person possessing, receiving or making use of it; and he had in his turn attempted to provide examples from political life (sensitivity to pressure from political authorities etc.) in order to demonstrate that [the law] had an even more universal significance. More generally, it is frequently asserted that the value theory of the so-called "Austrian School" ⟨232⟩ is based on "psychology"; and, on the other hand, the most prominent representatives of the "historical school" ⟨233⟩ also claim that they have helped "psychology" to achieve its proper status vis-à-vis the theoretical abstractions of "natural law". In view of the ambiguousness of the term "psychology", it would serve no useful purpose at all to bicker with the two camps as to which of them is justified in laying claim to it. [The result might be]: neither, or: both, depending on the point of view. However, what we are discussing here is the far more precise assertion by Brentano that the "theory of marginal utility"

1 Kaulla, *Historical Development*. See also: Kraus, *Value Theory*.

242

is based on the "fundamental law of psychophysics" and represents an application of that law. Here, we shall limit ourselves to the demonstration that *this* assertion is erroneous.

As Brentano himself mentions, the so-called fundamental law of psychophysics has undergone changes over time with respect to its formulation, its area of validity and its interpretation. For his part, Brentano initially (p. 66) summarizes its content, in quite general terms, as follows: Fechner has shown that "in all areas of sensation, the law governing the dependence of sensation on stimulus turns out to be *the same* as that formulated by Bernoulli with respect to [the finding that] the sensation of *happiness* occasioned by [receiving] an additional sum of money depends on the size of the fortune possessed by the person experiencing that sensation". Although the reference to Bernoulli can be found in precisely the same way in Fechner['s own work], it is nevertheless misleading. It is certain that Bernoulli's method has been one of Fechner's sources of inspiration. But to what extent two heterogeneous sciences have influenced each other in the course of developing [certain] conceptual constructions with related methodological purposes – that is purely a question of textual history. It has nothing to do with the problem that concerns us here: whether the Weber–Fechner law constitutes the *theoretical* basis of the theory of marginal utility. Take the example of Darwin: he was influenced by Malthus; but the theories of Malthus are not the same as those of Darwin; nor is either [set of] theories a special case of the other; nor are both [sets of] theories special cases of an even more general law. Our case is similar. "Happiness" is a concept that cannot be apprehended by psychophysics, nor is it even qualitatively uniform – in spite of what people were inclined to think in the age of utilitarian ethics. Psychologists would no doubt strongly object if it were identified with the concept of "pleasure" (and the question of the scope of that concept is in its turn the subject of much dispute among psychologists). But that apart, the parallel would be defective, even if it were formulated as a vague analogy, a mere image or a comparison. Even in that case, it would only hold for the external [aspect], and for part of the problem. Fechner's "stimulus" is always an "external" – that is to say: bodily[1] – process; it can therefore in principle, if not in actual fact, be measured directly in quantitative terms, and it is associated with certain conscious "sensations" [that are seen] as its "effect" or [as a] "parallel process". This "stimulus" would have to correspond to [receiving] an additional "sum of money" in Bernoulli's example – as that is also an "external" process – and could in fact, from a purely external point of view, correspond to it. But what, in the case of the fundamental law of psychophysics, correponds to the "fortune" already possessed by the person who, in Bernoulli's example, receives [an] additional [sum of] money? Apparently, it is easy to find an answer to this question as well, at least in its external aspect. [If we look at] Weber's well-known experiments on the differential sensitivity of individuals to *increases* in weight, the existing burden can be taken to correspond to the already existing monetary fortune. Let us also make that assumption. Then, according to the observations of Weber on which the fundamental law of psychophysics is based, the following simple proposition would hold: If someone who is already sustaining a weight of 3 ounces (for instance on the palm of his hand) is just able to register an increase of 1/30 [of this weight] (or 1/10 ounce), then the difference which that person will just be able to register if the burden already sustained is 6 ounces will also be 1/30 (or 1/5 ounce); and the situation with respect to other "sense-stimulations" is the same as that [described here] with respect to the "sense of touch". Accordingly, the difference between the increase in stimulus and the basic stimulus in any two cases would be consciously registered as being the same if the relation between the increase in stimulus and the basic stimulus is objectively the same. In other words:

---

1   Including of course a stimulus that *originates* "within" one's own body.

if the registered intensity of sensation is to increase arithmetically, then the intensity of the stimulus must be increased geometrically. We shall here completely leave aside [the question] to what extent the "law", formulated in these terms, has been confirmed empirically; the concepts of "stimulus threshold" and "stimulus limit", of "subliminal" and "supraliminal" stimuli ‹234› have been added to it, and a tangle of special laws (for instance that of Merkel ‹235›) has clustered around it. If we were to apply Weber's original, simple formula to economic phenomena, and if, like Brentano, we consequently – however risky that might be – equated increase in wealth with increase in "*stimulus*", then we would (as with Bernoulli) get the following result: if an increase of 100 Mark in the wealth of an individual who possesses 1,000 Mark is accompanied by a sensation of increased "happiness" that has a certain intensity, then [it follows] that, if *that same individual* (NB!) possessed 1 million Mark, an increase of 100,000 Mark in his wealth would be accompanied by a sensation of happiness with the *same* intensity. Let us assume that this would in fact be the case; and let us moreover assume that the concepts of "stimulus threshold" and "stimulus limit" – more generally: the curve [defined by] Weber's law – could somehow by analogy be applied to the "sensations of happiness" accompanying the acquisition of money. Would that really have any bearing on the questions to which economic theory seeks an answer? And does the validity of the logarithmic curve of psychophysics constitute a foundation without which the propositions [of economic theory] would not be understandable? It is no doubt a worthwhile undertaking to examine how various major groups of economically relevant "needs" react to the extent, but also, and above all, to the *way* in which they are "satisfied". ([The latter problem is] one concerning which the fundamental law of psychophysics has already nothing to contribute.) Quite a few discussions, for instance concerning the importance of the money economy for the qualitative expansion of needs, belong in this category, as well as, say, the investigations into nutritional changes under the pressure of economic transformations, and so on. But, apparently, none of these studies is in any way oriented towards the allegedly fundamental Weber–Fechner theory. And, if we were to [take] the various groups of needs – as for instance: nutritional needs, housing needs, sexual needs, needs for alcohol, and "spiritual", aesthetic needs – [and] analyse how they intensify and subside according to the *extent* of the supply of "means of satisfaction", we would indeed occasionally come across more or less far-reaching analogies to the logarithmic curve [defined by] the Weber–Fechner rule; but, on the other hand, the analogies would sometimes only be slight or completely non-existent; and, not infrequently, it would seem that the rule has been completely stood on its head (see below). Sometimes, the curves would suddenly break off completely; sometimes, they might become negative (and sometimes not); sometimes, they would run proportionally to the "satisfaction"; sometimes, they would approach zero asymptotically – and, for almost every kind of "need", [the curves] would be different. Still, [in this kind of analysis] we could at least find analogies here and there. Let us assume, without examining the matter, that such – always quite vague and fortuitous – analogies can also be found with regard to the very important possibility of changing the *way* in which – that is to say: the means with which – the needs are "satisfied". However, let us proceed further: The point of departure of the economic theory of marginal utility and of every "subjective" theory of value – to the extent that those theories concern themselves at all with the "states of mind" of the individual – is *not*, in total contrast to the [logic of] the fundamental law of psychophysics, an external "stimulus", but a "need". In other words (if we, for once, resort to "psychological" expressions): a complex of "sensations" and "affective situations", of "states" of "tension", of "discomfort", of "expectation" and the like, which may in any given case be extremely complex; and these, moreover, are combined with "memory images", "purposive ideas" and, in certain cases, with mutually conflicting "motives" of the most various kinds. And, while the fundamental law of psychophysics is meant to tell us how an *external* stimulus provokes psychical states ("sensations"), economics instead concerns itself with the fact that *external* conduct (action) with a certain orientation is provoked by such "psychical" states. Of course, this external conduct in its turn reacts on the "need" that was its source, by obviating it, or at least attempting to obviate it, by means of "satisfaction" – a process that is also, from a psychological point of view, most complex and not even unequivocal, and that can at any rate only in exceptional cases be equated with a simple "sensation" in the psychological sense. Psychologically speaking, the problem would therefore be the mode of *reaction*, not the mode of "sensation". Thus, these (here deliberately very roughly sketched) elementary processes of "action" constitute a sequence of occurrences that only in a small part – the last one – of their course may, at best, have a structure that is possibly "analogous" to that of the objects of the [above-mentioned] weight experiments of Weber's, and of any similar object; but it is evident that the structure of those occurrences in their totality is quite a different one. But, moreover, it is obvious that this elementary process – even in the form in which it has been depicted here – could never ever determine, or make possible, the development of economics as a science. For its part, it represents at most *one* component of those occurrences that our discipline deals with. In fact – and this is also the presupposition on which Brentano's own further exposition rests – economics has the task of investigating the configuration of human action (1) as a result of the competition between *different* "needs" that demand to be "satisfied"; (2) as a result of the *limited character*, not only of the "need capacity", but above all of the material "goods" and "labour force" that can be used for the "gratification" of those needs; (3) as a result of a quite definite kind of coexistence between *different human beings* who have been endowed with the same or similar needs, but who are at the same time in possession of different supplies of goods for the satisfaction of [those needs], and [as a result] of their competition with one another for th[ose] means of satisfaction. Not only is it *not* possible to regard the *problems* that arise here as special cases or complications of the "fundamental law of psychophysics", and not only do the *methods* for solving [those problems] *not* [fall into the category of] applied psychophysics or psychology: [the] simple[truth] is that both have nothing at all to do with that. The simplest reflection will show that the propositions of the theory of marginal utility are absolutely independent of whether Weber's law is valid to any extent at all (or, if so, to what extent); and not only that: [they are also completely independent] of whether it is at all possible to formulate *any* proposition with unconditionally general validity concerning the relation between "stimulus" and "sensation". For the theory of marginal utility to be possible, it is quite sufficient if the following [conditions hold]: (1) That our everyday experience is true, according to which human beings, when they act, are impelled, *among other things*, by "needs" that can only be satisfied by the consumption of commodities which are, in each given case, only available in limited quantities, or of outputs of labour or products of that labour. And (2) that our everyday experience is correct, according to which it is true of most needs, and particularly of those subjectively felt to be the most pressing ones, that with increasing consumption of the commodities and labour outputs [mentioned above], an increasing measure of "satisfaction" is attained, in such a way that *other*, as yet "unsatisfied", needs will now appear to be more pressing. And, finally, (3) that human beings have the ability – however much the extent to which they possess it may vary – of acting "purposefully", i.e. with the aid of "experience" and "advance calculation". That is to say: [they are able to act] in such a way that they apportion the available or obtainable, quantitatively limited "goods" and "labour force" between the various "needs" of the present or the foreseeable future, according to the *importance* that they ascribe to [those needs]. Now, it is obvious that this "importance" is not identical with, say, a "sensation" provoked by a physical "stimulus". Moreover, it may remain an open question whether the "satisfaction" of the "needs" will *ever* progress in a way that is in *any* way similar to the progression that, according to the Weber–Fechner law, holds with respect to the intensity of the "sensations" provoked by "stimuli". But *when* one reflects on the progression of "satisfaction" with Tiffany vases, ⟨236⟩ toilet paper, saveloy sausage, editions of the classics, prostitutes, medical or clerical assistance, and so on, then the analogy with the logarithmic curve of the "fundamental law of psychophysics" does appear to be quite problematical. And, if somebody attends to his "need" – which may, for instance, be [a "need"] to satisfy his "spiritual requirements" even to the detriment of his [provision with] nourishment – by acquiring books and paying for university lectures, while his hunger remains insufficiently appeased, then the application of a psychophysical "analogy" will at any rate not make [his action] any more "understandable" than it already is. For economic theory, it is quite *sufficient* that we can, on the basis of the [above-]mentioned, quite trivial, but indisputable facts of everyday experience, *theoretically conceive of* a plurality of human beings each of whom strictly "rationally" allots those "stores of goods" and that "labour force" which he can dispose of (physically, or by virtue of the protection afforded by a "legal order") for the sole and exclusive purpose of attaining, by peaceful means, an "optimal" satisfaction of his *various* competing "needs". Of course, every "psychologist" must surely turn up his nose at such "everyday experiences" as a basis for a scientific theory: Just take the concept of "need": what a crude category, borrowed from "popular psychology"! And what we call a "need" can set in motion such vastly different physiological and psychological chains of causation: Even the "need" to eat can (1) be based on a fairly complex psychophysical situation (hunger), which is perceivable in [our] consciousness, and which can, in its turn, to a major extent be determined by *various* kinds of circumstance operating as "stimuli": for instance a physically empty stomach, or simply the habit of eating at certain fixed hours of the day. But (2) the subjectively conscious disposition may also be lacking, and the "need" to eat [may be] "ideationally determined", ⟨237⟩ conditioned, for instance, by obedience to doctor's orders. The "need for alcohol" may be based on becoming "accustomed" to "external" stimuli, which in their turn create an "inner" state of "stimulation"; and [this "need"] can – Weber's logarithmic curve notwithstanding – be *intensified* by a supply of alcohol. Finally, the "needs" for certain kinds of "reading material" are determined by processes that – even though psychophysicists may perhaps, for their own ends, "re-interpret" them in terms of functional changes in certain cerebral processes – are in any case hardly elucidated by mere reference to the Weber–Fechner law. And so on. Psychologists [will] view this as a whole series of riddles that are extremely difficult from *their* perspective – while economic "theory" does not waste a single word on them – and, what is more, with an entirely easy scientific conscience! And to cap it all: "purposive action", "learning by experience", "advance calculation" – things that are, from a psychological point of view, the most highly complex, in part perhaps totally incomprehensible, and in any case among the most difficult to analyse – these and [other] similar concepts, without any sublimation through those familiar experiments with rotating drums or other laboratory equipment, ⟨238⟩ are [supposed to be] the "foundations" of a discipline! Yet this is in fact the case; and this discipline, which is not the least bit concerned whether materialism, ⟨239⟩ vitalism, ⟨240⟩ psychophysical parallelism, ⟨241⟩ any of the theories of interaction, [or] the "unconscious" of Lipps, or of Freud, or [in] some other [version], and so on, can be used to provide the foundations of *psychological* disciplines – indeed, which explicitly assures [us] that all this is *simply irrelevant* for *its own* purposes – this discipline, I say, nevertheless goes so far as to claim that it can arrive at *mathematical* formulas that express how economically relevant action takes place, as conceived by [economic] theory. And, more importantly: it actually makes good this claim. However fiercely the significance of its results may be disputed, for the most varied reasons connected with its *own* methods, the question of the "correctness" [of those results] is in any case absolutely independent of even the greatest possible upheavals affecting the fundamental hypotheses of biology and psychology – an independence just as absolute as the irrelevance [for the discipline of economics] of the question, for instance, whether it was Copernicus or Ptolemy who was right, ‹242› or what the situation is with respect to theological hypotheses, or, say, with the "alarming" implications of the second law of thermodynamics. ‹243› Changes, however far-reaching, in such fundamental theories of natural science simply cannot weaken even a single "*correctly*" constructed proposition of the economic theory of prices or ground rent.

Naturally, this (1) does not in any way mean to say that, within the domain of *empirical* analysis of economic life, there would be no point at which the *facts* established by the natural sciences referred to [above] (and by a large number of other [natural sciences]) could not acquire considerable importance; nor (2) does it mean to say that the kind of *concept* formation that has proved to be of use in those disciplines could not occasionally quite well provide a model for certain problems of economic inquiry. As far as the first point is concerned, I hope that I shall soon have the opportunity to examine how certain studies [in the field] of experimental psychology could perhaps be used in connection with, for instance, the investigation of certain conditions of factory work. ‹244› As for the second point, not only mathematical modes of thought (as has long been the case) but also, for instance, certain biological ways of thinking have their legitimate place [within] our [discipline]. And it is certainly a trivial commonplace for every economist that we at every step, on countless individual points in our discipline, have – and must have – a fruitful exchange of results and viewpoints with [those] work[ing] in other areas of research. But how, and in what sense, this happens in *our* domain is something that completely depends on the questions that interest *us*; and any attempt to decide a priori *which* theories from other disciplines should be "fundamental" for economics is futile, like all attempts [to establish] a "hierarchy" of sciences on the Comtean model. Not only [is it true that], at least generally speaking, precisely the most general hypotheses and assumptions of the "natural sciences" (in the usual sense of this term) are the most irrelevant ones for our discipline. But moreover, and above all: precisely on the point that is of decisive importance for the distinctive character of the approach of our discipline – i.e. in the theory of economics ("value theory") – we stand entirely on our own feet. The "everyday experience" that is the point of departure of our theory (see above) is of course the common point of departure of *all* specialized empirical disciplines. Every one of those disciplines wishes to go beyond ["everyday experience"] – and must have that aspiration, as that is precisely the basis of their right to existence as a "science". But in so doing, each of them "surpasses" or "sublimates" everyday experience in a different way and in a different direction. The theory of marginal utility, and indeed every economic "theory", does so not, say, in the manner and in the direction [taken by] psychology, but more or less in the exactly opposite way. It does not, for instance, break down *inner* everyday experiences into psychical or psychophysical "elements" ("stimuli", "sensations", "reactions", "automatisms", "feelings" etc.); instead, it attempts to "understand" certain "adaptions" of man's *external* conduct to conditions of existence, of a quite specific kind, that are *external* to man. This external world that is relevant for economic theory may, in the individual case, be "nature" (in the usual sense [of the term]) or "social environment"; but, in either case, the attempt will *always* be made to render the "adaptation" to [the external world] understandable by making the ad hoc, heuristic assumption that the action with which the theory deals runs its course in a manner that is strictly "rational" (in the sense discussed above). For certain cognitive purposes, the theory of marginal utility treats human action as if it ran its course from A to Z under the control of *business calculation* – that is to say: a calculation [made] on the basis of *all* the conditions that need to be considered. It treats the various "needs", and the goods available (or to be produced or acquired by exchange) for their "satisfaction", as "accounts" and "entries", which can be defined in numerical terms, in a continuous process of bookkeeping; [it treats] human beings as constant business managers, and their life as the object of this "business" of theirs, whose "accounts" are controlled. The approach [peculiar to] business calculation is therefore, if anything, the starting point of the constructions [of marginal utility theory]. Is the procedure [of accounting] in some way dependent on Weber's law? Is it an application of propositions concerning the relationship between "stimulus" and "sensation"? The theory of marginal utility, for its purposes, treats the "psyche" of all men, *conceived* of as isolated entities and including the man who is excluded from any act of buying or selling, as a *business mind* that is able to estimate the "intensity" of its needs, as well as the possible means by which they can be met, in numerical terms; this is the way in which it arrives at its theoretical constructions. Surely that is the very *opposite* of any psychology! – There is no doubt that those presuppositions of the "theory" developed on this basis are "unreal"; nevertheless, there is also no doubt that they have not simply been created out of nothing. The "value" of goods in the "isolated economy" constructed by the theory would be exactly equal to the *book value* that they would have in the ideally perfect accounts of an isolated household.[1] It contains just as many and just as few "unreal" [elements] as the accounts of any actual business. If a "share capital" of, say, 1 million Mark appears among the "liabilities" in a balance sheet, or if a building "has a book value" of 100,000 Mark, does that mean that this million, or those 100,000 Mark lie in some drawer? And yet, entering that item makes very good sense! Just as – mutatis mutandis! – the "value" in the isolated economy [postulated by] the theory of marginal utility [makes very good sense]. But it is not necessary to determine it by means of "psychology"! The theoretical "values" with which the theory of marginal utility works are supposed to make the processes of economic life understandable to us in a manner that is in principle similar to the way in which commercial book values of a business are meant to give the businessman information about the situation of his business and the conditions for its continued profitability. And the general theorems formulated by economic theory are simply constructs stating what the consequences of the action of an individual person, intertwined with [the actions] of all other persons, *must be if we assumed* that each individual person *were to* shape his conduct towards his environment exclusively according to the principles of commercial bookkeeping – in other words: "rationally", in *that* sense [of the word]. As everybody knows, that assumption does not hold; consequently, the empirical course of those processes that the theory was created to understand will only – to a degree that will vary widely, depending on the concrete case – exhibit an "approximation" to the theoretically constructed course of strictly rational action. The economic history of many epochs in the past has, not without reason, been called "the history of *un*economic behaviour". However, the distinctive historical character of the capitalist epoch, and consequently also the importance of the theory of marginal utility (and of any economic theory of value) for the understanding of that epoch, is rooted in the fact that, under today's conditions of existence, the approximation of reality to the theoretical propositions [of economics] *has continually increased*; that the fate of ever larger sections of humanity has been caught up in it; and that, as far as we can judge, this development will continue in the future. It is on this fact of *cultural* history, and not on the grounds of its ostensible dependence on the Weber–Fechner law, that the heuristic importance of the theory of marginal utility is based. For example, it is no accident that the fixing of the Berlin market rates under the system of the so-called uniform quotation ‹245› exhibited a particularly striking degree of approximation to the theoretical propositions concerning price formation, as developed by Böhm-Bawerk (following Menger); [the Berlin

1   Of course, this does not mean that the accounting "technique" should be imagined as being completely the same as that of an individual economy today.

system] might actually serve as a paradigm [for those propositions].[1] But the reason for this is certainly not, say, that those who come to the stock exchange are to some particularly specific degree (with respect to the relation between "stimulus" and "sensation") subject to the fundamental law of psychophysics. [The reason is rather] that transactions on the stock exchange are – or at least: *can* be – economically "rational" to an especially high degree. Not only does the rational *theory* of price formation have nothing to do with the concepts of experimental psychology; it has nothing to do with any "psychology" at all, of whatever kind, that aspires to be a "science" going beyond everyday experience. Take the example of someone who emphasizes the necessity of taking into account the specific "psychology of the stock exchange" *as a complement to* the purely abstract theory of price [formation]: the object of [such a "psychology of the stock exchange"] which that person will have in mind will precisely be the influence of factors that are *irrational* from an economic point of view, in other words: "disturbances" affecting the laws of price formation that are to be postulated theoretically. The foundation of the theory of marginal utility – indeed: of every subjective theory of value – is not psychological but (if we wish to find a methodological term for it) "pragmatic"; that is to say: it employs the categories of "ends" and "means". [I shall make] a few remarks on this point later.

As everybody knows (and as was mentioned above), the theorems that constitute specifically economic *theory* do *not* represent "the whole" of our science: they are only an instrument – albeit one that is frequently underrated – for the analysis of the causal interconnections of empirical reality. As soon as we seek to comprehend this reality as such, in its culturally significant components, and to explain it causally, economic theory reveals itself as a sum of "ideal-typical" concepts. That is to say: its theorems represent a series of *theoretically* constructed processes, which, with this "ideal purity", are seldom – and often not at all – to be found in the given historical reality; but, as their elements have been derived from experience and have only been subjected to an intellectual *accentuation* of their rationality, [these constructs] can on the other hand be used both as heuristic instruments for analysing the empirical multiplicity and as constructive means for presenting it.

Finally, let us return once more to Brentano. On p. 67, he proposes the following, more precise formulation of the Weber–Fechner law in the form in which it is, in his view, also the foundation of economics: For a sensation to be evoked at all, the stimulus threshold (see above) must be exceeded; once it has been exceeded, any further increase in the stimulus will intensify sensation at least proportionally, until the optimum (which varies with each individual) is reached; thereafter, the intensity of sensation will still increase in absolute terms, but less than proportionally with the increase in stimulus; if the stimulus continues to increase ever further, a point will eventually be reached beyond which the sensation will decrease even in absolute terms, until it completely disappears because the nerve has been deadened. He then goes on: "In economics, this law . . . had been accepted [in the form of] the law of *decreasing crop yield*, since it governs the growth of plants." One's first reaction is to ask in astonishment: Does arable land, and do plants, react according to *psycho*logical laws? However, at the top of p. 67, Brentano had made the somewhat more general statement that, according to a general *physio*logical law, every "life process" decreases in intensity when the conditions favouring it increase beyond a certain optimum; the example of decreasing crop yield apparently refers to this sentence and not to

---

1 I do not quite see why Brentano treats the "Austrians" with such disdain. ‹246› C[arl] Menger put forward ideas whose methodological implications were not fully thought out, but which were [in themselves] excellent; and as for the question of "style" (which is nowadays usually overrated, at the expense of the substantive intellectual content), Böhm-Bawerk is certainly also a master [in this field], while this is perhaps not Menger's strongest point.

the one immediately preceding [that example]. In any event, this does seem to indicate that Brentano regards the Weber–Fechner law as a special case of the general *optimum* principle [quoted immediately above], and apparently sees the theory of marginal utility as a sub-case of that special case. In this way, [the theory of marginal utility] is seemingly directly connected with a fundamental law of all life as such. Now, the concept of the "optimum" is indeed one that economic theory and the physiological and psychophysical approach have in common; and an *illustrative* reference to *this* analogy may very well, depending on the concrete didactic purpose, have *pedagogical* value. However, such "optima" are by no means restricted to "life processes". For instance, every machine usually has an optimum of performance for certain purposes: beyond that point, an increased supply of fuel, raw materials etc. will – at first in relative, then in absolute terms – diminish the result of its performance. In the case of the machine, a "heating threshold" corresponds to the psychophysical "stimulus threshold". Thus, the concept of the "optimum" – like the other concepts introduced by Brentano that are linked to it – has an *even* wider field of application and is *not* tied to the principles of "life processes". And, on the other hand, even a cursory reflection on the meaning [of the term] will immediately tell us that it contains a teleological "functional value": "optimum" – for what? [This "functional value"] is especially apparent in cases where we, explicitly or tacitly, operate with the category of a "purpose" (it does not interest us whether it is apparent everywhere, or only in such cases). What happens is that we conceive a certain complex multiplicity as a *unity*; that we relate this unity to a particular *result*; and that we then *evaluate* [the unity] *in relation to* this concrete result, as a "means" for achieving it – according to whether the result is achieved, is not achieved, is incompletely achieved, [and] whether few or many means are employed to achieve it. For example: for the purpose of making woven fabric out of yarn, we regard a given multiplicity of all sorts of differently shaped pieces of iron and steel as a "machine" of a certain kind, and we then consider *how much* woven fabric of a certain kind [this machine] "is able to" produce within a given span of time if a certain amount of coal and a certain amount of labour are used. Or, we investigate what the "function" is of certain structures consisting of "nerve cells", that is to say: how [those structures] "perform" for the "purpose" of transmitting certain sensations while being parts of a living organism. Or, we consider cosmic and meteorological constellations in the perspective of the following question: where and when will, for instance, a planned astronomical observation have the "optimal" chance of success? Or, we observe how economic man treats his environment from the perspective of the "satisfaction" of his needs. Let us not prolong this discussion any further, as I shall on another occasion revert to these problems of concept formation, to the extent that they lie within *our* area of knowledge (the "biological" questions are better left to the biologists). Concerning these matters, Gottl and O[thmar] Spann, for instance, have recently said much that is good, whereas there are other parts [of their contributions] (Gottl's in particular) with which I would not be able to agree. Moreover, by way of reassurance, the following remark should be made: the problems of "absolute" values or of "universal cultural values", which are the subject of so much dispute, not to speak of the alleged "opposition" of "causa and telos", which Stammler has postulated in such a terribly confusing manner, ⟨247⟩ have nothing whatsoever to do with the purely *technical* questions of concept formation that we are dealing with here – just as little as commercial accounting (a process that should without doubt be "interpreted" in "teleological–rational" terms) [has to do] with the teleology of a divine governance of the world.

Our intention here was merely to show the following: even the concept of an "optimum", which Brentano seems to regard as important for his thesis, has a nature that is neither specifically psychological, nor psychophysical, nor physiological or biological. On the contrary, it is common to quite a number of problems that are otherwise quite heterogeneous; it therefore states nothing about the foundations of economic theory, and certainly does not confer on the theory of marginal utility the character of a special instance of the application of the Weber–Fechner law or of any fundamental physiological law.

First published in *Archiv für Sozialwissenschaft und Sozialpolitik* 27 (1908), pp. 546–58.
Translated from: "Die Grenznutzlehre und das 'psychophysische Grundgesetz'", in
Max Weber, *Gesammelte Aufsätze zur Wissenschaftslehre* (ed. Johannes Winckelmann),
3rd ed., Tübingen: J.C.B.Mohr (Paul Siebeck) 1968, pp. 384–99.
The article is a review of Lujo Brentano's pamphlet *Die Entwicklung der Wertlehre*,
which was published in 1908. Brentano sent Weber the pamphlet at the end of May,
and the article was written in August–September of that year.

"ENERGETICAL" THEORIES OF CULTURE[1]

‹248› Even if we completely disregard the substantive significance of his works, Professor W[ilhelm] Ostwald in Leipzig is highly distinguished by the rare artistry [that characterizes] his exposition. This is not meant in the sense of the aesthetics of style, which is all too common nowadays. As far as questions of "style" are concerned, his artistry rather manifests itself in precisely the opposite way: in [his] ability (which is all too rare nowadays) to let the "substance" speak for itself and to take second place behind it, by using only a minimum of [stylistic] devices and [expressing himself] in simple terms, concisely and clearly. What is here meant by ["]artistry of presentation["] is rather the quality of the intellectual instruments that he has been able to use for "simplifying" the objects of thought, and the manner in which this has been done. Take somebody who has read the – mostly not very rewarding – general parts of older chemical compendia, for instance on atomic weights and compound weights and related matters; on the concept of "solutions" as opposed to "compounds"; on electrochemical problems; on isomerism; and so on. Faced with the astonishing reduction of effort (in comparison to [the effort required by those unrewarding expositions]) brought about by Ostwald's manner of presentation, which seeks to avoid hypotheses and restricts itself to the truly "general" aspects of chemical processes, that person – even if he is a total layman – will be delighted by the exceptional elegance of [Ostwald's] artistry. And when he considers the distinctive character of this accomplishment [of Ostwald's], [that person] will find it perfectly understandable that Ostwald – like Mach, with whom he has an intellectual affinity – is particularly prone to committing a [number of] error[s]. On the one hand, these errors are of a *logical* nature: (1) [That of] elevating certain forms of abstraction proper to the natural sciences into absolute standards for scientific thinking in general. (2) Accordingly, [Ostwald] regards heterogeneous forms of thinking, which the "economy of thought" (as Mach calls it) requires in relation to the problems of *other* disciplines, as being imperfect and underdeveloped, because they do not accomplish something that they are not at all meant to accomplish. Not only the "economy of thought" of history – in the widest sense of the term – but even that of biology displays such heterogeneous intellectual instruments; and it should be expressly noted that[, as far as biology is concerned], this is the case *irrespective* of whether the approach is "vitalistic" or (to any degree whatsoever) "mechanistic" ‹249›. On the other hand, this leads him to [commit] the *substantive* error (3) of trying to force as many occurrences as possible

---

1   Wilhelm Ostwald, *Energetical Foundations*.

– of any kind – into the mould of being "special cases" of "energetical" relations; and finally, (4) his passionate desire to use his conceptual instruments for the intellectual mastery of [the] objects [of his inquiry] is unabated when he enters the sphere of what *ought to* be, and tempts him into deriving value standards – characterized by pure "scientific parochialism" – from the facts found in his area of specialization. Nowadays, of course, it is quite customary to turn the "*image* of the world" [current within] a discipline upside down and transform it into a "world *view*", and it is common knowledge how this usually happens in Darwinian biology. (In the case of the scientific anti-Darwinists – a concept that is of course nowadays always a *relative* one – this [topsy-turvy process] usually, and characteristically, ends up as more or less extreme pacifism). Mach deduces altruistic imperatives from the "hopelessly lost condition" of the individual (this is also meant as a statement of logic, and not just of "thanatic" ‹250› fact). From certain views concerning the future course of the historical process, the historian L[udo] M[oritz] Hartmann, who in his metaphysical views is close to Mach and Exner-Ewarten, deduces the following categorical imperative: act in such a way that your action serves the process of (social) collective association. (Incidentally, from this would follow that Jay Gould, Rockefeller and Morgan, whose achievements have to be recognized by every consistent theory of evolutionary socialism as laying, to an eminent degree, the foundations of socialism, must necessarily be classified as brilliant *ethical* personalities.) And so on. In line with the immense technical and economic importance of chemistry, the ideals that, with untroubled authority, have pride of place in Ostwald's work are naturally technological ones.

In this respect, O[stwald] is to a large degree influenced by the (supposedly) "exact" sociological method – formulated along the lines of Comte's and Quetelet's ideas ‹251› – for the furtherance of which Ernest Solvay has founded his "Institut de Sociologie (Institut Solvay)" in Brussels. This is a place of research and publication, with reading rooms and every [kind of] material required for sociological work, and endowed with very considerable funds. As a creation of patronage it is just as magnificent and, in its way, exemplary, as the quality of the "scientific" method employed by Solvay in his works, and adopted by some of his collaborators, is deplorable. A cursory examination of any work of this kind, and particularly of those by Solvay himself, makes clear what sort of changelings result when violence is done to sociology by technologists trained exclusively in the natural sciences.[1] And the tragicomedy of this squandering of ample funds for purely dilettantish purposes is demonstrated most clearly by the following

---

1   As an example, let us make a summary analysis of E[rnest] Solvay, *Introductory Formulas*:
The energetical yield (rendement = R) of a living organism in each given case is the result of the following formula:

$$R = E_l/E_c = E_c - (E_f + E_r)/E_c$$

where E_c designates the primary energies consumed through respiration, nourishment, exposure to light etc. (E consommées), E_f the morphologically fixed [energies] in the given case (E fixées), E_r the unutilized residual [energies] (E rejetées), and, finally, E_l the energies liberated by the oxidization processes of the organism. The fraction E_l/E_c, which determines the rendement, improves from childhood (where E_f is very large) until it reaches its optimum when the person is fully grown; with increasing age, it then again sinks as a consequence of an increase in E_r (owing to a growing inability to utilize the energies consumed). From the "standpoint of sociology", however, only a fraction of the total free organic energies = E (Energies utilisables) is relevant for the calculation of the net energetical yield of an organism, and in particular of the individual *human being*: This is the share [of those energies] that can be utilized for *work*, as opposed to the fractional part E_t that is transformed into heat, and that, as in the case of every machine, remains unutilized. However, not all of this "useful energy" of the individual is *social*[ly] useful energy (E socio-énergétique), since individuals will first pursue their "physio-energetical" *self*-interest, so that only a fraction of their useful energy is made socially utilizable. Therefore, for any given period of time t, the "socio–utilisabilité" of the individual must be established by multiplying the individual useful energy with the coefficient u, which varies with the degree of socially useful energy. The result is then, for the span of time T covering the entire life of an individual, a quantity $SuE_u t$. By adding together the simple energetical rendements of all individuals in a society during a given time unit, determining the *average* fraction U, which more or less expresses their social utilizability, and dividing the product of U and the sum of the individual rendements by the sum of the energies consumed by the society during this time unit, one arrives at the formula for R_s (rendement social = social utilizability of *all* individuals in the given interval):

$$= U \, (E_c - [E_F + E_R + E_T])/E_c$$

Objects that do *not* have a physio–energetical character – that is to say: whose consumption does not consist in the *destruction* of energy in the interest of the organism – but that nevertheless influence the rendement relation, may in this connection, in principle, be included in this formula in the following way: They are regarded as corresponding increases or decreases in E_c (the primary energies available for use); i.e. they are equated with the energy consumed through the consumption of *nourishment* (the intrinsic type of energetical consumption). S[olvay] feels justified in claiming this even with respect to needs that are ["]purement d'ordre imaginatif ou moral["] ["purely imaginative or moral"] (p. 12). Even the "improper" consumptions – that is to say: those that diverge from the consumption by the "homme normal" [normal person], calculated as an average – can be included in the formulas. This can be done by taking into consideration [the following fact]: such an ["]énergétisme excessif["] ["excessive energeticism"] of [certain] individuals may occasionally manifest itself as an "énergétisme privatif" ["exclusive energeticism"] to the disadvantage of everybody; but under different circumstances – i.e. when we are dealing with "hommes capables" ["capable persons"], who in return for their additional consumption contribute a higher rate of energetical output – it may be anything but antisocial: on the contrary, it may have the effect of improving the energetical rendement of society. In other words: the energetical formulas, and the units of measurement (kilogrammetres, calories etc.) that are usually employed in energetics, are *generally* applicable.

Let us first comment briefly on this part of [Solvay's] exposition. We should above all be careful not to subscribe to the idea that the absolutely vapid character of Solvay's whole construction is somehow due to the fact that his formulas do not take the complicated nature of the phenomena sufficiently into account. Faced with this objection, S[olvay] would always be justified in answering that, if ever more variables were introduced, it would "in principle" be possible in the end to integrate any constellation, however complicated. Nor does the fact that many of [Solvay's] coefficients can never be measured quantitatively with exactitude – and some not at all – constitute an error "of principle". The theory of marginal utility, for instance, is, from a method[olog]ical point of view, entirely justified in making use of the fiction that needs can be measured in purely quantitative terms. (*Why* it is justified [in doing so] is a question that need not be discussed here.) The completely worthless character of the whole [of Solvay's] construction instead stems from the fact that he includes *value* judgements of a *purely subjective* character in those formulas, which are, on the face of it, so strictly "exact". The "point de vue social" ["social point of view"], the ["]socio-utilisabilité["] ["socio-usability"] of a person (that quality in itself, and of course even more: the degree to which it is present) and everything connected with [those concepts], can only be determined according to the entirely subjective ideals with which the individual approaches the question of what conditions in society *ought to be*. Countless nuances of the numerous possible value standards may become relevant in this respect, as may an even more infinite swarm of compromises between the innumerable possible, mutually competing value standards, or between value standards that are in direct conflict with each other in the form of undesirable means for the desired purpose, or unwanted side effects in addition to the intended result. [All these value standards] are of course absolutely equally justified, as long as neither of the two *belief* factors supposedly overcome by positivism – the "theological" or the "metaphysical" one – is allowed to enter through the back door. If this does not happen, the question whether an individual who generates an ["]énergétisme excessif["] – [Pope] Gregory VII, Robespierre, Napoleon, Augustus the Strong, Rockefeller, Goethe, Oscar Wilde, Ivan the Terrible, and so on – has nevertheless been "profitable" from the "socio-energetical point of view", can of course *only* be decided by means of a subjective value judgement. To an even greater extent, the same is true of the decisive further question: to what *degree* such types, and the innumerable persons who approximate them more or less closely, are "profitable" or "unprofitable". It is a ridiculous pastime to invent mathematical symbols for this value judgement: if [performing] such puny tricks had any sense at all, the coefficients corresponding to those symbols would have to be completely different for *every single valuating subject* (for instance, M. Solvay's [coefficient] would certainly be very different from mine)! – And the height of absurdity is of course reached when those who emit these puffs of hot air attitudinize as if they were offering something of a "scientific" nature. It was therefore necessary to demonstrate that Solvay's whole construction is utterly valueless, and to do so already at this point, although it is only here (p. 15) that Solvay himself starts to acknowledge the fact that the application of his formulas presents difficulties, since [he] now starts dealing with the "phénomènes d'ordre intellectuel" ["intellectual phenomena"]. [These phenomena], S[olvay] says, "considérés en eux-mêmes" ["considered by themselves"], do not correspond to any quantitative energy production that specifically characterizes them; instead, they actually ("essentiellement") represent a succession of given states of distribution of neuromuscular energy. (This way of looking at them is a well-known surrogate for strict "psychophysical parallelism".) The same quantitative consumption of energy may therefore represent achievements with widely differing *value* (valeur). Nevertheless, it *must* (NB: par ordre de qui? [on whose orders?]) be possible to integrate them into the formulas, and [the formulas] must be measurable – *since they of course* (sic!) play such a large role in sociology (and – it should be added in order to make this conclusion logically complete – [because] it has been decided a priori that sociology must accommodate itself to energetical formulas). And, in fact, the matter is quite simple: one *cannot* measure these achievements as such, and one does not *wish* to measure the energy production that (according to the usual psychophysical parallelism) accompanies them (concomitante) but is not characteristic of them; *however*, it *is* possible to measure *their effect* (effet). This is followed by a series of the most delightful hobgoblin leaps. How are we to "measure" the effect of, for instance, the Sistine Madonna ⟨252⟩ or of some piece of "art of the gutter"? Since S[olvay] shies away from openly confessing, to himself and others, that "effet" has simply, for devious purposes, replaced the ambiguous word "valeur" that was used previously, he [instead] constructs the following argument: The "normal" purpose of the "effort cérébral" ["cerebral effort"] in the "normal" individual *and therefore* (NB!) *in the (normal) collective individual* (society) is that of self-preservation, that is to say: of protecting oneself against harmful physical and "moral" (sic!) influences. *Consequently* (!), the normal *effect* of cerebral effort *always* results in an improvement of energetical rendement. This holds not only for technical inventions, and not only for the intelligent worker, as opposed to the unintelligent one, but also outside the intellectual sphere. Music, for instance, gives rise to cerebral states that cause modifications to occur in the processes of oxidization; and these in their turn serve the purpose of an improved utilization of the released organic energy (presumably an improved digestion or the like – although S[olvay] did, in an earlier passage, state that the effect of the ideo-energy on the size of E_r – i.e. the excretion of faecal matter – is insignificant. Therefore, the energetical significance [of music] has been proved; consequently, it is, like all similar phenomena, "in principle" measurable – and thus we have blissfully returned to the beautiful realm of the E_l and E_u formulas. Admittedly, there are still many coefficients for which the units of measurement would yet have to be established, as for instance – in Solvay's view – the number of possible ideas within a single unit of time etc. There are also intellectual or artistic creations where the profit remains potential, and still other ones that show a deficit – which are, in other words, socially harmful. (Here, S[olvay] is perhaps thinking of the suicides inspired by Werther, ⟨253⟩ which would have a negative influence on the energetical value [of that work]). But in any event, he thinks, *every* human being (sic!) can "in principle" be calculated (sic: "calquer"!) on the basis of the valuative *norm* (the direct or indirect improvement of the socio-energetical rendement), as to the extent (which will of course vary throughout the course of his life) of his psycho-energetical – positive or negative – social value, just as his physio-energetical value (see above) can be calculated. And it is extremely important that this is possible "in principle", the more so as it is also possible, "in principle", to calculate [a person's] "ideo-energies" which, because of the immature [judgement] of [his] contemporaries, have only become effective centuries later. Happily for the author, however, "it is *not* part of his task" to investigate the *method for* tackling the measurement of the valeurs physio-et psycho-énergétiques [physio- and psycho-energetical values]. At any rate, the broad outline traced on p. 21, which this – like any similar – [essay in] naturalistic self-delusion contents itself with, in his

facts: On the one hand, the Institute has, to take an example, published an utterly worthless work by Ch[arles] Henry.[1] (Not to publish it would run counter to the "tradition" established by Solvay.) Here, [Henry] presents voluminous calculations in a laborious attempt to determine, by means of "energetical formulas", the *social* (NB!) utility value of work, and *consequently* – like all "positivism" of *this* kind, even as early as in Comte's own work – to establish what the level of remuneration for the work *should be*. But on the other hand, the current director of the Institute, Professor Waxweiler, [has added] an Appendix in which he, within the space of a few pages, quite correctly – albeit with excessively polite consideration – points out the absurdity of this attempt (which any expert will regard as having been disposed of, ever since Thünen advanced his conception, ⟨255⟩ which was, after all, more profound and, above all, *economically* oriented). Since the Institute has, under the direction of Waxweiler, applied itself to genuinely worthwhile work – both popularizing and scientific – one may be allowed to hope that these "energetical" reminiscences will soon all be thrown into the [dark] corner where they belong.

The popular lectures that we have before us are dedicated to Ernest Solvay and demonstrate the merits of Ostwald's manner of thinking and presentation, as well as the consequences of

view includes "tout l'ensemble des recherches sociologiques proprement dites" ["the sum total of those investigations which can properly be called sociological"].

This is followed by the remark that underlying the "price" phenomena in today's exchange economy we find, as the "definitive" measure of value, the calories and oxidization processes that the organism is supplied with, directly or indirectly, in the form of goods exchanged. [But:] as long as there is an abundance of land, the oxygen in the air is not bought, not even indirectly (as part of the land value); on the other hand: when we purchase, say, a "genuine" Persian carpet, we are actually, according to Solvay, speculating in "oxidization processes"; but this is in fact a trick expression designating purely subjective estimations of value by *individuals* (just as all other "social" values also represent results of such estimations), and Solvay himself admits (see above) that no quantity of energy corresponds precisely to [such estimations]. But all this – and everything else that a first-semester student of economics would say when confronted with this nonsense – does not disturb our author. At the very beginning, we vaulted from [the] "valeur" of the work of art – which in that context must mean: its *aesthetic value* – to its "effet" (effects in terms of oxidization). In the same way, the argument here leads to the conclusion that the physio- and psycho-energetical improvement of the rendement of the "homme moyen" is the decisive means for improving the rendements of society itself. Consequently, the calculations of this "productivism" must guide the legislator in order [for him] to attain the "rendement normal" ["normal yield"], which in its turn depends on the existence of the "humanité normale"["normal humanity"] – that is to say: on the increase in the number of "hommes idéalement sains et sages" ["ideally sound and wise men"] who will not do *more* than is required for maintaining their own personal rendement normal, and at the same time make the "socially necessary" minimum of their energy available for social purposes.

Since every social group constitutes a unit of chemical reaction, and since it will not be long before every process in the universe will have been subjected to energetical evaluation (évaluation énergétique), Solvay believes that the time is approaching when such a normative "positive" sociology will become possible – "in principle", as we may also here be allowed to add! Here, we shall say nothing about S[olvay's] practical proposals. The intellectual content of his "productivism", as well as of his "accountabilism", is related to classical French utopianism (Proudhon's ideas, ⟨254⟩ for instance) in more or less the same derivative and philistine manner as that characterizing the relationship between his "achievements" – which we encountered above – and the lines of thought of Quetelet and Comte.

In his work under discussion here, Ostwald definitely lags behind *those* "achievements" as far as consistency is concerned, although – or rather: *because* – he is better endowed with "bon sens". For instance, Solvay's remarks on the lack of an unambiguous correlation between "intellectual" content and quantitative energy relations seem to be nowhere reflected in [Ostwald's] book.

1   Henry, *Measurement*.

the general proclivities (underlined in the foregoing) of "naturalistic" thinkers; even in their weakest parts they are, already as a "type", worthy of consideration. To the extent that they touch upon the domain of economics and social policy, they will be dealt with by a distinguished expert in social policy. ‹256› In the present context, I shall therefore omit a discussion of those [elements] (which I must admit that I consider as being among the worst things that Ostwald has ever written) and limit myself to a short résumé of the chapters presenting the substance of [Ostwald's] "energetical" conception of cultural processes – a conception that he has elaborated with consistency and, partly, in an elegant form. I shall also make a few remarks, either of a general nature or more particularly with regard to constructions that are farther removed from the domain of (economic and social) problems.

Chapter I (Work). Everything that we know about the external world can be expressed in energy relations: spatial and temporal changes in the existing energy relationships ("Energy" = work and all the products that work can be converted into). Every major cultural change has its basis in new energetical relationships (in particular: the discovery of new sources of energy or [a] different use of already known [sources]). (There follows a discussion of the distinctive character of the five kinds of energy, with special emphasis on the importance of chemical energy, as being the easiest to store and transmit.) Chapter II (The efficiency relation). The "efficiency relation" (the concept fundamental to the whole discussion) = the relation of the amount of useful energy B that is extracted from the primary energy A by means of an energy conversion, which we want for practical purposes; as a result of the unavoidable parallel creation of other energies besides the useful energy, [the efficiency relation] is always <1. The total work of culture aims at (1) an increase in primary energies; (2) an improvement in the efficiency relation: In particular, the legal order is meant [to further the achievement of] this latter [aim] (doing away with the waste of energy that takes place during fighting is quite analogous to the replacement of the paraffin lamp (efficiency relation 2 per cent) by the gas lamp with an incandescent mantle (efficiency relation 10 per cent). Only "free" energy – that is to say: energy that can be set in motion by means of differences of intensity within the existing mass of energy – can be utilized; and according to the second law of energetics, ‹257› this free energy will constantly decrease within every given closed corporeal system because of irreversible dispersion. Therefore, conscious cultural work can also be designated as the "endeavour to conserve free energy". The main factor that compels us to deviate constantly from this ideal is the value-determining one of "time": this is because only the acceleration of the slow (in the "ideal case": infinitely slow) conversions of energy makes it possible for us to utilize those conversions. But at the same time, this acceleration inevitably implies an accelerated destruction of free energy, in such a way that the desirable relation of both sides of the process to one another has an optimal value in any given case; if this value is exceeded, any further acceleration becomes uneconomical. The second law of energetics is therefore the guideline of cultural development. – Chapter III (The primary energies). "Almost everything that happens on this earth" has a cost in terms of the free energy radiated by the sun towards the earth. (The ebb and flow of the tides and the phenomena dependent on them are, in Ostwald's view, the only exception [to this] statement. This claim may to a certain extent be unsupported: O[stwald] completely denies the practical importance of the thermal energy of the interior of the earth; but while [this thermal energy] hardly influences the temperatures of the surface of the earth in general to any considerable degree in practice, it may possibly (as there are no absolutely watertight rock strata) be one of the factors determining the level to which seepage takes place at any given point, which would mean that it is one of the factors in determining the quantity of available surface water and all the occurrences depending on it.) In the long term, the economy must therefore be exclusively based on the regular utilization of the annual supply of radiation;

the efficiency relation of this utilization can still be so immensely enhanced that it should give us no cause for concern that the solar energy that has been converted into chemical energy and stored in the stocks of coal is being rapidly depleted – a depletion that admittedly constitutes a very serious breach of that principle, a "squandering of [our] heritage". The author does not mention the depletion – which, relative to the actual supplies, is only slightly less rapid – of the chemical elastic energies ‹258› [stored] in the stocks of iron, of the stocks of copper and zinc, which are so important for the products [connected with] electricity, and so on. It would perhaps have been apposite [for the author] to include a discussion of the question whether the chemical and elastic energy of aluminium – which is practically inexhaustible, and is at the same time remarkable for the constantly and rapidly decreasing costs [associated with it] – is able completely to replace the, at present indispensable, functions of those [other metals], [the supply of] which can, without doubt, in practice be exhausted. In an exposition that goes so far as to contemplate the future structure of our energy industry on the basis of concentrated and filtered solar energy that has been converted into chemical or electrical energy, such a discussion would, after all, have been natural. The more so, since Ostwald does not believe that the supply of energy through solar radiation has been lower in the past or will decrease in the future, within a span of time corresponding to a geological epoch. Thus, it apparently does not seem to be at all urgent, from a purely *energetical* point of view, to be particularly *economical* – with an eye to the future – with the mass of energy derived from that source. On the other hand, the chemical energy and elastic energy [stored in] the [above-mentioned] raw materials, which is indispensable for generating, transmitting and utilizing the most important of the useful energies, will, through use, be dispersed *just as* irretrievably as is the case with all free energies according to the law of entropy. *But*, in contrast to other [energies, these will be dispersed] within a *historically* foreseeable span of time: little more than a millennium, if the depletion continues to grow at the present pace. Generally speaking, the fact that Ostwald's discussion focuses exclusively on energetical relationships – that is: (1) obtaining new primary energies and (2) improving the efficiency relation of the generation of useful energies – means that he does not at all discuss the (after all quite important) role as an object of economy played by the given energy *conductors*, the supply of which is to a large extent not inexhaustible. It is fairly awkward to fit the qualities that make them useful [as conductors] into [either of] the two categories [cited above], and, in any case, this can only be done indirectly; however, no doubt Ostwald's terminology would be equal to that task as well. – But *if* the future prospects for the direct utilizability of new energies – and in particular for solar energy, which can at present almost exclusively be exploited through the medium of living or fossilized plants – are so exceedingly favourable as Ostwald confidently assumes, then the following question arises with respect to the energetical analysis of culture: Why is it, under those circumstances and in view of the generally decreasing birth rate [in our societies], that we attach any importance at all to the *efficiency relation*? Why does it not become increasingly irrelevant, instead of becoming ever more important? At most, it might be possible to find an answer to this question in Chapters IV (Living Beings), V (Man) and VI (The Mastery of Extraneous Energies ‹259›); but it would be fairly arduous, and the answer would [still] be incomplete. If Ostwald had posed and answered [this question] explicitly, this would have led him – in a manner from which his account would no doubt have benefited – to think through problems such as those that Sombart, for instance, raises in his critique of Reuleaux's concept of the machine. ‹260› These problems are touched on at the bottom of p. 82, but only briefly – and, moreover, misleadingly, since it is by no means correct that cultural "progress" (no matter which of the usual standards of "progress" is applied) is identical to an absolute "*reduction*" in the utilization of *human* energy. As far as the *relative* energetical importance of [human energy] is concerned, it may be true if we compare contemporary culture to that of Antiquity; but even in that relative sense, it does not hold for all "cultural progress" – unless one chooses to *designate* only "energetical progress" as "cultural progress", in which case we are in the presence of a tautology. Those reflections that Ostwald does not make might perhaps also have proved useful for him in connection with his somersault into the domain of the specialized discipline of economics (Chapter XI). They would also have prevented him from entertaining the quite erroneous idea – which is now clearly to be found in his exposition – that at least what we call *technical* progress will *always* stem from an improvement in the *efficiency relation*. Let us take the example of the transition from the manual to the mechanical loom. If the solar energy stored in the coal is added to the various kinetic, chemical (extra-human and human) and other energies that (of course including those parts of the energy that are dispersed without being utilized) proportionally fall to [the manufacturing of] a [certain amount of] textile produced by mechanical [means]; and if we then make the same calculation with respect to the [manufacture of that amount of textile on a] hand loom – [is it at all certain] that the purely energetical *efficiency relation* of the mechanical manufacture would *always* be greater than it was [when the textile was] hand-woven[?]. *Economic* "cost" is very far from simply running parallel to the expense of energy in the physical sense of the word; and in the exchange economy, the relationship between the *cost prices* determining the "competitiveness" is even farther removed from being equal to the relationship between the expended quantities of energy, although the latter will naturally in all cases – [and] often very "energetically" – play *some* role in this respect. O[stwald] himself has occasionally made reference to [certain] fundamental factors in the economics of life – [that one will] inevitably seek to accelerate the conversion of energy – which play a part in most "technical advances", and which directly require a *deterioration* in the energetical efficiency relation. And this is not just a single, isolated instance. Let us suppose that it actually proved possible, as Ostwald hopes, to invent a device that could convert solar energy directly into, for instance, electrical energy. In that case, the energetical *efficiency relation* might be many times lower even than [that obtained by] utilizing coal energy in a steam engine; but, nevertheless, the economic competitiveness of the energy generated in this new fashion could perhaps be overwhelming. Even the most "primitive" instrument with which man has been provided by nature: the human muscle, has a far greater "efficiency relation" in its utilization of the energy released by the biochemical processes of oxidization than even the best dynamo machine will ever have – and, nevertheless, the dynamo is superior [to the muscle] in the [field of] economic competition. No doubt, Ostwald knows quite well why this is so. But when the occasion arises, what happens again and again is that Ostwald attempts to demonstrate that "the whole cultural development" in its entirety stems from [just] *one* of the various energetical conditions: [that of] the "efficiency relation" – in spite of the fact that he himself began (see p. 257) by listing the discovery of *new* energies as a concomitant [factor]. From a purely energetical point of view, O[stwald] does not even contribute to the advancement of the purely *technological* problem, since we are not told anything significant about the really interesting point: the mutual *relationship* between the utilization of *new* energies and the demands of the "*efficiency* relation". And, of course, [he] is unable to do justice to the distinctive character of the approach of "economics" (in the institutional sense), although it is so closely related to the technological one.

Admittedly, Ostwald makes the preliminary reservation that he is conscious of treating only one aspect of the "cultural phenomena", and this is highly creditable in view of the urge for finding a "cosmic formula" ‹261› experienced by many other naturalistic thinkers. But, as ill luck will have it, he still believes in the long-outdated Comtean "hierarchy of sciences" and interprets it (bottom of p. 113) as meaning that the *concepts* of the "more general" disciplines, which occupy the lower rungs of the pyramid [of sciences], acquire validity for all the higher – i.e. "less general" sciences, and must therefore be "fundamental" for these latter sciences.

He will shake his head in disbelief if he is told that, as far as economic *theory* is concerned ([i.e.: with respect] to that specific part of the economic disciplines which distinguishes them from the other sciences), those *concepts* do not play any – not the tiniest – role; and, what is more, that precisely the most general *theorems* of the "more general" disciplines – that is to say: those [theorems] that have the highest degree of abstraction and therefore take us the farthest away from everyday experience – are completely irrelevant for economics in general. For instance, it is of no consequence for economics whether astronomy should accept the Copernican or the Ptolemaic system. ⟨262⟩ In the same way, it would be completely irrelevant for the validity of economic theory (which embodies certain hypothetical, "ideal-typical" ⟨263⟩ theorems) whether, say, the physical theory of energy will experience the most fundamental upheavals; [it would] even [be completely irrelevant] whether the law of the conservation of energy will – as can be expected – maintain its present range of validity, [which includes] the totality of physical, chemical and biochemical knowledge, or whether some "anti-Rubner" will one day overturn [Rubner's] experiments concerning the heat balance of [living] organisms ⟨264⟩ (which is of course extremely unlikely). Or we may illustrate the point by looking at the problem that for so long linked together physical research and economic interests: Let us assume the actual existence of a "perpetuum mobile", i.e. a source of energy that would at no cost pour free energy into a given energetical system. This would (1) in no way brand those hypothetical propositions of *abstract* economic *theory* as "erroneous". Moreover, (2) one might depict the technical significance of such a utopian source of energy as being ever so colossal (and one would have every reason to do so); but, nevertheless, the area within which those abstract and hypothetical theorems are valid in *practice* would only be reduced to zero if that source of energy had the effect that (a) every possible [kind of] energy would be available (b) everywhere and (c) at any time, (d) in unlimited quantities in any given span of time, however short, and (e) with any possible kind of effect. If just one of these conditions were just the least bit relaxed, this would immediately re-establish a corresponding infinitesimal possibility that the principles of marginal utility could have some directly practical importance. We have only dwelt for a moment on these utopian [matters] in order to make clear what is constantly forgotten, despite all modern methodological theory: Comte's hierarchy of sciences is a schema, far removed from real life, [conceived by] a grandiose pedant. Its author did not understand that there are disciplines that have totally different scientific objectives; and that *every one* of these disciplines takes as its point of departure certain immediate everyday experiences, and has to process and sublimate the substance of this "unscientific" knowledge from quite different and totally independent points of view. Self-evidently, the[se] various disciplines will very quickly arrive at some point where their objects intersect and come together (in the case of economics, this happens as soon as it takes a single step beyond "pure" theory). But anyone who – like Ostwald – fails to understand these fundamental facts, or who at the most tries to come to terms with them along the lines of Comte's system by merely keeping a small space open for the effects of "psychical energy" (p. 70), at least does not do justice to the distinctive character of the "cultural sciences" (for which O[stwald] actually wants to "lay the foundations").[1] That the pure

1 Incidentally, it is in itself questionable whether a modern chemist should speak of "psychical energy", as Ostwald is in the habit of doing. In any case, even those who accept [the idea of] psychophysical causality, and therefore reject "parallelism", ⟨265⟩ will hardly find themselves able to understand what Ostwald calls "psychological" processes (i.e. "thoughts") as something that can be evaluated in energetical terms – as Ostwald does, explicitly or implicitly. As for sentences such as the following (p. 97n): "Thoughts may (sic!) be grasped (sic!) non-spatially; but they do not exist (sic!) without time and energy, and they are (sic!) subjective" – it is best to draw a charitable veil over them. One may think what one likes about Münsterberg's *Outline* as a whole; but Ostwald would at least have profited

considerably from reading some chapters of that work. According to the nature of the methodology of the "energeticist", he can only deal with the "objective" performance – which [can be] represent[ed as] *quantitative* data – of the nervous system and the brain. In other words, he mainly has to deal with chemical energies, and not at all with "subjectivities", whose distinctive qualitative character (the "content" of the thought) cannot serve as a basis for establishing a definite *measure* of conversion between [those "subjectivities"] and quantitative "energetical" relations – [a "conversion rate"] that is, after all, part of the conceptual nature of all "energies". Let us assume that it would, for instance, become possible to establish that "mentally" determined processes had an effect on the balance of energy, and [let us further assume] that "introspective" cognition were deemed to be the specific "sense organ" for "psychical" energy and for the various "contents" of the "conversions" of that energy (this would be necessary, according to Ostwald (p. 98), already because psychical processes would otherwise not be classifiable as occurrences at all). In that case, even the most nonsensical babble and strange behaviour of a paranoiac could not in any way, as far as the energetical efficiency relation "*within* the epidermis" was concerned, be distinguished from the most sublime intellectual accomplishment; and what is more (and this obvious point again and again turns out to be the decisive one): there would be no kind of "*energetical*" efficiency relation [which could serve] as a standard, say, for [determining what was] a "correct" and an "incorrect" judgement. *Both* [kinds of judgement] require an energetical effort, and *nothing* at all makes it probable that, in the case of the "correct" judgement, this effort is different – with respect to the biochemical "efficiency relation" or in any other way – from the situation in the case of the "incorrect" judgement. To be on the safe side, it should also be noted already at this point that, contrary to the well-known position according to which the "true" is identified with the "useful" – an identification also made by Solvay (see above, p. 253n1) – the "efficiency relation" cannot, so to speak, be pulled in[to the equation] by being tested "energetically" in the "outside world". There are many undoubted truths whose utilitarian balance sheet has been so heavily burdened from an "energetical" point of view because of energy waste (chemical energy: burning at the stake; biochemical and kinetic [energy]: party organization and wars etc.) that they will be hard put to it to make up this deficit by improving some energetical efficiency relation – the more so since they also include truths that have *no* influence on that "efficiency relation" at all.

Apparently, Ostwald does not share those utilitarian epistemological [views]; however, he believes – quite rightly – that all purely historical, i.e. not *paradigmatic*, truths are technically worthless (p. 170), but also [believes that they are] *therefore scientifically* worthless. In line with this, his own, highly readable, book *Great Men* (1) only includes [in the category of] "great men" those who have significantly improved the energetical efficiency relation; and (2) he mainly treats them as paradigms for [the discussion of] the following *practical* question: What kind of education and study qualifies somebody to serve [the cause of] improving the efficiency relation? In other words, the aim of the book is not historical but didactic. (Incidentally, his purely "heroizing" account is on the whole unable to deal properly with the influence of the driving forces of scientific development: as everybody knows, it is increasingly becoming the rule that important discoveries are made, quite independently, by several different persons, and that [the question of] "coming first", which is [regarded] as being the only relevant goal [of research] and is [therefore] passionately disputed, is more and more decided by mere chance. Historians and others of their sort will probably be fairly unmoved by what they must regard as a somewhat naive philistinism on Ostwald's part; but at any rate, Rickert – to take an example – could not have wished for a better paradigm of specifically "natural-scientific" thinking (in the logical sense [of that term]).)

Enough. In the book [before us], Ostwald only hints (p. 70) at the possibility of incorporating the psychical [element] into energetics; and, on the other hand, he also emphasizes that the *limits* of his inquiry are to be found [at the point] where "psychological" factors become involved. But even if [the psychical element were in fact incorporated into energetics], this would probably be of precious little help for "laying the foundations of cultural science" (as Ostwald conceives them). And *how* would it be incorporated? Elsewhere, I have tried – as well as a layman can do that – on the basis of the work of Kraepelin and others, to make clear to myself and to the readers of the *Archive* how infinitely complicated, from an "energetical" point of view, is the role played by the "psychical" element in the psychophysics of work. ‹266› But Ostwald is apparently not at all referring to these aspects of the

"theory" of our discipline has nothing whatsoever to do with "psychology" is something that every theoretician who has been trained in modern methodology knows (or rather: *ought to* know).

In the three chapters on Living Beings (IV, V and VI), we first (p. 53) find a distinction between "anabionts" (that is: plants), which collect energy, and "katabionts" (that is: animals), which are, from an energetical point of view, parasitical consumers of the solar rays collected by [the anabionts]; man (for the time being still!) belongs to th[is] second group. Energetically speaking, man only differs from animals by virtue of the enormous, and constantly growing, amount of "extraneous" energies (i.e. [energies] that exist outside his epidermis) that he has brought under his control in the shape of tools and machines: The history of cultural development is identical with the history of the incorporation of extraneous energies into the field dominated by humans (so here this is [said to happen] even if there is *no* improvement of "efficiency relations"); this is followed by the proviso (which was briefly discussed in the footnote) that this approach is only feasible if it is "admissible" to speak of "psychical energy". [A number of] discussions are woven into [the exposition]: the energetical course of development of weapons of war (pp. 73–74); the energetical value of peace when compared to any kind of conflict, since [conflict] will always reduce the (energetical) efficiency relation; the domestication of animals (pp. 85–86; here, as in the discussion of slavery, knowledge of important results of specialized research [in these areas] is lacking); furthermore, a very nice energetical analysis of the importance of fire (p. 92); the transport and storage of energies and the behaviour of the different kinds of energy under these conditions (Chapter VII). The distinction between "tools" and "machines" (based on whether they [involve the] transformation of human or extra-human – including animal – energies – p. 69) is extremely superficial and almost completely devoid of sociological value. Then the author comes to the "collective societal association" (Chapter VIII). Its importance for culture is[, he says,] exaggerated nowadays, in that the whole of cultural science is equated (by whom?) with sociology: after all, the simplest tools were invented by individuals, and they could also be used by individuals. Society[, he goes on,] is only scientifically relevant to the extent that it is a "cultural factor" – that is to say: improves the "efficiency relation" (p. 112) (which here again becomes the *sole* standard); from the point of view of energetics, this is only the case to the extent that society influences the efficiency relation through order and division of functions. According to O[stwald], the decisive standard of "perfection" of living beings is the balance of energy, and *not* variety. (It is well known how a different version of this way of looking at things has already, quite justifiably, been ridiculed by K[arl] E[rnst] v. Baer. ⟨269⟩) Moreover, if we incorporate the

psychophysical problem. [On the other hand,] he may have in mind Wundt's theory of the "law of increasing psychical energy", ⟨267⟩ which has already been discredited from a scientific point of view, [and] which confusedly mixes up the "intensification" of what we call the "spiritual content" of a culturally relevant process – that is to say: a *valuation* – with the categories of the psychically existent. In that case, the mischief caused by Lamprecht's use [of that idea] ⟨268⟩ must be a warning to us. Finally, [we have] S[igmund] Freud's doctrines, which in their initial formulation seemed to establish a sort of "law of conservation of psychical (affective) energy". But since then – and irrespective of the psychopathological value that they might otherwise possess – their own author has reformulated them so that they have [now] lost all precision from an "energetical" point of view; at any rate, they will not (at least: not yet) be of any use for scientists with a strictly energetical approach. And, even if they did, at some [future] time, come to possess that usefulness, they would of course, in accordance with their distinctive character, under no circumstances legitimize the confiscation, to the profit of "psychology" as a common denominator, of all those viewpoints in the "cultural sciences" that had hitherto eluded the grasp of "energetics". Enough of all this. Our concern has been to determine in general the methodological point at which the author oversteps the boundaries of the area of *theory* (we have already dealt with the area of practice) within which his viewpoints are valid.

"extraneous" energies of human beings – energies of which, for the most part, only a small percentage is utilized, [since] the muscle, as already noted, is the best dynamo that we know of – then there is at any rate, at the present stage of technology, no question of a relatively favourable *balance* of energy (efficiency relation) of the human being. And if this is so, how about the "balance of energy" of culture?

If we are to take the exposition at the top of p. 112 even approximately literally, then Ostwald does not in any way include *art*, for example (in the widest sense of the term), among the "cultural factors". However, on pp. 88–89, Ostwald puts our minds at rest: [art may after all be a cultural factor] provided that it – at long last – avoids "mistakes" such as those that we still find grouped together (as paradigms of "the narrow outlook of the beginner") in Schiller's *The Gods of Greece*, ‹270› and [instead] takes as its subject matter the transformations and wanderings of energy. In so doing, it could serve the cause of enlightenment of the masses and combat the waste of energy. As we can see, here Ostwald's principled naturalism by far surpasses that evinced by du Bois-Reymond's anathema against the formation of winged creatures [in art] ‹271› (because they had an "atypical" or "paratypical" constitution and, as mammals with six extremities, were anatomically questionable). The only question is: how can art live up to this programm[atic demand]? The maximal conversion of energy per square metre of canvas is attained by painting explosions or pictures of naval battles. A colour sketch that I once saw in a private collection, done by the Emperor William II himself (in his youth) ‹272› [and depicting] two armoured vessels producing a colossal amount of gun smoke, represents a fairly close approximation to the ideal. But what use is that against the wasteful use of energy by civilians? Perhaps A[dolf] v. Menzel's famous rolling mill ‹273› has an even greater (energetical!) *efficiency relation*; however, its didactic effect on the masses – especially on the housewives, who would surely be very important in this connection – is hardly any stronger. Poetically and artistically decorated cooking recipes should be completely acceptable. But what else? And above all: *how?* It would probably only be possible to give a "symbolic" artistic portrayal of the law of the conservation of energy and the theory of entropy, and then all those annoying "irrealities" would of course be reintroduced! Ostwald's precursors on the path of "rational" definition of the purposes of art – for instance Comte, Proudhon and Tolstoy – were just as philistine as he is; but they did not approach their task as blindly as he does. In Leipzig, an unfortunate imbalance seems to prevail: for the purposes of science, Lamprecht (for instance) is far too much in touch with art, while Ostwald, on the other hand, is not quite enough [in touch with it] (quite irrespective of all his achievements in connection with the chemical analysis of the pigments used in painting); and, in accordance with an unfortunate characteristic of "psychical energy", it is difficult to "equalize" these differences in intensity, in spite of the fact that "contact" no doubt frequently occurs. In this way, Ostwald has not even succeeded [in elaborating] a genuinely "energetical" approach to art – and [it is difficult to imagine] what it would look like. In terms of the "energetical" efficiency relation, it would probably – very much against the "usual" opinion these days – above all be "Luca fà-presto" ‹274› who would gain the [laurel] wreath, since the criterion must surely be not some alleged absolute value of the finished result in itself, but the result *compared with* the "energy consumption" – in other words: the "efficiency relation". And genuine *artistic* "progress" would be constituted by the energy *saving* achieved by modern technology with respect to the production of paints for artists, hoisting stones for monumental buildings, the production of artistic furniture, etc. – as only *that*, and not the achievements of the architect, painter [or] cabinet maker, will improve the "efficiency relation". Apparently, all that "energetics" (the efficiency relation) can offer the so-called "artist" is a sermon, in the most magnificent fashion, about "simplicity" in [the choice of] artistic means. It is difficult to see why Ostwald, having gone so far as to formulate the postulates analysed above, did not not resolutely draw these last consequences as well. It would be high time! From an "energetical" point of view, it is really an unbearable thought that the production of, say, an artistically perfect table, has involved the consumption of vast amounts of kinetic, chemical, biochemical, elastic energy etc., which can *never* be reclaimed from that table. In energetic terms, [the table] does not represent a greater amount of potential calories than a block of wood of the same size: its specific "form" energy, ⟨275⟩ which distinguishes it as a work of art, is *valueless* for [the purposes of] energy production. How unfortunate that "art" *begins* precisely at the point where the technician's "way of looking at things" *ends*! But perhaps this is true, in general and everywhere, of what is called "culture"? If so, O[stwald] ought to have recognized this and *stated it* quite clearly. As it is, the relationship between his ideas and the "cultural sciences" remains completely obscure.

But let us return to [Ostwald himself]. – The highest form of improvement of the efficiency made possible by "society" is apparently (p. 122) that of establishing a tradition of experience by the formation of general concepts that – like, in the last resort, each and every science (pp. 169–70) – help in prophesying the future and controlling it by means of invention (pp. 121–22; incidentally, [it is claimed] that plants have already made "inventions" (p. 152) – a questionable "teleological" extension); language is the instrument utilized by the collective societal association for this purpose.

But oh! how miserable, even today, is the situation of language and the science of language (Chapter IX). Ever since the failure of the attempt to "formulate" phonetic laws (pp. 127–28 – here Ostwald seems not to be quite well informed concerning the nature and the present state of this problem), specialists in linguistics [are said] not to have made any serious attempt at all to reach the pinnacle of *every* science: [the construction of] an artificial synthesis of languages that meets the demands of energetics (these [demands] are [described] at the bottom of p. 126). Evidently, Ostwald has in mind the analogy with the importance of the synthesis of urea for organic chemistry. ⟨276⟩ As a consequence [of this lack of a synthetic language], tremendous amounts of energy are lost in direct conflicts between languages and in international language problems, since the natural languages have obviously shown themselves to be unequal to this task. ⟨277⟩ – This last claim cannot be proved. O[stwald] is obviously unaware of the sense in which his comments on the "philologists" are in fact "justified": It was in fact made impossible to preserve the position that Latin had attained as the universal language of scholars, because the Renaissance, with puristic zeal, destroyed the vigorous attempts to develop scholastic Latin, which was for that very reason denounced as "barbaric"; [and] the lack of such a language of scholars is indeed without doubt the most important weakness [in the area of language], as English is an adequate instrument for commercial purposes. As for the destruction of the natural languages, its consequences are not quite so simple as O[stwald] assumes. But, as Ostwald's sphere of interest is limited to the natural sciences (in the *logical*, not the substantive sense of the term), it would probably be impossible for him to understand the positive creative importance of *precisely* those – often so annoying – ambiguities of natural language systems, [ambiguities] that do in part result in a greater poverty, but also in a greater richness, of potential content, than is required and determined by the *abstracting* formation of concepts. – In the following chapters on "Law and Punishment" (Chapter X), "Value and Exchange" (Chapter XI) and "The State and its Power" (Chapter XII) the pace is lively – in certain parts even close to frantic; but the postulates underpinning [the argument] are often not very "energetical", and, as I have said, I shall pass them over except for a few scattered comments: Ostwald generally fails to appreciate the distinctive character of juridical concept formation, and [this is] also [evident] in his remarks concerning the "theft" of electricity (p. 12). ⟨278⟩ Jellinek has recently furnished by far the best discussion of the fact that, in [juridical concept formation], the question is absolutely not whether the "energetical" criteria are satisfied, but whether [the criteria] laid down by the legal norm (a movable "*object*" belonging to someone else) are met. Juridical [thinking] has a tendency – which in this case is perhaps exaggerated, but for which there are good practical reasons, and which is in no way due to ignorance of chemistry – to proceed along *formal* lines, and generally to leave to the legislator, and not to the judge, the extension of the legal norm to cover "new" facts. "Form is the enemy of the arbitrary and the twin sister of freedom". ⟨279⟩ But whether this state of affairs is "new" in the legal sense is something that never follows from natural–scientific considerations alone, but primarily from the *total* context of the indisputably valid *legal* norms in the given case. The combination of [these norms] into an internally consistent theoretical system is *one* of the tasks – the most elementary one – of jurisprudence, and also provides the primary standard for deciding cases where it is "prima facie" (and sometimes definitively) not clear how the norms are binding; in principle, this will not be disputed even by those who adhere to the idea of "free law". ⟨280⟩ To what extent a natural–scientific approach might upon occasion be useful for [the construction of such a system] will completely depend on the individual case. But precisely in cases that have *not* been "provided for", (value) considerations of a completely *non*-natural–scientific character will always be decisive in the final analysis – whether or not this seems "backward" to chemists. – Furthermore, as far as the remarks on the meaning of "equality before the law" (p. 142) and on the "proportionality" of the punishment (p. 143) are concerned – [with the conclusion that] *milder* prison sentences should be demanded for persons with socially higher status, since they will be more relatively affected – they can hardly be said to have an "energetical" character. [The argumentation with respect to "proportionality"] rather corresponds to the idea of "retribution", which naturalists otherwise decry so strongly as being obsolete. "Energetical" considerations may certainly lead to related conclusions, even if the consequences will often be quite different; but, then, one must establish the energetical "efficiency relation" of the *norm* of punishment in relation to its *result*. As Ostwald would have it, one must then, for instance, critically evaluate the "efficiency relation" of the energetical outlay involved in obtaining [not only] the elastic energy of the prison walls, but also the chemical energy [needed to] make the arrest and the biochemical energies [needed for] the administration of the prison; and then, [one must] ask what is the minimum outlay of energy necessary to fulfil the "energetical" purpose of punishment – that is to say: maintaining order by eliminating elements of disturbance. Ostwald recommends that persons harbouring homicidal instincts (why only those [instincts?]) should be castrated; [but] energetically [speaking], the "efficiency relation" would in this respect be more favourable if one limited oneself to the very small expenditure of kinetic and elastic energy involved in the alternative: corporal punishment or hanging. [And,] since Ostwald also lays particular stress on the necessity of preserving the work energy of the criminal for society, there would be no obstacle to making "energetical" distinctions according to the profession of the criminal: [Not only] pensioners, but also philologists, historians and other idlers of that kind, who do not improve the energetical efficiency relation, should be hanged (incidentally: as they are useless, why not [hang them] already now, before they make a nuisance of themselves as criminals?); but for workers, technicians, entrepreneurs who make an intellectual contribution and, above all, for those persons who make the greatest contribution to the improvement of the efficiency relation: *chemists*, corporal punishment should be the chastisement of choice. If O[stwald] refuses [to draw] these conclusions, he must realize that [his negative attitude] is probably determined by considerations other than the "energetical" ones – and, after all, his book [was meant to] offer nothing but ["energetical" considerations]. In the same way, the comments on "equality before the law" contain ideals that are certainly not "energetical", but entirely [derived from] "natural law"; as for [Ostwald's] remarks concerning the "meaning" of the legal order (p. 26), which also completely correspond to the old physiocratic "natural law", ⟨281⟩ the fact that they are based on "energetical" arguments will hardly make them more convincing to anyone who does not already agree with them for quite different reasons. The cheerful conviction (p. 38) that the "stupidity" of man is the only obstacle to the general success of the ambition to reach the optimal efficiency relation will – unfortunately – make social historians shake their head. – This mixing up of value judgements and empirical science appears simply everywhere, with fatal consequences. After all, even a dilettante such as Ostwald might be able to realize that the relationship between needs and cost just cannot be defined "energetically" ([although] one willingly makes every allowance for his discussions of the economic concept of value and the *justum pretium* (p. 152) ⟨282⟩ – they are completely worthless and identical to scholastic thinking, but professional economists often enough err in the same way). A final point: on p. 55, [Ostwald] writes that the "general problem of living beings" is that of "securing for itself the longest possible period [of existence]; *in this connection*, the species *is to be* (sic!) considered as a total entity". He himself will realize that this proposition does not have an energetical origin; but that being so, surely he might have asked himself where the categorical imperative in the sentence beginning "in this connection" will then find its legitimation? Why should I care about the "species"? A natural *science* really should not at all presume to be able to give an authoritative answer to this practical question; and least of all is it obvious how any sort of *ethical* duty to adopt a particular attitude to the "species" could be deduced from any energetical "efficiency relation".

In the discussion in the last chapter (Science), which is devoted to education, a certain lack of familiarity on Ostwald's part with the status of educational science manifests itself, beginning with the claims that he makes on p. 182. Anyone who is not bound by confessional or other authoritarian interests will of course agree with the remarks (p. 182, note) on religious instruction. As for the question of the position of classical languages, however, it is certainly – especially from his particular point of view – not as simple as he assumes. ⟨283⟩ It made a very strong impression on me when a particularly enthusiastic teacher with strictly clerical views explained to me – admittedly in contrast to the official Catholic position – that he preferred young people to be trained, to the largest extent possible, *purely* in the natural sciences (in addition to [receiving] religious instruction); he did not expect that [kind of training] to be in any way detrimental to his confessional interests, but rather to result in the extirpation of liberal–"subjectivist" ideals and their replacement by "organic" ones in the Thomistic sense. ⟨284⟩ ([And,] in my opinion, he had good reason to believe this, considering the whole spirit of modern Catholicism and its adaptability.) On the other hand, it is well known that highly distinguished scholars, whose interest in "technical progress" would fully satisfy even Ostwald['s requirements], and whose detailed arguments are based on their wide-ranging experience of university seminars with students coming both from "Gymnasien" and from "Realgymnasien", ⟨285⟩ have emphasized that students in the latter category are almost invariably less well trained in *thinking* – which is, after all, the crucial factor (from the "energetical" point of view as well). So, at any rate, these matters are not quite simple. When (p. 180) "character development" is identified with "development of *social* qualities", and if one in turn (as Ostwald undoubtedly does) equates this ambiguous concept with "qualities that are energetically (i.e. technically) useful", then this has consequences that are unfortunately far – very much farther than Ostwald thinks – from achieving that "freedom of thought and of mind" which [he, in] the final sentence of the book (p. 184)[,] believes will result from the dissemination of knowledge of the natural sciences. Ostwald is – and must be, if he wants to be consistent – an apostle of "order" and the avoidance of "energy-wasting" excitement over non-*technological* ideals; and such a figure – whether he wants to or not (and probably this would be very much against Ostwald's will) – will inevitably spread around him a mentality of compliance and adaptation towards the *given* social power relations

– a mentality that has been consistently characteristic of matter-of-fact men of every epoch. It is a fact that freedom of mind is certainly *not* an ideal that has technological or utilitarian value, and it cannot be established on "energetical" grounds. And it is not certain that, by subjecting all progress in scientific thought to the value standard of practical "control" of the external world, one will in the long run serve the interests of science – not even of science as defined according to that very same value standard. Surely, it was no accident that it was *not* Bacon – the patriarch of this standpoint in the theory of science – but thinkers with quite a different orientation in that respect who created the method[olog]ical foundations of the modern exact natural sciences. What is nowadays called "seeking scientific truth for its own sake" was formerly – by Swammerdam, for instance – in the language of those times called "the demonstration of the wisdom of God in the anatomy of a louse"; ⟨286⟩ and, at that time, the good Lord functioned quite well as a heuristic principle. On the other hand, it must of course be granted that it was *economic* interests that used to provide sciences such as chemistry (and many other natural sciences) with the necessary momentum, and [that they] still do so. But should we promote this agent, which is *in fact* the most important one in the field of chemistry, to the status of being the "meaning" of scientific work, as this was formerly done with the good Lord and his "glory"? In *that* case, I would be happier with the latter!

The foregoing remarks may have given the impression that I see the energetical approach as totally lacking in usefulness for our discipline; but that is not my opinion. It is completely acceptable to try to get a clear impression, in any given case, of the physical and chemical energy balances [resulting from] technical and economic developments. Ostwald mentions that Ratzel has benefited from discussions with him on such matters; no doubt he is quite right, and we shall have the same experience. In particular, his general remark (p. 3) that it is necessary to establish *all* the *particular* propositions that can be derived from the application of the laws of energy to social phenomena deserves our unreserved agreement. But when he then (p. 3) immediately adds that we are thereby "*laying the foundations*" of sociology from the standpoint of energetics, this is in fact a consequence of the misguided Comtean systematization of the sciences. What arouses our interest are the concrete *individual* results of chemical, biological and other kinds of research, when they have relevance for our approach; but, on the other hand, the fundamental theorems [will] – as already stated previously – [only interest us] in quite exceptional cases, and never as an essential "foundation". It is always peculiarly difficult for representatives of the natural sciences to grasp this fact – although it should actually come as no surprise to thinkers who base themselves on [the principle of] "economy of thought". Furthermore, it is undeniable that the terminology of many disciplines – as for instance our own, as far as the economic theory of production is concerned – would gain considerably in precision if it took into account the concepts of physics and chemistry. But Ostwald overestimates all these benefits in such a ridiculous manner that he frequently almost invites the scorn of everyone who is reasonably familiar with the real problems of the "cultural sciences". For its part, the preceding critique has here and there (but only to an extremely modest extent, considering the way in which our problems are dealt with by Ostwald) struck a somewhat facetious note; but this should not be misunderstood. I have good reason not to throw stones at people who make a few blunders when they venture beyond the boundaries of their narrow specialist field: nowadays, it is becoming increasingly unavoidable to experiment with one's own concepts in adjacent and neighbouring areas, although this so easily leads [one] to [make] mistakes. But in view of the immense arrogance with which representatives of the natural sciences usually regard the work of other disciplines (particularly the historical ones), which have other metho[olog]ical goals and therefore have to proceed in other ways, it is quite justified to point out that Chwolson's "Twelfth Commandment" ⟨287⟩ applies even to such an important

267

thinker as Ostwald. He has been badly advised with respect to his sources of information; moreover, he has only damaged his own cause by introducing his favourite practical *demands* from every possible political field (economic, criminological, educational policy, etc.) into the investigation – [an investigation] that, if its approach is purely scientific, should be strictly limited to its factual subject matter: the *causal* importance of energetical relations and the *method*[*olog*]*ical* scope of energetical concepts. Those demands simply cannot be decided on the basis of "energetical facts"; and [Ostwald] *himself* also decides them on the basis of quite different premises.

In spite of all differences of opinion, this is regrettable. The innumerable grotesque blunders committed on two-thirds of all the pages of this pathetically awful treatise (here, we have not even described 10 per cent of them) [deserve] the most brutally frank criticism; but, nevertheless, Ostwald is and will remain a thinker whose refreshing enthusiasm, as well as his sensitivity to modern problems, which has stayed unencumbered by any inflexible dogmatism, must make it a pleasure for anyone to work together with him on the widespread problems connected with "technology and culture". If his treatise has been dealt with so extensively here, this is owing, not only to the importance of its author, but also to the fact that [this work], with its merits and weaknesses, is "typical" of the way in which "naturalism" – i.e. the attempt to derive *value* judgements from the facts [established by] natural science – generally, *once and for all*, proceeds (whether crudely or finely). The errors of otherwise important scholars are often more instructive than the correctitudes of totally insignificant figures. This [book] is a failure; but it has been treated so thoroughly here because of the characteristic and typical *errors* [that it contains]. No historian, economist or other representative of the disciplines of the "cultural sciences" of our times would dream of presuming to prescribe to chemists and technologists what methods and points of view they should adopt. The representatives of those latter disciplines must gradually learn to limit themselves *in the same way*, if they wish to enter into a fruitful co-operation – a co-operation that nobody can desire more strongly than th[is] reviewer. A fruitful discussion [with them] is impossible as long as they do not even have a common awareness of the following [facts]: what first made the utilization of *technical* "inventions" possible at all, what still makes it possible and what will make it possible (or impossible) [in the future] were and are certain *historically* given and historically changeable *social* conditions – that is to say: certain kinds of constellation of *interests*; consequently, the future techn[ologic]al development depends on the evolution of these constellations of interests, and not at all on the purely "technical" possibilities by themselves.

First published in *Archiv für Sozialwissenschaft und Sozialpolitik* 29 (1909), pp. 575–98. Translated from: "'Energetische' Kulturtheorien", in Max Weber, *Gesammelte Aufsätze zur Wissenschaftslehre* (ed. Johannes Winckelmann), 3rd ed., Tübingen: J.C.B.Mohr (Paul Siebeck) 1968, pp. 400–26.
The article is a review of Wilhelm Ostwald's book *Energetische Grundlagen der Kulturwissenschaft*, which was published in 1909. Weber probably wrote it during the summer of that year.
Where the translation of a French term is not obvious from the context, it has been added in square brackets.

ADOLF WEBER, *THE TASKS OF ECONOMIC THEORY AS A SCIENCE*

(Excerpts)

The whole structure of [this] newly written pamphlet shows that it does not intend to put forward any new idea: it obviously springs from a need to make a profession of faith, and merits attention as a symptom of a certain "mood" that continues to manifest itself in the most varied forms. [The pamphlet] deals with (1) the discussion of the scientific character of economics; the relationship of the latter (2) to "ethics" and (3) to practical business; and, finally, (4) the task of "educating the nation", which falls to economics. In the discussion under (1), [the author] (arguing against Schmoller, pp. 26ff.) rejects historicism, and also (following Sombart, p. 5, and Diehl, p. 16) opposes the introduction of the methods of the natural sciences; [he then], after a few remarks on economic motives, proceeds to offer a short systematic exposition of economics, partly along the lines of Hasbach and Plenge, but mainly structured in his own fashion. Under (2), [the author] strongly insists that the question of "what ought to be" (which can only be answered subjectively – p. 34) should be kept separate from the scientific investigation of facts, and that the academic teacher should maintain a strict distinction between his scientific work and any activities in favour of *political* reform that he might pursue. On this basis, [the author], under (3), goes on to attempt to make peace between (academic) theory and (business) "practice" by choosing as his watchword the phrase: that the economic Ought should be "measured" by "the standard of the economic Is". And finally, under (4), [the author] allots to science – which must, however, at the same time strictly observe the limitations to its activity defined under (2) and (3) – the task of contributing to the economic education of the nation (in List's sense ⟨288⟩) by dispelling "prejudices" such as "the dogma that capital and labour are necessarily opposed to each other" (by demonstrating that increased productivity is accompanied by rising wages) or the biased criticism of property speculation (by making clear why rents are raised).

The author repeatedly refers to me, among others; and there is indeed, particularly in the discussion in section (3), but also in many other places, a concordance of views that is welcome to me. In view of this, I find it appropriate also to point out where [our] views do *not* coincide (at least if we are to judge from the way in which the author expresses himself).

[. . .]

The author himself is [. . .] still not completely free from the confusion between value judgements and the presentation of facts [. . .] In fact, whether one regrets it or not, the "opposition" between "capital" and "labour" is not simply a question of wages, and therefore cannot "objectively" – and certainly not "subjectively" – be removed by rising wages. The belief in the existence of a "purely economic Ought", which can be derived from, or measured by, the standards of the "economic Is", is a palpable error engendered by scientific parochialism.

[. . .]

I determinedly claim my right as a citizen to be an "academic socialist" ‹289› [when I take part] in public discussions of current problems; and, just as determinedly, I take pride in the fact that my former pupils embrace *every conceivable* "standpoint" in the field of economic and social policy. And I am *not* of the opinion that, when scholars occupy themselves with current problems, this does not benefit the interests of science. Constant experience has shown, and will continue to show, that when we want to disclose the ambiguity of apparently unambiguous concepts, we need to test them against *concrete* historical situations underlying practical problems [of] topical [interest]; [experience also shows] that the interest in purely scientific knowledge has been guided by purely practical questions [of] topical [interest]. This is inherent in the [very] nature of a large part of our store of concepts as being the product of "value-relation" [. . .] Of course, I also consider it as the summit of unjustifiable practice to attempt to present value *judgements* as scientific knowledge, and to force an evaluative "standpoint" – and of course: a *"moderate" just as much as* an "extreme" one – on one's students when one is speaking from the *lectern* and shielded from the public. However, opponents of the academic socialists indulge, and will continue to indulge, in these unjustifiable practices to *at least* the same extent as *some* academic socialists do. The remarks by the author (pp. 53 and 65) call for the additional comment that it is not sufficient (as Gothein, Sering and others do) simply to abstain from taking up purely *party* political positions; in fact, doing this makes the situation worse by giving the false impression that such a contradiction in terms as [the expression] "impartial evaluation" could make *sense* at all, or that ambiguous expressions such as "interest of the totality", "general good" etc. could ever constitute *less* "subjective" standards than any party line, however "extreme". As for the "relativistic" belief that it is possible to find historically oriented standards of *evaluation*, it simply contains – in a different version – the same illusions as the idea that it is possible to construct a "purely economic Ought" and to "measure" it against the standard of the "economic Is".

[. . .]

Among the points of detail, the following should be noted:

The distinction between "natural" and "human" sciences", or between the investigation of "body" and "soul" is a method[olog]ically obsolete position.

[. . .]

Evidently, the author has not yet completely clarified his "methodological" position; but this can go hand in hand with producing competent work within one's specialized discipline, just as one can have keen eyesight while lacking knowledge of the physiology of the eye. (This is something that must constantly be stressed these days, in view of the immoderate amount of methodological work [being produced]).

[If] principles of classification are to be completely exhaustive from a *logical* point of view, they cannot "take the individuality of the scholar into account" (p. 17): Here, [the author] seems to have succumbed to the erroneous view – which, by the way, is constantly propounded even by such an excellent author as Eulenburg – according to which a distinction concerning the *logical* character of the cognitive goals of science would (or could) prevent anyone from working in "border areas" [between the sciences], or from formulating, in one [and the same] scientific work or even in *one and the same* sentence, truths that, if analysed logically, would (for instance) partly have a nomothetic character ([belong to] "natural science", in the *logical* sense of the term) and partly an idiographic one ‹290› ([be] "historical", in the logical sense of the term). – I cannot go along with [the author's] maltreatment of jurisprudence (p. 36). The author's treatment of the distinctive character of that discipline is incorrect [. . .] But, admittedly, the jurists have only themselves to blame for judgements like [the author's], insofar as many of them, in a spirit of scientific parochialism, tend to make the following deduction: Since they are indispensable as "technicians", jurists as such have a specific vocation to give authoritative opinions concerning new legislation on the basis of their own *value* judgements, which are derived from and *justified by* their *professional* knowledge. In fact, however, the only vocation that their professional knowledge qualifies them for is that of demonstrating the *means* for reaching a certain goal.

The author protests against [the practice of] evaluating science by the sole standard of "savoir pour pouvoir" ‹291›, a practice that is, for instance, occasionally found in the work of Ostwald and of chemists and technologists in general. However, this protest – which is particularly valuable coming from a teacher in a business school – leads the author, in his admittedly quite short comments (p. 52–53), to characterize the so-called "pragmatism" ‹292› in a somewhat misleading manner. The confusion that is one of the fundamental qualities of this anti-philosophical "philosophy" has indeed led to the concept of "cash value" being used as a standard for the measurement of *truth*, ‹293› often in a purely *practical* and utilitarian sense. However, as used by W[illiam] James, the concept has not only this sense, but at least *also* another one: value for the (in Kirchhoff's sense) "simplest description" of empirical facts ‹294› whose *cognitive* content is the object of our (scientific) "interest"; and, *in practice*, [this "simplest description"] is quite obviously important to [James,] because the rejection of the thesis of a unitary conception of the world is meant to make room for his *religious*, mystically oriented assumptions. It is certainly no coincidence that these opinions are mainly found in America and – to the same, if not a greater, extent – in England; but the reasons for this are not those which the author apparently assumes. Since the era of nominalism and Bacon, ‹295› England has always been one of the strongholds of the theory of multiple truth[s]; and there, [this theory] has by turns had to serve [the cause of] the freedom of empirical scientific research, as opposed to dogmatic constraint, and [that of] securing the needs of religion faced with the advance of natural science. Formerly, it was sufficient for this purpose to place religious truth, as the summit of irrationality, alongside [but] completely separate from empirical science, so that it was removed from any complication and from all conflicts with [science]. Nowadays, this is no longer sufficient: the absolute irrationality of the *meaning* of all knowledge – that is, not only of the "world" conceived as an "object" – must be added in order to make sufficient room for religious interests. – Naturally, this motive, which was present in James' case, is no longer generally valid in that way *today*. Instead, together with its other roots, an additional and no doubt very strong foundation of "pragmatism" is normally to be found in certain peculiar characteristics of the lines of thought that physicists in England and America (as opposed to France and – with the exception of Mach – Germany) have for a long time been wont to pursue. One example of this, which is for instance also characteristically manifest in Maxwell's case, is the use of methods of *demonstration* that are, rationally speaking, mutually incompatible, but that have a high intuitive appeal from the point of view of sense perception, while they can never claim to represent the "actual" process. Duhem, for instance, has given a fine description of this method of treatment, as opposed to the indigenous continental one. It was particularly close to the way of thinking of the pragmatic "economy of thought", and its roots stretch back beyond the beginnings of modern natural science; but this is not the place to pursue this subject further. If it were to be investigated – something that only a specialized scholar could do – a point of particular interest would be the realization that the "internationality" of "culture", which is so often emphasized, has its *limits*, even in the domain of intellectual achievements. These limits can to a major degree be explained by the historical cultural tradition; but, in addition, their orientation may also be influenced by "dispositions" or geographical conditions. Of course, the fact that "pragmatism" can be made historically "explicable" to us does not make the philosophical evaluation of it any more positive; for the main part, I agree with the author in this respect.

First published in and translated from *Archiv für Sozialwissenschaft und Sozialpolitik 29* (1909), pp. 615–20.
Adolf Weber's pamphlet *Die Aufgaben der Volkswirtschaftslehre als Wissenschaft* was published in 1909. This review by Max Weber was published in September of that year.

ON SOME CATEGORIES
OF INTERPRETIVE
SOCIOLOGY[1]

I The meaning of an "interpretive" sociology

The course of human ("external" or "inner") behaviour exhibits interrelations and regularities, like all occurrences. But what is, at least in its fullest sense, peculiar to human behaviour is [that it exhibits] interrelations and regularities whose course can be interpreted so that it can be *understood*. An "understanding" of human behaviour that has been obtained by means of interpretation first of all possesses a specific qualitative "evidentness" whose strength may vary very considerably. The fact that an interpretation possesses this evidentness to a particularly high degree still does not in itself constitute any sort of proof of its empirical validity: Behaviour[s] whose external course and effects are identical may stem from the most varied constellations of motives; and the most intelligibly evident motive is not always the one that was actually involved. Instead, the "understanding" of the interrelation must still, to the extent possible, be subjected

---

1   Apart from Simmel's discussions (in *Philosophy of History*[2]) and previous essays of my own [*Roscher and Knies*, *Objectivity*, *Critical Studies*, *Stammler*, *Marginal Utility* and *Energetics*], reference should be made to the comments by Rickert (in *Limits of Concept Formation*[2]) and the various works by K[arl] Jaspers (now especially his *General Psychopathology*). The conceptualization differs from [that of] those authors and also from F[erdinand] Tönnies' work *Community and Society* (which is of lasting importance), as well as from the works of A[lfred] Vierkandt and others; but these differences [of conceptualization] need not always [imply] differences of opinion. From a method[olog]ical point of view, relevant works are, in addition to the above-mentioned ones, those of Gottl (*Dominance of Words*) and (with respect to the category of objective possibility) Radbruch; also, if more indirectly, those of Husserl and Lask. Moreover, it will be readily seen that the concepts show external similarities with (but are in substance as far removed as possible from) the constructions of R[udolf] Stammler (*Economy*[2]), whose outstanding qualities as a legal scholar are fully matched by his disastrous tendency to create confusion as a theoretician of society. This is quite deliberate. The way in which sociological concepts are formed is to an exceedingly large extent a question of how well it serves its purpose. It is in no way *necessary* for us to construct all the categories defined below (V–VII). They have partly been developed in order to show what Stammler "should have meant". The second part of the essay is a fragment of an exposition written quite some time ago, which was meant to serve as a method[olog]ical foundation for substantive investigations, including a contribution ("Economy and Society") to a forthcoming series of volumes; other parts [of that exposition] may well eventually be published elsewhere. The formulations are so pedantically detailed because of a wish to draw a sharp distinction between the *subjectively* meant meaning and the objectively valid one (in this respect, they deviate somewhat from Simmel's method).

to control by means of the usual methods of causal imputation, before an interpretation, how-ever evident, can become a valid "intelligible explanation". Now, purposively rational behaviour possesses the highest measure of "evidentness". By "purposively rational behaviour" we shall understand: behaviour that is exclusively oriented towards means which are (*subjectively*) considered to be adequate for the attainment of purposive goals which are (subjectively) unambiguously comprehended. It is by no means only purposively rational action that can be understood by us: we also "understand" the typical course of affects and their typical consequences for behaviour. From the point of view of the empirical disciplines, the boundaries of what is "understandable" are fluid. Ecstasy and mystical experiences – like (above all) certain kinds of psychopathic interrelations or the behaviour of small children (or, say, of animals – which do not concern us here) – are not accessible to our understanding and explanation through understanding, to the same extent as other processes and events. It is not, however, the "abnormal" as such that is inaccessible to explanation through understanding. On the contrary: it may precisely be the act of a person who towers above the average that – because it corresponds to a "correctness type" (a term whose meaning will be discussed shortly) – is absolutely "understandable" and at the same time the "simplest" to comprehend. As has often been said, one "does not have to be Caesar in order to understand Caesar". ‹296› Otherwise, all writing of history would be meaningless. On the other hand, we regard some processes as being quite ordinary human activities of a "personal", and indeed "psychical", nature; but, in their interrelation, they nevertheless completely lack that qualitatively specific evidentness that is the hallmark of the understandable. Just as in the case of many psychopathic processes, we are only partly able to "understand" how phenomena connected with, for instance, memory and intellectual exercise happen. The interpretive sciences therefore treat the ascertainable regularities of such psychical processes exactly as they treat law-like regularities in physical nature.

Of course, the fact that purposively rational behaviour possesses a specific evidentness does not entail that rational interpretation should be regarded as a special goal of sociological explanation. One might just as well make exactly the opposite claim, considering the role that "purposively irrational" affects and "emotional states" play in human action; and in view of the fact that, in any purposively rational interpretive approach, one constantly encounters purposes that in their turn can*not* be interpreted as rational "means" for other purposes, but must simply be accepted as goal orientations that cannot be subjected to further rational interpretation (even though their emergence as such may then still be the object of "psychologically" interpretive explanation). Nevertheless, rationally interpretable behaviour very often constitutes the most appropriate "ideal type" ‹297› for the sociological analysis of intelligible interrelations: sociology, like history, starts by making a "pragmatic" interpretation, on the basis of interrelations of action that can be understood in rational terms. Social economics, for example, proceeds in this way by making its rational construction of "economic man". And interpretive sociology in general does the same, since we regard it as having as its specific object, not just any kind of "inner state" or external behaviour, but *action*. By "action" (including deliberate omission and acquiescence), we shall always mean an understandable behaviour towards "objects" – understandable in the sense of being specified by some (*subjective*) *meaning* that it "has" or that is "meant" (though this may pass more or less unnoticed). Buddhist contemplation and Christian asceticism of inner conviction are, in terms of their meaning, related to "inner" objects (from the point of view of the acting person), while the rational economic actions of a person with material goods is related to "external" objects. That kind of action which is specifically important for interpretive sociology is, in particular, behaviour (1) that, in terms of the subjectively meant meaning of the acting person, is related to the *behaviour of others*; (2) whose course is *partially determined* by this meaning-relatedness; and (3) that can therefore, on the basis of this (subjectively) meant meaning, be intelligibly *explained*. Now, affective acts and those "emotional states" (such as "feelings of dignity", "pride", "envy" and "jealousy") that are relevant for the course of the action – i.e. indirectly relevant – are also, in terms of their subjective meaning, related to the external world and, more particularly, to the actions of others. But what are interesting about them for interpretive sociology are not their physiological and (what used to be called) psychophysical manifestations, for instance pulse rates or variations in reaction time and the like; nor is it the purely psychical facts that may characterize them, as for example the combination of feelings of tension, pleasure and aversion. Instead, [interpretive sociology] differentiates according to the typical meaning-relatedness (above all, towards the external [world]) of the action; and, consequently (as we shall see), it uses purposive rationality as an ideal type precisely in order to be able to estimate the importance of the purposively *ir*rational [elements of the action]. *Only* if we designated the (subjectively meant) meaning of the relatedness of human behaviour as its "inner aspect" – a terminology that is not unproblematical! – would we be able to say that interpretive sociology considers those phenomena exclusively "from within" – which would in that case mean that it does not enumerate its physical *or psychical* elements. This means that differences in the psychological qualities of behaviour are not directly relevant for us in themselves. Identical meaning-relatedness does not necessarily imply that the operative "psychical" constellations are also identical (although it is certain that differences in one may be determined by differences in the other). For instance, a category such as the "pursuit of profit" has no place in any kind of "psychology": If we consider two successive proprietors of the "same" business enterprise, the "same" pursuit of "profitability" within this enterprise may not only go hand in hand with absolutely heterogeneous "character traits"; its whole course and final result may even be completely identical, but [nevertheless] be directly determined by fundamental "psychical" constellations and character traits that are completely contrary to each other; and the (from a psychological point of view) ultimate "goal orientations" that are decisive in this respect may have no affinity at all to each other. If processes and events do *not* have a meaning that is subjectively related to the behaviour of others, this does not in itself make them *irrelevant* for sociology. On the contrary: they may well be the ones providing the decisive conditions – in other words: the reasons – for the action. After all, for the interpretive sciences, action is to a very considerable degree – even exclusively, in the case of the theoretically constructed action of isolated economic man, for example – related in terms of its meaning to the "external world", which is in itself devoid of meaning – that is to say: to natural objects and processes. But phenomena that lack a subjective "meaning-relatedness" – such as developments [over time] in the statistics of births and deaths and in the selection processes of anthropological types, as well as the way in which purely psychical facts occur – are only relevant for interpretive sociology in their role as "conditions" and "consequences" towards which meaning-related action is oriented, just like the role played in economic theory by the given facts of climate or of the physiology of plants.

The processes [by which qualities are] inherited, for instance, cannot be understood in terms of a subjectively meant meaning, and of course all the less so, the more exactly their conditions can be exactly established by the natural sciences. Let us suppose that it would somehow become possible (we are deliberately speaking in "non-professional" terms here) to link with approximate precision the degree to which certain sociologically relevant qualities and drives are present – for example those that (such as, say, the ability to orient one's action rationally, in general, or the possession of certain other specifiable intellectual qualities, in particular) favour either the development of the ambition to attain certain kinds of social power or the chance of actually attaining them – with a certain cranial index, or with descent from certain human groups specifiable by reference to certain characteristics, of whatever kind. In that case, interpretive sociology would evidently have to take those special facts into account in its work, just as it would [take into account] the fact, say, of the typical life cycle of human beings or of human mortality in general. But the specific task [of interpretive sociology] would only begin at the precise point where one had to explain by means of interpretation: (1) by what sort of meaning-related action – [meaning-related] to objects either in the external world or in their inner world – would the persons endowed with those specific inherited qualities then attempt to realize those objects of their ambition that those qualities had favoured or partly determined; and to what extent and why was this attempt successful or unsuccessful? And (2) what intelligible consequences for the meaning-related behaviour of *other* persons did this ambition, due to inherited traits, have?

II Relationship to "psychology"

The upshot of what has been said so far is that interpretive sociology is not part of a "psychology". That "kind of" meaning-related structure of action that is most immediately accessible to "understanding" is action that is, subjectively, strictly rationally oriented towards means (subjectively) deemed to be unambiguously adequate for attaining (subjectively) unambiguous and clearly comprehended ends. And [the accessibility to "understanding"] is greatest when those means also seem appropriate for [attaining] those ends in the eyes of the investigating scholar. But, when we "explain" such action, this certainly does not mean that we attempt to deduce it from "psychical" facts; evidently, the exact contrary is the case: we attempt to deduce [the action] quite exclusively from expectations that were subjectively held concerning the behaviour of *objects* (subjective purposive rationality), and that could be justifiably held according to valid experience (objectively correct rationality). The more unambiguously an action is oriented in accordance with the type of correct rationality, the less will psychological considerations of any kind contribute to a better understanding of the course of [that action] in terms of [its] meaning. On the other hand, in every explanation of "irrational" phenomena – that is to say: those where the "objectively" correct conditions of purposively rational action were ignored or (which is something different) the purposively rational considerations of the acting person were also subjectively excluded to a relatively large extent (for instance [in] a "panic on the stock exchange") – it is necessary, above all, to determine what the action *would have been* in the rational ideal-typical limiting case of absolute purposive and [absolutely] correct rationality. As even the most elementary consideration will show, it is only when this has been determined that it is at all possible to impute the course [of the event] causally to objectively as well as subjectively "irrational" components, because it is only then that one knows what components of the action can "only be psychologically explained" (to use the characteristic formulation that is commonly employed) – that is to say: have to be imputed to interrelations based either on an objectively erroneous orientation or on subjective purposive irrationality (in this latter case, [the interrelations are based] on motives that are either completely unintelligible and can only be grasped in the form of rules of experience, or [that can] be interpreted intelligibly but not in terms of purposive rationality). Thus, this is also the only way of determining what aspects of the "psychical" findings (which we shall assume to be completely known) have become relevant for the course of the action. This holds in absolutely every single case of historical and sociological imputation. However, when interpretive psychology encounters the most fundamental "goal orientations" that can be grasped with "evidentness" and can in *that* sense be "understood" ("empathetically re-experienced") – such as, say, the "sexual instinct" – they are nothing more than given facts which must in principle simply be accepted [as such], just like any other constellation of factual elements, even one that is totally devoid of meaning.

The middle ground, between absolutely (subjectively) purposively rational action and absolutely unintelligible psychical given facts, is occupied by what are usually termed "psychologically" intelligible (purposively irrational) interrelations, and these actually merge into each other by gradual transitions. (A casuistic treatment of them would be extremely difficult, and it would not be possible to give even a bare outline of it here.) – Action that is subjectively oriented in accordance with purposive rationality is in itself something quite different from action that is "correctly" oriented in accordance with what is objectively valid ("correct rational" action). The action which a researcher has to explain may seem to him purposively rational to a very high degree, but at the same time oriented according to assumptions on the part of the acting person that the researcher finds totally invalid. For example, action oriented according to conceptions of magic often has a character that is subjectively far more purposively rational than any non-magical "religious" behaviour, since religion is forced, precisely in a world progressively losing its magic, to make ever more (subjectively) purposively irrational meaning-related assumptions ("convictional" or mystical ones, for instance). But even apart from cases of [causal] imputation (see above), historical writing and sociology constantly *also* have to deal with the relationship between the actual course of an action whose meaning is intelligible and that type to which the action "must" conform *if* it were to correspond to what (from the researcher's point of view) is "valid" (or, as we would say: to the "correctness type"): The fact that a subjectively meaning-related behaviour (thought and deed) is oriented so that it corresponds to, contradicts or (more or less closely) approximates a [certain] correctness type may, for certain (but *not* all) purposes of historical writing and sociology, be extremely important "for its own sake" – in other words: because of the value relations guiding [the investigation]. Moreover, this [circumstance] will on the whole be a highly important causal determinant of the external course – the "outcome" – of the action. Thus, it is a circumstance whose concretely historical or typically sociological preconditions must in each case be determined up to the point where the degree to which the empirical course of events is identical with, deviates from, or contradicts, the correctness type seems to be explained intelligibly *and therefore* [to have been accounted for] through the category of "adequate causation in terms of meaning". Correspondence to the "correctness type" is the "most intelligible" causal relationship because it is the "most adequate" one "in terms of meaning". From the point of view of the history of logic, it seems to be "adequately caused in terms of meaning" that, if a thinker [finds himself] in a certain, subjectively meaning-related context of discussions of logical matters (the "problem situation"), an idea that approximates the correctness type of the "solution" will "occur" to him. In principle, this is just the same as when the orientation of an action towards what is, according to experience, [actual] reality, seems to us to be specifically "adequately caused in terms of meaning". However, the fact that the actual course of an action to a large extent approximates the correctness type (in other words: the *actual objectively* correct rationality) by no means necessarily coincides with action that is subjectively purposively rational – that is to say: action oriented towards clear and fully conscious goals, and [towards] means deliberately chosen as being "adequate". Indeed, nowadays, quite a large part of the work of interpretive psychology precisely consists in uncovering interrelations that have been insufficiently noticed, or have totally escaped notice, and are therefore, in this sense, not subjectively rationally oriented, but that nevertheless take a course as if they were in fact to a large extent intelligible as being objectively "rational". We shall in this connection completely disregard certain aspects of so-called psychoanalytical work; but a construction such as Nietzsche's theory of "ressentiment", ⟨298⟩ for example, also contains an interpretation by which an objective rationality of external or inner behaviour – of which [the person in question] is insufficiently or not at all aware, because he, for understandable reasons, "disavows" it – is derived from a given pragma of interests ⟨299⟩ (in quite the same (method[olog]ical) sense, incidentally, in which this was done decades earlier by the theory of economic materialism). ‹300› Of course, in such cases, the subjectively (even unconscious) purposive rational [element] and objectively correct rational [one] may quite easily get into a not always entirely transparent relationship; however, this will be of no further concern to us here. What was important was simply to indicate in a sketchy (and necessarily imprecise) way that precisely the "merely psychological" aspect of "understanding" is always problematical and limited. On the one hand, we have the unnoticed ("disavowed"), relatively extensive rationality of behaviour that is apparently purposively quite irrational: it can be "understood" because of that rationality. On the other hand, we have the fact substantiated by hundreds of examples, particularly in cultural history: that phenomena which have apparently been directly determined by purposively rational [considerations] actually came into being historically as a result of quite irrational motives and subsequently survived by virtue of being "[well] adapted", and in some cases became universal, because changing circumstances of life led them to acquire a large measure of technical[ly] *correct* rationality.

Naturally, sociology does not only take note of the existence of "pretended motives" of action, of "substitute satisfactions" of instinctual drives and the like: it is particularly aware that even completely "unintelligible" qualitative components of a motivational sequence may influence that sequence – including the orientation of its meaning and the nature of its consequences – in the most far-reaching manner. Action that is "identical" in terms of the orientation of its meaning may sometimes take a course that leads to radically different final outcomes already because of purely quantitative variations in the "reaction time" of the persons participating in the action. Such variations, and even more the qualitative emotive states, will often direct chains of motivations, which in terms of the orientation of their "meaning" arose in "similar" ways, into paths that are in effect heterogeneous, even as far as the orientation of their meaning is concerned.

From the point of view of sociology, there are quite gradual transitions between (1) the more or less approximately attained correctness type; (2) the type oriented according to (subjectively) purposive rationality; (3) behaviour whose purposive rationality is only to a certain degree conscious or perceived, and only to a certain degree unambiguous; (4) behaviour that is not purposively rational, but motivated in a context which is intelligible in terms of its meaning; (5) behaviour motivated in a context that is only to a certain degree intelligible in terms of its meaning, and that is more or less strongly broken up or co-determined by unintelligible elements; and finally, (6) completely unintelligible psychical or physical phenomena "in" or "pertaining to" a person. [Sociology] knows that not every action that takes a "correct rational" course was determined in a subjectively purposively rational manner; and, in particular, it regards it as self-evident that actual action is not determined by interrelations that can be logically and rationally inferred, but by "psychological" ones (as they are normally called). Logically, it is possible, for instance, to infer that mystical and contemplative religiousness "leads to" indifference to the salvation of others, and [that] the belief in predestination ‹301› ["leads to"] fatalism or ethical anomie. ‹302› But, in fact, [mystical and contemplative religiousness] may, in certain typical cases, lead to a kind of euphoria that one "has", subjectively, in the form of a peculiar objectless feeling of love (to that extent, we are confronted with a context that is at least *partially* "unintelligible"); and this feeling is then "abreacted" in social action, where it takes the form of "acosmistic love" ‹303› – a relationship that can be "understood" at least psychologically, but of course not in terms of "purposive rationality". As for the belief in predestination, it may even, under certain conditions (which are completely intelligible), in a specifically rationally understandable way allow the capacity for actively ethical action to become a cause of knowledge for the believer with respect to his personal salvation; thus, [the belief in predestination] can develop that capacity in a way that can be thoroughly understood, partly in terms of purposive rationality, partly in terms of its [intrinsic] meaning. On the other hand, the standpoint of believing in predestination may itself, in a "psychologically" understandable way, be the product of certain precisely definable circumstances of life (whose contextual elements can in their turn be understood in terms of their meaning) and of "character" traits that must be taken as given. – Enough of this. The relationship of interpretive sociology to "psychology" is different in each individual case. Objectively correct rationality can be used by [interpretive sociology] as an ideal type in relation to empirical action; purposive rationality [can be used] as an ideal type in relation to what is psychologically understandable in terms of its meaning; and what is understandable in terms of its meaning [can be used] as an ideal type in relation to action whose motivation is unintelligible. The comparison with the ideal type makes it possible to determine the causally relevant elements of irrationality (this term being defined differently on each level) for the purposes of causal imputation.

However, sociology would protest against the assumption that [interpretive] "understanding" and causal "explanation" have *no* relationship with another. It is true that they begin their work at opposite poles of what happens. In particular, the statistical frequency of a certain behaviour does not make it one jot more "intelligible" in terms of its meaning; and, in itself, a maximum of "intelligibility" [of an occurrence] in no way speaks in favour of its frequency – indeed, in the case of absolute subjective purposive rationality, it will mostly speak against it. But nevertheless, mental interrelations that can be understood in terms of their meaning, and in particular motivational sequences oriented according to purposive rationality, can certainly qualify as links in a chain of causation that, for instance, begins with "external" circumstances and at the end again leads to "external" behaviour. Of course, even for [sociology], interpretations of concrete behaviour "in terms of meaning" are in themselves, however highly "evident" they may be, to begin with only hypotheses of [causal] imputation. They therefore need to be verified to the largest possible degree, by means that are in principle exactly the same as [in the case of] any other hypothesis. We regard them as usable hypotheses when we [feel] justified in assuming that there is a certain "chance" (which may be of very different magnitude in the individual cases) that concatenations of motivations in terms of (subjective) meaning are present. This is because chains of causation into which motivations oriented according to purposive rationality have been inserted by means of interpretive hypotheses are, under certain favourable circumstances, and even with respect to precisely that rationality, directly amenable to statistical testing and thus, in these cases, to the (relatively) best proof of their validity as "explanations". Conversely, whenever statistical data (under which also fall many data of, for example, "experimental psychology") indicate the course or the consequences of a behaviour containing some element that may be interpreted intelligibly, we only consider them to be "explained" when they have also actually, in the concrete case, been interpreted in terms of their meaning.

Finally, for an empirical discipline, the degree of *correct* rationality of an action is an *empirical* question: Whenever they are concerned with the actual relations between their *objects* (and not with their own logical preconditions), empirical disciplines cannot avoid operating with "naïve realism" (in one form or another, depending on the qualitative nature of the object). Consequently, as objects of sociological investigation (for instance, if a statistical investigation wishes to establish the degree of their correct rational "application"), even mathematical and logical propositions and norms are for us, precisely in a "logical" sense, nothing more than conventional habits of practical conduct – even though their validity is at the same time a "precondition" of the work of the investigator. It is true that we in our work also deal with important problems where the relationship between empirical behaviour and the correctness type actually also becomes a causal *factor* [determining the] *development* of empirical phenomena.

But the demonstration of this state of affairs does not divest the object of its empirical character: it is a goal orientation of the investigation, determined by value relations and determining what kinds of ideal type are to be employed and what their function is to be. The important general problem of the "rational" in history – which presents difficulties even with respect to its meaning – does not need separate treatment here:[1] From a logical point of view, the use of the "correctness type" is, at least as far as the general concepts of *sociology* are concerned, in principle only *one* instance of the construction of ideal types (although often a very important one). Precisely in terms of [the] logical principle [governing it], it plays its role no differently (in principle) from how an expediently chosen "incorrectness type" may also play it, depending on the purposes of the investigation. For such a[n "incorrectness"] type, though, the deviation from what is "valid" is still of decisive importance. But from a *logical* point of view, it makes no difference whether the elements from which an ideal type is constructed are intelligible in terms of meaning or are specifically devoid of meaning. What is used to construct the ideal type is in the first case the valid "norm", and, in the second one, a factual state of affairs is empirically sublimated into a "pure" type. But even in the first case, the empirical *material* is not formed by categories belonging to the "sphere of validity": it is only the constructed ideal type that belongs to it. And it completely depends on the value relations [governing the investigation] to what extent the most expedient ideal type is a correctness type.

III Relationship to legal dogmatics

Finally, the aim of the approach: the "[interpretive] understanding", is the reason why interpretive sociology (in our sense) treats the single individual and his action as its most basic unit, its "atom" (if we for once allow ourselves this, in itself questionable, analogy). Other approaches may quite possibly have goals that perhaps involve treating the single individual as a complex of psychical, chemical or other "processes" of some kind. But for sociology, everything that lies below the threshold of behaviour that is interpretable in terms of meaning and related to (inner or external) "objects" is only relevant in the same way as phenomena in nature, which is "devoid of meaning" – that is to say: as a condition or as an object of subjective orientation of that behaviour. And for the same reason, for the approach [of interpretive sociology], the individual is also the upper limit and the only agent of meaning-related behaviour. No mode of expression that seems to deviate from this [principle] should be allowed to obscure it. It is a peculiarity not only of language but also of our way of thinking that, in the concepts comprehending action, that action appears in the guise of a persistent being, an objectified structure or one that is "personified" and lives its own life. This is also, indeed especially, true in sociology. For sociology, concepts such as "state", "co-operative association", "feudalism" and similar ones designate (generally speaking) categories of certain kinds of joint human action; and it is therefore

---

1   I hope at some appropriate time to illustrate, by means of an example (the history of music) the way in which the relation between the correctness type of a certain behaviour and the empirical behaviour "has an effect", and what is the relationship between this developmental factor and the sociological influences, for instance in the concrete development of an art. Precisely those relationships – in other words: the seams at which tensions between empirical [facts] and the correctness type may burst open – are of immense importance from the point of view of the dynamics of evolution, not only for a history of logic or other sciences, but in quite the same way in all other areas. The same is of course true of the situation that is to be found, albeit in individual and fundamentally different configurations, in every field of culture: That (and in what sense) it is *not* feasible [to define] an unambiguous correctness type; and that, instead, a compromise or a choice between several such bases of rationalization is possible or cannot be avoided. Such problems, which are of a substantive nature, cannot be discussed here.

the task of sociology to reduce them to action that can be "understood", which without exception means: the action of the participating individual human beings. For other approaches, this is by no means necessarily the case. Above all, there is a difference between the sociological and the legal approach in this respect. For instance, jurisprudence occasionally treats the "state" as a "legal person" just as if it were a single individual, because this procedure seems useful, perhaps indispensable, as a conceptual aid in its efforts to arrive at an objective interpretation of the meaning of legal provisions – that is to say: [to establish] what *should be* [regarded as] their valid content. In just the same way, legal provisions treat embryos as "legal persons", while the empirical interpretive sciences regard the transition, even in children, from the purely factual aspect of practically relevant behaviour to "action" which can be understood in terms of meaning, as being completely fluid. On the other hand, to the extent that "law" is relevant as an object for sociology, [that discipline] is not concerned with determining the logically correct "*objective*" meaning of "legal provisions", but with *action*, for which naturally – among other things – people's *ideas* about the "meaning" and the "validity" of certain legal provisions play an important role as determinants and resultants. Sociology only goes further than this (further, that is, than determining that such an idea of validity is actually present) in that (1) it also takes into account the *probability* of such ideas being current; and (2) it considers the following point: The empirical fact that, in any given instance, certain ideas concerning the "meaning" of a "legal provision" that is seen as being valid are prevalent in the minds of certain people, will under certain specifiable circumstances have the consequence that action can be rationally oriented according to certain "expectations", and will therefore give certain concrete individuals certain "chances". This may influence the behaviour [of those individuals] to a considerable extent. This is the conceptual sociological meaning of the empirical "validity" of a "legal provision". Therefore, from a sociological point of view, the word "state" – if, indeed, sociologists use it at all – *only* covers a course of human action of a particular kind. Sociology often, as in that case, has to use the same word as legal science; but, when it does, [that word] has another meaning for it than its juridically "correct" one. However, it is the inescapable fate of all sociology that, when it investigates actual action, which is everywhere characterized by constant transitions between the [various] "typical" cases, it very often has to use rigorous legal expressions (rigorous because they are based on a syllogistic interpretation of norms) and must then invest [these expressions] with a sociological meaning that is radically different from the legal one. Moreover, sociology must continually, in accordance with the nature of its object, proceed as follows: meaning-related phenomena that are "familiar" and well-known from everyday life are used to define other phenomena; and, later, they must then in their turn be defined with the aid of those [self-same] other phenomena. We shall pass a number of those definitions in review.

IV "Communal action"

We shall speak of "communal action" when human action, in terms of its subjective *meaning*, is related to the behaviour of other human beings. For instance, we shall not call an unintended collision between two bicyclists ["]communal action["]; but we shall use that term about their possible prior attempts to avoid colliding with each other or, after a collision, about their possible "scuffle" or their "negotiation" of an amicable "settlement". It is not just communal action that is important for sociological causal imputation. But it is the primary object of an "interpretive" sociology. An important normal – but not indispensable – component of communal action is, in particular, its orientation, in terms of meaning, according to the *expectation* of others behaving in a certain way and, as a consequence of that, [according to] the (*subjectively*) estimated chances of one's action achieving its objective. In that connection, an extremely understandable and important basis for the explanation of the action is the *objective* existence of those chances – that is to say: the greater or lesser probability (which can be formulated in a judgement of objective possibility) of this expectation being justified. More about this presently. To begin with, we shall continue to consider the situation where there is a subjectively held expectation. – All action – without exception – that is "purposively rational" (in the previously defined sense) is particularly oriented in accordance with [certain] expectations. Consequently, it would seem at first glance that, in principle, it makes no difference if the action is guided by the fact that the acting person expects certain processes in *nature* to occur (whether these processes have originated independently of that person, or whether they have come about as a reaction to action on his part that was precisely intended to bring them about), or that he expects a certain behaviour on the part of other *human beings*. But if the acting person acts purposively rationally, his expectation that other persons will behave in a particular way may also be based on his [further] expectation that the behaviour of these other persons will be subjectively *meaning-related*, so that he also (subjectively) believes that, on the basis of certain *meaning-related* elements [of the situation], he can, with a greater or lesser degree of probability, calculate in advance the chances of that behaviour [occurring]. In particular, this expectation may be subjectively based on the fact that the acting person has come to an "understanding" with the other person or persons: that he has made "agreements" with them which he believes that he has reason to expect them to "comply with", in accordance with the meaning that he himself ascribes [to those agreements]. This in itself gives communal action a specific qualitative character, because it very considerably enlarges the area of expectations according to which the acting person will believe that he is able to orient his own action in a purposively rational manner. However, the possible (subjectively meant) meaning of communal action is not just limited to the particular orientation according to "expectations" concerning the "action" of others. In limiting cases, that [orientation] may [even] be completely disregarded, and the action related to others in terms of its meaning may be solely oriented according to the subjectively held belief in the "value" of the meaning of that action ("duty", or whatever it might be) as such, so that the action is not oriented according to expectations, but value oriented. In the same way, when "expectations" are involved, what is expected must not necessarily be the action of another person, but may equally well, for example, simply be an inner attitude (a "pleasure", say) on his part. There is an empirically quite fluid transition from the ideal type of behaviour that, in terms of its meaning, is related to *meaning*-related behaviour of others, to the case where the other person (an infant, for example) is only considered as an "object". From our point of view, action oriented according to expectations of meaning-related action is simply the rational limiting case.

However, from our point of view, "communal action" is always the behaviour – either (1) *historically* observed or (2) constructed *theoretically* as being objectively "possible" or "probable" – of *single individuals*, [and] oriented according to the actual or anticipated potential behaviour or attitude of other single individuals. This must also be quite strictly kept in mind with respect to those categories that are now to be discussed.

V "Societization" and "societal action"

We shall use the term ["]societized action["] ("*societal action*") to designate communal action when, and to the extent that, [the communal action] is (1) oriented, in terms of its meaning, according to expectations based on [instituted] orders (2) whose "institution" has taken place in a purely purposively rational manner with a view to action expected on the part of the societized persons as a consequence [of the institution of those orders], and when (3) the meaning-related orientation is subjectively purposively rational. – An instituted order, in the purely empirical sense which that term is meant to have here, may be quite provisionally defined here as either (1) a unilateral request (which, in the rational limiting case, is explicit) addressed by [certain] persons to [certain] other persons, or (2) a mutual declaration that [certain] persons make to each other (and that, in the limiting case, is explicit) – in both cases with a content that is subjectively meant to hold out the prospect of, or expect, a certain kind of action. For the time being, a more detailed [discussion] of these matters will be left aside.

In cases where action is subjectively, in terms of its meaning, "oriented" according to an instituted order, the action of the societized persons may in fact objectively correspond to the action that is subjectively expected from them. However, the meaning of an instituted order – and consequently: the action that one has held out the prospect of on one's own part, as well as the action expected of others – may have been understood differently, or later be interpreted differently, by different societized persons. Consequently, [when] action is subjectively oriented [by different societized persons] according to what they subjectively consider to be the same [instituted] order, that action will not necessarily, objectively, be the same in identical cases. Moreover, the "orientation" of action according to an instituted order may also consist in a societized person deliberately acting *in contravention of* the subjectively comprehended meaning [of that order]. Even if someone consciously and intentionally plays in contravention of what he has subjectively understood to be the meaning of the [instituted] order of a card game – in other words: if he "cheats" – he continues to be societized as a "player", in contrast to someone who withdraws from further play. In just the same way, a "thief" or a "homicide", by concealing his activities or his person, in fact orients his behaviour according to the very same [instituted] orders that he subjectively consciously contravenes in terms of their meaning. Therefore, what is crucial for the empirical "validity" of an order that has been established in a purposively rational way is not that the individual acting persons continually orient their actions *in conformity with* the meaning of [that order], as they subjectively interpret it. [That an instituted order is empirically "valid"] may instead mean one of two things: (1) that individuals will in fact (subjectively) on average – like the cheat and the thief – expect that the *other* societized persons will, on average, behave "as if" they were guided by the wish to comply with the instituted order; [or] (2) that individuals *could* objectively have that expectation – based on an (on average) applicable estimation of probable human conduct (a particular variety of the category of "adequate causation"). Logically, (1) and (2) should in principle be strictly distinguished from each other: one is an expectation that is *subjectively* held – that is to say: the researcher assumes that it is "on average" held – by the acting person who is the *object* of investigation; the other is a probability to be calculated *objectively* by the *subject* seeking knowledge (the researcher), taking into account the *probable* knowledge and ways of thinking of the participants. However, when constructing general concepts, sociology also attributes to the acting persons the average subjective intellectual "capacity" required for estimating that probability. That is to say: [sociology], once and for all, ideal-typically assumes that the objectively existing average probabilities will also, on average, be taken approximately into account by persons acting with purposive rationality. Therefore, we, too, shall regard the empirical "validity" of an [instituted] order as consisting in those average expectations being objectively well founded (the category of "objective possibility"), in the special sense that, on the basis of [our] average probable assessment of the facts in any given case, we shall deem action to be "adequately caused" if it is subjectively, in terms of its meaning, *on average* oriented according to [those facts]. In this connection, therefore, the *objectively* calculable probability that [certain] possible expectations [are justified] also functions as a sufficiently intelligible cause of *knowledge* with respect to the probability that the acting persons hold those expectations. In fact, the expressions used to designate [each of] those two [situations] will almost inevitably coincide; but, naturally, [this] should not blur [the awareness of] the logical chasm [between them]. [The statement] that the [above-mentioned objective] probability can, on average, in terms of its meaning serve as an appropriate basis for the subjective expectations of the acting persons, "*and therefore*" in fact (to a relevant degree) did serve as such a basis, is of course only meant in the first sense: as a judgement of objective possibility. It has already become clear from what has been said so far that what appears to be a logically exclusive alternative between the continued and discontinued existence of a societization – [an alternative] that is apparently, from a logical point of view, an exclusive one – actually comprehends an unbroken range of transitions. It is certainly true that, from the moment when all the players participating in a card game "know" about each other that the agreed rules of the game are no longer being respected at all, then the empirical existence of the [instituted] order [constituted by the card game] is no longer given, and the corresponding societization no longer exists; and the same is true when no normally relevant probability objectively exists "and therefore" is no longer subjectively taken into account – for example, [the probability] that a murderer will *normally* worry at all about the [instituted] order that he is deliberately violating, *since* his violation will not entail any foreseeable consequences for him. A [societization] exists as long as, and to the extent that, actions oriented towards its orders, in terms of their average meant meaning, are still taking place on a practically *relevant* scale. But this situation is a fluid one.

From what has been said, it also follows, for example, that individual action may actually in terms of its subjective meaning be oriented towards *several* [instituted] orders that, according to conventional ways of thinking in that particular context, "contradict" each other in terms of their meaning, but are nevertheless empirically "valid" alongside each other. To take an example: according to the average prevalent view of the "meaning" of our legislation, duels are absolutely forbidden. According to certain widely held conceptions of the "meaning" of [certain] supposedly valid conventions[1] in society, [duels] are required. By engaging in a duel, the individual orients his action according to those conventional orders. But, by concealing this action, he orients it towards the orders [instituted by] the laws. In this case, therefore, the practical effects of the empirical "validity" of the two [instituted] orders (the term ["empirical"] being here, and everywhere else, [understood as] that which can *on average* be expected with respect to the subjective meaning-related orientation of action) are different. But we attribute empirical "validity" to both orders – that is to say: [in both cases], the action is oriented, in terms of meaning, according to the subjectively comprehended meaning of [the instituted order], and influenced by it. However, we shall regard the probability of an [instituted] order "being complied with" as the normal expression of the empirical "validity" [of that order]. That is to say: the societized persons will, on average, probably count on others behaving in a way that will, on average, be regarded as being "in accordance with the [instituted] order"; and they will also, on average, adjust their own action in accordance with the similar expectations of other persons ("societal action in accordance with an [instituted] order"). It should at once be emphasized that there is more to the empirical "validity" of an [instituted] order than the fact that the "expectations" of the societized persons in relation to their actual behaviour are, on average, well founded. This is only the most rational sense [of the term], and at the same time – sociologically speaking – the most directly comprehensible one. But a situation where the

---

1   We shall not provide a special discussion of this concept here. It should only be noted that, sociologically, we regard as "law" an order whose empirical validity is guaranteed by a coercive apparatus (in a sense that will be discussed shortly) of the group societized as a "legal" community, [while] we regard as ["]convention["] [an order] that is only guaranteed by "social disapproval" on the part of the group societized as a "conventional" community. Naturally, in actual fact the borderline [between the two] may be fluid.

behaviour of each and every participant would *exclusively* be oriented only according to "expectations" concerning the behaviour of *others* would constitute the absolute limiting case in relation to "communal action" and would imply the absolute instability of those expectations in themselves. On the contrary: the average probability that those expectations are "well-founded" will be the greater, the more one may, on average, count on the action of the other participants being *not* only oriented according to the[ir] expectations concerning the actions of others, and the more widespread (to a relevant degree) the subjective view among the[se other participants] that the "legality" (comprehended in terms of its subjective meaning-relatedness) of the [instituted] order is "binding" upon them.

We shall use the term (subjectively) "order-infringing" societal action to designate the behaviour of the "thief" and the "cheat", while [we shall use the term] objectively "abnormal" societal action to designate action that is, in terms of its subjective intention, in accordance with the [instituted] order, but that nevertheless deviates from the average interpretation of the order. Beyond these categories, we find the cases of purely "societization-determined" action: A person will, when acting in other contexts, feel constrained to take into consideration, in a purposively rational manner, the obligations that he has imposed on himself through societization (for instance he may, in order to [be able to] meet expenses entailed [by the societization], refrain from spending money for other purposes). Or, when acting in other contexts (for instance developing his "friendships" or his whole "lifestyle"), he may – without having the corresponding, purposively rational intention, and [even] unconsciously – be influenced by the fact that certain aspects of his action are oriented in accordance with orders instituted by mutual agreement (for example, those of a religious sect). In reality, all these distinctions are fluid. In principle, it makes no difference at all whether societal action takes the form of relations (in terms of meaning) to other societized persons or to third parties: relations of this latter kind may even constitute the principally meant meaning of the agreement [on which the societal action is based]. On the other hand, it is possible to make the following distinction within the [category of] action oriented towards the orders of the societization: [That action] may either be "societally related" – that is to say: it may directly express a position with respect to the orders of the societization (as always, interpreted in terms of their *subjective* meaning); in other words: [the action is] aimed, according to its meant meaning, at the methodical, general implementation of the empirical validity [of those orders] or, conversely, at their alteration or enlargement . Or [the action] may merely be "societally regulated" – that is to say: oriented in accordance with those orders without being "societally related" in the sense just defined. This distinction, too, is fluid.

The rational ideal type of societization is for us, provisionally, the "*purposive association*": societal action where both the content and the means of [such] action have been ordered in a purposively rational manner by *agreement* among *all* the participants. In the agreement on the order ([the] "ordinance"), the persons acting societally will, in the ideal-typical rational case, also have stipulated, in a subjectively unambiguous manner, what action shall be "imputed to the association", in what forms [such action shall be] carried out, by what persons ("organs of the association") [shall act in this manner] or how it is to be determined who those persons are, and what "meaning" – that is to say: what consequences for the persons entering into the societization – this is to have. Further: whether – and if so, which – material goods and services ("purposive assets") shall be available for achieving the agreed purposes of societal action ("purposes of the association"). Similarly: what organs of the association shall dispose of [those assets] and how [they shall do so]; what services the participants must offer for the purposes of the association; what action on their part shall be "prescribed", "prohibited" or "permitted"; and what advantages they themselves can expect by reason of their participation. Finally: whether organs of the association – and if so, which ones – shall stand ready to enforce compliance with the agreed order; and under what conditions and by what means they shall do so ("coercive apparatus"). Every participant in societal action to a certain extent relies upon the other participants conducting themselves (approximately and on average) in conformity with the agreement, and he takes this expectation into account in the rational orientation of his own action. For the empirical existence of the association, it is immaterial on what grounds an individual believes that he can have this reliance, as long as he is objectively *justified* in assuming that, judging from the actual conduct [of others], interests of *some* sort will (on average and to a sufficient extent) make it advisable for them to comply with the agreed order. But the probability (which he assumes) that physical coercion or psychical pressure (however mild, for instance simply [in the form of] the Christian "brotherly admonition") will be brought to bear in case of non-compliance, may of course, considerably strengthen both his subjective [feeling of] certainty that he will, on average, not be disappointed in his reliance, and the objective probability that those expectations are well founded. Action that, according to its subjectively *averagely* assumed meant meaning, constitutes an "agreement" will be called "societizational action", in contradistinction to "societal action", [which is] oriented towards this agreement. – Within [the category of] action oriented towards the agreement, the most important kind of "societally related" societal action is, on the one hand, the specific societal action of the "organs" and, on the other hand, the societal action of the societized persons that is, in terms of its meaning, related to that action of the organs. Especially within the societizational category of "institutions" (which will be discussed later), in particular the "state", those orders that have been created for the purpose of orienting this latter action [of the societized persons] (the "institutional law" – in the state: "public law") are usually distinguished from those orders that regulate other actions of the societized persons. But the same distinction applies within the purposive association ("associational law" as opposed to those orders that have been created *by* the association). However, we shall not concern ourselves with these (fluid) distinctions here.

When fully developed, the purposive association is not a transitory "social structure", but a lasting one. This means that it is regarded as retaining its identity, in spite of the turnover of participants in the societal action – that is to say: in spite of the fact that persons who previously participated no longer do so and that new participants continually appear (naturally, in the ideal-typical limiting case, always by virtue of new, special agreements). This will be the case as long as one may in fact, in spite of the turnover of persons, to a sociologically relevant extent expect action to occur that is oriented towards the "same" orders of the associative grouping; and a (subjectively comprehended) order [remains] the "same" in the sociological sense as long as the average ways of thinking of the societized persons assume this sameness [to be present] with respect to those points that are, on average, regarded as important. This may be assumed more or less unambiguously and more or less approximately: from a sociological point of view, "sameness" is a completely relative and fluid state of affairs. The societized persons in the association may deliberately change [instituted] orders through new societizational action; alternatively, the nature of the practical significance of those orders for action may change ("changed significance" – also, imprecisely, called "change of purpose") or [that significance may] be completely lost, without new societizational action, because of a change in the prevailing average conception of its "meaning" or – in particular – because of changed circumstances. Whether, in such cases, it is most expedient for sociology to regard the societal action that is now taking a different course as a "continuation" of the old ["social structure"] or as a "new" one, will depend on both (1) the degree of continuity of the changes; (2) the relative importance of those old orders that empirically continue to exist, in the form of action oriented towards them; and (3) whether the organs of the associative grouping and the coercive apparatus continue to exist in the shape of the same persons or of persons selected in the same way, or at least act in the same manner. We are therefore again faced with a situation characterized by quite gradual transitions. Similarly, [the following] question must in all respects be decided in the individual case (and, consequently: according to what serves the purposes of the concrete investigation): when is a societization to be regarded as an "independent" structure, and when is it to be viewed as "part" of a more general societization [?]. In principle, the latter distinction may occur in two varieties: Either (1) the empirically "valid" *orders* of a societal action have not been exclusively instituted through an ordinance by the participants in that action (autonomous orders): the societal action has been partly determined by the fact that the participants also (as always: normally) orient that action towards the orders of another societization in which they participate (heteronomous ‹304› orders, such as, say, the [orientation of] the societized action of the church towards the orders of the political powers, or vice versa). Or (2) the organs of a societization are in their turn in a particular way societized within a more general structure of organs of the associative groupings of another societization (such as, for instance, the organs of a "regiment" within the general apparatus of an "army administration" (a heterocephalous, as opposed to an autocephalous, ‹305› purposive associative grouping, such as a free association or an independent "state"). When orders are heteronomous, organs are often, but not necessarily, heterocephalous. Nowadays, societal action in an autocephalous association is normally partly determined by the orientation of the [association] members towards the ordinances of the political associative grouping; it is therefore heteronomous. Each individual "enterprise" is at present in principle autocephalous, and a considerable part of its societal action is nowadays already heteronomous – that is to say: oriented towards the orders of other associative groupings, above all political ones. The socialist "socialization" of the means of production would mean that [its societal action] would become heterocephalous in relation to the organs of (some sort of) "totality". –

However, not every agreed societization leads to the creation of a purposive association, which is definitionally constituted by (1) agreement on *general* rules and (2) having its own *organs* of the associative grouping. A societization can also be meant to be quite transitory ("ad hoc societization" – [persons] acting together in a revenge killing to be carried out immediately, to take an example); consequently, all the elements mentioned above as characteristics of purposive associations may [in that case] be lacking, apart from the rationally agreed "order" of the societal action, which is by definition the constitutive characteristic [of purposive associations]. A useful example of the range [of activities lying] between ad hoc societization and purposive association is that of industrial "cartels", with the simple one-time agreement between individual competitors on minimum price levels at one end of the scale, and the "syndicate", with its own huge assets, sales offices and an extensive organizational apparatus, at the other. The only thing that the[se "cartels"] have in common is the agreed order, which – if we here make the ideal-typical assumption that all the points have been explicitly specified – will at least contain an agreement on what action on the part of the participants is to be regarded as prescribed (or, conversely, as prohibited), and, moreover, what action on their part is permissible. If we take the case of an isolated [act of] exchange (conceived as [taking place] in the absence of any "legal order"), the agreement must at least – if we take the ideal-typical case of complete explicitness as our example – (1) prescribe the transfer of the goods to be exchanged, and possibly also the duty of guaranteeing their ownership vis-à-vis third parties; (2) prohibit the repossession [of the goods]; and (3) permit either side to dispose as it pleases of the goods that it has received as part of the exchange. – Such an isolated rational "exchange" of this type is one of the limiting cases of the "organ-less" societization. Except for the agreed order, it lacks all the specific characteristics of a purposive association. It can be heteronomously ordered (by a legal order or by convention), or it may exist quite autonomously, its "expectations" being determined by the mutual belief that the *other* party will conduct itself in accordance with the agreement (no matter what interests underlie this conduct). But it is neither an autocephalous nor a heterocephalous societal action, because it does not have the character of a lasting "structure". Nor, of course, do acts of exchange occurring as mass phenomena (even as mass phenomena that are in themselves causally interconnected – "market") in any way constitute a purposive associative structure; on the contrary, such an occurrence is fundamentally different from that kind of structure. The example of the exchange also usefully illustrates the fact that the action *bringing about* the societization (societizational action) is not necessarily only oriented in accordance with expectations concerning the action of the societizing persons themselves. On the contrary: in the example [of the exchange], they are also oriented according to expectations that third, non-participating parties will "respect" the result of the exchange, the "change of ownership". To that extent, it is pure "communal action" of the kind that we shall later call "consensual action".

Historically, we often find the stages of a gradual development beginning with ad hoc societization and progressing towards a lasting "structure". The societization that we today call the "state" typically originated in free ad hoc societizations of booty hunters to a military campaign under a leader chosen by themselves, on the one hand, and the ad hoc societization of those threatened, for purposes of defence, on the other hand. The "purposive assets" and the lasting character are wholly lacking. After a successful (or unsuccessful) booty campaign (or defence) and the distribution of the booty, the societization ceases to exist. From that state of affairs, a long series of seamless transitions leads towards the permanent societization of the warriors, with systematic taxation of women, the unarmed and the subjugated, and continues to the usurpation of judicial and administrative societal action. On the other hand, it is also possible – and this is one of the various processes playing a role at the origin of the "national economy" – that the amorphous structure of the "market", which represents a "communal action", may emerge as a result of the decline of the permanent societizations existing for the satisfaction of needs.

The "psychical" attitude of the participants – in other words: the question of the "inner state" on the basis of which they, in the last resort, societize themselves and then orient their behaviour towards the agreed orders: whether they comply with the[se orders] merely out of sober considerations of expediency; or because of their passionate attachment to the agreed or presumed purposes of the societization; or based on a reluctant acknowledgement that those purposes are a necessary evil; or because [the agreed purposes] correspond to what is customary; or for any other reason – that question is of no importance for the existence of the societization as long as it is in effect probable, to a sociologically relevant extent, that the [participants] will actually orient themselves towards the agreement. The various participants may of course pursue completely different, contradictory and antagonistic goals through their participation in the societal action, and very often do so. The associative grouping supporting the regulation of war by international law, and the legal societization for communal action on the market, with its conflicts over exchanges and prices, are only particularly clear examples of this universally recurrent state of affairs. All societal action is of course the expression of a constellation of interests on the part of the participants, which in itself involves the orientation of action (both that of others and their own) towards its orders, but *nothing at all* apart from that, and which therefore takes quite varied forms. The substance of that constellation of interests can, quite generally, only be characterized in a purely formal sense, as has already been done several times: the individual believes that he has an interest in being able to count on the action of one or more *other* persons, agreed upon through the societization, and to orient his own action accordingly.

VI "Consensus"

There are complexes of communal action that, in the *absence* of an order agreed upon in a purposively rational way, nevertheless (1) in effect take place as if such [an order] had been agreed upon, and in relation to which (2) this specific effect is partly due to the nature of the meaning-relatedness of the action of the individual. – Every purposively rational exchange involving "money", for example, implies not only the individual act of societization with the exchange partner, but also a relation, in terms of meaning, to the future action of indistinctly imagined and imaginable persons who, actually or potentially, possess or desire to possess money or wish to engage in exchange involving money: One's own action is oriented according to the expectation that others, too, will "accept" money – an expectation that is [a] necessary precondition for the use of money. In this connection, the orientation is in general, in terms of its meaning, related to one's own interest in the satisfaction of one's own needs, and indirectly also to the presumed interest of other individuals in the satisfaction of theirs. But it is not an orientation towards an instituted order concerning the way in which the needs of the imagined participants are to be satisfied. On the contrary: it is precisely only because such an ordering ("in common") of the satisfaction of the [economic] needs of the users of money is (at least relatively) absent that the use of money becomes relevant. Nevertheless, the total result [of the use of money] normally in many respects has a character "as if" it had been obtained as a result of orientation towards an ordering of the satisfaction of the needs of all participants. And this is the case *because of* the meaning-relatedness of the action of the user of money, who, like any participant in an exchange when engaging in that exchange, is within certain limits, on average, in a situation where his interests will normally require him to show a certain measure of consideration for the interests of others, because these latter interests will normally determine the grounds for the "expectations" that he can justifiably hold concerning the actions of others. The "market", as an ideal-typical complex of such actions, therefore has the character introduced above with the "as if" formulation.

In the ideal-typical "purposively rational" limiting case, a *language* community consists of numerous individual instances of communal action oriented according to the expectation that some other person can be made to "understand" one's meant meaning. This occurs massively among a multitude of persons, through similar use (in terms of meaning) of certain externally similar symbols, and somehow approximately "as if" the speakers oriented their [verbal] behaviour in accordance with purposively agreed grammatical rules; and since this phenomenon is determined by the meaning-related character of the [speech] acts of the individual speakers, it is another instance corresponding to the "as if" characteristic mentioned [at the beginning of this section].

However, that characteristic is almost the only thing that those two cases have in common. The way in which the total effect is achieved can in both cases be illustrated in a way that exhibits some superficially parallel [features]; but [those parallels] have no significant cognitive value. Therefore, all that the "as if" can do here is to serve as a foundation for defining a sociological *problem* that is present in both cases; but [when we start investigating that problem], this immediately leads to conceptual developments that are quite different in substance [in the two cases]. All analogies with the "organism" and similar biological concepts are doomed to remain sterile. Furthermore, it is by no means *only* human communal action that can produce a total result looking "as if" the action has been determined by an order [instituted by] agreement. This can also – and far more drastically – come about through different forms of "similar" and "mass" action that do not fall under [the category of] communal action.

This is because "communal action", as we have chosen to define it, must exhibit the characteristic that the action of one person is, in terms of its meaning, related "to" that of another. In other words, the "similarity" of the behaviour of a number of people is not sufficient; nor is every kind of "interaction"; nor is "imitation" purely as such. No matter how similar the behaviour of the members of a "race" is on some particular point, we shall only regard that "race" as a "racial community" when action by its members has its origins in a mutual relatedness in terms of meaning – for instance (to take an example representing the absolute minimum), if members of the race in some respect "segregate" themselves from the "racially alien" surrounding world *with reference to* the fact that other members of the race do the same (no matter whether the[se others] do so in the same way and to the same extent). When a mass of people passing in the street react to a rain shower by opening [their] umbrellas, that is not communal action (but "massively similar" action). Nor does it [qualify as] communal action when action is taken under the non-meaning-related "influence" of the action of others, as for instance in a panic, or when a mass of people passing in the street are crowded together and succumb to some [form of] "mass suggestion". In such cases, when the behaviour of individuals is influenced by the *mere fact* that others participating in the same situation also behave in a certain way, we shall speak of "mass-conditioned behaviour". For there is no doubt that the mere fact that a "mass" acts simultaneously – even when geographically separated but linked to others, for instance through the press – can influence the way in which all the individuals behave. (How this happens shall not be discussed here; it is the object of investigations in the field of "mass psychology"). In reality, the transition from "mass-conditioned action" to communal action is of course completely fluid. Evidently, even a panic contains elements of communal action in addition to mass-conditioned ones. The behaviour of the above-mentioned people in the street develops into [communal action] when, say, an armed drunkard exhibits threatening behaviour and a number of them rush at him and collectively seize and detain him, possibly by a "division of labour". Or when the same happens in order to administer joint emergency treatment to a seriously injured person. Since the action is here characterized by a "division of labour", this is an instance of the obvious fact that communal action has nothing to do with "similar" action as such, and in fact often means the opposite. This also constitutes the difference between [communal and] "imitative" action. "Imitation" may simply be "mass-conditioned" action, or it may to a greater extent be oriented in accordance with the action of the imitated person, in the sense of "copying" it. And this may in its turn be owing more to a positive appreciation – purposively rational or of some other kind – of the value of the imitated action as such, or it may simply, in terms of its meaning, be related to expectations. (It may, for example, be owing to the necessities of "competition".) A wide scale of transitions leads to the following case of very specific community action: a certain behaviour is copied because it is seen as a distinctive sign of belonging to a group of people who – for whatever reason – lay claim to a specific "social honour" and are, to a certain extent, treated accordingly. However, this last case obviously transcends the boundaries of merely "imitative" action and is not exhaustively characterized by that category.

For us, the existence of a "language community" does not mean that the production of certain sound complexes is characterized by mass-conditioned similarity (that is not at all necessary); nor does it simply mean that one person "imitates" what others do; instead, it indicates a behaviour in connection with "utterances" that is, in terms of its meaning, oriented towards certain average chances of making oneself "understood" within a [certain] group of people, and that "may" therefore also, on average, expect [to have] this meaning-related effect. In the same way, "domination" does not mean that a stronger force of nature somehow prevails, but that the action ("command") of [certain] people is related in terms of its meaning to the action ("obedience") of [certain] other people, and vice versa, so that one *may*, on average, count on the realization of the expectations according to which the action of both sides is oriented.

We can conclude that the "as if" phenomenon described [above] does not provide [us with] a category of phenomena with distinctive characteristics that are applicable in practice. Instead, further to what has just been said concerning "imitation" and "domination", we shall introduce another distinction into this multiplicity of situations: By "*consensus*", we shall understand: that an action oriented according to expectations concerning the behaviour of other persons has an empirically "valid" chance of seeing those expectations realized, because there is an objective probability that these other persons will in practice treat those expectations as being, in terms of meaning, "valid" for their behaviour, even though no agreement to this effect exists. The motives of those other persons on the basis of which one may expect that behaviour on their part are conceptually immaterial. If, and to the extent that, the course of communal action is determined by the orientation in accordance with such chances of "consensus", it shall be called "consensual action".

The objectively "valid" consensus – in the sense of the calculable chances – should naturally not be confused with the fact that an individual acting person will subjectively count on other persons treating his expectations as valid in terms of meaning – just as the empirical validity of an agreed order [should not be confused with] the subjective expectation of compliance with [it in terms of] its subjectively meant meaning. But, in both cases, there is a reciprocal relationship of intelligibly adequate causation between the *average* objective validity – which, logically speaking, falls under the category of "objective possibility" – of the chance and the *average* subjective expectations in each individual instance. – As in the case of agreement, the subjective orientation of action in accordance with consensus may in the individual case only be ostensible, or may be only approximative; and this will affect the degree and the unambiguousness of the empirical probabilities of validity. Consensually communitized individuals may deliberately act in contravention of the consensus, just as societized persons act in contravention of the[ir] agreement. In the example [that we gave above], the "thief" oriented his action towards the subjectively comprehended meaning of societization. In the case of consensual domination (to take another example), the "disobedient" person will in the same way orient his action towards the subjectively comprehended meaning of consensual domination, by concealing his disobedience. Therefore, the concept of "consensus" should not be confused with the "satisfaction" of the participants with its empirical validity, even in a subjective respect. The fear of unpleasant consequences may determine "submission to" the average meaning of a relationship of despotic domination, just as well as [it may determine] entering into a "free" agreement that is [in fact] not wanted by the individual. Although persistent dissatisfaction may jeopardize the chances of its empirical continuation, it will not dissolve the consensus as long as there is, objectively, a relevant probability that the ruler can count on his commands being obeyed (as the meaning of [this term] is, on average, comprehended). The question why [this is so] is of importance, inasmuch as an orientation *purely* towards the "expectations" concerning the behaviour of one or more *other* persons (simple "fear" of the "master" on the part of those who "obey" him) will – just as in the case of societization – constitute a limiting case and will imply a large measure of instability: Here, too, the "expectations" will have more of an objective "basis", the greater the probability that one may count on the "parties to the consensus", on average, *regarding* themselves as being "obliged" (for whatever reason) to act in subjective "accordance with the consensus". In the last resort, agreements, too, are "valid" by virtue of this consensus (concerning their legality). In this context, however, an existing consensus should not be identified with a "tacit agreement". Naturally there is a range of transitions from the explicitly agreed order to the consensus; and within this range, we shall *also* find behaviour that the participants will in practice, on average, mutually treat as being a tacitly agreed order. However, in principle this does not distinguish it from the explicit agreement. And an "unclear" agreement is, empirically speaking, an order with respect to which it will, in accordance with the prevailing manner of interpretation that is usual in the individual case, be particularly *probable* that it will have different practical consequences. On the other hand, the "valid" consensus in its pure type contains no elements of ordinance or, especially, of agreement. The persons communitized by consensus may in certain cases never have had any personal knowledge of one another; nevertheless, the consensus may in such cases represent an empirically almost unshakeable "norm". This is the case, for instance, with respect to the sexual behaviour of members of an exogamous clan ⟨306⟩ who meet for the first time, [since such tribes] may often extend widely, through [different] political and even linguistic communities. The same is the case with the use of money, where the consensus is constituted by the probability that the object treated, according to its meant meaning, as money in the course of the relevant act of exchange will be treated by an unknown multiplicity [of persons] as a "valid" instrument for the payment of debts – that is to say: for performing a communal action regarded as "obligatory".

Not every communal action falls under the category of consensual action, but only that [communal] action whose orientation is precisely, on average, based on the probability of consensus. Thus, for example, the social segregation of members of a racial group [is consensual action] when the participants may to some relevant degree be counted on to treat [that segregation] in practice, and on average, as *obligatory* behaviour. Otherwise, it is – as the case may be – either mass-conditioned or simple communal action of individuals without consensus. The fluid character of the transition is obvious. [The fluidity] is particularly marked in cases such as the detaining of the drunkard or the emergency aid. From the subjective point of view of the individual participants, it is more than mere de facto *co-operation* in the form of simple communal action only when the action is oriented towards some consensus that is presumed to be empirically "valid" – as for instance [the consensus] that everybody participating in that actual joint action will feel obliged to continue participating to the extent that, and for as long as, this corresponds to the averagely comprehended "meaning" of [that joint action]. On average, there is a degree of difference between those two examples in this respect: action to provide emergency aid will tend to have the sense that there is a probability of consensus – that is to say: [it will] tend to be consensual action – while the other form of action will tend to be simple, actual, co-operative community action. And, of course, not every behaviour by a number of persons that has the outward appearance of "co-operation" is communal, let alone consensual, action. And on the other hand, [the element of] external joint action is in no way a necessary component of the concept of consensual action: for instance, it is completely lacking in all cases of relatedness, in terms of meaning, to the action of unknown other persons. As in the examples [of the drunkard and the emergency aid], there is also a degree of difference between the consensual action of the members of the same clan and the communal action related to the potential action of other prospective exchange participants. In the latter case, the expectations only constitute a consensus to the extent that they are based on the chance that the action of others is, on average, oriented in accordance with [situational elements] assumed to be *valid* – and that normally only occurs when [these expectations] are "expectations of legality". Therefore, it is only to that extent that the action is consensual action: otherwise, it is only consensually *conditioned* communal action. On the other hand, the example of the emergency aid already shows that the substance of the "consensus" can also be a quite concrete purposive relation that lacks the abstract character of a "rule". And in cases where we assume that one and the same consensual communitization – a "friendship", say – has a "lasting" character, the substance of [the consensus] may also be constantly changing, and only be specifiable by reference to a permanent *meaning* that can be constructed ideal-typically and that the acting persons in the concrete instance somehow treat as valid. But even this substance may change while the persons remain the same, and, then, it is also purely a question of usefulness whether one will speak of a changed "continuation" of the relationship or of a "new" one. Moreover, this example, and even more that of an erotic relationship, shows that, evidently, the relationships in terms of meaning, and the "expectations", constituting the consensus need not in the least have the character of a purposively rational calculation and of an orientation towards "orders" that can be rationally constructed. In the case of consensus, what the "actual" orientation in accordance with "expectations" means is simply this: that one person, on average, has a *chance* of being able to adapt his own behaviour according to a certain meaning – which is more or less often assumed to be "valid", but may at the same time perhaps be highly irrational – of the (inner or external) behaviour of another person. Therefore, just as [we saw it in the discussion of] societization, it completely depends on the individual case whether the meaning of the consensus, which can (more or less) be specified in the form of "rules", will lead to averagely general *regularities* of practical behaviour: Here, too, consensus-*conditioned* action is not identical with consensual action. A "status convention", for example, is a consensual action constituted by that behaviour which is on average, in any given case, empirically "deemed" to be obligatory. By virtue of this consensus on "validity", the "convention" differs from mere "custom" based on some sort of "practice" and habitual "disposition", just as it differs from "law" by virtue of the fact that a coercive apparatus is lacking (both distinctions being of course fluid). However, a status convention may very likely have actual consequences for the behaviour of the participants that are not, from an empirical point of view, "deemed" to be consensually obligatory. For example, feudal conventions may prompt the view that trade is unethical and therefore lead to a lower degree of legality in dealings with merchants.

Completely different subjective motives, purposes and "inner states", whether intelligible as being purposively rational or "only psychologically" understandable, may result in communal action that is identical in terms of its subjective meaning; and they may also create a consensus that is identical in terms of its empirical validity. The actual basis of consensual action is simply a constellation of "external" or "inner" interests working in favour of the validity – [which is] more or less unambiguous, as the case may be – of the "consensus", and nothing else; and the existence [of these interests] may be due to (otherwise very heterogeneous) inner states and purposes of individuals. This is not to deny that it is quite possible to give an indication of the substance of the motives, interests and "inner states" that, on average, most often constitute the grounds for the emergence and continued existence of the various kinds of communal action (and especially of consensual action) that can be distinguished according to the prevalent subjective "orientation" of their "meaning". Precisely [such indications] are one of the tasks of every substantive sociology. Quite general concepts, such as those that were to be defined here, necessarily have little substantive content. Naturally, there is a fluid transition from consensual action to societized action (which is of course simply the special case of an order being instituted by means of an ordinance). Thus, the consensual action of passengers on a tram who "take the side" of another passenger in a dispute between him and the conductor turns into societized action if they later combine to write a joint "complaint". And whenever an order is instituted in a purposively rational way, "societization" is certainly present, although its extent and meaning may vary very considerably. Thus, it already constitutes a "societization" when, say, a "journal", with "publishers", "editors", "collaborators" and "subscribers", is founded for members of a race "segregating" themselves consensually, but without a [formal] agreement [to do so]: their previously amorphous consensual action will now receive "directives" – with varying chances of validity – from [the columns of] that journal. [This is] also [the case] when an "academy" such as the Crusca, ⟨307⟩ and "schools" teaching the rules of grammar, are created for a linguistic community. Or when an apparatus of rational orders and officials is created to serve the purposes of "domination". And conversely, almost every societization will engender some ("societationally *conditioned*") consensual action among the societized members that transcends the limits of its rational purposes. Every bowling club has "conventional" consequences for the behaviour of its members towards one another – in other words: it gives rise to communal action that lies outside the societization and is oriented towards "consensus".

When he acts, an individual constantly participates in numerous and always varying [forms of] communal, consensual and societized action. Every communal act [that he performs] may conceivably be related, in terms of its meaning, to a different set of actions on the part of others, and to different [forms of] consensus and societization. The more numerous and diverse (in terms of the nature of the probabilities constitutive for them) the sets [of actions] towards which the individual *rationally* orientates his [own] action, the further advanced is the "rational societal *differentation*"; and the more [his action] assumes the character of *societization*, the more advanced is the "rational societal *organization*". And, naturally, the individual can through one and the same act (as part of his action) participate in numerous kinds of communal action: An act of exchange that somebody carries out with X, who is the legal representative of Y, who in turn is an "organ" of a purposive association, includes (1) a verbal and (2) a written societization; an exchange societization (3) with X personally; (4) with Y personally; and (5) with the societized action of the participants in that purposive association; [moreover,] (6) the act of exchange has, in its conditions, in part been oriented towards expectations concerning the potential action of other prospective exchange participants (competitors on both sides) and towards the corresponding instances of consensus concerning legality, and so on. An act must be an instance of communal action in order to qualify as consensual *action*, but not in order to be consensus-*oriented*. Any disposition of someone's stores of goods and possessions will normally only become possible if it is probable that it will enjoy the protection provided by the coercive apparatus of the political community. But, even apart from that, every such disposition is also consensus-oriented when, and to the extent that, it is made with a view to the possibility of changing one's own stores of goods through an exchange with others. [This is true] to an even greater extent of "private economic management" in a money economy, which encompasses both societized, consensual and communal action. ⟨308⟩ Only the purely limiting case of the Robinsonade ⟨309⟩ completely lacks all communal action, and therefore also all consensus-oriented action, since it is, in terms of its meaning, only oriented towards expectations concerning the behaviour of natural objects. Therefore, the very fact that [the Robinsonade] is conceivable is sufficient to illustrate clearly that not all "*economic*" action, already from a purely conceptual point of view, includes *communal* action. The situation is rather, speaking quite generally, the following: precisely the conceptually "purest" types in the various spheres of action lie beyond communal action and consensus. This holds for the domain of religion, as for that of the economy [and] of scientific and aesthetic conceptions. "Objectivization" will – not necessarily, but as a rule – quickly lead to communal action, and especially – again: if not necessarily always, at least as a rule – to consensual action.

After all that has been said, one should on no account somehow identify communal action, consensus and societization with the idea of [being] "with and for one another", as opposed to being "against one another". For us, not only the completely amorphous communitization (as is quite evident) but also "consensus" are in no way identical with "exclusiveness" towards others. It depends on the individual case whether a consensual action is "open" – in other words: anyone who wants it can join it at any time – or whether, and to what extent, it is "closed" – in other words: the participants make the participation of others impossible, either purely consensually or by agreement. A concrete language community or market community has (mostly fluid) boundaries at some point. That is to say: normally, not every human being can be taken into consideration in the "expectations" as an actual or potential participant in the consensus, but only a certain number of people, who can often only be delimited quite vaguely. But the participants in a language community, for instance, normally have no interest in excluding other persons from the consensus (but, of course, occasionally from a concrete conversation); and the persons who are interested in a market are also often interested in an "enlargement" of the market. Nevertheless, both a language (which can be sacred, status-linked or secret) and a market may be monopolistically "closed" by consensus and societization. And on the other hand, even the participation (normally closed by societization) in the specific communal action of concrete political power structures may, precisely in the interests of power, be kept largely open (for "immigrants").

The participants in the consensual action *may*, by that action, pursue a common interest directed against outsiders. But this is not necessary. Consensual action is not the same as "solidarity"; nor is societal action by any means exclusively opposed to that communal human action that we call "*conflict*" (by which we shall, quite generally, understand the effort to succeed in letting one's own will prevail against that of another person who resists it, [the effort being] oriented in accordance with expectations concerning the behaviour of the other person). On the contrary: conflict potentially pervades all possible kinds of communal action. It depends on the individual case to what extent, for instance, an act of societization is an expression of solidarity directed against other persons, or of a compromise of interests, or whether it simply means a shift – desired by the participants for some reason – in the forms and the objects of the conflict, according to the average (but perhaps individually varying) subjectively intended purpose. Often, it is a combination of elements of each of the three. All consensual communities, including those linked to a feeling of the most boundless devotion (such as erotic or charitable relationships), may, in spite of that feeling, involve compelling another person in the most ruthless manner. And on the other hand, the majority of all "conflicts" involve some measure of societization or consensus. Here, as is often the case with sociological concepts, the states of affairs that they designate partly overlap, and they even do so with respect to the same characteristics, which are simply viewed from different perspectives. A conflict where no kind of communitization with the adversary is present is only a limiting case. We find ever greater fragments of a consensual communitization between the conflicting parties [when we consider a range of possible conflicts] – first, say, the assault of a [horde of] Mongols; then, the present methods of warfare, which are, however, precariously, also determined by the "law of nations"; then the knightly feud governed by regulations concerning the weapons and means of conflict ("Messieurs les Anglais, tirez les premiers!"); ‹310› then the regulated legal duel; and, finally, the friendly, unprovoked student duel, ‹311› which already falls under [the category of a] "sporting competition". And when the violent conflict is transformed into a "competition" – be it for Olympic wreaths, or electoral votes, or other instruments of power, or for social honour, or for gain – it is in its entirety played out on the basis of a rational societization, whose orders serve as "rules of the game", which determine the forms of conflict, but thereby also shift the chances [of success] in the conflict. The gradual increase in "pacification", in the sense of the decreasing importance of the use of physical force, only reduces it, but never entirely eliminates the appeal to the use of [such] force. But in the course of historical development, the use of force has increasingly been monopolized by the coercive apparatus of *one* particular kind of societization or consensual community – the political one – and has been transformed into the ordered threat of coercion by those in power and, finally, to a force that, in formal terms, acts neutrally. We shall now briefly – but only to the extent necessary in order to complement the ideal-typical concepts discussed above – have to occupy ourselves with the fact that almost every communitization is in one way or another based on (physical or psychical) "coercion".

VII "Institution" and "associative grouping"

In the examples that we have occasionally used, we have already, several times, encountered a circumstance on which we must now more particularly focus our attention: that someone becomes and remains a participant in a consensual community "without his own doing". When we are dealing with amorphous consensual action – "speaking", for instance – this need not be discussed further: in any given case, one "participates" in it when one's action fulfils the condition – that of consensus – that we have chosen as our criterion. But otherwise, the situation is not always so simple. Above, the rational "purposive association" – based on an explicit agreement on means, ends and orders – was taken to be the ideal type of a "societization". In that connection, it was already established that, and in what sense, such a "purposive association" can be regarded as a lasting structure, even though the participants change. Still, it was assumed that the "participation" of the individuals – the (on average) well-founded expectation that each of them would orient his action towards the [instituted] order – was based on specific rational agreement among all of them. However, there are very important forms of societization where the societized action is, to a large extent, just as in the case of the purposive association, ordered by human ordinances with regard to [its] ends and means – i.e. "societized" – but where it is nothing less than a fundamental condition of its existence that the individual will normally become involved in participation in the societized action – that is to say: that he, too, will be affected by expectations concerning the orientation of his action towards those orders instituted by human beings – *without* his own doing. The communal action constituting [such societizations] is precisely characterized by the fact [(1)] that, when certain objective circumstances are present with respect to a particular person, it is expected of him that he should participate in the communal action, and therefore, in particular, that he should orient his action towards the [instituted] orders; and, moreover, [(2)] that this expectation will, on average, be justified because the individuals in question are empirically regarded as being under an "obligation" to take part in the communal action constituting the community, and because there is a chance that they may, even if they resist it, be constrained to do so by a "coercive apparatus", however moderate the form of that constraint. The circumstances to which that expectation is linked in a particularly important case – that of the political community – are above all, for example: the descent from certain persons, or birth (in certain cases even just residence, or at least certain acts [committed]) within a certain territory. The normal way in which the individual enters the community is then that he is "born into" and "educated to be" a participant. We shall use the term "*institutions*" to designate communities where this is the case – that is to say: (1) where participation is ascribed to the participants, independently of declarations on their part, on the basis of purely objective circumstances (in contrast to the rational purposive association) and (2) where *one* of the factors determining action is the existence of such rational orders, instituted by human beings, and of a coercive apparatus (in contrast to those consensual communal relationships that have no intentional rational order and are therefore in that respect amorphous). Consequently, not every community into which one is normally born and educated is an "institution": not the language community, for example, nor the household community, as neither of them have such rational ordinances. On the other hand, the structural form of the political community that is usually called "state" and, for instance, the [structural form] of the religious [community] that is usually, in the strictly technical sense, called "church" [are "institutions"].

The relationship between the institution, with its rational ordinances, and the "*associative grouping*" is the same as that between societized action, oriented towards a rational agreement, and consensual action. By associative group action we shall understand action that is consensus-oriented and not oriented towards ordinances – in other words: consensual action – where

(1) the participation of the individual is ascribed consensually, and is not of his own, purposively rational doing to that effect; where, moreover, (2) despite the absence of an order [formally] instituted for that purpose, consensually *effective* orders, regulating the action of the participants consensually regarded as belonging to the associative grouping, are laid down by certain persons (the power-holders); and where, in addition, (3) those persons themselves, or others, are ready, if necessary, to exert physical or psychical coercion (no matter of what kind) against participants whose behaviour contravenes the consensus. We are, of course, as with all "consensus", dealing with the *average* unambiguously understood meaning and with the variable *average* probabilities of empirical validity. [Examples of] fairly pure types of "associative grouping", with their power-holders, are: the primeval "household community", with its "master of the house"; a "patrimonial" political structure lacking any rational ordinance, with its "lord"; the community of a "prophet" (the power-holder), with his "disciples"; [and] a religious "community" based solely on consensus (with, perhaps, a hereditary "hierarch"). Otherwise, the [associative grouping] presents no differences of principle compared to other kinds of "consensual action", and the whole casuistry pertaining to the latter [type of action] can with the same sense be applied to [the associative grouping]. In modern civilization, nearly all associative group action is nowadays, in one way or another, at least partially ordered through rational [instituted] orders (for example, the household community is heteronomously ordered through "family law" instituted by the state institution). Consequently, the transition to the "institution" is fluid, the more so since there are only very few "pure" types of institution: The more varied the institutional action that constitutes them, the more it is the rule that [this action] is not in its entirety ordered in a purposively rational fashion by ordinance. Those ordinances, for instance, that are created – let us assume in this case: [created] in a completely purposively rational manner – for [the regulation of] the societized action of political institutions and that are called "laws" will, in the first instance, at least as a general rule, only in a fragmentary manner single out situations whose rational ordering is, in the given case, desired by any interested party. Thus, the consensual action that actually constitutes the lasting existence of the structure is not only, normally, more comprehensive than the societized action within the structure that is oriented towards purposively rational ordinances (the same is the case with most purposive associations); it also, normally, precedes that [societized action] in time. The "institutional action" is the rationally ordered part of the "associative group action", and the institution is a partly rationally ordered associative grouping. Or (since the transition is, from a sociological point of view, completely fluid), [we might say] that even though the institution is a completely rational "new creation", it is not [created] in a sphere of validity that is completely "empty of associative grouping": [What happens is rather that] already existing associative group action, or action regulated by associative groupings, is transformed into a new institutional whole by "annexation" or by an integration of the existing associative groupings, and subordinated, by means of a series of ordinances to that effect, to completely new [instituted] orders applying to the action related to, and/or regulated by, the associative groupings. Or [alternatively], the associative grouping is simply replaced [by another] to which action is henceforth to be related (or, respectively, whose orders will henceforth regulate it); or only the personnel of the institutional organs – and especially of the coercive apparatus – is replaced.

It is extremely rare for new *institutional* ordinances of any kind to come into being – whether in connection with a process that can be regarded as the "fresh creation" of an institution or in the normal course of institutional action – as a result of an autonomous "agreement" among all the participants in the future action where loyalty towards the ordinance is expected, according to its average meant meaning. Instead, they almost without exception [come into being] through "*imposition*". What this means is that certain persons proclaim an ordinance as being valid for action related to or regulated by the associative grouping, and that the members of the institution (or those subject to the institutional power) actually more or less completely conform to it by loyally orienting [their] action (in terms of its meaning) more or less clearly in accordance with it. That is to say: in institutions, the order instituted by ordinance acquires empirical validity in the form of "consensus". Here, too, this [latter concept] should be carefully distinguished from "consent" or something like "tacit agreement". Here, too, it should rather be understood as the average *probability* that those persons who are "meant" to be affected by it, according to an (average) interpretation of the meaning [of the imposed ordinance], will actually in practice *treat* it as being "valid" for their behaviour – that is to say: will, on average, orient their action in conformity with it. (It is conceptually immaterial whether they do so out of fear, religious belief or reverence towards the ruler, or on the basis of purposively rational considerations, or from any other motive.) – The imposition may be autonomous – that is to say: accomplished by "institutional organs", by means of their specific institutional action in conformity with ordinances (this action being empirically valid on the strength of consensus): such as, say, the laws of an institution that is, externally, completely or partly autonomous (a "state", for instance). Or [the imposition] may be done "heteronomously", from outside, for example with respect to the societized action of the members of a church or congregation or some other institution-like associative grouping, through imposition by another (for instance, a political) associative grouping – [an imposition] to which the participants in the community conform in their heteronomously ordered communal action.

The quite overwhelming majority of all ordinances, *both* by institutions *and* by associations, do not originate in agreements; they are imposed [from above] – that is to say: imposed on communal action, on the basis of a "consensus expectation", by persons or groups of persons who have, for whatever reason, actually been able to influence that action according to their will. This actual power of imposition may in its turn be (consensually) empirically "valid" as being the prerogative of certain persons, either in their personal capacity, or determined on the basis of [certain] criteria, or to be selected according to [certain] rules (for instance by election). In such cases, these pretensions and ideas concerning a "valid" power of imposition – which are empirically valid because they actually, on average, determine the action of the participants to a sufficient extent – can be called the "constitution" of the institution in question. The extent to which [this "constitution"] is set down in rational, explicit ordinances varies very considerably. Often, precisely those questions that have the greatest practical importance are not set down [in that fashion]; indeed, this is sometimes deliberate (for reasons not to be discussed here). Consequently, ordinances are only an uncertain guide to the empirically valid power of imposition, which, in the last resort, always rests on associative group "consensus". Actually, the decisive substance of the "consensus" representing the *actually* empirically valid "constitution" is one of *probability* – [a probability] that can in each case only be estimated: what persons would those compulsory participants [of the institution] who, according to the usual interpretation, are in any given case meant to be affected by [the constitution], in the last resort, in practice and on average, [probably] "*obey*", and to what extent and in what respects would they do so? The authors of purposively rational constitutions may stipulate in them that the imposition of binding ordinances should also, for instance, be contingent on the approval by a majority of the members, or by a majority of persons designated according to certain criteria or to be selected according to [certain] rules. Of course, from the perspective of the minority, even this is still in all respects an "imposition"; and this fact was reflected in the view – which was also widespread in our country in the Middle Ages and which predominated in the Russian Mir, for example, ‹312› up until the present time – that, strictly speaking (and in spite of the officially established majority principle), a "valid" ordinance requires the approval of all those who are to be bound by it.

In substance, any power of imposition rests on "*domination*": a specific influence (which may in the concrete case vary in extent and kind) of concrete persons (prophets, kings, patrimonial lords, masters of the house, elders or other dignitaries, officials, party or other "leaders" whose sociological character exhibits highly significant *differences*) on the associative group action of others. This influence in its turn rests on characteristically varied motives, *one* of which is the probability that physical or psychical coercion, of whatever kind, may be applied. But here, too, consensual action oriented exclusively in accordance with expectations (especially of "fear" on the part of those who obey) only represents a relatively unstable limiting case. Here, too, the estimated probability that the consensus is empirically valid will be the greater (other circumstances being equal), the more one may, on average, reliably expect that those who obey do so for *one particular* reason: because they, also *subjectively*, regard the relationship of domination as "*binding*" for them. To the extent that this is (on average or approximately) the case, the relationship of domination will rest on the "*legitimacy*" consensus. Here, we encounter the problems connected with [the analysis of] domination, which is the most important foundation of nearly all approximative group action and which must necessarily be considered separately. This cannot be done here, as a crucial part of the sociological analysis [of domination] is concerned with the various possible foundations (in terms of their subjective meaning) of that "*legitimacy*" consensus, which is of fundamental importance for the specific character of the domination whenever the compliance is not determined by naked fear of directly threatening force. However, this problem cannot be discussed [simply] in passing, and consequently, we shall not now – as would otherwise have been natural – attempt to deal with the "real" problems (which begin at this point) of the sociological theory of associative groupings and institutions.

As we have seen, there has also, time and again, in individual cases been a development from concrete rational orders of purposive associative groupings to the creation of "comprehensive" consensual action. But taken as a whole, although the course of historical development that we can observe does not clearly show that consensual action is "replaced" by societization, it does indicate an ever wider-ranging purposively rational ordering of consensual action through ordinance[s] and, in particular, the increasingly frequent transformation of associative groupings into institutions ordered in a purposively rational manner.

What are the practical consequences of the rationalization of the orders of a community? In order to "know" the rules of accounting and to orient his action towards them by applying them correctly – or even incorrectly, in the individual case, because of error or for fraudulent purposes – an office clerk, or even the head of an office, obviously does not need to be aware of the rational principles on the basis of which those norms were devised. In order to calculate "correctly", we do not need to have a rational understanding of the arithmetical principles underlying, for instance, the maxim of subtraction: "2 minus 9: that is not possible, so we have to borrow 1". The empirical "validity" of elementary arithmetic is an instance of "consensual validity". But "consensus" is not the same as "understanding". The principles of arithmetic are "imposed" upon us when we are young in quite the same way as the rational instruction of a despot is imposed on [his] subject; and this is true even in the innermost sense: at first, the foundations and even the purposes [of arithmetic] are quite incomprehensible to us, but, nevertheless, it is ["imposed"] on us as being bindingly "valid". To begin with, "consensus" is therefore simply "conformity" to the customary, *because* it is customary. And this is, more or less, what it remains. To check whether our calculation is consensually "correct", we do not resort to rational considerations, but make empirical cross-checks that we have learned by practice ([i.e. have] had imposed upon us). This recurs in all areas, as when we make proper use of an electric tram, a hydraulic lift or a gun, without knowing anything about the scientific principles underlying their construction – into which even the tram conductor and the gunsmith can only be imperfectly initiated. No ordinary consumer will nowadays have even a rough knowledge of the production techniques of the goods that he uses daily, and he will mostly not even know what materials they are made of and what industry has produced them. All that he is interested in are those expectations concerning the performance of these artefacts that are of practical importance for him. The situation is no different with respect to social phenomena – money, for example. A person using money does not know how it actually acquires its peculiar characteristics (since, in fact, even professional specialists have heated arguments about that). The same [is true] of orders created in a purposively rational way. As long as the creation of a new "law" or a new paragraph in the "statutes of the association" is [still] being discussed, at least those interested persons who will in practice be especially affected by it will usually under- stand what the "meaning" of [the proposed] new order is actually meant to be. But, once it has become "familiar" practice, that meaning which its authors originally – more or less uniformly – wanted it to have may have been forgotten, or obscured by a "change of significance", so that only a minute fraction of judges and lawyers are really capable of understanding the "purpose" for which complicated legal norms were at that time agreed upon or imposed, while the "public" is [only] cognizant even of the [mere] fact that the legal norms have come into existence and are empirically valid – and therefore of the resulting "probabilities" – just so far as is absolutely necessary in order to avoid the most drastic unpleasant consequences. With the growing complexity of the [instituted] orders and the progressive differentiation of societal life, this state of affairs is becoming more and more generalized. There is no doubt that the persons best acquainted with the empirically valid meaning of instituted orders – that is to say: with the average probable "expectations" following from the fact that [those orders] were once created and are now, on average, interpreted in a certain way and guaranteed by the coercive apparatus – are precisely those who have the intention of acting systematically in *contravention* of the consensus, in other words: to "violate" or to "circumvent" those [instituted orders]. Thus, the rational orders of a societization, whether it is an institution or an association, are imposed or "suggested" by a first group of people for certain purposes (which may perhaps be conceived quite differently by different members of that group). A second group of people, the "organs" of the societization, subjectively (and more or less uniformly) interpret [the orders] – although they are *not* necessarily aware of those purposes underlying their creation – and implement them actively. A third group of people will, to the extent absolutely necessary for their private purposes, subjectively acquaint themselves (more or less closely) with the way in which [the orders] are thus usually implemented, and will orient their (legal or illegal) action towards them, because [the orders] give rise to certain expectations concerning the behaviour of other persons (the "organs", as well as the members of the institution or the association). A fourth group of people, however (the "mass"), will "traditionally" (as we usually call it) be trained to act in a way that corresponds (more or less closely) to the averagely understood meaning [of the orders], and will act in that way, mostly without knowing anything about the purpose and meaning – or even the very existence – of the orders. The empirical "validity" *precisely* of a "rational" order therefore in its turn mainly rests on consensual conformity to what is habitual, what is familiar, what one is brought up to do, what constantly recurs. If we look at its subjective structure, that type of behaviour is often even that of more or less approximately uniform mass action without any meaning-relatedness. The progressive societal differentiation and rationalization therefore – if not in absolutely every case, at least as a normal effect – mean that, on the whole, the persons affected in practice by the rational techniques and orders will be at an ever greater distance from the rational basis [of those techniques and orders]; and they will on the whole know less about that rational basis than the "savage" will know about the meaning of the magical procedures of the sorcerer [in his community]. Thus, the rationalization of community action will most certainly not result in a universalization of the knowledge about its conditionalities and interrelations, but mostly in the exact opposite. The "savage" knows infinitely more about the economic and social conditions of his own existence than "civilized man" (in the usual sense [of that term]). Nor is it universally true in that connection that the action of "civilized man" proceeds throughout in a manner that is subjectively more purposively rational. Here, the situation varies between the individual spheres of action: it is a separate problem. Instead, what gives the situation of "civilized man" its specifically "rational" flavour in this respect, in contrast to that of the "savage", is that (1) he has generally accustomed himself to *believe* that the conditions of his everyday life, whether they are called trams, or lifts, or money, or law courts, or armed forces, or medicine, are *in principle* rational in nature – that is to say: that they are human artefacts which can be rationally known, rationally created and rationally controlled. (This has certain important consequences for the character of the "consensus"). Moreover, (2) he is confident that [these conditions of life] function rationally – that is to say: according to known rules – and not irrationally, like the powers that the savage wishes to influence through his sorcerer; [confident] that one can, at least in principle, "count" on [these conditions], "*calculate*" their performance and orient one's action according to unambiguous expectations formed on the basis that they furnish. This is the reason why the rational capitalist "enterprise" has a specific interest in "rational" [instituted] orders, whose probable practical functioning can be calculated like that of a machine. More about that elsewhere.

First published in *Logos* 4 (1913), pp. 253–94.

Translated from: "Über einige Kategorien der verstehenden Soziologie" in Max Weber, *Gesammelte Aufsätze zur Wissenschaftslehre* (ed. Johannes Winckelmann), 3rd ed., Tübingen: J.C.B.Mohr (Paul Siebeck) 1968, pp. 427–74.

Max Weber originally planned to write a sociological introduction to a volume that he was to contribute to the large collective work *Grundriß der Sozialökonomik* (Outline of Social Economics) of which he had become the de facto lead editor in 1909 (see p. 273n1). He later decided against including it there; instead, he combined it with some sections on methodology (which probably included material from his earlier, also abandoned, "logical/methodological" introduction to the *Grundriß*) and published it separately as *Categories*. In its turn, *Categories* can be seen as an early version of the *Basic Concepts* with which Weber opens the first part of *WG*. There are important variations between the two texts, however, above all in terminology.

DECLARATION

The remarks in the article of our co-editor concerning our position with respect to so-called "theoretical" economics might give rise to misunderstandings. We should therefore like to declare, with all desirable clarity, that, within the framework of economics, we both attach the greatest imaginable importance to so-called "theory" – which, as we conceive it, means the rational construction of concepts, types and systems, and naturally includes the "discussions of value, price etc." which [according to our co-editor] are lacking. But we are at one in opposing *bad* theories and erroneous conceptions of their methodological *implications*. In the work that we have already published, there is sufficient evidence (even though it does not conform to the usual textbook categorizations) to show that we are actively involved precisely in [the discussion of] the problems of theoretical investigations within our science. [Our work] certainly does not imply that we "wholly renounce a science which stands on its own feet, that is to say: which works according to its own method"; on the contrary, [our work] precisely has the aim of providing our science with secure foundations. But, admittedly, we believe that our work has demonstrated that it is time to replace the alternative: "historical" or "theoretical" – [an alternative] that has governed the discussion for too long – by another and more profound characterization of the different "schools of thought" within our science.

Werner Sombart   Max Weber

First published as and translated from: "Erklärung", *Archiv für Sozialwissenschaft und Sozialpolitik* 44 (1917), p. 348.

The "Declaration" was prompted by remarks made by Edgar Jaffé (who was co-editor of the *Archive* together with Werner Sombart and Max Weber) in a review in the *Archive* of a book by Robert Liefmann (*Principles*). Here, Jaffé wrote that "the positions taken so far by the adherents of the historical school of thought – [a group] which has until now included almost every leading personality within the discipline [of economics] in Germany – in the last resort imply nothing less than the complete renunciation of a science which stands on its own feet, that is to say: which works according to its own method", and went on: "A characteristic example of this is the position taken by men like Max Weber and Werner Sombart. In spite of the extraordinary range of his knowledge and the extension of his work into a large number of adjacent fields (legal science, epistemology, sociology), [Weber] has completely neglected economic theory and also from time to time expressed a minimum of expectation with respect to the possible results of purely theoretical investigations". As for Sombart, he had emphasized the importance of placing historical research on theoretical foundations; but his conception of theory in fact only included the construction of types, and "he rejected discussions of value, price etc. as being completely superfluous".

In this connection, it is interesting to note that Weber, in a letter to Robert Liefmann of 12 December 1919 (GStA Berlin Rep. 92, Nl. Max Weber, no. 30/8) writes:
"I myself regret that I have been able to do so little – almost nothing – for theory, but one cannot do everything. I do not hold theory in less esteem. But the other things also demand to be done."

THE MEANING OF "VALUE FREEDOM" IN THE SOCIOLOGICAL AND ECONOMIC SCIENCES[1]

In what follows, except where something different is either explicitly stated or obvious from the context, the term "valuations" is to be understood as: "*practical*" evaluations of a phenomenon that is capable of being influenced by our actions, as being reprehensible or worthy of approval. The problem of the "freedom" of a particular science from this kind of valuation – i.e. the validity and meaning of that logical principle – is not in any way identical with a quite different question that will be discussed briefly right away: whether or not one *should* in *academic teaching* "profess" one's practical valuations, rooted in ethics, cultural ideals or some other world view. This [latter] question cannot be submitted to scientific discussion, since it is in itself completely dependent on practical valuations and therefore cannot be definitively settled. One can find proponents of both the following standpoints (if we only take the extreme ones): (a) it is justified to distinguish between, on the one hand, facts that are purely empirical or can be deduced logically, and, on the other hand, valuations that are practical, ethical or based on some world view; but, nevertheless (or perhaps even for that very reason), problems concerning both categories belong on the podium; (b) even if that distinction can*not* be carried through consistently, it is nevertheless advisable to keep all practical value questions as much as possible in the background in one's lectures.

Standpoint (b) seems unacceptable to me. – In particular, it seems to me that it is simply impossible to maintain the distinction, not infrequently made in our disciplines, between practical valuations of a "*party* political" nature and those which have a different character; it only serves to conceal the practical implications of the position suggestively conveyed to the audience. But if one does actually include valuations in one's lectures, only a bureaucrat would maintain that the academic platform requires a "lack of passion" and that one should therefore avoid subjects which threaten to arouse "heated" debate – a position that should be rejected by any

1   Revised version of a memorandum submitted in 1913 for an internal discussion in the Committee of the "Association for Social Policy" and printed for private circulation. As far as possible, all [the elements] that were only of interest for that body have been deleted, [while] the general methodological reflections have been expanded. Among the other memoranda submitted for that discussion, that written by professor Spranger has been published (Spranger, *Value Judgements*). I must confess that I find that work – by a philosopher whom I, too, hold in high esteem – curiously weak, because it has not been sufficiently clearly developed; but already considerations of space have led me to avoid any polemics with him and to restrict myself to presenting my own position.

independent[-minded] lecturer. Of the scholars who felt that they did *not* have to forgo making practical valuations in empirical discussions, the most passionate ones – such as Treitschke, for example, and (in his own way) also Mommsen – were actually the easiest to put up with. Precisely because of the intensity of the emotion affecting [the lecturer], the student is at least put in a position where *he* is able to evaluate the extent to which the subjectivity of the lecturer's valuation may have resulted in a possible distortion of his statements; thus, the student can do for himself what the lecturer was temperamentally incapable of doing. In that way, it would be possible to preserve the effect of genuine pathos on youthful minds which the advocates of valuations in academic teaching would like those valuations to achieve; at the same time, the student would not be misled into confusing different spheres with each other – [a confusion] which must arise when the statement of empirical facts and the exhortation to [take] a practical stand on great existential problems are both tempered by the same cool lack of passion.

Standpoint (a) seems to me (viewed, it should be noted, from the subjective standpoint of its own proponents) to be acceptable *if*, and only if, the academic teacher sets himself the absolute duty of making relentlessly clear to the audience and, above all, to himself – in every single case, and even at the risk of making his lecture less elegant – *what* parts of his lecture represent either purely logical deductions or purely empirical statements of fact, and *what* parts of it contain practical valuations. But it does seem to me that it is a clear dictate of intellectual integrity to do this, once the disjunction between the [two] spheres is conceded; in that case, it is the absolute minimum of what is required.

On the other hand, the question whether or not practical value judgements are *at all* admissible in academic teaching (even subject to [the foregoing] proviso), is one of practical university policy. It can therefore only, in the last analysis, be settled with reference to the tasks that each individual, on the basis of *his* valuations, wishes to assign to the universities. If someone claims that the universities – and therefore also he himself, *by virtue of* his qualifications as an academic teacher – should still today assume the universal role of forming personalities and of propagating political, ethical, artistic, cultural or other opinions, his attitude to [the question of the admissibility of value judgements in university teaching] will be different from [the attitude] of someone who believes that he must acknowledge the fact (and the consequences of the fact) that the really valuable effects of academic lectures are actually only achieved when persons with *specialist* qualifications provide *specialist* instruction, and that "intellectual integrity" is therefore the only specific virtue which [academic instruction] should seek to inculcate. The first standpoint may be propounded on the basis of just as many different ultimate positions as the second one. As for the second standpoint (which I personally accept), it can be derived both from an overwhelmingly positive and from a thoroughly modest assessment of the importance of "specialist" training. For instance, it is not necessarily [held] because one hopes that everybody should become, in the inner sense, as much of a pure "specialist" as possible. On the contrary, [it may be held] because one does *not* want to see the most fundamental, completely personal decisions that a person has to make on his own regarding his life lumped together with *specialist* training (however highly one may rate the importance of [specialist] training, not only for the general intellectual education of young people, but also – indirectly – for their self-discipline and moral attitude); and [because one does not wish to see] the students prevented, by suggestive comments made from the academic platform, from solving those [fundamental questions] according to their own conscience.

Personally, I find Professor v. Schmoller's prejudice in favour of [the profession of] value judgements in academic teaching quite intelligible as the echo of a great epoch that he and his friends helped to create. But, in my opinion, even he surely cannot have failed to notice that, in actual fact, the situation of the young generation has changed considerably in one important respect. Forty years ago, it was widely believed in the scholarly circles of our disciplines that, in the domain of practical and political valuations, one of the possible positions must in the last resort be the only *ethically* correct one. (Admittedly, Schmoller himself has always only to a very limited extent been of that opinion.) However, it can easily be ascertained that, particularly among those in favour of [the profession of] value judgements in academic teaching, this is nowadays no longer the case. When it is claimed today that such professions of value judgements are legitimate, that claim is no longer made in the name of ethical demands [based on] (relatively) straightforward postulates of justice – postulates whose ultimate basis, and whose consequences, either were or seemed to be (relatively) simple, and above all (relatively) impersonal because of their indisputable, specifically *supra*personal character. Instead, [the profession of valuations in academic teaching is nowadays,] as the result of an inevitable development, [claimed to be legitimate in the name of] a motley bunch of "cultural valuations" – which actually express subjective expectations *from* culture – or, quite openly, the alleged "right of the personality" of the teacher. [My own] position – which may be shocking to some, but which can hardly be refuted, as it, too, contains a "practical valuation" – is that, among all kinds of prophecy, the only completely intolerable one is the (in this sense) "personally" coloured *professorial prophecy*. Surely, this is an unexampled situation: [We have] large numbers of officially certified prophets who do not do their preaching publicly: in the streets, or in churches, or in some other way; nor, if they [do it] privately, do they do so in personally selected, self-professed conventicles of faith. Instead, [these prophets] arrogate to themselves the right, "in the name of science", to deliver themselves of authoritative rulings on world views from the academic platform, in the ostensibly objective, uncontrollable, discussionless and quiet [atmosphere] of the officially privileged lecture hall, and thus carefully shielded against any contradiction. It is an old-established principle (vigorously defended by Schmoller on one occasion) that what takes place in the lecture hall should not become the object of public discussion. It is quite possible to hold the opinion that this [principle] can occasionally have certain negative consequences, even in the field of empirical science; however, the assumption – which I share – is that the "lecture" ought, after all, to be something else than a "talk", and that the strict, matter-of-fact, sober impartiality of an academic exposition would suffer, to the detriment of [its] pedagogical purpose, if the public – the public media, for instance – [were able to] interfere. But, in any case, this privilege of freedom from [outside] control only seems appropriate as far as the purely *specialist* qualifications of the professor are concerned. But there is no specialist qualification for personal prophecy, which therefore should not benefit from that privilege. At present, students are *forced to* attend certain institutes of higher education, and therefore also [the lectures given by] the teachers there, in order to get on in life. But [the "prophet"] should on no account exploit this situation by providing the students, not only with what they need for that purpose – that is to say: the awakening and training of their faculty of understanding and their intellect, and along with that: [a certain amount of factual] knowledge – but also with his own so-called "world view", which is no doubt occasionally quite interesting, but often quite trivial, and which he can offer without fear of contradiction.

The professor, like everybody else, has other opportunities for propagating his practical ideals; and, if they are lacking, he can easily create them in an appropriate form: experience shows that every honest attempt to do this [will succeed]. But the professor should not claim to possess, *as a professor*, particular gifts for being a statesman or a cultural reformer – and he does just that when he uses [his] untroubled position on the academic platform [to express] his sentiments concerning statesmanship or cultural policy. In the press, in public meetings, in associations, in essays – [in short:] in any form that is also available to any other citizen – [the professor] may (and should) do what his god or his daemon ‹313› calls upon him to do. But what the student should above all learn from their professor in the *lecture hall* is: (1) the ability to content himself with simply carrying out a given task; (2) to face facts – including (indeed: above all) those that are uncomfortable for him personally – and to distinguish between stating [such facts] and taking an evaluative stand with regard to them; (3) to rate his own person less highly than the task [before him]; and, consequently, to suppress the desire to parade, unbidden, his personal tastes or other feelings. In my opinion, this is today vastly more urgent than, say, forty years ago, when this particular problem really did not exist in that form. It has been claimed that "personality" is, and should be, a "unity" in the sense that it would, so to speak, be lost if it did not manifest itself on every [possible] occasion; but this simply *is not true*. In any *profession*, the *task* as such has its claims and must be performed in accordance with its own inherent laws. Any person who has to carry out a professional task must confine himself [to it] and eliminate everything that is not *material* [to it] – and especially his own loves and hates. And it is *not true* that a strong personality reveals itself by first looking, on every occasion, for its own unique, completely "personal touch". Instead, one would wish that, in particular, that generation which is now reaching manhood will again, more than anything else, get accustomed to the idea that "being a personality" is not something that one can set as a deliberate goal, and that there is only one way in which one can (perhaps!) become [a personality]: by committing oneself unreservedly to a "cause", whatever [that cause] and the "claims of the day" ‹314› entailed by it may look like in the individual case. It is in poor taste to mix up one's personal affairs with dispassionate discussions of professional matters. And the "vocation" loses the only really significant meaning that it still retains today if one does not fully exercise that specific form of self-restraint which it requires. The fashionable cult of the personality – whether it endeavours to live itself out on the throne, in the public office or in the academic chair – almost invariably achieves an outward effect; but its intrinsic pettiness is always apparent, and it is always detrimental to the cause. I hope that I do not have to emphasize that worshipping personality in *this* way: simply because it is "personal", is something that is quite certainly completely foreign to precisely those persons whose views I oppose here. Some see the responsibilities of the [academic] teacher in another light; and some have other educational ideals, which I respect but do not share. However, we must consider, not only their intentions, but also how [the views] that they legitimate by their authority must *affect* a generation which in any event, inevitably, has a pronounced predisposition to take itself [too] seriously.

Finally, it should hardly be necessary to point out that many of the pretended *opponents* of (political) value judgements in academic teaching certainly have no justification at all when they invoke the principle of the elimination of "value judgements" (a principle, moreover, that they often thoroughly misunderstand) in order to discredit discussions of cultural and social policy which take place, quite publicly, *outside* the universities. There is no doubt that such spuriously value-free, tendentious elements exist and, moreover, that they are, within our own discipline, supported by the obstinate and deliberate partisanship of strong interest groups. Against this background, it is undoubtedly understandable that a considerable number of academics – precisely among those who are of independent mind – nowadays persist in making valuations in academic teaching, because they are too proud to participate in this mimicry of a purely feigned "value freedom". In spite of this, my personal view is that one should do the (in my opinion) right thing: The practical valuations of a scholar who restricts himself to professing them, on suitable occasions, outside the lecture hall, will have even greater weight if it is known that, in his lectures, he is disciplined enough to do nothing but his "professional duty". However, all this raises questions of practical valuations, to which no answer with binding force can therefore be given.

In any case, if the right to profess valuations in academic teaching is invoked *in principle*, this [position] can in my opinion only be consistently held when it is at the same time guaranteed that *all* partisan valuations will have an opportunity to assert themselves on the academic platform.[1] In Germany, those who underline the right of academic teachers to profess valuations usually advocate the exact opposite of the principle of equal representation of all – even the most "extreme" – tendencies. For instance, given Schmoller's personal position, it was of course logical for him to declare that "Marxists and Manchesterites" ‹316› were disqualified from holding academic chairs – although he, in particular, was never so unjust as to ignore the *scholarly* accomplishments of precisely those circles. But it is on just these points that I have personally never been able to agree with our esteemed master. Surely it is obvious that one cannot in the same breath demand the acceptance of value judgements in academic teaching and then, when the consequences of this position have to be drawn, stress that universities are state institutions for the training of civil servants who are "loyal to the state". As a consequence [of this reasoning], the universities would not become "colleges for professional training" (which many university teachers find so degrading): instead, they would become theological seminaries, but without the religious dignity attaching to [such seminaries]. Admittedly, attempts have been made to construct certain barriers by means of "logical" inference. One of our foremost jurists has occasionally, while declaring himself to be *opposed to* the exclusion of socialists from the academic platform, stated that he, too, would at least not be willing to accept an "anarchist" as a teacher of law, since [an "anarchist"] denied the validity of law in general – an argument that he apparently regarded as conclusive. I hold precisely the opposite view. An anarchist can certainly be a good legal scholar. If so, then precisely that (so to speak) Archimedean point which he occupies by virtue of his objective convictions (provided they are genuine) and which lies *outside* the conventions and assumptions that are so self-evident to us, may enable him to see that the basic tenets of ordinary legal theory contain problems which will be overlooked by everybody who takes [those tenets] too much for granted. The most radical doubt is the father of knowledge. The jurist is no more responsible for "proving" the value of the cultural goods whose existence is bound up with the existence of "law" than the doctor is responsible for "demonstrating" that the prolongation of life is desirable under any circumstances. Indeed, neither is at all able to do so with the means at his disposal. But if one wanted to use the academic platform as a forum for practical value discussions, then it would obviously be one's duty to lay the most fundamental questions of principle, in particular, open to unfettered discussion from every point of view. Can this be done? Today, precisely the most decisive and important questions of practical–political values are *excluded* from [discussion in] the lecture halls of German universities by the very nature of the political situation. Anyone who puts the interests of the nation above *all* its concrete institutions, without exception, will, for instance, regard it as a question of central importance whether the prevailing view of the position of the monarch in Germany ‹317› is compatible with the global interests of the nation and with the instruments for safeguarding those interests (war and diplomacy). Those who would today be inclined to answer this question in the negative, and to doubt whether lasting success in those two areas can be achieved as long as there have not been thorough changes in that respect, are not always the worst patriots, nor are they in any way anti-monarchists. But everybody

---

1   For that purpose, it is certainly not enough to apply the Dutch system: [in the Netherlands], even the theological faculty has been released from confessional requirements; but there is full freedom to found universities, provided their financing is guaranteed and standards of qualifications for the appointment of professors are respected; and private persons may found university chairs and propose candidates ‹315› for appointments to them. That [system] simply gives an advantage to those who have money, and to authoritarian organizations already in power, and it is well known that only clerical groups have made use of it.

knows that those vital national questions cannot be discussed completely freely in the lecture halls of German universities.[1] However, in view of that fact – the permanent exclusion from free discussion on the academic platform of just those valuational questions that are the crucial ones in terms of practical policy – it seems to me that the only [course of action] consonant with the dignity of a representative of science is to *keep silent* about even those value problems that he is obligingly allowed to discuss.

The question – which has an evaluative basis and therefore cannot be bindingly answered – whether one may, or must, or should, profess practical valuations in [*academic*] *teaching* should on no account in any way be mixed up with the purely *logical* discussion of the role played by value judgements in empirical disciplines such as sociology and economics. Otherwise, this would make it more difficult to have an unbiased discussion of the actual logical position; and the conclusions [of this latter discussion] will in themselves give no indications concerning the [first] one, apart from the purely logical requirement that the teacher should be clear and strictly distinguish between the [two] heterogeneous problem spheres.

Another point that I do not wish to discuss is whether it is "difficult" to separate empirical statements of fact from valuation. It is difficult. All of us, [including] the undersigned advocate of this demand, offend against [that principle], time and again. But at least the adherents of so-called "*ethical*" economics should be aware that the moral law, too, cannot be fulfilled, but is nevertheless regarded as a "duty". And if we examine our consciences, we may find that the main reason why it is so difficult to live up to [the principle of separation between the two problem spheres] is that we are reluctant to deny ourselves [the pleasure of] entering the highly interesting domain of valuations, in particular if they have that titillating "personal touch". Every university teacher will naturally [have] notice[d] that the faces of his students light up in anticipation when he begins to "profess" [his beliefs], and also that the expectation [of such "professions"] has an extremely favourable influence on the size of the audience at his lectures. It is also common knowledge that, because of the competition for students, ‹318› a prophet – however minor – who can fill an auditorium will often, when it comes to advancements, have an advantage over others whose scholarship may be much weightier and whose teaching may be much more *sober* – unless the[ir] prophecy happened to be too far removed from the valuations that are, politically or conventionally, regarded as normal in the concrete case. Only the *pseudo-value-free* prophet representing material interests has even better chances, because of the influence [of those interests] on the political powers. In my opinion, all th[ese phenomena] are undesirable, and I shall therefore abstain from examining the claim that the demand for the exclusion of practical valuations is "narrow-minded" and would make the lectures "boring". I shall leave open the question whether the academic teacher should above all endeavour to make lectures dealing with factual, empirical subjects "interesting"; but, for my own part, I fear that, if students are stimulated by too many personal touches, this might at any rate eventually make them lose their taste for simple work on the allotted task.

Another point, which I do not want to discuss but to recognize explicitly, is the following: precisely by *pretending* to eliminate all practical valuations and by "letting the facts speak for themselves" in the well-known fashion, it is possible to evoke such [practical valuations] particularly strongly and suggestively. The better varieties of rhetoric deployed in parliament and on the hustings make use – quite legitimately, for their purposes – of just that device. It is not necessary to waste a single word to stress that, if [that device] were employed on the academic

---

1 That [situation] is not peculiar to Germany. In practice, [such] barriers exist, openly or tacitly, in almost every country. They only differ with respect to the character of the value problems thus excluded [from discussion].

rostrum, this would, from the perspective of the demand for distinguishing [between statements of fact and valuations], constitute the most reprehensible of all [possible] abuses. But the fact that it is possible to make a deceptive pretence of actually living up to an imperative surely does not imply any criticism of the imperative in itself. And that imperative is as follows: *if* the teacher does not feel that he should abstain from [professing] practical valuations, he should make [their valuational character] absolutely *clear,* to the students *and to himself.*

And finally: what must be combated with the greatest possible determination is the idea (which is not infrequently met with) that one can come closer to scientific "objectivity" by weighing the different valuations against each other and [finding] a "statesmanlike" compromise. Not only is it *just as impossible,* with the means of empirical disciplines, to prove the [correctness of the] "middle course" as [that of] the most "extreme" valuations. On the contrary: within the sphere of *valuation,* [the "middle course"] is the least unambiguous one from a *normative* point of view. It does not belong in the lecture halls, but in political programmes, party headquarters and parliaments. The normative and empirical sciences can only render the political actors and the warring parties *one* invaluable service: that of saying to them: (1) With respect to this practical problem, the following different "ultimate" positions are *conceivable;* and (2) such and such are the facts that you have to take into account when choosing between those positions. That brings us to the "matter" before us. ‹319›

The term "value judgement" has given rise to endless misunderstanding and to controversy, above all of a terminological (and therefore utterly sterile) nature, and this has obviously contributed nothing at all to the substance of the matter. As was said at the beginning of this article, it is perfectly clear that in these discussions, as far as our discipline is concerned, the issue is that of *practical* valuations of social facts as being practically desirable or undesirable, whether on ethical or on cultural grounds or for some other reason. In spite of all that has been said on this subject,[1] it has, in all seriousness, been "objected" that science wishes to achieve results that are "valuable" – both in the sense (1) that, logically and factually, [they are] judged to be *correct* and (2) that they are *significant* from the point of view of scientific interest – and, furthermore, that the selection of the material already implies a "valuation". There is another, almost incredibly strong and constantly recurring misconception: as though it were claimed that empirical science cannot treat "subjective" human valuations as an *object* [of investigation] – although sociology, and the whole theory of marginal utility ‹320› in the field of economics, are based on the opposite assumption. But all that [our position] amounts to is the demand – which is in itself quite trivial – that, in his research and exposition, the scholar should keep [two things] completely *apart:* [on the one hand,] statements concerning empirical facts (including the "valuational" conduct that he observes in empirical human beings investigated by him); and[, on the other hand], his *own* practical, valuational position – that is to say: his *judgement* of those facts (including any "valuations" by empirical human beings, if [those valuations] are made the object of an investigation by him) as being desirable or undesirable – [a position] that is, in that sense, an "evaluating" one. [He should make that strict distinction] because those two [sets of] problems are simply heterogeneous. In an – otherwise valuable – treatise, [its] author argues that a scholar can also take his own valuation as a "fact" and then draw conclusions

---

1   I must refer to what I have said in preceding articles [*Objectivity, Critical Studies* and *Stammler*]. (Quite possibly, the specific formulations may occasionally not be sufficiently correct, but this should not concern any point of substantive importance.) With respect to the impossibility of resolving [the conflict between] certain ultimate value judgements concerning an important group of problems, I should like to refer in particular, among other [works], to G[ustav] Radbruch's *Introduction to Legal Science*[2]. My position differs from his on certain points; but they are not germane to the problem under discussion here.

from it. What is meant by this statement is indisputably correct; but the expression chosen is just as certainly misleading. When holding a discussion, it is of course possible to agree beforehand that a certain practical measure – for instance, that the cost of increasing the size of the armed forces is to be borne by the propertied [classes] – should be taken as a "presupposition" in the discussion and that only the *means* of bringing it about should be discussed. This is often quite practical. But, surely, such a practical aim, which has been agreed on in advance, is not called a "fact" but a "goal that has been set a priori". And the discussion of the "means" would very quickly show that those two things are different, not only terminologically but also in substance – unless the "goal set in advance" and not to be discussed were as concrete as that of lighting a cigar. In that case, though, it is hardly ever necessary to discuss the means. On the other hand, in almost *every* case where one is dealing with an aim couched in more general terms (for instance that which was just chosen as an example), experience will show that the individual participants in the discussion have quite different conceptions of that goal which was supposed to be unambiguous. Moreover, and in particular, one may find that the ultimate reasons for desiring exactly the *same* end may differ widely, and that this has an influence on the discussion of the means. But let us leave this aside. At least, it has not yet occurred to anyone to dispute the fact that one *can* take as one's point of departure a certain agreed goal and only discuss the means for achieving it, and that this *can* result in a discussion in purely empirical terms. But the whole of [this] discussion precisely concerns the choice of goals, not of "means" [towards] a given goal – in other words: in what sense it is possible *not* just to accept the valuation on which the individual bases himself as a "fact", but to make it the object of scientific *criticism*. If this [point] is not kept in mind, then any further debate is useless. –

What is actually not at all under discussion is the question whether practical valuations, and in particular ethical ones, may lay claim to a *normative* status, and therefore have a different character than, say, the question – which has been quoted as an example – whether one should prefer blondes to brunettes, or similar subjective questions of taste. Those are problems for a philosophy of values, not for the methodology of the empirical disciplines. The only important point for that [methodology] is that the validity of a practical imperative as a norm, on the one hand, and the truth value of an empirical statement of fact, on the other hand, belong on absolutely heterogeneous levels of the problem, and that the specific dignity of *each* is impaired if one fails to appreciate this and tries to force the two spheres together. In my opinion, this [error] has been committed to a considerable extent, in particular by Professor v. Schmoller.[1] Particularly in view of my esteem for our [great] master, I cannot pass over the points where I feel unable to agree with him.

[It has been argued that] the advocates of "value freedom" regard the fact that the evaluative positions prevailing at a given time vary historically and from one person to another as sufficient proof that ethics, for instance, can necessarily only have a "subjective" character. Let me first of all say that this is not correct. Statements of empirical fact, too, are frequently subject to great controversy; and there may often be far more general agreement that somebody is to be considered a scoundrel than (especially among specialists) concerning the question of how to interpret a damaged inscription. Schmoller believes that there is a growing conventional consensus among all religious denominations and individuals concerning the main elements of the practical valuations; however, this stands in sharp contrast to my own impression, which is the opposite one. But anyway, that is irrelevant to our problem. What should in any case be opposed is the view that science can content itself with the fact that a certain practical position of this kind, however widely accepted it might be, is conventionally viewed as self-evident. The specific

1   In his article (*Theory*[3]) in the *Handwörterbuch der Staatswissenschaften*.

function of science is in my opinion exactly the opposite one: it should see a *problem* in anything that is conventionally self-evident. After all, this was what Schmoller and his friends themselves did in their day. Again, one may investigate the *causal* effect that the *actual* existence of certain ethical or religious convictions has on economic life, and possibly estimate it as being considerable; but surely this does not imply that, because those convictions have perhaps been causally very effective, one therefore has to *share* them or at least to regard them as "valuable". On the other hand, even if one acknowledges the great value of some ethical or religious phenomenon, this does not in any way imply that [one] would also regard the unforeseen consequences of realizing this phenomenon [in practice] as being equally positive. Statements of fact are immaterial to those questions; and [different] individuals would necessarily reach quite different conclusions concerning [those questions], on the basis of their own practical valuations concerning religion and other matters. All this has nothing to do with the matter in dispute. On the other hand, I most emphatically deny that a "realistic" science of ethics – that is to say: [one that] demonstrates how the ethical views prevalent at a given time within a certain group of people have been influenced by the other conditions of life [of those people], and have in their turn influenced [those conditions] – can for its part produce an "ethics" that can ever say anything about what *ought to be* the case. In just the same way, a "realistic" description of the astronomical ideas of, say, the Chinese – in other words: one that demonstrated their practical motives for pursuing astronomy, how they did so, what their results were, and how they arrived at them – could never aim at proving the correctness of that Chinese astronomy. And, in the same way, by demonstrating that the Roman agrimensors, ‹321› or (even when dividing very large estates) the Florentine bankers, ‹322› with their methods, quite often arrived at results incompatible with trigonometry or the multiplication table, one cannot put into question the validity of the latter. Empirical–psychological and historical investigation of a particular valuational position, with a view to determining its individual, social and historical causes, can never, under any circumstances, lead to anything else than *the explanation of it by means of understanding*. That is by no means [a] negligible [result]. [First of all], it is desirable because it has the incidental personal (albeit not scientific) effect of making it easier to "do justice", from a personal point of view, to somebody who – in fact or apparently – holds other views. But, moreover, it is extremely important from the scientific point of view, in two respects: (1) for learning about the *real* ultimate *motives* of human action, when the aim is to make an empirical causal study of such action; and, (2) for determining one's own and the opponent's real valuational positions when one is engaged in discussion with someone whose values are (in fact or apparently) different from one's own. The true purpose of a discussion of *values* is to grasp what the opponent (or oneself) really means – the value, that is, which is the real, not just the apparent, concern of each the two parties – in order to make it at all possible to define a position with respect to [that value]. From the point of view of the demand for the "value freedom" of empirical analysis, it is therefore far from sterile, let alone absurd, to discuss valuations: but if discussions of that kind are to be useful, one has to realize what their true purpose is. The elementary precondition of such discussions is to understand that [certain] ultimate valuations may in principle and irreconcilably *diverge*: "To understand all" is not "to forgive all"; ‹323› and, in itself, an understanding of the other person's position does not in any way lead to an acceptance of it. It may just as easily, and often with far greater probability, lead one to realize that agreement is *not* possible, as well as why – and where – it is not possible. That [kind of] knowledge *is* true knowledge, and "discussions of valuations" *do* precisely have the aim [of attaining it]. But what one certainly does not arrive at in this way – since it lies in just the opposite direction – is any kind of normative ethics or, more generally, [the demonstration of] the binding force of any "imperative". On the contrary: it is common knowledge that the – at least apparent –

"relativizing" effect of such discussions will rather make it more difficult to reach that goal. On the other hand, this of course does not mean that one should avoid them. Quite the contrary: an "ethical" conviction that can be unseated by the psychological "understanding" of other valuations has been *worth* no more than religious beliefs that (as sometimes also happens) are destroyed by scientific knowledge. Finally, when Schmoller assumes that the advocates of "value freedom" in the empirical disciplines would only be able to acknowledge "formal" ethical truths (by which he apparently means: in the sense of [Kant's] *Critique of Practical Reason* ‹324›), this calls for a few comments, although the problem is not necessarily germane to our [main] subject.

First of all, Schmoller's view according to which ethical imperatives can be identified with "cultural values" (even the most lofty ones) must be rejected: There may be positions where cultural values are "duties", even where they are in inevitable and irremediable conflict with every possible kind of ethic. Conversely, an ethic may without any internal contradiction reject all cultural values. In any case, the two value spheres are not identical. It is also a grave, but widespread, misunderstanding that "formal" propositions – such as those, say, of Kantian ethics – do not contain any *substantive* directives. The possibility of a normative ethic, however, is by no means called into question merely because there are problems of a *practical* kind for [the solution of] which such a normative ethic cannot by itself provide any unambiguous directives. (In my opinion, certain problems of an institutional – and therefore "social–political" – nature quite specifically belong to the group [of such problems]). Nor [is the possibility of a normative ethic called into question] because [of the fact that] ethics is not the only thing that has "validity" in the world, and that other value spheres exist besides it – [spheres] whose values can perhaps only be realized by assuming ethical "guilt". This applies particularly to the sphere of political action. In my view, it would be a sign of weakness to deny the tension between political action, in particular, and the ethical [sphere]. But this is not something that is peculiar to [the political sphere], contrary to the impression given when "private" morality is customarily opposed to "political" morality. – Let us examine some of the "limits" of ethics mentioned above.

Among the questions that *no* ethics can decide unequivocally is [that concerning] the consequences of the fundamental principle of "justice". Whether, for instance, much is owed to those who accomplish much (this would probably correspond most closely to the views that Schmoller once put forward), or [whether], on the contrary, much is demanded of those who can accomplish much; in other words: whether one ought, in the name of justice (as other points of view – for instance [the need for] sufficient "incentives" – must then be ruled out), to offer great opportunities to great talents, or whether, on the contrary, (as Babeuf [thought] ‹325›), one should balance out the injustice of the unequal distribution of mental capacities by rigorously ensuring that talents – which in themselves give those who possess them an exhilarating feeling of prestige – should not also be able to exploit their better opportunities in the world to their own advantage, these [questions] cannot be bindingly decided on the basis of "ethical" premises. However, this is the type of *ethical* problem relevant to most of the questions concerning social policy.

But in the sphere of personal conduct, too, there are quite specific, fundamental ethical problems that ethics cannot settle on the basis of its own presuppositions. They include, above all, the fundamental question whether the intrinsic value of ethical conduct (usually referred to as the "pure will" or the "conviction") is in itself sufficient to justify this conduct, in accordance with the maxim "The Christian acts rightly and leaves the outcome to God", ‹326› as it has been formulated by Christian moralists; or whether the responsibility for those *consequences* of the action that can be foreseen as possible or probable, because this action is enmeshed in the ethically irrational world, should also be taken into account. In the social sphere, all radically revolutionary political attitudes, especially so-called "syndicalism", ‹327› are based on the first [of those] principles, while all "Realpolitik" ‹328› is based on the second one. Both invoke ethical maxims. But these maxims are in eternal conflict with each other, a conflict that no ethic can, in and of itself, provide the means for resolving.

These two ethical maxims have a strictly "formal" character; in that respect, they resemble the well-known axioms from [Kant's] *Critique of Practical Reason*. It is widely believed that those [Kantian] axioms, because of their formal character, do not contain any substantive indications at all for the evaluation of conduct. As I have already said, this is by no means the case. Let us deliberately choose an example as far removed as possible from all "politics", which may perhaps make clearer what that much-discussed "merely formal" character means. Let us suppose that a man says of his erotic relationship with a woman: "At first, our relationship was only a passion; now, it is a value". In the cool and dispassionate terms of Kantian ethics, the first half of that sentence would be expressed as follows: "At first, we were *only means* for each other". This would amount to a claim that the whole sentence was a special case of the well-known [Kantian] principle, ‹329› which is, strangely enough, often interpreted as a purely historically conditioned expression of "individualism", although it is in fact a quite brilliant formulation [covering] an immense multitude of ethical situations, but which must of course be correctly understood. In its negative version, and in the absence of any indication of what might, in positive terms, be the opposite of the – ethically reprehensible – treatment of another person "only as a means", [that statement] obviously contains (1) an acknowledgement of the existence of independent value spheres separate from [the] ethical [one] and (2) a demarcation between the ethical sphere and those [other ones]; and, finally, (3) it affirms that, and in what sense, the ethical status of actions oriented towards values other than ethical ones may be different [in different cases]. In fact, those value spheres that allow or prescribe the treatment of another person "only as a means" are heterogeneous to [the sphere of] ethics. This [point] cannot be developed further in this context; but, at any rate, one finds that, even in the case of the extremely abstract [Kantian] ethical principle, its "formal" character does not mean that it remains indifferent to the *substance* of the action. – However, the problem becomes even more complicated. The negative evaluation implied by the words "only a passion" may, from a particular point of view, be regarded as an insult to what is, in the deepest sense, most genuine and real in life – as a denigration of the only, or at any rate the high, road leading away from those value mechanisms that are impersonal or supra-personal, and therefore inimical to life; away from the enslavement to the stony lifelessness of everyday existence; away from the pretentiousness of unreal "obligations". [The proponents] of this view would probably scorn the term "value" as a designation of the extremely concrete experience to which it refers; but it is at any rate possible to imagine a version of that view which would nevertheless constitute a sphere that was equally foreign and hostile to everything sacred or good, to every ethical or aesthetic law, to every cultural significance or valuation of personality, but would still – and perhaps even for that reason – claim an independent and, in the most extreme sense of the word, "immanent" status. Whatever may be our atttude with respect to that claim, it is at least impossible to prove or "refute" it with the means afforded by any "science".

As old [John Stuart] Mill has remarked, any empirical observation of these facts would make one realize that the only metaphysics that fits them is [that of] absolute polytheism. ‹330› Moreover, if a consideration that was not empirical but aimed at the interpretation of meaning – in other words: a genuine philosophy of values – went one step further, it would have to acknowledge that no conceptual scheme of "values", however well ordered, would be able to do justice to the crucial aspect of the situation: Values are in fact, in the last resort, everywhere and always, not just alternatives; [they are] engaged in an irreconcilable struggle to the death [with each other] – as it were, between "God" and the "Devil". Between those [positions], no relativization or compromise is possible. At least not if we consider their [intrinsic] *meaning*. For, in our daily lives, we all constantly encounter such relativizations and compromises in practice, and therefore believe that they are also possible [in principle]. The different value spheres intersect and intertwine in almost every single important position taken by persons in real life. People's humdrum "everyday lives", in the truest sense of that expression, make them shallow precisely in that they do not become aware [of the fact] that irreconcilably antagonistic values are thus [in practice] mixed up with each other, partly for psychological reasons, partly for pragmatic ones. Above all, they do not *want* to become aware of [that fact]: on the contrary, they evade the choice between "God" and the "Devil", and the fundamental personal decision as to which of the conflicting values belongs to the realm of one, and which to the other. The fruit of the tree of knowledge, disturbing to human complacency yet inescapable, is precisely this [insight]: that we cannot avoid knowing about these conflicts, and must therefore realize that every single important act – and to an even much greater extent: life as a whole, if it is to be lived in full awareness and is not just to unfold like a natural event – involves a series of fundamental decisions through which the soul, as Plato [describes it], *chooses* its own fate, ‹331› – the meaning, that is, of its activity and being. It is therefore a gross misconception of the intentions of the representatives of the theory of value collision when their standpoint continues, from time to time, to be interpreted as "relativism" – as a conception of life, that is to say, that is based on the diametrically opposite view of the interrelations of the value spheres, and is only meaningfully tenable (if it is to be consistent) on the basis of a very special ("organic") type of metaphysics.

Let us return to our special case. [Here] it can, in my opinion, be asserted without any possible doubt that if, within the domain of practical–political valuations (in particular those dealing with economic and social policy) one wishes to deduce guidelines for valuable action [from those valuations], all that an *empirical* discipline can demonstrate with the means at its disposal are the following: (1) the unavoidable means; (2) the unavoidable side effects; (3) the resulting competition between a number of different *possible* valuations [on the basis of] their practical consequences. Beyond this, *philosophical* disciplines may, with their analytical instruments, elucidate the "meaning" of the valuations – that is to say: their fundamental structure, and their consequences, in terms of *meaning*. Thus, [those disciplines] may assign [to the valuations] their "place" within the totality of all possible "ultimate" values and delimit their spheres of validity in terms of meaning. But the question: (1) to what extent a goal may justify the unavoidable means, or: (2) to what extent the unwanted side effects may be acceptable, let alone: 3) how to resolve conflicts between a number of goals that one has set for oneself or that are regarded as obligatory, and that collide in the concrete case – even such simple questions are entirely matters of choice or compromise. No (rational or empirical) scientific procedure of any kind whatsoever can decide them. *Our* strictly empirical science can least of all presume to relieve the individual of [the burden of] his choice, and it should therefore not give the impression of being able to do so.

Finally, it should be explicitly noted that the recognition of *this* state of affairs in *our disciplines* is completely unrelated to the position that one may adopt with respect to the very briefly outlined value–theoretical arguments set out above. For there is simply no logically tenable standpoint from which it could be denied [that this is the situation for our disciplines], with the exception of a hierarchy of values unambiguously prescribed by *ecclesiastical* dogmas. Take the following questions: Are the concrete facts like this or like that? Why did those facts turn out this way and not differently? Is a given set of facts usually, according to a rule of what actually happens, followed by another set of facts, and with what [degree of] probability? I have yet to see anybody asserting that those questions are *not*, in terms of their meaning, fundamentally different from the questions: What should in practice be *done* in a concrete situation? What are the viewpoints from which that situation might seem desirable or undesirable in practice? Can we find propositions (axioms) – of any kind – that can be formulated in general terms and to which those viewpoints can be reduced? Now take the following [pair of] questions: On the one hand: in what direction *will* a concretely given factual situation (or generally, a situation of a certain, sufficiently precisely defined, type) probably develop, and with what probability? (or respectively: what is its usual, typical course of development?). And on the other hand: should one *contribute* to the development of a certain situation in a certain direction – whether it be the probable one, the exact opposite or any other direction? Or finally, [take another pair]: On the one hand: what view concerning a problem (of whatever kind) *will* probably, or even with certainty, be formed by certain persons under [certain] concrete circumstances, or by an indefinite number of persons under similar circumstances? And on the other hand: is this view, which (probably or with certainty) will be formed, *correct*? – [Is there really anybody who will maintain] that the questions in each of these pairs have even the least to do with each other, in terms of their meaning? That, in actual fact (as people go on claiming), th[ose questions] "cannot be separated"? Or that this last claim is *not* inconsistent with the requirements of scientific thinking? But whether somebody who acknowledges that the two kinds of question are absolutely heterogeneous will nevertheless claim the right to comment on both one and the other of the two heterogeneous problems in one and the same book, on one and the same page, even in the principal and the subordinate clause of one and the same syntactic unit – that is his affair. All that can be demanded of him is that he does not – unintentionally, or in order to give his remarks added flavour – *deceive* his readers with respect to the absolute heterogeneity of the problems. Personally, I hold the view that every means – however "pedantic" – should be utilized in order to avoid confusion.

Thus, the discussion of the *practical valuations* ([made by] those persons who *participate* in a discussion) can only mean the following:

(A) The explication of the ultimate, internally "consistent" value axioms on which the differing opinions are based. All too often, one is wrong not only about those of the adversary, but also about one's own. In essence, this procedure is an operation that takes the individual valuation and the analysis of its meaning as its point of departure and then ascends ever higher towards ever more fundamental valuational positions. It does not operate with the instruments of an empirical discipline and does not produce any knowledge of facts. It is "valid" in the same sense in which logic is valid.

(B) The deduction of the "implications" of certain ultimate value axioms for *valuational* positions, if [those axioms], and they alone, were made the basis of the practical evaluation of factual situations. The argument [as such] proceeds purely in terms of meaning; however, the deduction is dependent on statements [of] empirical [fact] because it involves a casuistic analysis, as exhaustive as possible, of those empirical situations that *may* be at all relevant for a practical evaluation.

(C) Determining the *factual* consequences that the realization in practice of a certain practical valuational position with respect to a [certain] problem would have: (1) as a result of being bound to certain unavoidable *means*; (2) as a result of the unavoidability of certain, not directly desired side effects. This purely empirical operation may, among other things, lead to the following conclusions: (a) That it is absolutely impossible to realize even the most remote approximation of the evaluative position, because no way of carrying it out can be found. (b) That it is more or less *improbable* that [the valuational position] can be completely or even approximately realized, either for the same reason or because it is probable that unwanted side effects will appear which are liable, directly or indirectly, to make the realization illusory. (c)

That it will prove necessary to accept [certain] means or side effects which the proponent of the practical [valuational] demand had not taken into account, so that his value decision concerning [the balance between] the goal, the means and the side effects will become a fresh problem for himself, and less compelling for others. – Finally, [the discussion of practical value judgements] can mean that:

(D) *New* value axioms, and demands that can be derived from them, will be advocated – [axioms and demands] which the proponent of [another] practical demand had not been aware of, and towards which he had therefore not defined his position, even though the realization of his own demand conflicts with those other ones, either (1) in principle or (2) as a result of their practical consequences – in other words: either in terms of their meaning or in actual practice. Further discussion of the first case involves problems [of the kind referred to above] under (A), while further discussion of the second one involves [problems] of type (C).

Therefore, this type of discussion of valuations is far from being "meaningless"; it is extremely meaningful, particularly if its purpose is understood correctly – indeed only, in my view, if this is the case.

However, the *usefulness* of a discussion of practical valuations, at the right place and in the correct sense, is by no means restricted to such direct "results" that it may produce. If it is conducted correctly, it may moreover provide a strong and lasting stimulus for empirical research by providing it with the *problems* for investigation.

Certainly, the problems addressed by the empirical disciplines must be solved in a "value-free" way. They are not "value problems". But, within our disciplines, they are influenced by the relation of elements of reality "to" values. As for the meaning of the term "value relation", I must refer to my own earlier writings and above all to the well-known works of H[einrich] Rickert. I must refrain from repeating it in this context. Suffice it to recall that the term "value relation" simply represents the philosophical interpretation of that specifically scientific "*interest*" which governs the selection and formation of the object of an empirical inquiry.

In any case, this purely logical fact does not legitimize any kind of "practical valuations" in the field of empirical inquiry. It does imply, however, (as historical experience also shows) that even purely empirical scientific research is *guided* by cultural interests – that is to say: *value* interests. Now, it is clear that value discussions can be a means of developing the casuistic analysis of these value interests. Such [discussions of value] may to a large extent relieve the scientific investigator, and in particular the historian, of the task of "*value interpretation*", or at least make it easier for him to perform [that task], which is extremely important for him as a preparation for his actual empirical work. Not only is the distinction between valuation and value relation often not clearly made; the same is also true of [the distinction] between valuation and value interpretation (i.e. the development of *possible* positions, in terms of meaning, towards a given phenomenon); and this gives rise, in particular, to a lack of clarity with regard to the proper understanding of the logical nature of history. In this respect, I can therefore refer to my comments on pp. 157ff. [above] – without pretending, however, that they are in any way conclusive.

Instead of entering yet again into a discussion of these fundamental methodological problems, I prefer to address more fully certain individual points that are of practical importance for our disciplines.

It is still widely believed that guidance for the formulation of practical valuations ought to be, must be, or at least may be, derived from "developmental trends". But from such "developmental trends", however clear, one can only derive unambiguous imperatives for action with regard to the means that can be expected to be the most appropriate for realizing a certain given position, but not with regard to that position itself. In this respect, the concept of "means" is of course used in its widest possible sense. For instance, if somebody took the power interests of the state as his ultimate goal, then both an absolutist and a radical–democratic constitution might, depending on the given situation, appear to him as the (relatively) most appropriate means; and, if he changed his evaluation of these purposive instruments of the state, as means, it would be quite ridiculous to regard this as a change in the "ultimate" position itself. But it is evident that, as mentioned earlier, the individual is also constantly faced with the following problem: Should he abandon his hopes of realizing his practical valuations if he has to acknowledge the existence of an unambiguous developmental trend that makes the realization of his goal conditional on the employment of new means, which he may regard as problematical from a moral or some other point of view, or on accepting side effects that are abhorrent to him? Or if [the developmental trend] makes it so unlikely that the goal can be realized that his endeavours in that direction, judged by its chances of success, is bound to look like sterile tilting at windmills? – But the knowledge of the existence of such more or less unalterable "developmental trends" is by no means a special case. It is equally true of *every* single new fact that it may call for a new balancing of the end against the unavoidable means [and] of the intended goal against the unavoidable side effects. But not only is it impossible for an empirical science to answer the question of whether such a rebalancing should take place, and what practical conclusions it should lead to; as already mentioned, *no* science of any kind can answer that question. To take an example: one may demonstrate to the convinced syndicalist that his actions are not only socially "useless" – in other words: that no change in the external class situation of the proletariat can be expected to result from it – but that it will also inevitably bring about a worsening of that class situation because it engenders "reactionary" sentiments. No matter how concrete [that demonstration] is: for [the syndicalist], it proves *nothing at* all, provided that he really commits himself to the ultimate consequences of his viewpoint. And this is so, not because he is a madman, but because he may, from his own point of view, be "in the right" – as we shall discuss shortly. On the whole, people are sufficiently strongly inclined to adapt their inner attitudes to whatever is successful or promises to be successful. [They do so] not only by [adapting] the means, or by [modifying] the extent to which they endeavour, under the given circumstances, to realize their ultimate ideals – that goes without saying – but also by sacrificing those ideals themselves. In Germany, people feel justified in glorifying this as "Realpolitik". But, at any rate, it is difficult to see why representatives of an empirical science should feel a particular need to support this tendency by setting themselves up as a claque applauding any given "developmental trend", nor why they should transform the "adaptation" to such trends from being a fundamental *valuational* problem, which can only be resolved by each individual in each individual case, and which is therefore also the responsibility of each individual, into a principle ostensibly protected by the authority of a "science".

In a sense, it is true that successful political action is always "the art of the possible". However, it is equally true that, very often, the possible has only been attained by reaching for the impossible that lay beyond it. After all, it was not the only really consistent ethic of "adaptation" to the possible – the bureaucratic morals of Confucianism ⟨332⟩ – that created those specific qualities of *our* culture to which all of us probably, in spite of all [our] other differences of opinion, subjectively attach a (more or less) positive value. I, for one, would regret it if [our] nation were systematically weaned away, particularly in the name of science, from [acknowledging] the fact (which I have gone into above) that action has not only a "result value" but also a "convictional value". In any case, a failure to appreciate that fact will impede [our] understanding of realities. Let us again take the example of the syndicalist: if [somebody's] conduct, in order to be consistent, must let itself be guided by [its] "convictional value", it is pointless – from a logical point of view as well – to confront it solely with its "result value" for the purposes of "criticism": *All* that the really consistent syndicalist wants is to preserve, within himself, a certain conviction that he regards as unconditionally valuable and sacred, and, if possible, to awaken it in others. His external action, particularly that which is in advance doomed to failure – even total failure – has only one purpose: that of giving him, in his own mind, the certainty that this conviction is genuine – that is to say: [that it] is not idle boasting, [but] has the power to "prove itself" in action. In fact, such action *is* – perhaps – the only means of achieving that purpose. Apart from that (if he is consistent), his kingdom, like the kingdom of any ethic of conviction, is not of this world. All that can be said from a "scientific" point of view is *that* this conception of his own ideals is the only one which is internally consistent, and that it cannot be contradicted by external "facts". I believe that [this statement] renders a service both to the followers and to the opponents of syndicalism – indeed, just that service which they can rightly demand from science. On the other hand, it seems to me that nothing can be gained, from the viewpoint of *any* kind of science, by [arguing] "on the one hand – on the other hand", with seven arguments "for" and six "against" a certain phenomenon (say, the general strike ‹333›), and balancing them against each other after the fashion of former theories of public finance and administration ‹334› and, for instance, modern Chinese memoranda. ‹335› On the contrary: science, at least in its *non-valuational* form, has done everything that it can with respect to the syndicalist position when it has reduced it, as described, to its most rational and internally consistent form, and has established [not only] the preconditions of its empirical development, [but also] its chances and – based on experience – its practical consequences. That one ought to be, or ought not to be, a syndicalist, can never be proved, except on the basis of very definite metaphysical premises that are undemonstrable and that, in the present case, cannot be demonstrated by *any possible kind* of science. That an officer prefers to be blown up together with his redoubt instead of surrendering *may* also, in the individual case, be absolutely useless in *every* respect, measured in terms of results. But surely it is not a matter of indifference whether or not the conviction that impels such an action, without asking what use[ful purpose it serves], actually exists. In any event, such a conviction need not be "meaningless", any more than the conviction harboured by the consistent syndicalist. Admittedly, it would not appear to be in the best of taste if a professor, from the comfortable heights of his academic lectern, were to exhort his audience to follow the example of Cato the Younger ‹336› in this fashion. But nor is he obliged, after all, to praise the opposite standpoint and to proclaim it a duty to adapt one's ideals to the chances afforded by the existing developmental trends and situations.

In the foregoing, I have repeatedly used the term "adaptation"; and, considering the formulations that I have chosen in [each] given case, [its meaning] should perhaps be sufficiently clear. But the term turns out to have a double meaning: [either] adaptation of the means for the realization of a given ultimate position to the given situation ("Realpolitik" in the narrower sense of the term); [or], when choosing from among the possible ultimate positions themselves, adaptation to the real or apparent momentary chances [of success] of one of them (the kind of "Realpolitik" with which [Germany] has [since 1890] ‹337› achieved such strange results). But this by no means exhausts the number of possible meanings [of the term "adaptation"]. Therefore, I think that it would be better if this much misused concept were left completely out of any discussion of our problems, concerning both "valuational" and other questions: It is completely misleading as the expression of a scientific *argument*; and it crops up again and again with that function, for the purpose of "explanation" (for instance, of the empirical fact that certain groups of people have, at certain times, held certain ethical views) as well as of "evaluation" (for instance, of those actually existing ethical views as being objectively "appropriate" *and therefore* objectively "correct" and valuable). In neither of those respects does [the concept of "adaptation"] contribute anything, as it always needs a preliminary interpretation. It has its home in [the field of] biology; and, in biological terms, it refers to the chance – which is given, on the basis of the [prevailing] circumstances, and can be stated in relative terms – that a group of people has of preserving its specific *inherited* psychophysical traits by means of ample reproduction. If it were actually used with this meaning, then – to take an example – those social strata that had the most ample economic means and regulated their life in the most rational fashion would, according to the well-known empirical data in the birth statistics, be the "least well-adapted" ones. Those few Indians who lived in the Salt Lake area before the Mormon migrations ‹338› were just as well and just as poorly "adapted" – in a biological sense, but also in any other of the numerous possible, truly and purely empirical, alternative senses of the term – to that environment as the later populous Mormon settlements. Thus, the concept [of "adaption"] does not in the least help us to gain a better empirical understanding of anything, although we may easily imagine that it does. And it should be clearly stated already at this point that, *only* if we are dealing with two organizations that are otherwise absolutely similar in *every* conceivable respect is it possible to say that a particular concrete difference [between them] creates an *empirical* situation that, for one of them, is more conducive to its continued existence, and is in that sense "better adapted" to the given conditions. If [the situation] is to be *evaluated*, one person may take the position that the greater numbers of people that the Mormons brought to [the Salt Lake area], and the material (and other) accomplishments and characteristics of those people, are proof of the superiority [of the Mormons] over the Indians. Another person, who finds the means and side effects of the Mormon ethic (which is, at least in part, responsible for those accomplishments) utterly abhorrent, may prefer the steppe even without Indians, and certainly the romantic existence of [the Indians] on [those steppes]; and no science *of any kind whatsoever* could presume to convert [either of] them. Here, [we are] already [confronted] with the irresolvable [problem] of *balancing* ends, means and side effects against each other.

It is only when one is looking for the appropriate means for achieving an absolutely unambiguously given goal that [this] question can really be decided empirically. The statement: "x is the only means for achieving y" is in fact simply an inversion of the statement "x is followed by y". However (and this is the main point), the concept of "adaptedness", and all related [concepts], at any rate does not provide any information at all about the valuations on which it is ultimately based; on the contrary, it merely covers them up, and the same is true, for instance, of the concept of "human economy", ‹339› which has lately become fashionable and which is in my opinion thoroughly confused. Depending on the meaning that one gives to the concept [of "adaptation"], either everything or nothing is "adapted" in the domain of "culture". This is because *conflict* is an ineradicable element of all cultural life. One can change the instruments of conflict, its object, even its fundamental direction and its agents; but it cannot be eliminated. Instead of being an external struggle of antagonistic persons for external objects, it may be an inner struggle of mutually loving persons for inner values; therefore, instead of external compulsion, there may be an inner one (in particular in the form of erotic surrender or charitable devotion). And finally, [the conflict] may be the inner struggle of an individual with himself within his own soul. But it is always present, and its effects may be the greater the less one is aware of it – in other words: the more it takes the form of letting things slide, through obtuseness or complacency, or deceiving oneself with illusions, or operating a "selection". "Peace" means a shift in the forms of the conflict, or the parties to the conflict, or the objects of the conflict or, finally, in the chances of selection – and nothing else. And it is obvious that absolutely nothing of a general character can be said as to whether, and when, such shifts are able to stand the test of an ethical or some other evaluative judgement. Only one conclusion can be drawn with certainty: if one wishes to *evaluate* any ordering (of whatever kind) of societal relationships, one must in the last resort, without exception, also examine it with respect to *the type of human being* that it gives the best chances of becoming dominant, by way of external selection or inner selection (of motives). Otherwise, the empirical investigation is not really exhaustive; and, moreover, the necessary factual basis for an evaluation – whether deliberately subjective or claiming objective validity – will simply be lacking. These facts should at any rate be kept in mind by the large number among [my] colleagues who believe that it is possible to apply unambiguous concepts of "*progress*" when one determines [the course of] social developments. That leads us to a closer examination of this important concept.

Of course it is possible to use the concept of progress in an absolutely value-free way: in that case, it is identified with the "progression" of some concrete process of development, viewed in isolation. But, in most cases, the situation is considerably more complicated. Here, we shall examine a few cases, taken from heterogeneous fields, where the interweaving with valuational questions is especially intimate.

When we are dealing with the irrational, emotional, affective content of our mental attitudes, the quantitative increase of *possible* attitudes and – what is usually bound up with it – their qualitative diversification can be designated in a value-free manner as [constituting] a progress in psychical "differentiation". But this is very quickly combined with a valuational concept: the increased "span" [or] "capacity" of a concrete "mind", or (as in Simmel's *Schopenhauer and Nietzsche*) of an "epoch" – a construct that is already less than unambiguous.

Of course, there is no doubt that, in fact, the "progressive differentiation" does take place; but it has to be added that it is not always present where one believes it to be. At present, increased *attention* is being paid to nuances of feeling, owing both to the increasing rationalization and intellectualization of all spheres of life and to the increasing subjective importance attached by the individual to all his manifestations of life (which often seem extremely trivial to others); and this may easily be taken for an increase in differentiation. The [increased attention] may indicate [that an increase in differentiation has occurred], or may [even] promote that process. But appearances are deceptive, and I admit that my estimate would be that, in actual fact, [the belief in the existence of such an increased differentiation] is to a fairly large extent mistaken. Still, the fact exists. Now, whether one uses the *term* "progress" to describe progressive differentiation is in itself a question of terminological convenience. But whether one should *evaluate* [that process] as a "progress" in the sense of an increase in "inner richness" cannot, at any rate, be decided by any empirical discipline. [Those disciplines] are not concerned with the question whether, in any given case, the possibilities of feeling that have recently emerged or been raised to the level of consciousness, perhaps accompanied by new "tensions" and "problems", should be acknowledged as "values". On the other hand, if someone wishes to take an evaluative stand with respect to the fact of differentiation as such (it is obvious that no empirical discipline can prohibit anybody from doing so) and looks for a standpoint on which to base it, he may also be prompted by many contemporary phenomena to ask [the following question]: If [the process of differentiation] is at present anything more than an intellectualistic illusion, what is the price to be "paid" for it? For instance, he must recognize that the chase after "experiences" – the really fashionable value in Germany nowadays – can to a very large degree be the result of a diminished ability to live up to the inner demands of "everyday existence". And he must also recognize that, when individuals increasingly feel the need to publicize their "experiences", this might also be judged to be [testimony of] a diminished sense of detachment, and therefore also of a diminished sense of style and dignity. In any case, within the sphere of valuations of subjective experiencing, "progressive differentiation" can initially *only* be identified with an increase in "value" in an intellectualistic sense: either [(1)] as an increase in the amount of ever more *conscious* experiencing or [(2)] as an increasing capacity for expression and communication.

The situation is somewhat more complicated with respect to the applicability of the concept of "progress" (in an *evaluative* sense) in the domain of *art*. Occasionally, it is vehemently denied. (Whether rightly or wrongly depends on the sense in which it is meant). No *evaluative* approach to art would have found the exclusive dichotomy between "art" and "non-art" sufficient [for its purposes]. In addition, [those evaluative approaches] have distinguished between attempt and realization; between the values of different realizations; [and] between a complete realization and one that failed on a particular point or on a number of points – even important ones – but nevertheless was not entirely worthless. And it has applied that distinction not just to a concrete will to form but also to the will to art ‹340› of whole epochs. When it is applied in such contexts, the concept of "progress" certainly seems trivial, because it is ordinarily employed in connection with purely technical problems. But it is not intrinsically meaningless. The problem has yet another character in the purely empirical *history* of art and the empirical *sociology* of art. [The history of art] of course does not recognize a "progress" in art with respect to the aesthetic evaluation of works of art as meaningful realizations: an empirical inquiry cannot, with the instruments at its disposal, produce that evaluation, which therefore lies completely beyond its tasks. On the other hand, the history of art, in particular, can employ a concept of "progress" that is in every respect simply technical and rational, and therefore unambiguous. That [this concept] – which will be discussed immediately below – can be used in the empirical history of art is a consequence of the fact that it is entirely limited to the determination of the technical *instruments* employed for a given, definite purpose in the service of a particular will to art. It is easy to underestimate the significance for the history of art of these strictly limited investigations, or to misinterpret them in the manner of those fashionable but totally insignificant persons who are supposedly "connoisseurs", but not genuinely so, and who claim to have "understood" an artist when they have peeped into his studio and made a careful inventory of his external means of expression: his "manner". But properly understood, "technical" progress is the [true] domain of the history of art, because it is precisely [such progress], and its influence on the will to art, which constitutes that part of the development of art that can be determined purely empirically – that is to say: without aesthetic evaluation. Let us take a few examples that illustrate the real importance of the "technical" [element] – in the true sense of the word – for the history of art.

The development of the Gothic style ‹341› was first and foremost the result of the technically successful solution of an, in itself, purely architectural problem [in connection with] the building of vaults over spaces of a particular kind, namely the question of the technically optimal way of creating abutments for the support of a cross-arched vault, together with some further details that will not be discussed here. [Certain] quite concrete constructional problems were solved. When it was realized that this also meant that a certain kind of vaulting of non-quadratic spaces had also become possible, this awakened the passionate enthusiasm of those architects – who are as yet unknown and will perhaps always remain so – to whom we owe the development of the new architectural style. Their technical rationalism applied this new principle with thoroughgoing consistency. Their will to art used it as a means of realizing hitherto undreamt-of artistic projects and then led sculpture towards a new "sense of body" that had its main origins in the totally new methods of treating spaces and surfaces in architecture. The fact that this revolution, which was primarily determined by technical considerations, converged with the content of certain feelings – [which must] to a large degree [be explained] sociologically and by the history of religion – supplied an important part of the body of problems on which the creative artists of the Gothic period worked. In uncovering those material, technical, social and psychological conditions [influencing] the new style, the history and sociology of art have done all that they can do purely empirically. But, in so doing, these disciplines do not "valuate" the Gothic style compared, say, to the Romanesque or to that of the Renaissance (which in its turn was very strongly oriented towards the technical problems of the cupola and, in parallel, to the partly sociologically conditioned changes in the field of activity of architecture); nor does [the history of art] – as long as it remains an empirical discipline – "valuate" individual buildings aesthetically. On the contrary: the *interest* in works of art and in their aesthetically relevant individual peculiar characteristics – and therefore [also] the *object* of the history of art – is heteronomously ‹342› given, as an a priori, by the aesthetic value [of those works of art] – a value that the history of art is incapable of determining with the instruments at its disposal.

[The situation is] similar in the field of the history of music ‹343›. Its central problem, from the standpoint of the *interest of the modern European* ("value relatedness"!), is probably the following: Why was it only in Europe, and during a certain epoch, that the polyphony which had almost everywhere emerged in the area of folk music developed into harmonic music, whereas everywhere else the rationalization of music took another, and mostly quite the opposite, direction, namely that of developing the intervals by divisions of distance (particularly of the fourths) and not by harmonic division (of the fifths)? Thus, the following problems are central: the origin of the third in its harmonic conception, i.e. as a unit in the triad; furthermore: that of harmonic chromaticism; and, further: that of modern musical rhythm (with heavy and light beats), instead of metronomic beat – a rhythm without which modern instrumental music is inconceivable. Here, again, we are primarily dealing with problems of "progress" in terms of purely technical rationality. For instance, the antique chromatic (supposedly even enharmonic) music for the passionate dochmiac verses in the recently discovered Euripides fragment ‹344› demonstrates that chromaticism was known well before harmonic music, as a means of expressing "passion". Therefore, what distinguishes that antique music from the chromaticism created by the great musical experimenters of the Renaissance, who had a tempestuous, rational striving for new discoveries, and in fact had the same purpose of giving musical form to "passion", is not the *will* to artistic expression but the technical *means* of expression. What was technically new was that this chromaticism developed into the one characterized by our harmonic intervals, rather than on the melodic half- and quarter-tone *distances* used by the ancient Greeks. And this development, in its turn, was based on already existing solutions of technical, rational problems. [These included], in particular, the creation of the rational notation of music (without which no modern composition would be at all conceivable); [the invention,] even earlier, of certain instruments calling for a harmonic interpretation of musical intervals and, above all, [the development] of rationally polyphonic vocal music. To a major extent, these accomplishments were due to the monks in the mission fields of north-western Europe in the early Middle Ages: Without having any idea of the long-term implications of what they were doing, they rationalized the polyphony of folk music for their own purposes, rather than letting their music be arranged for them (as did the Byzantine monks) by a Melopoios ‹345› schooled in the Hellenic tradition. If this set of intrinsically "technical" musical problems emerged out of a rationalism peculiar to occidental monasticism, this was owing to the concrete special characteristics (explainable sociologically and by the history of religion) of the external and internal situation of the occidental Christian church. On the other hand, the adoption and rationalization of the dance measure – the source of those musical forms of which the sonata is the final expression – was determined by certain forms of social life in Renaissance society. Finally, the development of the piano – one of the most important technical vehicles of the development of modern music and its propagation within the bourgeoisie – had its roots in the specific indoor character of the culture of northern Europe. All these [developments] constitute "progress" in the *technical* means available to music and have had a very strong influence on its history. The empirical history of music can and must describe these components of its historical development without performing, for its part, an *aesthetic* evaluation of the musical art works. Technical "progress" has quite often produced its first manifestations in works that, judged by the standards of aesthetics, were highly imperfect. The focus of *interest* – the *object* that is to be explained historically – is hetero-nonomously given for the history of music by its aesthetic significance.

As regards the development of painting, the elegant modesty that characterizes Wölfflin's definition of the problem in his *Classical Art* is a quite outstanding example of what can be achieved by empirical investigations.

It is a characteristic manifestation of the complete dichotomy between the sphere of values and the empirical [one] that the utilization of a certain *technique*, however "advanced", says nothing at all about the *aesthetic* value of the work of art. Even if a work of art has been elaborated with an extremely "primitive" technique – such as, for instance, paintings [made] without any knowledge of perspective – it may be aesthetically equal to other, highly accomplished ones created with rational techniques – provided that the will to art [underlying it] has been confined to forms of expression adequate for that "primitive" technique. The initial result of the creation of new technical means is merely an increase in differentiation, and merely offers a *possibility* of increasing "richness" (in the sense of enhanced value) of art. In fact, it is not unusual for it to have the opposite effect, so that the sense of form is "impoverished". But in an empirical–*causal* perspective, changes in "technique" (in the widest sense of the term) are precisely the most important generally determinable factors in the development of art.

Not only art historians but historians in general will usually object that they are not willing to allow themselves to be deprived of the right to make political, cultural, ethical [or] aesthetic evaluations, and that they cannot do their work without [having resort to such evaluations]. Methodology has no power to prescribe to anyone what he [should] intend to offer in a literary work, and no intention of doing so. For its part, it only claims the right to state the following: that certain [kinds of] problems are heterogeneous to each other; that *mistaking* one [kind] for the other will result in a discussion at cross-purposes; and that one kind can be meaningfully discussed with the means of empirical science or of logic, while this is impossible with respect to the other one. I may further add a general observation, without attempting to prove its correctness here: a careful review of historical works will soon show that, when the historian begins to "valuate", the relentless and thoroughgoing unravelling of the empirical–historical causal concatenation will almost invariably be interrupted, to the detriment of the scientific results. In such cases, historians run the risk, for example, of "explaining" as the result of an "error" or a "decline" what was in fact the consequence of [the influence] on the acting person of ideals foreign to themselves; and they thereby fail in their most essential task: that of "understanding". There are two reasons for this misunderstanding. First of all – if we continue to take the example of art – the reality of art can be subjected not only, on the one hand, to purely aesthetic valuation and, on the other hand, to purely empirical and causal explanation, but also to a value *interpreting* approach. I shall not repeat here what has been said elsewhere (see pp. 157–67) about the nature of this approach. There is no doubt at all that it has intrinsic value and that it is indispensable for every historian. Nor is there any doubt that the ordinary *reader* of art-historical works also – indeed: in particular – expects this kind of approach to be part of what he is offered. As far as its logical structure is concerned, however, it is not identical to the empirical approach.

And then, [second:] anybody who wants to accomplish something, however purely empirical it may be, in the field of the history of art, must for that purpose have the ability to "understand" [the process of] artistic production; and that [ability] is of course inconceivable without the capacity for making aesthetic judgements – in other words: without the *ability* to evaluate. Naturally, the same holds for political historians, historians of literature, [and] historians of religion or philosophy. But this fact has no implications for the logical nature of historical studies.

I shall revert to this later. Here, I merely wished to discuss the question of the sense in which art historians can speak of "progress", *apart* from aesthetic evaluations. As it turned out, in the field of the history of art, that concept acquires a technical and rational meaning that refers to the *means* for the realization of artistic intentions, and that may in fact become important precisely for the empirical history of art. But what was said above is just a special case of a quite universal phenomenon; and it is therefore time to examine [the application of] the concept of "rational" progress in the field where it most particularly belongs and to consider its empirical or non-empirical character.

Windelband defines the subject of his *History of Philosophy* (Windelband, *History⁴* §2, p. 8) in the following manner: "the process by which *European* humanity has embodied its view of the world . . . in scientific concepts". This makes it necessary for him, with his (in my opinion) quite brilliant pragmatic approach, to employ a specific concept of "progress" that follows from this relatedness to cultural values. On the one hand, this concept of "progress" (the consequences of which are drawn *History⁴*, pp. 15–16) is by no means self-evident for every "history" of philosophy; but on the other hand, if the corresponding relatedness to cultural values is taken as a base, [the concept] applies not only to a history of philosophy, and to every other history of any other science, but also – contrary to Windelband's own assumption (*History⁴*, p. 7, no. 1, para 2) – simply to every [kind of] history. Nonetheless, in what follows, I shall only discuss those rational concepts of "progress" that play a role within our sociological and economic disciplines. Our European–American social and economic life is "rationalized" in a specific way and in a specific sense. Consequently, it is one of the main tasks of our disciplines to explain this rationalization and to construct the concepts appropriate to it. In this connection, the following problem – which was touched on, but left open in [the discussion of] the example of the history of art – arises again: What does it really mean when a process is designated as "rational progress"?

Here, too, we find that different meanings of [the word] are mixed up: (1) the mere differentiating "progression"; (2) the increase over time in the technical rationality of the *means*; and, finally, (3) the enhancement of *value*. To begin with, *subjectively* "rational" conduct is not identical with rationally "correct" action – that is to say: [action] utilizing those means that are, according to scientific knowledge, the objectively correct ones. It only means that the *subjective* intention is to orient oneself systematically towards [the utilization of] means that one *believes* to be the correct ones, in order to [attain] a given goal. A progressive subjective rationalization of action therefore does not necessarily also constitute objective "progress" in the direction of rationally "correct" action. For instance, magic has been just as systematically "rationalized" as physics. Almost everywhere, when an intentionally "rational" therapy was first applied, this meant that the cure of empirical symptoms with herbs and potions, which had simply been tested empirically, was set aside in favour of exorcizing the (supposedly) "real" (magical, demoniacal) "cause" of the ailment. Formally speaking, [the new magical therapy] therefore had precisely the same structure – characterized by increased rationality – as many of the most important advances in modern therapy. Nevertheless, in *valuational* terms, we will not be able to see those magical priestly therapies as constituting "progress" towards "correct" action, compared with the [empirical] ones. And on the other hand, by no means every "progress" towards utilizing "correct" means has been brought about by a "progression" in the subjectively rational sense mentioned above. That action which becomes subjectively more rational leads to action that is objectively more "appropriate" to the goal is only one of several possibilities – something that can, with greater or lesser probability, be expected to happen. But if, in a given case, the proposition holds that the measure x is a means (let us assume: the only one) for achieving the result y (this is an empirical question, and is in fact simply the inversion of the causal statement "x is followed by y"), and if people deliberately make use of this proposition when they orient their action towards achieving the result y (this can also be established empirically), *then* the orientation of their action is "technically *correct*". If any single element of human conduct, of whatever kind, becomes technically "more correct" (in this sense) in its orientation than before, then that constitutes "*technical progress*". *Whether* that is the case is indeed – always provided, of course, that the given goal is absolutely unambiguous – something that an empirical discipline can establish with the means of scientific experience; that is to say: something that can be established empirically.

In this sense, therefore, it is actually possible – provided, that is, that the goal is *un*ambiguously given – to define with precision concepts of "technical" correctness and "technical" progress, as far as the means are concerned. (In this context, "technical" is understood in its widest possible sense as [indicating] rational conduct in general and in all fields, including the political, social, educational and propagandistic manipulation of, and domination over, human beings). In particular (I shall confine myself to those areas that are closest to us), it is possible to speak with approximate precision about "progress" in the specialized field that is ordinarily called "technology", but also in the field of commercial and legal technique, *provided* that an unambiguously defined status of a concrete entity is taken as the starting point. But only with approximate precision, since – as any knowledgeable person will know – the various technically rational principles will come into conflict with each other – a conflict that can in each case be solved from the standpoint of the actual interested parties, but never "objectively". And, if we assume that the needs are *given*; further, that all these needs in themselves, as well as their subjective ranking, should be *exempt* from criticism; and finally, moreover, that the economic order is settled and of a *given* kind; – and if we again make the proviso that[, in connection with the satisfaction of the needs,] the [respective] interests regarding, for instance, the duration, the reliability and the degree of satisfaction of those needs may come into conflict, and in fact do so – then [we can also speak of] "economic" progress towards a relative optimum of satisfaction of needs, when the possibilities of acquiring the means [to cover them] are *given*. But [this is true] *only* under those assumptions and limitations.

Attempts have been made to deduce from [these facts] the possibility of unambiguous, and at the same time purely *economic*, valuations. A characteristic example of this is the model case once quoted by Professor Liefmann, where the profitability interests of the producers of consumer goods [are said to] dictate that these goods should be destroyed when their price sinks below the cost price. This destruction must, in his opinion, be judged to be even objectively "correct" from an economic point of view. However, that exposition and (which is the relevant point here) any similar one assumes a number of preconditions as being self-evident, which they are not: First of all, that the interests of the individual not only in fact often reach beyond his death, but that they *should* once and for all be deemed to do so. Without this shift from the "Is" to the "Ought", the supposedly purely economic valuation in that case cannot be formulated unambiguously. For instance, without [that shift] it is impossible to speak of the interests of "producers" and "consumers" as if they were the interests of persons who live on indefinitely. But, from a purely *economic* point of view, one cannot take it for granted that individuals take the interests of their *heirs* into consideration. [In economic thinking], living persons are replaced by interested parties who invest "capital" in "business" for profit and who exist for the sake of that "business". This is a fiction that is useful for theoretical purposes. But, even as fiction, it does not correspond to the situation of the workers – especially not the childless ones. Second, [Liefmann's example] ignores the fact that there is a "class situation" that, under the predominant influence of the market mechanism, may – but need not – result in certain strata of consumers being (in absolute terms) less well supplied with goods. This may happen not just in spite of, but even *as a consequence of*, the "optimal" distribution (to be defined, in the concrete case, on the basis of considerations of profitability) of capital and labour among the different branches of trade and industry. This is because the "optimal" distribution of profitability, which is the precondition of constant capital investment, is in its turn dependent on the constellations of power between the classes; and those constellations may – but need not – in the concrete case lead to a weakening of the position of those [consumer] strata in the price war. – Third, [Liefmann's example] ignores the possibility of permanent, irreconcilable conflicts of interest between members of different political units and thus takes an a priori position in favour of the "free trade argument"; ‹346› and, whenever that argument is used as a basis for demands as to how things *ought to be*, it is immediately transformed from an extremely useful heuristic instrument into a, by no means self-evident, "valuation". In order to avoid this conflict, [Liefmann] may posit the political unity of the world economy – something that is theoretically entirely permissible. But this does not eliminate the possibility that, if those consumable goods are destroyed – for the sake, we may assume, of the *permanent* optimum of profitability (for producers *and* consumers) under the given circumstances – this will provoke criticism. The scope of that criticism will change, however: In that case, it will be directed at the general *principle as such*, according to which the market provision is governed by directives such as the one furnished by the optimum of profitability (expressed in monetary terms) of the individual economic units involved in the exchange. If the organization of the provision of goods were not based on the market principle, there would be no reason for it to take into account at all the constellation of interests of the individual economic units (a constellation that was due to the market principle); nor, therefore, would it be necessary to prevent those consumable goods that were actually available from being consumed.

Professor Liefmann's proposition is only correct, even in a theoretical sense (but in that case, self-evidently so) under the following strictly defined presuppositions: (1) Persons assumed to be unchanging, with needs assumed to be constant, have as their guiding purpose profitability interests that are exclusively of a permanent kind; (2) there is a complete dominance of private capitalist methods of providing for needs by means of completely free market exchange; (3) the state is disinterested and only serves as a guarantor of the law. [If those conditions hold,] the valuation only concerns the rational means for the optimal solution of a particular technical problem of distribution of goods. But the fictions of pure economic theory, which are useful for theoretical purposes, cannot serve as a basis for practical valuations of situations in real life. The fact remains that economic theory can say absolutely *nothing* but the following: given a technical goal x, the only way of attaining it is by doing y, or by doing either y, y^1 or y^2; in the latter case, there are the following differences with respect to the ways in which y, y^1 and y^2 achieve their effect and – perhaps – with respect to their rationality; and if one attains the goal x by [doing y, y^1 or y^2] one will have to take into account the "side effects" z, z^1 and z^2. These are all simply inversions of causal propositions, and "valuations" can only be associated with them to the extent that they concern the degree of rationality of an imaginary act. The valuations are unambiguous if, and only if, the economic goal and the social structural conditions are strictly defined, and the only choice to be made is that between a number of economic *means*; and if, moreover, those means only differ as to the reliability, the speed and the quantitative degree of fulfilment of the goal, while they function completely identically in every other respect that might possibly be relevant to human interests. Only in that case can a means be *valuated* as being quite unconditionally the "technically most correct one", and only in that case is that valuation unambiguous. In every other case – and that means: in every case that is not purely technical – the valuation will cease to be unambiguous, and [other] valuations, which can no longer be defined in purely economic terms, will also play a part.

But establishing the unambiguousness of a *technical* valuation within the purely economic sphere would obviously *not* be enough to achieve an unambiguous, definitive "valuation". On the contrary: after these first discussions, one would be confronted with a jumble of infinitely manifold, possible valuations that could only be reduced to manageable proportions by tracing [those valuations] back to [their] ultimate axioms. Let me just mention [one factor explaining] this [situation]: behind the "action" stands a human being. He may hold the view that an enhancement of the subjective rationality, and of the *objective, technical* "correctness", of an action above a certain threshold – or even, from certain perspectives: any such enhancement at all – will endanger important valued goods (for instance of an ethical or a religious kind). The (maximalist) Buddhist ethic, for example, rejects every purposive action already because it is a purposive action and therefore leads away from redemption. [This ethic] would hardly be espoused by any of us; but it is simply impossible to "refute" it in the sense [in which one refutes] an incorrect calculation or a wrong diagnosis. And even if we do not resort to such extreme examples, it is easy to see that, however "technically correct" economic rational-izations might be, that [kind of] correctness *in itself* does not provide them with any kind of legitimacy if they have to be evaluated. This is true of all rationalizations without exception, including such apparently wholly technical fields as banking. Those who oppose such rationalizations are not necessarily fools, far from it. On the contrary: if one wishes to *valuate*, one must take into consideration the influence of technical rationalizations on all external and inner conditions of life. In our disciplines, the *legitimate* concept of progress will always and everywhere be connected with the "technical" – which, as was said previously, should here be understood as the "means" for attaining an unambiguously *given* end: it never rises to the level of "ultimate" *valuations*.

To sum up: in my opinion, the use of the expression "progress" is extremely *inopportune*, even within the limited field where it can be used without empirical misgivings. But one cannot prevent people from using some particular expression, and, in the last resort, possible misunderstandings can be avoided.

Before winding up, I must discuss one last group of problems, concerning the place of the rational within the empirical disciplines.

When the normatively valid becomes the object of an *empirical* inquiry, it loses, as an object, its normative character: it is treated as "existent", not as "valid". To take an example: If [we] wanted to establish statistically the number of "miscalculations" in a certain field where calculations are carried out professionally – [a task] that it might quite well, from a scientific point of view, make sense to undertake – then the fundamental principles of arithmetic would be "valid" for those statistics in two completely different senses. On the one hand, the normative validity of [those principles] would of course be an absolute presupposition for *our own* calculations. But, on the other hand, when the degree of "correct" application of the rules of arithmetic becomes relevant as the *object* of the investigation, the situation is, from a purely logical perspective, quite different. Here, the application of certain arithmetical rules by the persons whose calculations are the object of statistical investigation is treated as an actual procedural maxim that [their] education has made it a *habit* for them [to follow]. What has to be established is the frequency with which that maxim is actually followed – just as, say, [the frequency with which] certain symptoms of madness manifest themselves can be established statistically. In that case, where their application is an "object", their normative "validity" – in other words: their "correctness" – is not at all part of the discussion and is completely irrelevant from a logical point of view. For his part, the statistician who checks the calculations of the investigated persons must of course also conform to the convention of calculating "according to the rules of arithmetic". But, in quite the same way, he would also have to apply a certain method of calculation that, judged normatively, was "wrong", if a certain group of people regarded that method as being "correct", and if he had to investigate statistically the [question of the] frequency with which that method of calculation was actually (and, from the standpoint of that group of people, "correctly") applied. In other words: for the purposes of every empirical, sociological or historical approach, the rules of arithmetic must, if they are made the *object* of an investigation, be regarded as maxims of practical procedure that are *conventionally* accepted within a certain group of people and adhered to more or less closely – and nothing else. Every exposition of the Pythagorean theory of music ‹347› must simply accept the calculation (which, according to our knowledge, is "wrong") that 12 fifths equal 7 octaves. In the same way, every history of logic [must accept] the historical existence of logical constructions that are (in our view) contradictory; and[, although] it is understandable from a human point of view, it is not a scientific achievement to respond to such "absurdities" with explosions of anger, as a particularly distinguished historian of medieval logic once did.

Every product of the mind, including logical or mathematical ideas, is liable to be affected by this metamorphosis of normatively valid truths into conventionally accepted opinions, as soon as it becomes the object of reflections concerning its empirical *existence* and not its (*normatively*) correct *meaning*; and this is quite independent of the fact that, on the other hand, the normative validity of logical and mathematical truths is the a priori of every single empirical science. – The logical structure [of these truths] is less simple when they – as already mentioned above – perform a special function in connection with empirical investigations into interrelations in the [human] mind – a function that must be carefully distinguished from the two other positions [that these truths may have]: as objects of investigations and as the a priori of such investigations. Every science dealing with interrelations in the [human] mind or in society is a science of *human* behaviour (a term that, in this case, includes every act of thought in the mind and every psychical disposition). It has the aim of "understanding" this behaviour and, by that means, to give an "explanatory interpretation" of it. Now, the difficult concept of "understanding" cannot be dealt with in detail here. In the present context, we are only interested in a particular kind [of "understanding"]: the "rational" interpretation. We obviously have no difficulty in "understanding" that a thinking person "solves" a particular "problem" in a way that we ourselves consider to be normatively "correct" – for instance, that somebody makes a "correct" calculation, [or] that he uses the (according to our own knowledge) "right" means to reach [his] intended goal. And our understanding of these phenomena is particularly evident *because* it concerns the realization of something that is objectively "valid". Nevertheless, we must be careful not to believe that, in this case, the normatively correct [element] has, from a logical point of view, the same structure as in its general position as the a priori of all scientific investigation. Instead, its function as a means of "understanding" is exactly the same as that provided by purely *psychological* "empathizing" when the aim is to attain knowledge, by means of understanding, of (logically speaking) irrational emotional and affective interrelations. Here, the instrument employed in the explanation by means of understanding is not the *normative* correctness, but instead, on the one hand, the fact that researchers and teachers are *conventionally* in the habit of thinking in a certain way and not otherwise; and, on the other hand, that they are able, if necessary, to "empathize", by virtue of understanding, with a manner of thinking that deviates from their own and that, judged by their habitual standards, seems to them to be normatively "erroneous". In itself, the fact that the "erroneous" way of thinking, the "error", is in principle just as accessible to understanding as the "correct" one proves that what is considered to be normatively "correct" is taken into consideration *not as such*, but only as a *conventional* type that is particularly easy to understand. This leads to a final statement concerning the role played by normatively correct [elements] in the context of sociological knowledge.

It is clear that, in order to "understand" an "incorrect" calculation or logical statement, and to be able to determine and describe its influence, as it manifests itself in the consequences which [that error] actually had, one must not only [take the] self-evident [step of] checking it oneself, by means of a "correct" calculation or logical construction: one must also explicitly designate, by means of "correct" calculation or "correct" logic, precisely that point where the investigated calculation or logical construction diverges from what the author writing the account for his part regards as normatively "correct". [If this must be done], it is not necessarily just for the practical pedagogical purpose to which Windelband, for instance, devotes particular attention in his *History* ([putting up] "signs of warning" against "false tracks"), since that is after all only a desirable side effect of historical work. Nor [would it be] because every historical problem concerning, among other things, some kind of logical or mathematical or other form of scientific knowledge could inevitably only be based on the "truth value" that we accept as valid – and therefore also on "progress" towards that "truth value" – as the only possible ultimate value relation guiding the selection of the material. (And even if that were actually the case, one would still have to bear in mind the point made so often by Windelband: that the route taken by that kind of "progress" has very often not been the direct one, but instead – to use an expression from economics – that of "fruitful roundabout production" ‹348› passing through "errors" – that is to say: a conflation of problems). [The precise designation of the divergences would be necessary] because (and therefore only to the extent that) the points at which the theoretical construct constituting the object of the investigation diverges from what the author himself must regard as "correct" will regularly turn out to be among those which seem to him specifically "characteristic" – that is to say: in his eyes, they are either directly value-related or they are *important* because of their causal connection to other value-related phenomena. Normally, however, it is more likely that this will be the case to the extent that the guiding value of a historical account is constituted by the truth value of ideas – in particular in the case of a history of a particular "science" (such as philosophy or theoretical economics). But it is by no means necessarily restricted to such cases. On the contrary, a situation that is at any rate similar arises whenever the [scientific] account has as its object action that is subjectively (according to its intent) rational, so that erroneous "thoughts" or "calculations" may be [among] the *causal* components [determining] the course of action. For instance, if we are to "understand" the conduct of a war, we must necessarily – even if this is not done explicitly or in detailed form – imagine an ideal commander-in-chief, on each side, with [full] knowledge and constant awareness of the total situation and the distribution of the military resources on both sides, and of all the possibilities that this afforded of achieving the goal (which would be precisely defined in the concrete case) of destroying the military power of the adversary, and whose action on this basis would have been free from all mistakes or logical "errors". Only then will it be possible to establish precisely how the fact that the actual commanders-in-chief did not possess that knowledge, and did make mistakes – that they were, in fact, far removed from being purely rational thinking machines – causally influenced the [actual] course of events. In other words: the rational construction is valuable here because it functions as an instrument of correct causal "imputation". The utopian constructions of strictly and faultlessly rational action that we find in "pure" economic theory have exactly the same purpose.

For the purposes of causal *imputation* of empirical events, we do in fact need rational constructions – empirical–technical or logical, as the case may be – that furnish an answer to the following question: what *would* a particular pattern of external action or, say, a theoretical construct (for instance a philosophical system) look like (or have looked like) under the assumption of total rational, empirical and logical "correctness" and "consistency"? From a logical point of view, however, the construction of such a rationally "correct" utopia is only *one* of the various possible forms of the "ideal type" (as I have called such concepts – although I am not at all wedded to that particular terminology). Not only is it, as already stated, possible to imagine cases where it would actually be more useful to construct an ideal type of a characteristic way of drawing *incorrect* conclusions, or of a certain kind of conduct that was typically *not* conducive to the intended purpose, but, above all, there are whole spheres of behaviour (the sphere of the "irrational") where the purpose is better served by [an ideal type] that simply has the precision yielded by [a process of] isolating abstraction, rather than a maximum of logical rationality. It is true that, *in actual fact*, investigators especially often use "ideal types" that have been constructed as normatively "correct". But, from a *logical* point of view, that special quality of normative "correctness" is not an essential feature. On the contrary: For instance, if an investigator wishes to characterize a specific typical attitude possessed by persons living during a certain epoch, he may construct both a type of disposition that he regards as being in accordance with his own ethical norms – and in that sense as being objectively "correct" – and one that he regards as being completely contrary to his own ethical norms, and then compare the behaviour of the investigated persons with them; and, as a further possibility, he may construct a type of disposition that he personally does not in any way evaluate as being positive or negative. In other words, normatively "correct" [behaviour] does not have a monopoly of any kind for the purpose [described]: Whatever the substantive character of the ideal type – whether it represents an ethical, a legal–dogmatic, an aesthetical or a religious norm of belief, or a technical or economic maxim, or a maxim of legal or social or cultural policy, or any sort of "valuation" that has been given the most rational form possible – the *only* purpose of constructing it in an empirical investigation is to "compare" empirical reality with it, to establish how it contrasts with reality, how far removed or relatively close it is to [reality], in order to describe it with the help of *concepts that are as unambiguously intelligible as possible*, and to understand and explain it in a process of causal imputation. Rational, legal–dogmatic concepts, for example, perform the same functions for the empirical discipline of the history of law (see pp. 212ff.); and the principles of rational calculation have that function with respect to the analysis of the actual behaviour of the individual economic units in a productive economy. In addition, both of those dogmatic disciplines are naturally of eminent normative–practical use as "doctrines of good procedure". [But] in that capacity, as a dogmatic science, neither one is an empirical discipline (in the sense discussed here) – no more than, say, mathematics, logic, normative ethics or aesthetics. (Otherwise, and for other reasons, they are just as utterly different from those disciplines as the latter are from each other).

A final point: obviously, economic theory is a dogmatic science in quite a different logical sense than, say, legal dogmatics. The concepts of economic theory have a relationship to economic reality that is specifically different from the relationship that the concepts of legal dogmatics have to the actual reality of the objects of the empirical history and sociology of law. But, just as the history and sociology of law can, and must, make use of the concepts of legal dogmatics as "ideal types", the almost *exclusive* purpose of pure economic theory is to [use concepts] in this way in order to gain knowledge of the social reality of the present and the past. [Pure economic theory] makes certain assumptions, which hardly ever correspond completely to reality but approximate it more or less closely, and then asks: What would human social action look like under these assumptions, if it were strictly rational? In particular, it assumes the dominance of purely economic interests: in other words, it excludes the influence of power political, as well as other non-economic, orientations of action.

However, the theory has experienced a typical process of "problem conflation". The pure theory – which, thus conceived, was "independent of the state", "independent of morals" and "individualistic" – was and will always be indispensable as an instrument of economic method.

But, in the eyes of the radical free trade school, it gave an exhaustive picture of a reality that was "natural" (that is to say: not distorted by human foolishness); and, moreover [it was seen], on this basis, as an "Ought": not as an ideal type to be used in the empirical investigation of facts, but as an ideal valid in the sphere of values. The subsequent change in the assessment of [the role of] the state in the field of economic and social policy had repercussions in the sphere of valuations, which in their turn spread to the empirical sphere and led to the rejection of pure economic theory, not only as the expression of an ideal – [a status] that it should never have been allowed to claim in the first place – but also as a method for investigating facts. Rational pragmatism was to be replaced by all manner of "philosophical" considerations, and because of the identification of the "psychologically" existent with the ethically valid, a clear distinction between the sphere of valuation and empirical work became impracticable. The eminent contributions made in the field of history, sociology and social policy by the representatives of this scientific tendency have been generally recognized; but to the unbiased observer, it is equally clear that not only theoretical but in fact all strictly scientific work in the field of economics has been in a state of complete decay for decades, as a natural consequence of the problem conflation [described above]. One of the two main theses advanced by the opponents of pure theory was that the rational constructions of that theory were "pure fictions", which did not tell us anything about actual facts. Properly understood, this claim is correct: the theoretical constructions are in no respect anything more than instruments for gaining knowledge of actual reality; they do not in themselves yield any such knowledge, and since other circumstances and sequences of motives, which do not form part of the assumptions [on which those constructions are based], also play a part, reality will, even in the most extreme cases, only manifest an approximation to the constructed course of events. As was said above, however, this does not in the least speak against the usefulness and necessity of pure theory. The second [main] thesis [advanced by the opponents of pure theory] was that, at any rate, a valuation-free theory of economic *policy* as a science was an impossibility. Naturally, [this thesis] is absolutely wrong – in fact, wrong to such an extent that "freedom from valuations" (in the sense given above) is[, on the contrary,] the precondition of *every* purely scientific approach to questions of policy, and in particular to social and economic policy. It should not be necessary to repeat that it is evidently both possible, scientifically useful and necessary to formulate propositions of the type: γ is the only, or (under the conditions b^1, b^2, b^3, γ^1, γ^2, γ^3) are the only, or the most effective means of producing the (economic policy) outcome x. Only one point should once more be emphasized: the problem is whether [the goal] that one wishes to attain can be defined with complete *precision*. If so, then the problem is simply that of inverting causal propositions, and therefore a purely "technical" one. For precisely this reason, there is in all these cases no binding reason at all why science should be precluded from formulating these technical, teleological propositions as purely causal ones, i.e. in the form: γ is always followed (or: γ^1, γ^2, γ^3 is, under the conditions b^1, b^2, b^3, always followed) by the outcome x. The meaning is exactly the same, and the "practitioner" can easily formulate his "prescriptions" on that basis. But, besides the task of putting forward purely ideal-typical formulas (on the one hand) and (on the other hand) that of establishing such economic *individual* causal relationships – for that is what we are always dealing with when "x" needs to be sufficiently *precise*, and the imputation of the outcome to the cause, and thus of the means to the end, needs to be sufficiently strict – the scientific theory of economics does also have certain other tasks. It also has to investigate the totality of social phenomena with respect to the way in which they are, in part, influenced by economic causes – that is to say: it must apply an economic interpretation of history and society. And furthermore, it has to show how economic processes and economic forms are determined by social phenomena of various kinds and in various stages of development – that is to say: [it has to perform] the task of economic history and economic sociology. Among those social phenomena, we evidently find the political actions and structures (indeed, they hold pride of place) and, first and foremost, the state and the legal order guaranteed by the state. But – equally evidently – [we find] not just the political [actions and structures], but the totality of all those structures that influence the economy *to a degree that is sufficiently relevant* for the scientific interest. The term "theory of 'economic *policy*'" would of course be quite unsuitable for designating the sum total of these problems. If it is nevertheless used in this sense, this can only be explained by the practical importance of studies in [public] policy – an importance that is due, in an external sense, to the character of universities as establishments for the education of public officials and, in an internal sense, to the fact that the state possesses enormous instruments of power that are particularly suitable for exerting an intensive influence on the economy. It should hardly be necessary to point out once again that, in all these investigations, it is possible to convert "cause and effect" statements into "means and ends" [statements] whenever the relevant *outcome* can be defined with sufficient precision. Nor does this, of course, in any way alter the logical relationship between the sphere of valuations and the sphere of search for empirical knowledge. Only one more, final point should be made in this context.

The developments of the last decades, and in particular the unprecedented events that we are witnessing at present, have enhanced the prestige of the *state* tremendously. Among all the social communities, the state alone is accorded "legitimate" power over life, death and freedom; and its agencies make use of that power: against external enemies in wartime, and against internal opposition in both peace and war. In peacetime, it is the greatest economic entrepreneur and the most powerful collector of tributes from the citizenry, while, in time of war, it has unlimited disposal of all available economic goods. In numerous areas, its modern, rationalized entrepreneurial management has made it possible to achieve results the like of which could certainly not, even approximately, have been obtained by any other kind of collaborative action in collective societal associations. This almost inevitably led to the conclusion that [the state] must also – and particularly with respect to valuations in the domain of "politics" – be the ultimate "*value*", and that all social actions must in the last resort be measured in terms of the interests connected with its [continued] existence. However, this is a completely inadmissible way of transforming facts belonging to the sphere of the existent into norms belonging to the sphere of valuations – quite apart from the fact that the consequences of that valuation are not precisely defined, as every discussion of the "means" (the "preservation" or "support" of the "state") will soon show. If we, for a start, stay within the sphere of actual facts, we can – as against the above-mentioned prestige – point out that there are certain things that the state *cannot* do – even in the military field, which is regarded as its special domain. When we observe many of the phenomena that the present war has provoked within the armed forces of *nationally* mixed states, we can draw the lesson that the voluntary devotion – which the state cannot achieve by compulsion – of the individual to the cause defended by his state is not without importance for the military success. And, as for the economic domain, we can only hint at the fact that, if the economic forms and principles adopted during the war were to be continued as *permanent* features of [the] peacetime [economy], this could very quickly have consequences that would be a keen disappointment, not least to those who advocate expansive state ideals. However, this cannot be further discussed here. And [if we move to] the sphere of *valuation*, it may well make sense for someone [– on the one hand –] to advocate the view that the power of the state should be increased to the fullest extent in the interest of its usefulness as a means of compulsion [to be employed] against opposition, while denying [– on the other hand –] that [the state] has any *intrinsic* value at all, and qualifying it as a purely technical instrument for the realization of quite different values – an instrument whose dignified status would merely be derived from those values, and could therefore only be retained as long as the state did not attempt to elude that ancillary function.

Obviously, this is not the place for developing – let alone defending – this, or indeed any possible, valuational standpoint. I simply wish to point out that if anyone, then professional "thinkers" are under a special obligation to keep a cool head when confronted with the dominant ideals – even the most majestic ones – at any given time; and this means that they should continue to be able to "swim against the current" if necessary. The "German ideas of 1914" ⟨349⟩ were produced by the "literati". The "socialism of the future" ⟨350⟩ is a cliché that really means that the economy [should be] rationalized by means of a combination of further bureaucratization and administration by vested interests in single-purpose organizations. ⟨351⟩ When the parochialists in the field of economic policy, in their fanatical enthusiasm for these purely technical measures, invoke on them the blessings not only of German philosophy but also of religion – a phenomenon that nowadays occurs on a massive scale – instead of soberly discussing their appropriateness (which to quite some degree is based on cool considerations of financial policy), then that is nothing but a nauseating aberration, in the worst possible taste, on the part of conceited "literati". The returning warriors will have a major say in the formulation of the real "German ideas of 1918"; and today, it is probably too early for anyone to predict in advance what [those ideas] could or should look like. But they will be significant for [our] future.

First published in *Logos* 7 (1917), pp. 40–88.
Translated from: "Der Sinn der 'Wertfreiheit' der soziologischen und ökonomischen Wissenschaften" in Max Weber, *Gesammelte Aufsätze zur Wissenschaftslehre* (ed. Johannes Winckelmann), 3rd ed., Tübingen: J.C.B.Mohr (Paul Siebeck) 1968, pp. 489–540. (The subtitles given in the Table of Contents of that volume are not original and have not been retained here.)
The original version of this essay was a contribution by Weber, elaborated in August 1913 in the form of a memorandum, to a debate in the Association for Social Policy in January 1914 on "Value Freedom". The memorandum, together with contributions by other participants in the debate, was printed and circulated privately. Weber later decided – possibly in connection with discussions with his publisher about the collection of his methodological writings into a separate volume to be published after the war – to revise and expand the text into an article for publication, which ran to some fifteen pages more than the original memorandum. In this expanded form, it appeared in November 1917.

SCIENCE AS A PROFESSION
AND VOCATION

‹352› You have asked me to speak about "Science as a profession and vocation". Now, economists like myself have a somewhat pedantic custom, which I should like to observe: we always start by considering the external circumstances, which in this case means asking the following question: What is science like as a profession in the material sense of the word? In practice, this nowadays essentially amounts to asking: What is the situation of a graduate student who is determined to enter academic life and devote himself to science as his profession? In order to understand the peculiarities of our conditions in Germany, it is useful to proceed by way of comparison and to look at the situation in the country abroad that differs most strongly from us in this respect – that is to say: in the United States.

In our country – as everyone knows – a young man who devotes himself to science as a profession normally begins his career as a "private lecturer". After having consulted the full professor responsible for that area of specialization, ‹353› and with his approval, he acquires the right to teach at a particular university ‹354› on the basis of a thesis and an examination – which is mostly something of a formality – by the faculty. He can then give lectures on subjects chosen by himself within the limits of his *venia legendi*; ‹355› he receives no salary and no other remuneration than the lecture fees paid by the students. ‹356› In America, the career normally begins quite differently, namely with an appointment as "assistant". This more or less corresponds to the usual situation in the large institutes of the faculties of natural science or medicine in our own country, where only a fraction of the assistants aim at becoming a private lecturer, and even then in many cases only at a late stage. This difference has the following implications in practice: In our country, the career of a man of science is on the whole built on plutocratic premises. It is extremely risky for a young scholar with no private means to expose himself to the conditions of an academic career. He must be able to put up with it at least for a number of years without having any way of knowing whether he will then have any prospects of taking up a position that will enable him to support himself. In the United States, on the other hand, they have the bureaucratic system. There, the young man receives a salary right from the beginning. Admittedly, it is a modest one: in most cases, the salary is a little lower than the wages of a not entirely unskilled worker. Still, since he has a fixed salary, he begins with an apparently secure position. However, the rule is that he can, like our assistants, be dismissed, and he must be prepared for this to happen, and without compunction, if he does not live up to expectations. And what is expected is that he makes "full houses". That cannot happen to a German private lecturer. Once you have him, you can never get rid of him. True, he has no "rights". But at least, he has the understandable expectation that, if he has lectured for years on end, he has some sort of moral claim to consideration. That [expectation] also – and this is often important – applies to the question whether to admit new private lecturers. The question is whether all scholars of proven worth should, as a matter of principle, be given the right to teach, or whether the "teaching needs" should be taken into account – in other words: whether the private lecturers already in place should have a monopoly of teaching. This is a painful dilemma that is connected with the dual aspect of the academic profession to be discussed shortly. In most cases, the second option is preferred. However, this increases the risk that the professor responsible for that subject, however conscientious he may be subjectively, will nevertheless give preference to his own pupils. Personally – to make that clear – I have made it a rule that a scholar whom I have supervised for his doctorate must prove his worth and acquire his teaching rights under someone *else* and at another university. But this has led to one of my best pupils ‹357› being rejected at another university because no one *believed* him [when he told them] that this was the reason.

There is a further difference between Germany and America: the private lecturer in Germany is generally *less* involved in lecturing than he would wish. True, he has the formal right to lecture on any subject within his discipline. But that would be regarded as an unseemly manifestation of disrespect vis-à-vis the more senior lecturers in the field; so, as a rule, the full professor in the discipline gives the "big" lectures, and the private lecturer restricts himself to the less important ones. The advantage is that he is – albeit not quite voluntarily – free to devote his early years to scholarly work.

In America, these matters are organized on a different principle. In his early years, the lecturer is absolutely overloaded, precisely because he is *paid.* In a department of German studies, for example, the full professor may give a three-hour lecture [every week] on Goethe – that is all; while the young "assistant", who has twelve hours of teaching every week, will consider himself fortunate if, in addition to drumming German language into the students' heads, he is assigned the task of lecturing on poets of (at most) Uhland's calibre. ‹358› This is because the syllabus is prescribed by the departmental authorities, and the "assistants" are bound by it, just like the assistants in German [faculty] institutes.

Here in Germany, we can clearly see that, in broad areas of science, the university system has recently been moving in the direction of the American one. The large institutes of medicine and the natural sciences are "state capitalist" enterprises. It is impossible to administer them without disposing of resources on a major scale. And this creates the same situation as in all other cases involving capitalist enterprises: "the separation of the worker from the means of production". ‹359› The worker – that is to say: the assistant – is dependent on the means of work put at his disposal by the state; consequently, he is just as dependent on the institute director as a worker in a factory [on the factory owner] (since the institute director, in completely good faith, regards that institute as "*his*" institute and acts at his discretion in it), and his position is often as precarious as that of every "proletaroid" ‹360› existence, and as that of an "assistant" in an American university.

In very important respects, our German university life – like our life in general – is becoming Americanized; and I am convinced that this development will spread to those disciplines where – as is still very largely the case today in my own discipline – the artisan himself owns his means of work ([which] in essence means: his [private] library), just like the old craftsman of the past [owned his tools] within [the framework of] his trade. That development is well under way.

The technical advantages are beyond any doubt, as in all capitalist and, in addition, bureaucratized enterprises. But the prevailing "spirit" within them is different from the traditional historical atmosphere of the German universities. Both inwardly and externally, an extremely deep chasm separates the head of a large capitalist university enterprise of this kind from the ordinary, old-style full professor. This is also true of their inner attitude (a point that I do not want to go further into here). In an inner as well as an outward sense, the old *constitution* of the university ⟨361⟩ has become a fiction. But what has remained, and even grown much more prominent, is a factor peculiar to the university *career*: whether a private lecturer [like the one I have described], let alone an assistant, will ever succeed in obtaining a position as a full professor, or even as head of an institute, is purely a *gamble*. Chance is certainly not the only factor, but it does have an unusually large influence. I can hardly think of any other career in this world where chance plays such an [important] part. I feel all the more justified in saying this because it was owing to a number of absolutely fortuitous circumstances that I myself, at a very early age, ⟨362⟩ was called to a full professorship in a discipline in which people of my own age had at that time undoubtedly achieved more than I had. And I actually believe that this experience has given me a keener eye for the undeserved fate of the many whom chance has treated, and still treats, in precisely the opposite way and who cannot, in spite of all their ability, within this apparatus of selection reach the position that they would deserve.

The fact that chance, and not just ability as such, plays such an important role is not solely, or even mainly, owing to human factors, which of course manifest themselves in this selection [process], just as they do in any other one. It would be unjust to attribute to the inferior personal qualities of faculty members or ministry officials the responsibility for the indisputable fact that so many mediocrities play a prominent role in the universities. Instead, that fact is due to the laws of human co-operation as such – in particular, the co-operation between several corporate bodies (in this case: between the Faculties, who make proposals [for nominations], and the Ministries). ⟨363⟩ By way of comparison, we can take the proceedings in connection with the elections for the Papacy, which constitute the most important verifiable example of a similar selection of [individual] persons, and which we can observe through many centuries. Only rarely does the cardinal who is said to be the "favourite" stand a chance of being selected. Instead, it is as a rule the second or third most favoured candidate who is successful. The same is the case with the President of the United States: only exceptionally does the top man – that is to say: the most outstanding one – win the "nomination" in the party conventions and go on to contest the election. Instead, it is mostly the number two, and often the number three [who is "nominated"]. The Americans have already coined technical sociological terms for these categories, ⟨364⟩ and it would be quite interesting to use these examples to study the laws governing selections through the formation of a collective will. We shall not do this here today. But [those laws] also hold for collegiate university bodies; and what is surprising is not so much that [those bodies] often make the wrong choice, but rather that the number of *correct* appointments is nevertheless, relatively speaking, very considerable. In a few countries, the parliament or – as in our own country up till now – the monarch (both have quite the same effect) or, at present, revolutionary power-holders ⟨365⟩ intervene for *political* reasons; and in those cases, one can be sure that the only people who stand a chance are complacent mediocrities or careerists.

No university teacher thinks back with pleasure on discussions of appointments, for they are seldom pleasant. Nevertheless, I can say that, in the numerous cases that I know about, the sincere *intention* to decide the matter on its merits was always present, without exception.

One should be clear about this: If decisions on academic destinies are to such an extent a "gamble", it is not just because selection through the formation of a collective will is [an] inadequate [procedure]. Every young man who feels that he has a vocation to be a scholar must realize that the task awaiting him has a dual aspect. He must have qualifications not only as a scholar, but also as a teacher; and the two are by no means identical. One can be a quite outstanding scholar and an absolutely awful teacher. Let me remind you of how men such as Helmholtz and Ranke did their teaching – and they are not just rare exceptions. Now, it is a fact that our universities, the small ones in particular, are competing for students in the most ridiculous manner. The narrow-minded landlords in the university towns celebrate the arrival of the thousandth student, and they would like nothing better than to organize a torchlight procession for the two thousandth. ⟨366⟩ It should be frankly admitted that it has a positive influence on the income from student fees if the neighbouring disciplines have teachers who "bring in the crowds". And, even apart from that, the number of students [attending a course of lectures] does, after all, constitute tangible proof, measurable in figures, of the lecturer's teaching qualities, whereas scholarly quality is imponderable and often, quite naturally, a matter of dispute, especially in the case of bold innovators. Consequently, almost everyone succumbs to the idea that a large attendance at lectures brings immense benefits and is of immeasurable value. If it is said of a lecturer that he is a bad teacher, that usually amounts to an academic death sentence, even if he is the greatest scholar in the world. But the answer to the question whether someone is a good or a bad teacher is found in the frequency with which the gentlemen of the student body honour [his lectures] with their presence. However, the fact is that, if the students flock to a [particular] teacher, this is to a very large extent owing to purely extraneous factors – his exciting delivery, even the tone of his voice – to a degree that is scarcely credible. On the basis of my experience (which is after all quite extensive), coupled with sober reflection, I have a deep distrust of mass lectures, even if they, too, cannot of course be wholly dispensed with. Democracy has its proper place. But academic training, of the kind that we should provide at our German universities, in keeping with their traditions, is a matter of *intellectual aristocracy*, and we should be under no illusions on that score. On the other hand, it is also true that perhaps the most difficult pedagogical task of all is that of presenting scientific problems in such a way that an untrained but receptive mind can understand them and – this is the only important point for us – think about them in an independent manner. That is certainly so. But whether that task has been accomplished is something that cannot be decided on the basis of the number of students attending a lecture. And – to come back to our theme – that [pedagogical] art is a personal gift which by no means coincides with the scientific qualities of a scholar. And, unlike France, we have no body of "immortals" of learning; ⟨367⟩ instead, according to our tradition, the universities must satisfy both demands: for research and for teaching. But, whether the abilities necessary for doing both can be found within a single individual is a matter of pure chance.

Academic life, then, is a wild gamble. When young scholars come to ask one's advice about applying for admission as private lecturers, the responsibility, if one encourages them, is almost too much to bear. If he is a Jew, one will of course say to him: *lasciate ogni speranza.* ⟨368⟩ But one must ask all the others, too, to examine their conscience and answer the question: Do you think that you can bear to see one mediocrity after the other getting ahead of you, year after year, without becoming embittered and a broken man? Naturally, one gets the same answer every time: "Of course I can: I live only for my 'vocation'". But I, for one, have known only a very few who were able to live with [that experience] without damage to their own soul.

This was what [I felt it] necessary to say about the external conditions of the scholarly profession.

However, I believe that you really want to hear about something else: about the *inner* vocation for science. Nowadays, the inner attitude towards the pursuit of science as a profession is first of all determined by the fact that science has entered a stage of unprecedented specialization, and that this will continue in the limitless future. This situation does not simply concern [science in its] external aspect; no, precisely in its internal aspect it means that an individual can only feel certain of achieving something completely perfect in the scientific domain [if he is working] under conditions of rigorous specialization. Whenever our work spreads into the domain of neighbouring disciplines (this happens from time to time, and sociological work in particular, to take an example, must necessarily do so again and again), we must resign ourselves to the realization that, at best, we are providing the specialists with useful *questions* that they may not so easily become aware of from the vantage point of their own discipline, but that our own work must necessarily remain highly imperfect. Only through strict specialization can the academic worker in the field of science really and fully, once and perhaps never again in his entire life, get the feeling: "Here, I have achieved something that is going to *last*". Nowadays, a truly definitive and excellent achievement is always a specialist achievement. Therefore, if someone is not able to, so to speak, put on blinkers and get completely caught up in the idea that the fate of his soul depends on whether he makes the correct conjectural reading of this, precisely this, passage in this manuscript – then he should stay well away from science. He will never within himself live through what may be called the "inner experience" of science. If one does not know this strange exhilaration, which all outsiders only smile at, this passion, this feeling that "millennia had to pass ere thou camest to life, and other millennia wait in silence" ‹369› to see whether this conjecture is correct, then one does *not* possess the vocation for science, and one should do something different. For nothing is worth anything for a human being, as a human being, unless he is *able to* do it with *passion*.

However, it is [also] a fact that any amount of such passion, however genuine and deep it may be, cannot even come close to forcing the result. It is true, though, that [passion] is a precondition of the decisive factor: the "inspiration". Among young people nowadays, the idea is apparently very widespread that science has become a matter of calculation; that it is produced as if "in a factory": in laboratories and statistical card indexes, not with the whole of one's "soul", but only with cool reason. This above all invites the comment that [those young] people on the whole have no clear idea of what goes on in a factory, or in a laboratory. In one, as in the other, some idea – and moreover: the right idea – has to *occur* to a person if he is to achieve anything worthwhile. But that [process of] inspiration cannot be forced; and it has nothing to do with cool calculations of any kind. True, [such calculations] are also an absolute precondition. For instance, no sociologist – even if he is advanced in years – should actually consider himself to be above making many tens of thousands of quite trivial calculations in his head, perhaps for months on end. ‹370› And if he wishes for [those calculations] to yield anything, he will pay a penalty for trying to rely solely on mechanical aids. In any case, what one does get [out of those figures] is often precious little; but he will not even achieve that "little" if some definite idea does not "occur" to him concerning the orientation of his calculations and (in the course of performing them) concerning the significance of the individual results that he obtains. As a rule, for an idea to ripen, very hard work is needed. Not always, of course. The idea [that occurs] to an amateur can be just as important for science as that of the expert – or [even] more important. Indeed, it is to amateurs that we owe many of the very best problem formulations and insights in our field. The only difference between the amateur and the expert is that the working methods of the amateur – as Helmholtz said of Robert Mayer ‹371› – are not sufficiently sound and secure, so that he is mostly not in a position to check the viability and assess the importance of the idea, or to pursue it in practice. A flash of inspiration is no substitute for work. And on the other hand, work does not eliminate the need for inspiration, nor can it force it to appear – any more than passion can. Both of them – and especially both *together* – can entice it. But it comes when it chooses, not when we choose. It is certainly true that the best ideas do not come while one is sitting at one's desk, brooding and pondering. They come, as Jhering has described it, while one is sitting on a sofa and smoking a cigar; or, as Helmholtz observes of himself with the precision of the natural scientist, during a walk on a gently rising road; or in similar circumstances – at any rate: when they are not expected. But on the other hand, they would not have presented themselves to someone who had not sat brooding at his desk, and who had not passionately pursued those problems. Be that as it may: if one does scientific work, one has to accept that all such work has an element of pure chance: will the "inspiration" come or not? Someone may be an excellent worker and yet never have had a valuable idea of his own. But it is a grave error to suppose that [all] this is true only of science, and that, in an office (to take an example), things are different from a laboratory. A businessman or a big industrialist who does not possess a "business imagination" – that is to say: who does not have ideas, brilliant ideas – is a man who, for the whole of his life, would have been better suited as a clerk or a technical official: he will never be an innovator in his organization. In spite of what conceited scholars may imagine, the role played by inspiration in the domain of science is not more important than it is in those areas where modern entrepreneurs tackle the problems of practical life. And on the other hand – and this is often not appreciated – its role is no less important than in the domain of art. It is childish to imagine that a mathematician could arrive at any scientifically valuable result by sitting at a desk with a ruler or with other mechanical tools or calculators. Of course, the mathematical imagination of a scholar such as Weierstrass is quite differently oriented, in terms of its nature and its results, from [the imagination] of an artist; and qualitatively, the two are fundamentally different. But not as far as the psychological process is concerned. Both are intoxication (in the sense of Plato's "manía" ⟨372⟩) and "inspiration".

Now, whether someone has flashes of scientific inspiration depends on fates that are hidden from us, but also on [having] the "gift". It is not least this undoubted fact that has led to an outlook which is – quite understandably – especially popular among young people, and which nowadays puts itself at the service of certain idols whose cult is now spreading on every street corner and in every periodical. Those idols are: "personality" and "experiencing". The two are closely connected, and the idea is prevalent that "experience" constitutes "personality" and is a necessary part of it. People work hard to have "experiences" – since that is of course necessary for a conduct of life in keeping with [one's] personality – and if they do not succeed, then they must at least act as if they possess that gift of grace. Formerly, that [sort of] "experience" was in plain language called a "sensation", and people had – so I think – a more appropriate idea of what a "personality" was and what it signified.

Ladies and gentlemen! In the realm of science, the only persons who have "personality" are those who are *wholly devoted to the task* [*before them*]. And this does not only apply to the domain of science. We know of no great artist who has ever done anything other than to serve his art and that alone. Even a personality of Goethe's stature had to pay a price, as far as his art was concerned, for having taken the liberty of wanting to turn his "life" into a work of art. You may be inclined to disagree with that; but, in any case, only a Goethe could be allowed to take such a liberty. And at least no one will dispute that even for [Goethe] – who only appears once in a thousand years – there was a price to be paid. The situation is no different in the political sphere, but I shall not speak of this today. But, in the domain of science, someone is quite definitely not a "personality" if he walks on to the stage himself, acting as an impresario for the task that he should devote himself to; if he tries to legitimize himself by what he "experiences"; and if he asks [himself]: "How can I prove that I am something other than a mere 'expert'[?] How can I manage to say, in form or in substance, what nobody has ever said before quite like that[?]". This phenomenon occurs on a massive scale nowadays. It always gives an impression of pettiness, and it demeans the person who asks such questions, whereas his inner devotion to his task, and to that alone, could have raised him to the height and dignity of the cause that he purports to serve. In this respect, too, the situation of the artist is no different.

While our work shares these preconditions with [the sphere of] art, it is subject to a fate that makes it vastly different from that of the artist. Scientific work is harnessed to the course of *progress*; but there is – in this sense – no progress in the domain of art. It is not true that a work of art from a period where new techniques had been acquired – or, say, the laws of perspective had been mastered – should therefore from a purely artistic point of view be superior to [a work of art] that had not benefited from any knowledge of those techniques and laws – *provided* that this [more "primitive"] work of art was appropriate both in substance and in form – that is to say: [provided] that it selected and shaped its object in a way that was in conformity with artistic norms, given the absence of those conditions and techniques. A work of art that achieves true "fulfilment" will never be surpassed; it will never become obsolete. Each individual may have a different assesssment of its significance for himself personally; but nobody will ever be able to say of a work [of art] that, in an artistic sense, achieves true "fulfilment" that it has been "surpassed" by another work of art that also achieves "fulfilment". But in the field of science, every one of us knows that what he has accomplished will be obsolete in ten, twenty or fifty years. That is the fate – indeed, that is the very *meaning* of scientific work; and it is subject to and dedicated to [that meaning] in a quite specific sense, compared to all other cultural elements of which the same might otherwise be said: Every scientific "fulfilment" implies new "questions" and *demands* to be surpassed and rendered obsolete. Everyone who wishes to serve science will have to resign himself to this. Undoubtedly, [a piece of] scientific work can remain important because its artistic qualities make it "enjoyable", or as a didactic tool. But let me repeat: To be surpassed in the field of science is not only the fate that we all share, it is the goal that we all work towards. We cannot work without hoping that others will go further than we [have done]. In principle, this progress is unlimited. And this brings us to the problem of the *meaning* of science, since it is not at all self-evident that something subject to such a law can in itself have meaning and sense. Why does one engage in something that, in actual fact, never comes to an end, and never can? Well, first of all for purely practical purposes – technical purposes, in the wider sense of that term: in order to be able to orient our practical action according to the expectations that scientific experience provides us with [knowledge of]. Well and good. However, that is only important for someone who engages in practical action. So what is the inner attitude of a man of science towards his own profession (provided, of course, that he feels the need to have [such an attitude])? He will maintain that he engages in scientific work "for its own sake" and not just because other people may use [scientific knowledge] to achieve positive results in the field of business or technology – because they can get better food, better clothing, better lighting and better government [in that way]. But in what sense does he believe that it is meaningful to achieve those results, which are always doomed to obsolescence – in other words: [how can it be meaningful for him] to let himself be harnessed to this specialized enterprise, which goes on for ever? That calls for some general considerations.

Scientific progress is a fraction – indeed, the most important fraction – of that process of intellectualization to which we have been subject for thousands of years, and which usually provokes such extraordinarily harsh reactions these days.

Let us first of all get a clear picture of what this intellectualistic rationalization, through science and scientifically oriented technology, actually means in practice. [Does it mean], for instance, that we – let us say: everyone sitting in this hall – know more about the conditions determining our lives than an Indian or a Hottentot? Hardly so. If one of us goes on the tram, he has not the faintest idea – unless he is a physicist by profession – about how that tram is able to move. Nor does he need to know anything about it. For him, it is enough to be able to "count on" the tram behaving [in a certain way]; he orients his [own] behaviour accordingly. But how to build a tram so that it will move – that is something which he knows nothing about. In that respect, the savage knows incomparably more about his tools. Today, if we spend money, I am willing to bet that almost everyone [in this room] – and this even goes for those fellow economists who might be present – will have a different answer to this question: "What is it about money that enables it to buy something – sometimes a lot, sometimes a little?". The savage knows how to manage to get something to eat every day, and what institutions can help him to do so. In other words, increased intellectualization and rationalization do *not* bring with them a general increase in our knowledge of the conditions under which we live our lives. What they bring with them is something else: the knowledge, or the belief, that *if we wished to*, we *could* at any time learn about [the conditions of our life]; in other words: that, in principle, no mysterious and unpredictable forces play a role in that respect, but that, on the contrary, we can – in principle – *dominate* everything by means of *calculation*. And that, in its turn, means that the world has lost its magic. Unlike the savage, for whom those forces existed, we no longer need to resort to magical means in order to dominate or solicit the spirits. That can be done by technology and calculation. This, above all, is the meaning of intellectualization as such.

This process of loss of magic, which has been going on continually in Western culture for thousands of years, and more generally, this "progress", to which science belongs both as a constituent part and as a driving force – do they have any meaning over and above the purely practical and technical? This question is raised in its most fundamental form in the works of Leo Tolstoy. He arrived at it in a peculiar way. To an increasing extent, the problem that he was pondering revolved around the question whether *death* was a meaningful phenomenon or not. ‹373› For him, the answer was negative, as far as the culturally developed human being was concerned. And the reason that he gave was that the individual life of civilized man has its place within an infinite "progress", and should therefore never, in terms of its own inherent meaning, come to an end, since anyone who has his place within such progress always has further progress ahead of him: No one dies at the pinnacle [of life], because that pinnacle lies in infinity. Abraham, or any peasant who died in olden days, died "old and full of years" ‹374› because he was part of the organic cycle of life; because his life, even in terms of its [inherent] meaning, had given him what it had to offer when its evening came; because there were no more riddles that he wished to solve; thus, he could have [had] "enough" of [his life]. But the culturally developed human being, who is placed within the continual [process of] enrichment of his civilization with ideas, knowledge and problems – [that] man can become "tired of life", but not grow ["]full of years["]. For he will only catch hold of the tiniest part of what the life of the spirit constantly begets, and it will always be something provisional, never anything definitive; consequently, death is a meaningless occurrence for him. And because death is meaningless, cultural life in itself will also be meaningless, since it is the senseless "progressive character" of cultural life that brands death as meaningless. One finds this idea as a keynote of Tolstoy's art in all his later novels.

What do we think of that [way of reasoning]? Does "progress" as such have a discernible meaning that goes beyond the merely technical, so that it might be a meaningful occupation to work in the service of progress? This question must be raised. But this is no longer just a question of [someone's] vocation *for* science – that is to say: the problem of what science as a profession means to those who devote their lives to it – but also another [question]: What is the *vocation of science* within the totality of human life? And what is its value?

Here, the contrast between past and present is immense. You may recall the wonderful image at the beginning of Book Seven of Plato's *Republic*: ‹375› The men in the cave, chained, with their faces turned towards the wall of rock in front of them; the source of light is behind them and they cannot see it; therefore, they only occupy themselves with the shadows which it casts on the wall, and try to understand how they relate to each other. And then one of them succeeds in breaking his chains; he turns around – and sees the sun. Dazzled, he gropes around and speaks stammeringly of what he has seen. The others say that he is mad. But gradually, he learns to look into the light, and then his task is to go down to the men in the cave and to lead them up to the light. He is the philosopher, and the sun is the truth of science – that science which alone does not grasp at illusory constructions and shadows, but seeks true being.

But who takes that view of science nowadays? Today, the general feeling of young people in particular is probably rather the opposite one. [They see] the theoretical constructions of science as an unreal world where artificial abstractions try to grasp the lifeblood and sap of real life with their wizened hands, but never succeed in catching hold of them. Instead, the[se young people] find true reality pulsating here in life, in what was for Plato the play of shadows on the walls of the cave: that other world consists of lifeless phantoms abstracted from reality, and nothing else. How did this transformation come about? Ultimately, the passionate enthusiasm of Plato in the *Republic* can be explained by the fact that, for the first time, the meaning of one of the great instruments for all attainment of scientific knowledge: the *concept*, was found and raised to full awareness. It was Socrates who discovered its full importance. He was not the only one in the world to discover it. In India, you can find the first beginnings of a logic quite similar to that of Aristotle. But nowhere else was there this awareness of its importance. Here, for the first time, there seemed to be an instrument with which you could grip someone in a logical vice so that he could not escape without admitting either that he knew nothing, or that this and nothing else was the truth, the *eternal* truth that was imperishable, unlike the doings of those blind people [in the cave]. That was the tremendous insight experienced by the pupils of Socrates. And from this it seemed to follow that if you could just find the right concept of beauty, of goodness, perhaps of courage, or of the soul – or whatever it might be – then you could also grasp its true essence; and that, in its turn, seemed to show the way towards knowing and teaching how to act rightly in life – and especially as a citizen, [since] that was the crucial thing for the ancient Greeks, whose thinking was political through and through. That was why they engaged in science.

To this discovery by the Hellenic mind was added the second great instrument of scientific work, born of the Renaissance: the rational experiment, as a means of controlling experience reliably; without [this instrument], modern empirical science would be impossible. There had been earlier experiments: for instance, physiological [experiments were conducted] in India in order to enhance the ascetic techniques of the yogi; ⟨376⟩ mathematical experiments were made in Ancient Greece for purposes of military technology; and, in the Middle Ages, there were experiments, for example in the field of mining. But it was the achievement of the Renaissance to elevate the experiment to the status of the principle of research as such. And the pioneers were the great innovators in the realm of *art*: Leonardo and others like him – above all, characteristically, the musical experimenters of the sixteenth century with their experimental claviers. ⟨377⟩ From these men, the experiment moved into the field of science (especially through Galilei) and of theory (through Bacon); and then it was adopted by the exact specialized disciplines in the continental universities, beginning with Italy and the Netherlands in particular.

Now, what did science mean to these people living on the threshold of the modern age? For the experimenters in art, such as Leonardo, and for the musical innovators, it meant the path to *true* art, which for them also meant: the path to true *nature*. Art was to be raised to the status of a science, and that also – and above all – meant that the artist was to be raised to the status of a learned doctor [of sciences], both socially and in terms of the meaning of his life. That ambition also underlies Leonardo's "Treatise on Painting", ‹378› for example. And today? "Science as the path to nature" – that would sound like blasphemy to young people. No, [for them] it is the other way round: [they want] to be released from the intellectualism of science, in order to return to their own nature, and hence to nature itself! Or perhaps even: science as the way to art? Here, no criticism is needed. – But in the age when the exact sciences emerged, even more was expected of science. Perhaps you recall the words of Swammerdam: "I bring you here the demonstration of divine providence in the anatomy of a louse"; ‹379› this shows you what the scientist of those times, under (indirect) Protestant and Puritan influence, felt to be his special task: [that of finding] the way to God. At that time, it was no longer to be found in the [works of the] philosophers, with their concepts and deductions; every Pietist theologian of those days (Spener in particular) knew that God could not be found by that method, which the Middle Ages had employed in their search for him. God is hidden; his ways are not our ways, his thoughts are not our thoughts. ‹380› But people hoped to find clues to his intentions for the world in the exact natural sciences, where his works were physically tangible. And today? Apart from a few overgrown children (who are especially to be found in the natural sciences), does anybody still believe that astronomical or biological or physical or chemical knowledge can teach us anything about the *meaning* of the world, or at least about the way in which one could find clues to such a "meaning" – if indeed there is one? If anything, scientific knowledge is likely to ensure that the belief that the world *has* something like a "meaning" will wither at the root! Or even: science as the path "to God"? Science, the power which is specifically alien to God! This fact – [that science is alien to God] – is something that no one today, whether he admits it to himself or not, will really doubt in his heart of hearts. The fundamental prerequisite of living in communion with the divine is to be liberated from the rationalism and intellectualism of science: this, or something of a similar nature, is one of the fundamental points that emerge when young people with a religious disposition, or who are in search of religious experience, express their feelings. And not just with respect to religious experience, but to experience of any kind. What is strange, though, is the course that they adopt: The spheres of the irrational – the only ones that intellectualism had so far left untouched – are now raised to the level of consciousness and brought under its magnifying glass . That is what the modern intellectualistic and romanticized [cult of the] irrational amounts to in practice. This way of liberating oneself from intellectualism is likely to bring with it the exact opposite of what those who choose it believe that it will achieve. – A final point: Naïve optimists have celebrated science – that is to say: the techniques of mastering life that are based on science – as the road to *happiness*; but I think I may be allowed to ignore this [idea] completely, in view of Nietzsche's devastating criticism of those "ultimate men" who have "invented happiness". ‹381› Who believes it, apart from a few overgrown children occupying academic or editorial chairs?

Let us return [to our subject]. Given these inner conditions, what is the meaning of science as a profession, since all those earlier illusions – "the path to true being", "the path to true art", "the path to true nature", "the path to the true God", "the path to true happiness" – have evaporated? The simplest answer was that given by Tolstoy ‹382› with the words: "[Science] is meaningless because it does not furnish an answer to the only question of importance to us: 'What should we do? How should we live?'". It is simply an indisputable fact that [science] does not give that answer. The question is, though, in what sense it "does not" give an answer, and whether it might not nevertheless perhaps be of some assistance to those who put the question in the right way. – Nowadays, it is common to speak of a science "without presuppositions". Does that exist? It depends on what is meant by it. In any piece of scientific work, one always has to assume the validity of the rules of logic and method[ology] – those general foundations of our orientation in this world. Well, those presuppositions are the least problematical ones, at least in the context of the particular question that we are asking. But, moreover, any scientific activity is based on the presupposition that its results will be *important* in the sense of "being worth knowing". And, obviously, that is where all our problems begin, as this presupposition itself cannot be proved by scientific means. It can only be *interpreted* with respect to its ultimate meaning, which one may then reject or accept, according to one's own ultimate attitude to life.

Futhermore, the relationship between scientific work and these presuppositions varies very considerably according to their structure. Natural sciences such as physics, chemistry and astronomy assume as a matter of course that the ultimate laws governing cosmic occurrences – to the extent that science is able to formulate them – are worth knowing. Not just because that knowledge makes it possible to achieve technical results; but also "for the sake [of those sciences] in themselves" – if they are to be a "vocation". That presupposition in itself simply cannot be proved. And even less is it possible to prove whether the existence of the world that they describe is valuable – whether that world has a "meaning", and whether it is meaningful to live in it. That is a question that [these sciences] do not consider. Or take a practical art such as modern medicine, which is so highly developed scientifically. The general "presupposition" of medical practice is, trivially formulated, that one must accept the task of preserving life as such and of reducing suffering as such to the extent possible. And that is problematical. A patient who is terminally ill may beg to be released from life; in the eyes of his relatives, that life may have lost all its value; they may wish for him to be released from his suffering; the cost of preserving that worthless life (perhaps he is a wretched lunatic) may be unacceptably high for them; and, whether they admit it to themselves or not, they may therefore wish for his death; but [nevertheless], the doctor will keep the patient alive with the means at his disposal. The presuppositions of medicine, and the Criminal Code, will prevent him from taking a different course. Medical science does not ask whether or when life is worth living. All the natural sciences provide us with an answer to the question: "What should we do *if* we want to have *technical* mastery of life?". But *whether* we should have such technical mastery, whether we want to have it, and whether it actually, in the last resort, makes sense to have it – those are questions that [those sciences] do not concern themselves with, or that they assume as given for their purposes. Or take a discipline such as aesthetics. It is a given for that discipline that works of art exist, and it tries to establish under what conditions this is so. But it does not pose the question whether the realm of art is perhaps a realm of diabolical splendour, a kingdom of this world and therefore in its innermost depths inimical to the divine and, with its profoundly aristocratic spirit, inimical to the fraternity [of man]. Thus, it does not ask whether works of art *should* exist. – Or take jurisprudence. [That discipline] determines what is valid [law] according to the rules of legal thought, which is based partly on logically binding [conclusions], partly on conventionally established constructions; in other words: [it determines what is legally valid] *provided that* certain legal rules and certain methods of interpreting [those rules] are accepted as binding. But it does not tell us *whether* law should exist [at all] and *whether* these particular legal rules should be established. It can only indicate that, if one wants a certain result, then this [or that] particular legal rule is, according to the norms of our legal thinking, the appropriate means of achieving it. Or take the historical sciences of culture. They teach us to understand political, artistic, literary and social phenomena of a culture as resulting from the conditions that gave rise to them. But they do not as such furnish an answer to the question whether those cultural phenomena were, and are, *worthy* of existence; nor do they give an answer to another question: whether they are worth knowing. [These sciences] are based on the assumption that it is interesting to participate, by this procedure, in the community of "cultural beings". But they are unable to prove "scientifically" to anybody that this assumption is correct; and the fact that they make it does not in any way prove that it is self-evident. In actual fact, it is nothing of the kind.

But I should like to focus on those disciplines that I am most closely concerned with: sociology, history, economics, political science and those varieties of cultural philosophy that see it as their task to interpret them. It is often said that politics has no place in the lecture room; and I subscribe to that statement. [That principle] should be respected by the students. For example, I should regret it just as keenly if, say, pacifist-minded students were to gather around the podium in the lecture hall of my former colleague Dietrich Schäfer in Berlin and produce the same sort of commotion that anti-pacifist students are reported to have made ‹383› [during the lecture of] Professor Foerster, whose views are in many respects as far removed as possible from my own. But the university teacher, too, should respect the principle that politics has no place in the lecture room, particularly in a scientific discussion of politics – indeed: above all in that case. Taking a stand on practical political issues is one thing; the scientific analysis of political structures and of how parties stand is quite a different one. A person who speaks about democracy at a public meeting will make no secret of how he himself stands; in that forum in particular, he has the damned duty and obligation of taking a clear partisan position. In that case, the words that he employs are not instruments of academic analysis, but tools for political campaigning to win over others to his position. They are not ploughshares for lightening the soil of contemplative thought, but swords to be used against the opponent: weapons in the struggle. But in a lecture or an auditorium, it would be an outrage to use words in that way. In those [academic] settings, if someone is speaking on the subject of, say, "democracy", he will take its different forms, analyse how they function, determine the different consequences of this or that [form] for the conditions of life, and then contrast th[ose forms] with the other, non-democratic forms of political order, and attempt to get so far that *the student* will be able to find the point from which he can adopt a position towards [these forms of government] on the basis of *his own* ultimate ideals. But the genuine teacher will take great care to avoid forcing any sort of opinion on the student from the height of the rostrum, either explicitly or by suggestion (the most dishonest method being, of course, that of "letting the facts speak for themselves").

But why should we not do that? Let me say right at the outset that many highly esteemed colleagues [of mine] take the view that it is totally impossible to exercise that kind of self-restraint, and that, if it were possible, it would be ludicrous to do so. Now, it is impossible to demonstrate scientifically to an academic teacher what his duty is in that position. What we can demand of him is simply that he has the intellectual honesty to recognize that the problem of establishing facts, demonstrating what is true in mathematics or logic, or uncovering the internal structure of cultural values is entirely *heterogeneous* from the problem of furnishing an answer to the question of [what is] the *value* of culture and of its individual elements, and how one should accordingly *act* within the cultural community and political groupings. If he then goes on to ask why he should not deal with both [sets of problems] in the lecture room, the answer must be: because the lectern of an academic lecture room is not the proper place for the prophet or the demagogue. Both for the prophet and for the demagogue, it is written that "they should go forth into the streets and speak publicly". ‹384› In other words: speak where criticism is possible. In the lecture room, where one faces the audience, it is for them to keep silent and for the teacher to speak. And I find it irresponsible for an academic teacher to exploit this situation, where the students have to go to his lectures in order to get on in their [academic] careers, and where there is nobody present who [can] respond to him critically – exploit it so that, instead of giving his students, as is his duty, the benefit of his knowledge and academic experience, he imposes his personal political views on them. No doubt, an individual [lecturer] may find it impossible to suppress his subjective sympathies as much as he ought to. In that case, he must face the sharpest criticism in the forum of his own conscience. And [anyway], [his insufficient fulfilment of the demand] proves nothing: it is also possible to make errors of fact, but this does not in any way disprove that it is one's duty to seek the truth. If I therefore object to this [practice], it is not least – indeed: above all – in the interests of science. I am willing to demonstrate, with the writings of German historians as my evidence, that whenever the man of science introduces his own value judgement, complete understanding of the facts *ceases*. However, that goes beyond the limits of this evenings's topic, and would call for lengthy discussion.

I only ask how a devout Catholic and a Freemason, who follow the same course of lectures on the forms of church and state or on the history of religion, can ever be made to agree on the same *valuation* concerning those subjects?! That is out of the question. Nevertheless, the academic teacher must wish, and must demand of himself, to be of use to both of them through his knowledge and methods. Now, you will be quite justified in saying that the devout Catholic will also refuse to accept the factual account of the process by which Christianity emerged [if it is] propounded by a teacher who does not share his dogmatic assumptions. Undoubtedly so! But there is the following difference: It is indeed true that science "without presuppositions" – in the sense of rejecting religious ties – does not acknowledge "miracles" or "revelation". If it did, it would be untrue to its own "presuppositions". [But] the [religious] believer acknowledges both. And this "presuppositionless" science expects no less – but also *no more* – from [the believer] than the acknowledgement that, *if* that process had to be explained without the intervention of those supernatural elements (which cannot be taken into account as causal factors in an empirical explanation), then it must be explained in the way that science attempts to do. And the believer can acknowledge this without betraying his faith.

But, we may now ask, do the achievements of science have no meaning at all for those who are indifferent to facts as such and for whom only practical positions are of importance? Perhaps they do, after all. Let me just make this initial point: The first task of any competent teacher is to teach his students to acknowledge *uncomfortable* facts – by which I mean facts that are uncomfortable for his partisan views; and for every partisan view – including my own – there are certain facts that are extremely uncomfortable. I believe that when an academic teacher compels his listeners to make a rule of this, this is more than just an intellectual achievement; I would even be immodest enough to call it a "moral achievement", even though that may sound like using rather too much pathos to describe something that should simply go without saying.

So far, I have only discussed the *practical* reasons for not imposing one's personal views [on others]. But there is more to it than that. The "scientific" advocacy of practical standpoints is impossible for much more profound reasons (except in cases where one is discussing the means for achieving a goal that is presupposed as a fixed *given*). It is meaningless, in principle, because the different value orders of the world are in irresolvable conflict with each other. Old [John Stuart] Mill (whose philosophy I do not otherwise find praiseworthy, but he is right on this point) has made the remark that, if we start from pure experience, we arrive at polytheism. ‹385› That is a superficial formulation, and it sounds paradoxical, and yet there is truth in it. Today, if we know anything, we know once again that not only can something be sacred although it is not beautiful, it can also be sacred *because* and *insofar as* it is not beautiful. You can find evidence of that in the 53rd chapter of the Book of Isaiah ‹386› and in the 21st Psalm. ‹387› And not only can something be beautiful although it is not good – it can also be beautiful because of what is not good about it: Nietzsche has reminded us of that; ‹388› and, before him, you can find [the same idea] expressed in the "Fleurs du Mal", as Baudelaire called his volume of poems. And it is a commonplace that something can be true although, and because, it is not beautiful and not sacred and not good. But those are just the most elementary cases of this conflict between the gods of the different orders and values. I do not know how one could make a "scientific" judgement concerning the [respective] *value* of French and German culture. Here, too, different gods are in conflict – unceasing conflict – with each other. It is as it was in the ancient world, which had not yet lost the magic of its gods and demons, only in a different sense: The ancient Greeks brought sacrifices now to Aphrodite, now to Apollo; and, above all, each one of them sacrificed to the deities of his own city. This is how it still is today; but the magic is no longer there, nor the mythical, but deeply genuine plasticity which that conduct of the ancient Greeks possessed. And it is fate, but certainly not any kind of "science", that reigns over those gods and decides their struggle. What is accessible to understanding is only *what* the divine is for one or the other of these orders, or within each of them. That is the end of the matter as far as discussions in lecture rooms and by professors are concerned, although it naturally by no means brings to an end the tremendous problem of *life* involved in this matter. But in that respect, other forces prevail than the opinions of university professors. Who would presume to provide a "scientific refutation" of the ethic of the Sermon on the Mount ‹389› – for example, the dictum "Do not resist evil" or the image of turning the other cheek? ‹390› Nevertheless, it is clear that what is preached there is, from an innerworldly perspective, an ethic of debasement: one has to choose between the religious dignity bestowed by this ethic and the manly code of honour, which preaches something entirely different: "Resist evil – otherwise you will bear part of the responsibility for its dominance". For each individual, depending on his ultimate position, one [ethic] is the Devil and the other one is God; and each individual must decide which one is God and which one the Devil *for him*. And this holds good for all the orders of life. The grandiose rationalism of the ethical and methodical conduct of life that flows from every religious prophecy had dethroned this polytheism in favour of the "One thing that is needful". ‹391› – But, confronted with the realities of external and inner life, it was then forced to accept those compromises and relativizations with which we are all familiar from the history of Christianity. But, today, we live an "everyday existence" from the religious point of view. The numerous gods of former times, who have lost their magic and have therefore assumed the aspect of impersonal powers, rise up out of their graves, seek to dominate our lives and resume their eternal struggle among themselves. But what becomes so difficult for modern man in particular, and most of all for the young generation, is to meet the challenge of such an *everyday* existence. All the chasing after "experiences" stems from this weakness. For it is a weakness to be unable to face up to the grave fate of the age.

It is the fate of our culture, however, that we are again becoming more clearly aware of this situation, after a millennium during which our (allegedly or supposedly) exclusive orientation towards the sublime fervour of the Christian ethic eyes had blinded us to this situation.

But enough of these very far-reaching questions. The response of some members of our young generation to all this might be: "Yes, but after all we come to lectures in order to experience something more than just analyses and statements of fact". But that is a mistake on their part: in the professor, they are looking for something that is not to be found there – for a *leader*, not a *teacher*. But we have only been put on the academic platform for the purpose of *teaching*. Those are two different things, and it is easy to satisfy oneself that this is so. Let me take you back once more to America, since that is where such things can often be seen in their most clear and naked original form. An American boy learns far, far less than a German boy. He is subjected to an incredible number of examinations; but in spite of that, he has not yet, in terms of the *meaning* of his school life, become an absolute examination creature like the German boy. This is because the bureaucracy that requires an examination certificate as an entry ticket into the realm of the rewards of office is still in its early stages over there. A young American respects nothing and nobody, no tradition and no office, apart from the personal achievement of an individual; *that* is what Americans call "democracy". This is their conception of the meaning of that term, and that is what matters, however distorted reality may look when compared to that conception. His view of the teacher standing in front of him is as follows: He sells me his knowledge and his methods and is paid with my father's money, just as the woman at the greengrocer's sells my mother a cabbage, and that's that. However, if the teacher is, say, a football champion, then he is the student's leader in that field. But if he is not a football champion (or something comparable in another sport), then he is just a teacher and nothing more; and no young American would dream of letting [such a teacher] sell him "world views" or authoritative rules for the conduct of his life. This [conception] is unacceptable to us, formulated in that manner. But one may ask whether there is not a grain of truth in this way of looking at things (which I have deliberately exaggerated somewhat in this context).

Fellow students! You come to our lectures with these expectations concerning our leadership qualities without saying to yourselves beforehand that, out of a hundred professors, at least ninety-nine will not be football champions in [the game of] life – and that, on the contrary, they do not, and should not, claim to be "leaders" in matters concerning the conduct of life. You should bear in mind that the worth of an individual does not depend on whether he possesses leadership qualities. And, at any rate, *those* qualities that make someone an outstanding scholar and academic teacher are not the same as those that [would] make him a leader with respect to the practical orientation of life or, more particularly, in the political domain. If someone also possesses those [leadership] qualities, it is purely a matter of chance; and it is very problematical if everyone giving an academic lecture feels that it is expected of him that he should claim to possess them. And it is even more problematical if every academic teacher can play the leader in the lecture room at his own discretion: Those [teachers] who are most ready to see themselves in the role of a leader will often be the ones least suited to play that role; and above all, academic lecturing does not give them the slightest possibility of *proving* whether they can in fact play it. A professor who feels called upon to advise young people and who enjoys their confidence should show his worth in personal contacts, man to man. And if he feels called upon to intervene in the struggles of world views and partisan opinions, he should do so in the open, in the marketplace of life: in the press, in public meetings, in associations, wherever he likes. Surely it is a little too easy for him to demonstrate the courage of his convictions in places where those present – who perhaps hold different convictions – are condemned to silence.

Finally, you will ask: If that is the case, what is in fact the positive contribution of science to practical and personal "life". And that brings us back to the problem of the "vocation" [of science]. First of all, [science can] of course [give us] knowledge of the techniques for controlling life – the external world as well as human actions – by calculation. Well, you may say, that is merely the woman at the greengrocer's [in the example] of the young American. I quite agree. Second – and this, after all, is something that the woman at the greengrocer's does not [provide us with] – methods of reasoning: the instruments [of thought] and intellectual training. You may reply: well, this is not vegetables, but it is nothing more than the means of procuring vegetables. All right; I will not argue about this tonight. But fortunately, science can contribute even more than that; we are able to offer you a third benefit: achieving *clarity*. Provided, of course, that we possess it ourselves. Insofar as this is the case, what we can make clear to you is this: In practice, it is possible to take this or that position with regard to the value problem at issue in each given case (for the sake of simplicity, I will ask you to take social phenomena as examples). *If* you take this or that position, then scientific experience tells us that you must apply such and such *means* in order to implement your position in practice. Now, these means may in themselves have such a character that you feel that you must refuse to employ them. Then, you simply have to choose between the end and the unavoidable means. Does the end "justify" those means, or not? The teacher can lay before you the necessity of [making] this choice; but he cannot do more than that, as long as he wishes to remain a teacher and not to become a demagogue. Moreover, he can of course say to you: If you want [to achieve] this or that end, then you must accept such and such side effects that experience tells us will then occur. Here, we again have the same situation. However, all these problems are still of the kind that any technician may be faced with, since he, too, must in numerous cases make decisions according to the principle of the lesser evil or of what is, relatively speaking, the best option. But, for him, one main thing – the *goal* – is usually given, while this is precisely *not* the case for us, as soon as truly "ultimate" problems are involved. And this brings us to the last contribution that science as such can make in the service of clarity; and at the same time, we reach its limits. We can – and we should – also tell you this: In terms of its *meaning*, this or that practical standpoint can be derived with inner consistency, and therefore with honesty, from such and such an ultimate fundamental position (possibly from one, possibly from several different ones) based on a world view, but not from such and such other [fundamental positions]. Figuratively speaking, you serve this god *and offend that other god* when you decide in favour of a certain standpoint, since, if you remain true to yourself, you will necessarily arrive at such and such ultimate, inner *consequences* in terms of meaning. At least in principle, it is possible to make such statements; and the discipline of philosophy, as well as the essentially philosophical discussions of principle within the specialized scientific disciplines, attempt to do so. In that way, we can, if we are competent enough (which I shall assume here), compel the individual – or at least help him – to *give an account to himself of the ultimate meaning of his own conduct*. It seems to me that this is not such a small contribution, and [it is] also of value in one's personal life. Here, too, I am tempted to say that a teacher who succeeds in doing this is acting in the service of "moral" forces – that is to say: assuming the duty of creating clarity and a sense of responsibility; and I believe that the more conscientiously he can avoid seeking to force a position on his listener or to convey it to him by suggestion, the better he will fulfil that duty.

Admittedly, the assumption that I am putting forward here is always based on this one fundamental fact: a life that is self-contained and understood on its own terms can only acknowledge that those gods are forever warring with each other – or, in non-figurative language: [it must acknowledge] that the ultimate *possible* standpoints towards life are irreconcilable, and that the struggle between them can therefore never be bindingly resolved; – in other words, that it is necessary to *decide* which one to choose. Whether, under those circumstances, it is worth having science as one's "vocation", and whether science itself has an objectively valuable "vocation" – that is again a value judgement about which nothing can be said in the [academic] lecture room, since it is a *precondition* of academic teaching to answer [those questions] in the affirmative. As far as I myself am concerned, my own work constitutes an affirmative answer to that question. [The acceptance of that "vocation"] is also – even particularly – required from those who hate intellectualism like the worst of devils, as young people nowadays do (or, on the whole, only imagine that they do). In their case, the old saying applies: "Reflect: The devil is old; grow old to understand him". ⟨392⟩ That is not meant as a reference to the birth certificate, but to the fact, that if you want to get the better of this devil, you should not – run away from him (as so often happens nowadays); on the contrary: you must start by acquainting yourself fully with his ways, in order to see his power and his limitations.

Science today is a "vocation" that is pursued as a *profession*, in the service of knowledge of oneself and of relationships between facts; it is not a gift of grace, possessed by seers and prophets and dispensing salvation goods and revelations; nor is it a constituent part of the meditation of sages and philosophers on the *meaning* of the world. That is an ineluctable given of our historical situation, from which we cannot escape if we wish to remain true to ourselves. And if Tolstoy rises up within you once more and asks: "Since science does not do so, who, then, gives an answer to the question: What should we then do? and: How should we organize our lives? – or, in the language that I have employed here this evening: Which of those warring gods should we serve? or perhaps a completely different one, and who would that be?" – then the answer must be: only a prophet or a saviour. And if he is not to be found, or if his message is no longer believed, then you will certainly not bring him back to this earth by having thousands of professors attempt to usurp his role by carrying on in their lecture rooms as officially remunerated or privileged minor prophets. All that this will accomplish is that the knowledge of one crucial fact will never be brought home, with the full force of its significance, to so many in our youngest generation who are yearning for a prophet: that the prophet simply *is not* there. I believe that it can never, under any circumstances, be to the advantage of a truly religiously "musical" person, in particular to his inner needs, if this fundamental fact: that he is fated to live in an age alien to God and bereft of prophets, is concealed from him and from others by means of surrogates – and all these academic prophecies are such surrogates. It seems to me that the integrity of his religious sensibility must rebel against this. Now, you may be inclined to say: But in that case, what are we to think of the fact that there is something called "theology" that claims to be a "science"? Let us not evade the answer. "Theology" and "dogmas" are not a universal phenomenon; but they are certainly not unique to Christianity. On the contrary: they are also to be found (if we move backwards in time), in highly developed form, in Islam, in Manicheism, in Gnosticism, in Orphism, in Parseeism, ‹393› in Buddhism, in the Hindu sects, in Taoism and in the Upanishads, ‹394› and of course also in Judaism. (Admittedly, though, the extent to which they have been developed systematically does vary greatly.) And it is no accident that Western Christianity – in contrast to what Judaism, for example, contains in the way of theology – has developed [its theology and its dogmas] more systematically, or attempts to do so, nor that it is here that [their] development has had by far the most important historical consequences. This was a product of the Hellenic spirit, to which all theology of the West goes back – just as all theology of the East (apparently) goes back to Indian thought. All theology is an intellectual *rationalization* of the [sense of] possessing religious salvation. No science is completely without presuppositions, and no science can substantiate its own value to someone who rejects these presuppositions. But every theology does add [to these general presuppositions] some specific ones that are necessary for its work, and hence for the justification of its own existence. [It does so] in various senses and to various degrees. *Every* theology (including, for instance, that of Hinduism) has as its presupposition that the world must have a *meaning*; and it asks how that meaning must be interpreted so that this is conceivable. Just as Kant's epistemology proceeded from the presupposition that "scientific truth exists, and it is *valid*" ‹395› and then went on to inquire under what presuppositions of thought that would be (meaningfully) possible. Or, as modern philosophers of aestheticism (explicitly – such as, for instance, G[eorg] v. Lukács – or in fact) proceed from the presupposition that "works of art *exist*" and go on to ask: How is that (meaningfully) possible? However, as a rule, theology does not content itself with the [above-mentioned] presupposition (which in essence belongs to the philosophy of religion). Instead, it regularly bases itself on a further presupposition: that it is simply necessary to believe in certain "revelations" as facts that are important for salvation (that is to say: [as facts] without which a meaningful conduct of life is not possible), and that certain states and actions have a holy quality, and hence: that they constitute a religiously meaningful way of conducting one's life, or that they are at least constituent components of such a conduct of life. And theology then again asks: How can these presuppositions (which simply must be accepted) be meaningfully interpreted within the framework of a total view of the world? In that connection, those presuppositions themselves lie beyond what is "scientific" from the point of view of theology. They do not constitute "knowledge" in the usual sense [of that term]: they are something that one "has". Whoever does not "have" faith or ["is not in"] those other holy states cannot obtain them through any theology, let alone through another science. On the contrary: in every "positive" theology, ⟨396⟩ the believer will reach the point where the saying of Saint Augustine applies: "Credo non quod, sed *quia* absurdum est". ⟨397⟩ The ability to achieve this virtuoso performance of "sacrificing the intellect" is the crucial characteristic of a positively religious person. And the fact that this is so shows that the tension between the value spheres of "science" and religious salvation cannot be resolved, in spite of (or rather: as a consequence of) the theology, which after all reveals [that tension].

Properly speaking, the "sacrifice of the intellect" can only be made by the disciple to the prophet, or by the believer to the church. But, as yet, a new prophecy has never come into being simply because (I deliberately repeat the following metaphor, which many have found offensive ⟨398⟩) many modern intellectuals feel the need to furnish their souls, as it were, with objects that are guaranteed as being genuinely antique, among which they remember that religion was also to be found. Admittedly, they don't have any religion; but by way of a substitute, they decorate a sort of private chapel and amuse themselves with decking it out with little images of saints from all sorts of places. Or they find a surrogate in all kinds of experience, which they invest with the dignity of possessing a mystical sanctity. And then – they go and peddle it on the book market. That is simply either fraud or self-deception. [On the other hand], it is certainly not a fraud, but something very serious and genuine – although it may sometimes express a mistaken interpretation of the meaning of one's own actions – when many of those communities of young people that have quietly grown up in recent years interpret their own human relationships in the community as having a religious, cosmic or mystical character. While it is true that every genuinely fraternal act can be accompanied by the knowledge that it contributes something of lasting value to a supra-personal realm, it seems to me questionable whether the dignity of purely human relations in communities is enhanced by those religious interpretations. But the further discussion of this question does not belong in this context.

It is the fate of our age – with the rationalization, the intellectualization and, above all, the disenchantment peculiar to it – that precisely the ultimate and most sublime values have withdrawn from the public sphere, either into the realm of mystical life in a world beyond the real one or into the fraternity of personal relations between individuals. It is no accident that our greatest art is intimate rather than monumental; nor [is it accidental] that it is today only in the smallest circles of the community, from one human being to another, pianissimo, that a pulse beats as a faint echo of that prophetic spirit which in former times swept through the great congregations ⟨399⟩ as a fire storm and welded them together. When we attempt to force through and "invent" a monumental conception of art, this results in those pathetic monstrosities that we find in the numerous monuments [erected during] the last twenty years. If one tries to create new religious constructions by brooding rumination but without new, genuine prophecy, then the result is similar – in an inner sense, which must have an even worse effect. And as for academic prophecy, that will certainly only create fanatical sects, but never a genuine community. If someone cannot endure this fate of the age like a man, he must be told that he should rather return to the merciful, wide open arms of the old churches – silently, purely and simply, without the usual publicity of the renegade. After all, they do not make it difficult for him. In the process, he must inevitably somehow, one way or another, make the "sacrifice of the intellect". If he is actually able to do so, we should not blame him for it. After all, such a sacrifice of the intellect in order to achieve unconditional religious devotion is still, from a moral point of view, not the same as shirking one's plain duty to be intellectually honest – which is what happens when one lacks the courage to make up one's mind about one's ultimate standpoint, but instead resorts to feeble relativization in order to make that duty less onerous. And for me, [the sacrifice of the intellect] ranks more highly than that sort of academic prophecy which does not realize that, within the confines of the lecture room, the only virtue is that of plain intellectual honesty. And that honesty demands that we should openly state that all those many who are longing for new prophets and saviours are in the same situation as that which emanates from the beautiful Edomitic watchman's song from the time of exile, which has been included among the oracles of Isaiah: "One is calling to me from Seir, 'Watchman, how long will the night still last?'. The watchman says: 'Morning comes, but it is still night. If you will inquire, come back another time.'" ‹400› The people to whom this was said has been inquiring and waiting for much longer than two thousand years, and we know its calamitous fate. This should teach us that it is not enough simply to yearn and wait; we should act differently: attend to our work and face up to the "demands of the day", ‹401› both personally and professionally. And those demands are plain and simple, as long as each of us finds and obeys the daemon ‹402› who holds the threads of *his* life.

First published as *Wissenschaft als Beruf,* Munich/Leipzig: Duncker und Humblot 1919.
Translated from: "Wissenschaft als Beruf" in Max Weber, *Gesammelte Aufsätze zur Wissenschaftslehre* (ed. Johannes Winckelmann), 3rd ed., Tübingen: J.C.B.Mohr (Paul Siebeck) 1968, pp. 582–613.
This essay is the revised and printed version of a lecture given by Max Weber in Munich to members of a Bavarian student organization on 7 November 1917.
The lecture was the first in a series planned by the organization on "'intellectual' / 'artistic' work as a profession and vocation" (see endnote 352). The lecture was to be published together with three other lectures (among them a second one, also by Max Weber, on "Politics as a profession and vocation"). But, since the two other lectures (on Education and Art, respectively) were delayed (in fact, they may never have been delivered at all), it was decided in January 1919 to publish the two lectures by Weber separately, and the two volumes appeared in July 1919. Weber was not altogether satisfied with his original lecture, which had been taken down in shorthand and typed out, and revised it fairly thoroughly before publication, although the essential structure and much of the original wording seem to have been retained.

CONTRIBUTIONS AND INTERVENTIONS

(Excerpts)

All the following contributions to, and interventions in, debates by Max Weber were originally printed in the *Verhandlungen des Vereins für Sozialpolitik 1905* (no. 1), *Verhandlungen des Vereins für Sozialpolitik 1909* (no. 2) or *Verhandlungen des ersten Deutschen Soziologentages 1910* (nos. 3–5). They have been translated from *Gesammelte Aufsätze zur Soziologie und Sozialpolitik* (ed. Marianne Weber), Tübingen: J.C.B.Mohr 1924, with the exception of Intervention 1, which was republished in *MWG* I/8 and has been translated from that text.

1 Association for Social Policy, Mannheim 1905

Intervention in debate after G. Schmoller's lecture on
"The relationship of cartels to the state"

[. . .]

I shall [. . .] now enter into [a discussion of] rather more fundamental viewpoints, where we are [. . .] in the last resort, dealing with differences between value judgements. I must therefore [. . .] state that no science, and least of all jurisprudence, is able to demonstrate the validity of any value judgement, or to prove that a legal rule, of whatever kind, should exist. I consider those jurists who have tried to claim such a role for themselves, as jurists, to be the most godforsaken bunch of people that one can imagine. If anyone is unsuited to make decisions about what *ought to* be, it is the jurist, who, if he wants to be a man of legal science, is obliged to be a formalist. I have all the more right to say this because I myself, as a professor of jurisprudence, have had the dubious pleasure of examining junior lawyers and therefore feel that I have some first-hand experience of jurists and their psychology. What we can say to the jurist ‹403› is never more than this: If you want to do such and such, then the following technical–juridical means can be employed for that purpose. That modest position is what the jurist should be confined to, just as we should confine ourselves to that position when we speak in our capacity as economists. But, gentlemen, I should have to protest if I were told that, when I speak in this forum, I speak as a man of science. Here, it is the human being as such who speaks, and no one else. What I know by virtue of my scientific work is working material that I only use when considering whether an ideal can be realized and what the probable consequences of its realization would be. The value of that ideal in itself can never ever be deduced from that working material.

[. . .]

MWG I/8, pp. 270–72.

2 Association for Social Policy, Vienna 1909

Intervention in discussion on "The productivity of the national economy"

The concept of "national prosperity" obviously implies all conceivable kinds of ethics. In order to eliminate that [aspect], one has recourse to the idea that "national prosperity" is identical with [a situation where] all individual participants in an economic group have the greatest possible income. Against this, I should like to point to the [example of] the Roman Campagna. It is owned by a handful of enormously rich landowners. They are confronted with a handful of enormously rich tenant farmers. They are [in their turn] confronted with a few handfuls of shepherds (I exaggerate somewhat), who *could* easily be paid so [well] by these pecuniary powers that they would not have to steal and to starve – so that they, too, would be "satisfied". If that were so, the sparse group of people populating this "desert" *might* enjoy a measure of prosperity in their private economy that [would] satisfy all their own demands. But if you, gentlemen, choose an evaluative position, of whatever kind – [provided] it is *not* absolutely identical with the egoistic interests of these few people, with their purely *private* interests in economic profit – then let me ask you: Are you satisfied with this situation? Is it consistent with your ideal of "productivity", in view of the fact that – leaving aside other points of view – there would be room on these huge estates for masses of farmers, with cash incomes the sum of which would be far greater than the sum of the incomes that this desert generates at present? But if one criticizes the present state of affairs from any such point of view, then one presupposes *another* concept of "prosperity" than that which has been developed here. Therefore, I believe that the concept of national prosperity that our colleague Liefmann has just *ü*developed has exactly the same implications as those which we reject, except that the wording is slightly different. This can be demonstrated by looking at just that example which was used [by Liefmann] concerning the destruction of currants and rice. ‹404› Liefmann says that the entrepreneurs realized that they must reduce the amount of capital and labour [expended on the procurement of rice and currants] to the extent necessary in order to retain an appropriate private income. Well and good – but the destruction of the rice was nevertheless harmful to certain interests that were without doubt present, namely the interests of those social strata [whose members] would have been very happy to acquire the currants or the rice at the cheapest possible price in order to use them for nourishment; the destruction was harmful to the private "prosperity" of [the members of] those strata. The interests that have here been taken as a basis are exclusively those of the entrepreneurs.

[. . .] To mix up prescriptive demands with scientific questions is the work of the Devil – which th[is] Association has, however, quite often carried out in generous measure.

This brings me to the real problem. It is certainly true that an empirical science can only be based on how [things] are, and it tells us *nothing* about how [they] ought to be. Nevertheless, I should not like this to be understood as if there could be no scientific discussion touching on the domain of the Ought. The question is only in what sense [this is possible]. To begin with, I can say to someone who confronts me with a certain value judgement: My dear fellow, you are mistaken about what you yourself really *want*. Look here, I take your value judgement and analyse it dialectically for you, by means of *logic*, in order to trace it back to its ultimate axioms, in order to show you what are the *possible* "ultimate" value judgements that it implies – value judgements that you simply have not been aware of, that are perhaps completely incompatible, or only compatible if compromises are made, and between which you consequently have to *choose*. That is not empirical work, but *logical* intellectual work. Then, I can go on to say: If you wish to act in accordance with this precise, really unambiguous value judgement in the interest of a particular Ought, *then* scientific experience shows that you must use such and such *means* in order to reach the end which corresponds to your value judgement. If those means are unacceptable to you, then you must *choose* between the means and the end. And finally, I can say to him: You must take into consideration that according to scientific experience, the means that are indispensable for carrying your value judgement into effect will also have other, unintended *side effects*. Do you also find those side effects desirable – yes or no? *Science* can take that man to the threshold of this "yes" or "no": up to that point, we are dealing with questions to which answers can be given by an empirical discipline, or by logic, that is to say, [they are] purely scientific questions. But the "yes" or "no" *itself* is *no longer* a question of science, but one to be answered according to [one's] conscience or subjective taste; in any case, the answer to it lies in a different intellectual sphere. Nevertheless, it is not in itself completely absurd to have discussions of practical questions even in a *scientific* association, as long as one is conscious of the fact that, in the last resort, the only questions that one can pose [are the following]: What are the [necessary] means and the side effects that must be accepted if one acts in accordance with this or that fundamental principle – those are questions of empirical science; and, in addition: What are the *ultimate* positions implicit in the value judgements that fight against each other – that is a [question to be answered by] logical discussion, [whose results are] also binding on everybody who thinks theoretically. The fall from grace only begins when those purely empirical or purely logical trains of thought are mixed up with subjective practical value judgements. [. . .]

Now, today we have been presented with a concept that in this respect is one of the worst possible ones; and instead of consigning it to the oblivion that it deserves, attempts have been made to save it. Admittedly, worthy attempts were made to analyse what a plethora of quite different "problems" we are dealing with when we employ the concept of economic productivity, which every demagogue adorns himself with these days. In the end, however, this again left us with "average judgements" that were to function as standards; and finally, the concept [of productivity] was accepted [. . .] in this form. I have to say, though, that I can't accept this. I hope that, in the long run, nobody will accept it; and, in fact, I regret that a *theoretical* question is discussed here in this manner. [The positions] are so inconsistent! In Herr v. Philippovich's excellent, limpidly clear paper, we find the totally correct statement that "*We have no* unitary value judgement". But no sooner has this been said than "productivity" bobs up again, and we are told that "average judgements" are made everywhere concerning what must happen. Exactly! and the task of science *ought to be* to criticize precisely those average judgements, to demonstrate the problems that lie hidden in them – and nothing else. If I constantly, with a certain amount of pedantry if you like, object so very vehemently when "what ought to be" is mixed up with "what is", it is not because I hold matters of "what ought to be" in low esteem, quite to the contrary: it is because I find it unbearable when problems of world-shaking importance, of the greatest ideal significance, in a sense the most exalted problems that may move the human heart, are transformed into a technical and economic question of "productivity" and made the object of discussions within a *specialized* discipline such as economics. Let us ask ourselves why those simple principles are so often sinned against, especially by members of our Association. The Association for Social Policy came into being not as a scientific but as a *practical* association – a small fighting body faced with formidable opponents. In that historical situation, it went without saying that, above all, it had to begin by demolishing all sorts of partisan talk posing as science. In so doing, it was confronted in *scientific* circles with the following prejudiced opinion: a science that has to deal with the pursuit of economic profit as the motive cause of social life must *therefore* also regard that striving as the only standard for the evaluation of human beings, of things, or of events. In their fight against this confusion between science and value judgement, what befell our academic mentors was that they committed exactly the same sin, but in reverse. In order to refute the claim to exclusive validity of that *standard of evaluation*, they tried to demonstrate that *other* causes of human action, besides the individual pursuit of economic profit, could be economically relevant. Naturally, they were completely justified in doing so! *But*: the result was that now, scientific investigation and value judgement were *even more strongly* intertwined in an intimate embrace, [and that] attempts were still made to support judgements concerning what *ought to be* with statements concerning facts and their interconnections. It was a sin that was extremely easy to explain, a "pardonable" one, almost unavoidable, and committed again and again by all of us and even more by all our opponents. But when this frequent [but still] occasional sin becomes an intellectual habit and is even made into a virtue, then we have to protest against it, particularly since we have over and over again been confronted with its many unpleasant consequences. It has happened again and again that if somebody did not share our *ethical* judgements, it was *therefore* believed that his *scientific* [point of view] could be dismissed. That is [an] impossible [position]. It is unacceptable for us, in spite of our deep respect for the generation that fought the great battles of the past, the generation whose epigones we are and who provide the massive foundations indispensable for our own work. This is the point where we must make the attempt to find a different basis; [. . .] and it is only to the advantage both of science and, *especially*, of *practical* striving when we make a clear distinction between the two. And when we observe, with a certain regret, that value judgements, even within our midst, are today more differentiated than they formerly were, honesty demands that we state this openly. We know of no ideals that can be demonstrated scientifically. And it is certainly more difficult to have to find [those ideals] within ourselves at a time that is already characterized by a subjectivist culture. But we are totally unable to promise a land of milk and honey, and a paved road leading to it, both in this world and in the next, both in thought and in action; and our human dignity is branded with [the realization] that our peace of mind cannot be as profound as that enjoyed by those who dream of such a [promised] land.

[. . .]

Dr. Goldscheid has tried to show that, in two cases, empirical science contains value problems. As for the first of these cases, I grant him that he is right; I can even claim to have said the same for years already: The question of *what* problems we decide to investigate – that is to say: what we shall interest ourselves in, what is *worth* knowing about – is a question of values and can only be answered on the basis of subjective value judgements. But naturally, this has nothing to do with [the other] question: When we deal with problems that interest us, do we have to treat them in such a way that every single *judgement* – because it lies in another intellectual sphere – is kept far removed from the *scientific* discussion? That, and only that, is the point. – The second case discussed by Dr Goldscheid has a different character. He has recommended that economics, too, should accept what is [otherwise] generally accepted and take the most highly regarded science, natural science, as its guide – [a recommendation that he sees as] particularly relevant to questions of what *ought to be*. Well, to begin with, I have to admit that those guides already in existence which are allegedly based on "natural science" are, in my opinion, perfectly useless. May I in this connection refer to a comment by our colleague [Professor] Zwiedineck. He has drawn my attention to the most recent form of the eternally popular and widespread practice of using the discoveries of the natural sciences as a basis for judgements concerning what ought to be: nowadays, this is done with reference to the laws of energy conversion, to the theory of entropy, [and] to the constant tendency of free energy to assume a static form. ‹405› There have even been attempts to formulate judgements on this basis as to what paint[ers] should take as [their] subject matter, and more of this kind. In my opinion, a true natural scientist would positively shudder if he were told that it was expected of him to introduce such practical value judgements into his work, or to pass them off as resulting from it. It was precisely from the natural sciences that we hoped for support when we formulated the idea of re-evaluation and reflection in our own discipline; we did not expect them to regard it as their duty to sin even more grievously than we ourselves have done.

[. . .]

Verhandlungen des Vereins für Sozialpolitik 1909, Leipzig: Duncker und Humblot, 1910, pp. 580–85 and 603–04.

3 German Sociological Society, General Meeting, Frankfurt 1910

Business Report

The Business Report of our Society, which it has fallen to me to deliver, must in the main deal with (1) the constitutional changes made by the Society during the past year and (2) the scientific tasks that the Society has set itself for the near future. Considering the varied meanings of the concept of "sociology", it is useful for a Society carrying that name – which is so unpopular in our country – to make it as clear as possible what it wants to stand for by giving quite concrete information concerning its present constitution and the next tasks that it now wants to take up.

As far as [the constitutional changes] are concerned, the following [principle] [. . .] has only found expression in our statutes during the last year: [. . .] That within the Society, in principle and definitively, no propaganda for *practical* ideas will be tolerated. The Society is "impartial", but not simply in the sense that it tries to be fair to everybody and to understand everybody, or to draw the popular "median line" between partisan views – political, social–political, ethical or aesthetic or other value judgements of any kind whatsoever. [Its "impartiality" means that] it has nothing at all to do with those positions: it is simply *of no* party in any domain. Consequently, the existence, the distinctive character, the demands and the successes of political, aesthetic, literary, religious and other partisan viewpoints can of course perfectly well become the object of an *analysis* that concerns itself with *the fact that they exist*, with the supposed and actual reasons for their existence, with their success and chances of success, and with their consequences in "principle" and in "practice" – and that establishes [its results in these respects] purely objectively and without any value judgement of its own. But paragraph 1 of our statutes now states that our Society may never discuss the For and Against, the value or lack of value of such a [partisan] viewpoint. For instance: If the Society organizes an inquiry into the situation of the press [. . .] this means, according to our principles, that the Society does not have the least intention of sitting in judgement on the actual state of affairs which it is to discuss, and that it will not ask whether this state of affairs is desirable or undesirable; it will do nothing more than establishing what the state of affairs is; why it is just the way it is; and what are the historical and social reasons for this.

[. . .]

Verhandlungen des Ersten Deutschen Soziologentages, Tübingen: J.C.B.Mohr (Siebeck), 1911, pp. 39–40.

4 German Sociological Society, General Meeting, Frankfurt 1910

Intervention in the debate on W. Sombart's paper on "Technology and culture"

[. . .]

Let me only make one remark: Of course, it is certainly correct [to say] [. . .] that the belief in the value *of science* is a precondition for all our work; nor have [we] disputed that. But what [we] did say was that in this forum, we want to exclude *practical* value questions concerning [our] *life*. Not because we hold them in lower esteem. On the contrary. I believe that each of us attaches *specific* importance to these practical problems, which involve [our] whole subjectivity, but which, for that very reason, are treated in quite another intellectual sphere. And a major consequence of this is precisely that we do *not* treat those problems as dry questions of fact, and therefore do not mix them up with the strictly objective, cool statements of fact that we discuss in this forum. Otherwise, [the treatment of] *both* kinds of problems will suffer.

[. . .]

Nowadays, the so-called materialist conception of history ‹406› is advanced in a way that completely obscures its real meaning. For instance, the discussion of the materialist conception of history has been hopelessly confused by the fact that an eminent scholar, Stammler, interprets it in a way that would indeed have astounded Marx greatly. ‹407› According to Stammler's interpretation, everything that belongs to the *substance* of social order – for instance religious interests, just as much as economic ones – constitutes the "*matter*" of social life; and a "materialist" conception of history is one according to which the matter of social life is taken to be the cause of the form of life, that is to say, the way in which life is *ordered* externally. Of course, this [construction] makes the materialist conception of history, in Marx's sense, completely pointless.

[. . .]

How is the artistic development (to take an example) affected by the evolution of the modern proletariat as a class, by its attempt to portray itself as being, in itself, a cultural community – for that was of course what was magnificent about this movement . . . (The President [Sombart] tries to interrupt the speaker) . . . I frankly admit that the word "magnificent", which I just used, expresses a value judgement, and I take it back . . . (Great merriment) . . . What I want to say is: that is what is *interesting* for us about this movement [. . .]

[. . .]

In the past [. . .] quite heterogeneous elements, originating in spheres quite different from that of technical needs, have played a role in the development of those sciences that are today the most important ones from a technical point of view – elements of a purely irrational kind that had no direct connection at all with any sort of economic or technical interest. Such questions are dealt with by the "sociology of science". But I should like to register a protest against the expression that was used by one of the speakers here (I don't know who): that something, whether it was called technology or economy, was the "final" or "definitive" or "real" cause of something [else]. If we examine the causal chain, the result is always the same: sometimes, the chain runs from technological to economic and political phenomena; at other times, it runs from political to religious and then to economic phenomena, etc. It never comes to rest at any point. As for that version of the materialist conception of history which after all is not infrequently met with, and according to which the "economic [element]" is in some sense (no matter what) something "final" in the causal chain, that point of view has in my opinion been completely invalidated scientifically.

Verhandlungen des Ersten Deutschen Soziologentages, Tübingen: J.C.B.Mohr (Siebeck), 1911, pp. 95–98.

5 German Sociological Society, General Meeting, Frankfurt 1910

Intervention in the debate on H. Kantorowicz's paper on "Legal science and sociology"

I am partly responsible for the exclusion of the so-called value judgements; and it has been said that, during the whole of this Meeting, we have talked about things that cannot be discussed without value judgements. I would therefore remind you that, for example, yesterday, a theologian spoke in this forum about things that certainly move him as deeply as anything, and that he spoke about them in an absolutely – I call everyone to witness who listened [to him] – in an absolutely "value-free" manner, and that yesterday, we were able to discuss [his paper] in a value-free manner, and that I would find it disgraceful if [this] Society were to profess the view that only a theologian is able to speak in a value-free manner and that a value-free discussion is only possible with a theologian. In my personal opinion, those value-judgements which are excluded from the discussion according to our statutes are not simply the political ones. In this forum, the value of a work of art, the value of a legal norm – including a legal norm in the past – cannot be discussed, either. It is quite true that we shall discuss here what *effect* legal norms have had, for instance on the peasants at this or that stage [of historical development]. But whether that effect was desirable, whether that was good or not from some historical–philosophical point of view, is something that we cannot deliver a judgement on in this forum, because those are matters relating to the subjective, practical, personal opinion of the individual scholar, and which cannot be resolved by the kind of work that we want to pursue. Of course, if we *find* "value judgements", and to the extent that those manifestations of life are important for our findings, we shall also treat them as *objects* of our investigation, and attempt to "understand" them by way of explanation. And this "understanding" is evidently impossible unless we ourselves are *capable* of taking up an inner, valuational position concerning the question to which those "value judgements" relate. But we ourselves do not want to "take up" valuational "positions"; we want to determine and explain *facts* and – this is the only kind of value judgements which have a place in our forum – to discuss *logical* and *method*[*olog*]*ical* questions concerning the way in which science is pursued. We find that other [academic] societies already to a sufficient degree see to [the formulation of] practical value judgements concerning legal *policy*; what distinguishes us from them is precisely that we demand of ourselves that we exercise restraint in that respect: that we limit ourselves to the description and explanation of facts, on the one hand, and to the logical foundations of our scientific work, on the other hand. But that we can do!

Gentlemen! Underlying Dr Kantorowicz's paper, there was an assumption with which I am in full agreement, and which I should like to point out once again. I may, as I have already done on previous occasions, summarize it as follows: We can consider a certain legal rule – for instance, a paragraph in the Civil Code – in two completely different ways; or, more correctly: it *is* something quite different, depending on the question that we wish to get an answer to when we consider it. On the one hand, we can ask what the "meaning" of this legal rule is; that is to say: We can assume that we are in the presence of a general, hypothetically formulated norm, and ask: as [this norm] is formulated, is it applicable to the cases X, Y and Z, in the sense that a judge who wishes to deliver a "*correct*" judgement would have to rule in such and such a way? That is a question of dogma and not of fact; not a sociological question in any sense of the word, but a pure question of law. On the other hand, we can look at this same legal rule sociologically. In that case, it not only immediately changes its meaning, but becomes something else entirely. What "*is*" a legal rule, sociologically speaking? It means the following: if the facts X, Y, Z (which I just mentioned) are present, then there is a certain actual *probability*, a "chance", that *factual* consequences of a certain kind will occur, and that an actual compulsion will be exerted in a certain direction in favour of [any] person who turns to certain authorities established by the state – the "courts" – and who is willing and able to pay the required amount of money and to accept whatever further repercussions [these actions] could have. This chance that – considering what is, on average, the "*usual*" "interpretation" of a printed rule contained in a Code – the power of the state *will in fact* support the economic or other interests in question, this chance is a possibility whose "probability" can in principle (not in fact, but in principle) be calculated in just the same way as [the probability] of any possible occurrence in dead or living nature. The meaning, in sociological language, of the legal–*dogmatic* assertion that a legal rule with a certain content is "*valid*" is simply the following: There is a certain *probability* that certain *actual* circumstances will lead to a certain compulsory intervention by the state. It has been said that somehow, in the sociological domain, the calculation could be replaced by an "evaluation"; but that is out of the question. I simply cannot understand what that is supposed to mean. On the contrary: What we have learnt from the natural sciences – and will, I hope, learn to an even greater degree – is the way in which they treat facts simply as facts. It is not in this area that the empirical sciences differ from each other.

Whether, in the individual case, those legal rules actually materialize in a judgement that is "*correct*" if we look at the *meaning* of the rule[s] – that is to say: if we ask a question which is quite different from the sociological one – well, *that* depends on a vast number of sociological conditions and quite concrete things. In certain cases, it may certainly also [depend on] whether the judge has already refreshed himself rather heavily. It depends on the kind of preliminary training that the jurist has had, it depends on a thousand [different] concrete circumstances which in any event, whether they are of a social nature or not, have a purely factual character. The "validity" of a legal rule in the *sociological* sense represents an empirical probability of facts; its validity in the juridical sense is a logical Ought. Those are two quite different things. The import of what I have, perhaps not quite clearly, demonstrated here may perhaps become clearer if I choose another example. Admittedly, I have already used it elsewhere; ‹408› but, as you could hardly have read it, I shall produce it again, with your permission. Let us consider the following sentences: "The United States, in contradistinction to [its] individual states, has the right to conclude commercial treaties" – first sentence; second sentence: "Accordingly, the United States has concluded a commercial treaty with Mexico"; third sentence: "That commercial treaty is not in accordance with the interests of the United States"; fourth sentence: "since it has influenced the balance of payments of the United States negatively"; "It would rather have been in the interest of the United States to do such and such"; "It is the fault of the Constitution of the United States that something like that could happen"; "Consequently, the mood in the United States is such and such"; etc. You will see, if you put these individual sentences next to each other and ask yourselves what is *meant by* the concept of the "United States" in each case – if you do that, you will, I say, come to the following conclusion: In each case[, that concept means] something different; and [it] never [means] the United States in the *legal* sense [of the term]. The United States in the legal sense of the term is a complex of legal norms whose *meaning* must be interpreted by jurisprudence; while the "United States", in the sense in which we have to deal with it in the science of economics, in sociology, in politics – generally speaking: apart from legal science – is a practically infinite complex comprising parliamentarians of all kinds, the President and the bureaucracy, the military, coal pits, gold mines, blast furnaces and iron that is or could be produced there, workers, and I don't know what else besides. In each of the cases referred to, it perhaps means something different; and, in any event, in almost every case it has been merged into a concept from a different perspective. The legal concept of the United States, however, has the immense advantage, compared with this sociological concept of the United States, that its content is in principle *logically* clear. Consequently, the sociological concepts and the collective concepts of other disciplines are regularly oriented towards precisely that legal concept, in spite of the fact that the *juridical* conceptual system "United States" is a purely ideal theoretical construct, which as such corresponds to nothing empirical in real life, but is precisely something which is "valid", as one usually says. But it is only "existent", *empirically* existent, to the extent that jurists *usually* think of it as corresponding to its *valid* sense, that is to say: more or less as corresponding to the juridical *norm* of thought; not because it is *valid* as an ideal norm, but because there is a certain *chance* that people, and in particular judges, will *act* in a certain way which corresponds to it.

To sum up: the dogmatic consideration – that is to say: the consideration of norms of constitutional and public law – is something quite different from the consideration of a legally ordered community for which [these norms] are "valid" from the dogmatic point of view.

The question now is: *how is it logically possible* that sociological findings can nevertheless become important for legal considerations? As a first instance, Dr Kantorowicz has pointed to the fact that the legal system is necessarily imperfect from a logical point of view, that it is not a logically closed system. Granted! But does it already follow from that premise by itself that such a heterogeneous approach as the sociological one would be an appropriate substitute for it? That is certainly not what [Dr Kantorowicz] wants to say; he only wants to say the following: Knowledge of the actual structure of society, or, for instance, of the communities that I have just referred to and that are, for the sake of brevity, described by that juridical term (which, as such, belongs to a quite heterogeneous category), may in certain cases be the only meaningful, and consequently the only possible, basis for determining the *purpose* of legal norms. As a classic example of what he finds logically correct, [Dr Kantorowicz] himself has cited the passage from the Swiss Civil Code which stipulates that the judge must decide each individual case in accordance with what he himself, if he were the legislator, would lay down as the legal norm covering that case. ‹409› Gentlemen, that is evidently not a sociological, but a strictly Kantian principle, which could almost word for word have been taken from the *Critique of Practical Reason.* ‹410› (Interruption from the audience:) I only say that it *could* have been taken from [that work], not that it is actually taken from it. (Dr Kantorowicz: But one must have recourse to sociological considerations in order to follow the injunction.) Certainly, we are in full agreement on that point; I only wanted to state that what I say here was in accordance with the sense of your own remarks. From the very beginning, I had no doubts on that score.

[. . .]

I [. . .] should now like to make a few short remarks concerning the history of law. [. . .] On the whole, what has been said [in that respect] only concerned the following points: The ways in which sociology can be of service to the history of law; and [the demand] that the history of law should be pursued sociologically, that is to say: that it should take as its object the factual aspects of jurisprudence – the way in which law was put into living practice – and not the legal [system] that might be constructed on the basis of some legal norms of the past. I should like to make one comment on that: The fundamental question of what is really relevant from a legal–historical viewpoint, and what therefore becomes the object of the history of law – that question can only be answered on the basis of systematic considerations. Moreover: investigations into the history of law can only be pursued, and are actually pursued, in the following manner: If I have before me a "source of law" – [by which] I mean a source of knowledge concerning law, be it a Code of Law, a precedent, a judgement, a deed under private seal, or whatever – the first thing I need to do is to form a legal–*dogmatic* picture of it. [I have to ask myself] what is the legal rule whose *validity* is a *logical* precondition of [this "source of law"]. I must therefore, as far as possible, transport myself back into the mind of a judge of that time [and ask myself] how a judge of that time must *logically* have decided a given case before him, if he took this legal rule, which I construct dogmatically, as the basis of his decision. [Although] you may not immediately believe so, this is actually the way in which the history of law proceeds: if you look [closely], there is no doubt about it. It is only on the basis of these dogmatic considerations that I will then be able to note that – as so often happened – in this or that case, the actual, living sentiment of justice did *not* function like that, [that is, was *not*] in accordance with the sense that I had derived and that could be constructed ideally. And only then am I at all able to see *what* the living law of those times – that is to say: the law as it manifested itself in actual compulsion – in fact looked like; [it will] perhaps – even probably – [be] filled with inconsistencies and differ from one court to the other. In other words: A legal–dogmatic construction is indispensable as a heuristic principle, even for [looking at] the law of former times, [and] even for the history of law. That is why I would not find it justified to make a distinction like the following: the law that is no longer valid is regarded only as a fact, not as a "norm"; and the law that is still valid [is regarded] as a norm, not as a fact. Both [kinds of law] can be examined both concerning their meaning . . . (Interruption: By the judge) – No, not only by the judge. I, too, can immerse myself scientifically in [that question], and so does every legal dogmatist. And, in the same way, I can immerse myself in the question of what might, juridically constructed, be the actual content of one of the many strange regulations of English law in former times, if its juridical consequences were carried to their conclusion by means of logic. Those questions are not necessarily uninteresting, and, above all, they are useful from a heuristic point of view.

As already said, a legal–*dogmatic* construction and analysis are also the principle for selecting what is scientifically *relevant* for the history of law. And, Gentlemen, the same holds – since we are anyway involved in this discussion about "value judgements" – the same holds for the relation of *values* to the problems that we have to deal with scientifically in the Sociological Society. This is because the question whether a certain fact is to become the object of our discussions – that is to say: whether it has become scientifically "interesting" – is in the last resort identical with the question whether it is significant [from the point of view of] *cultural values*. But when we, as empirical scientists, deal with an "interesting" fact, then we have left the question: *why* it *is* interesting, behind us, as our task is now solely and exclusively that of determining the facts – and nothing more than that. And it is also in the interest of the parties who quarrel about the value or lack of value of [those facts] that somebody is there to tell them: I don't say if you are right or wrong; I cannot do that with the instruments furnished by empirical science. But I can simply tell you that those *are* the facts – perhaps he does not even know them – those are the conditions, those are the consequences of that state of affairs. That is to say: if what you want were to happen, then such and such means and such and such side effects would have to be accepted. Those are questions that can be answered on the basis of the model: X is followed by Y. But all the other questions, which *cannot* be answered on the basis of that model, do not belong within our domain. It is of no importance to us here whether or not the answer to those other questions is *called* scientific; in any event, its place is not in the arena of a science purely concerned with facts, as we want to pursue it. That [view] should never have been disputed, and we ought to stick to it.

And finally: [. . .] in the domain of economics, the so-called economic principle plays a role similar to that of dogmatic law. The economic principle – what does that imply? It formulates its judgements as follows: *If* somebody, with divine omniscience, knew the totality of his present and future needs and were in a position to balance them against each other, on the one hand; and *if*, [on the other hand], he also, with divine omniscience, had knowledge of [all] existing supplies and of the expenditure of labour necessary for the fulfilment of these needs for goods – potential and actual, [something] that in turn also depends on what are the needs of so and so many *other* persons who also want those goods – if he knew all that, *how would he then* act in accordance with the principle of fulfilling as many of his needs as possible with the means at his disposal? As you can see, Gentlemen: in real life, in actual life, nobody is ever in that position; that is simply impossible. Such a person, who not only acts absolutely and purely rationally but who is also omniscient, does not exist. Nevertheless, Gentlemen, this theoretically fabricated action – a purely intellectual construct – is heuristically useful for the analysis of actual action. Experience shows that actual action has a certain tendency to approximate such purely rational action; and that tendency is particularly evident in times like ours – [times] of economic rationalism. We would not at all be in a position to analyse actual human action in the economic domain unless we had previously imagined [what] a strictly rational human action – which never occurs in real life, not even on the stock exchange [. . .] – what such a strictly rational action would be. It is not only in the economic domain that we find something like that. It is impossible to understand the Austrian campaign and Moltke's actions, ‹411› even purely historically, unless one has – unconsciously – made the following construction: *If* Moltke had been omniscient; if he had therefore known what was the disposition of the Austrian army, what were the chances of getting so and so quickly to such and such a place, quite precisely; if he had been omniscient with respect to *every* circumstance that was at all relevant for a successful outcome, the successful outcome which he wanted to achieve and which in this case was clearly that of defeating the enemy – *if* he had known all that, and [if he] had been able to act strictly with only this aim in mind, untroubled by faulty reasoning and mistakes, by insufficient information, by whatever else, *how would* he then have had to act? That is the heuristic principle that we apply in order to understand Moltke's actual actions, as Moltke's actual actions were rational to the extent that he succeeded in making them rational. Naturally, he would like to act according to this principle; [but] he could not do so because he was a human being subject to making mistakes and with insufficient information about the situation. But in order to understand his actual actions, which were partly determined by those irrational elements, we must be able to construct an imaginary picture of strictly rational action and of his [criteria of] success. Otherwise, we can indeed understand human social life and historical phenomena no more perfectly than [we can understand] what goes on in a beehive. It is quite certain that we can today to a very large degree describe and analyse what goes on in a beehive, and we have extensive knowledge of it; but when we are dealing with human social life, this gives us an immense advantage that we do not want to throw away, since we can in principle, with the aid of those instruments of rational construction, go much further in our reflections on, and [our] knowledge of, the causal concatenations than we have ever been able to, and will ever be able to, when dealing with animal colonies.

Verhandlungen des Ersten Deutschen Soziologentages, Tübingen: J.C.B.Mohr (Siebeck), 1911, pp. 323–30.

LETTERS

Excerpts

All the known Weber letters from the period 1906–1917 have been published in the *MWG*. For letters before or after that date, the translator has relied on his own transcripts from letters now in the German State Archives in Berlin (GStA I, Berlin) and in the Bavarian State Library (BSB Munich) and, in a few cases, on transcripts in the Düsseldorf Max Weber Centre, which have kindly been put at his disposal by the editors of the *MWG*. The original provenance of each letter is given after the letter, together with summary information about the recipient (when his/her name appears for the first time in this main section) and, wherever necessary and possible, about its context.

The excerpts translated here contain only those passages which, in the editors' view, are of general methodological interest.

The sequence of the letters is chronological.

To Lujo Brentano
1 January 1897

[...]

Even though it would be most unscientific to see it as possible, even in principle, that the analysis and causal *explanation* of economic phenomena could subjectively [come to] conclusions that would differ because they were coloured by partisan opinions, we on the other hand saw it as self-evident that, when it comes to the *judgement* of these phenomena, the ideals on which the person formulating the judgement bases himself (consciously or unconsciously) will be decisive; consequently, [that judgement] will almost inevitably be blurred by subjective and even partisan factors, and this is no bad thing. Therefore, the only demand that one can make is that the standard according to which the judgement is made should be *made clear*. Now, since it seems inevitable that in the lecture room the student will meet not only with *explanations* but also with *judgements* of economic phenomena – at least, this is *in fact* invariably the case – it also seems useful that he should be confronted with the possibility of examining [the phenomena] on the basis of *different* ideals.

[...]

Federal Archives, Koblenz, Nl. Lujo Brentano, no. 67, 171–72.
Lujo Brentano (1844–1931) was a German economist.

To Marianne Weber
(Five postcards)
7 April 1902

[. . .] I don't do much, but read Rickert, ⟨412⟩ who is quite good, but here and there gives rise to objections. [. . .]

10 April 1902

[. . .] Otherwise, I mostly read Rickert, who is *very* good, apart from the terminology ("value"). [. . .]

11 April 1902

[. . .] I have finished Rickert. He is *very* good; to a large extent, what I find in [his book] is something which I myself had thought of, although I had not elaborated it from a logical perspective. Here and there, I have reservations concerning the terminology.[. . .]

2 January 1903

[. . .] I hope that I shall at least be able, sometime, to finish this wretched patchwork, ⟨413⟩ in which [I] in fact work almost exclusively with other people's ideas.

3 January 1903

[. . .] At least, I hope to finish the outline of the rest of this confounded piece of work before returning home. [. . .]

BSB Munich, Ana 446
Marianne Weber (1870–1954) was the wife of Max Weber; she was a writer in her own right, above all on feminist subjects.

To Heinrich Rickert
14 June 1904

[. . .]

I am very pleased that you can accept the idea of the "ideal type". ⟨414⟩ I feel that a category of this kind is indeed necessary to distinguish between "valuation" and "value relation". How it is termed is of course a minor consideration. I chose the term [ideal type], because in ordinary usage, the terminology "ideal limiting case", "ideal clarity" of some typical process, "ideal constructions", etc. is employed *without* the implication of an *Ought*), and moreover, because [the concept] which *Jellinek* ([in] *The General Theory of the State*) calls an "ideal type" is meant to be perfect only in a logical sense, not as an *ideal*. ⟨415⟩ Anyway, the concept must be further clarified; it contains all kinds of problems which were not analysed in my presentation.

[. . .]

GStA Berlin I, Rep. 92, Nl. Max Weber, no. 25.
Heinrich Rickert (1863–1936) was a German philosopher and close friend of Max Weber.
The letter from Rickert to which the present one is a reply must have been a (first) reaction to Weber's *Objectivity* article, which came out around the middle of April 1904.

To Georg v. Below
17 July 1904

[. . .]

With the exception of the last third – which is, however, in my opinion the most important part ‹416› – the article [on *Objectivity*] really only contains an application of the ideas of my friend Rickert.

[. . .]

GStA Berlin Rep. 92, Nl. Max Weber, no. 30/4.
Georg v. Below (1858–1927) was a German constitutional and economic historian.

To Heinrich Rickert
2 April 1905

[. . .]

It has been both stimulating and pleasant for me to read your "Philosophy of History". ⟨417⟩ Of course, [I] also [read it] with approval – particularly your objections to "historicism as a *world view*", since certain remarks in your *Limits of Concept Formation* could still leave some doubts about your position in that respect.

I have reservations concerning the following points:

(1) P. 71, last sentence. Even if one *only* accepts causality in the form of "conformity to laws", history, which uses "laws" as a means of *imputation*, does *not* become a science of laws.

[. . .]

(2) P. 88. I see *no* compelling need to introduce the concept of the "systematic cultural sciences". ⟨418⟩ Your concept of the "*relatively* historical" ⟨419⟩ yields everything that one could wish for. And above all: the concept "systematic" is of course *anything but unambiguous*. Our science is a prime example of that. And *even less* is it possible to establish a *necessary* relation between "systematic" and "generalizing". A *cross-section* of the *modern* capitalist economic culture is *eminently* historical, but assumes a *systematic form*. A "system" which in that case wanted to *free itself* from what is "observable" would become an "ideal type" of the *unique* and *uniquely* specific economy of the present [. . .] but *certainly* not a system of *generic* concepts (although it would of course *make use of* such concepts).

In jurisprudence, the logical problems that present themselves are surely quite *heterogeneous* ones. They are not completely covered by the example: science of laws – historical science.

(3) P. 108. There is no foundation for identifying "victory of the proletariat" with an "*economic* good". The relevant ideals are *not* of an economic kind – that is precisely the characteristic feature.

[. . .]

GStA Berlin Rep. 92, Nl. Max Weber, no. 25.

To Willy Hellpach
5 April 1905

[. . .]

When you give a more precise formulation of your standpoint with respect to Windelband, Stammler etc. by saying that what is *common* to all those scholars is that they negate that dogma[tic affirmation] of the one and only acceptable method which you apparently profess, *then* you are admittedly quite right. But in that case, you would in my opinion have to add to that group of scholars every cultural historian (in the broadest sense of the term) of any note – with the exception of Lamprecht, and of Breysig who works in a similarly amateurish way – and, from [the ranks of] the theoreticians, Simmel (to take an example). Personally, I would then also have to be counted among those who are damned in this fashion, and this *in spite of and because* I want our journal to define as its most essential task the conceptual structuring of the historical material and the advocacy of the rights of "theory" – as is made clear in an introductory article (*Objectivity*) in the *Archive*, although the treatment of the problems in [that article] only has a very narrow focus. If one wishes to be of service to the method[ology] of the cultural sciences (or whatever else they might be called), one must, in my opinion, from the beginning and above all rid oneself of that value judgement and openly resign oneself to the *fact* that the "only possible vertical tripartition" [to which you refer] ‹420› simply *does not* exist within broad and important branches of our knowledge – in *any* sense, not even as an "ideal". It is not at all evident why this would be inconsistent with the view – which *all* those scholars would accept – that it is justified to treat the *whole* field of phenomena characterized by the so-called "human spirit" in accordance with that "three-stage" method *as well.*[1] Here, the "scientific parochialism" [exhibited by] the gentlemen of the natural sciences – [a category] that also includes the psychologists – plays a role, to the detriment of methodological openness.

[. . .]

As you can see, dear Sir, our views frequently diverge, *perhaps* more apparently than in actual fact. But I must admit that, *as far as* I am competent to judge, I am fairly (and increasingly) sceptical with respect to a "social psychology" as the *general* basis for work within the "cultural sciences". I was *all the more* pleased by your subtle explanation of your approach to the problem; but in my view, that approach does not in any way need to be anchored to a new "science" ("social ps[ychology]"). *In spite of* the fact that I fundamentally disagree with much of what you say, I am pleased with your approach. Therefore, I *must* be all the more strongly in favour of keeping it apart from those other, quite different problems. The *Archive* mainly concerns itself with the "cultural sciences", and it is part of our *programme* to adhere to the principle of defending the *distinctive character* of the historical method *alongside* the right to "formulate laws"; therefore we could not (in my opinion) open our columns to a glorification of L[amprecht], even if he were still a "man of science" – which is not the case.

[. . .]

GStA Berlin Rep. 92, Nl. Max Weber, no. 17.
Willy Hellpach (1877–1955) was a German medical scientist, psychologist and politician. This and the next letter form part of a dialogue between Weber and Hellpach concerning an article that Hellpach had submitted for publication in the *Archive*; it appeared there in the autumn of 1905 (Hellpach, *Social Pathology*).

1   The simple fact is that in this field, answers to some problems can be found by [using] that method, and [answers to] other problems must be found by [using] a completely heterogeneous one.

To Willy Hellpach
9 April 1905

[. . .]

The *historical* science of today *is* not "description", but something completely different; [and] any future [historical science] *must* work towards a goal that is quite different from the "construction of laws": for [historical science], "laws" are one *instrument* – and a very important one – among others, but never the *goal* of [its] research. The two "lines of development" [described in] Lamprecht['s work] ‹421› are in effect identical *because* he does not realize this and arranges the historical [material] in "laws", "stages" and so forth, instead of regarding such conceptual constructions as *one* among *several means* of acquiring knowledge (and [one] of quite relative value). Any such attempt to arrange [facts] will *with necessity* lead to doing violence to them, unless it is limited to purely formal elements – which are *also* relevant for history, but quite certainly not to the *exclusion* of all others.

[. . .]

GStA Berlin Rep. 92, Nl. Max Weber, no. 17.
See the Editorial Note to the previous letter.

To Franz Eulenburg
16 April 1905

[. . .]

By the way: I don't know that anybody – myself, for example – considers Rickert to be a "great man". Anyway, that would be of no consequence. But, admittedly, I consider him to be *one of our most competent logicians*. The points of view that he tries to assert afresh are self-evident; but nonetheless they are often forgotten.

[. . .]

GStA Berlin Rep. 92, Nl. Max Weber, no. 30/4.
Franz Eulenburg (1867–1943) was a German economist and one of Weber's collaborators on the large collective work *Grundriß der Sozialökonomik* (Outline of Social Economics).

To Heinrich Rickert
28 April 1905

[. . .]

My paternal vanity is saddened by the fact that you have *terminological* doubts concerning the ideal type. However, I, too, am of the opinion that *when* we speak of Bismarck *not* as the "*ideal*" but as the ideal *type* of the Germans, this does *not* in itself imply that we see him as an *exemplary* character; instead, it means that he possessed certain – in themselves indifferent, possibly even unpleasant – German characteristics, as for instance *thirst*, to a specifically *intensified* degree, in [their] "conceptual purity". You really should accept the *terminology*, which is in my view natural, [to designate] the intermediate step – which is necessary *in substance* – between "ideal" and "generic concept". After all, everything can be "misunderstood", most of all, for instance, your concept of the "natural sciences". Or: propose another name. But these are minor matters; more importantly, the concept still contains logical problems.

Your concept "systematic sciences of culture" raises problems of *substance*. In that respect, I still stand by my reservations. If the account of *successive* [events] were the only [proper] "history", then the historian would *immediately* become a "systematizer", whenever he made a *cross-section* for the purposes of summing-up, [or] when he *describe*[*d*] the starting point, an intermediate stage, or the end point of a development in terms of its "state". But surely, the question of *when* [the historian] resorts to [such a description] is a purely *aesthetic* one. The *description* of a concrete, valid *legal regime* is in itself completely historical: [it is] the formation of an "individual". The situation is *different* when the legal regime is analysed *dogmatically*, that is to say, when the validity and the *meaning* of the norm are examined by means of an *interpretation*. But *then*, problems are involved that are logically heterogeneous and lie *beyond*, or rather *elsewhere than*, the dualism "natural science" – "history". In *economics*, the "systematic" approach – when it is not simply a classification of theorems for the purposes of *instruction* – is *either concept formation* (construction of ideal types), that is to say (logically speaking) *preliminary* historical work, *or a historical* cross-section of an individual stage of development. In the *latter* case, it is "history" in the same sense as Jacob Burckhardt's *Culture of the Renaissance*.

[. . .]

GStA Berlin I, Rep. 92, Nl. Max Weber, no. 25.

To Willy Hellpach
10 September 1905

[. . .]

I shall not here elaborate further on the many doubts that I *always* have when the concept of the "type" is brought into play without more detailed comment. ["Type"] may of course mean either (1) "norm", in the sense of what *ought* to be (logically "*correct*" thinking, for instance); [or] (2) the most "consistent" expression of a "characteristic trait" in [its] "ideal purity" ("individuality" in certain cases, conceptual "ideal types" etc.); [or] (3) a *cross-section* through the empirical material – that is to say: a statistical average. For the time being, I cannot judge whether it is also possible to introduce the ["type"] concept into the conceptualization of being *psychically* "ill" *without* defining it in more detail; in the field of physical [illness], the concept is of course sufficiently (but certainly not quite unequivocally) precise.[1] After all, the "*values*" that, from the point of view of logic, are a precondition of the concept of being "inimical to the community", ‹422› have a *substantive* content which is extremely heterogeneous, and now and then mutually conflicting. Therefore, the problem is surely how the concept of being "inimical to the community" can *nevertheless* attain the *degree* of relative precision which is (and therefore must be) sufficient in this case.

[. . .]

The letter is one of a series of letters from Weber to Hellpach commenting on the MS for Hellpach's Habilitationsschrift (second doctoral dissertation). (Hellpach, *Methodology of Psychopathology*).

---

1   In particular, I have noticed that, contrary to what you did in your *Psychology of Hysteria*, you do not make use of the concept of the "meaninglessness and excessiveness" (of certain psychical reactions) when defining the pathological. I suppose that there are *substantive* or *method*[*olog*]*ical* reasons for this?

To Willy Hellpach
10 October 1905

[. . .]

Many thanks for your remarks concerning Wundt. I am pleased that you recognize that the formulations in question – which are, however, *typical* of Wundt – contain metaphysics, not psychology. But what you say about the "creative synthesis" ‹423› only strengthens my convictions. I agree that *if* that concept, as used by Wundt (not to mention Lamprecht and others of that kin) meant nothing but the "fusion", the emergence of something qualitatively "new" – that is to say, in other words, if it coincided with the concept of the causal *inequation!* ‹424› – then any comment on the *terminology* would be a waste of time. But the fact is that if *that* were the case, whenever *qualitative* changes *as such* became the *object* of scientific inquiry, the situation would be exactly the same as in your [example of] the chord c–e–g; the "qualitatively new" character of water (respectively: of its combination with sulphur) would also "be" a "creative synthesis" in absolutely the same sense as the "fusion" of two psychical elements, "feelings", or however you want to designate the ultimate noëtically given ‹425› "elements" of psychical processes. Your statement: that this circumstance (concerning water) "does not 'in the last resort' (i.e.: for its own sake) *interest* the '*natural sciences*' at all" – a formulation that is completely consonant with *Rickert*'s disparaged account – is precisely what I myself emphasize as the crucial point. If you place all qualia ‹426› within the "psyche", and say that the process in the water is only relevant to "bodies" in their capacity of being "objects of 'our' imagination" – all right! But then – as you will agree with me – there will not be the *tiniest* difference between that process in the "object" water, which we "see" "*outside* ourselves" and a process which, because it deals with, say, "fusions", etc., of "images in memory", we "introject" "*into* ourselves". If – as I actually believe – we agree on this, then we are in agreement on the main point, since you have acknowledged that the idea of increasing "differentiation" as the specific characteristic of the psychological domain – a conception that in my opinion lies perilously close to Spencer's evolutionary theories ‹427› – is not exclusively a characteristic of "spiritual" (or "psychological") objects. *Exactly* the same ["differentiation"] can of course be found in connection with the "evolution" of any "planetary system"; and moreover, *as soon as* we "regard" such a system – for instance the solar system – as "evolution" and "*system*", it, too, is certainly not "just" an "addition" of its "constituent parts". (By the way, I have reservations with respect to your formulation concerning the triad: as I see it, if one wants to be precise, one cannot in any way say that there is a "sum of the old qualitative elements" *to* which the "new qualitative element" is added.) The really *important* point – and this is *also* true of the "development" or "sifting out" of the "intellectual functions" from the "psychical whole" – is to realize that the concept of differences of "complexity" (which does not and cannot have an "objective" meaning considering the intensive infinitude of any, even the smallest and most "homogeneous", section of the cosmos) is brought about by a specific form of *abstraction* on the basis of an act of "valuation": it is completely out of the question [to maintain] that the "primitive psyche" (understood as the sum of all its manifestations) is something that is "objectively" "less *complex*"; [but] the moment we look in isolation at certain *individual* elements – *the only ones that matter to us* – of the "developed" psyche, and "*measure*" the primitive psyche with respect to *those*, and *only* those, elements, [then the primitive psyche] *becomes* [less complex], as we "regard" it. If somebody formulates the result of this measurement as "growing psychical energy", and is – like yourself – always conscious of the meaning of that expression, no one has the right to prohibit him from doing so, even if that were possible. But one should in my opinion remain alert not only to the risk of misunderstanding [that expression] (cf. Lamprecht), and to the fact that it is equivocal, being reminiscent partly of valuational and partly of naturalistic concepts; but above all (at least precisely from your point of view) to the fact that it employs *quanti*fying terms ("growth", "energy") in areas that, in your opinion (which I completely share), by their very nature *only* and *essentially* base themselves on the category of the causal *in*equation, that is to say, of purely *quali*tative *"change"*.

Surely you must see that this throws the door wide open to misrepresentation – not by professional psychologists (although *Wundt* himself has fallen victim to it), but by those who operate with these categories in the areas where psychology, in your opinion, aspires to be a "fundamental science" – and *must* operate with them *if* your opinion is correct. And finally, the concept as *you* define it (= "fusion" or "causal inequation") is inadequate for the purposes of *history*, since *historical* concepts (that is to say, those concepts that are *specific* to it – for instance, the concept of "culture") – *are* precisely *valuational* concepts.

GStA Berlin Rep. 92, Nl. Max Weber, no. 17.

To Ladislaus v. Bortkievicz
12 March 1906

[. . .]

My most sincere thanks for your letter. Nowadays, it is a very rare occurrence, and a real pleasure, to receive such a thorough discussion of an article that one has written. ‹428› Since I am in the process of moving house, *I* must today be more brief than I should have liked. First of all: the word "statistical" is a slip of the pen, and I cannot understand how it came about: of course one cannot speak of the "statistical theories" of Kries. ‹429›

Against your objection to the "Baden School" ‹430› (incidentally, you *only* find the *essence* of Rickert's theory in his second volume, ‹431› *not* in the first volume *by itself,* and definitely not in Windelband['s work]), I should like to start by referring to my article in Vol. XIX of the *Archive* ("The 'Objectivity' of Knowledge in Social Science"). The degree of *frequency* is [either] a "historical" fact (because it is of historical interest) *or* a "heuristic instrument", depending on the "sense" of the cognitive *aim,* and the same is true of all other "statistical" products of knowledge. On the other hand, the sentence "bimetallism does not guarantee . . ." ‹432› has a character that belongs *purely* to "natural science", as that term is understood in Rickert's terminology (with which I am *not* in complete sympathy); that is to say: it is, *logically speaking, in no way* different from a "law of nature", provided one does not demand that the concept be absolutely "rigorous". Here, there is *no* "relation" to values, in the sense in which this is a precondition for *history.* On the other hand, it is *completely* correct, as you point out, that the concepts "heuristic instrument" and "generic specimen" are *not* congruent. ‹433› I assumed that I had disposed of possible objections of this kind by saying that I would later deal specifically with the case mentioned under (2) ‹434›. However, in reply to your argument, I must very strongly emphasize that *logic* has the duty *strictly* to *distinguish between* contradictory positions that may sometimes get blurred in *practice* in science. Without any doubt, "teleological" knowledge can be generalizing: *all* the examples that you cite show this, as does the everyday practice of our science. But "value relation", in *that* sense in which it is invariably part of the *historical* approach (in the widest sense of the term), is the exact opposite of all generalization. I hope that when I enlarge on the subject – God knows when that will be ‹435› – I shall remove your objections in this respect. *Eulenburg* has simply *not understood* Rickert. ‹436›

[. . .]

University Library, Uppsala (Ladislaus v. Bortkievicz, 7).
Printed in part in *MWG* II/5, pp. 45–47 from a typescript copy.
Ladislaus v. Bortkievicz (1868–1931) was a Polish–Russian economist and statistician.

To Friedrich Gottl
27 March 1906

[. . .]

You are *quite right* in saying that Rickert has *not* provided a sufficient formulation of the *logical* character of "value-*relating*" (although *he* was the one who *discovered* that concept). As I see it, it is precisely this task that you will fulfil.

[. . .]

GStA Berlin, Rep. 92, Nl. Max Weber, no. 11. Printed *MWG* II/5, pp. 59–60.
Friedrich Gottl (from 1907: v. Gottl-Ottlilienfeld) (1868–1958) was an Austrian economist and sociologist.
This and the two subsequent letters to Gottl contained Weber's editorial comments on a Gottl manuscript to be published in the *Archive*. (It appeared in the second 1906 issue.)

To Friedrich Gottl
28 March 1906

[. . .]

(1) The *one-sidedness* of the *perspective* is *not* a distinctive characteristic of the *idiographic* ‹437› disciplines; on the contrary: in [the idiographic disciplines], it is always provisional, whereas it is *empirically* definitive in the natural sciences. But your account gives the impression that these "one-sided" perspectives are identical with the "values" to which the "individual" is related.

[. . .]

(3) Your reference to *Rickert* is mistaken in so far as he has made it quite plain that the expression "generally accepted values" – which he does use here and there – only refers to positions *ascribed* to everybody (that is to say: it implies a *demand that a position should be taken* from the point of view of the *historian*, not the *fact* of "validity" as a *value*), so that there is a *complete* absence of *metaphysical* premises.

[. . .]

You seem to proceed from the assumption that what is important in logical investigations is to delimit "*areas*"; from a *logical* perspective, however, cognitive goals that are fundamentally different and can only be differentiated *logically* may be coupled in *one and the same* sentence of a scientific work.

[. . .]

GStA Berlin, Rep. 92, Nl. Max Weber, no. 11. Printed *MWG* II/5, pp. 62–63.

To Friedrich Gottl
29 March 1906

[. . .]

Moreover, I do *not* accept that "value" stands on the same level as "interest" or "importance" in relation to the servitude to *words* ‹438› that determines the use [of those concepts]. Under *all* circumstances, "valuation" takes us into another world (that of the "subject taking a stand", as Münsterberg terms it). The guiding function of "interest" and the "important" are also found in the *nomothetical* sciences, but *not* the anchoring to "values".

[. . .] I have objections from *my* point of view to [your description of] the relationship between logic and *methodology. Logic* does not care a damn whether its results are useful for giving *practical* directions.

[. . .] The expressions [. . .] "viewed from the standpoint of the *universal* context", [. . .] "transcend the *whole* of reality", [. . .] "*disclose* the "personal dignity" of the individual", and others like them, must in my opinion give rise to strong misgivings, because they give the impression (1) that we actually intended to obtain knowledge about the *entire*ty of the "given", [and] (2) that "individuals" in the *logical* sense of the word are something that exists *independently* of our *value* relations, even though [you later] deny this (albeit in fairly vague terms). I *doubt* whether it is simply "economy of thought" rather than the *cultural* significance of Europe that can lead to distinguishing it as a "continent" from Asia [. . .]. What do you mean by the "*unfolding*" of the "universal context" [. . .]? Surely, this raises all those problems of "significance" which can only be explained by means of the "value relation". Or are there independent "*natural significances*"? – It seems to *me* that Rickert was quite right in "stating the obvious", as you put it; *without* it, *all* discussions of the principles of individuation remain completely *up in the air*: something is always still *missing*, one does not see *why* we are actually interested in the *individual* configuration of those "mountain ranges" etc. – whether the reason is, in the last resort, the naïve circumstance that they "catch our eye", or something else; again and again, one gets the impression that it is the *material* which produces the "individual".

[. . .]

"[P]erspective", in the sense in which it is discussed *here*, is in no way a distinctive characteristic of the "idiographic"; on the *contrary*, it is *precisely* in the *nomothetical* search for knowledge that it is absolutely *essential*, and it only affects the "idiography" *because* [the "idiography"] needs general [forms of] knowledge as a means of *imputation* and must therefore make use of [general] "laws", which are *always* one-sided.

[. . .]

GStA Berlin, Rep. 92, Nl. Max Weber, no. 11. Printed *MWG* II/5, pp. 64–67.

To Willy Hellpach
18 April 1906

[. . .]

Since I completely agree with you on every point of your account and find it extremely clear, I am already for that reason tempted [to have it published] in the *Archive*. The main *objection*: our readership is protesting (in letters to the publisher) against enlarging even further [the space allotted to] "methodological" discussions in the journal; and, accordingly, the publisher is also protesting. And although I myself will for the present, in the interest of the journal, remain silent on these issues, we already have heavy commitments precisely with respect to articles of that sort (Gottl – 3 articles! – Eulenburg, Lask).

[. . .]

It seems to me (and surely you hold the same view) that, even in the eyes of the strictest "somaticist", ⟨439⟩ the [category of] "social pathology" (as you define it) is *already* justified *because* no somaticist *can* deny that the *content* of the pathogenic psychical manifestations is determined by the "environment". The *only* thing that the somatically oriented psychiatrist will find "important" is simply that the content in question, irrespective of what it consists of, is pathogenically and "somatically" determined – so that the actual "content" is only relevant for him as a *heuristic instrument*; but for somebody who is investigating *social* relationships, it is precisely the *content* that is "*important*" for him, either because it has a "value in itself" (is a "historical individual") or because it became causally important. This means that a "social pathology" (in your sense) would under *all* circumstances become an auxiliary science for "history" (in the widest sense, including social history) as well as for "sociology" (the nomothetic social sciences), and could only be practised by a *professional* in the field of psychiatry. [The social pathology] would have a say *both* in the analysis of concrete "personalities" *and* in the analysis of concrete events (for instance in the history of religion), *as well as* in the formulation of *laws* of "social psychology". Thus, its *existence* is independent of the extent of the dominance of *somatic* theories; but of course, its significance, *even* in the field of purely cultural science, and *particularly* in the clinical field, is not [independent of the extent of that somatic dominance].

[. . .]

At one point you have briefly referred to the distinction between "the intrinsic historic value" and "*causal*-historical importance"; but you do not take it up later on – probably because you do not wish to complicate the discussion any further. (The manner in which the historical *interest* would be affected by the demonstration of the pathogenic character [of the historical phenomenon] is not necessarily the same in the two cases, but this takes one beyond the scope of your essay. I only mention it for the sake of completeness.)

[. . .]

I believe that there must be a mistake in your *formulation* at the middle of p. 41. Surely the social–psychical origin of pathological phenomena does *not* awaken [our] cognitive interest because the *causes* are historically relevant, but [rather] *either* (a) from a *clinical* point of view; or

(b) from a *historical* point of view (that is to say: because the concrete pathological phenomenon in question is *in itself* historically relevant); or (c) from a *sociological* point of view (because it is possible to construct "laws" concerning the connection between the pathological phenomena in question and certain social phenomena that have caused them). I think your formulation must be a slip of the tongue.

[. . .]

GStA Berlin, Rep. 92, Nl. Max Weber, no. 17. Printed *MWG* II/5, pp. 80–83.
The comments in this letter refer to the manuscript for an article by Hellpach submitted by him to Max Weber for possible publication in the *Archive*. The article did not appear there, but in another journal (Hellpach, *Application*).

To Robert Liefmann
15 July 1907

[. . .]

It goes without saying that I shall be very glad to acquaint myself with your formulations concerning the theory of value, precisely because I have at the moment already for a long time had very little to do with those matters. It all depends on what one understands by "a completely subjective theory of value". For instance, I do *not* accept it if it is formulated so that its basis is the "intensity of a pleasurable sensation" (while it is of course quite correct that this concerns relations of *degrees* of "value", although it "is" not a "judgement of degree"): the aim of a theory of value is not to establish psychological facts, but to demonstrate "ideal-typically", in a conceptual and therefore unreal form, how we adjust that part of our behaviour which is relevant from the point of view of economics to certain external and internal typical *situations*.

[. . .]

When tackling the problem of values, above all one has to ask the question: what are the phenomena in [empirical] reality that we wish to elucidate by forming the concept of "value"? [. . .] How does [that concept] help us to obtain knowledge of reality – or, put in another way: if we imagine that it does not exist, what gap in our acquisition of knowledge will then force us to formulate it? Only in *that* way [. . .] is it possible to say what value "is" (or, more correctly: what can be understood by it).

[. . .]

GStA Berlin Rep. 92, Nl. Max Weber, no. 30/7. Printed *MWG* II/5, pp. 333–34.
Robert Liefmann (1874–1941) was a German economist who had written his doctoral thesis in Freiburg under Weber's supervision. His views on the theory of value were part of a book published in the autumn of 1907. He seems to have sent Weber at least parts of the manuscript – or an abstract of the main ideas – in advance, and the present letter contains Max Weber's preliminary reaction to them.

To Else Jaffé
13 September 1907

[. . .]

Specialist knowledge is *technical* and teaches *technical* means. But where *values* are being fought over, the problem is projected onto an entirely different level of the intellect, removed from any "science"; more precisely: the *problem* is posed in a completely different manner. *No* specialized science, and *no* scientific knowledge, *however* important [. . .] can provide a "world view".

[. . .]

BSB Munich, Ana 446. Printed *MWG* II/5, pp. 393–403.
Else Jaffé-Richthofen (1874–1973) wrote her doctoral dissertation in economics in
Heidelberg in 1901, co-supervised by Weber, who later became her intimate friend.
She was married to Weber's co-editor of the *Archive*, Edgar Jaffé.
The present excerpt is from a long letter where Weber critically discusses the ideas of the
psychiatrist Otto Gross and of Sigmund Freud.

To Heinrich Rickert
3 November 1907

[. . .]

What [you have], in my opinion, *not demonstrated*, is [. . .] what makes [the "individualizing cultural science"] different from the "*individualizing natural sciences*" ⟨440⟩ – a major trump card for [your] opponents (Eulenburg in a new article [*Philosophy*], just published in the *Archive*, Hettner [*Sciences*] and others, Tchuprov [*Statistics*]); I wish that you would, at some appropriate time, directly state your views on that point, and [that you would] in particular counter [the view that] "uniqueness" can in the last resort only be determined in simple *spatio-temporal* terms. *I* agree with you, of course; but although there are excellent elements in your exposition [in the *Festschrift*] (and in Lask's as well), the [concept of] the "systematic cultural sciences" is in my opinion a rather questionable category; and, if biology is viewed as value-*free*, things start getting – at the very least – serious for *sociology*, particularly *economic* sociology: in that discipline, too, it *might* be possible to claim that the focus on what is *relevant* from the point of view of the – purely physiological – *sustenance of life* constitutes what is significant; and *in that case*, things are (*in principle*) no different than they are in [the field of] biology.

[. . .]

GStA Berlin Rep. 92, Nl. Max Weber, no. 25. Printed *MWG* II/5, pp. 414–18.
In this letter, Weber is commenting on Rickert's contribution to the second edition of a *Festschrift* to the philosopher Kuno Fischer (Rickert, *Philosophy²*, 1907), which Rickert had sent him.

To Robert Michels
4 August 1908

[. . .]

Oh – you still have to endure *so* much resignation! For me, concepts such as "will of the people", "*true* will of the people" etc. have already long ago ceased to exist. They are *fictions*. It is precisely as if one wanted to talk of a "will of the boot consumers", which must determine *how* the bootmaker should organize his [bootmaking] technique.[1] There are *two* possibilities. Either: (1) "my kingdom is not of this world" ‹441› (Tolstoy, or *syndicalism* ‹442› carried to its *logical conclusion*, which is *nothing more* than the sentence "for me, the goal is nothing, the *movement* everything", ‹443› translated into *revolutionary–ethical*, *personal* terms, but which *you*, too, in *fact* do not carry to its logical conclusion [. . .] – *or*: (2) the *affirmation* of culture (that is to say, *objective* culture, which manifests itself in *technical* etc. "achievements") accompanied by *adaptation* to the sociological conditions of *all* technical phenomena, be they economic, political or of any other kind (precisely in "collective societies", such technical phenomena would be embodied to the *highest* degree). In the *second* case, all talk of "revolution" is farcical, and *any* idea of *doing away with* the "domination of man over man" by means of *any* social system, *however* "socialist", or of any form of "democracy", *however* ingenious, is a *utopia*. But your own criticism does not nearly go far enough. Someone who wants to live as a "modern human being", if only in the sense of having a newspaper every day, railways, trams etc. etc., *renounces* all those ideals that *you* dimly cherish as soon as he *leaves* the sphere of those who want revolution *for its own sake*, *without* any "goal", even without any *conceivable* goal. [. . .] You are a thoroughly honest fellow, and will carry through to its conclusion, as far as you yourself are concerned, [. . .] the critique that long ago led me to [adopt] that way of thinking and that has *therefore* branded me as a "bourgeois" politician, *as long as* even the little that one is *able to* strive for in that role does not recede into the infinite future.

[. . .]

AFLE Turin, Nl. Robert Michels, Box Max Weber, 60. Printed *MWG* II/5, pp. 615–20.
Robert Michels (1876–1936) was a German–Italian social scientist; his book on the *Sociology of Parties* (1907) made him one of the founders of modern political sociology.
In this letter, Weber is commenting on an article by Michels on "The Oligarchic Tendencies of Society", published in the *Archive* in early 1908.

---

1   The shoe consumers *do* know where the shoe *pinches* them, but *never* how it should be made [to fit] *better.*

To Robert Michels
16 August 1908

[. . .]

Your article could be *two things*: (1) a "*profession of faith*" and an "*appeal*". That was what I took it to be. *Generally, we don't publish that kind of stuff.* But precisely in *this* case, I found it awkward to say "no" to it – because I could appear to be "prejudiced", and *above all*, because it might perhaps otherwise *not* have been *easily* accommodated, either in bourgeois *or* in socialist publications in Germany, the way they are. *Consequently, I stated that I would remain neutral with* respect to the question of its acceptance. I only expressed my reservations concerning the *factual* aspect of certain details, but *without* "*demanding*" any alterations. Or (2) [the article] was meant to be a *scientific* analysis and *not* just an ad hoc "examination" – so to speak *ad usum Delphini* ‹444› – for practical political purposes. In *that* case, I would have *rejected* it. For that is not what it *is*, although you now write that that is what it should be *taken to be*. A *scientific* work is not one that "distributes light and shade" – as you put it – and there is *no* place in it for "justice" – only for *facts* and their *causes*. Admittedly, in the work of *every one* of us, "description" and "evaluation" are *always* in danger of being mixed up with each other, – but one must *seek one* [*of the two*]. You *want to* do the one – but *do not* accomplish it (I shall come back to that) – on the other hand, you *accomplish the other*, but *ineffectually* (because *that* reader to whom the appeal is directed will *either* say, "I have known that (at least *almost* all of it) for a long time", *or* he will feel: "he does not understand *me*, and the 'gods' that he serves are *so* absolutely 'different' from mine that the whole thing leaves me unmoved"). For example, the colossal problems that underlay the "Kulturkampf" ‹445› are not exhausted with [the use of] the term "illiberal"; and there is certainly more to the "national idea" than would appear from the vituperation that you (*quite properly*, from *your* point of view) direct against it. If you do not succeed in making clear to the reader – or at least *attempt* to make it clear – that, in order to be consistent, he should, even on the basis of *his* ideals, come to *your* conclusions, *then* the criticism *only* makes sense if you say the opposite: "We *serve* different gods, you are right, we have nothing in common". But you don't say that *either*; instead, you "make accusations", even though the reader will have the feeling that here, there *is* nothing to "make accusations against". Here there is only *struggle*. The *only accusations* that would make an *impression* on that kind of reader would concern the *lack of freedom of science*, and even then *only* if the accusations were not *mixed up with* questions concerning "Bismarck", "the Navy", "patriotism" etc. The latter group of questions can only be judged *subjectively*,[1] while the *former* (the lack of freedom of science in the universities) can be verified *objectively*. But, because the two are mixed up, *neither* of the[se approaches] is effective. But, as I said, if one looks at the article as an "*appeal*", that is *your* business, not *mine*.

[. . .]

AFLE Turin, NI. Robert Michels, Box Max Weber, 61. Printed *MWG* II/5, pp. 637–42.
The "article" to which Weber refers in this letter is probably the manuscript of an article on "University and Socialism" submitted by Michels to Weber as editor of the *Archive*. The article was not published in the *Archive*.

---

1   Because *nobody* can *prove* that one *should not* be "loyal" to one's "nation", just as nobody can *prove* that one *should* be "*loyal*" to one's *class*. On the other hand, the duty to pursue *science* in a non-*partisan* manner is *in theory* (but that is what matters) conceded by *everyone*.

To Lujo Brentano
30 October 1908

[. . .]

I am of the opinion (1) that Menger expresses what he wants to say without embellishment, plainly and clearly, albeit somewhat awkwardly – (2) that it is completely *un*justified to regard him simply as a poor imitation of Gossen or *of anybody else* (it would take me too long to substantiate that assessment here). He overrates himself enormously, that's true, but he has *very* considerable merits, and in the quarrel with Schmoller he was *right* in *substance* on the main points. ‹446›

[. . .]

BA Koblenz, Nl. Lujo Brentano, no. 67, 83–84. Printed *MWG* II/5, pp. 688–89.
The letter was a reply to Brentano, who had commented on a number of points in Weber's review (*Marginal Utility*) of his book on psychophysics.

To Robert Michels
19 February 1909

[. . .]

What *interested* me most was the strike "ethic". But I must say that I shook my head vigorously. Surely, you cannot be unaware that *quite* a considerable number of all strikes (as, for instance the failed dock strike in Hamburg) ‹447› not only set back the unions . . . but retarded *any* progress for the class movement by years, or even by decades, and had an *effect* that was directly *contrary* to what must seem desirable to somebody who measures the *value* of the strike by what it contributes towards moving closer to "socialization", or to the unification of the proletariat as a class, or *whatever* (provisional) socialist "goal" one may choose. Against the background of *these* experiences, the claim that *every* strike has an *effect* in the *direction* postulated by socialism, and that *therefore every* strike is "just", is the most bizarre statement that one can possibly formulate. And generally, [as far as] measuring "ethics" by their "effects" [is concerned]: have you completely forgotten your Cohen? ‹448› *That*, at least, was something that he could [have] cure[d] you of. Particularly [when you define yourself] as a *syndicalist*! The *syndicalist* Michels would perhaps have the right (and the duty) to say that the *conviction* which drives a strike *is always* the "true" conviction: it is the *militaristic* (class-militaristic) conviction; it is *patriotic* (class-patriotic) – *consequently*, etc. But [then], it is *so* weak to look for *effects*! And then to do violence to the facts!

[. . .]

AFLE Turin, Nl. Robert Michels, Box Max Weber, 62. Printed *MWG* II/6, pp. 60–62.
It has not been possible to identify the article by Robert Michels on which Weber is commenting in this letter (and in the letter of 12 May 1909 quoted below).

To Ferdinand Tönnies
19 February 1909

[. . .]

(1) . . . *No*, my dear friend, you cannot "scientifically" prove that monarchy – to which my attitude as a *politician* is the same as yours – is "bad". You cannot even do that with regard to the Russian or Chinese monarchy, or that of Genghis Khan. This is because the claim that something is "bad" is always based on weighing up values against each other and, in addition, on weighing up ends against means and ends against side effects; and, in such cases, a *scientifically* demonstrable result is impossible a priori.

(2) Certainly, I am also (at least as strongly as yourself and perhaps even more so), of the opinion that, if someone accepts the general necessity, as far as his own actions are concerned, of letting oneself be guided by "values", value judgements or whatever you want to call them – if he is not "unmusical" in that respect, then it is possible to demonstrate in a *compelling* way that he is bound by all the consequences of the Kantian imperative ‹449› (no matter in what more or less modernized form – the substance remains the same as before). To demonstrate this dialectically (or rather, more accurately, to discuss this as a problem) *is* the task of ethics as a science – a science whose procedures, by way of an "internal" critique, of the uncovering of what is *logically* implicit – "posited" – in a thesis, are dialectical in quite the same way as logic [is]. But, in my opinion, that can never go beyond demonstrating the *formal* characteristics of a moral *attitude*. This formal critique of attitudes can never demonstrate that a social, supra-personal structural system, whatever it may be, *is ethically binding*. In this category belong all metaphysical dogmatisms – whether religious or not, clerical or anti-clerical; an individual may embrace them, but he should never believe that he has the right to pass them off as science. Our thought does not have to keep within the limits of science, but it should not pass itself off as science, unless it is either (1) analysis of facts (including abstraction and all empirically verifiable syntheses and hypotheses) or (2) conceptual critique.

(3) Self-evidently, to the extent that religions claim that empirical facts or causal influences on empirical facts have their origin in some sort of "supernatural" [force] [these religions] must come into conflict with every scientific truth. On the other hand, a study of modern Roman Catholic literature, which I carried out in Rome a number of years ago, has taught me how completely hopeless it is to believe that any kind of knowledge produced by any kind of science is "indigestible" for that Church. With the greatest ease, it appropriates the idea of the evolution [of species] and derives very great benefit from it – and it is completely impossible to prevent and "disprove" that by honest scientific means. The steady and slow influence of the *practical* consequences of our conception of nature and history will perhaps over time lead to a fading away of these ecclesiastical powers . . . but no manner of anti-clericalism, oriented towards a "metaphysical" naturalism, can bring that about.

[. . .]

GStA Berlin Rep. 92, Nl. Max Weber, no. 30, Vol. 7. Printed *MWG* II/6, pp. 63–66.
Ferdinand Tönnies (1855–1936) was a German philosopher, sociologist and economist. He, Werner Sombart and Georg Simmel were, together with Weber, co-founders of the German Sociological Society in 1909.
The letter was prompted by remarks by Tönnies concerning an article by Weber on "Academic Freedom in the Universities" (in *Hochschul-Nachrichten* 19 (1909), pp. 89–91), where Weber foreshadows many of the views on value freedom that he later formulated in more detail in *Value Freedom*.

To Robert Michels
12 May 1909

[...]

The strike ethic? Well, dear friend, at the end of your article you *do* actually write that *every* strike *is* justified *because* it lies on the road towards the future goal. (1) This last statement is demonstrably *untrue*: the effect of failed strikes is a setback that may sometimes almost last for decades (Hamburg!), and (2) surely that *is* an "ethic of consequences": the *means* are "justified" *because* the *result* that one hopes to achieve is "justified". – But syndicalism is either a fanciful nothingness found in [the heads of] intellectual romantics and undisciplined workers unfit to make financial sacrifices, *or* it is a religion based on *conviction*, a religion whose existence is justified *even if no* future goal is *ever* "achieved", and even if science can *demonstrate* that there is no chance of this ever happening.

[...]

AFLE Turin, Nl. Robert Michels, Box Max Weber, 66. Printed *MWG* II/6, pp. 124–26.
It has not been possible to identify the article by Robert Michels on which Weber is commenting in this letter (and that of 19 February 1909 quoted on the previous page).

To Franz Eulenburg
(After 12 July 1909)

[. . .]

I was convinced that you would not remain with the "old Adam", sticking to your narrow psychologistic position, and I could see symptoms of a change. I [was] only waiting for your "Preliminary Questions", ⟨450⟩ so that, in a review of that work, I could confront you with the sum total of your misinterpretations in the field of epistemology and the philosophy of history and say: that *can*not be the last word of a man of this quality: Two paths are open: Hegel or – *our* way of treating things. He will have his Damascene conversion ⟨451⟩ to one of those two positions, but probably to that of Hegel. Now you have robbed me of that pleasure! Now, I shall only be interested in the quality of the "real" Hegel, since everyone has his own version! We shall then see how far I can follow you, but you can be assured of my great interest in the road that you are following; and, above all: thank God that you have progressed beyond the philistinism (if you will excuse the term!) of the old Adam.

[. . .]

GStA Berlin Rep. 92, Nl. Max Weber, no. 30, Vol. 7. Printed in *MWG* II/6, pp. 172–75.

To Heinrich Rickert
25 July 1909

[. . .]

In substance, this work of yours ‹452› has *surprised* me more than any of your previous ones. What? *You* as a man "who runs with the hare and hunts with the hounds"? And can it really be said with *any* sort of justification that one is taking the "first" (transcendental–*psychological*) path when one analyses each of the different *genera* of possible judgements in order to establish what *categories* they presuppose? Surely no more than when you determine the concept of "pure meaning", since you have accomplished *that* determination by means of extremely concrete *examples*! You *yourself* say that *in the last resort* one cannot *conceive of* "pure meaning" without a subjectivity that is oriented towards it. Surely, it is in actual fact a *limiting* category that we arrive at by means of an extreme *logical* abstraction. To what extent would the situation be different *in principle* when we look at other and more specific categories? I still don't really see that. The *historical* merits (of transcendental psychology) don't prove anything! Surely, every *logical* analysis goes in the opposite direction – in a *logical* sense – whatever the way in which it is *described* in practice.

Now, I am eagerly waiting to see whether Lask, whose *main* point, as I see it, is at least partly anticipated, ‹453› will still have his own say.

[. . .]

GStA Berlin Rep. 92, Nl. Max Weber, no. 25. Printed in *MWG* II/6, pp. 202–04.

To Marianne Weber
13 October 1909

[. . .]

Yesterday, at the General Meeting [of University Teachers], it was from the outset regarded as certain that the position that *we* had taken, ‹454› and which was "crucified", last year, would [now] be accepted as "self-evident". I wanted to wring *even more* out of them – the acceptance [of the view] that, in university teaching, one may not force "value judgements" on one's students – but that was too difficult for that bunch, and nobody lifted a hand to applaud.

[. . .]

BSB Munich, Ana 446. Printed in *MWG* II/6, pp. 288–89.

To Heinrich Rickert
(Around 24 July 1911)

[. . .]

What the "axiophobia" ‹455› of sociologists means is (in my case) simply this: I find it *unacceptable* when the highest problems concerning *values* are mixed up with the question *why* the price of pork in Berlin today is x pfennig; – when it is claimed that the ultimate standpoints that have the power to move the human soul can be read into woolly concepts of "productivity" (or something similar); – and when [those ultimate standpoints] are inseparably welded together with purely *empirical* questions. Only when we have rendered to *our* king – the realm of the empirical – the things that are his can we render unto "God" – the philosophy of value – the things that are his.

[. . .]

GStA Berlin Rep. 92, Nl. Max Weber, no. 25. Printed in *MWG* II/7, pp. 250–51.

To Robert Liefmann
(Between 23 and 28 October 1912)

[. . .]

(2) In your critique of Philippovich's "economic" concept of productivity, I find that a central argument is lacking: When you say that this cannot be accomplished by *theory* [and] that it is the business of statistics etc., this has no force. Philippovich would be justified in answering: "I had not been told that I was only allowed to do theoretical work; the decisive point is whether we are dealing with questions of scientific fact". And if statistics can tell us something about the degree of "productivity" of a branch of industry (for instance, the production of powdered marble for the purpose of adulterating flour, something that actually happens in American industry, in Knoxville, Tennessee), *then* that is a "fact", and there is no reason why it should not also be possible to formulate general statements, that is to say: "theory", covering this fact. The crucial point was the following: these gentlemen could not distinguish between two different things: first, looking at the "subjective valuations" of economizing subjects as *objects of science* – here, the theory sometimes (but not always) for methodical purposes builds on the fictive assumption that we are dealing with quantities which can be measured and numerically expressed; and, second, the influence of evaluations – which are necessarily "subjective" (that is to say, dependent on political, religious and ethical positions) – formulated by *the man of science who is analysing the facts* – an influence that can be found in almost *all* judgements which we men of science would formulate concerning the activity of *any* individual as being "productive" or "unproductive". We object to the latter, not to the former.

[. . .]

GStA Berlin Rep. 92, Nl. Max Weber, no. 30, 6. Printed in *MWG* II/7, pp. 716–22.
Weber's comments refer to a recently published article by Liefmann (*Productivity*).

To Hans Gruhle
8 March 1913

[. . .]

What is specific about all kinds of psychology or psychopathology based on "understanding" (including that of Freud), and the specific transformation of the concept of a "symptom", is that, as the (psychical) events are "related to *meaning*", the "symptom" has a *substantive* "*significance*": this constitutes a fundamental difference from *all* concept formation in the natural sciences, in the proper sense of that term, irrespective of whether the object of [that concept formation] is a physical or a psychological attitude (the latter being established by means of "introspection"). *This*, surely, is where [we find] the transition to the concept of a "symbol". You wanted to cover that by means of the concept of "association". I believe that this concept – which is really quite a difficult one, more difficult than it seems – is *not* adequate, as psychiatry obviously cannot avoid speaking of "*meaningless*" associations, "*mere*" associations of sounds etc. So, underlying this is the concept of "*having* a sense", and even the (valuational) concept of "being meaning*ful*" (which is something different). Surely, the "*meaning*" of Freud's theses lies precisely in the claim that *this* variety of "symptoms" has a (hidden) "sense" and that, because and to the extent that [the symptoms] have this sense, they are "symbols".

[. . .]

BSB Munich, Ana 612. Printed in *MWG* II/8, pp. 112–14.
Hans Gruhle (1880–1958) was a German psychiatrist and psychologist who had just received his Habilitation (second doctorate) in Heidelberg.
Weber's comments refer to the lecture that Gruhle had given as part of the process giving him the right to teach at Heidelberg University.

To Robert Wilbrandt
2 April 1913

[. . .]

We would, I think, differ when it comes to your belief [that is is possible to elaborate] a general theory of the "means". By the way, it is not quite clear to me what (the broad features of) such a theory might look like. I hold the view that what dominates the sphere of values is the irresolvable *conflict*, and consequently the necessity of constant *compromises*; no one, except a *religion* based on "revelation", can claim to decide in a *binding* form how those compromises should be made. The parallel [between economics and] *medicine* is so questionable because [in medicine] it is at least possible to construct a *conventional* concept of "health" that is more or less unequivocal, while *we* [economists] *cannot* do so. *Which* would it be? Consequently, I do *not* believe in an *autonomous* economic value judgement, even concerning the "means": for means, too, can only be unambiguously determined with respect to *concrete*, given goals. To take an example: what is "human economy"? (*Goldscheid*'s concept seems to me to be *nothing more than* a new word for something that is well known.) *What* human *qualities* is [the "human economy" ‹456›] designed to develop? Surely not just physical ones. But then: *what* spiritual ones? Perhaps even some whose nature and consequences are *anti*-economic?

[. . .]

GStA Berlin Rep. 92, Nl. Max Weber, no. 27. Printed in *MWG* II/8, pp. 165–66
Robert Wilbrandt (1875–1954) was a German economist. Apparently (his letter is not known), he wanted to discuss his and Weber's positions in the planned discussion on "Value Freedom" in the Committee of the Association for Social Policy (see p. 304n1).

To Heinrich Rickert
5 September 1913

[. . .]

From my personal point of view, I am pleased to hear that you are entering a prophetic phase, although, as you know, I "in principle" fulminate against the lecture-room prophets. But these days, both the students and the professors are of a different mind. *I* shall therefore, to the best of my ability, contribute to getting almighty, massive "eschatological" prophecies into the lecture rooms, so that the universities, for their chastisement, will "experience Jesus Christ".

[. . .]

GStA Berlin Rep. 92, Nl. Max Weber, no. 25. Printed in *MWG* II/8, pp. 318–20.

To Heinrich Rickert
End of November 1913

[. . .]

Many thanks for giving me the pleasure of reading your article. Both the idea of the "open system" and the sixfold division and the parallelism ‹457› are most apt and valuable – precisely *because* values are, in our *empirical* work, interconnected in such absolutely heterogeneous and irrational ways. I have the following reservations, which I feel sure that you *agree with*:

(1) The "ranking" which you speak of is only of a formal *logical* nature. (In fact, you yourself say this.)
(2) This is only *one* – particularly successful – systematization among others. (That can in my view be demonstrated.)
(3) Ethics is *not* identical with "social ethics", that is to say, it is *not* [necessarily] tied to behaviour towards *others* – even when [this behaviour] merely consists in a certain attitude. (You *might* be interpreted in that sense.) Even a human being on the loneliest of islands makes "ethical" demands on himself.

And then – here you do *not* agree with me – the *conclusion* ‹458› is, first of all, a metabasis eis allo genos ‹459› [and], second, it appropriates something for *philosophy* that holds for *all* scientific accomplishments.

The histories of Thucydides, Tacitus, Ranke etc. are "outdated" and nevertheless perfect accomplishments in *exactly* the same *sense* as any closed philosophical system (and are therefore not "outdated" just because [our] knowledge of the *facts* has advanced). What is valuable about the fact that something is *perfectly accomplished* and finished – *if* in the concrete case this is a *value* at all (and not just a *technical* advantage for subsequent "users") – is that this is no longer a "scientific" or a "philosophical" value, but belongs in a quite different – either a purely personal, or an aesthetic or ethical – value *sphere*, as defined in your system.

It would be possible to demonstrate with binding force – on *quite formal* grounds, based on the [implicit] *meaning* – that the path of a *scientific* philosopher is *always* the exact opposite of that of a *prophet*. And only "revelation" *can* make – or rather, offer – binding *choices*.

Your conclusion is (*much against* your *will*) grist to the mills of *Schmoller* and the *relativists* = "Aha! in the last instance, '*evolution*' decides".

[. . .]

UB Heidelberg, Heid. Hs. 2740 Erg. 93, 1.2 (Nl. Heinrich Rickert). Printed in *MWG* II/8, pp. 408–10.
The comments in Weber's letter refer to an article by Rickert that had just appeared in the journal *Logos* (Rickert, *System*).

To Heinrich Rickert
[Before 31 October 1915]

[. . .]

I am looking forward with impatience to even the smallest part of your future logic. ‹460› If [you produce] something in *that* area, I shall take up methodological work again. *That* is where something is waiting for you now, particularly since Lask's death.

[. . .]

GStA Berlin Rep. 92, Nl. Max Weber, no. 25. Printed in *MWG* II/9, pp. 149–53.

To Robert Liefmann
9 March 1920

[. . .]

If *I* have now become a sociologist (according to my documents of appointment!) it is to a large measure because I want to put an end to the whole business – which still has not been laid to rest – of working with collective concepts. In other words: sociology, too, can only be pursued by taking as one's point of departure the actions of one or more (few or many) *individuals*, that is to say, with a strictly "individualistic" method.

[. . .]

As I see it, it is a simple terminological error when you say that the *rational* constructions that theory must perform [in order to judge whether a particular price can be obtained in the marketplace] are psychological. If I say that 2 × 2 = 4, that is not something "psychological", but an intellectual act. And the more rational, the more undisturbed by error, emotion and extra-economic irrationalities are the economic considerations – as theory assumes it to be the case in the ideal types – the more the opposition between the "subjective" and the "objective" is reduced.

[. . .]

[You claim that] I have asserted that theory has little cognitive value. *Where* did I make that assertion? Theory creates ideal types, and this contribution is, precisely in my eyes, the most indispensable. One of my fundamental convictions is that sociology and economic history are *no* substitutes for theories.

[. . .]

What I cannot understand is that you, as a strictly rational theoretician (any other kind [of theoretician] is inconceivable!) hope for any contribution from psychology. Theory is an ideal-typical construction, to which the realities conform to varying degrees. Psychology might perhaps be useful [when we are dealing with] irrational deviations from the rational, but what contribution can be expected from any kind of "psychology" [to understand] an action that is strictly determined by [the relation between] means and end[s], and that we *understand* rationally?

[. . .]

GStA Berlin Rep. 92, Nl. Max Weber, no. 30/8, 76–80.
The comments in Weber's letter refer to Liefmann's work on the theory of economics (Liefmann, *Principles*).

NOTES AND DRAFTS

The Berlin State Archives contain a number of manuscript notes in Max Weber's handwriting, most of them probably written during his stay in Nervi (near Genoa) from late December 1902 to early January 1903. They range from simple jottings to longer drafts of inserts for the article on *Roscher and Knies*, which he was working on at the time. Their source value is of course questionable, inasmuch as they did not make it to the final, published version. But echoes of them can be found both in *Roscher and Knies* and in *Critical Studies*; and, in any event, they provide valuable insights into Weber's immediate reactions and reflections on reading works of such central importance for his methodological writings as Rickert's *Limits of Concept Formation* (1902), Eduard Meyer's *Theory and Method* (1902) and Gottl's *Dominance of Words* (1901).

This section also contains the unfinished draft of a review by Weber of Georg Simmel's *Sociology* (1908) and a fragment of a note or letter on formal ethics found in the Berlin State Archives.

All the items in this section have been translated from the original texts.

1 Handwritten note from an envelope with the imprint "Schickert's Parc-Hôtel, Nervi", marked "Rickerts 'Werthe'" (Rickert's "values")

When R[ickert] says: ___, ‹461› it would be more fair to say that in the place of a number of admittedly trivial, but completely *understandable* terms, we get a most dangerously shimmering and ambivalent expression, which positively invites misunderstanding. As a test, one can try, *wherever* R[ickert] speaks of "values", to replace that term by "___". ‹462› A large part of his exposition would then acquire a significantly more trivial outward hue; but, if phil[osophy] is the "s[cience of the][?] obvious" (Windelband), ‹463› then it should not shy away from expl[icitly] stating the obvious as such, in form as well [as in substance].

However much you shake Rickert's concept of "value", with the meaning which it is given on p. ___, ‹464› all that emerges is the sense of "worth knowing about"; consequently, the "necessity" of relating [historical material] to a value can be reduced to the statement, which *on the face of it* appears quite trivial, that history should describe those parts of empirical *reality* that are *worth knowing about*. This in itself implies that Rickert's strict – at least strictly *formulated* – demarcation between "historical" individuals (those related to a value) and other [individuals] *must* in fact be conceived as a historically and individually *fluid* one; and, above all, we should not ignore the infinite gradations of the *extent* to which elements of reality are worth knowing.

In reality, the selection [of elements] depends on these constantly fluid and varying *differences* in the interest taken in the elements of empirical reality by the *individuals* ‹465› who are in each case the historian's *public*; thus, it is *not* only dependent on the degree to which that interest is *universal*, let alone conforms to a *norm*. Given the limitations of our receptive capacity, the selection is carried out according to the "principle of economy"; that is to say: the *most intensive* interest is satisfied first. The [different] interest[s] may in turn have, if not an infinity, at least a practically *inexhaustible* variety of causes. This is also true in the field of cultural phenomena, [where they can range] from the interest of the collector of stamps [or] slippers to the loftiest impulses that move [the human] heart.

Once the most pressing questions have been answered, and since our receptive capacity is limited and the multiplicity of the world is infinite, our interest in the remaining questions will quite quickly dwindle towards naught; and in fact, when we look at what it is *actually possible* to investigate scientif[ically], *practically* reach zero. But all this only modifies [what was said above] if and to the extent that we accept the idea of quantities "turning into" qualities. The *fact* that there is *general* interest in many parts of reality and a *lack* – perhaps in fact a *general* lack – of interest in most of the other parts, is quite easy to explain *psychologically*, and the same holds for at least the general features of the *gradations* [of interest]; but, in my opinion, the attempt to *formulate norms* not only leads into metaphysics, that is [text unfinished]. As soon as one tries to look for something different, something *objective*, behind the *fact* that, in any given instance, historical interest will be limited and graduated, one enters into the domain of *norms*; that is to say: one is then looking for a principle from which it would be possible to deduce not only *what* should, once and for all, be the object of our interest, but [also] to what *degree* we sh[ould] graduate our interest in the various el[ements] of reality. Precisely that is in fact the meaning – translated into everyday terms – of the "value metaphysics" with which R[ickert] concludes. ‹466› Here it must suffice to express doubts as to the possibility of grasping the *substance* of such norms, and simply to add that such doubts might be consistent with the view that the "absolute validity" of certain "values" (what we would call "interests") could be taken to be more than simply a *limiting* concept. The *logical* possibility of a "formal ethics" ‹467› at least shows us that the *concept* of *norms* [covering] the infinite multiplicity of the object of these norms does not in itself guarantee that [such norms] can be formulated in *substance*.

GStA Berlin Rep. 92, Nl. Max Weber, no. 31/6, 12–18.
The note, which was obviously written with a view to publication (possibly as part of *Roscher and Knies*) has, since it first appeared in English in 2001, ‹468› been referred to as "the Nervi fragment".

---

2 Handwritten note marked "Neue Wissenschaften" (New sciences)

Objects enter into the realm of that which is *worth knowing* when they become *problems*, when *new questions* arise. When we *realize* that there is something that we *don't* know. Economy was already in Antiquity "related to values". But not seen as a *problem*.

GStA Berlin Rep. 92, Nl. Max Weber, no. 31/6, 20.

---

3 Handwritten note

Simple hist[orical] "immediate experience" in Gottl's sense ‹469› *does not exist*. It always already contains *meaning* and *purpose*. From our earliest years, we find ordering principles in it, [and] thus, we *learn* to "have immediate experience". Only in *that* sense does history consist of memorized images. Only [text undecipherable], who have not yet learnt to think, are exceptions from this. We see *ideas* everywhere and search for them. Our "immediate experience" can no longer be at all separated from *speech* and *words*. Memorized images have an intellectual *structure*, *language* is not without importance.

Somebody who "immediately experience[d]" history, as we describe it, would not be an *individual*, but an "ideal collective consciousness".

[. . .] Human "action". "Action" is already a *concept*; the "act" is delimited according to certain *principles*.

GStA Berlin Rep. 92, Nl. Max Weber, no. 31/6, 58–60.

4 Part of a handwritten note on Wilhelm Roscher

What Roscher would have found most congenial would therefore have been [the] peculiar combination of ethics and history belonging to that [kind of] ethical relativism that, on the one hand, rejects Kant's ethics because of its (supposedly!) purely formal character but[, on the other hand,] nevertheless does not want to forgo ethical principles with a status equal to that of the *norms* of thought, and is therefore forced to [employ] emanationist constructions. ‹470› The most highly developed type is *Fichte's* ethical principle, which could be formulated more or less as follows: "become valuable as a member of a 'valuable whole'". ‹471›

While the consistent proponents of [Roscher's] emanationist ethics are by necessity forced into metaphysical constructions and, at least, to make the assumption that the value of the ideal to which the individual must submit is an *absolute* one – this is now also Rickert's position ‹472› – others, among them most historians, usually ignore these metaphysical consequences [. . .].

GStA Berlin Rep. 92, Nl. Max Weber, no. 31/6, 71.

5 Handwritten note

To elevate the histor[ical] *method* into a histor[ical] *world view* ‹473› [is to commit] the same error as that [represented by] the "w[orld] v[iew] of natural sc[ience]". One should not become a slave to one's method a[nd] one's concepts.

GStA Berlin Rep. 92, Nl. Max Weber, no. 31/6, 75.

6 Handwritten note

There is nothing more *intelligible* than the effect of feelings of patriotism. [This only became] problematic when common sense was made into a "psychology" (even by Schmoller). Certainly, science makes *all* that is self-evident into a problem. But it should not be the slave of its own approach when entering into areas where there are *no* problems. ‹474›

That reality is intelligible and can be "immediately experienced" is, in a *scient[ific]* sense, only true of the *ideas* that we bring into it and try out within it. (Contrary to Gottl['s view]), *Rickert's* achievement is to have demonstrated this (couched in different terms).

Irrespective of the answer to the question whether the "psychical" processes are more "immediately given" for us than the "physical" ones – as Dilthey believes – or whether both are, in quite the same sense, [part of the] "content of consciousness" – as Rickert states – it will probably still be true that at least the course of human *thoughts* can be made "intelligible" to us in a qualitatively *different* sense compared to any construct, be it called "physical" or "psychical", *not* covered by that category. It is certainly true – as Simmel states – that we can only ever uncover the *thoughts* of others by means of an *interpretation* among the motives underlying a course of events; but what gives the interconnections of human motives their distinctive character, which *even logic* has to take into account, is the simple fact that there is a *possibility* of interpreting the immediately given – *intelligibly*, not just in *formulaic* terms. [When we consider] the course of human thoughts, "intuitability" and "intelligibility" are identical.

GStA Berlin Rep. 92, Nl. Max Weber, no. 31/6, 132–34.

---

7 Handwritten note

Cosmos character of hum[an] institutions.

The basis is a *selection* of the purposeful strivings of individuals towards objective purposiveness.

Every cosmos is susceptible to *concept*[*ual*] analysis in the manner of the natural sc[iences]. But this should not be transformed into conceptual realism (mysticism). Nor [?] is the *concept* ever scient[ifically] definitive. But *here*, the *arche*types have their place in the world of the existent. What *ought* to be (in a type sense) is *selected*.

How the cosmos comes into being and operates is something that we want to, and are able to, *look into in an inner sense* (Gottl).

"Development"

That *with respect to* which we let some development unfold itself is an *intellectual* construct.

Development – subjective

But it is necessary always to keep in mind that when the [term] "development", in the above sense, is used with respect to social institutions, it is a concept that *we* apply to the material [and?] that we use as a criterion for selecting what is "significant and important" from the chaos of causal interconnections, and as a form for the structuring and description [of those interconnections] when we, under the given circumstances, regard this as expedient and harmless. It is not some hidden agent behind the course of history, so that our foremost task would then be to ferret it out everywhere and without exception and to extract its essence from the material. The question whether we should make use of the concept can *only* be answered case by case, and in every case according to the state of the material; and, when our knowledge advances, this may in any given case lead us to demonstrate the empirically observed facts structured in a developmental sequence, but may just as well lead us in the opposite direction, to [regard] a developmental construction as being outdated and to abandon it in favour of a purely classificatory structuring of the material.

GStA Berlin Rep. 92, Nl. Max Weber, no. 31/6, 142–44.

---

8 Handwritten note

Development

v. Below/E[duard] Meyer

(1) I am not sure − for reasons that would lead us too far afield − whether it is advisable to make use of the concept of dev[elopment] here. But v. Below's objections to Ed. Meyer['s views] ‹475› on this point do not, in my view, preclude making use of the concept of "development", provided that the other conditions for using it are present. The "development" of budding life − [a case] where even v. Below would surely not question the appropriateness of using that concept − may miss its goal because of "accidental" disturbances; [indeed], the "development" of any organism at all may be broken off before "maturation". Here, too, we are dealing not with the opposition between "accidental" and "necessary", but − something that v. Below fails to appreciate − with that between "accidental" and "adequate", which has a markedly different logical character. What E[duard] M[eyer] means is this: As a matter of fact, we today regard the emergence of German statehood, whatever form it may have [taken], as [an] *adequate* consequence of the originally given historical situation in its totality, just as we regard the full maturation of a foetus as "normal"; and we treat a *disturbance* of this "natural" process as an "accident". It is quite true that this way of looking at things represents a synthesis that *we* perform on the basis of "subjective" needs; but v[on] B[elow] himself − like innumerable others before and after him − has quite correctly emphasized that syntheses of that kind are simply indispensable for attaining historical knowledge.

(2) We "get knowledge" of the intensive infinity of hist[orical] relationships by again and again introducing "*thoughts*" into it − that constitutes the "subjectivity" of history − and − that constitutes the "objectivity" [of history] − by again and again conscientiously testing, on the basis of the *material*, whether these thoughts represent an "*adequate*" picture, or *which* form of thought and combination of thoughts, among several imaginable ones, represents the most adequate picture of the event that is at all possible. It is quite true that history in this way consists of, so to speak, a sequence of "vaticinationes post eventum". ‹476› It is not [the case?], however, that the idea of the adequate development only arises as a garnishing of what has in actual fact occurred (for whatever reason). On the contrary: When (to take an example) Ed[uard] Meyer makes his inspired demonstration of the tendency in Hellenic culture towards theocratization, which was disseminated under the rule of the Persians and which accorded with their political maxims (as shown by the example of the Jews), ‹477› we are dealing with a "development" where it actually "happened differently". From the point of view of "developmental history", [that "development"] was broken off because of the world-historical "accident" [represented by] the battle of Marathon, and the way was kept open for other budding developments. In this case, it seems to me that the use − explicit or tacit − of the concept "developmental tendency" is the *only* means of shedding light on the grandiose importance of that insignificant brawl. It is our *subjective view* that [this] importance is so enormous: we regard it from the point of view of the high value that we accord to our culture; and to that extent, the same is true of the whole "conception" [of the "historical development"]. But this is harmless as long as we remain conscious of those elements in the historical account that belong to *us*. But, admittedly, when we become the slaves of our own concepts and ideas and begin to canonize them as realities − as happens all too often − then we need a devil's advocate (and not just in [the field of] history), like the one possessed by jurisprudence in the shape of E. I. Bekker,

‹478› or like v. Below, who has emerged in the discipline of history [with the same function] (see the remarks in his *Method*).

GStA Berlin Rep. 92, Nl. Max Weber, no. 31/6, 145–47.
Part of the note has the form of an actual draft passage for publication.

---

9 Handwritten draft fragment entitled "Georg Simmel als Soziologe und Theoretiker der Geldwirtschaft" (Georg Simmel as a sociologist and theoretician of the money economy)

When one is obliged to evaluate the work of G[eorg] Simmel from a position that is, on the whole, antagonistic to his own; more particularly: when one cannot accept important aspects of his method[ology]; when one unusually frequently has reservations concerning his substantive results, and quite often takes a negative view of them; and, finally, when one occasionally finds his mode of exposition strange, and often at the very least uncongenial – and when, on the other hand, one feels simply compelled to acknowledge that this mode of exposition is nothing short of brilliant and (what is more important) achieves unique results that cannot be imitated; that there is an absolute abundance of new ideas of fundamental importance, and of the most subtle observations, in almost every single one of his works, and that almost every one of these works belongs among those books where not only the valid, but even the erroneous results contain a wealth of stimulation for one's own further reflections, compared to which the majority of even the most worthy achievements of other scholars often have a peculiar air of feebleness and poverty; finally, that this is also completely true of the epistemological and method[olog]ical foundations [of those works], and here again, even when [those foundations] are likely to be untenable in the last resort; generally speaking: that Simmel on the whole, even when he is on the wrong path, fully deserves his reputation as one of [our] foremost thinkers and as one of the main inspirations for academic youth, and for [his] academic colleagues (provided that their intellect is not too obtuse, or their vanity or their bad conscience (or both in combination) are too acute to allow them to be "inspired" at all by somebody who at the age of fifty has not advanced beyond an associate professorship and must therefore quite obviously be [counted] among the "failures") – faced with these contradictions, one must ask how they can be reconciled. The following account will provide a critique of Simmel's distinctive scientific character as it emerges from his two main sociological works, and should thereby contribute to answering that question, and also to an evaluation of Simmel's position as a scientist, which is peculiarly problematic in so many respects. Of course, it is *not* a problem that Simmel has still not been accorded "official" recognition – which he has amply deserved for more than fifteen years – by having a full professorship conferred upon him. As far as Berlin and Prussia are concerned, the reasons for this, petty as they are, are known to anyone at all who wishes to know them. And outside Prussia, experience has shown that every effort by other faculties to recruit Simmel will remain fruitless for as long as the competent authorities lack the resolve to emancipate themselves from the influence of those Prussian decision makers who would feel slighted if Simmel were offered a full professorship. A more serious problem is the following: Alongside [some] uncritical (and substantively insignificant) enthusiasm for Simmel, and alongside the (substantively very significant) existence of a group of extremely gifted and highly competent judges who, though they may be critical of many details of Simmel's work, have the most unqualified praise for him, not only do we find a large number of specialists in *philosophy* who harbour an outright loathing for him – this is unfortunately only too easy to understand in view of the typical sectarian character of the philosophical "schools" of our time (to *none* of which Simmel belongs), quite apart from other contributing motives; but there are also, in the disciplines adjacent to Simmel's *sociological* field of activity, scholars who must be taken very seriously and who, at least in response to a summary inquiry, tend on the whole to take a negative view of Simmel as a scholar, even though they may praise certain details [of his work]. Among economists, for instance, he may provoke veritable fits of rage – such reactions have even now and then appeared in print – and the same professional circles coined the phrase that, in the final analysis, Simmel's art can be summed up as that of dividing the air and uniting it again. It is characteristic that this fairly widespread attitude, which at times comes close to being malicious, has *never* found firm expression as some kind of *systematically* coherent critique of Simmel. On the contrary: *all* serious critics of Simmel on grounds of principle have so far ended up in a position similar to the one in which I, for my part, have admitted above that I find myself; but nevertheless, there must be adequate grounds for the existence of that attitude [as such], if not for its justification as a value judgement. In this case, the undertone of animosity that an attentive observer will clearly notice cannot be explained simply by reference to the ridiculous disapproval of the [very] term "sociology" that other scholars in Germany with indisputable first-rate achievements have also continually had to endure, and must still put up with. In this connection, it may be sufficient to make one quite general point: As we shall see, Simmel's way of constructing his argument involves the quotation of innumerable examples from the most diverse areas of knowledge for the purpose of illustrating some sociological phenomenon, not infrequently in the form of an "analogy"; this [procedure] will be criticized below because it raises major and fundamental doubts – [doubts that are] particularly pronounced in the case of Simmel's treatment of sociological problems. Now, it is quite often the case that the "analogy" may be reasonably useful for Simmel's particular purposes, but that the specialist, who has to treat those phenomena according to their intrinsic nature or in their specific context, *must* inevitably from *his* point of view regard as "contingent" that aspect of a phenomenon which is selected as being "analogous", and [*must* find] that the [analogous] use leads to a "distorted" view of the "essence" of the phenomenon and to a misjudgement of its causal components; [moreover], this is not accidental, but happens – as will be discussed later – for reasons that are a necessary consequence of the way in which Simmel, for his purposes, finds it useful to draw [his] "analogies". And precisely *because* that (from the specialist's point of view) improper procedure is applied with a considerable degree of brilliance; and furthermore, because he often does not find it very easy to analyse the ultimate reasons *why* he feels that the procedure is "improper", the professional economist, after a number of such experiences, will indignantly fling away the book and be finished with his judgement of it. The crucial point will usually – at least very often – be that where the specialist deals with problems of "facticity" – of "what is" – Simmel is looking for the "meaning" that we can find (or can [*sic*] believe that we can find) in the phenomenon. – Here, we shall not examine whether Simmel's use of difficult logical and other philosophical problems as "analogies" in order to illustrate quite heterogeneous subject matters does not provide his philosophical colleagues – who will surely often regard this procedure as a [mere] "pastime" – with a legitimation for not occupying themselves seriously with him, without taking into account whether that procedure helps Simmel to reach *his* goal. Simmel's ultimate *interests* are directed towards metaphysical problems, [towards] the "*meaning*" of life; and because this is so clearly noticeable in the way in which he treats the questions of the specialized sciences, it is all too easy to overlook the fact that he may well – albeit this sometimes rather has the nature of a "by-product" – also have made a greater contribution to the advancement of the specialized interests of his discipline than [the] total contribution made by a considerable number of "full professors" of philosophy, of the quality that is nowadays becoming the standard.

But enough of that. The preceding remarks had to be made; but they should not be taken to imply that we here intend to try to convince people whose minds are already made up of Simmel's importance; ignoring that aspect completely, the aim is rather to try to examine the way in which Simmel works sociologically, with respect both to method and to substance, on the basis of his two major works.

There was no intrinsic reason why we should dwell for long on Simmel's *own* explanations concerning the nature of sociology and the meaning of his sociological method; we should prefer to get an idea of it from the manner in which he treats individual problems. However, at a time when sociologists who must be taken very seriously go so far as to propound the thesis that the *sole* task of a theory of society is to define the concept of society, we must also go into those questions beforehand.[1]

For Simmel, "sociology" is (if we start by speaking quite generally) a science concerned with "interactions" among individuals. Now, the concept of "interaction" is clearly to some extent an ambiguous one. In its widest possible sense: as the *reciprocal* influencing of several "entities" (however defined), "interactions" can, for instance, be found in the most varied nuances in mechanics, physics, chemistry and all the disciplines of natural science, to such an extent that their general existence has even been regarded as counting among the "axioms". Gravitation is always reciprocal gravitation; not only the collision between two bodies moving in different directions, but also the impact of a moving body upon a body at rest influences them both (transmission of kinetic energy (changes of speed and direction), generation of heat energy). Indeed, it may be said generally that, in the world of *physical* reality, it is hardly possible to conceive of an influencing that is not in some sense "reciprocal" in the strictest sense of the term and as a *general* phenomenon: Although the earth only receives a tiny fraction of the heat and light energy of the sunrays, even the irradiation of the earth by the sun must, because of the reflected radiation, exert a reciprocal influence on the sun compared with those masses of [sun]rays that stream into the open universe – an influence that may be immeasurably small, but will at any rate not be equal to zero. On p. 134 of his *Sociology*, Simmel informs us that even the condition of an "abstract desire to dominate" which is satisfied by [the knowledge] that the action or suffering of others (no matter *what* character it has) is a product of his (the dominating person's) will, already constitutes an "interaction"; [and] as this must necessarily be interpreted to mean that already the mere *potential ability* to decide (the fate of others) plays the same role – and that this is even true [when we are dealing with] others whose existence is totally unknown to the dominating person, [just as], conversely, the person influenced in this way may have no inkling (as one may often enough convince oneself during the instruction of recruits) of the name and concrete existence of the "commander", but only knows policemen, mayors, non-commissioned officers and so on – then one is led to conclude (as in the example

---

1   In this connection, we may on many important points base ourselves on the penetrating critique formulated (albeit before the appearance of Simmel's latest work) by Dr O[thmar] Spann with respect to Simmel's concepts of "society" and "sociology". I refer to [Spann's] exposition in his book *Economy and Society*, in particular pp. 192ff.; it should be noted that, in the following, I shall not make renewed reference to that exposition after each individual sentence. I shall touch on the more important points of agreement and disagreement [between us]. Simmel's *Sociology*, which has appeared in the meantime, contains some appreciable, but not fundamental, modifications compared to his earlier standpoint criticized by Spann.

from the realm of physics quoted above) that this concept of "interaction" is at any rate so comprehensive that one could only by an extremely artificial process of thought conceive of an influencing of one human being by another which would be purely "one-sided", that is to say: which did *not* contain some element of "interaction". [. . .]

Original in the Arbeitsstelle of the Max Weber Gesamtausgabe in the Bavarian Academy of Sciences, Munich.

---

10 Marianne Weber's typewritten, incomplete copy of a lost original – probably a draft letter or comment on some text by Helmut Kaiser

Fragment on formal ethics

Someone who evades the duty of defining his own position concerning the substantive problem should not be so derogatory as Kaiser is in his criticism.

To proceed by first defining what guilt means and then deducing from this that a conflict of duties is therefore a logical contradiction and thus cannot arise, is a purely scholastic piece of work. It is a simple fact that human action at the service of a general idea or a concrete purpose is tied to unavoidable means and unintended but unavoidable side effects that can (probably or possibly) be expected. In this connection, the acting person may regard that idea or that purpose as being absolutely, or to the highest conceivable degree, obligatory, [while he] on the other hand [views] those means and those side effects as negative values that it is equally necessary [for him] to reject. In that case, no formal rule can decide the matter. It is equally impossible to find formal rules [that can decide] to what extent an individual should orient his action according to a responsibility for the result of *that* [action], or, conversely, [to what extent] he can or should instead ascribe that responsibility to the way the world is [constituted], or to God, and content himself with the purity of his own *intentions*.

It is even less possible to find formal rules that might be able to determine the relative status of values engaged in a conflict with one another that cannot be decided – values all of which it may be an equally ineluctable duty to realize. And least of all is it possible for a formal ethics to decide in cases where the realization of extra-ethical values means that ethical norms are violated. On the other hand, however, although its purely formal character would seem to demand this, [a formal ethics] cannot even stipulate that every similar violation of an *ethical* norm must be equally negatively judged from an ethical point of view, as the ethical judgement, too, will vary, according to whether the violation is the result of [action] in the service of a value that is extra-ethical, but regarded as supra-individual, or is motivated in some other way.

Enough: formal ethics has to face the fact that its propositions do not enable it to deduce substantive conclusions – even within the ethical domain itself, let alone concerning conflicts between value spheres. An attempt to [perform such a deduction] would be just as sterile as if one wanted to deduce, say, substantive chemical facts from logical propositions. The Kantian imperatives, too, are valid analyses of certain elementary facts concerning the way in which ethical *judgements* are made. Irrespective of the function that they may consequently have in connection with substantive decisions in the field of ethics, they in any case do not support any kind of decision concerning the ethically irrational conflicts of the value sphere. ‹479›

It is [a manifestation of] shallow thinking when the idea of an "*individual vocation*" – an idea, that is, which certainly does not primarily belong within the sphere of ethics – is identified with the concept of an "exception from an ethical rule", like the rules of school grammar; or, conversely, when one draws conclusions concerning the importance of ethical facts from the observation that one cannot demand with binding force that someone who does not have the vocation to be an artist should realize artistic values.

The attempt to use purely formal means to make the discussion of substantive value conflicts conclusive has intolerable consequences when one is dealing with the problems of sexuality. It is quite characteristic that, if anything at all is to be achieved in this respect, the problem must be transferred to the formal–juridical sphere; marriage identified with [what goes on at the] registry office; the belief in the eternal value of love, and the attendant paradoxical hope that it will last forever, are levelled down to a contractual promise of duration; and, finally, the lover's and the loved one's responsibility for the soul of the other are reinterpreted as a sort of legal damage liability. One can hardly imagine a more devastating criticism of ethical formalism than those platitudes, which it cannot avoid. The hair-splitting can safely be completely ignored. But one may find it astonishing that, in [Kaiser's] less than profound criticism of the expression "alien to nature", he rejects the obvious meaning of [the word] "nature" in that context – that which has an adequate correspondence with the specific value in question – in favour of a superficial analogy drawn from the sphere of technology. That amounts to saying that meaning and purpose are identical [concepts]. All in all, it is no accident that ethical discussions are only fruitful when they are given an object by means of the confrontation of [different] concrete substantive judgements with each other. I find *this* critical discussion sterile, and any discussion of it [must be] equally sterile. When methodological discussions are put before a substantive exposition, this is turning the logic of the matter upside down. First, it must be established whether a certain proposition is factually correct or incorrect; then, one can raise the question of method.

GStA Berlin Rep. 92, Nl. Max Weber, no. 30/9.
The copy has been edited in handwriting by Marianne Weber in certain places. Where it is not obvious that her changes are rectifications of mistakes, the translation is based on the unedited typewritten text.
The copy has the handwritten "title": "Fragment über normative Ethik" (Fragment on normative ethics). But, as a reading of the text itself makes clear, it really concerns the limitations of *formal* ethics, and it has therefore here been given the title "Fragment on Formal Ethics".

ENDNOTES

If the same explained word or passage occurs several times in one article or in one of the three subsequent main sections (Contributions and Interventions, Letters, Notes and Drafts), only the first occurrence is noted and explained. But if it occurs in more than one article or subsequent main section, it is noted and explained once in each article or main section.

Articles

1 A publication on the occasion of the 1903 centenary of the refoundation of Heidelberg University (Schöll, *Professors*). See Editorial Note, p. 99.

2 The reference is to Knies, *Economy*.

3 These include, in particular, Roscher, *Antiquity* (1849); Roscher, *Corn Prices* (1847); Roscher, *Ideas* (1845); and Roscher, *State Theory* (1847).

4 The German text has "Kameraldisziplin" ("Cameral discipline"). Cameralism is an old-fashioned term designating the science of government, particularly that dedicated to reforming society and promoting economic development in the lands of eighteenth-century Germany.

5 The German historical school of jurisprudence was a branch of legal philosophy founded by Friedrich Karl v. Savigny. Its central idea was the identification of law with custom, tradition and the "national genius" (Volksgeist): law was "found" by the jurist and not "made" by the state or its organs.

6 Herbart held that the individual could only be understood in his or her social context.

7 At the beginning of the 1850s, Moritz Lazarus, applying the laws of the psychology of the individual to the nation and to mankind, established a new branch of research which he termed "national psychology" (Völkerpsychologie). Together with his brother-in-law Heymann Steinthal, Lazarus in 1860 founded the journal *Zeitschrift für Völkerpsychologie und Sprachwissenschaft* (*Journal of National Psychology and Linguistics*).

8 The "chasm of irrationality". The immediate source of this terminology is no doubt Lask, *Fichte's Idealism*, p. 57: "When the isolating activity of reflection and abstraction has divided the absolute totality into the 'products of reflection': the infinite (the concept) and the finite, the chasm of irrationality is ineluctable". The Latin term "hiatus irrationalis" is found in Fichte's *Wissenschaftslehre* ("Theory of Science").

423

9 Emanationism in the general sense is the principle according to which creation is a gradual process of emanation and descent from a transcendental absolute to mundane reality. In his dissertation on Fichte's idealism, Emil Lask used the term to describe a theory of concept formation in which concrete reality emanates from abstract concepts, which are therefore more "real" and have a higher ontological status (as opposed to the "analytical" theory of concept formation, where concepts, being formed by abstraction, are the more remote from reality, the more general the concept is).

10 Discursive (as opposed to intuitive) knowledge is based on empirical data and logical inferences; it is mediate, while intuitive knowledge is immediate. Discursive cognition is the process by which discursive knowledge is acquired.

11 In his book *Laokoon* (1766), G.E. Lessing argues that sculpture is fundamentally different from poetry: sculpture should above all depict physical beauty, while poetry can deal with moral, spiritual and symbolic subjects.

12 An epic poem, in nine songs, from 1797.

13 The *History of the Peloponnesian War* of Thucydides includes a number of set speeches, some of which, according to Thucydides himself, had to be reconstructed so that the speakers "say what, in my opinion, was called for by each situation". (Tr. Rex Warner, Penguin Books 1954.)

14 This is a partial quotation from F.H. Jacobi, "Vorbericht" (*Jacobi Gesamtausgabe* IV,1, xiii).

15 To Thucydides, τύχη (Tyche) represents chance, in the sense of an inexplicable situation that occurs regardless of foresight or planning.

16 According to Hegel, logos or reason informs absolute reality. "The real is rational, the rational is real."

17 In his essay on "The Historian's Task" (Humboldt, *Historian's Task*), Wilhelm v. Humboldt sets out, as one of the basic presuppositions of idealist historiography, the "doctrine of ideas" according to which historical phenomena are merely the external manifestations of underlying eternal ideas.

18 In his Introduction to *The Knights* by Aristophanes (1837), Droysen had expressed some reservations concerning the ability of Thucydides to treat Cleon impartially in his *History of the Peloponnesian War*, since Cleon had been the man who proposed the resolution banishing Thucydides from Athens. Roscher claims that Droysen has no actual evidence to back up his doubts, which are only based on "vague possibilities", and adds that Thucydides' "great name and historical status" should in themselves have been enough to shield him from such allegations.

19 In his *Institutio Christianae Religionis* (*Institutes of the Christian Religion*) (1536), Jean Calvin asserts that God has pre-ordained who it is that He will graciously save.

20 In his book *L'homme machine* (*Machine Man*), published in 1747, Julien Offray de la Mettrie propounds the doctrine that man is an organic machine composed of matter endowed with the ability to think.

21 This no doubt refers to the Marxist idea that the world is moving irresistibly towards increased suffering of the working classes and increased contradictions within capitalism, ending in world revolution.

22 "It will be enough for me, however, if these words of mine are judged useful by those who want to understand clearly the events which happened in the past and which (human nature being what it is) will, at some time or other and in much the same ways, be repeated in the future." (Thucydides, *History of the Peloponnesian* War, tr. Rex Warner, Penguin Books 1954).

23 Spinoza taught that man should, as much as possible, free himself from dependence on his passions and live a life of reason as a free person, who neither hopes for any eternal, otherworldly rewards nor fears any eternal punishments.

24 In his book *Die kulturhistorische Methode* (*The Method of Cultural History*) (Berlin 1900), Karl Lamprecht says that any given phase of civilization is paralleled by a "collective psychical condition" controlling the period, "a diapason which penetrates all psychical phenomena and thereby all historical events of the time".

25 In a speech before the Berlin Academy of Sciences in 1880, Emil du Bois-Reymond outlined seven transcendent problems or "world riddles", some of which – such as the origin of motion or sensations – neither science nor philosophy could ever explain.

26 The reference is probably to 1309b14–1310a2, which, in modern texts (for instance, Oxford Classical Texts), is placed in Book 5, Chapter 9, but which in older German texts is to be found in Chapter 7. The pertinent passage is the following: "the adherents of the deviation-form [of constitutions], thinking that this form is the only right thing, drag it to excess, not knowing that just as there can be a nose that although deviating from the most handsome straightness towards being hooked or snub nevertheless is still beautiful and agreeable to look at, yet all the same, if a sculptor carries it still further in the direction of excess, he will first lose the symmetry of the feature and finally will make it not even look like a nose at all." (Tr. H. Rackham, Harvard University Press 1944.)

27 Heteronomy generally refers to action that is influenced by a force outside the individual. In this instance, Weber uses the term more specifically, to designate the action of non-economic causal factors on the human economy.

28 In his *System,* §11, n6, Roscher describes how the "materialists" of the eighteenth century base themselves on the conception of the reasonable character of the "instinctual" self-interest of the individual.

29 The reference is to the following passage in Schmoller's *Open Letter* to Treitschke (1874–75), p. 268: "A person advocating free competition does not say that everyone should be able to do what he likes; on the contrary, he expects that everybody will be forced by the price movements to act in a way which furthers the common good. What is proper or improper behaviour in a competitive situation is decided by [feelings of] common decency."

30 In his *System,* §11, n6, Roscher describes how the "materialists" of the eighteenth century base themselves on the conception of the reasonable character of the "instinctual" self-interest of the individual.

31 Bernard Mandeville's book *The Fable of the Bees* (1714, with a second volume in 1732) builds on the principle that "private vices" (following one's desires) will lead to "public benefits". It illustrates a number of key principles of economic thought, including "the invisible hand" and the "paradox of thrift" (if people save too much, the general economy will decline and people will in fact grow poorer).

32 Milton, *Paradise Lost*, Book II, lines 229–83. Weber is probably referring to Mammon's exhortation to "seek/our own good from our selves", with the corollary: "Our greatness will appear/then most conspicuous, when great things of small,/useful of hurtful, prosperous of adverse/we can create".

33 A quotation from Goethe's *Faust* (see endnote 79), Part I, line 1335–36 (tr. David Luke, Oxford University Press 1987).

34 A quotation from Friedrich Schiller's poem "Resignation" (first published 1786). The tenor of the poem, and of the quotation, is that one cannot expect that one's misfortunes or privations in this world will be compensated in the next one.

35 See Dilthey, *Ideas*, pp. 1326–27.

36 What is meant is the claim by Roscher (*Thucydides*, pp. 200–01) that, in a "philosophical" explanation, the "explained" concept is always subordinate to the "explaining" one, "and the beauty of [such a 'philosophical'] explanation is essentially based on the strictness of this distinction".

37 This is probably a reference to Jellinek, *Theory*, Chapter 6 ("The Evolution of the Concept of State"), pp. 132–44.

38 In his "Preface" to a book by one of his pupils, Hermann Hinrichs, Hegel formulated a sarcastic critique of Schleiermacher's argument that the "feeling of absolute dependence" on God experienced by sentient beings proves the divine existence. Hegel says that, if this were the case, then the *dog* must be the best Christian, since it would experience the strongest feeling of dependence: if it were thrown a bone when it was hungry, it might even have intimations of salvation.

39 In books and articles around the turn of the century, particularly *Introduction* (1901), Johannes Reinke advocated a "theoretical biology", as opposed to the "traditional" empirical biology. Here, he attempts to explain the evolutionary processes of life along vitalistic lines through a theory of "dominants".

40 Drews, in an article in the *Preußische Jahrbücher* 1902, (Drews, *Reinke*) had objected that Reinke's revision of his own theory of dominants (so that these dominants were no longer structuring forces (forma formans) but only structured ones (forma formata)) meant that they could not be the cause of life. Reinke's rejoinder (Reinke, *Dominants*) came later in the year in the same journal.

41 In his book *Treatise on Man*, Adolphe Quetelet describes the statistical concept of the "average man" (l'homme moyen), who is characterized by the mean values of measured variables that follow a normal distribution.

42 Chrematistics is the science or art of acquiring wealth, including money-making and exchange. The concept goes back to Aristotle, who contrasts it with "economics" (oikonomik), which deals with wealth consumption in the satisfaction of human wants and the provision of commodities to meet such wants.

43 In the passage referred to, Roscher, in opposition to the view that a genius like Goethe can have its own, "home-made", set of morals, argues: "Could confectioners also have their own morals?".

44 This is not a direct quotation from any classic, but a formulation that was apparently fairly widespread at the end of the nineteenth century.

45 Theodicy (literally: the justice, or justification, of God) is a term introduced by Leibniz in 1710, denoting the conception that the idea of a benevolent God is compatible with the existence of evil in this world.

46 In the original, this subtitle is numbered "I" and italicized. However, no title appears later with a "II", so the "I" has been left out; but the title has been given a separate place, since it can in fact be said to cover the whole of the two *Knies* essays.

47 "Academic socialists" ("Kathedersozialisten" – literally "socialists of the academic platform") was a term coined disparagingly by the German liberal politician H.B. Oppenheim in 1872 to characterize professors of economics committed to an active government policy of social reform. Prominent among these academics were adherents of the "historical school" such as Gustav Schmoller and Adolph Wagner.

48 The "quarrel about methods" was a controversy over the methodology of economics, carried on in the late 1880s and early 1890s between the supporters of the Austrian school of economics, led by Carl Menger, who favoured a theoretical approach, and the proponents of the (German) historical school, led by Gustav Schmoller. The controversy started with

Menger's attack on the historical school in his *Investigations into the method of the social sciences* (1883), Schmoller's sharp review ("On the methodology of the political and social sciences", 1883) of Menger's work, and Menger's no less sharp rejoinder (*The errors of historicism in German economics*, 1884).

49 Apart from an essay from 1850 on "Statistics as an independent science", these essays seem to deal with concrete subjects such as railways or telegraphs.

50 The definitions are found in Helmholtz, *Relationship*. The discussion of the distinction between these two kinds of science had already begun in the 1840s, but gathered momentum with the emergence of a more mechanistic conception of science, typified by Helmholtz.

51 On 5 August 1810, Napoleon promulgated the Trianon Decree, which raised tariffs on colonial goods to an exorbitant degree.

52 This unusual neologism ("charakterogenetisch" in German) should apparently be taken to indicate "that which exerts an influence on human character". Although it is related in meaning to "characterological", the two concepts are not identical.

53 In his *Logic²*, Vol. II, 2, in particular pp. 267–81, Wundt deals with the methodology of the sciences of the human spirit. Here, he describes the concept of the "creative synthesis" (which is, in his view, "a principle [. . .] that dominates the formation of the individual psychic entities") as follows: "[. . .] the psychic entities are causally related in a certain manner to the elements that constitute them; but at the same time, they always possess *new* qualities which are not present in the individual elements. In this sense, therefore, all psychic entities are products of a *creative* synthesis" (Wundt, *Logic²*, Vol. II, 2, pp. 268–69).

54 In his *Limits of Concept Formation* (p. 422), Rickert introduces the concept of a causal inequation on the basis of the following argument: "All causes considered by an absolute historical account are different from each other. In the same way, the historical effect is always different from the cause which produces it: if it were nothing else than [its cause] and did not have a different character [. . .] it could not become historically significant by virtue of its uniqueness. Consequently, the concept of the causal equation is foreign to history; on the contrary: if one has to describe the causal interconnection between two individual historical processes, this can only be done by means of causal inequations."

55 "The cause equals the effect." This principle was incorporated by Leibniz into his theory of motion (kinetic energy), and gave rise in physics to the idea of conservation of kinetic energy (see immediately below).

56 The law of conservation of energy is an empirical law of physics, first formulated by Mayer and Helmholtz, stating that the total amount of energy in an isolated system remains constant over time.

57 Herostratos was a young man in Ancient Greece, who in 356 BC set fire to the temple of Artemis in Ephesos in order to become famous. He did become – negatively – famous, in that such acts are commonly referred to as "herostratic".

58 The Black Death was a deadly pandemic of a plague-like infection which reached its peak in Europe between 1348 and 1350. It killed about one half of the European population. (The fact that the pandemic can be said to have "invaded" Europe from Asia puts this example on a par with the three other examples given by Weber of "invasions".)

59 The Dollart is a bay between the Netherlands and Germany. It is believed that dikes holding back the waters of the Dollart from the surrounding low country collapsed in the early fifteenth century, so that the Dollart overflowed the land.

60 King Gustavus Adolphus II of Sweden (1594–1632) invaded Germany in 1630 on the Protestant side during the Thirty Years' War and rapidly reversed the declining fortunes of the Protestants. He died in the battle of Lützen in 1632.

61 Forces under generals of Genghis Khan (*c*.1162–1227), Emperor of the Mongols, invaded Georgia, Armenia and parts of Russia 1220–25, but, strictly speaking, Genghis Khan himself did not take part in these actions.

62 This is probably a reference to the German naturalist Ernst Haeckel who, in opposition to Emil du Bois-Reymond (see endnote 25), maintained that all aspects of human consciousness could be explained in purely physiological terms.

63 Phylogenetics is the study of evolutionary relatedness among various groups of organisms.

64 Psychometrics is the field of study concerned with the theory and technique of psychological measurement.

65 The Peruzzi were bankers in Florence in the fourteenth century. Their account books from the years 1335–43 survive and provide an indispensable primary source for the economic history of Florence.

66 In the "Third Antinomy" discussed in his "Critique of Pure Reason", Kant argues for the possibility of a "causality through freedom" independent of the normal chain of "causality through nature", because the chain of causation under the law of nature presupposes a first cause which is not itself caused by a preceding natural cause. The ability to posit and work towards ends therefore constitutes human freedom. A similar argument is found in the "Critique of Practical Reason", where Kant argues that moral obligation presupposes an ability to act independently of all prior determination.

67 This detailed discussion never materialized.

68 A famous painting by the Renaissance painter Raphael, *c*.1513, of the Virgin, Child and Saints. The painting is called "Sistine" because one of the Saints depicted is Saint Sixtus; it was also placed in the convent of Saint Sixtus in Piacenza for some time.

69 Nomological knowledge is knowledge of general laws, as opposed to knowledge of individual events. The term is closely connected with "nomothetic", a word used – first by the German philosopher Wilhelm Windelband – to characterize the group of (typically natural) sciences seeking laws, as opposed to what Windelband called the "idiographic" sciences, seeking knowledge of what is individual and unique.

70 In probability theory, the law of large numbers is a theorem that describes the result of performing the same experiment or test a large number of times. According to the law, the average of the results obtained from a large number of trials should be close to the expected value, and will tend to become closer as more trials are performed.

71 In 1756, King Frederick II ("the Great") of Prussia, having secured an alliance with Great Britain, invaded the neutral Kingdom of Saxony. This was Prussia's first move in the Seven Years' War (1756–63), which pitted Britain and Prussia against France, Austria and Russia.

72 The source of this reference may be Schopenhauer, *The World as Will and Representation* (Vol. 2, Supplements to Book 1, Second Half, On the Theory of the Laughable) who tells the story of two lions who broke down the dividing wall between them and, in their rage, devoured each other so that only the two tails remained.

73 The term "introjection" was coined by R. Avenarius in the 1890s. As discussed by him, it covers the process by which our "natural" relationship to reality is "falsified" so that all the perceived elements of our environment are taken to be nothing but "perceptions within us". The object of perception is transferred ("introjected") into the brain of human beings. "Elements of the real world become elements of ideal thought." According to Münsterberg, the psychical is introjected into the body and takes over the temporal and spatial coordinates of the body. "The psychological impulse to action must take effect on the central motor apparatus at a certain place in space and at a certain time" (Münsterberg, *Outline of Psychology*, p. 256).

74 The reference is to Rickert, *The Universal*.

75 This refers to a passage in Schopenhauer's doctoral dissertation from 1813, *On the Fourfold Root of the Principle of Sufficient Reason* where he says: "The law of causality is [. . .] not so obliging as to let itself be used like a cab which one sends away after having arrived at one's chosen destination."

76 Weber is probably referring to elements of the "personal rule" of King Frederick William IV of Prussia (1795–1861) towards the end of his reign. For instance, his will contained an injunction on all future kings to abolish the constitution of Prussia.

77 Probably a reference to the "energistic" theory of Wilhelm Ostwald, according to which differences and changes of energy are the fundamental elements of physical nature. See Weber's critique of Ostwald's theories in *Energetics*, pp. 252–68.

78 Fluids are guttiform when they can form droplets.

79 Goethe's major play. Part I was published in 1808, Part II in 1832.

80 The reference is to Schleiermacher, *Hermeneutics*, Schleiermacher, *Concept*, and Boeckh, *Encyclopedia*.

81 The Lisbon earthquake occurred in 1755 and had a profound impact on thinking all over Europe because of the widespread destruction and large toll of human life (30–40,000 inhabitants are believed to have died).

82 In his *Philosophy of History²*, pp. 51–52, Simmel comments on Ranke. Although Ranke is known for his empirical approach to history, there are those who maintain that he also looked for the "essence" behind the facts.

83 This quotation seems to have originated with Simmel himself.

84 In Plato's dialogue *Meno*, Socrates develops the idea that the soul is repeatedly incarnated. All knowledge is in the soul from the beginning, but, with each new reincarnation of the soul, knowledge is again forgotten. Learning is therefore recovery of what one has forgotten.

85 In *The Stalwart Cavalry Captain* (1890), a novel by Hans Hoffmann, there is no mention of a "sick horse". What Weber is referring to is the painting of a "faulty horse", which, on p. 236 of the novel, is described in the following terms: "The artist of Ancient Greece, when sculpting a marble goddess, was able to extract and synthesize from a hundred living models a representation of the ultimate and pure epitome of every perfection; in just the same way, the horse depicted by the skilful creator of this work of art represents a pure, complete ideal picture, marred by no contingent detail, of all the imperfections found in real life."

86 "Ein jeder sieht, was er im Herzen trägt". Goethe, *Faust I*, Prologue.

87 Probably a reference to p. 58.

88 Versified story by the German humorist Wilhelm Busch of the adventures of two young puppies, Plisch and Plum ("Splash" and "Plop" – named after the sound they made when their original owner tried to drown them by throwing them into the millpond).

89 Pseudo-spherical space is a space (in non-Euclidean geometry) where the measure of curvature is everywhere negative.

90 According to Rickert, man, by virtue of having the capacity of taking a stand concerning values, has constitutive importance for history. Therefore, man is the subject of history and stands at the centre of the historical account: man is "the historical centre".

91 "Causa cessante cessat effectus" (when the cause ceases, the effect ceases) is a scholastic proposition formulated by Saint Thomas Aquinas (*Summa theologiae* I, 96, 3). Robert Mayer, in his essay "Die organische Bewegung in ihrem Zusammenhange mit dem Stoff" (Organic Movement in its connection with Matter), 1845, encapsulates the principle of the law of the conservation of energy in the expression "nil fit ex nihilo, nil fit ad nihilum" (nothing

comes from nothing, nothing becomes nothing), which implies the existence of potential energy. (See also endnote 55.)

92 In fact, among the points mentioned by Weber, the axiom "cessante causa cessat effectus" is the only one discussed by Wundt in that work.

93 The theoretical and "marginalist" school of economics, whose leading figure was Carl Menger (see endnote 48 above).

94 "Ein jeder sieht, was er im Herzen trägt". Goethe, *Faust I*, Prologue.

95 This is, indisputably, what Weber writes. But, equally indisputably, he means the opposite: that their scientific value is inversely proportional to their aesthetic charm.

96 The concept of the "historical individual" was one that Weber borrowed from Heinrich Rickert (*Limits of Concept Formation*). It designates, in Weber's own words (from the *Protestant Ethic*) "a complex of interconnections in historical reality which we unite into a conceptual whole from the point of view of their cultural significance".

97 See p. 61.

98 Emanationism in the general sense is the principle according to which creation is a gradual process of emanation and descent from a transcendental absolute to mundane reality. In his dissertation on Fichte's idealism, Emil Lask used the term to describe a theory of concept formation in which concrete reality emanates from abstract concepts, which are therefore more "real" and have a higher ontological status (as opposed to the "analytical" theory of concept formation, where concepts, being formed by abstraction, are the more remote from reality, the more general the concept is).

99 Probably a reference to the idea that history is "essentially" the result of the interplay of certain innate racial qualities.

100 The German historical school of jurisprudence was a branch of legal philosophy founded by Friedrich Karl von Savigny. Its central idea was the identification of law with custom, tradition and the "national genius" (Volksgeist): law was "found" by the jurist and not "made" by the state or its organs.

101 "Ich bin kein ausgeklügelt Buch/Ich bin ein Mensch mit seinem Widerspruch" ("I am not a book whose mysteries have been worked out/I am a human being with its contradictions") – From the poem "Homo sum" in the collection *Huttens letzte Tage* by Conrad Ferdinand Meyer.

102 Theodicy (literally: the justice, or justification, of God) is a term introduced by Leibniz in 1710, denoting the conception that the idea of a benevolent God is compatible with the existence of evil in this world.

103 According to Hegel, logos or reason informs absolute reality. "The real is rational, the rational is real."

104 Heinrich Braun's *Archiv für soziale Gesetzgebung und Statistik* (Archive for Social Legislation and Statistics) started publication in 1888.

105 The *Finanzarchiv* was a periodical first published in 1884 and dedicated to all aspects of financial questions.

106 The *Accompanying Remarks* are translated on pp. 95–98.

107 See endnote 104. For more details, see the *Accompanying Remarks*.

108 "Homo sum; humani nil a me alienum puto" – "I am a human being; nothing human can be foreign to me". Quotation from the comedy *Heautontimorumenos* by the Roman poet Terentius (*c*.200–159 BC).

109 Since 1845, it had been possible for every municipality in Prussia to organize courts of arbitration to deal with conflicts between workers and employers, with an equal number of judges representing the two sides.

110 In its broader sense: the idea that material circumstances, rather than human thought, determine the basis and the limits of history. The idea has become especially influential within the Marxist philosophy of history ("economic" or "historical" materialism), where historical development is seen as determined by the opposition between the productive forces (labour, tools, knowledge) and the social conditions under which the means of sustenance of life are produced.

111 *Manifest der Kommunistischen Partei* ("Manifesto of the Communist Party") (1848), written by Karl Marx and Friedrich Engels as the programme for the Communist League.

112 Possibly a reference to the ideas and activities of the German physician and biologist Alfred Ploetz, who in 1904 founded the journal *Archiv für Rassen- und Gesellschafts-Biologie* ("Archive of Racial and Social Biology") and the following year the *Berliner Gesellschaft für Rassenhygiene* ("Berlin Society for Racial Hygiene"). Weber made a long, critical intervention in a sharp debate in 1910 in the German Sociological Society about a paper presented by Ploetz.

113 In his essay on the *Protestant Ethic* (Part I, n40), Weber mentions that "in former times, wide clerical (in particular Lutheran) circles were motivated by their general sympathy for authoritarianism to let themselves be used by businesspeople as "black police" whenever there was a need to brand strikes as a sin or labour unions for encouraging "cupidity".

114 A famous painting by the Renaissance painter Raphael, *c*.1513, of the Virgin, Child and Saints. The painting is called "Sistine" because one of the Saints depicted is Saint Sixtus; it was also placed in the convent of Saint Sixtus in Piacenza for some time.

115 Probably Emil du Bois-Reymond in his speech on "The Limits of our Knowledge of Nature" (1872).

116 The reference may be to E. de Laveleye, who in his book *De la propriété et de ses formes primitives* ("On Property and its Primitive Forms") (1874) postulated an evolutionary process of ownership of land, originating in "primitive agrarian communism". Laveleye's book, translated and supplemented by Karl Bücher, was published in German in 1879 under the title "Das Ureigentum" ("Original ownership").

117 This may be a reference to the ideas of J.J. Bachofen, who in his book *Das Mutterrecht* ("The Mother Right") (1861) postulated a theory of cultural evolution according to which man originally lived in a state of sexual promiscuity (what he called the "hetaerism" stage).

118 The concept of the "historical individual" was one that Weber borrowed from Heinrich Rickert (*Limits of Concept Formation*). It designates, in Weber's own words (from *The Protestant Ethic*), "a complex of interconnections in historical reality which we unite into a conceptual whole from the point of view of their cultural significance".

119 A reference to Rudolf Stammler's book *Economy and Law according to the Materialist Conception of History* (1896). Weber subjects the second edition of the book, which came out in 1906, to an extensive critical discussion in his essay *Stammler*.

120 According to Hegel, logos or reason informs absolute reality. "The real is rational, the rational is real."

121 The German historical school of jurisprudence was a branch of legal philosophy founded by Friedrich Karl von Savigny. Its central idea was the identification of law with custom, tradition and the "national genius" (Volksgeist): law was "found" by the jurist and not "made" by the state or its organs.

122 The German historical school of economics was a group of German economists who saw economics as resulting from careful empirical and historical studies and took a correspondingly negative view of abstract economic theorems. The historical school can be divided into the Older school, led by Wilhelm Roscher, Karl Knies and Bruno Hildebrand, and the Younger school, led by Gustav v. Schmoller. Max Weber is often

categorized as a member of the Younger school, but in many respects took up an intermediate position between the historical school and the Austrian "marginalists".

123 The Austrian economist Carl Menger (see endnote 48).

124 The Austrian school of economic theory was called "marginalist" because it taught that people decide whether to effect any given change on the basis of the marginal utility of that change, with rival alternatives being chosen according to which has the greatest marginal utility. (The marginal utility is defined as the utility gained (or lost) from an increase (or decrease) in the consumption of that good or service.) In general, preferences display diminishing marginal utility.

125 An intellectual process of ordering that first indicates a broader category to which the item in question belongs, and then distinguishes that item from other items in the category by indicating one or more properties possessed by that item, but not by other items in the category. This method goes back to the Greek philosopher Aristotle.

126 Discursive (as opposed to intuitive) knowledge is based on empirical data and logical inferences; it is mediate, while intuitive knowledge is immediate. Discursive cognition is the process by which discursive knowledge is acquired.

127 In Greek mythology, the innkeeper Procrustes would force his customers to fit his iron bed by stretching them or lopping off the extra length.

128 It is not entirely clear what specific phenomenon, if any, this general formulation is meant to refer to. In the context, however, it seems likely that Weber was thinking of the chain of reasoning that led Scholastic philosophers to justify the activities of "middlemen" – who were in fact already a feature of the economic system of the time – by recognizing that the incentive of the middlemen to render their services depended on a margin between the price at which they bought and the price at which they sold, without which it would be impossible for them to meet their incidental costs and provide for their subsistence.

129 Robinsonades are stories or examples where a person finds himself in an isolated position and has to survive by his own wits and by husbanding such resources as he can get access to. The basic reference is to the fictional figure of Robinson Crusoe, whose life for 28 years as a castaway on a tropical island, partly in complete solitude, is described in Daniel Defoe's novel *Robinson Crusoe* (1719). His solitary condition was a favourite subject of economists because conditions on his island were the closest one could get to those of a "laboratory", so that he could be seen as a kind of rational "economic man". Economists who insisted on the importance of the historical conditions of the economy would obviously be critical of this approach, and the German historical school therefore characterized their "theoretical" opponents, above all the Austrian school, for their lack of realism, their "Robinsonades".

130 In his *Institutio Christianae Religionis* (*Institutes of the Christian Religion*) (1536), Jean Calvin asserts that God has pre-ordained who it is that He will graciously save.

131 Methodism is a branch of Christianity that has its origins in the revival movement in the Anglican Church led by John Wesley (1703–91) and Charles Wesley (1707–88).

132 To the German historian F.C. Schlosser, history was a school for morals: in his works, he sat sternly in judgement upon men and events.

133 See Weber's description of Gierke's conception of the state, p. 24n115.

134 In Weber's lecture *Politics as a Profession and Vocation*, he describes the American political system with special emphasis on the "spoils system", which, in his opinion, means that the American political parties are exclusively focused on the Presidential and the gubernatorial election campaigns, because that is where the "spoils" are to be found. See also Weber's description, both in *Politics as a Profession and Vocation* and in his long article on *Parliament*

and *Government in Germany under a new Political Order*, of the American political "boss", who is devoid of principles and exclusively interested in harvesting votes. (In the latter article, the "boss" is directly described as an "entrepreneur").

135 The concept of "Augenblicksgötter" ("momentary gods") was introduced by the German scholar Hermann Usener in his book *Götternamen* (1896) as the first stage in a sequence of different kinds of deities: "Something that approaches us suddenly, as if sent from above, and makes us happy, or sad and bowed" (Usener).

136 This was a literary academy founded in Florence in 1582 for the purpose of purifying the Tuscan dialect.

137 In a famous essay from 1819, *De la liberté des anciens comparée à celle des modernes* ("On the liberty of people in Antiquity compared with that enjoyed by people of the present day"), Benjamin Constant repeatedly singles out Sparta as the *typical* Greek city state (polis), while Athens is taken to be the exception.

138 "Ein jeder sieht, was er im Herzen trägt". Goethe, *Faust I*, Prologue.

139 The direct reference is probably simply to the idea of free trade. But it is likely that this is also an indirect reference to Lujo Brentano's lecture *Das Freihandelsargument* (1901), in which Brentano argues that it is entirely possible for a state, under conditions of free trade, to develop into an industrial state, even if its production costs may be higher than in the other industrial countries with which Germany competes. (The argument is the old Ricardian one of comparative advantage.)

140 In his literary parody *Faust, Part III* (1862), the influential Goethe scholar Fr. Th. Vischer made fun not only of Goethe's *Faust, Part II*, (see endnote 79) but also of those Goethe scholars who over-interpret the poet. Vischer divided this group into "Stoffhuber" ("material-seekers") and "Sinnhuber" ("meaning-seekers").

141 Goethe, *Faust, Part I*, lines 1085–89 (tr. John R. Williams).

142 See pp. 121–37.

143 The German historical school of economics was a group of German economists who saw economics as resulting from careful empirical and historical studies and took a correspondingly negative view of abstract economic theorems. The historical school can be divided into the Older school, led by Wilhelm Roscher, Karl Knies and Bruno Hildebrand, and the Younger school, led by Gustav v. Schmoller. Max Weber is often categorized as a member of the Younger school, but in many respects took up an intermediate position between the historical school and the Austrian "marginalists". ("Our discipline" is a reference to the science of economics.)

144 In this connection, Meyer (*Theory and Method*) refers to Barth, Bernheim, Lamprecht and Breysig.

145 This was Windelband's doctoral thesis (*The Theories of Chance* (1870)).

146 In its classical form, this principle holds that there is an adequate reason to account for the existence and nature of everything that could conceivably not exist. It is normally attributed to the seventeenth-/eighteenth-century philosopher Leibniz. However, the "principle of sufficient reason" referred to by Weber is probably that discussed by John Stuart Mill. In this formulation, it states that "a phenomenon must follow a certain law, because we see no reason why it should deviate from that law in one way rather than another" (J.S. Mill, *System of Logic* (1886), p. 496).

147 "*The essential achievement of the will, in short, when it is most voluntary, is to ATTEND to a difficult object and hold it fast before the mind. The so-doing is the fiat . . . Effort of attention is thus the essential phenomenon of will*" (William James, *The Principles of Psychology*, Chapter XXVI, pp. 561–62).

148 With regard to a possible war with Austria.

149 Weber is probably referring to elements of the "personal rule" of King Frederick William IV of Prussia (1795–1861) towards the end of his reign. For instance, his will contained an injunction on all future kings to abolish the constitution of Prussia.

150 Czar Paul I of Russia (1754–1801) succeeded his aunt, the Empress Catherine the Great, in 1796. His actions as Czar were often eccentric and unpredictable, and he was reputed to be actually mad. He was assassinated in 1801.

151 This is the most famous chapel in the Vatican Palace in Rome. It takes its name from Pope Sixtus IV, who ordered it to be built on the site of an earlier chapel. It was constructed between 1473 and 1481. After its completion, the chapel was decorated with frescoes by a number of the most famous artists of the day, including Botticelli, Ghirlandaio, Perugino and Michelangelo.

152 The Spanish Armada was a large Spanish fleet sent against England in 1588. After initial, unsuccessful engagements, it was scattered and largely destroyed by a storm in the Atlantic.

153 See p. 55.

154 The dispute concerned Meyer's book *The Origins of Judaism* (1896), in which he argued that Judaism had originated in the Persian period (fifth century BC).

155 The concepts of "evolutionary" and "epigenetic" interpretation do not come from Meyer, but from Wundt (*Logic*).

156 King Frederick William IV of Prussia adopted a wavering stance towards the March Revolution of 1848. He did, however, remain dedicated to German unification for a time, which led the Frankfurt Parliamentary Assembly to offer him the crown of Germany on 3 April 1849. However, the king refused it, purportedly saying that he would not accept "a crown from the gutter".

157 In 1895, the German physicist Wilhelm Röntgen discovered a new and different form of ray, produced by the impact of cathode rays on a material object. Because their nature was then unknown, he gave them the name X-rays.

158 The passage in question is found in Breysig, *Uniqueness*, p. 8 (Weber's confusion may be explained by the fact that there were no less than three articles by Breysig in the 1904 volume of *Schmollers Jahrbuch*).

159 The "Persian Wars" were fought between the invading Persians and the Ancient Greeks from 499 to 449 BC. The battle of Marathon (490) was the first major battle in these wars. Here, the Persians were decisively defeated by the Athenians.

160 Instances of valour.

161 During the first ten years or so that Goethe spent in Weimar (1775–86), he developed a strong and very intimate friendship with Charlotte v. Stein, who was locked in a loveless marriage. We possess more than 2,000 letters and notes from Goethe to Frau v. Stein, but none from her to him.

162 That is to say, during Goethe's subsequent voyage to Italy (1786–88), which led to a marked cooling-off in his relationship with Frau v. Stein.

163 In eighteenth- and nineteenth-century Italy, the Cicisibeo was the acknowledged gallant (and often lover) of women of high social standing.

164 Weber uses the term "Ottecento", current in the history of art as a designation of *nineteenth*-century Italian art, apparently in the mistaken belief that this expression designates the *eighteenth* century – which is obviously the period that he wishes to refer to.

165 Rousseau's *Confessions*, one of the first major works of autobiography, was published in 1782, four years after the death of its author. They include detailed and unvarnished descriptions of Rousseau's emotional life.

166 This was a sermon given, as described in St Matthew's Gospel, ch. 5–7, by Jesus on a mountainside to his disciples and a large crowd of people.

167 The principal assembly of the city-state of Athens in Ancient Greece.

168 A trilogy of tragedies written by the Ancient Greek playwright Aeschylus.

169 The German philologist Johann Heinrich Düntzer invented a new method of interpretation, which was, however, seen as so narrow and pedestrian that he is now forgotten, except for the fact that it was he who formulated the famous criticism "hier irrt Goethe" ("Here, Goethe is mistaken") – concerning Goethe's own estimation of who was the greatest love of his life!

170 Goethe, *Faust I* (Faust's Study) ("Then the parts in his hand he may hold ... but the spiritual link is lost, alas!").

171 A list of newly published books.

172 A reference to the Provençal poetry of "courtly love" (eleventh–twelfth century).

173 Romulus Augustulus (reigned 475–76) was the last of the Western Roman emperors; Justinian (reigned 527–65) was one of the first of the Eastern Roman emperors, who partly recovered the Western Roman Empire, including the city of Rome; Diocletian (reigned 284–305), in 286 established Nicomedia as the Eastern capital city of the Roman Empire, so that Rome was no longer the capital of the whole of the Empire.

174 Drews, in an article in the *Preußische Jahrbücher* 1902 (Drews, *Reinke*), had objected that Reinke's revision of his own theory of dominants (so that these dominants were no longer structuring forces (forma formans) but only structured ones (forma formata)) meant that they could not be the cause of life. Reinke's rejoinder (Reinke, *Dominants*) came later in the year in the same journal.

175 This is a reference to what was probably meant to be part of a further essay, planned by Weber, which never materialized.

176 "For educational purposes."

177 The Second Punic war (218–201 BC) between Carthage and the Roman Republic; the Seven Years' War (1756–63) involving all the major European Powers (Prussia, Great Britain and a coalition of smaller German states against Austria, France, Russia, Sweden and Saxony); the war of 1866 between Prussia and Austria.

178 In the course of the public proclamation, on March 18, 1848, of a Patent Royal concerning reforms in Prussia, two shots were fired – whether intentionally or by some sort of mistake has never been definitively established. The mood of the public demonstration turned ugly, and armed soldiers intervened. The result was intense street fighting leaving hundreds of dead.

179 In a letter to Bortkievicz (p. 385), Weber writes as follows: "First of all: the word 'statistical' is a slip of the pen, and I cannot understand how it came about: of course one cannot speak of the 'statistical theories' of Kries".

180 An "offence by causation" ("Erfolgsdelikt") is an act that becomes an offence because of its subsequent effects (e.g. manslaughter), in contradistinction to the "offence by commission" ("Tätigkeitsdelikt"), where the act in itself constitutes the offence (e.g. giving false statements under oath).

181 Caesar, who had been proclaimed dictator for life, was assassinated on 15 March 44 BC, by a group of senators led by Brutus.

182 The "Persian Wars" were fought between the invading Persians and the Ancient Greeks from 499 to 449 BC. The battle of Marathon (490) was the first major battle in these wars. Here, the Persians were decisively defeated by the Athenians.

183 (See the preceding endnote). The estimate of the number of soldiers involved is necessarily uncertain. There seems to be wide agreement that there were 10–11,000 soldiers on the Greek side. Numbers given for the Persian forces vary wildly, but an estimate of about 25,000 soldiers may not be too wide of the mark.

184 The Persian army withdrew and only returned ten years later.

185 In his Foreword to the *World History* of which he was the editor, Hans F. Helmolt wrote that he had intentionally avoided defining value standards for the evaluation of the cultural evolution, since such standards would be "arbitrary". One had to look at the whole course of world history in order to form an opinion concerning it.

186 Having proclaimed himself King of Sicily, Duke Conradin of Swabia, on 23 August 1268, encountered the army of Count Charles of Anjou at Tagliacozzo in Central Italy. His (Italian, Spanish, Roman, Arab and German) troops were too eager to obtain plunder after a preliminary success and finally lost the battle. Conradin was caught, and beheaded by Charles later that year.

187 See Goethe, *Maximen und Reflektionen*, no. 575: "The most sublime would be to comprehend that every fact is already theory."

188 "Problematic judgements are judgements where the assertion or negation is only . . . assumed to be possible. In assertorical judgements, [the assertion or negation] is regarded as actual (true). In apodictical judgements, it is regarded as necessary"(Kant, *Critique of Pure Reason*, §9).

189 A quotation from Busch's illustrated versified story *Abenteuer eines Junggesellen* ("Adventures of a bachelor"), 1875.

190 Shakespeare, *Hamlet*, Act III, scene 1.

191 A reference to M. Jourdain, the main character in Molière's comedy *Le Bourgeois Gentilhomme* ("The Bourgeois Gentleman").

192 Less than three months before the Austro-Prussian war broke out, Prussia had made a treaty with Italy committing the latter to fight on the Prussian side if war broke out between Austria and Prussia within three months. As a result of the war, Austria ceded the Veneto province to France, and France in her turn, in accordance with a secret agreement with Prussia, gave the Veneto to Italy. There was no coalition between Austria and France during the war because of skilful Prussian diplomatic manoeuvering vis-à-vis France.

193 "Nobody is perfect" (literally: "There are faults within the city walls as well as outside them"), Horace, *Epistles*, 1.2.16.

194 Critical idealism is the philosophical tendency according to which the primary subject of philosophy is the character and foundations of experience, rather than reality as such. Kant was the most prominent exponent of this tendency, and the term "critical idealism" is often used to characterize Kant's philosophy in general.

195 As opposed to idealism, philosophical naturalism holds that nature is all there is, and all basic truths are truths of nature.

196 No source has been found for this (apparent) quotation.

197 In its broader sense: the idea that material circumstances, rather than human thought, determine the basis and the limits of history. The idea has become especially influential within the Marxist philosophy of history ("economic" or "historical" materialism), where historical development is seen as determined by the opposition between the productive forces (labour, tools, knowledge) and the social conditions under which the means of sustenance of life are produced.

198 The computation of indices based on skull measurements was widely used in cultural anthropology at the end of the nineteenth and beginning of the twentieth century.

199 *Manifest der Kommunistischen Partei* ("Manifesto of the Communist Party") (1848), written by Karl Marx and Friedrich Engels as the programme for the Communist League.

200 Nomothetic knowledge is knowledge of general laws, as opposed to knowledge of individual events. The term "nomothetic" was used – first by the German philosopher Wilhelm Windelband – to characterize the group of (typically natural) sciences seeking laws, as opposed to what Windelband called the "idiographic" sciences, seeking knowledge of what is individual and unique.

201 See Weber's explication of this distinction, p. 151 above.

202 The law of conservation of energy is an empirical law of physics, first formulated by Mayer and Helmholtz, stating that the total amount of energy in an isolated system remains constant over time.

203 In his book *The World View of Modern Physics* (1902), pp. 29–31 Eduard v. Hartmann tries to show that the second law of thermodynamics is only valid for a finite world. (The second law of thermodynamics states that the entropy of an isolated system that is not in equilibrium will tend to increase over time, approaching a maximum value at equilibrium.)

204 In its classical form, this principle holds that there is an adequate reason to account for the existence and nature of everything that could conceivably not exist. It is normally attributed to the seventeenth-/eighteenth-century philosopher Leibniz. However, the "principle of sufficient reason" referred to by Weber is probably that discussed by John Stuart Mill. In this formulation, it states that "a phenomenon must follow a certain law, because we see no reason why it should deviate from that law in one way rather than another" (J.S.Mill, *System of Logic* (1886), p. 496).

205 The reference is to the idea of the French mathematician Laplace that "an intellect which at a certain moment would know all forces that set nature in motion, and all positions of all items of which nature is composed, if this intellect were also vast enough to submit these data to analysis, it would embrace in a single formula the movements of the greatest bodies of the universe and those of the tiniest atom". This formula is also known as "Laplace's demon".

206 Some historians in the late eighteenth century (Stammler mentions Justus Möser) offered "materialistic" (economic) reasons for the Crusades, viewing them as early examples of the economic expansion of Europe.

207 Stammler points to the development of trade in Western Europe in the late Middle Ages as a factor favouring the introduction of Roman law, which was a legal system based on the specification of possession and exchange of goods.

208 The reference is to the so-called "Bauernlegen", i.e. the process by which large landowners expropriated and incorporated the land of deserted farmsteads, or bought up free peasant holdings, possibly by pressurizing the owners. Stammler's example is more specific, however, and concerns the English enclosures, for which, according to the German sociologist Paul Barth (quoted by Stammler), the feudal system was a relevant factor.

209 "Carmina non prius audita". Horace, *Odes*, Book III, 1.

210 Robinson Crusoe was a fictional figure whose life for 28 years as a castaway on a tropical island, partly in complete solitude, is described in Daniel Defoe's novel *Robinson Crusoe* (1719). His solitary condition was a favourite subject of economists because conditions on his island were the closest one could get to those of a "laboratory", so that he could be seen as a kind of rational "economic man". Economists who insisted on the importance of the historical conditions of the economy would obviously be critical of this approach, and the German historical school therefore characterized their "theoretical" opponents, above all the Austrian school, for their lack of realism, their "Robinsonades".

211 This case concerns the "unnatural acts of indecency committed by human beings with animals".

212 The Austrian school of economic theory was called "marginalist" because it taught that people decide whether to effect any given change on the basis of the marginal utility of that change, with rival alternatives being chosen according to which has the greatest marginal utility. (The marginal utility is defined as the utility gained (or lost) from an increase (or decrease) in the consumption of that good or service.) In general, preferences display diminishing marginal utility.

213 This seems to refer to the general notion that people come together in a political association (state) with some kind of regulative idea in mind. There may be an indirect reference to Hobbes, *Leviathan*, §§17–19 (although Hobbes speaks of a "Commonwealth").

214 Weber's expression is "Metabase", which in logic means an impermissible jump in an argument from one area into another, logically different, one.

215 The game of skat was developed in the first decades of the nineteenth century from previous card games including "lhombre" and "tarok". A "skat congress" held in August 1886 established the "General German Rules of Skat". The rules of skat are extremely complicated. But since Weber's argument can in fact be understood without knowledge of these rules, there will be no attempt to explain them in the endnotes.

216 The concept of the "historical individual" was one that Weber borrowed from Heinrich Rickert (*Limits of Concept Formation*). It designates, in Weber's own words (from the *Protestant Ethic*) "a complex of interconnections in historical reality that we unite into a conceptual whole from the point of view of their cultural significance".

217 A famous painting by the Renaissance painter Raphael, *c.*1513, of the Virgin, Child and Saints. The painting is called "Sistine" because one of the Saints depicted is Saint Sixtus; it was also placed in the convent of Saint Sixtus in Piacenza for some time.

218 A famous restaurant in Paris. It had in fact ceased to exist when the Addendum was written: it was closed in 1905 and only re-opened in 1947.

219 Telos (from the Greek τέλος) means "end" or "purpose". The term has been used, with the sense of a "final cause", by philosophers since the times of Aristotle. It is the root of the term "teleology".

220 In its classical form, this principle holds that there is an adequate reason to account for the existence and nature of everything that could conceivably not exist. It is normally attributed to the seventeenth-/eighteenth-century philosopher Leibniz. However, the "principle of sufficient reason" referred to by Weber is probably that discussed by John Stuart Mill. In this formulation, it states that "a phenomenon must follow a certain law, because we see no reason why it should deviate from that law in one way rather than another" (J.S.Mill, *System of Logic* (1886), p. 496).

221 Nomological knowledge is knowledge of general laws, as opposed to knowledge of individual events. The term is closely connected with "nomothetic", a word used – first by the German philosopher Wilhelm Windelband – to characterize the group of (typically natural) sciences seeking laws, as opposed to what Windelband called the "idiographic" sciences, seeking knowledge of what is individual and unique.

222 Rümelin (as quoted by Stammler) sees "society" as covering the communal existence of a number of persons without the ordering authority of a "state".

223 This is a term originating in Roman law, meaning "gross negligence" (as opposed to simple negligence).

224 Robinsonades are stories or examples where a person finds himself in an isolated position and has to survive by his own wits and by husbanding such resources as he can get access

to. The basic reference is to the fictional figure of Robinson Crusoe, whose life for 28 years as a castaway on a tropical island, partly in complete solitude, is described in Daniel Defoe's novel *Robinson Crusoe* (1719). His solitary condition was a favourite subject of economists because conditions on his island were the closest one could get to those of a "laboratory", so that he could be seen as a kind of rational "economic man". Economists who insisted on the importance of the historical conditions of the economy would obviously be critical of this approach, and the German historical school therefore characterized their "theoretical" opponents, above all the Austrian school, for their lack of realism, their "Robinsonades".

225 This was a native American ("Indian") whose life was saved by Robinson Crusoe (see endnote 224) and who became his devoted companion.

226 Bräsig is an estate steward in *Ut mine Stromtid*, a three-volume novel (1862–64) in Low German dialect by Fritz Reuter.

227 Allgemeines Preußisches Landrecht – an important Civil Code of Prussia promulgated in 1794. The code covered wide fields of civil, family, penal and administrative law.

228 According to Brentano, "usability" ("Brauchbarkeit") denotes the general usefulness of something, without reference to a specific purpose, whereas "utility value" ("Gebrauchs-wert") sees the usability in relation to a specific subjective need.

229 The Austrian school of economic theory was called "marginalist" because it taught that people decide whether to effect any given change on the basis of the marginal utility of that change, with rival alternatives being chosen according to which has the greatest marginal utility. (The marginal utility is defined as the utility gained (or lost) from an increase (or decrease) in the consumption of that good or service.) In general, preferences display diminishing marginal utility.

230 The Weber–Fechner law (originally formulated by Ernst Heinrich Weber and later elaborated by Gustav Theodor Fechner) describes the relationship between the physical magnitudes of stimuli and the perceived intensity of the stimuli. Generally speaking, according to the Weber–Fechner law, the relationship between stimulus and perception is logarithmic.

231 Daniel Bernoulli had formulated the so-called "St Petersburg Paradox" according to which a naïve decision criterion, taking into account only the expected value, would recommend a course of action that no (real) rational person would be willing to take. His own proposed solution of the paradox was based on the supposition that "the determination of the value of an item must not be based on the price, but rather on the utility it yields . . . There is no doubt that a gain of one thousand ducats is more significant to the pauper than to a rich man though both gain the same amount". This is an early expression of the notion of marginal utility (see endnote 229) taking into account the finite resources of the participants.

232 The theoretical and "marginalist" school of economics, whose leading figure was Carl Menger (see endnote 229 above).

233 The German historical school of economics was a group of German economists who saw economics as resulting from careful empirical and historical studies and took a correspondingly negative view of abstract economic theorems. The historical school can be divided into the Older school, led by Wilhelm Roscher, Karl Knies and Bruno Hildebrand, and the Younger school, led by Gustav v. Schmoller. Max Weber is often categorized as a member of the Younger school, but in many respects took up an intermediate position between the historical school and the Austrian "marginalists". See also note 48.

234 "Stimulus threshold": the limit below which the stimulus is too weak to be perceived; "stimulus limit": the limit above which an increase in the stimulus is no longer perceived;

"subliminal" stimulus: a stimulus that is not sufficient to be perceived; "supraliminal" stimulus: a stimulus that is just sufficient to be perceptible. The first, third and fourth of these concepts are already to be found in Fechner's *Psychophysics*; the first and second concept are further elaborated by Wundt (*Psychology*).

235 In 1888–94, Heinrich Merkel published a reformulation of the Weber–Fechner law, according to which a certain amount of the energy in the stimulus is not transferred to the perceived sensation.

236 The reference is to the glass vases in art nouveau style produced by the American artist–designer Louis Comfort Tiffany (1848–1933).

237 The German term ("ideogen") is found in Breuer and Freud's *Studies in Hysteria* (1892), in the sense of "determined by representations".

238 This is a reference to a system of graphic notation, for instance of blood pressure, by means of moving pens on rotating drums.

239 The philosophical theory of materialism holds that the only thing that exists is matter; and that all phenomena (including consciousness) are the result of material interactions. In other words, matter is the only substance. See also endnote 110.

240 Mechanistic explanations of natural phenomena were extended to biological systems by Descartes and his successors. Descartes maintained that animals, and the human body, are "automata", mechanical devices differing from artificial devices only in their degree of complexity. Vitalism developed as a contrast to this mechanistic view. Vitalists hold that living organisms are fundamentally different from non-living entities because they contain some non-physical element or are governed by principles different from those that govern inanimate things.

241 Descartes had postulated that there were two kinds of substance: material and spiritual, and that one could have an effect on the other (for example: the idea of hitting another person could cause the movement of the striking arm). Leibniz took up the opposite position, that of psychophysical parallelism: The dualism postulated by Descartes was true, but the two substances could have no causal influence on each other. In order to explain how this was possible, Leibniz had recourse to the idea of a pre-established harmony instituted by God. Physical and mental processes ran alongside each other like two completely synchronized watches. In the nineteenth century, Fechner proposed a different version of this view: there was still no causal connection between the two substances, but they should be seen not as two separate watches, but as two different perspectives from which one and the same watch (say, a particular person) could be viewed: from outside (the material aspect) and from inside (the spiritual aspect).

242 The Greek astronomer Ptolemaeus (*c.*100) constructed an astronomical model with the Earth at the centre of the planetary system (geocentric). It was replaced in the sixteenth century by the heliocentric model elaborated by Copernicus, with the Sun at the centre of the planetary system.

243 This is probably a reference to the idea of William Thomson (Lord Kelvin) that the second law of thermodynamics would eventually lead to general diffusion of heat, cessation of motion, and exhaustion of potential energy in the universe ("heat death").

244 This is a reference to Weber's work on *The Psychophysics of Industrial Work* (published 1908–09, now *MWG* I/11).

245 This is a procedure by which a single quotation is established for each quoted share, on the basis of offers and demands, in advance of actual operations on the stock exchange.

246 In a letter to Lujo Brentano of 10 October 1908, Weber apologizes for this footnote, which was based on the assumption that Brentano had voiced his disparagement of Böhm-Bawerk

in the book under review. This assumption was erroneous, although Weber reminds Brentano that the latter had privately uttered such disparaging judgements concerning the whole Austrian marginalist school.

247 See the posthumously published Addendum to Weber's criticism of Stammler (*Addendum*, pp. 227–41).

248 In general, energetics is concerned with seeking principles that accurately describe the useful and non-useful tendencies of energy flows and storages under transformation.

249 Mechanistic explanations of natural phenomena were extended to biological systems by Descartes and his successors. Descartes maintained that animals, and the human body, are "automata", mechanical devices differing from artificial devices only in their degree of complexity. Vitalism developed as a contrast to this mechanistic view. Vitalists hold that living organisms are fundamentally different from non-living entities because they contain some non-physical element or are governed by principles different from those that govern inanimate things.

250 Connected with death ("thanatos" in Greek).

251 Comte believed that mankind had progressed to the third and last phase of its quest for truth: the scientific one, where science could begin answering the questions that had presented themselves in the earlier, metaphysical phase. He devised a hierarchical ordering of the sciences. At its apex stood (together with anthropology) the science of the social. Comte saw this new science, for which he (re)invented the term "sociology", as the last and greatest of all sciences, one that would include all other sciences and integrate and relate their findings into a cohesive whole. Quetelet was among the first who attempted to apply statistics and concepts of probability to social science, planning what he called a "social physics". His goal was to understand the statistical laws underlying social phenomena, and to explain the values of these variables by other social factors. (See also endnote 41.)

252 A famous painting by the Renaissance painter Raphael, *c.*1513, of the Virgin, Child and Saints. The painting is called "Sistine" because one of the Saints depicted is Saint Sixtus; it was also placed in the convent of Saint Sixtus in Piacenza for some time.

253 The novel *Die Leiden des Jungen Werther* ("The Sorrows of Young Werther") by Goethe, which ends with the suicide of its hero, Werther, was said to have inspired actual suicides of young persons gripped by the "Werther fever".

254 The French liberal socialist Proudhon was critical of the utopian thinking of Saint-Simon and Fourier, but his own vision of socialism was, in the words of Martin Buber, a continuation, on a higher plane, of the line of development begun by those thinkers.

255 v. Thünen developed the basics of the theory of marginal productivity – allotted to the productive factors labour and capital, respectively – and worked out models of spatial economics.

256 The reference is to Lujo Brentano.

257 Ostwald formulated the "second law of energetics" in a number of different ways. In his *Energetical Foundations* (p. 31), he offers the following formulation: "[Within a given, closed system], free energy can only decrease or be consumed, but never increase".

258 Elastic ("potential") energy ("Formenergie" in Ostwald's terminology) is the energy that causes or is released by the elastic distortion of a solid or liquid (e.g. when the spring of a watch is wound up).

259 In *Energetical Foundations* (pp. 82–83), Ostwald explains that he is talking about both inorganic and organic energies, and among the latter both animal/plant energies and energies of other human beings (slaves, for example).

260 In his *Capitalism* (1902), Werner Sombart supplemented Reuleaux' kinematic principle of the machine with the idea of the machine as substitute labour.

261 The reference is to the idea of the French mathematician Laplace that "an intellect which at a certain moment would know all forces that set nature in motion, and all positions of all items of which nature is composed, if this intellect were also vast enough to submit these data to analysis, it would embrace in a single formula the movements of the greatest bodies of the universe and those of the tiniest atom". This formula is also known as "Laplace's demon".

262 The Greek astronomer Ptolemaeus (*c.*100) constructed an astronomical model with the Earth at the centre of the planetary system (geocentric). It was replaced in the sixteenth century by the heliocentric model elaborated by Copernicus, with the Sun at the centre of the planetary system.

263 See pp. 121–37.

264 The German physiologist Max Rubner performed a number of experiments to determine the fundamental character of the metabolism of living creatures. In 1883, he introduced the "surface hypothesis", which stated that the metabolic rate of birds and mammals maintaining a steady body temperature is roughly proportional to their body surface area. See Rubner, Laws.

265 Descartes had postulated that there were two kinds of substance: material and spiritual, and that one could have an effect on the other (for example: the idea of hitting another person could cause the movement of the striking arm). Leibniz took up the opposite position, that of psychophysical parallelism: The dualism postulated by Descartes was true, but the two substances could have no causal influence on each other. In order to explain how this was possible, Leibniz had recourse to the idea of a pre-established harmony instituted by God. Physical and mental processes ran alongside each other like two completely synchronized watches. In the nineteenth century, Fechner proposed a different version of this view: there was still no causal connection between the two substances, but they should be seen not as two separate watches, but as two different perspectives from which one and the same watch (say, a particular person) could be viewed: from outside (the material aspect) and from inside (the spiritual aspect).

266 A reference to Weber's work on *The Psychophysics of Industrial Work* (1908–09), now in *MWG* I/11.

267 See pp. 36–40.

268 In the Second Supplementary Volume (1902) to Lamprecht, *History*, p. 23.

269 In his *History*, v. Baer had held up to scorn the anthropomorphic belief in progress and values in nature by describing the developmental history as it would be written from the standpoint of birds.

270 A poem by Schiller from 1788. Ostwald's formulation is probably a misprint. What he is describing as having a "narrow outlook" is not Schiller, but primitive man, who could only picture anorganic energies in the shape of humans.

271 In his *Natural Science*, pp. 414–16, du Bois-Reymond criticizes those artists who produce pictures or sculptures of winged mammals because such creatures are "para-typical": incompatible with the natural types as defined by the theory of biological evolution.

272 It is not possible to determine with certainty what drawing this might be – possibly a drawing by the Emperor (when still a Prince) from 1885 of a fight between armoured vessels and torpedo boats.

273 This was a famous painting of a steel rolling mill from 1875 (in the Old National Gallery in Berlin) by the German painter Adolph v. Menzel.

274 The reference is to Luca Giordano (1634–1705), a Neapolitan painter who was given the nickname Luca fà-presto ("Luca makes-quickly") because he painted so fast.

275 Weber is probably making a ponderous joke here: Ostwald has spoken of "form energy" as the equivalent of "elasticity", which is in accordance with the usual terminology of energy theory. Weber now says: the beautiful table has its "artistic" value by virtue of its "form energy", which is, however no different from the "form energy" (in energy terms) of a shapeless block of wood.

276 The synthesis of urea by Friedrich Wöhler in 1828 from an inorganic precursor was an important milestone in the development of organic chemistry.

277 Wilhelm Ostwald was active in the movement for establishing an artificial language and contributed to the development of Ido (a derivative of Esperanto).

278 The remarks concern a court case in the 1890s, where the court refused to accept that a person who had surreptitiously connected his electrical system to the main cable without a meter could be convicted for "theft" because the definition of "theft" in the Criminal Code spoke of stolen "objects" – and electrical current was not an "object".

279 This is a (slightly abridged) quotation from Jhering, *Spirit*, Vol. 2.

280 This is the idea that the pronouncements of the judge, not written law, are the main source of law. One of the German jurists who, up to a certain point, supported the idea of "free law" as a supplement to written law was Hermann Kantorowicz, whose presentation at the 1910 meeting of the German Sociological Society Weber criticized (see pp. 365–67).

281 The Physiocrats were a group of economists in eighteenth-century France whose main thesis was that government policy should not interfere with the operation of natural economic laws and that land is the source of all wealth.

282 "The just price." This expression refers to the idea that any product should have a price that is no greater than the actual value of the product. This idea was first put forward by Thomas Aquinas and for a long time had a prominent place in Roman Catholic economic and social doctrine.

283 Ostwald claimed that the influence of "philologists with no knowledge of the world or of science" had done immense harm to culture, and underpinned this statement by referring to the classical language bias of the "Gymnasien", which, in his view, only enabled the pupil to be at home in the classical world. This harmful influence, he felt, was very noticeable, especially among jurists and bureaucrats, and "[was] the root cause of a major part of the evil at present besetting Germany". (See also endnote 285.)

284 Thomism (the philosophy based on the teachings of Thomas Aquinas) maintained an "organicist" conception of society which demanded that all parts of society should work together for a common good and be subordinated to higher moral principles.

285 "Gymnasium" was, from 1812, the official term for a secondary school qualifying its students directly for university. It was characterized by a strong emphasis on classical languages and culture. Towards the end of the nineteenth century, the need for more practically and commercially oriented students led to the institution of parallel "Realgymnasien" focusing on the natural sciences and modern languages.

286 This is a (slightly free) quotation from the German translation of Jan Swammerdam's *Bible of Nature* (1752), p. 30.

287 "Thou shalt not write about something that thou dost not understand." See O.D. Chwolson's *Hegel*, p. 13 (Ostwald had reviewed this book).

288 List's fundamental doctrine was that a nation's true wealth is the full and many-sided development of its productive power. Therefore, its economic education should be more important than immediate production of value, and it might be right that one generation

should sacrifice its gain and enjoyment to secure the economic strength and skill of the future.

289 "Academic socialists" ("Kathedersozialisten" – literally "socialists of the academic platform") was a term coined disparagingly by the German liberal politician H.B. Oppenheim in 1872 to characterize professors of economics committed to an active government policy of social reform. Prominent among these academics were adherents of the "historical school" such as Gustav Schmoller and Adolph Wagner.

290 The term "nomothetic" was used – first by the German philosopher Wilhelm Windelband – to characterize the group of (typically natural) sciences seeking laws, as opposed to what Windelband called the "idiographic" sciences, seeking knowledge of what is individual and unique.

291 The direct translation of this French expression is "to know [something] in order to be able to do [something]". The origins of the expression are unknown. The sense in this connection is "knowledge not for its own sake but for the sake of its usefulness".

292 Pragmatism proceeds from the basic premise that theory and practice are not separate spheres. The pragmatist philosopher John Dewey criticized what he called "the philosophical fallacy": that philosophers often take categories (such as the mental and the physical) for granted because they don't realize that these are merely nominal concepts, invented to help solve specific problems.

293 William James, in his book *Pragmatism* (1907), p. 200, precisely talks of "truth's cash value".

294 The renowned German physicist Gustav Kirchhoff is quoted as having written, around 1874, in his *Vorlesungen über mathematische Physik* (1876–94), that "the task of mechanics is to describe movements in nature completely and in the simplest possible way".

295 Nominalism is the philosophical view – which counted Francis Bacon among its adherents – that abstract concepts, general terms or universals have no independent existence but exist only as names.

296 This quotation seems to have originated with Simmel himself.

297 See pp. 121–37.

298 Nietzsche develops his theory of ressentiment in his book *The Genealogy of Morals* (1887). Ressentiment is not resentment, but resentment that has (unconsciously) become internalized, in which the weak have rationalized their own weakness by inversely privileging it as morally superior to the strong. There is still resentment in the petty sense, but it is systematized in an (inverse) transvaluation of values.

299 "Pragma" (from the Greek word πρᾶγμα) generally means "action", "practice" or "business" (cf. "pragmatic"). Weber, however, uses the word with the slightly different meaning of "unavoidable fact" or "fundamental condition". The "pragma of interests" is therefore to be understood as "the given interests of the person or group of persons concerned".

300 In its broader sense: the idea that material circumstances, rather than human thought, determine the basis and the limits of history. The idea has become especially influential within the Marxist philosophy of history ("economic" or "historical" materialism), where historical development is seen as determined by the opposition between the productive forces (labour, tools, knowledge) and the social conditions under which the means of sustenance of life are produced.

301 In his *Institutio Christianae Religionis* (*Institutes of the Christian Religion*) (1536), Jean Calvin asserts that God has pre-ordained who it is that He will graciously save.

302 (From the Greek word ἀνομία ("lawlessness")): The conviction that one is not bound by ordinary ethical laws.

303 Acosmistic love is a "total" love of everything, where the focus is not on any particular object of love but on the generalized surrender to the feeling of loving as such.

304 From outside (as opposed to: autonomous).

305 If an organization appoints its own leadership, it is autocephalous; if outsiders do so, it is heterocephalous.

306 That the clan is exogamous means that its members share and respect the norm that they should not marry other members of the same tribe.

307 This was a literary academy founded in Florence in 1582 for the purpose of purifying the Tuscan dialect.

308 The German text has "eitel", which (in this context) has no other normal meaning in English than "purely" or "nothing but". From a substantive point of view, however, there seems to be no doubt that "both . . . and" is what Weber intends to say.

309 Robinsonades are stories or examples where a person finds himself in an isolated position and has to survive by his own wits and by husbanding such resources as he can get access to. The basic reference is to the fictional figure of Robinson Crusoe, whose life for 28 years as a castaway on a tropical island, partly in complete solitude, is described in Daniel Defoe's novel *Robinson Crusoe* (1719). His solitary condition was a favourite subject of economists because conditions on his island were the closest one could get to those of a "laboratory", so that he could be seen as a kind of rational "economic man". Economists who insisted on the importance of the historical conditions of the economy would obviously be critical of this approach, and the German historical school therefore characterized their "theoretical" opponents, above all the Austrian school, for their lack of realism, their "Robinsonades".

310 In his *Précis du règne de Louis XV* ("Short Account of the Reign of Louis XV"), Voltaire describes how, during the battle of Fontenoy (1745), French and British/Hanoverian troops that had encountered each other by chance shied away from being the first to shoot, the French with a turn of phrase like the one quoted by Weber ("English Gentlemen, please commence firing").

311 The German term is "Bestimmungsmensur". Originally, the "ritualized" duels of members of the German student associations had to be initiated by some sort of provocation or insult. Later on, this element retreated into the background, and the duels were "arranged" ("bestimmt") with other student associations.

312 In the Russian Mir, or peasant community, the land was owned jointly by (or, if the peasants were serfs, assigned to) the Mir. The Mir had an assembly, obligations and rights; it was responsible for allocating the arable land to its members and for reallocating such lands periodically. Woodlands, pastures and waters were used jointly.

313 The term "daemon" does not have the ordinary meaning of the word "demon" here. It is probably inspired by Schopenhauer (*The World as Will and Representation*) or by Goethe (the poem ΔΑΙΜΩΝ ("Daimon") in the cycle *Urworte. Orphische*). This "daimon" (daemon) is present "as 'fate', as the characteristic and preformed essence of individual identity, the unchanging and self-directive 'law' of destiny" (Lawrence Scaff).

314 Goethe, *Maximen und Reflektionen*, II, 31.

315 The German term used by Weber, "Präsentationspatronat" ("right of presentation"), has clerical origins. In Germany, if the patron who had the "right of presentation" proposed a candidate for a clerical living, the bishop was obliged to accept the proposal unless the candidate was obviously unsuitable. According to certain canonical lawyers, the presentation in itself even gave the candidate a right to be appointed. Weber comments in more detail

on the Dutch system in an intervention at the Third German Conference of Teachers in Institutions of Higher Education, held in Leipzig in October 1909.

316 A reference to the adherents of Manchester Liberalism – a political, economic and social movement of the nineteenth century with its origins in Manchester. The Manchester Liberals argued that free trade would lead to a more equitable society, making essential products available to all. As well as being advocates of free trade, they were radical opponents of war and imperialism and proponents of peaceful relations between peoples. Manchesterism can therefore more generally be seen as a belief in free and consensual relations among individuals and groups at all levels.

317 A reference to the "personal rule" which the German Emperor, William II, tried to implement, particularly in the field of foreign policy, after the resignation of Bismarck in 1890.

318 German universities competed keenly for the maximum of enrolled students. See also endnote 366.

319 The "Memorandum" from 1913 on which this article is based was a written contribution to a debate in the Association for Social Policy on "Value judgements".

320 The Austrian school of economic theory was called "marginalist" because it taught that people decide whether to effect any given change based on the marginal utility of that change, with rival alternatives being chosen based upon which has the greatest marginal utility. (The marginal utility is defined as the utility gained (or lost) from an increase (or decrease) in the consumption of that good or service.) In general, preferences display diminishing marginal utility.

321 The agrimensors were the land surveyors in ancient Rome. In all questions concerning the determination of boundaries by means of marks, the area of surfaces, and explaining maps and plans, the services of the agrimensor were required.

322 In the fourteenth and fifteenth century, Florence was a centre of banking. See also endnote 65.

323 A reference to a French proverb ("Tout comprendre, c'est tout pardonner") of uncertain origin. The proverb is found in that form, inter alia, in Tolstoy's *War and Peace*.

324 According to Kant, the content of the universal moral law, the "categorical imperative", must be nothing over and above the law's form, otherwise it will be dependent on desires. The only law whose content consists in its form, according to Kant, is the statement: "Act in such a way that the maxim of your will could always hold at the same time as a principle of a universal legislation".

325 During the French Revolution, "Gracchus" Babeuf advanced a number of radically egalitarian propositions, including the following: "Nature has given to every man the right to the enjoyment of an equal share in all property", which may well be the one that Weber is thinking of.

326 This is probably a reference to one of Luther's lectures on Genesis, in which he says: "fac tuum officium, et eventum Deo permitte" ("Do your allotted work and leave the outcome to God").

327 Syndicalism endeavoured to bring about an alternative economic system, based on collectivized trades unions ("syndicats" in French). Its adherents often viewed it as a potential force for revolutionary social change, replacing capitalism and the state with a new society democratically self-managed by workers. (See also endnote 333.)

328 Realpolitik is a policy which does not base itself on values or ideological positions, but seeks to attain concrete and relatively short-term goals formulated on the basis of the interests of one's own party or state.

329 The Kantian categorical imperative has three formulations (of which the first, from the *Critique of Practical Reason*, is quoted in endnote 324). The second formulation, to which Weber is obviously referring in the passage on p. 314, is found in Kant's *Groundwork of the Metaphysic of Morals*, and runs as follows: "Act in such a way that you treat humanity, whether in your own person or in the person of any other, never merely as a means to an end, but always at the same time as an end."

330 This is a reference to John Stuart Mill, *Three essays on Religion*, 1874, p. 130: "There is the amplest historical evidence that the belief in Gods is immeasurably more natural to the human mind than the belief in one author and ruler of nature."

331 At the end of Plato's *Republic*, Socrates tells the story of Er, a man who has returned from the dead to tell what goes on there. Er describes how the souls of the dead have to choose their next life, along the following lines: "Your genius will not be allotted to you, but you will choose your genius [. . .] Virtue is free, and as a man honours or dishonours her he will have more or less of her; the responsibility is with the chooser" (tr. Benjamin Jowett).

332 As Weber himself wrote in his treatise on Confucianism: "Confucianism was [. . .] adaptation to the world, its orders and conventions. Indeed, it was in fact nothing but an enormous codex of political maxims and rules of social decorum for cultured men of the world" *MWG* I/19, pp. 345–46.

333 The general strike was seen by syndicalists as the most effective means of bringing about radical social change.

334 The German text has "Kameralistik" ("cameralism") (see endnote 5).

335 The reference is unclear.

336 Marcus Porcius Cato (called Cato the Younger to distinguish him from his great-grandfather, Cato the Elder)(95–46 BC), who was among those opposing Caesar's bid for power in Rome, committed suicide after Caesar's victory in the battle of Thapsus. Cato himself had not taken part in the battle, but did not wish live under Caesar's rule and by virtue of his pardon.

337 Bismarck was dismissed as Reich Chancellor by the Emperor William II in 1890.

338 The first group of Mormon pioneers settled in the area of the Salt Lake (Utah, USA) in 1847.

339 This is probably a polemical swipe at the work of the Austrian sociologist Rudolf Goldscheid, who was, together with Weber, among the founders of the German Sociological Society in 1910, but whose views on value freedom diverged so sharply from those of Weber that the latter quit the Society after a couple of years. Goldscheid had, in 1911, published a major "social–biological" work on *Höherentwicklung und Menschenökonomie* ("Higher Development and Human Economy") in which he propounded the thesis that the existing economy was anti-human and should be replaced by a wholly new economic system, that of the "human economy".

340 The German term ("Kunstwollen") was probably borrowed from the art historian Alois Riegl (1858–1905), who coined it in opposition to the purely mechanistic view of art as "a mechanical product consisting of a particular purpose, raw material, and technique".

341 The Gothic style developed in the twelfth and thirteenth centuries.

342 From outside (as opposed to: autonomously).

343 Weber is referring to studies, which he had already begun, and later resumed, but which only appeared after his death (in 1921) as *The Rational and Sociological Foundations of Music* (see now *MWG* I/14).

344 Only a few scraps of Ancient Greek music are known. Prominent among these is a small papyrus fragment of the tragedy *Orestes* by Euripides. This fragment, published by Karl

Wessely in 1892, included notations of the accompanying music. The verses in question, which are among the most passionate ones in the whole play, are written in the Dochmiac metre (basic metrical scheme: short-long-short-short-long), which was used in Greek tragedy to express extreme agitation or distress. In ancient Greece there were three standard tunings of the four-string lyre. These three tunings were called diatonic, chromatic and enharmonic. The enharmonic tuning was seen as an expression of particular musical refinement.

345 This Greek term designated, in Classical times, a "poet of songs", i.e. a poet whose creations were intended to be accompanied by music.

346 The direct reference is probably simply to the idea of free trade. But it is likely that this is also an indirect reference to Lujo Brentano's lecture *Das Freihandelsargument* (1901), in which Brentano argues that it is entirely possible, under conditions of free trade, to develop into an industrial state, even if its production costs may be higher than in the other industrial countries with which Germany competes. (The argument is the old Ricardian one of comparative advantage.)

347 The Ancient Greek philosopher Pythagoras taught that all things and concepts could be represented numerically. This teaching found seemingly strong support in the fact that the musical pitch depends on the length of the vibrating string producing the sound, and that musical intervals were connected with relations between whole numbers.

348 This term was coined by the Austrian economist Eugen v. Böhm-Bawerk to describe the process whereby capital goods are produced first and then, with the help of the capital goods, the desired consumer goods are produced.

349 The concept of the "ideas of 1914" was formulated in Germany at the beginning of the First World War, by a number of writers. These ideas elevated "German-ness" to an almost metaphysical value, in explicit opposition to English Liberalism and French Democracy.

350 Weber is probably referring to currents of thought demanding "socialism without parliament". In his essay *Parliament and Government in Germany*, Weber argues that this system would mean that "interest groups legitimated and (allegedly) controlled by the state bureaucracy would actively carry out the duties of self-government in the syndicates and passively bear the burdens imposed by the state. The officials would then be controlled by these syndicalised vested interests intent on commerce and profit" (tr. Ronald Speirs).

351 A "single-purpose organization" ("Zweckverband") is an organization that brings together various groups or communities for the realization of major projects.

352 The German title is "Wissenschaft als Beruf". The term "Beruf" covers a whole scale of meanings, from "job" or "occupation" through "profession" to "vocation" and even "calling". However, it has been the almost invariable custom to translate it in the title of this lecture as "vocation", which emphasizes the "inner" aspect of "Beruf". This is perhaps understandable, as the lecture does to a considerable extent deal with what Weber calls the "inner" vocation for science. However, it also contains a discussion of the external, "material" aspects of academic work; and the historical background to the lecture makes it clear that a translation different from "vocation" is called for. Weber was invited to give this lecture by a student association as part of a series of talks on the particular problems of "intellectual" or "artistic" work as a profession – in other words of living *for* something that one also had to live *off*. This duality dictated the title of the lecture and should be reflected in the translation. This can best be done (as in the excellent recent translation of Weber's political writings) by rendering "Beruf" in the title as "profession and vocation". In the body of the text, the appropriate single term will be used whenever possible.

353 The German universities in Weber's time were not organized in institutes, but according to subjects, each under an "Ordinarius" or "full professor". The full professors made up

the Faculties, of which there were not many (e.g.: Legal and Economic Sciences, Humanities, Medicine, Natural Science). The Faculties, under the chairmanship of a Dean chosen by the Faculty members, would in principle administer their own affairs with little outside interference.

354 The so-called "Habilitation", or "second doctorate", entered upon some years after the "Dissertation" (which is roughly equivalent to a Ph.D.).

355 "Permission to lecture."

356 For each course of lectures or seminar that they attended, the students paid a fee to the University, which passed it on to the university teachers.

357 The reference is probably to Robert Liefmann, who in fact had to apply to several universities before finding one that would accept him as a private lecturer (and then on the basis of an explanatory letter from Weber).

358 Uhland wrote on lyrical and patriotic subjects, and his works became immensely popular in Germany. But their intrinsic quality did not suffice to lift him above the status of a minor poet.

359 This is probably a reference to Karl Marx, who writes in *Das Kapital* that "the so-called primitive accumulation is simply the historical process of divorcing the producer from the means of production".

360 Werner Sombart, in his book on *The Proletariat* (1906), distinguished between "proletarian" and "proletaroid" existences, the latter being that of independent "have-nots".

361 The traditional constitution of German universities, inspired by Wilhelm v. Humboldt (1767–1835), was based on the unity of science, the unity of research and teaching, and the unity of teachers and students.

362 Weber was barely thirty years old when he was appointed to the chair of "economics and financial science" at the University of Freiburg.

363 Professors were appointed by the Ministry of Education. The relevant Faculty drew up a shortlist of candidates, but the Ministry often overrode the first choice of the Faculty, and occasionally even preferred a candidate who was not even on the shortlist.

364 Weber may be thinking of James Bryce, who in his *The American Commonwealth* (1888) divided the candidates for the Presidency into the "favourites", the "favourite sons" and the "dark horses".

365 Weber's lecture was given in November 1917, but only published, with his revisions, in the spring of 1919, when left-wing revolutionaries held the reins of power across Germany. In fact, Weber's own appointment as Professor in Munich was in part due to a decision by the left-wing government to disregard the person heading the Faculty shortlist and start negotiations with Weber, who shared second place on the list with another academic.

366 At the end of the nineteenth century, there was strong competition between the universities of Freiburg and Heidelberg as to which would get the most students; in Freiburg, regular festivities were organized at the university in July 1904, and a commemorative coin struck, on the occasion of the enrolment of the two thousandth student.

367 This is a reference to the Académie Française, whose members are known as "the Immortals".

368 "Abandon all hope." Part of the inscription over the gates to Hell in Dante's *Divine Comedy*. There were no formal restrictions on Jews in German academic life, but in practice, they were usually passed over for appointments, or had to be content with "minor" professorships.

369 Weber is fond of this quotation, which he uses more than once. He ascribes it to Carlyle, but no relevant passage has been found in Carlyle's work (although Carlyle does say of Dante that he was "the voice of ten silent centuries").

370 This reflects Weber's own experience with the data for his study on *The Psycho-physics of Industrial Work*. In that connection, Weber writes to his publisher that he has had to do "50,000 calculations in the space of six weeks".

371 The quotation cannot be located. Robert Mayer discovered the law of conservation of energy (see endnote 56) while he was a ship's doctor in the 1840s. But, because of his lack of formal training as a physicist, it took him so long to publish his discovery that Helmholtz had published similar results in the meantime (Helmholtz later gracefully acknowledged Mayer's priority).

372 See Plato, *Phaedros*, 244–45, where Socrates describes the madness (manía) of poetry: "he who, having no touch of the Muses' madness in his soul, comes to the door and thinks that he will get into the temple by the help of art – he, I say, and his poetry are not admitted; the sane man disappears and is nowhere when he enters into rivalry with the madman" (tr. Benjamin Jowett).

373 This theme is discussed in Tolstoy's "Three Deaths" (1859) and *The death of Ivan Ilyich* (1886).

374 Genesis, ch. 25, v. 8: "Then Abraham gave up the ghost, and died in a good old age, an old man, and full of years."

375 Plato, *The Republic*, 514–17.

376 The yogi are adepts of the Indian philosophical system of yoga, which teaches the liberation of the self through meditation and asceticism.

377 The main purpose of these experiments was to construct well-tuned keyboard instruments for polyphonic music.

378 The reference is to the *Trattato della Pittura*, a book published around 1530 on the basis of manuscripts by Leonardo da Vinci, in which he devotes much discussion to the question whether painting is one of the sciences.

379 This is a (slightly free) quotation from the German translation of Jan Swammerdam's *Bible of Nature* (1752), p. 30.

380 Isaiah, ch. 55, v. 8: "For my thoughts are not your thoughts, neither are your ways my ways, saith the Lord."

381 "Alas! The time of the most contemptible man is coming, the man who can no longer despise himself. Behold! I shall show you the Ultimate Man. 'What is love? What is creation? What is longing? What is a star?' Thus asks the Ultimate Man and blinks . . . 'We have discovered happiness' say the Ultimate Men and blink" (Nietzsche, *Thus Spoke Zarathustra* (tr. R.J. Hollingdale), London: Penguin 1969, p. 46).

382 The following lines in Weber's text are a free version of what Tolstoy writes in his tract *What Then Must We Do?* (1886).

383 Dietrich Schäfer was a university professor with pronounced nationalistic and expansionist views. Professor F.W. Foerster was a radical pacifist who in October 1917 was prevented from lecturing by 500 nationalist students making "an infernal din" in the auditorium "with the aid of various musical instruments", as Foerster himself later described the incident.

384 This is an allusion to Jeremiah, ch. 2, v. 2: "Go and cry in the ears of Jerusalem".

385 This is a reference to John Stuart Mill, *Three essays on Religion*, 1874, p. 130: "There is the amplest historical evidence that the belief in Gods is immeasurably more natural to the human mind than the belief in one author and ruler of nature."

386 "He is despised and rejected of men; a man of sorrows, and acquainted with grief; and we hid as it were our faces from him; he was despised, and we esteemed him not", Isaiah, ch. 53, v. 3.

387 The reference should probably have been to the 22nd Psalm: "But I am a worm, and no man; a reproach of men, and despised of the people."

388 This is a constant theme in Nietzsche's work. See, for instance: "[. . .] the greatest of all swindles and self-deceptions [is] to equate good, true and beautiful, and to portray that unity"(*Fragments*, 1886, group 7, 20).

389 This was a sermon given, as described in St Matthew's Gospel, ch. 5–7, by Jesus on a mountainside to his disciples and a large crowd of people.

390 Gospel of St Matthew, ch. 5, v. 39: "But I say unto you, That ye resist not evil: but whosoever shall smite thee on thy right cheek, turn to him the other also."

391 Gospel of St Luke, ch. 10, v. 42: "But one thing is needful . . ."

392 Goethe, *Faust II*, Act II, end of Scene in a Gothic Chamber.

393 *Manicheism* was a religion founded in Mesopotamia by Mani in the third century. Central in its teachings was the dualistic view of the world as being divided between the forces of good and the forces of evil. *Gnosticism* is a general term for various belief systems present around and just after the birth of Christianity. It is uncertain whether they should be classified as a religion, a mystic sect or as a heretical movement within the Christian church. Gnosticism focuses on the attainment of a redeeming insight ((Greek) "gnosis": "knowledge") that can liberate body and soul from their bonds to this world. *Orphism* is the modern term for religious movements in Ancient Greece centred around a set of myths, ascribed to the poet Orpheus, in which the death and resurrection of Dionysos showed the believer the way to a life after death through mystical rites and a holy life. *Parseeism* or Zoroastrianism was the largest pre-Islamic religion in Iran, originally preached by the (possibly mythical) prophet Zarathustra in the sixth century BC. Central in Zoroastrian belief is the ethical dualism: man must choose between good and evil. Fire is a sacred element. There are today around 20,000 adherents of Zoroastrianism in Iran and around 100,000 in India (Parsees).

394 *Taoism* stands alongside Confucianism as one of the two great religious and philosophical systems of China. It is traditionally traced to the mythical character Lao-Tse (sixth century BC), whose writings include the book Dao De Jing ("The Way to Virtue"), which advocates humility and piety. The *Upanishads* are Hindu scriptures that constitute the core teachings of Vedanta (a group of philosophical traditions concerned with self-realization leading to an understanding of the ultimate nature of reality). They do not belong to any particular period. The oldest date to the middle of the first millennium BC, while the latest were composed in the Middle Ages.

395 The quotation has not been identified, but an argument in this sense can be found in the "Preface" to Kant's *Critique of Pure Reason* (1787).

396 That is, a theology explicitly based on historical revelation.

397 "I believe not what is absurd, but because it is absurd." This saying is now seen as a short version of a longer argument by the eminent early theologian Tertullian (*c.*160–*c.*225) in his *De Carne Christi* (On the Body of Christ), Book 5, ch. 4. Weber very probably found the saying in (more or less) the form quoted here in Windelband, *History*[4], p. 187.

398 Weber had already used this metaphor in the "Introduction" to his treatise on Confucianism (*MWG* I/19, p. 101).

399 This is a reference to the early Christian congregations, where the sense of community was awakened by those who were divinely inspired. (See 1 Corinthians 14.)

400 This is Weber's abbreviated adaptation of Isaiah, ch. 21, v. 11–12 in Luther's Bible. It diverges somewhat (and positively, in terms of intelligibility) from the King James Bible version.

401 A quotation from Goethe, *Wilhelm Meisters Wanderjahre* (Complete Edition, Vol. 42, Section II (1907), p. 167).

402 The term "daemon" does not have the ordinary meaning of the word "demon" here. It is probably inspired by Schopenhauer (*The World as Will and Representation*) or by Goethe (the poem ΔΑΙΜΩΝ ("Daimon") in the cycle *Urworte. Orphische*). This "daimon" (daemon) is present "as 'fate', as the characteristic and preformed essence of individual identity, the unchanging and self-directive 'law' of destiny" (Lawrence Scaff).

Contributions and interventions

403 This is what the German text literally means. But substantively, it does not make perfect sense. Weber would not say to the jurist: if you want to do this or that, you must employ the following means. On the contrary, that is what he would expect and want jurists to say to the politician. Although the text has been accepted by the scrupulous *MWG* editors, it may therefore be a case of wrong transcription by the stenographer at the 1905 Conference.

404 See pp. 326–28 for a closer description and discussion of Liefmann's argument.

405 For a thorough critique by Weber of this line of thinking, see pp. 252–68.

406 In its broader sense: the idea that material circumstances, rather than human thought, determine the basis and the limits of history. The idea has become especially influential within the Marxist philosophy of history ("economic" or "historical" materialism), where historical development is seen as determined by the opposition between the productive forces (labour, tools, knowledge) and the social conditions under which the means of sustenance of life are produced.

407 For Weber's thorough critique of this aspect of Stammler's work, see pp. 186–90.

408 See p. 219.

409 The reference is to Article 1, 2nd sentence in the Swiss Civil Code of 1 December 1907: "If no command can be taken from the statute, then the judge shall pronounce in accordance with the customary law, and failing that, according to the rule which he as a legislator would adopt" (tr. Robert B. Schick, Boston 1915 (Official Publication of the Comparative Law Bureau of the American Bar Association)). In substance, the provision is still in existence.

410 According to Kant, the content of the universal moral law, the "categorical imperative", must be nothing over and above the law's form, otherwise it will be dependent on desires. The only law whose content consists in its form, according to Kant, is the statement: "Act in such a way that the maxim of your will could always hold at the same time as a principle of a universal legislation".

411 The reference is to the war of Prussia against Austria in 1866 and the actions of General v. Moltke, the Commander-in-Chief of the Prussian forces.

Letters

412 The reference is to the second volume of Rickert's *Limits of Concept Formation*, which had just come out.

413 This is a reference to the article on Roscher and Knies.

414 See pp. 121–37.

415 It may be of interest to note that Weber was mistaken about the character of Jellinek's concept of the "ideal type", which was not in fact the same as Weber's. As Marianne Weber relied on her husband's letters in writing her biography of him, it is probable that this letter was responsible for her perpetuation of the mistake in the biography. The true state of affairs was only established by the German sociologist Fr. Tenbruck in 1959 (see Bruun, *Methodology*, pp. 214–15).

416 Weber is referring to the part dealing with the concept of the ideal type.

417 This was Rickert's contribution – a chapter on "The Philosophy of History" – to a *Festschrift* to Kuno Fischer (Rickert, *Philosophy*).

418 "Quite apart from psychology, many of the so-called sciences of the human spirit – for instance linguistics, jurisprudence and economics – are, at least in part, certainly not historical [sciences], but rather systematic cultural sciences, whose method is not necessarily the same as that [employed by] the generalizing natural sciences; for that reason, their logical structure is one of the most difficult and interesting problems of methodology" (Rickert, *Philosophy*, p. 88).

419 "Not only is it possible to have an absolutely historical approach, which considers reality with respect to what is individual and singular in [that reality]; we would also call an approach historical when it is oriented towards something general, but regards this general thing as something particular compared with something even more general. Thus, the concept of history becomes [. . .] relative" (Rickert, *Limits*, p. 266).

420 As there is no reference to this concept in the published version of Hellpach's article, he seems to have taken Weber's comments to heart.

421 The specific reference to Lamprecht's work was probably contained in Hellpach's letter to Weber, which has not been preserved. However, the following excerpt from Lamprecht's *German Economic Life in the Middle Ages* may serve as an example of his method: "It was our task to conduct an investigation of certain lines of development in the history of material culture in certain areas and, in so doing, to design the study in such a way that, in the sequence of the individual accounts, those main developmental stages would at any rate be highlighted whose existence a subsequent, pure historical account would have to posit" (Vol. 1, 1485–86). See Roger Chickering, *Karl Lamprecht. A German Academic Life*, Atlantic Highlands: Humanities Press (1993), pp. 109, 139.

422 The concept of "social pathology" or of being "inimical to the community" is a central one in Hellpach's second doctoral dissertation.

423 See pp. 121–37.

424 In his *Limits of Concept Formation* (p. 422), Rickert introduces the concept of a causal inequation on the basis of the following argument: "All causes considered by an absolute historical account are different from each other. In the same way, the historical effect is always different from the cause which produces it: if it were nothing else than [its cause] and did not have a different character [. . .] it could not become historically significant by virtue of its uniqueness. Consequently, the concept of the causal equation is foreign to history; on the contrary: if one has to describe the causal interconnection between two individual historical processes, this can only be done by means of causal inequations."

425 This means: given in the mind itself (see also next endnote).

426 The term "qualia" used by Weber had direct philosophical connotations. It was used in English by C.S. Peirce as early as 1867 to describe the immediate or given ("qualitative") elements of experience. Basing himself on Peirce's view that these "qualia" were the most basic constituents of the totality of sensory experience, the psychologist William James used the term some years later to denote the "irreducible data" of perception. Without using the term, the German physiologist Emil du Bois-Reymond (see endnote 25) included the question of the nature and origins of such qualitative elements among his seven "world riddles".

427 Herbert Spencer posited (first in his essay "Progress: Its Law and Cause" (1857)) that all structures in the universe develop from a simple and undifferentiated homogeneity to a complex and differentiated heterogeneity, this development being accompanied by a process

of greater integration of the differentiated parts. This evolutionary process could be found at work, Spencer believed, throughout the cosmos.

428 This is a reference to *Critical Studies*.

429 A reference to a formulation in Weber's *Critical Studies* (p. 171n267).

430 The neo-Kantian philosophers of this period are usually assigned either to the "Marburg School" (for instance Hermann Cohen, Ernst Cassirer, Paul Natorp) or to the "Baden School" (Wilhelm Windelband, Heinrich Rickert).

431 The second volume of Rickert, *Limits*.

432 This is probably a (truncated) quotation from Bortkievicz' letter, which we unfortunately do not possess.

433 This may have prompted the marginal comment by Weber recorded on p. 152n251.

434 The reference is probably to p. 156n254.

435 The last substantive discussion by Weber of the concept of "value relation" is to be found in *Critical Studies* (see pp. 157–67), which was published in 1906.

436 See p. 161n258.

437 In the terminology of the German philosopher Wilhelm Windelband, the "idiographic" sciences are those seeking knowledge of what is individual and unique, as opposed to the law-seeking ("nomothetic") disciplines.

438 The term "servitude to words" (Wortknechtschaft) is naturally coupled with that of the "dominance of words" (Herrschaft des Worts); both were coined by Fr. Gottl (in *Dominance of Words*, published in 1901). The "dominance of words" designates the situation where words are understood and treated as if they were in themselves concepts corresponding to reality.

439 A somaticist is a person who attributes mental diseases to bodily rather than psychical causes.

440 Rickert's argument at this point is that (1) the various scientific disciplines may, irrespective of the nature of their material, apply both individualizing and generalizing methods; therefore, (2) one may find not only "generalizing", but also "individualizing" natural sciences, and conversely, an account of cultural life may be "generalizing"; (3) "history", however, can only be characterized as an "individualizing cultural science", as "its purpose is always to describe a unique [. . .] developmental sequence in its uniqueness and individuality" (*Philosophy²*, p. 370).

441 Gospel of St. John, ch. 18, v. 36.

442 Syndicalism endeavoured to bring about an alternative economic system, based on collectivized trades unions ("syndicats" in French). Its adherents often viewed it as a potential force for revolutionary social change, replacing capitalism and the state with a new society democratically self-managed by workers. (See also endnote 333.)

443 This formulation can be attributed to the critique of the German Social Democrat Eduard Bernstein.

444 Literally "for the use of the Dauphin [i.e. the son of King Louis XIV of France]". Used of Classical texts expurgated in order to make them acceptable reading for the youthful Crown Prince. Here in a wider sense: "fit for everybody to read".

445 "Kulturkampf" ("cultural struggle") is an expression designating the measures taken by Bismarck in the 1870s to curb the influence of the Roman Catholic Church (and Roman Catholicism in general).

446 C. Menger and G. Schmoller were the main figures in the "quarrel about methods" (see endnote 48).

447 This strike lasted from November 1896 to February 1897, but failed, in spite of widespread public sympathy, because of the intransigence of the employers.

448 This is a reference to the neo-Kantian philosopher Hermann Cohen who, in the spirit of Kant, stood for a strictly normative conception of ethics without consideration of the effects of the "ethical" action.

449 According to Kant, the content of the universal moral law, the "categorical imperative", must be nothing over and above the law's form, otherwise it will be dependent on desires. The only law whose content consists in its form, according to Kant, is the statement: "Act in such a way that the maxim of your will could always hold at the same time as a principle of a universal legislation".

450 Since 1905, Eulenburg had regularly announced the imminent publication of a book by him on "Preliminary Questions of Social Philosophy". The book never appeared, however; instead, Eulenburg published a series of articles in the *Archive* in 1910, 1911 and 1912 which contained large extracts from the planned book.

451 This term designates a sudden and complete change in one's beliefs (the reference is to the conversion of St Paul to Christianity on the road to Damascus).

452 A reference to Rickert, *Paths*.

453 Rickert's pupil, the philosopher Emil Lask, who had shown Rickert the manuscript of his next book, had complained that Rickert had, in *Paths*, "anticipated" (in plain words: stolen) Lask's main point.

454 At the Second General meeting of University Teachers in 1908, Weber, together with his brother Alfred, had proposed a resolution according to which no university teacher could be dismissed because of his political beliefs or "world view".

455 "Fear of values." This highly unusual expression was probably used in a letter (which we do not possess) from Rickert to Weber.

456 This is probably a polemical swipe at the work of the Austrian sociologist Rudolf Goldscheid, who was, together with Weber, among the founders of the German Sociological Society in 1910, but whose views on value freedom diverged so sharply from those of Weber that the latter quit the Society after a couple of years. Goldscheid had, in 1911, published a major "social–biological" work on *Höherentwicklung und Menschenökonomie* ("Higher Development and Human Economy") in which he propounded the thesis that the existing economy was anti-human and should be replaced by a wholly new economic system, that of the "human economy".

457 Rickert proposes a three-level ranking of the realization of values: with respect to future, present or eternal goods. There is a hierarchization between those levels insofar as the two first ones are finite, while the third one is an "infinite" synthesis between them. Cultural goods are realized in either of two types of behaviour or conduct: contemplation or action ("theory" and "practice"). As a result of the combination of these two distinctions, six "value areas" can be defined: On the "contemplative" side: science, aesthetics and mysticism; and, on the "active" side: ethics (or "social ethics"), "perfect" personal life and religion ("theism"). The "parallelism" is not explicitly discussed as such by Rickert, but it is obvious that the combination of the two distinctions can be interpreted as presenting "parallelisms".

458 Section 5 of *System*, where Rickert suddenly declares in favour of philosophy itself as a *closed* system.

459 This term is a loan from Aristotle, meaning: the illegitimate transfer of a method from its proper science to another; here probably in the wider sense of contradicting oneself or making a logical "category mistake". See also endnote 214.

460 A reference to a manuscript on the "Fundamental Problems of Logic as a Science of Theoretical Values" elaborated by Rickert in 1908 but never brought to completion or publication.

Notes and drafts

461 The blank reference is probably to the following passage in Rickert's *Limits of Concept Formation*, p. 368: "The words 'essential', as well as 'interesting', 'characteristic', 'important' or 'significant' – terms that must always be applicable to history – require the assumption of some accepted value in order to have any stable meaning at all. So when we claim that any object which is to be the subject of history must be related to a value, we are in fact only converting into logical terminology the quite trivial truth that everything that the historian describes must be interesting, characteristic, important or significant."

462 The blank can most probably be filled out with the words "essential", "interesting", "characteristic", "important" and/or "significant" from the passage quoted in endnote 462.

463 The text is nearly illegible, and the reading is therefore conjectural. No clear reference to a statement of this sort has been found in Windelband's work; but there is a passage in the Foreword to Rickert's Habilitationsschrift (second doctoral dissertation) *Der Gegenstand der Erkenntnis* ("The object of cognition") from 1891 that says something similar ("Not only the 'old', but also the 'new' epistemology can – if it is to remain in any way important alongside the psychology of cognition – have no other task than that of seeing a problem where other sciences regard something as being obvious").

464 The reference is not entirely clear, but may be to the following passage in Rickert, *Limits of Concept Formation*, p. 358: "From this we can infer that the relation to a universal value enables us not only, in any given [part of] reality, to distinguish between two kinds of individual, but also to carry out this distinction in such a way that we can claim that its correctness must be accepted by everyone. The objects that, from this viewpoint, are classified as 'in-dividuals' are those that will form the stuff of history, which, as a science, has to distinguish the essential from the inessential in a way which is universally valid, and to shape that which is [selected as] essential into a necessary unity." (The hyphened word "in-dividual" is a Rickertian terminological creation.)

465 The word "individual" is used here in the ordinary sense of "single person", not in the philosophical sense in which it is discussed by Weber in the preceding paragraph.

466 This is probably a reference to the discussion of "metaphysical objectivity" in the last chapter of Rickert's *Limits of Concept Formation*.

467 See *Fragment on Formal Ethics* (pp. 421–22) and *Value Freedom*, pp. 313–14.

468 In Bruun, *Rickert*.

469 See p. 61n179.

470 Emanationism in the general sense is the principle according to which creation is a gradual process of emanation and descent from a transcendental absolute to mundane reality. In his dissertation on Fichte's idealism, Emil Lask used the term to describe a theory of concept formation in which concrete reality emanates from abstract concepts, which are therefore more "real" and have a higher ontological status (as opposed to the "analytical" theory of concept formation, where concepts, being formed by abstraction, are the more remote from reality, the more general the concept is).

471 Weber may have found the basis for this formulation in the philosopher Emil Lask's *Fichte's Idealism*, which was published in 1902. The following example may serve as an example of Lask's argument on this point: "The supra-empirical element of our individual nature is always [. . .] conceived as being a component having its proper place in a comprehensive valuational [set of] interconnection[s]" (Lask, *Fichte's Idealism*, p. 153). See pp. 8–9.

472 As an illustration, we may take the following passage from the last chapter of Rickert's *Limits of Concept Formation*: "The ethical individual, like the historical one, always accepts

its proper place within an individual whole; and it has the duty to support the individuality of [that] whole" (*Limits of Concept Formation*, p. 720).

473 The last section of the last chapter of Rickert's *Limits of Concept Formation* has the title: "The world view of natural science and of history".

474 It is tempting to connect this note with Rickert's argument, towards the very end of *Limits of Concept Formation*, that the nation has an absolute ethical value; see, for instance, the passage *Limits of Concept Formation*, p. 722: "It is [. . .] an ethical duty to be, above all, a member of a nation, since we are only able to fulfil most of our duties as members of a nation."

475 See pp. 147–48.

476 "Prophecies after the fact." The expression, which is found in Virgil's *Aeneid*, Book VI, is most often applied to statements by Old Testament prophets, or in the Gospels, which have the form of predictions but have in fact been written with the knowledge that the predicted event actually occurred.

477 See pp. 148 and 175.

478 E[rnst] I[mmanuel] Bekker was a German jurist who, although he belonged to the German historical school, was critical towards many of its tenets: in particular, he rejected the concept of natural law, and proposed applying the methods of the inductive natural sciences to the field of legal studies.

479 This (or "conflicts within the value sphere") is the literal sense of the uncorrected German typewritten text. Marianne Weber corrects this to "conflicts between the different value spheres". It is impossible to determine whether this correction represents a better reading of the original handwritten letter or a "clarifying" insertion on Marianne Weber's part.

ENGLISH KEY
TO GLOSSARY

The Glossary is the main reference point for explaining German terms and their English equivalents. The English key to the Glossary indicates the first word of the heading(s) under which the translation of the English term in question is discussed in the Glossary. (It should be noted that these headings do not necessarily represent a direct translation of the relevant English term into its German equivalent.)

Academic socialism/academic socialist	*Kathedersozialismus/Kathedersozialist*
Accentuate	*steigern*
Accidental	*Zufall*
Accordance with laws	*Gesetzmäßigkeit*
Accustomed	*einleben*
Achievement	*Leistung*
Acknowledge	*erkennen*
Acquire knowledge	*erkennen*
Acquisitive instinct	*Erwerbstrieb*
Act	*Handlung; wirken*
	see also Performatory act
Act economically	*Wirtschaften*
Action	*Handeln; Handlung*
	see also Coming into being; Joint action; Societal action; Societizational action
Actions	*Tun*
Activities	*Tun*
Actual/actuality	*aktuell; faktisch; real*
Adequate	*adäquat*
Adopt a position	*Stellung nehmen*
Affect	*Hereinragen*
Affect/affective	*Affekt*
Alarmingly	*bedenklich*

Ambition	*Streben*
Analyse	*auflösen; zerlegen*
Analytically	*zerfällend*
Apparent/apparently	*offenbar*
Appreciate/appreciation	*Würdigung*
Approach	*Betrachtungsweise; Problemstellung*
Appropriate	*brauchbar; zweckmäßig*
Arbitrary/arbitrariness	*Willkür*
Art	*see* Will to art
Articulate	*artikulieren*
Ascertainable	*erkennbar*
Ascribe/ascription	*zurechnen; Zumutung*
Aspect	*Färbung; Wendung*
Assets	*see* Purposive assets
Association	*Verein*
	see also Collective societal association; Purposive association
Associative grouping	*Verband*
Assumption	*Voraussetzung*
Atmosphere	*Stimmung*
Attitude	*Verhalten*
Attribute	*zurechnen*
Average	*Durchschnitt*
Aware/awareness	*bewußt*
Basis	*anknüpfen; begründen*
Behaviour	*Handeln; Tun; Verhalten*
Being	*Sein*
	see also Coming into being; Cultural being; Generic being; Human being
Bind	*zwingen*
Body	*see* Sense of body
Break down	*auflösen; zerlegen*
Bring about	*bewirken*
Business	*Betrieb*
Calculate/calculation/calculable	*berechnen*
Call forth	*suggerieren*
Category	*Gattung*
Causal equation/causal inequation	*Kausalgleichung*
Causal explanation	*see* Need for causal explanation
Causal regression	*kausal*
Causation	*Verursachung*
	see also Chain of causation
Cause/causal/causality	*bedingen; bewirken; kausal; Ursache*
	see also Real cause; Law of causality
Cause	*Sache*
Cause of knowledge	*Erkenntnisgrund*

Certain	*bestimmen*
Chain of causation	*Kausalreihe*
Chance	*Chance; Zufall*
Character	*see* Distinctive character
Characteristic form	*Ausprägung*
Circumstances	*Tatbestand*
Claim to validity	*Geltenwollen*
Clear	*eindeutig*
Climate of opinion	*Stimmung*
Coercive apparatus	*Zwangsapparat*
Cognition	*erkennen*
Cognitive goal	*Erkenntniszweck*
Cognitive instrument	*Erkenntnismittel*
Cognitive purpose	*Erkenntniszweck*
Cognitive value	*Erkenntniswert*
Collective societal association	*Vergesellschaftung*
Colouring	*Färbung*
Combination	*Einheit*
Coming into being	*Werden*
Common	*see* Life in common
Common good	*see* Sense of common good
Communal action	*Gemeinschaftshandeln*
Communal relationship	*Vergemeinschaftung*
Community/communitized	*Gemeinschaft*
	see also Household community
Compel	*zwingen*
Complete interconnectedness	*Allzusammenhang*
Component	*Bestandteil*
	see also Reduce to components
Composition	*Gliederung*
Comprehend	*begreifen*
Comprehensive intuition	*Gesamtanschauung*
Comprehensive phenomenon	*Gesamterscheinung*
Concatenation	*Ablauf*
Conceive	*vorstellen*
Conceive/conceivable/conceivability	*begreifen; Denken; Denkmöglichkeit; vorstellen*
Concept	*Begriff*
Concept/conceptual	*Begriff; Gedankenbild*
	see also Law concept; Object concept;
	Relational concept
Concept of an object	*Dingbegriff*
Conception	*Auffassungsweise; Bewußtseinsinhalt*
Conceptual content	*Begriff*
Conceptualization	*Begriff*
Concern	*ankommen*
Concurrent	*Nebeneinander*
Conditionality	*bedingen*

Conditioned	*bedingen*
Conduct	*Handeln; Tun; Verhalten*
Conduct of life	*Lebensführung*
Configuration	*Gebilde*
Conscious/consciousness	*bewußt*
Consensus/consensual	*Einverständnis*
Consequence	*Erfolg*
Consistent	*Einheit*
Constituent part	*Bestandteil*
Constrain	*zwingen*
Construct	*Gebilde*
	see also Mental construct
Construction	*Aufstellung; Bildung; Gebilde; Schema*
Construction of concepts	*Begriff*
Contacts	*Verkehr*
Contained	*stecken*
Content	*Inhalt*
Content of feelings	*Gefühlsinhalt*
	see also Conceptual content; Cultural content;
	Empty of content
Context	*Zusammenhang*
	see also Total context
Contingent	*Zufall*
Contribute	*mitbedingen*
Convenient	*zweckmäßig*
Conviction	*Gesinnung*
Copy	*nachbilden*
Correct rationality	*Richtigkeitsrationalität*
Course	*Ablauf*
Course of events/course of history	*Geschehen*
Course of life	*Lebensprozeß*
Criticism	*see* Epistemological criticism
Cultivation	*Pflege*
Cultural being	*Kulturmensch*
Cultural content	*Kultur*
Culturally developed nation	*Kulturvolk*
Culture	*Kultur*
Customs	*see* Manners and customs
Dangerous	*bedenklich*
Deal with	*Pflege*
Dealings	*Verkehr*
Deduce	*ableiten; erschließen*
Deliberate	*bewußt*
Delimit	*stecken*
Demand	*Postulat*
Departure	*see* Point of departure
Dependence	*bedingen*

Deplete	*entleeren*
Derive	*ableiten; erschließen*
Desire	*Bedürfnis*
Detachment	*Distanz*
Determine	*bedingen; bestimmen*
	see also Partly determine
Development	*entwickeln; Gewordensein; Werden*
Different	*besondert*
Differentiation	*Besonderung*
Dignity	*Dignität*
Discover	*erschließen*
Discredit	*erledigen*
Dispassionate	*sachlich*
Dispose of	*erledigen*
Disposition	*Gesinnung; Habitus*
Dissolve	*auflösen*
Distinctive character	*Eigenart*
Distinctive quality	*Eigenart*
Doctrine of good procedure	*Kunstlehre*
Dominance	*Herrschaft*
Domination	*Herrschaft*
Driving force	*Trieb; Triebfeder*
Earning	*Erwerben*
Economic activity	*Erwerben*
	see also Act economically
Economics	*Nationalökonomie*
	see also Social economics/social-economic;
	Market economy; Political economy
Effect	*bewirken*
	see also Take effect
Effective	*wirken; zweckmäßig*
Element	*Bestandteil; Moment*
Elements of culture	*Kultur*
Emanate/emanation/emanationism	*emanieren*
Embedded	*stecken*
Emergent	*Werden*
Emotion/emotive	*Affekt; Gefühl*
Emotional content	*Gefühlsinhalt*
Empathize/empathy	*einfühlen/Einfühlung*
Empirical experience	*erfahren*
	see also Science of empirical experience
Empty of content	*entleeren*
End	*Zweck*
Endeavour	*Streben*
Enter into the spirit	*einleben*
Enterprise	*Betrieb*

Entity	*Einheit; Gebilde*
	see also Total entity
Epistemological criticism	*Erkenntniskritik*
Epistemology/epistemological	*Erkenntnistheorie*
Equation/inequation	*see* Causal equation/causal inequation
Essence/essential	*Wesen*
Establish	*begründen*
Establishment of social relations	*Vergesellschaftung*
Estimate	*Würdigung*
Ethic/ethics/ethical	*Ethik; sittlich*
Evaluate/evaluation	*bewerten; Wertung*
Event/events	*Hergang; Vorgang; Geschehen*
	see also Course of events; Natural event
Everyday existence	*Alltag*
Evident/evidentness	*evident/Evidenz*
Evoke/evocation	*provozieren*
Evolution	*entwickeln; Werden*
Evolutionary law	*entwickeln*
Example	*Exemplar*
Existence	*Sein*
	see also Everyday existence
Existence in common	*Zusammensein*
Existential judgement	*Existenzialurteil*
Existing	*zuständlich*
Expectation	*Zumutung*
Expedient	*zweckmäßig*
Experience/experiencing	*erfahren; Erleben*
	see also Immediate experience; Reproduce immediate experience; Science of empirical experience
Expert	*Fachdisziplin*
Explain/explanation	*erklären*
Expression	*Äußerung*
External	*äußer*
External manifestation	*Äußerung*
Fact	*see* In fact
Factor	*Moment*
Facts	*Tatbestand*
Factual	*faktisch*
Familiar	*einleben*
Feel	*Gefühl*
Feeling	*Fühlen; Gefühl*
	see also Content of feelings
Feeling of possessing salvation	*Heilsbesitz*
Finish off	*erledigen*
Finite/finiteness	*endlich*
First of all	*zunächst*

463

Focus	*anknüpfen*
Folk	*Volk*
Force	*see* Driving force
Form	*Schema*
	see also Characteristic form; Will to form
Formation	*Bildung; Gebilde*
Formulation	*Aufstellung; Bildung; Wendung*
Fortuitous	*Zufall*
Free	*unbefangen*
Fundamental	*letzt*
Furtherance	*Pflege*
General/generality	*allgemein; generell*
General concept	*allgemein*
Generic	*Gattungsmäßig*
Generic being	*Gattungswesen*
Genus	*Gattung*
Give rise to	*anknüpfen*
Goal	*Zweck*
	see also Cognitive goal; Postulated goal
Grasp	*begreifen*
Gravely	*bedenklich*
Ground rent	*Rente*
Group	*Verband*
Grouping	*Verband*
Habit of mind	*Habitus*
Haphazard	*unbefangen*
Heterogeneous	*heterogen*
Heuristic instrument	*Erkenntnismittel*
History	*see* Course of events/course of history
Household/householding	*Haushalt*
Household community	*Hausgemeinschaft*
Hue	*Färbung*
Human being	*Mensch*
Human spirit	*see* Sciences of the human spirit
"I"	*Ich*
Idea	*Gedanke; Vorstellung*
Ideal type	*Idealtypus*
Identify/identifiable	*erkennen; erkennbar*
Image	*Abbild*
	see also Mental image
Imagine	*vorstellen*
Immediate	*unmittelbar*
Immediate experience	*anschaulich; Erleben*
	see also Reproduce immediate experience

Impartial	*unbefangen*
Implications	*Tragweite*
Importance/important	*ankommen; Bedeutung; Tragweite; Wesen*
Imposition	*Oktroyierung*
Impressions	*Einsicht*
Impute	*zurechnen*
In fact	*faktisch*
Inanimate nature	*tote Natur*
Incidental	*Zufall*
Indistinct	*ungeschieden*
individual	*Individuum*
Industrial tribunal	*Gewerbegericht*
Infer	*erschließen*
Information	*Wissen*
Inner	*Innen-*
Innerworldly	*innerweltlich*
Inquiry	*see* Purpose of inquiry
Inseparably	*ungeschieden*
Insight	*Einsicht*
Inspiration	*Geist*
Instinct	*Trieb*
	see also Acquisitive instinct
Institute/institution	*satzen; Anstalt*
Institutional action	*Anstalt*
Instrument	*Mittel*
	see also Cognitive instrument; Heuristic instrument
Intellect/intellectual/intellectually	*Denken; Gedankenbild; Geist; geistig*
Intelligible	*verständlich*
Intend	*meinen*
Interaction	*Wechselwirkung*
Interconnectedness	*Zusammenhang*
	see also Complete interconnectedness
Interconnection	*Zusammenhang*
Intercourse	*Verkehr*
Internal	*Innen-*
Interpret/interpretation/interpretive	*deuten; Interpretation*
Interpretive sociology	*verstehen*
Interrelation	*Wechselwirkung; Zusammenhang*
Intrinsic value	*Eigenwert*
Intuit/Intuition/intuitable/ intuitability	*anschaulich; Erleben*
Intuition	*see also* Comprehensive intuition
Inward	*Innen-*
Is	*Sein*
Joint action	*Zusammenhandeln*
Jointly	*ungeschieden*

Judge/judgement	*bewerten; Urteil*
	see also Existential judgement; Value judgement
Justify	*begründen*
Juxtaposed	*Nebeneinander*
Knowledge	*Einsicht; Erkenntnis; Wissen*
	see also Acquire knowledge; Value as knowledge
Law	*Gesetz; Gesetzmäßigkeit*
	see also Evolutionary law; Science of laws
Law concept	*Gesetzesbegriff*
Law of causality	*Kausalgesetz*
Law of nature	*Naturgesetz*
Law of thought	*Denkgesetz*
Law-like character	*Gesetzlichkeit*
Law-like regularity	*Gesetzmäßigkeit*
Lead with necessity	*zwingen*
Life	*see* Conduct of life; Course of life
Life in common	*Zusammenleben*
Likelihood	*Chance*
Limiting case	*Grenzfall*
Literati	*Literat*
Logic/logical	*Logik; Gedankenbild*
Lose	*entleeren*
Loss of magic	*Entzauberung*
Magic	*see* Loss of magic
Man	*Mensch*
Manifestation	*Erscheinung*
	see also External manifestation
Manifold	*Mannigfaltigkeit*
Manners and customs	*Sitte*
Market economy	*Verkehr*
Mass-conditioned	*massenbedingt*
Material	*dinghaft*
Matter	*ankommen*
Maxim	*Maxime*
Mean	*meinen*
Meaning	*Bedeutung; Sinn;*
	see also Meant meaning
Meaningful	*sinnhaft*
Meaningless	*sinnhaft*
Meaning-related	*sinnhaft*
Means	*Mittel*
Meant meaning	*meinen*
Mental	*Gedankenbild; geistig*
Mental construct	*Gedankenbild*

Mental image	*Gedankenbild*
Mental state	*Inhalt*
Mentality	*Gesinnung*
Method/methodical	*Methode*
	see also Quarrel about methods
Methodology/methodological	*Methode*
Milieu	*Milieu*
Mind/mental	*Denken; Geist; geistig; Seele*
	see also Habit of mind
Misgivings	*bedenklich*
Model	*Schema*
Moment	*Moment*
Mood	*Stimmung*
Moral/morals	*sittlich; Sitte*
Motive	*Bestimmungsgrund*
Multiplicity	*Mannigfaltigkeit*
Nation/national	*Volk*
	see also Culturally developed nation
National psychology	*Völkerpsychologie*
Natural event	*Naturvorgang*
Natural occurrence	*Naturvorgang*
Natural process	*Naturvorgang*
Nature	*Sinn; Wesen*
	see also Inanimate nature; Law of nature
Necessary element of thought	*Denknotwendigkeit*
Necessity	*see* Lead with necessity
Need	*Bedürfnis*
Need for causal explanation	*Kausalbedürfnis*
Non-material	*geistig*
Object	*Objekt*
Object concept	*Dingbegriff*
Objectified	*dinghaft*
Objective	*Objekt*
Objectivity	*Objekt*
Objectivize	*Objekt*
Obvious/obviously	*offenbar*
Occurrence	*Geschehen*
	see also Natural occurrence
Omission	*Unterlassung*
Opinion	*anschaulich; Einsicht*
	see also Climate of opinion
Opportunity	*Chance*
Order/ordering	*Ordnung*
Ordinance	*satzen*
Organization	*Gliederung*

Organization of trade and industry	*Gewerbeverfassung*
Orient	*orientieren*
Ought	*Sollen*
Parallel	*Nebeneinander; Parallelismus*
Parallelism	*Parallelismus*
Part	*see* Constituent part
Particular	*besondert*
Partly determine	*mitbedingen*
People	*Mensch*
Perceive/perception/perceivable	*erkennbar; wahrnehmen*
Perform	*erledigen*
Performance	*Leistung; Verhalten*
Performatory act	*hantieren*
Personality	*Persönlichkeit*
Persons	*Mensch*
Perspective	*Gesichtspunkt; Problemstellung*
Phenomenon/phenomena	*Anstalt; Erscheinung; Vorgang; Tatbestand*
	see also Comprehensive phenomenon
Phraseology	*Wendung*
Point of departure	*anknüpfen*
Point of view	*Betrachtungsweise; Gesichtspunkt*
Political economy	*Nationalökonomie*
Positing	*Setzung*
Position	*see* Adopt a position
Postulate	*Postulat*
Postulated goal	*Postulat*
Precept	*Postulat*
Precise/precision	*Bestimmtheit; eindeutig*
Precondition	*Voraussetzung*
Predominance	*Herrschaft*
Presumption	*Zumutung*
Presupposition	*Voraussetzung*
Prevailing	*Geltung*
Principle	*Postulat; Satz*
Probable/probability	*Chance; wahrscheinlich*
Problem	*Problemstellung*
Problematical	*bedenklich*
Procedure	*see* Doctrine of good procedure
Process	*Ablauf; Hergang; Vorgang*
	see also Natural process; Vital process
Process of life	*Lebensprozeß*
Profession	*Beruf*
Professional	*Fachdisziplin*
Project into	*Hereinragen*
Proposition	*Aufstellung; Satz*
Provoke	*provozieren*
Psyche/psychical	*Psyche; Seele*

Psychological	*Psyche; Seele*
Psychology	*see* National psychology
Purpose	*Zweck*
	see also Cognitive purpose
Purpose of inquiry	*Erkenntniszweck*
Purposeful	*zweckvoll*
Purposive	*zweckmäßig; zweckvoll*
Purposive assets	*Zweckvermögen*
Purposive association	*Zweckverein*
Purposive system	*Zwecksystem*
Purposively rational/purposive rationality	*zweckrational*
Pursuit	*Betrieb*
Quality *see* Distinctive quality	*Eigenart*
Quarrel about methods	*Methodenstreit*
Question	*Problemstellung*
Questionable	*bedenklich*
Quote	*zitieren*
Rationality	*see* Correct rationality; Purposively rational/ purposive rationality
Real/reality	*real; Wirklichkeit*
	see also Science of reality
Real cause	*Erkenntnisgrund; Realgrund*
Realize/realization	*verwirklichen*
Reason/reasonable	*begründen; Bestimmungsgrund; Denken; Vernunft*
Recognizable	*erkennbar*
Reduce/reduction	*auflösen*
Reduce to components	*zerlegen*
Re-experience	*nacherleben*
Re-feeling	*Nachfühlen*
Refer to	*zitieren*
Reflect/reflection	*Abbild*
Refrain from	*Unterlassung*
Regarded as	*Geltung*
Regression	*see* Causal regression
Regularity	*Regel*
	see also Law-like regularity
Relation/relatedness	*Beziehung; Verhältnis*
	see also Value relation; Value relatedness
Relational concept	*Relationsbegriff*
Relationship	*Verhältnis*
Relevance	*Hereinragen; ankommen*
Rent	*see* Ground rent
Replicate	*nachbilden*
Represent/representation	*vorstellen; Vorstellung*
Reproduce immediate experience	*nacherleben*

Reproduce/reproduction	*Abbild; nachbilden*
Requirement	*Bedürfnis*
Result	*Erfolg*
Reveal	*erschließen*
Rise	*see* Give rise to
Rule	*Regel*
Salvation	*see* Feeling of possessing salvation
Schema	*Schema*
Scheme	*Schema*
Scholarship	*Wissenschaft*
Science	*Wissenschaft*
	see also Specialized science
Science of empirical experience	*Erfahrungswissenschaft*
Science of laws	*Gesetzeswissenschaft*
Science of reality	*Wirklichkeitswissenschaft*
Science of society	*Gesellschaftswissenschaft*
Sciences of the human spirit	*Geisteswissenschaften*
Scope	*Tragweite; Umfang*
Search for knowledge	*erkennen, Erkenntnis*
Secular	*diesseitig*
Self-interest	*Eigennutz*
Self-seeking	*Selbstsucht*
Sense	*Sinn*
Sense of body	*Körpergefühl*
Sense of common good	*Gemeinsinn*
Sensuous	*sinnlich*
Sentence	*Satz*
Sentiment	*Gefühl; Stimmung*
Separate	*besondert*
Sequence	*Ablauf*
Servitude to words	*Wortknechtschaft*
Settle	*erledigen*
Shuffle around	*hantieren*
Significance/significant	*Bedeutung; Tragweite; Wesen*
Simultaneous	*Nebeneinander*
Situation	*Tatbestand*
Sober	*sachlich*
Social	*Gesellschaft; social*
Social-	*social*
Social economics/social-economic	*Sozialökonomik*
Social relations	*see* Establishment of social relations
Socialism/socialist	*see* Academic socialism/academic socialist
Societal	*Gesellschaft*
Societal action	*Gesellschaft*
Societization	*Vergesellschaftung*
Societizational action	*Vergesellschaftung*
Societized	*Gesellschaft*

Society	*Gesellschaft*
	see also Science of society
Sociology	*see* Interpretive sociology
Soul	*Seele*
Specialist/specialized	*Fachdisziplin*
Specialized science	*Wissenschaft*
Species	*Gattung*
Specific	*spezifisch*
Specimen	*Exemplar*
Spirit	*Geist; Stimmung*
	see also Enter into the spirit; Sciences of the
	human spirit
Spiritual	*geistig*
Stage	*Stand*
Stand	*see* Take a stand
Standpoint	*Gesichtspunkt*
State/static	*Stand; zuständlich*
	see also Mental state
State [political organization]	*see* Theory of the state
State of affairs	*Tatbestand*
Statement	*Äußerung; Satz*
Status	*Dignität; Geltung*
Status group	*Stand*
Stratum	*Schicht*
Striving	*Streben; Wollen*
Structure	*Gebilde; Gliederung*
Stuck	*stecken*
Study	*Wissenschaft*
Subdivide	*zerlegen*
Subjectivize	*subjektivieren*
Substance	*Inhalt*
	see also Void of substance
Substantive	*sachlich*
Substantive content	*Begriffsinhalt*
Succeed/succession	*Ablauf; Aufeinanderfolge; Nebeneinander*
Success	*Erfolg*
Suggest	*suggerieren*
Suitable	*zweckmäßig*
Supra-individual	*überindividuell*
System	*Gebilde; Schema*
	see also Purposive system
Take a stand	*Stellung nehmen*
Take effect	*wirken*
Task	*Sache*
Theoretical	*Gedankenbild*
Theoretical construct/intellectual construct	*Gedankenbild*

Theory of the state	*Staatslehre*
Thesis	*Satz*
Think/thought	*Denken*
Thinker	*Geist*
This-wordly	*diesseitig*
Thought	*see* Law of thought; Necessary element of thought
Tinge	*Färbung*
Total context	*Allzusammenhang*
Total entity	*Gesamtwesen*
Totality	*Gesamtheit*
Trace back	*kausal*
Trade and industry	*Erwerben*
	see also Organization of trade and industry
Transactions	*Verkehr*
Tribunal	*see* Industrial tribunal
Turned out the way it did and not otherwise	*Gewordensein*
Type	*see* Ideal type
Ultimate	*letzt*
Unambiguous	*eindeutig*
Unbiased	*unbefangen*
Uncover	*erschließen*
Underpin	*begründen*
Understand	*verstehen*
Understandable	*verständlich*
Undifferentiated	*ungeschieden*
Uniform	*Einheit*
Unique/uniqueness	*einmalig; einzigartig*
Unit	*Einheit*
Unity of life	*Lebenseinheit*
Unity/unitary	*Einheit*
Universal	*universell*
Unprejudiced	*unbefangen*
Unreal	*hinterweltlich*
Unworldly	*übersinnlich*
Urge	*Bedürfnis*
Usability	*brauchbar*
Use/useful	*brauchbar; zweckmäßig*
Usual	*Pflege*
Utility value	*brauchbar*
Valid/validity	*gültig; Geltung*
	see also Claim to validity
Valuate/valuation/valuational	*Wertung*
Value	*Wert*
	see also Cognitive value; Intrinsic value; Utility value

Value as knowledge	*Erkenntniswert*
Value judgement	*bewerten; Werturteil*
Value relatedness	*Wertbezogenheit*
Value relation	*Wertbeziehung*
Version	*Wendung*
View	*anschaulich*
	see also Point of view; World view
Viewpoint	*Gesichtspunkt*
Visualization	*vorstellen*
Vital process	*Lebensprozeß*
Vocation	*Beruf*
Void of substance	*inhaltsleer*
Volition	*Wollen*
Way	*Wendung*
Whole	*Einheit*
Will to art	*Kunstwollen*
Will to form	*Formungswollen*
Willing	*Wollen*
Wish	*Bedürfnis*
Within	*Innen-*
Words	*see* Servitude to words
Work	*Betrieb*
World beyond the real one	*hinterweltlich*
World view	*Weltanschauung*
Worth knowing about	*Erkenntniswert*

GLOSSARY

The references are illustrative, not exhaustive. "NT" means "non-technical", ordinary. "T" means "technical", "specialized".

Abbild; abbilden: "Reproduction" or "reflection" (rather than "representation"); sometimes "image".

Ablauf: Almost one half of the occurrences are in *Roscher and Knies*, and more than one third in *Categories*. The normal translation is "course", but, according to the context, other translations may be preferred, such as "process", "sequence" or "succession". Combined with "kausal", "Ablauf" has been translated as "concatenation".

ableiten: "Derive" or "deduce" (the latter for instances resembling "logical" deduction) cover most of the field. In a few cases, other translations are appropriate, according to context.

adäquat: "Adequate", particularly, of course, in its "technical" sense (adäquate Verursachung). The translation "adequate" is occasionally used NT for "hinlänglich" or "zulänglich".

Affekt; affektuell; Affekt: Most of the passages where these expressions occur deal with something that is contrasted with, or impairs, rational action. Therefore, in order to maintain the link with Weber's categories of action, which include "affective" action, it seems most appropriate to use the slightly stilted, but acceptable translation "affect"/"affective". Occasionally, "Affekt-" is best translated as "emotion"/"emotive".

aktuell; Aktualität: Used above all in the discussion (in *Knies I*) of Münsterberg, who employs the term to indicate an immediate, as opposed to a reflective, state of the psyche. The "stellungnehmendes Subjekt" – the "subject taking a stand" – is in a state of "Aktualität". When one considers Weber's use of the term "aktuelles Verstehen" for immediate understanding that is not dependent on reflection or knowledge of causal connections, there might be a case for translating "aktuell" as "immediate". This solution, however, would compete with the translation of "unmittelbar", which also very definitely has to be rendered as "immediate". "Actual"/"actuality" have therefore been preferred; this choice is supported by the further consideration that, where Weber's language is plainly an echo of that employed by the scholars on whom he comments, it is even more indicated to keep close to the terminology used. There is another, rather more NT, sense of "aktuell" – the opposition to "potentiell" – and here, the translation "actual" is also quite natural. See also *Realität*.

allgemein: Weber mainly uses "allgemein" (1) in a NT sense; (2) for extensive (generic) generality of concepts (in one passage, (p. 191) he equates this usage with "generell"); and (3) in connection with "validity" (*allgemeingültig*), again with a clear connection to sense (2)). In all three senses, "allgemein" is normally translated as "general". There seems no reason to bring in "universal" as a translation of (2) or (3) to distinguish between them, the more so since "universell" is used both to denote extensiveness (of interconnections) and intensiveness (of significance). The context (often adverted in the form of quotation marks) usually in itself yields the necessary distinctions.

When "allgemein" (or "generell", which is always translated as "general") occurs in its substantivized, abstract form ("das Allgemeine/das Generelle"), the translation ("the General") will have a capital G in "General", for the sake of consistency with the similar capitalization of "the Individual" (see *individuell*), and to make quite sure that there is no confusion with "the [officer with the rank of] general". *Allgemeinbegriff* is translated as "general concept". It either has the sense under (2) above, or is a reference to the specific Hegelian terminology; in the latter case, this is obvious from the context. *Allgemeinheit* only occurs infrequently, with a sense that certainly permits the translation "generality" or "general character". See also *universell*.

Alltag: "Everyday existence".

Allzusammenhang: "Complete interconnectedness". This may not be standard English; but it sounds more natural to "experience" the "interconnectedness" of elements than their "interconnection". In one instance (p. 199), it seems more natural to translate "Allzusammenhang" by "total context".

alsbald: NT. Old-fashioned. Indicates that something happens *immediately* after something else. Becomes increasingly frequent in the articles from 1904 and 1905. Sometimes almost a stylistic tic.

alsdann: NT. Indicates sequence of time. Need not always be translated if sense is given by context. Otherwise, "then" or equivalent translations.

anknüpfen: Obviously a NT term. "Take as basis" or similar expressions; or "focus on", "take as point of departure" or "give rise to" – all depending on context.

ankommen: "Concern" and "matter" are appropriate in most cases; sometimes some version of "importance" or "relevance" fits better. Once or twice, "focus on" seems to be the best solution.

anschaulich; *Anschaulichkeit*; *Anschauung*:   In some cases, "Anschauung" is clearly NT and means "view", "opinion". The question is whether, apart from that, "Anschauung"/ "anschaulich"/"Anschaulichkeit" should always be translated as "intuition"/"intuitable"/ "intuitability", in accordance with standard philosophical terminology.

This is one of the few cases where Weber himself discusses the T meaning of a term ("anschaulich") (p. 74n200). Unfortunately, his main point is that the term is ambiguous. It covers, he says, the "immediate experience" which has *not* been subjected to logical treatment ("logisch unbearbeitete Erlebnis"), but also (he does not state this, but the implication is clear) inner experience which has to some extent been subjected to logical treatment, the "inner intuitability of the processes of consciousness" ("innere Anschaulichkeit der Bewußtseinsvorgänge"). In order to avoid that ambiguity, Weber says that he prefers to use the term "evidentness" ("Evidenz", q.v.) for the "processed" experience. At the same time, Weber mentions that "logicians" use "Anschaulichkeit" in the sense of "insight into the reasons on which a judgement is based" ("Einsicht in die Gründe eines Urteils"). And, to compound the complications, he then, one page later, uses "anschaulich" in *both* those senses. At any rate, this demonstrates that Weber is not consistently tied to the standard philosophical sense. Moreover, he uses "anschaulich" in a further sense, which basically goes back to Kant, but which in practice has the NT function of indicating that something is or can be demonstrated or seen directly and in a clear form.

The upshot of all this is that "anschaulich" should not invariably viewed as being burdened with its various "philosophical" implications. The context should decide whether one of the NT senses of the term or the "philosophical" one ("intuition" etc.) is the most appropriate one.

Anstalt: This term mostly occurs, in a T sense, in *Categories*, where it has been translated as "institution" throughout. There is a slight difficulty, though, when the *German* word "Institution" appears (once only, p. 300) in a sense that is obviously not the same as that of "Anstalt". This has been handled by translating "Institution" – in this one instance – as "phenomenon", which is substantively appropriate in that particular context. In the rest of the *Meth. Writings*, both "Anstalt" (few occurrences, all NT) and "Institution" have been translated as "institution". *Anstaltshandeln*: "institutional action".

artikulieren; artikuliert: "Artikulieren" is always "(to) articulate", but "artikuliert" as an adjective is sometimes rendered as "articulate" rather than "articulated".

Aufeinanderfolge; aufeinanderfolgen: Succession; succeed

Auffassungsweise: Only two occurrences, both in *Roscher*. "Conception".

auflösen; Auflösung: "Reduce(d) to"/"reduction" or "break down into"; "resolve itself into"; "dissolve into" ("sich auflösen") – all according to context. Since "analysieren" occurs quite frequently in Weber's methodological writings, "analyse" has been reserved as a translation for that word.

Aufstellung: NT. With a substantive sense: "construction"; with a verbalized one: "formulation". Sometimes: "proposition".

Ausprägung: Three occurrences only, all in *Critical Studies*, two in inverted commas. "Characteristic form".

äußer: Consistently translated as "external".

Äußerung: Two main senses: (verbal or written) "statement"; and a more general "expression" or "(external) manifestation".

bedenklich: "Questionable"; "problematical"; occasionally: "dangerous", "giving rise to misgivings"; as an adverb: "gravely", "alarmingly".

Bedeutung; Bedeutsamkeit; bedeutsam; bedeuten; bedeutend; unbedeutend: These are central terms. There is a NT sense of "meaning" ("meaningless" etc.). But "Bedeutung" will only occasionally be found with the sense of "meaning". Instead, there is a constant choice to be made between "importance" and "significance". The choice is made both easier and more difficult by the fact that there is an overlap in the sense of those two terms, inasmuch as it is *possible*, in contexts of causality, where "importance" would ordinarily be the best choice, to speak of "(causal) significance". But even if one adopted a principle of preferring "significance" wherever possible, one would still be left with a residue of passages where "importance" was the only natural translation. In view of this, the guideline has been as follows: "Bedeutung" is translated as "importance" when the *causal* aspect seems to be the dominant one, and "significance" when the connection with *values* is more prominent. In a number of instances, it has been impossible to make that choice unambiguously. There, the inelegant but safe solution has been to translate as "significance/significant and importance/important". (In one instance, "Bedeutungen" has been translated as "significant meanings" to get the aspects of "meaning" and "significance" into one term). When we are dealing with *bedeutungslos*, there is an added complication in that "insignificant" is not an exact negation of "significant"; therefore, "not significant" is a better rendering of "bedeutungslos". *Bedeutsam* may mean either "significant" or "important" (or both) according to the criteria just set out, and has been dealt with in accordance with them.

bedingen; bedingt; Bedingung; Bedingtheit: "Bedingen" can be rendered both by "conditioned" and by "determined". "Conditioned" is difficult to avoid in cases where "Bedingung" is also present, since "condition" is clearly the right translation for that term. *Bedingtheit* is most often translated as "conditionality" (this term seems to have acquired the sense of "being conditioned" after having originally only meant "being conditional"), but also as "dependence", "being determined", "having causes" or the like.

Bedürfnis: Normally translated as "need", particularly in passages dealing with economic needs. Occasionally also as "requirement", "wish", "desire" or "urge", according to the context. See also *Kausalbedürfnis*.

begreifen; begreiflich: In *Knies I*, there is a definite "technical" use of "begreifen". For a number of reasons, the best solution in that context seems to be "find comprehensible". In many other cases, too, "comprehend/comprehensible" for "begreifen/begreiflich" seems appropriate. "Conceive" – which is linguistically close to "concept" – has also occasionally been used; but "conceivable" does not really correspond to "begreiflich". Elsewhere, in a slightly more NT sense, "grasp" and similar translations have been used.

Begriff; begrifflich; Begriffsbildung; Begriffenes: "Begriff" has been translated as "concept", and "begrifflich" as "conceptual". *Begriffsbildung* seems to have an "active" and a more "passive" form. In the "active" form, it is translated as "concept formation", "conceptualization" or "construction of concepts", etc. In the "passive" form, it simply seems to mean "concept" and has been translated accordingly. *Begriffenes* has usually been rendered as "conceptual content": it is in substance not distinguishable from "Begriffsinhalt" (q.v.).

Begriffsinhalt: Normally: "conceptual content". Sometimes (in *Objectivity*), "substantive content" looks more appropriate. (The term is not found outside *Roscher* and *Objectivity*.)

begründen: Can be rendered by some sort of construction with "reason" or "basis", as well as "justify", "underpin" and "establish".

berechnen; berechenbar; unberechenbar: Calculate, calculation, calculable, incalculable.

Beruf: "Profession" has been used for the "secular" sense of the term (with an easy bridge to "professional") and "vocation" for the "higher" sense. (See also endnote 352.)

Besonderung; besondert: Old-fashioned (only in Grimm's *Dictionary* (1854): "secretio, disjunctio") and rare (only in *Roscher* and *Objectivity*). "Besonderung": "differentiation"; "besondert": "separate", "particular", "different".

Bestandteil: "Component (part)"; "constituent part"; "element".

bestimmen: The standard translation is "determine". In the many occurrences of "bestimmt" in the sense of "certain", (parallel with "gewiß": "ein bestimmtes/gewisses Verhältnis" – "a certain relationship"), "bestimmt" is translated as "certain".

Bestimmtheit: Translated as "precision" throughout.

Bestimmungsgrund: An old-fashioned word that occurs relatively seldom. According to Grimm (1854), it means something like "ratio" in latin. It has therefore been translated as "motive" or "reason".

Betrachtungsweise: The normal translation is "approach". If the visual element is more pronounced, "point of view" or similar formulations have been used instead.

betreiben: See *Betrieb*.

Betrieb: This is a multi-faceted concept. Swedberg, who has commented on it both in his *Max Weber Dictionary* and in the Glossary to his selection of Weber's *Essays in Economic Sociology*

(1999), gives two separate senses: (1) "continuous rational activity" and (2) "(noneconomic) enterprise". In neither sense does the term *necessarily* describe something economic. It should be noted that these definitions are taken from *WG*, part I, and are therefore subsequent to virtually all the texts in the *Meth. Writings*.

In most cases, "Betrieb" is used in the *Meth. Writings* in a NT sense quite close to (1) above, and directly derived from the verb "betreiben" ("pursue/engage in/carry on some activity"). It designates the, more or less rational and systematic, pursuit of an activity, and is translated correspondingly as "pursuit" or "work". In some cases, the sense is clearly economic – rather along the lines of what Weber later calls "Erwerbsbetrieb" – and is translated as "business" or "enterprise".

bewerten; Bewertung: "Evaluate"/"evaluation" and "judge"/"judgement" ("value judgement", in one case).

bewirken: The sense is "effect", "bring about" or "cause", and the translations reflect this. Many of the occurrences are in *Stammler* and reflect Stammler's formulations, where "Handlungen" are "bewirkt", rather than Weber's more "active" verbalized formulations ("Handeln").

bewußt; Bewußtsein: "Conscious(ness)" is of course the normal translation of the term in its stricter sense. But "aware"/"awareness" and "deliberate" have been used in the more general sense.

Bewußtseinsinhalt: The literal translation, "content of consciousness" is clumsy and unsatisfactory. Instead, the word has been translated as "conception" – a free translation that seems to correspond to the sense in which the German word is used.

Beziehung: "Relation". See also *Wertbeziehung*.

Bildung: For concepts: "formation". For laws: "formulation". Otherwise often: "construction".

brauchbar; Brauchbarkeit. Brentano has a discussion (referred to on p. 242) of the distinction between "Brauchbarkeit" ("usability") and "Gebrauchswert" ("utility value"). There are virtually no other occurrences in the *Meth. Writings* of "Gebrauchswert"; "Brauchbar(keit)" can be found elsewhere, but in a NT sense. However, in order to distinguish, if possible, "brauchbar" from "nützlich", "brauchbar" has, whenever possible, been translated as "of use", "appropriate" or the like, reserving "useful" for "nützlich".

Chance: "Chance" frequently occurs in Weber's methodological work; in particular, the concept holds a central place in *Categories*. It is therefore reasonable to try to retain the "chance" terminology in the translation, if this can be done without detriment to the sense. As noted by Swedberg (*Weber Dictionary*), the German "Chance" can mean both "opportunity" and "probability"/"likelihood". Both senses are covered in the OED definition of "chance" in English ("an opportunity that comes in any one's way" and "a probability or possibility of anything happening, as distinct from a certainty"); so, in principle, it should be possible to use "chance" as a translation for both aspects. Swedberg (and Parsons in his translation of *WG*) choose a different route, however; they translate one aspect as "opportunity" and the other one as "probability" (Swedberg) or "likelihood/probability" (Parsons). It should be noted that Swedberg is specifically dealing with Weber's economic sociology, where "opportunity" may well be easier to accommodate as a translation. It should also be noted that Weber, in the *Meth. Writings*, quite frequently uses "Wahrscheinlichkeit" ("probability") (q.v.) in parallel with, and as more or less equivalent to, "Chance". When one analyses the occurrences of "Chance" in the *Meth. Writings*, one notes that the two senses tend to merge, so that it is often quite difficult to make the choice between "opportunity" and "probability" when assigning its proper place to a particular occurrence of "Chance".

It therefore seems advantageous to keep "chance" as a consistent translation of "Chance". This will pinpoint Weber's terminological peculiarity without much risk of actual confusion between the two aspects (and if there is some confusion in certain cases, it may in fact, as just noted, be inherent in the German text).

This conclusion is beset with another complication, however, in that Weber also, quite often, uses the term "Zufall" and "zufällig" in discussions where the natural English translation would also be "chance", both as a noun and as an adjective (cf. the OED definition "casual or fortuitous circumstance"). By retaining "chance" as a translation of "Chance", one gets an extra load of "chances" covering "zufällig/Zufall". Again, however, there is little risk of substantive confusion; and again, there is a certain tendency for some of the "Zufall" "chances" to shade over into the "opportunity" or "probability" "chances". It should also be noted that there is in many cases no adequate substitute for "chance" in the "accidental" sense.

The overall conclusion is therefore to accept "chance" both for "Zufall/zufällig" – whenever appropriate – and for "Chance" in both aspects. See also *Zufall*.

Denken; denkend; denken: In many instances, "Denken/denkend" clearly means "(by way of) conscious reflection" and is translated as "intellect(ually)". But there seems no reason to try to standardize the translation completely, the more so as "denken" often has a quasi-NT function. According to the context, there are therefore a number of other translations, e.g. "thought" and "mind" (for "Denken") and "think", "reason" and "conceive" (for "denken").

Denkgesetz: "Law of thought". Only a few hits. A German Philosophical Dictionary from 1904 distinguishes between psychological and logical "Denkgesetze", and this is probably a sufficient reason for rejecting the possible alternative translation: "law of logic".

Denkmöglich(keit):   Rare. "Conceivable/conceivability".

Denknotwendigkeit: The two main possibilities are "necessary element of thought" and "necessary principle of thought". The former has been preferred as being more adequate to the specific context. (The term is only found in one passage, but with multiple occurrences there.)

deuten; Deutung: Normally, "interpret/interpretation" seems to fit well. "Deutend" (very frequent in *Knies I*) is often rendered as "interpretive". "Deutung" occasionally has a NT sense of "analysis". See also *Verstehen; Interpretation*.

diesseitig: "This-wordly" or "secular".

Dignität: Although "status" does not in itself have the "dignified" connotations suggested by "Dignität", it is in many cases the most adequate translation of the German term. In other cases, "dignity" is perfectly appropriate as a translation.

Dingbegriff: Only occurs in *Roscher and Knies*. "Concept of [an] object" fits nicely, except in two cases (pp. 6 and 61n180 [63]), where "object concept" seems more appropriate.

dinghaft: Three occurrences only, of which two in a discussion in *Knies II* of Lipps, but not as a quotation from him. This very German construction has been translated as "material" (*Knies II*) or "objectified" (*Categories*), although "thingly" was a tempting alternative in the first passage.

Distanz: In its "inner" sense, there is only one occurrence (in *Value Freedom*) of this term, which has been translated as "detachment". Scaff (*Iron Cage*, p. 184) says that "detachment" is a misguided translation, and replaces it with "distance", but it is difficult to see the difference, and to the extent that there is one, it seems, if anything, more misleading to use "distance".

Durchschnitt; durchschnittlich: Literally "(on) average". Very frequent in *Categories*. It might have been rendered as "usually", "normally" and the like, which makes for easier reading. But, on the assumption that there is a reason for Weber's choice and persistent use of that particular term in cases where other German terms, such as "pflegen", "normalerweise" etc., were readily available, "durchschnittlich" has consistently been translated as "average"/ "on average" in *Categories*. Very few and unproblematical occurrences in other essays in the *Meth. Writings*.

Eigenart; eigenartig: "Eigenart" (a term which is very common in all Weber's writings) is, with a few exceptions, consistently translated as "distinctive character". The exceptions are usually explained by the context, for instance if the German text speaks of "charakteristische Eigenart"; in such cases, "Eigenart" is usually translated as "distinctive quality".

Eigennutz: Only occurs in *Roscher* and *Knies II*. "Self-interest". ("Selfishness" or the like would be too pejorative for the actual connotations of "Eigennutz". Moreover, Roscher actually gives the English term "self-interest" parallel to the German one in *System*, §11). It shares this translation with the – infrequent – "Eigeninteresse", but this is acceptable, since the two concepts are used interchangeably by Weber himself (pp. 21–22).

Eigenwert: "Intrinsic value".

eindeutig; Eindeutigkeit: "Unambiguous" is usually the most apposite translation of "eindeutig"; "clear" or "precise" have also been used. "Precision" for "Eindeutigkeit" is a little more elegant than "unambiguousness" and has therefore been preferred in some cases.

Einfühlung; einfühlen: Consistently rendered as "empathy" and "empathize".

Einheit; einheitlich; Einheitlichkeit: In some of the discussions, notably of Knies' thought, these concepts have a T character, and it is therefore useful to try to standardize their use as much as possible, at least in those instances. "Einheit" has normally been translated as "unity" and, occasionally (this is also a "regular" dictionary translation), as "unit". Very rarely, when the emphasis is not on the unity but on the existence of something as such, the translation is "entity". There are also a (very) few instances of "combination" and "whole". *Einheitlich* logically has the translation "unitary". When it is occasionally clear that the element of uniformity or consistency is central, it is translated as "uniform" or "consistent". (Other translators have chosen "homogeneous"; but although this is a regular dictionary translation, it rarely, if ever, makes good sense in the *Meth. Writings*.) *Einheitlichkeit* is translated as "unitary character" throughout.

einleben: Three occurrences in *Knies*. "Enter into the spirit of." A few more in *Categories*, in the form "eingelebt", which has been translated as "familiar" or (in one case) "accustomed".

einmalig; Einmaligkeit: "Unique(ness)." See also *einzigartig*.

Einsicht: The consistent translation of this is simply "insight" (occasionally "knowledge"). In a few cases, the context makes it clear that Weber is talking about "impressions" or "opinions" concerning facts, and the translation will then reflect this.

Einverständnis: This term only, but very frequently (110 occurrences!), appears in *Categories*. It is consistently translated as "consensus". *Die Einverstandenen*: "the parties to the consensus". *Einverständnishandeln*: "consensual action". *Einverständnisbedingtes Handeln* (two occurrences only): "consensually conditioned action".

einzigartig: "Unique" throughout. (There seems to be no reason for distinguishing it from the translation of "einmalig".)

emanieren: "emanate"; *Emanation*: "emanation"; *emanatistisch*: "emanationist"; *Emanatismus*: "emanationism".

endlich; Endlichkeit: "Finite"; "finiteness" or "finite character"

entleeren; Entleerung: Only occurs in *Roscher*. "Empty of (substantive) content"; "deplete"; sometimes simply "lose".

entwickeln; *Entwicklung*:   The balance between "development" and "evolution" as a translation of "Entwicklung" is not definitionally clear. But "evolution" has biological overtones that Weber wanted to avoid for himself, while he obviously wished to pinpoint them in the authors whom he criticized. (Scaff, *Iron Cage*, p. 42n17). There will therefore be a tendency for "Entwicklung" to be translated as "evolution" in more critical and polemical contexts. *Entwicklungsgesetz* occurs only in *Roscher* and with a corresponding critical tinge, and has therefore been translated by "evolutionary law" or "law of evolution".

Entzauberung is a crucial concept for Weber, particularly in his writings on religion. In the *Meth. Writings*, it only occurs in *Science*, and once in *Categories*. Literally, the German term means "loss of magic". The usual English translation has been "disenchantment", but this term has connotations of simple disillusionment that tend to water down the starkness of the German word. Therefore, the literal translation ("loss of magic") has been preferred.

erfahren; *Erfahrung*:   "Erfahrung" is very common and has "experience" as its normal translation. When contrasted with "Erleben" or "Erlebnis" (q.v.), or with "Verstehen" (q.v.), it is translated as "empirical experience". When it is the first part of composite words such as "Erfahrungssatz", it may also, but will not necessarily, be rendered as "empirical". "Erfahren" is used in a very few cases (e.g., pp. 73–74) as a substantivized infinitive; in order to respect as far as possible Weber's tendency to "verbalize" his substantives (cf. "Handeln" etc.), these instances have been translated as "experiencing".

Erfahrungswissenschaft: "Science of empirical experience" throughout. This translation is supported by the fact that Weber constantly uses "empirisch" in the context of "Erfahrungswissenschaft".

Erfolg: May be "success", but will in a number of cases simply be "result" or "consequence".

erkennbar: With one exception, the term is NT, and translations are therefore quite variable: "recognizable", "identifiable", "can be ascertained", etc. The T translation is "perceivable".

erkennen: The verb as such mostly has a NT sense that may be translated variously, most often as "acquire knowledge (of)", but also as "acknowledge" or "identify". As a substantivized infinitive ("Erkennen"), its "active" sense of "search for knowledge" is retained everywhere. Where the reference is clearly epistemological (as in "diskursives Erkennen" – see endnote 10), it is rendered as "cognition".

Erkenntnis: The core translation is simply "knowledge". However, the word can in German have a more "active" or "processual" meaning than "knowledge" in English; in such cases, "search for knowledge" or similar constructions have been preferred.

Erkenntnisgrund: This term is used in constant conjunction with its conceptual opposite *Realgrund* (q.v.). They are burdened with a heavy load of philosophical tradition. Among the many available solutions, a fairly simple one has been adopted: *Erkenntnisgrund* is translated as "cause of knowledge", and "*Realgrund*" as "real cause". The hallowed philosophical translation of *Erkenntnisgrund* is "cognitive cause"; but in Weber's main discussion of these concepts (*Critical Studies*), he is not discussing cognition but acquisition of structured knowledge.

Erkenntniskritik: "Epistemological criticism."

Erkenntnismittel: There are a number of possibilities here, but the choice has been "heuristic instrument". It works well in almost every case, sometimes combined with "for uncovering . . ." or "for grasping . . .". It is almost exclusively confined to discussions of historical method. In one instance, it occurs in an epistemological context and is translated there as "cognitive instrument" – a translation that would, on the other hand, be inappropriate when dealing with historical method and established "facts".

Erkenntnistheorie; erkenntnistheoretisch: The standard translations are "epistemology" and "epistemological".

Erkenntniswert has been translated as "cognitive value", "value as knowledge" (see *Erkenntnisgrund*)
or "worth knowing about", as appropriate.

Erkenntniszweck; Erkenntnisziel: Both words – in particular "Erkenntniszweck" – have both a
more "abstract" and a rather more "concrete" sense. In the abstract sense (discussion of
general categories), the translation is "cognitive goal" or (a little more concretely) "cognitive purpose(s)". In the more concrete sense, the translation is some variation of "purpose
of the inquiry". It should be noted that "Erkenntniszweck" has a separate sense: that of
"knowledge being the purpose of something". But here as well, "cognitive purpose" can,
in the given context, give the right impression.

erklären; Erklärung: Very frequent in the *Meth. Writings*. "Explain/explanation" is the consistent
translation.

Erleben; Erlebnis; Erlebung: Particularly frequent in *Knies I* and *Knies II*. There is a NT sense,
which is rendered as "experience". When contrasted with "Erfahren/ung", or in connection with "understanding", the consistent translation is "immediate experience" or in
a very few cases "intuiting" (while "Erfahren/ung" is in these cases translated as "empirical
experience"). See also *erfahren, Erfahrung*.

erledigen: Usually pejorative: "dispose of", "finish off", "discredit". Sometimes neutral: "settle"
or "perform".

Erscheinung: The ordinary translation is "phenomenon". Weber is very liberal with his
"phenomena" in a NT sense. The very few instances where "Erscheinung" has a more
T character, it is translated either as "phenomenon" or as "manifestation" (which also
covers *Erscheinungsform*).

erschließen: The term is used both in a more logical sense ("infer" – the most usual translation
of all – "deduce", or "derive") and, occasionally, in a more "empirical" one ("uncover",
reveal", "discover"). It acquires a T meaning in the discussion of Gottl in *Knies II*, since
Gottl puts it at the centre of his theory of history. Unfortunately, this does not mean that
it is possible to be quite consistent in the translation. Although "infer" on the whole
seems to work well in this context, there is at least one passage where "uncover" is more
natural.

Erwerben: There is a lively debate (Keith Tribe, J.-P. Grossein, Richard Swedberg)
about the T (*WG*) translation. But in the *Meth. Writings*, the sense is NT and simply
has to do with somebody's economic activity or interest. The translations of the
(very few) occurrences are correspondingly varied: "economic", "earning", "trade and
industry".

Erwerbstrieb: "Acquisitive instinct".

Ethik: Normally: "ethics"; but "ethic" when Weber is talking about a "scheme of moral
science". See also *sittlich* and *Sitte*.

Evidenz: "Evidentness". The word is not elegant, but it is at least recognized by the OED
(with the sense of "quality or state of being evident; clearness; obviousness; plainness"),
and it preserves a direct link to "evident", which seems a natural translation of the German
evident.

Many other translations of this term have been proposed over the years, including
"verifiable certainty" (Swedberg), "certainty" (Burger) and "evidentiality" (Tribe).

Weber has his own gloss (p. 74n200) on his use of "Evidenz" rather than "Anschaulichkeit"; but that does not seem to speak against "evidentness".

Exemplar: The standard translation here is "specimen". In a few cases, "example" is more appropriate. "Exemplar" has been avoided, as it has the fairly fixed meaning of "model problem" in physics and, not least, because it has apparently been utilized with a special sense in Kuhn's theory of scientific development.

Existenzialurteil: "Existential judgement" seems to be the received English translation of this philosophical term. It has been consistently used here.

Fachdisziplin; fachmäßig; fachlich; fach . . . : These terms have been translated as "specialist/ized" or "professional" (the two most common choices), or as "expert". No attempt has been made to unify the translation, which varies with the context.

faktisch: "Factual" and "in fact" cover most of the cases; but where "faktisch" is opposed to the imaginary, it may be translated as "actual" (cf. "in actual fact").

Färbung: "Colouring" (or "hue"/"tinge") is a natural translation in most cases. In one instance, "aspect" seems to be the only acceptable one.

Formungswollen: One occurrence only (in *Value Freedom)*. Translated as "will to form" on the analogy of "will to art" for *Kunstwollen* (q.v.).

Fühlen: "Feeling" (not "emotion") throughout. See also *Affekt*.

Gattung; gattungsmäßig; Gattungsbegriff: In abstract discussions, "Gattung" is rendered as "genus" (linking it with "generic concept" for "Gattungsbegriff"); in more concrete contexts, as "species" or (once) "category".

Gattungsmäßig: "Generic" throughout; *Gattungsbegriff*: "Generic concept" throughout.

Gattungswesen: There are two aspects to be considered: the "Gattung" ("genus" or "species") and the "Wesen" ("(living) being" or "(usually not living) entity"). Weber uses the term very sparingly, in discussions of the conceptions of Roscher and Knies; and his focus, particularly in the Roscher discussion, is very definitely on the "biological" aspect. The translation is therefore "generic being", rather than the more biologically neutral "member of a species".

Gebilde: The usual translation of "Gebilde" is either "structure" or, in cases where the artificiality of the "Gebilde" is evident, "construct"/"construction". In a few cases, "entity" has seemed more appropriate; and there are single instances of "formation", "configuration" or even "system" (language system).

Gedanke has almost invariably been translated as "idea".

Gedankenbild; Gedankengebilde; gedanklich: "Gedankenbild", which has a sense of "picture in one's mind", has everywhere been rendered as "mental image". ("Intellectual image" will not do, nor will "image in one's mind" or some similar clumsy construction). Constructions with "idea" have been avoided in this connection, except in one case, where "Bild" and "Gebilde" almost seem to fuse, and "idea" fits the context. In *Gedankengebilde*, on the other hand, the emphasis is not on "in one's mind", but on the theoretical/intellectual character of the construct. The term has therefore been consistently translated as "theoretical/ intellectual construct", except in one case, where the diffuseness of the "construct" seemed to point to "mental construct" as a more appropriate rendering. *Gedanklich* is a difficult term. It has zones of contiguity with "geistig", and, as with that term, context must decide what translation is the most appropriate. "Intellectual" in many cases turns out to be the best solution. In a number of other cases, particularly when there is an explicit or implicit distinction between theory and substance, or theory and reality, "theoretical" seems to work better. When Weber is dealing with the implications of a normative proposition, "logical" sometimes seems more natural than "theoretical". Occasionally, yet other translations suggest themselves: "conceptual" and even, now and then, "mental" or "in . . . mind" – which otherwise fall within the ambit of "geistig".

Gefühl; gefühlsmäßig: "Feeling" and "emotion" share most of the – fairly wide – field, with "feeling" tending to be used for the more structured aspects of the "Gefühl". Occasionally, "sentiment" is more appropriate. When Weber is discussing the "heuristisches Gefühl" of the historian, it is tempting to use "feel" instead of "feeling", whenever this cannot be misunderstood.

Gefühlsinhalt: Rare. "Emotional content" or "content of feelings/sentiments".

Geist is less of a problem than one would think. In some cases, "spirit" is entirely appropriate in English. In others, "mind" or "intellect" remain true to the sense of the German text, and this is also true in isolated cases where other translations ("inspiration"; "thinker") have been used.

Geisteswissenschaften: This is a classic conundrum, and no ideal solution can be found. After very careful consideration, the translation chosen is that of "sciences of the human spirit". When one considers the contexts in which Weber uses the term, it is clear that a construction is needed which, like the German term, includes an *object*. "Humanities" therefore does not fit (it also has too many "institutional" connotations). "Human sciences" – which would do nicely as a counterpart to "natural sciences" – has to be eliminated for the same reason. On the other hand, "sciences of the mind" represents an unwanted step in the direction of psychology; and "sciences of the spirit" sounds odd. "Sciences of the human spirit" combines the object and at least an echo of the distinction "human/natural"; it also has the advantage of containing the direct translation of the German term ("spirit").

geistig is more difficult than *Geist*. It occurs quite frequently, and in contexts that make a consistent translation impossible. "In . . . mind" or "of . . . mind" has often proved to be a serviceable translation, "mental" less often so. In a number of cases, "intellectual" is the obvious choice. "Spiritual" in fact turns out to be a kind of residual category where the other possibilities mentioned are not appropriate. Occasionally, but only reluctantly, "spiritual and intellectual" has been used to make sure that both aspects (the "creative" and the "rational") are covered. Twice (in connection with "culture"), "non-material" has seemed to be the most reasonable rendering.

Geltenwollen: One occurrence only. "Claim to validity."

Geltung; gelten; geltend: "Geltung" often means "validity" in a normative sense; but sometimes, the "validity" – unlike "Gültigkeit" (q.v.) – has a more or less pronounced element of "empirical prevalence", and "geltend" has in such cases instead been translated as "dominant" or "prevailing". "Gelten" can be even more "general" and simply mean "be regarded as" or "having the status of".

Gemeinschaft: Very frequent, particularly in *Categories*. "Community." *vergemeinschaften* (no direct entries, but two for *die Vergemeinschafteten*: "the communitized (persons)").

Gemeinschaftshandeln: Since "Gemeinschaft" is rendered as "community", "community action" or "communal action" are the natural candidates. There has to be some sort of symmetry with "Gesellschaftshandeln" (q.v.), which is also solely to be found in *Categories*, and for which "society action" or "societal action" seem to be the best alternatives. It is true that Weber often emphatically delivers himself of the opinion that only individuals can act. But the German terms that he employs here very definitely give the opposite impression, and there is a point in transmitting these instances of Weber's penchant for paradoxical terminology to the English-speaking reader. "Gemeinschaftshandeln" is therefore translated as "communal action" (and "Gesellschaftshandeln" as "societal action").

Gemeinsinn: Only in *Roscher* and (once) *Knies I*. "Sense of common good."

generell: "General." See also *allgemein*.

Gesamtanschauung: "Comprehensive intuition."

Gesamterscheinung: "Comprehensive phenomenon."

Gesamtheit: With one or two exceptions, consistently translated as "totality". It shares that translation with "Totalität", which is, however, much less frequent.

Gesamtwesen: Rare. "Total entity."

Geschehen: A portmanteau, NT term, broadly covering "what happens". "Events", "course (of events, of history)" or "occurrences" have all been frequently used as translations.

Gesellschaft: "Society." *Gesellschaftlich*: In *Categories*, "gesellschaftlich" has a definite systematic and T character, and is therefore in that essay translated as "societal" (in order to avoid confusion with "social" as a translation of the – occasionally occurring – "sozial"). In the other essays, the considerations underlying the translation of "gesellschaftlich" are different: Weber, in more than one passage, treats "gesellschaftlich" and "sozial" as quite parallel, if not identical, terms; and here, "gesellschaftlich" has therefore generally been translated as "social" (rather than "societal"). In *Stammler*, however, there is a definite emphasis on the fact that Stammler's concept of "gesellschaftlich" *differs* from "sozial", and in order to bring out this, "gesellschaftlich" has in that connection been translated as "in society".

A number of related terms also only occur in *Categories*: *Gesellschaftshandeln*: "societal action" (see also *Gemeinschaftshandeln*). *Vergesellschaften*: "societize" (mostly occurs in the construction "die Vergesellschafteten" – "the societized persons"). *Vergesellschaftetes Handeln*: "societized action". (Actually, this term only occurs in the definition on p. 282, where it is seen as identical with "Gesellschaftshandeln" ("societal action"). But since Weber uses two terms for making the identification, this construction and the terminological distinction have been retained.)

Gesellschaftswissenschaft(en): "Sciences of society."

Gesetz: "Law."

Gesetzesbegriff occasionally seems to reflect the use of that term in the work of Heinrich Rickert, and is in those cases accordingly translated as "law concept".

Gesetzeswissenschaft: "Science of laws" has been used throughout. It has the advantage of being parallel with "science of reality" for *Wirklichkeitswissenschaft* (q.v.). There is no real danger of confusion with "legal science".

Gesetzlich(keit) is most often used by Weber in parallel with "Gesetzmäßig(keit)" and mostly with an empirical reference. It is translated as "law-like (character)" or by a number of other apposite expressions ("covered by a law" etc.). There are few instances of "normative" "Gesetzlichkeit".

Gesetzmäßig(keit) is a very complicated term in the *Meth. Writings*. This is not the fault of Weber, but of Rudolf Stammler, whose terminological jugglings with it form the core of a whole section in *Stammler*. The central ambiguity is that between the empirical "law-likeness" and the normative "accordance with laws". In *Stammler*, an attempt has been made to vary the translation so that the points made by Weber are illustrated by the terminology. There will therefore be many instances of "law-like (regularity)" (empirical), but also some instances of "accordance with laws" (empirical or normative), and, once or twice, simply "law" (empirical or normative). Apart from the *Stammler* discussion, the term is mostly unproblematical. When used empirically, it is translated as "law-like (regularity)" or – in case of developments – "in accordance with laws".

Gesichtspunkt: An attempt has been made to distinguish between "Gesichtspunkt" ("point of view", "viewpoint", "perspective") and "Standpunkt" ("standpoint"). But Weber uses these terms in a NT sense, and there has been room for corresponding variation in the translations as well.

Gesinnung: "Conviction" in connection with the discussion of "Gesinnungsethik" (in *Value Freedom*) and now and then elsewhere, where appropriate. Otherwise, "disposition" or "mentality".

Gewerbe: A difficult word to render accurately. It oscillates between "trade", "industry" and "business". When it occurs (not often), it must be interpreted according to the concrete context. "Gewerbegericht" is definitely an "industrial tribunal" (for the settlement of conflicts between workers and employers). "Gewerbeverfassung" is an "organization" (in the vague, "framework" sense) of business-in-general. Weber can talk of the ideal type of a "capitalist" Gewerbeverfassung abstracted from certain traits of large-scale industry, but also of a "Schneidergewerbe". All things considered, "organization of trade and industry" probably covers "Gewerbeverfassung" best.

Gewordensein; So-und-nicht-anders-Gewordensein: "Gewordensein", in principle, has a double aspect: how something developed, and what it has now become as a result of that development. Sometimes, it has been possible to render both those aspects ("as it has evolved" or the like); but in some cases, the "developmental" aspect is clearly the dominant one, and the translation "development" seems adequate. *So-und-nicht-anders-Gewordensein* is a classic Weberianism, with only one occurrence. It has been rendered as "as having turned out the way it did and no differently".

Gliederung: Normally "structure"; occasionally "composition" or "organization".

Grenzfall: "Limiting case."

gültig; Gültigkeit: "Valid(ity)" in the strict, "intrinsic" sense, as opposed to the possible wider sense of "Geltung" (q.v.).

Habitus: "Disposition" or "habit of mind".

Handeln: A tentative distinction has been applied between a T and a NT sense of "Handeln". The T sense applies when Weber is discussing conceptual categories, or fundamental concepts, of social action. Here, consistency is essential. However, the "infinitive" version ("acting"), which would ideally be used in order to underline the active character of the word – as opposed to "Handlung" – is really not acceptable as a translation, so the translation has to be "action", in spite of its more "reified" character. In more NT contexts, no consistency has been sought: although "action" will be the most frequent choice, there are also instances where "conduct" or "behaviour" has been used.

Handlung is a more static or reified German word than "Handeln". Therefore, it is often (particularly in the singular) translated as "act". ("Act" has also been used as a translation of "Akt" or "Tat"). But the OED accepts both an "active" and a "static" sense of "action", and when it has seemed appropriate (particularly in the plural forms), "action(s)" rather than "act" has been chosen to render "Handlung(en)".

hantieren is, as such, a fairly "ordinary" word, meaning "handle", "potter around with", "busy oneself with", etc. It is not often met with in *Meth. Writings*. But when it does occur, we either have "hantieren mit" with what seems a definitely pejorative tinge ("shuffle something around aimlessly"); or, in Weber's discussion (in *Stammler*) of the game of skat, the word takes on a definitely T sense, so that "Hantieren" or "Hantierung" is best rendered by "performatory act". (Not "performative", since no speech is involved.)

Hausgemeinschaft: (Only in *Categories*.) "Household community."

Haushalt; haushalten: The traditional translation is "household(ing)", and, in the very few occurrences of the term in the *Meth. Writings*, this translation has been retained, the more so as at least one occurrence is a quotation from Knies, who would hardly have used the term in the more recent sense of "budgetary management".

Heilsbesitz only, in the *Meth. Writings*, occurs in *Science*. Tribe (*Essential Weber*) translates it as "possession of salvation", but this seems to leave out a certain subjective element. What is meant is the *feeling of* possessing salvation, and this is how the term has been translated here.

Hereinragen; Hineinragen: NT. "Project into", "affect", "have relevance for".

Hergang: Like *Vorgang* (with which Weber implicitly equates it on p. 43), "Hergang" can mean both "event" and "process", and performs flexible functions around those ideas. No T translation has been sought for.

Herrschaft: In the *Meth. Writings* (apart from the *Categories* essay), "Herrschaft" hardly ever has the T sense of "domination"/"rule"/"authority", but rather the general one of "dominance" or "predominance"; and those are therefore the English terms usually employed in the translation. In a couple of instances, though (pp. 174 and 394), the sense is the "traditional" one, and the word is translated as "domination". There are also a number of references to Gottl's book "Die Herrschaft des Wortes", which has been translated as "The Dominance of Words". See also *Wortknechtschaft*.

heterogen: The straight one-to-one translation is "heterogeneous". It is debatable whether the consistent adherence to this makes the English text more "academic" and unreadable than necessary, the more so as a large number of alternatives ("intrinsically different", "disparate" etc.) are available. However, "heterogen" has many occurrences and is quite obviously the term of preference for Weber, even in passages where the natural sense would seem less extreme than that implied by "heterogen". There seems to be a point in retaining such idiosyncratic, "extreme" wordings, rather than running the danger of watering down the text in the interests of accessibility. So: "heterogeneous" has been used throughout (with two exceptions, pp. 166 and 324).

hinterweltlich: Two occurrences only, both in *Science*. Probably a loan from Nietzsche, who coined the word, and whose use of it was often pejorative. The reference is to something beyond the real world. In one case, this is rendered as "unreal", in the other as "belonging to a world beyond the real one".

Ich: In *Knies I–II*, "Ich" is used in a T sense (the "I") in a number of cases. It has been translated as I; but as a naked I looks very bare and strange on the printed page, it has, *in this technical function*, always been provided with quotation marks. (In other languages, a capitalization would have done the trick; but this is not feasible in English, where "I" is capitalized in any case.) In many, but not all of the relevant German passages, Weber already puts "Ich" in quotation marks. But it has been done consistently in the English translation, even though this means obscuring a possible differentiation in the text between I with and I without quotation marks.

Idealtypus: "Ideal type." Some translators prefer "ideal-type" (with a hyphen), but this seems to shift the emphasis towards the "ideal" aspect, and thus to increase the possibility of misunderstanding the ideal type as having in any way the character of a normative ideal.

in: Weber often speaks of something "in seiner . . .". There is no single adequate way of dealing with this construction, which is meant to indicate that a certain attribute of something is the focus of attention when we look at that something. Sometimes, "in . . ." is possible; but not always. "With . . ." occasionally seems to work well. In a number of instances, treating the construction as a "concealed genitive" also makes sense. But no consistency has been attempted across the many hundreds of occurrences.

individuell; Individuum: "individual". *Historisches Individuum*: "historical individual". Thus, both the substantive and the adjective share the same translation. Normally, this should not create confusion. But when the adjective is used in a substantivized form ("das Individuelle"), the translation ("the Individual") has been given a capital I in "Individual" to distinguish it from "the individual [person or thing]" as a translation of "das Individuum".

Inhalt; inhaltlich: "Content" is of course often an obvious possibility (for instance in the construction "Begriffsinhalt" = "conceptual content"). But quite frequently, "Inhalt" carries the sense of "substance" and is translated accordingly. In one place (p. 77), "seelische Inhalten" has been translated freely as "mental states".

inhaltsleer: "Void of substance."

Innen: "Internal" and "within" ("von Innen heraus"); *inner:* "inner" whenever the reference is to the opposition "external"/"inner". Elsewhere, "inward" has also been used; *innerlich:* various solutions have been adopted, both "inner", "internal" and "within oneself".

innerweltlich: One occurrence only. "Innerworldly."

Interpretation; interpretieren: This word, which occurs quite frequently, has consistently been translated as "interpret(ation)". It presents no difficulties, and the only reason why it is included in this Glossary is that Weber himself, after having defined in *Critical Studies* the procedure of "Wertinterpretation" (value interpretation), says that he will use the German word "Deutung" instead to describe it. "Deutung" (q.v.) is also translated as "interpretation", but it is noteworthy that there are two separate words in German covering the single English one in this way.

Kathedersozialismus; Kathedersozialist: "Academic socialism"; "academic socialist".

kausal; Kausalität: "causal(ity)"; *kausaler Regressus:* This is standard language for Weber, and an attempt has therefore been made to translate it by "causal regression" wherever possible (although "regression", in modern scientific parlance, has a number of different connotations). But in some cases, "causal regression" works less well, and alternative translations such as "trace back . . . causes" have been used. See also *Ablauf.*

Kausalbedürfnis; kausales Bedürfnis: "Need for [a] causal explanation".

Kausalgesetz: "Law of causality".

Kausalgleichung; -ungleichung: "Causal equation/inequation". See also endnote 54.

Kausalreihe: "Chain of causation".

Körpergefühl: One occurrence only (in *Value Freedom*). "Sense of body."

Kultur: "Culture". *Kulturinhalt:* In the singular: "cultural content"; in the plural: "elements of culture". See also *Kulturmensch* and *Kulturvolk.*

Kulturmensch: "Cultural being".

Kulturvolk; Kulturnation: There are two problems here: "Volk" and "Kultur". "Volk" is consistently rendered as "nation" (see *Volk*). The problem with "Kultur" is that the English language does not readily lend itself to the most natural constructions ("culture nation" or "cultural nation" are no good). Consistency should be sought. There are two ways out: either "civilized", which is not so antithetical to "culture" as it appears, but which does break any link in the text with the term "culture" on its own; or some slightly awkward construction with "culture", of which "nation of culture" and "culturally developed nation" seem to be the most obvious ones. The latter has been chosen.

Kunstlehre: "Doctrine of good procedure".

Kunstwollen: A few occurrences, all in *Value Freedom*. The term may have been borrowed from the Austrian art historian Alois Riegl (see endnote 340), but it is used in a sense different from Riegl's, as the striving of an artist to produce art. Since there is a "standard" translation of Riegl's term as "will to art", this has been retained here, the more so as no obvious alternative presented itself. See also *Formungswollen.*

Lebenseinheit: A term borrowed from Otto Gierke. One occurrence only (in *Roscher*). "Unity of life."

Lebensführung: "Conduct of life" throughout. Tribe notes, in connection with the translation of the *Protestant Ethic*, that this English translation lacks "intensity", compared with the connotations of the German term. This lack does not appear to be so marked in the methodological writings.

Lebensprozeß: Only in *Roscher*, as direct or indirect quotation from Roscher. "Vital process", "process(es) of life", "course of life", according to context.

Leistung covers, as Keith Tribe has said, "a wide range of performative qualities". It does not, in the methodological essays, have a more T sense, except in the *Energetics* essay, where Weber several times refers to "Leistungen" in an "energetical" sense. However, in these cases, and in many of the other occurrences, "achievement" or "performance" cover the sense well, according to context.

letzt: In the sense of "fundamental", "letzt" has been translated as "ultimate" wherever possible, to retain the linguistic flavour of the German term. In *Categories*, though, "fundamental" often seems to be the most natural translation.

Literat: Only two occurrences (in *Value Freedom*). This term has distinct pejorative overtones in Weber's work. The term has been carried directly over into English, as "literati".

Logik; *logisch*: "Logic" and "logical" (or equivalent constructions) throughout.

Mannigfaltigkeit has been consistently translated as "multiplicity", *mannigfaltig* often as "manifold".

massenbedingt: (Only in *Categories*.) "Mass-conditioned."

Maxime: Used – sparingly – as a NT term in the early essays. But, in *Stammler*, it acquires a very specific, T meaning as an imperative of conduct. As such, it is invariably translated as "maxim".

meinen: "Mean", "intend". *Gemeinter Sinn* is a difficult problem for the translator. "Sinn" (q.v.) is normally translated as "meaning". Weber's idea, when speaking of "gemeinter Sinn", is obviously to stress that the meaning is not one applied *by an outside observer* to, for instance, an action: it is the actor's *own* meaning. The usual translation is "intended meaning". But there is a rational (purposive) bias in that translation, since "intention" is often something more than the ascription of a particular "sense" or "meaning". Therefore, the translation of "gemeinter Sinn" will here be the – admittedly unlovely – term "meant meaning", which has the merit of underlining more precisely the implications of the word "gemeint". (It may be noted in this connection that Joseph Schumpeter employs the same translation: "And he [Weber] emerged from gigantic labors with a definite and positive doctrine. The doctrine turns out to be two concepts: The Ideal Type and the Meant Meaning", J. Schumpeter, *History of Economic Analysis*, p. 818.) Occasionally, it is possible to rewrite the sentence so that the construction dissolves into something aesthetically more pleasing.

Mensch: According to context, "man" or "human being"; in the plural: "human beings", "men", "people" or even "persons".

Methode; *Methodologie*; *methodisch*; *methodologisch*: "Methode/Methodik" and "methodisch" occur far more frequently in the *Meth. Writings* than "Methodologie" and "methodologisch". However, when read in their context, there is no doubt that in the overwhelming majority of cases, the terms "methodisch"/"Methode"/"Methodik" have the sense of "methodological/methodology". We are dealing with the *principles underlying* the methods of the social sciences. Strong indirect corroboration of this line of interpretation is found in the fact that Weber himself, writing to his publisher in 1917 about the contents of a projected volume of essays (more or less coterminous with those later collected in *GAW*) uses the term "essays on the methodology (Methodologie) of the social sciences" and, two years later, speaks of these essays as "methodological–logical (methodologisch–logische)". We may safely conclude that, except where "methodisch"/"Methode" must definitely be taken to mean "methodical/method", those German terms may without distortion be translated as "methodological/methodology"; and that Weber's own usage is simply unsystematical. (For an example of this unsystematical usage, see Introduction, p. xxiii). However, in principle, square brackets have always been put around "olog(y)", when "methodisch"/"Methode" is translated as "methodological/methodology".

Methodenstreit: One occurrence only. "Quarrel about methods."

Milieu: May be "environment" or "background", and it is often not easy to discern which of the two aspects is meant. Since "milieu" is a possible translation, this has been preferred – the more so as Weber often puts the word in inverted commas.

mitbedingen: Not many occurrences. "Partly/in part determining" or "contributing" usually covers the logic.

Mittel: Although "Mittel" is very frequent as part of a "Zweck-Mittel" construction, it has not always been translated as "means" – just as "Zweck" has not always been translated as "end" – in both cases because "means" and "end" are "weak" and misunderstandable words as soon as one leaves the specific "means–end" framework. Instead, "instrument" is a frequent translation of "Mittel".

Moment: This word has two entirely separate meanings: (1) "moment" (in time); (2) "factor" or "element". The second one is most frequently relevant.

nachbilden; Nachbildung: Normally "reproduce"/"reproduction". In a few NT cases: "replicate" or "copy".

nacherleben: "Reproduce immediate experience" is the long form, but "re-experience" is a short alternative translation which is usually adopted and works well, without risk of misunderstanding.

Nachfühlen: Only occurs twice. "Reproduction of feelings" would be the long form, but "re-feeling" has been adopted as an adequate short alternative.

Nationalökonomie; Nationalökonomik; Volkswirtschaftslehre; Staatswirtschaftslehre; Volkswirtschaft: "Nationalökonomie" is very common in the *Meth. Writings*, while there are only a few occurrences of "Nationalökonomik". Technically speaking, the "-ik" form should designate the science; but in fact, both terms are used almost interchangeably, and "Nationalökonomie" covers both the practice and the science of economics. Both terms have been consistently translated as "economics". So has "Volkswirtschaftslehre" (few occurrences, and only in quotations from other authors). "Staatswirtschaft" and "Staatswirtschaftslehre" (very few occurrences, only in *Roscher* and as direct or indirect quotations from him) have both been translated as "political economy".

Naturgesetz: Always "law of nature", *not* "natural law" (which would be *Naturrecht*).

Naturvorgang: In the majority of cases, "natural event". But total consistency has not been aimed at, and sometimes the translation is "process of nature", "natural process" or "natural occurrence" – all according to context.

Nebeneinander; Nacheinander: *Nebeneinander* has a variety of translations: "simultaneous(ly)", "concurrent(ly)", "juxtaposed", "parallel". *Nacheinander* is invariably translated as "successive(ly)"/"succession".

Objekt: "Object" – a translation that it shares with "Gegenstand" (which occurs much less often); *objektiv*: "objective" – a translation that has been jealously guarded from occupation by any other German term. *Objektivität*: "Objectivity". For *objektivieren*, the OED gives two possibilities: "objectify" and "objectivize". "Objectify" has a clear sense of "making into an actual object", whereas Weber uses the term in the sense of creating distance between a phenomenon and its conceptualization. Therefore, "objectivize" is preferable, the more so as it seems useful to have isomorphism not only with "objectivity" but also with "subjectivize" and "relativize" (which does not admit "relativify").

offenbar: This may mean either "obvious(ly)" or "apparent(ly)". The choice is not always easy, and may depend on one's estimation of the degree of rhetorical irony involved. On the whole, "apparent(ly)" has often seemed the best translation.

Oktroyierung: "Imposition".

Ordnung: There are few occurrences outside *Categories* (where the term is, on the other hand, quite frequent). They may have different senses: order as opposed to disorder; order as ranking; order as command from above = "Anordnung"; and (social) order. "Order" normally covers all four. (In *Categories*, "order" is sometimes complemented by "instituted", in square brackets, to distinguish it from the order-as-command).

While "Ordnung" will usually have a "static" sense, there may occasionally be a more "active" one, which is translated as "ordering".

orientieren: The obvious translation is "orient". But, in *Categories*, "orientieren an" can be a problem. In many cases, the "orientation" means that the acting person somehow relates his action to something, without specifying whether that "orientation" represents conformity or the reverse. (Indeed, Weber specifically discusses the case of criminals "orienting" themselves towards an established order, not by conforming, but by trying to conceal their crime.) In these cases, "orientieren an" has been translated as "orient towards". But there are instances where the orientation is very definitely meant to represent conformity. In those cases, "orientieren an" has been translated as "orient in accordance with" or "orient according to".

Parallelismus: Normally: "parallelism" (but "parallel" can be perfectly acceptable).

Persönlichkeit: "Personality" has been chosen as the consistent translation, in spite of the fact that "person" might serve equally well in some cases. Weber is quite insistent in his use of "Persönlichkeit" (it occurs much more frequently than "Person" in his writings).

Pflege; *pflegen*:   "Pflegen" is common in Weber's work, usually with a meaning that comes close to "being usual"; the translation follows suit. "Pflege" in the sense of "care" or "cultivation" occurs a few times. Occasionally, it can be left untranslated; occasionally, "deal with" seems strong enough; at other times, "cultivation" or "furtherance" seem appropriate.

Postulat: Has two basic meanings in German: (1) a demand or even commandment, a principle of conduct; (2) a fundamental theoretical principle necessary to some theory, a thesis. The second sense is close to that of "postulate" in English. In practice, the two senses may coalesce. According to context, "demand", "principle", "fundamental principle", "precept", "postulate" or "postulated goal" have been employed as translations.

Problemstellung; *Fragestellung*:   "Problem" and "question", respectively, take care of most of these. "Approach" and "perspective" cover almost all of the rest. "Problematic" as a substantive – a recent academic word formation – has been avoided throughout.

provozieren; *Provokation*:   "Evoke"/"Evocation" (occasionally: "provoke").

Psyche; *psyche*; *psychisch*:   The main choice is "psychic" or "psychical". OED defines them as, essentially, equivalent, but "psychical" has a formal symmetry with "physical", and "psychic" has unwanted associations with the world of spiritualism. Both considerations are relevant here, and "psychical" has therefore been used throughout. There are a few cases where "psychisch" has been translated as "psychological" because the context ("motives", "rational action" etc.) made it clear that the text referred to something more than the merely psychical. On the other hand, "psychisch" has on the whole not been translated as "mental" – in order to reduce possible ambiguity when "mental" is used as a translation of other terms such as "geistig". *Psychologisch* is always rendered as "psychological".

real; *Realität*:   "Real" may, according to context, be translated as "real" or "actual". In cases where there is an affinity to the logic of the "real cause" (see *Realgrund*), "real" is normally preferred. "Realität(en)" is normally translated as "reality"("realities"); but in some cases, where the translation "reality" is "usurped" by "Wirklichkeit", "actuality" (and, once, "substance") have been used instead. See also *Aktualität*.

Realgrund: "Real cause". See also *Erkenntnisgrund*.

Rechtsinstitut: "Legal instrument".

Regel: The sense – and translation – of this word is unproblematical outside the *Stammler* essay. "Rule" covers most cases; where empirical regularity is involved, "regularity" may be employed instead. In large sections of *Stammler*, the whole argument concerns Stammler's confusion between normative rules and empirical regularities. "Regel" may therefore in some cases be translated as "rule" and in others as "regularity", according to the polemical context, and there will be no *terminological* consistency, but hopefully a conformity to the demands of Weber's argument.

Regressus, kausaler: see *kausal*.

Relationsbegriff: "Relational concept".

Rente: In *WG*, Weber regards "Rente" as the "passive" form of interest, contrasted with "profit". However, in the *Meth. Writings*, "Rente" most naturally means "ground rent".

Richtigkeitsrationalität: Only found in *Categories*. Literally, this term translates as "correctness rationality". But this is not the sense; and it can be confidently assumed that Weber uses "Richtig*keit*" because "richtige Rationalität" would be misunderstandable in German ("genuine rationality"). "Richtigkeitsrationalität" has therefore been translated as "correct rationality".

Sache: This term is used in an almost colourless way in the methodological writings, until we come to the "ethical" essays: *Value Freedom* and, above all, *Science*. The "Sache" is here a duty or task to which one should devote oneself without vanity, indeed with humility. It is a term which, in these essays, has a definite sternness about it. It has been translated as "task" or "cause".

sachlich: There is an interesting break in Weber's usage of this term. Until *Value Freedom*, it is normally contrasted with "formal" and therefore appropriately translated as "substantive" or some similar construction. In *Value Freedom*, however, the term is suddenly used with the sense of "cool", "dispassionate", "sober", and is translated accordingly.

Satz: This term has a purely linguistic reference ("sentence") but also a more general, "philosophical" one, which is, according to context, rendered as "thesis", "proposition", "principle" or "statement".

satzen: "Institute". This gives "instituted order" for "gesatzte Ordnung" and the occasional "institution" for the "active" verbal noun (*Satzung*) when no risk of confusion with "institution = Anstalt" exists; the "static" noun *Satzung* is translated as "ordinance".

Schema: A term whose translation is slightly complicated. In a few instances, where the reference to the Kantian notion of "Schema" seems apparent, it is translated as "schema" (the English term is defined in the OED with explicit reference to the Kantian concept). In a number of cases, "scheme" or "conceptual scheme" fits well. Sometimes, "form" or "construction" (as in: "juristisches Schema") is the obvious solution. But now and then, there is a strong case for using either "model" or "system" – both of them almost taboo words because they transport us into the conceptual realm of later sociological thought. If "model" and "system" have nevertheless been accepted in a few instances, the reasoning has been the following: "model" is used when "Schema" refers to rational teleological constructs (in *Knies II*); "system" is acceptable when referring to comprehensive theoretical schemes that Weber is *attacking* ("biologism" and Stammler).

Schicht: Rare. "Stratum."

Seele; *seelisch*:   There is an occasional sense of "soul". Otherwise, "mind"/"mental" is appropriate in most of the cases. Very occasionally, "psychical" or "psychological" seem, from the context, to be the best solution.

Sein: As opposed to "Sollen", "Sein" is "Is" or "what is". Taken by itself, it is "being" or, in certain contexts, "existence".

Selbstsucht: Only in *Knies II*. "Self-seeking."

Setzung: Only in *Knies II*. "Positing."

Sinn: A very important term, with many occurrences. There are two main translations: "sense" (NT; example: "in that sense of the word"), and "meaning". Very occasionally, the context calls for another translation than one of these two (for instance "nature", p. 123, where there is no possibility of ascribing false essence to that term).

sinnhaft; *sinnvoll*:   "Sinnhaft" indicates, in a neutral way, that something has meaning attached to it, but without any necessary (positive) connotation of being "full of" meaning. "Sinnvoll", on the other hand, definitely carries this positive connotation. Since "meaningful" carries the same positive connotation (or at least implies "fullness"), it seems obvious that the main translation of "sinnvoll" has to be "meaningful", and this has been fairly consistently adhered to. (*Sinnlos*, however, calls for a larger variety of translations than just "meaningless", although this – in the sense of "absurd" – has been the translation of choice in many cases.)

  The question then arises how to deal with "sinnhaft". First, it should be noted that this word is most frequently found in *Categories*, whereas "sinnvoll", on the other hand, *never* occurs in that essay. It might therefore be possible to translate "sinnhaft", like "sinnvoll", as "meaningful", and, in fact, this has been done by a previous translator. But, in terms of actual sense, "meaningful" is not a precise rendering of "sinnhaft", which is, moreover, such a central term in *Categories* that it seems to need a separate translation.

  The best solution seems to be "meaning-related", which (1) is reasonably precise, and (2) cannot reasonably be taken as being the translation of any other German term. Therefore, "meaning-related(ness)" will be used as a translation of "sinnhaft"/"Sinnhaftig-keit", whenever appropriate, in *Categories* (and in one or two instances in *Value Freedom*).

sinnlich: Rare (in *Knies II*, and once in *Adolf Weber*). As the *Knies II* occurrences are direct references to Husserl, the word should probably not be regarded as "indigenous" in Weber's methodology. The standard Husserl translation is "sensuous", and this has been adopted here as well. "Sinnlich-anschaulich" in *Adolf Weber* smacks so strongly of Husserl that the Husserlian terminology has been extended to that passage as well.

Sitte: The term has a wide reference, not only to morals (see *sittlich*) but also, more generally, to manners, customs and good behaviour. The usual translations are: "morals" or "manners and customs".

sittlich: "Ethisch" and "sittlich" should in principle be distinguished so that "ethisch" is "ethical" and "sittlich" is "moral". There may not be that much difference between them, however, as actually used by Weber (which is natural, since, in philosophical parlance, it is obvious that "moral" can cover at least part of what we would normally call "ethical"). Therefore, there may be an occasional divergence from the principle mentioned above.

"small words":   An effort has been made to translate all of these words, even though they sometimes represent little more than rhetorical tics on Weber's part. They do have an important function in situating the phrase in the context of the general argument and calibrating it. Individual words: *aber*: "but", "however" – or nothing; *also*: "thus" – but very often this word introduces a summing-up, and is rendered by ": in other words" or ": that is to say"; *denn*: it is a great pity that English has nothing better than "for" or "since" to offer as a translation of this exceedingly common conjunction. "For" often leads to misunderstanding, and has largely been ignored. In many cases, "denn" can be rendered by a colon. Occasionally, the whole sentence has been turned upside down to make sure that the logic is expressed properly. And sometimes, "denn" has had to be simply ignored, if the sense did not seem to suffer; *doch*: Often "surely" or "after all"; sometimes, it has been difficult to find a separate word for it; *eben*: Often: "precisely". Sometimes: "even". Italicizing the relevant word might give the sense of "eben", but this solution would be impractical in texts so strongly marked by Weber's own habit of italicizing words. *etwa*: often "say", sometimes "for example"; sometimes simply ignored; *freilich*: "though", "admittedly", "of course", "it is true", etc.; *hier*: often "here", but sometimes "in this context"; *ja*: indicates that something is taken as already given or obvious. "After all" sometimes gives the sense, but there is no standard solution; *so*: quite frequently functions and is translated like *also*; *zwar*: "although", "true", "admittedly" or other words indicating the restriction implied.

Sollen; *Seinsollen(d)*:   The consistent translation of "Sollen" is "Ought". In certain cases, however, when Weber is talking about the "Gelten-Sollen" of juridical norms, "ought to be valid" would give a rather too wistful impression ("ought to . . . but isn't"). In those few cases, it has been replaced by "should be valid". "Seinsollen" is translated as "ought to be/happen".

sozial; *sozialpolitisch*; *sozialpsychisch*; *sozialpsychologisch*; *sozialanthropologisch*; *sozialwissenschaftlich*: "Sozial" is translated as "social". For the composites, the following general principle has been applied: When the second part of the composite has the first part as its object or is an aspect of it (as in "sozialpsychologisch" or "sozialwissenschaftlich"), a composite translation is avoided in favour of rewrites like "in the field of . . .". The same holds for composites with "-politisch" where the first part is an area of policy, as in "sozialpolitisch". In other cases – such as "sozialpsychisch" and "sozialökonomisch" – the composite form is carried over into the translation, with or without a hyphen.

Sozialökonomik; *sozialökonomisch*:   This term originated in France and became part of German terminology towards the middle of the nineteenth century. Around 1900, it was current as an alternative designation of what might otherwise have been called "Volkswirt-schaftslehre", and with a similarly general sense of "economics" or "political economy". In the *Meth. Writings*, Weber above all uses it in the *Objectivity* essay, but certainly not to the same extent that he uses "(National)ökonomie" with its verbal derivatives both in *Objectivity* and in the other essays. According to Richard Swedberg, there is a tendency for the term to be used when Weber is talking of a complex of disciplines comprising (theoretical) economics, economic history and economic sociology, the reason being that the *social* aspect is stressed more strongly than in "Nationalökonomie".

K. Borchardt notes that the sense in which "Sozialökonomik" is used by Weber is not consistent. This may be seen as an argument for varying the translation, according to the interpretation of the term in the concrete context. However, it is also possible to see the inconsistency as an argument for keeping to a consistent translation, as this will enable the English-speaking reader to discuss meaningfully the question of the interpretation of the term, which is, in any event, significant as an indication of the thrust of Weber's interests. "Sozialökonomik/isch" has therefore been consistently translated as "social economics" and "social–economic". ("Socio-economic" would have been highly misleading.)

spezifisch: An attempt has been made to translate "spezifisch" consistently as "specific" and, at the same time, wherever possible, to avoid "specific" as a translation of other German words like "bestimmt".

Staatslehre: In some cases, "theory of the state" is the obvious choice. In others, alternatives might be considered ("political theory", "political science"), but, as there is no single instance where "theory of the state" will not fit as well, that translation has been used consistently.

Stand: Only five occurrences altogether with the T sense of "status group", plus a few with the uncomplicated NT sense of "stage" or "state".

stecken: "Is" or "is contained" usually cover the general sense; in some other cases, the translation is "delimit", "be stuck" or "be embedded".

steigern; *Steigerung*:   On the whole, this term is used in NT senses, with varying translations as appropriate. In Weber's discussion of the ideal type, however, there is an element of "technicality" in the use of "steigern", which in these instances has been rendered by "accentuation" (since Weber is describing a "Steigerung" of certain conceptual elements).

Stellung nehmen: This means "take a stand" or "adopt a position". In general, it is NT. But Weber devotes some care to the discussion of the term in connection with his treatment of Münsterberg in *Knies I* – where it is translated as "take a stand"; and the Münsterberg discussion seems to influence Weber's use of the term in general, so the slightly dramatic version "take a stand" has been adopted in many other places. In *Science*, however, the colloquial style often calls for less drama. See also *aktuell*.

Stimmung: Quite variable, and wholly NT: "mood", "atmosphere", "sentiment", "spirit", "climate of opinion".

Streben: Often "striving", but also "endeavour" or "ambition".

subjektivieren(d):   "Subjectivize/vizing". See *objektivieren*.

suggerieren; *Suggestion*:   "Suggest" (and in one instance "call forth") are acceptable translations, both in the more general sense of the terms and in the more T one associated with the discussion of "suggestive" historical accounts in *Knies II* . Outside these T instances, there is often a distinct sneer in Weber's use of the term – he much prefers the open stand to the "suggestive" one.

Tatbestand: The dictionary alternatives are: "state of affairs", "circumstances", "facts". All of these have been used, but often the reference is to a "situation" or to "phenomena", so the translations vary, although the sense is usually quite clear.

tot: "Tote Natur" – "inanimate nature".

Tragweite: "Scope", when used of concepts or the like; otherwise, "significance" or "importance" – the choice being made much along the lines of the different translations of "Bedeutung" – or, quite often, "implications".

Trieb: Basically, it would have been nice to have a consistent translation of "Trieb" as "instinct". In many cases, this also turns out to be possible. But sometimes, the "Trieb" seems a little too complex to be a simple "instinct", and in those cases, "driving force" has been preferred. The same holds for instances where the "Trieb" has elements of rational calculation in it (the economic "Trieb").

Triebfeder: "Driving force".

Tun: Translations range over the whole spectrum of action, from "conduct" (rarely) to "behaviour", "actions" and "activities".

überindividuell: "Supra-individual".

übersinnlich: "Unworldly".

Umfang: For concepts: "scope".

unbefangen; Unbefangenheit: "Impartial(ity)", "unbiased", "unprejudiced" and the like; also, in one or two instances, "free" and even "haphazard" (which is covered by the dictionary).

ungeschieden; Ungeschiedenheit: The term has two aspects: "inseparability" and "indistinctness". For the first aspect, the translations are "inseparably" and "jointly", shading over via "undifferentiated" into "indistinctness" for the second one.

universell: "Universal". See also: *allgemein*.

unmittelbar: "Immediate" is the standard translation.

Unterlassung: "Omission" or "refraining from".

Ursache; ursächlich: "Cause"; "causal"; often used by Weber for concrete causes of events, especially historical ones.

Urteil: In order to retain the conceptual link with neo-Kantian terminology, this term is in principle consistently translated as "judgement", even where the context may lead to some linguistic awkwardness.

Verband: Apart from *Categories*, only two, NT, occurrences (of which one is a quotation from Gierke). The "general", NT sense is "group" or "grouping" – the latter being best adapted to Gierke's very broad scope.

In the T sense in which "Verband" is found (very frequently) in *Categories*, other translators have often translated it as "grouping". However, since "Verband" is frequently used in *Categories* as a loose substitute for "Verein" ("association"), the "association/Verein" terminology has in the *Meth. Writings* been combined with the "grouping" terminology into the translation: "associative grouping", which is used throughout. *Verbandshandeln* accordingly translates as "associative group action", and *verbandsmäßiges Einverständnis* as "associative group consensus".

Verein: "Association".

Vergemeinschaftung is only, and infrequently, found in *Categories*. There is a question of principle as to whether the processual aspect of "-ung" is strong enough to be expressed in the translation, at least in certain cases. But the context shows that the "static" aspect is predominant in all cases. Hence: "Communal relationship".

Vergesellschaftung: Very frequent in *Categories*, but rare elsewhere. In *Categories*, "Vergesellschaftung" has been translated as "societization". It is debatable whether there should be a differentiation in the translation according to whether the sense of "Vergesellschaftung" is processual rather than structural. However, the line is difficult to draw in the concrete instance, and "societization" has therefore been adopted throughout. Other related terms are also confined to *Categories*: *Gelegenheitsvergesellschaftung*: "occasional societization". *Vergesellschaftungshandeln*, according to Weber's definition, designates the action *constituting* the societization. It has therefore been translated not as "societal action" but as "societizational action".

The five non-*Categories* occurrences are NT, and three of them are indirect quotations from Ostwald, who uses the term simply for the evolution towards the creation of society. There is some merit in avoiding the T term "societization" in these NT cases, in order to avoid the impression that we are dealing with the same strictly defined reference as in *Categories*. Instead, "Vergesellschaftung" has been translated as "collective (societal) association" in the Ostwald passages, and "establishment of social relations" in the *Roscher* context.

Verhalten: No attempt has been made to distinguish systematically between "behaviour" and "conduct", even in the *Stammler* essay, which has a very large number of occurrences of "Verhalten". However, whenever there seems to a more rational or general sense to "Verhalten", "conduct" has been preferred to "behaviour". For machines, "Verhalten" is translated as "performance". *Sich-Verhalten* (or *Sichverhalten*), which is quite frequent in *Categories*, indicates both more "active" and more "passive" stances, "inner" as well as "external" ones. "Attitude" has therefore been used to translate "Sich-Verhalten" in a number of cases. Otherwise, both "conduct" and "behaviour" may be appropriate translations of "Sich-Verhalten", according to context.

Verhältnis: "Relation" and "relationship".

Verkehr; Verkehrswirtschaft: *Verkehr* has a central conceptual core of "dealings"/"transactions"/ "contacts", but may demand quite different specifications in the individual instances. "Transactions" has been used in economic contexts, "intercourse", "contacts" and "dealings" in social ones. The translation of *Verkehrswirtschaft* has been much discussed. "Economy of exchange" has been proposed, but other translators prefer "market economy", which has also been adopted here.

Vernunft; vernünftig: "Reason(able)". Weber is very sparing in the use of these terms. In fact, "Vernunft" only occurs in references to Kant's *Critiques* (and in a Roscher quotation).

verständlich: "Understandable", and quite often "intelligible", whenever "understandable" would give rise to misunderstanding.

verstehen; Verstehen: This is a central term, and it is crucial to get the translation right and to be clear about the reasons behind it. The "obvious" translation is "understand(ing)", and this has been consistently adhered to.

One major exception to this, however, is the composite term *verstehende Soziologie*, which is so to speak constitutive for *Categories* – indeed for Weber's sociology as a whole. Here, "understanding" becomes unwieldy and may give rise to misunderstanding and misreading, and the "traditional" way of dealing with "verstehende Soziologie" is therefore to translate it as "interpretive sociology". This solution is understandable: In *Categories*, sociology is "verstehend", but the human behaviour which is its object is described as "verständlich deutbar", so that "deuten" and "verstehen" are brought together in a kind of methodological amalgam. There would therefore seem to be no obstacle to translating "verstehende Soziologie" as "interpretive sociology". Admittedly, at the start of *Categories*, there is a definite sequentiality in the procedure: first, one "deutet" ("interprets"), and by that means, one acquires "Verständnis" ("understanding"), but this should not in itself constitute an obstacle, since "deuten" seems to be more or less a *necessary* means of obtaining that "Verständnis".

Nevertheless, careful thought has here been given to the possibility of *avoiding* "interpretive sociology" as the rendering of "verstehende Soziologie", precisely because any deviation from the consistency in translating "verstehen" as "understand", and – to take the other half of the problem, so to speak – "deuten" as "interpret", muddies the waters. There will be places where Weber speaks of "verstehen" – in the sense of "understanding" – as being somehow connected with "verstehen" in "verstehende Soziologie", or vice versa. If "interpretive sociology" is chosen as the translation of "verstehende Soziologie", the English-speaking reader will not be able to make that connection. However, no other acceptable solution seems to be available. (The translation by Parsons of *WG* is inconsistent and unsatisfactory in this respect.) But great care has been taken in ensuring that *everywhere else*, the situation is quite clear. Thus, "understand" *always* goes back to "verstehen", and "interpret" *always* goes back to "deuten", *except* in the case of the term "interpretive sociology", which *always* goes back to "verstehende Soziologie" (as do "related" usages such as "interpretive sciences" or "interpretive psychology"). In the – relatively few – other cases of "verstehend" in Weber's methodological works, other translations than "interpretive" have been chosen ("by", "by means of" or something similar).

It should be noted, incidentally – and this may almost be a separate argument in favour of "interpretive sociology" as the translation of "verstehende Soziologie" – that "deuten" "thins out", and in fact almost disappears in its more T applications, after 1907–08. Thus, by the time *Categories* is published, the field has so to speak been cleared for "interpretive" getting a new meaning. *Nowhere* in *Categories* will the reader have any cause for confusion: "Interpretive" in that essay *only* goes back to "verstehend", *never* to "deutend".

Verursachung: "Causation". This term has otherwise been reserved for the translation of *Kausalreihe* (q.v.).

verwirklichen; *Verwirklichung*: Consistently: "realize"; "realization".

Volk: The translation of this term into English is always a problem. The most literal translation is "people", but the German term has strong connotations of unity and ethnic essence which are entirely absent from "people"; on the other hand, the English word "people" also carries the weak collateral meaning of "plurality of persons". These difficulties have led a number of translators to leave "Volk" untranslated – a solution that does, on the other hand, seem to over-emphasize the peculiarly German connotations. Instead, the translation "nation" has been adopted here. It is perhaps not ideal, but it has more of the "ethnic" and "unity" connotations. Moreover, it is not uncommon in other contexts (cf. "law of nations" for "Völkerrecht"). Possible confusion with the translation of the German terms "Nation" and "national" is only relevant in a few passages, where constructions have been found to avoid it. *Volkstümlich* (few occurrences) has either been translated as "folk" – as in "folk music" – or (according to the Duden definition; "in seiner Art dem Denken und Fühlen des Volkes entsprechend"/"dem Volke eigen") simply as "national"; *Volksgeist* (few occurrences, all as quotations from Roscher) has been translated as "genius of the nation", and *Volksseele* (few occurrences) as "soul of the nation". *Volksgemeinschaft* (quotation from Savigny) has been rendered as "national community".

Völkerpsychologie: "National psychology".

Voraussetzung: No systematic distinction has been made between "precondition", "presupposition" and "assumption".

Vorgang: This very frequent word has an almost portmanteau function, covering both "process" and "event", indeed, anything that "goes on" ("vor sich geht"). No consistent translation has been applied: the context decides. "Phenomena" may turn out to be the most reasonable solution in some cases. See also *Hergang*.

vorstellen is usually translated as "imagine" or "conceive"; in connection with the T sense of "Vorstellung", it is translated as "represent". "Sich-Vorstellen" (two occurrences only) has been rendered as "visualization".

Vorstellung has a general, NT, sense of "idea", and this is the general translation. In one T case (in *Knies II*), the translation is "representation".

wahrnehmen; *Wahrnehmung*: "Perceive/perception" throughout.

wahrscheinlich; *Wahrscheinlichkeit*: "Probable" and "probability". See also *Chance*.

Wechselwirkung; *-beziehung*: "Interaction" and "interrelation".

Weltanschauung: "world view".

Wendung: There is a linguistic sense ("formulation", "phraseology") and a more abstract one, which is translated as "way", "version" and, occasionally, as "aspect".

Werden (substantive):   "Coming into being"; "development"; "evolution". *Werdend*:   In the substantive form, most often "coming into being"; also "emergent", "what will happen".

Wert: "Value".

Wertung: Wertung is almost invariably translated as "valuation". There is a choice here between "valuation" and "evaluation", but the OED definitely gives its preference to "valuation" in this sense ("appreciation or estimation of anything in respect of excellence or merit"). *Werten* is accordingly translated as "valuate" (or "perform a valuation"), and *Wertungs-* as "valuational" or "valuative". However, we also have *bewerten/Bewertung*, which is in many cases in German somewhat closer than "werten"/"Wertung" to "evaluate" and has therefore been translated by "evaluate" (or, occasionally, "judge"). There may be occasional inelegancies brought about by this consistency (Weber sometimes uses "Werten" and "Bewerten" as interchangeable terms). But it has been adhered to, with very few exceptions where the context obviously dictated a departure from it. *Werturteil* is always "value judgement"; *Wertbeurteilung* (three occurrences only): "evaluative judgement"; *Wertbeziehung* (a central term in the early essays): "value relation"; *Wertbezogenheit* (one occurrence only): "Value relatedness".

Wesen; wesentlich: Weber is an "anti-essentialist", and the translation of *Wesen* as "essence" has therefore on the whole been restricted to cases where he is quoting other authors for whom that "essentialism" would be natural. Otherwise, "nature" has normally been chosen for *Wesen* in that sense. (There is of course also the sense of *Lebewesen*: "living creature"). *Wesentlich* is often translated as "important", but also, when the context permits it, as "in essence" or (in *Roscher* in particular) "essential(ly)" (and occasionally as "significant").

Willkür; willkürlich: "Arbitrariness", "arbitrary".

wirken; Wirken; wirksam; Wirksamkeit: Although it might be said that "Wirken" has a T flavour in some of Weber's accounts of the emanationist or essentialist thought of others, it does not seem necessary or warranted to try to look for consistency in translation. Context leads one to employ a large variety of terms ("act", "have/take effect", "be effective" etc.).

Wirklichkeit; wirklich: The normal translation is "real(ity)". See also *Erkenntnisgrund* and *real*.

Wirklichkeitswissenschaft: "Science of reality".

Wirtschaften: Two occurrences only. "Act economically."

Wissen: "Knowledge" and, in one instance as opposed to "Wissenschaft": "information".

Wissenschaft: In German, the term can refer to any organized and systematic academic study. In spite of the fact that the reference of the English term "science" is narrower, it has been used throughout as a translation of "Wissenschaft", with occasional variations ("scholarship", "study", etc., as appropriate). *Einzelwissenschaft*: "specialized science".

Wollen: This is different from "the will" (in one instance, "Freiheit des Wollens" has also been distinguished from "Freiheit des Willens"). "Willing" is unfortunately only rarely an acceptable translation, if only because of the risk of misunderstanding. Instead, "volition" has been used for the more theoretical contexts, and "striving" for the less T ones. (But see *Kunstwollen* and *Formungswollen*).

Wortknechtschaft (a Gottl coinage):   One occurrence only (in a letter). "Servitude to words." See also *Herrschaft*.

Würdigung; würdigen: Only a few occurrences. A NT sense ("estimate" or "appreciate"), plus a T use in *Knies I* (together with *Einfühlung, Nacherleben* and the like), where the translation is consistently "appreciation".

zerfällend: One occurrence only (in *Roscher*). "Analytically."

zerlegen; Zerlegung: "Break down", "subdivide", "reduce (to components)". Also, occasionally, "analyse" or "analyse in terms of".

zitieren: May mean either "refer to" or "quote", according to context.

Zufall; Zufälligkeit; zufällig: In the larger number of cases, "chance" seems to be the most adequate translation (see also *Chance*). This is the case, in particular, with the discussion of the role of "chance" in history, and of games of chance, in *Critical Studies*. Other choices have been: "accidental" and "fortuitous", as well as "contingent" and "incidental". The individual decisions have been taken on grounds of context and style, with "incidental" and "contingent" being the terms of choice when there is an element of the "non-essential" in "Zufall"/"zufällig".

Zumutung; zumuten: Only a few occurrences, but difficult to translate. The dictionary sense (both Grimm and Duden) of *Zumutung* has to do with ascribing or expecting *too much* from somebody. This is clearly not the sense in which Weber normally uses the term (in the one passage in which he does so, "presumption" fits nicely). Instead, what is implied seems to be a strong *expectation* that somebody will do something, an "imperative ascription". In different contexts, this may find expression in different translations: "expectation", "presumption" or "ascription". The term is methodologically important, cf. Weber's letter to Gottl of 28 March 1906 (p. 387).

zunächst: Something of a linguistic tic in Weber's writings, and many occurrences. Indicates some sort of priority, in time or in logic, or simply as a sign that we are starting a new argument. Usually translated by "first", "first of all" or the like.

zurechnen; Zurechnung: There are three possibilities: "impute", "ascribe" and "attribute", with their substantivizations. In the OED, they are more or less defined in terms of each other, and as such seen as equivalent. The first two are perhaps slightly more apposite in a T discussion of causality. The first one, moreover, has a negative tinge (one "imputes" crimes and faults), and, by implying guilt, also implies motivation. "Zurechnen" has etymological links with "impute", and has a similar negative tinge in German. However, Weber uses it in contexts where motivation is lacking. There is an important point here: Weber applies to the analysis of historical causation the legal reasoning apportioning guilt and responsibility; and, in so doing, he employs a term that, as is so usual with him, "goes against the grain" of its etymological logic, since guilt or responsibility is not relevant in the case of the establishment of empirical causes. "Impute" is therefore used for "zurechnen", even when it sounds odd. This line of translation has been adhered to as consistently as possible. Whenever a relationship of attribution is designated by some other verb or substantive than "zurechnen"/"Zurechnung", however, "impute" is replaced by "attribute" or "ascribe".

Zusammenhandeln: "Joint action".

Zusammenhang is used very widely, not least in *Categories*, and with diverse and sometimes almost impenetrable meanings. "Context" is appropriate when the meaning is "background"; otherwise "interrelation" or "interconnection" (together with "interconnectedness" for "Allzusammenhang"). "Nexus" might be a possible translation in cases where the reference is not to a general background but to a relationship between specific elements that is obviously causal. However, it has not been retained, since it has no acceptable plural, and since Weber himself uses the same word in German in a couple of cases ("Kausalnexus"), and it is preferable, when possible, to reflect his own choice of terms. See also *Allzusammenhang*.

Zusammenleben: "Life in common".

Zusammensein: "Existence in common".

zuständlich; *Zuständlichkeit*: Rare and – as far as "Zuständlichkeit" is concerned – archaic or philosophical (Husserl describes "Zuständlichkeit" as "a phase in some changeable being"). The reference is obviously "Zustand", and "state" or "static" is an appropriate translation in some cases. "Existing" has been used in other instances.

Zwangsapparat: "Coercive apparatus".

Zweck; *Ziel*: The normal translation of "Zweck" is "purpose". But in many cases, "goal" or "end" ("Zweck"– "Mittel" translates as "ends"– "means") is more appropriate. "Ziel" is normally "goal", but, again, "end" or "purpose" may, according to the context, be more appropriate.

zweckmäßig; *Zweckmäßigkeit*: A number of translations are possible, according to context: "suitable", "convenient", "appropriate", "useful", "expedient", "effective" (for card players). Also, occasionally, "purposive" (see *zweckvoll*).

zweckrational; *Zweckrationalität*: Only found in *Categories*. "Purposively rational" and "purposive rationality" throughout. (Other translators often use "instrumentally rational"/"instrumental rationality", but this concentrates too narrowly on the means–end aspect of *zweckrational*, ignoring the wider, purposive implications.)

Zwecksystem: "Purposive system".

Zweckverein: "Purposive association".

Zweckvermögen: "Purposive assets".

zweckvoll: In accordance with OED, "zweckvoll" has been translated as "purposeful" when the intention is obvious from the context, but as "purposive" when the "functional" or "appropriateness" aspect is dominant.

zwingen: "Compel" is the most usual translation; others are "constrain", "bind" and "lead with necessity".

BIBLIOGRAPHY

The bibliography covers all books and articles mentioned or quoted in the main text (with the exception of a few purely literary references), but not necessarily all those quoted in the endnotes. When no reference to a specific edition is given or intended by Weber, the reference in the Bibliography is to the first or to a standard edition of the work in question.

Each entry comprises:

- the full relevant bibliographical reference;
- the English translation of the title (if the work is in a foreign language);
- the short reference, in italics (preceded by "Q:") for quotation in the main text.

Where the Bibliography contains more than one work by the same author, the works of that author are ordered alphabetically according to the first word of the short reference.

Adair-Toteff, Christopher, "Max Weber as Philosopher: The Jaspers–Rickert Confrontation", *Max Weber Studies* 3 (2002), pp. 15–32.
Q: Adair-Toteff, *Confrontation*

Adler, Max, "Kausalität und Teleologie im Streite um die Wissenschaft", in: Adler/Hilferding, *Marx Studien. Blätter zur Theorie und Politik des wissenschaftlichen Sozialismus*, Vol. 1 (1904), pp. 193–433.
("Causality and teleology in the dispute about science")
Q: Adler, *Causality and Teleology*.

Adler, Max and Hilferding, Rudolf (eds), *Marx-Studien. Blätter zur Theorie und Politik des wissenschaftlichen Sozialismus*, Vol.1 (1904).
("Marx studies")
Q: Adler/Hilferding, *Marx Studies*.

Des Aristophanes Werke. 3 Theile (ed. Gustav Droysen), Berlin: Veit & Comp. 1835, 1837, 1838.
Aristotle, *Politics* (tr. H. Rackham), Cambridge, MA: Harvard University Press, 1944.
Q: Aristotle, *Politics*.

v. Baer, Karl Ernst, *Über die Entwickelungsgeschichte der Thiere I-II*, Königsberg 1828–37.
("On the developmental history of animals")
Q: Baer, *History*.

Baier, Horst, "Die Gesellschaft – ein langer Schatten des toten Gottes", *Nietzsche-Studien* 10–11 (1982), pp. 1–22.
("Society – a long shadow of the dead God")
Q: Baier, *Society*

v. Below, Georg, "Die neue historische Methode", *Historische Zeitschrift* 81 (1898), pp. 193–273.
("The new historical method")
Q: Below, *Method*.

Bernheim, Ernst, *Lehrbuch der Historischen Methode und der Geschichtsphilosophie*, Leipzig: Duncker & Humblot, 1894.
("Textbook of historical method and philosophy of history")
    3rd/4th edition 1903.
    Q: Bernheim, *Historical Method*³.

Biermann, Wilhelm Eduard, "Natur und Gesellschaft", *Jahrbücher für Nationalökonomie und Statistik* 82 (1904), pp. 681–87.
("Nature and society")
Q: Biermann, *Nature and Society*.

Biermann, Wilhelm Eduard, "Sozialwissenschaft, Geschichte und Naturwissenschaft", *Jahrbücher für Nationalökonomie und Statistik* 83 (1905) pp. 592–613.
("Social science, history and natural science")
Q: Biermann, *Social Science*.

Biermann, Wilhelm Eduard, "W. Wundt und die Logik der Sozialwissenschaft", *Jahrbücher für Nationalökonomie und Statistik* 80 (1903), pp. 50–64.
("W. Wundt and the logic of social science")
Q: Biermann, *Wundt*.

Binding, Karl, *Die Normen und ihre Übertretung*, Leipzig: Engelmann, 1872.
("The norms and their violation")
Q: Binding, *Norms*.

Boeckh, August, *Encyklopädie und Methodologie der philosophischen Wissenschaften* (ed. Ernst Bratuscheck), Leipzig: B.G. Teubner, 1877.
("Encyclopedia and methodology of the philosophical sciences")
Q: Boeckh, *Encyclopedia*.
    2nd edition 1886.

v. Böhm-Bawerk, Eugen, *Rechte und Verhältnisse vom Standpunkte der volkswirtschaftlichen Güterlehre*, Innsbruck: Wagner, 1881.
("Rights and relationships from the standpoint of the economic theory of goods")
Q: Böhm-Bawerk, *Rights and Relationships*.

v. Bortkievicz, Ladislaus, "Die erkenntnistheoretischen Grundlagen der Wahrscheinlichkeitsrechnung", *Jahrbücher für Nationalökonomie und Statistik* 72 (1899), pp. 332–49.
("The epistemological foundations of probability calculus")
Q: Bortkievicz, *Epistemological Foundations*.

v. Bortkievicz, Ladislaus, "Die Theorie der Bevölkerungs- und Moralstatistik nach Lexis", *Jahrbücher für Nationalökonomie und Statistik* 82 (1904), pp. 230–54.
("The theory of demographic and moral statistics according to Lexis")
Q: Bortkievicz, *Theory of Statistics*.

Brentano, Lujo, *Die Entwicklung der Wertlehre*, München: Verlag der Akademie, 1908.
("The development of value theory")
Q: Brentano, *Value Theory*.

Breysig, Kurt, "Die Entstehung des Staates aus der Geschlechterverfassung bei Tlinkit und Irokesen", *Jahrbuch für Gesetzgebung, Verwaltung und Volkswirtschaft im Deutschen Reich* 28 (1904), pp. 483–527.
("The genesis of the state from the kinship constitution among the Tlinkit and Iroquois")
Q: Breysig, *Genesis*.

Breysig, Kurt, "Einzigkeit und Wiederholung geschichtlicher Tatsachen", *Jahrbuch für Gesetzgebung, Verwaltung und Volkswirtschaft im Deutschen Reich* 28 (1904), pp. 1–45.
("Uniqueness and repetition of historical facts")
Q: Breysig, *Uniqueness*.

Bruun, Hans Henrik, *Science, Values and Politics in Max Weber's Methodology*, London: Ashgate, 2007.
Q: Bruun, *Methodology*.

Bruun, Hans Henrik, "Weber on Rickert. From Value Relation to Ideal Type", *Max Weber Studies* 1 (2001), pp. 138–60.
Q: Bruun, *Rickert*.

Bücher, Karl, *Die Entstehung der Volkswirtschaft*, Tübingen: Laupp, 1893.
("The origins of national economy")
Q: Bücher, *Origins*.

Bücher, Karl, "Wilhelm Roscher", *Preußische Jahrbücher* 77 (1894), pp. 104–23.
Q: Bücher, *Roscher*.

Burckhardt, Jacob, *Die Cultur der Renaissance in Italien*, Basel: Schweighauser, 1860.
("The Culture of the Renaissance in Italy")
Q: Burckhardt, *Culture of the Renaissance*.

Calkins, Mary Whiton, *Der doppelte Standpunkt in der Psychologie*, Leipzig: v. Veit & Comp., 1905.
("The double standpoint in psychology")
Q: Calkins, *The Double Standpoint in Psychology*.

Caygill, H. *A Kant Dictionary*, Oxford: Blackwell, 2005.
Q: Caygill, *Dictionary*.

Chwolson, Orest D., *Hegel, Haeckel, Kossuth und das zwölfte Gebot*, Braunschweig: Vieweg, 1906.
("Hegel, Haeckel, Kossuth and the Twelfth Commandment")
Q: Chwolson, *Hegel*.

Croce, Benedetto, *Aesthetik als Wissenschaft des Ausdrucks und allgemeine Linguistik: Theorie und Geschichte*, Leipzig: Seeman, 1905.
("Aesthetics as science of expression and general linguistics: theory and history")
Q: Croce, *Aesthetics*.

Croce, Benedetto, *Lineamenti di una logica come scienza del concetto puro*, Napoli: F. Giannini, 1905.
("Outline of logic as a science of the pure concept")
Q: Croce, *Outline of Logic*.

Defoe, Daniel, *The Life and Strange Surprizing Adventures of Robinson Crusoe, of York, Mariner*, London: Taylor, 1719.
Q: Defoe, *Robinson*.

Dilthey, Wilhelm, "Studien zur Grundlegung der Geisteswissenschaften" in: *Sitzungsberichte der Königlich Preußischen Akademie der Wissenschaften*, Vol. 1, Berlin: Verlag der Königlich Preußischen Akademie der Wissenschaften (1905), pp. 322–43.
("Studies on the foundation of the sciences of the human spirit")
Q: Dilthey, *Foundation*.

Dilthey, Wilhelm, "Die Entstehung der Hermeneutik", in: *Philosophische Abhandlungen. Christoph Sigwart zu seinem 70. Geburtstage 28. März 1900*, Tübingen: J.C.B. Mohr (Paul Siebeck), 1900, pp. 185–202.
("The origins of hermeneutics")
Q: Dilthey, *Hermeneutics*.

Dilthey, Wilhelm, "Ideen über beschreibende und zergliedernde Psychologie", in: *Sitzungsberichte der Königlich Preußischen Akademie der Wissenschaften zu Berlin*, Vol. 2, Berlin: Verlag der Königlichen Akademie der Wissenschaften (1894). pp. 1309–407.
("Ideas concerning descriptive and analytical psychology")
Q: Dilthey, *Ideas*.

Dilthey, Wilhelm, "Beiträge zum Studium der Individualität" in: *Sitzungsberichte der Königlich Preußischen Akademie der Wissenschaften*, Vol. 2, Berlin: Verlag der Königlichen Akademie der Wissenschaften (1896), pp. 295–335.
("Contributions to the study of individuality")
Q: Dilthey, *Individuality*.

Dilthey, Wilhelm, *Einleitung in die Geisteswissenschaften*, Duncker & Humblot, 1883.
("Introduction to the sciences of the human spirit")
Q: Dilthey, *Sciences of the Human Spirit*.

Dippe, Alfred, *Untersuchungen über die Bedeutung der Denkform Idee in der Philosophie und Geschichte* (Dissertation), Jena: Ant. Kämpfe, 1892.
("Investigations concerning the importance of the concept of the idea in philosophy and history")
Q: Dippe, *Investigations*.

Drews, Arthur, "Reinke's 'Einleitung in die theoretische Biologie'", *Preußische Jahrbücher* 116 (1902), pp. 101–20.
("Reinke's 'Introduction to theoretical biology'")
Q: Drews, *Reinke*.

Du Bois-Reymond, Emil, "Naturwissenschaft und bildende Kunst" (1890) in: *Reden*, 2nd ed., Vol. 2, Leipzig: Veit und Comp., 1912, pp. 390–425.
("Natural science and the fine arts")
Q: du Bois-Reymond, *Natural Science*.

Ebbinghaus, Hermann, "Über erklärende und beschreibende Psychologie", *Zeitschrift für Psychologie und Philosophie der Sinnesorgane* 9 (1896), pp. 161–205.
("On explanatory and descriptive psychology")
Q: Ebbinghaus, *Psychology*.

Elsenhans, Theodor, *Die Aufgabe einer Psychologie der Deutung als Vorarbeit für die Geisteswissenschaften*, Gießen: J. Ricker (Alfred Töpelmann), 1904.
("The task of a psychology of interpretation as preliminary work for the sciences of the human spirit")
Q: Elsenhans, *Psychology of Interpretation*.

Eulenburg, Franz, Review of Gottl, *Domination*, in: *Deutsche Litteraturzeitung* XXIV, Nr. 7 (1903), Col. 425–29.
Q: Eulenburg, *Gottl*.

Eulenburg, Franz, Review of Hartmann, *Development*, *Deutsche Literaturzeitung* XXVI, Nr. 24 (1905), Col. 1500–05.
Q: Eulenburg, *Hartmann*.

Eulenburg, Franz, "Neuere Geschichtsphilosophie. Kritische Analysen. I", *Archiv für Sozialwissenschaft und Sozialpolitik* 25 (1907), pp. 283–337.
("The philosophy of history in recent years")
Q: Eulenburg, *Philosophy*.

Eulenburg, Franz, "Gesellschaft und Natur. Akademische Antrittsrede", in *Archiv für Sozialwissenschaft und Sozialpolitik* 21 (1905), pp. 519–55.
("Society and nature. Inaugural lecture")
Q: Eulenburg, *Society*.

Fechner, Georg Theodor, *Elemente der Psychophysik*, Leipzig: Breitkopf und Härtel, 1860.
("Elements of psychophysics")
Q: Fechner, *Psychophysics*.

Fichte, Johann Gottlieb, *Wissenschaftslehre. Fichte Gesamtausgabe I/2*, Stuttgart: Frommann-Holzboog, 1965.
("Theory of Science")
Q: Fichte, *Theory of Science*.

Gerhardt, Ute, *Idealtypus*, Frankfurt: Suhrkamp, 2001.
("Ideal type")
Q: Gerhardt, *Ideal type*.

Gervinus, Georg Gottfried, *Grundzüge der Historik*, Leipzig: Wilhelm Engelmann, 1837.
("Outline of the theory of history")
Q: Gervinus, *Theory of History*.

Ghosh, Peter, "Max Weber, Werner Sombart and the *Archiv für Sozialwissenschaft*: The authorship of the 'Geleitwort' (1904)", *History of European Ideas* 36 (2010), pp. 71–100.
Q: Ghosh, *Authorship*.

Gierke, Otto, *Das Wesen der menschlichen Verbände*, Leipzig: Duncker & Humblot, 1902.
("The nature of human groupings")
Q: Gierke, *Groupings*.

Goethe, Johann Wolfgang v., *Faust* (tr. John Williams), London: Wordsworth, 1999.
Q: Goethe, *Faust*.

Gomperz, Heinrich, Über die Wahrscheinlichkeit der Willensentscheidungen, Wien: Gerold, 1904.
("On the probability of willed decisions")
Q: Gomperz, *Probability*.

Gottl, Friedrich, *Die Herrschaft des Wortes*, Jena: Gustav Fischer, 1901.
("The dominance of words")
Q: Gottl, *Dominance of Words*.

Gottl, Friedrich, *Die Grenzen der Geschichte*, Leipzig: Duncker & Humblot, 1904.
("The limits of history")
Q: Gottl, *Limits of History*.

Hampe, Karl, *Geschichte Konradins von Hohenstaufen*, Berlin: Wagner, 1893.
("History of Conradin von Hohenstaufen")
Q: Hampe, *Conradin*.

Hartmann, Eduard v., *Die Weltanschauung der modernen Physik*, Leipzig: Haacke, 1902.
("The world view of modern physics")
Q: Hartmann, *World View*.

Hartmann, Ludo Moritz, *Über historische Entwickelung*, Gotha: Friedrich Andreas Perthes, 1905.
("On historical development")
Q: Hartmann, *Historical Development*.

Hellpach, Willy, *Grundlinien einer Psychologie der Hysterie*, Leipzig: Engelmann, 1904.
("Fundamental traits of a psychology of hysteria")
Q: Hellpach, *Psychology of Hysteria*.

Hellpach, Willy, *Grundgedanken zur Wissenschaftslehre der Psychopathologie*, Leipzig, 1906.
("Fundamental thoughts on the methodology of psychopathology")
Q: Hellpach, *Methodology of Psychopathology*.

Helmholtz, Hermann, *Über das Verhältnis der Naturwissenschaften zur Gesammtheit der Wissenschaft*, Braunschweig: Fr. Vieweg und Sohn, 1862.
("On the relationship of the natural sciences to science as a whole")
Q: Helmholtz, *Relationship*.

Helmolt, Hans Ferdinand (ed.), *Weltgeschichte I-VIII*, Lepizig/Berlin: Bibliographisches Institut, 1899–1905.
("World history")
Q: Helmolt, *World History*.

Henry, Charles, *Mesure des capacités intellectuelle et énergétique*, Bruxelles/Leipzig: Misch&Thorn, 1906.
("Measurement of intellectual and energetical capacity")
Q: Henry, *Measurement*.

Hettner, Alfred, "Das System der Wissenschaften", *Preußische Jahrbücher* 122 (1905), pp. 251–77.
("The system of sciences")
Q: Hettner, *Sciences*.

Hildebrand, Bruno, *Die Nationalökonomie der Gegenwart und Zukunft*, Vol. 1, Frankfurt a.M.: Literarische Anstalt J. Rütten, 1848.
("Economics of the present and in the future")
Q: Hildebrand, *Economics*.

Hinneberg, Paul, "Die philosophischen Grundlagen der Geschichtswissenschaft", *Historische Zeitschrift* 63 (1889), pp. 18–55.
("The philosophical foundations of the science of history")
Q: Hinneberg, *Foundations*.

Hintze, Otto, "Roschers politische Entwickelungstheorie", *Jahrbuch für Gesetzgebung, Verwaltung und Volkswirtschaft im Deutschen Reich*, N.F. 21 (1897), pp. 767–811.
("Roscher's theory of political development")
Q: Hintze, *Roscher*.

v. Humboldt, Wilhelm, "Über die Aufgabe des Geschichtsschreibers", in: *Abhandlungen der Königlichen Preußischen Akademie der Wissenschaften zu Berlin aus den Jahren 1820–1821*, Berlin: Georg Reimer, 1822, pp. 305–22.
("The historian's task")
Q: Humboldt, *Historian's Task*.

Husserl, Edmund, *Logische Untersuchungen I-II*, Halle a.S.: Max Niemeyer, 1900–01.
("Logical investigations")
Q: Husserl, *Logical Investigations*.

James, William, *The Principles of Psychology*, Boston: Henry Holt, 1890.
Q: James, *Principles*.

Jaspers, Karl, *Allgemeine Psychopathologie*, Berlin: Springer, 1913.
("General psychopathology")
Q: Jaspers, *General Psychopathology*.

Jellinek, Georg, *System der subjektiven öffentlichen Rechte*, Tübingen: J.C.B. Mohr (Paul Siebeck), 1892.
("System of subjective public law")
    2nd edition 1905.
    Q: Jellinek, *System*^{2}.

Jellinek, Georg, *Allgemeine Staatslehre*, Berlin: O. Häring, 1900.
("General theory of the state")
Q: Jellinek, *Theory*.
    2nd edition 1905.
    Q: Jellinek, *Theory*^{2}.

v. Jhering, Rudolf, *Geist des römischen Rechts auf den verschiedenen Stufen seiner Entwicklung*, Leipzig: Breitkopf und Härtel, 1865.
("The spirit of Roman law at various stages of its development")
Q: Jhering, *Spirit*.

Kant, Immanuel, *Anthropologie in pragmatischer Hinsicht*, Akademie-Ausgabe, Vol. 7, Berlin, 1907.
("Anthropology from a pragmatic point of view")
Q: Kant, *Anthropology*.

Kant, Immanuel, *Grundlegung zur Metaphysik der Sitten*, Akademie-Ausgabe, Vol. 4, Berlin, 1903.
("Groundwork of the metaphysic of morals")
Q: Kant, *Metaphysic.*

Kant, Immanuel, *Kritik der Urtheilskraft*, Akademie-Ausgabe, Vol. 5, Berlin, 1908.
("Critique of judgement")
Q: Kant, *Critique of Judgement.*

Kant, Immanuel, *Kritik der praktischen Vernunft*, Akademie-Ausgabe, Vol. 5, Berlin, 1908.
("Critique of practical reason")
Q: Kant, *Critique of Practical Reason.*

Kant, Immanuel, *Kritik der reinen Vernunft*, Akademie-Ausgabe, Vol. 3, Berlin, 1904.
("Critique of pure reason")
Q: Kant, *Critique of Pure Reason.*

Kaulla, Rudolf, *Die geschichtliche Entwicklung der modernen Werttheorien*, Tübingen: Laupp, 1906.
("The historical development of the modern theories of value")
Q: Kaulla, *Historical Development.*

Kautz, Julius, *Theorie und Geschichte der National-Oekonomik*, Wien: Gerold, 1858.
("Theory and history of economics")
Q: Kautz, *Theory and History.*

Kistiakovski, Theodor, "The Russian School of Sociologists and the Category of Possibility in the Perspective of the Social Sciences" in: *Problems of Idealism* (ed. Novgorodzev), Moscow (1902). [Original in Russian.]
Q: Kistiakovski, *School.*

Knies, Karl, *Die politische Ökonomie vom Standpunkte der geschichtlichen Methode*, Braunschweig: C.A. Schwetschke und Sohn (M. Bruhn), 1853.
("Political economy from the standpoint of historical method")
   Q: Knies, *Economy.*
   2nd edition 1883:
   Die politische Ökonomie vom geschichtlichen Standpuncte.
   ("Political economy from the historical standpoint")
   Q: Knies, *Economy².*

Knies, Karl, *Geld und Credit*, Berlin: Weidmann, 1873/79.
("Money and Credit")
Q: *Money and Credit.*

Knies, Karl, Review of Roscher, *System*, *Göttingische gelehrte Anzeigen* 1 (1855), pp. 89–101.
Q: Knies, *Roscher.*

Kraus, Oskar, "Die aristotelische Werttheorie in ihrer Beziehung zu den Lehren der modernen Psychologenschule", *Zeitschrift für die gesamte Staatswissenschaft* 61 (1905), pp. 573ff.
("The Aristotelian theory of value in its relationship to the theories of the modern school of psychology")
Q: Kraus, *Value Theory.*

v. Kries, Johannes, "Über den Begriff der objectiven Möglichkeit und einige Anwendungen desselben", *Vierteljahrsschrift für wissenschaftliche Philosophie* 12 (1888), pp. 179–240, 287–323 and 393–428.
("On the concept of objective possibility and some of its applications")
Q: Kries, *Objective Possibility*.

v. Kries, Johannes, *Die Principien der Wahrscheinlichkeitsrechnung*, Freiburg i.Br.: J.C.B. Mohr (Paul Siebeck), 1886.
("Principles of probability calculus")
Q: Kries, *Probability Calculus*.

Lamprecht, Karl, "Was ist Kulturgeschichte? Beitrag zu einer empirischen Historik", *Deutsche Zeitschrift für Geschichtswissenschaft* 7 (N.F., 1) (1896/97), pp. 75–150.
("What is cultural history? Contribution to an empirical theory of history")
Q: Lamprecht, *Cultural History*.

Lamprecht, Karl, *Deutsche Geschichte*, Berlin and Freiburg i.B.: Hermann Heyfelder/Berlin: Weidmann, 1891–1909.
("German history")
Q: Lamprecht, *German History*.
Ergänzungsbände: Zur jüngsten Deutschen Vergangenheit.
("Supplementary volumes: On the most recent German past").
Erster Ergänzungsband: Tonkunst – Bildende Kunst – Dichtung – Weltanschauung. – Berlin: R. Gaertners Verlagsbuchhandlung, Hermann Heyfelder, 1902.
("First Supplementary Volume: Music; the fine arts; literature; world views")
Zweiter Ergänzungsband, Erste Hälfte: Wirtschaftsleben – Soziale Entwicklung.
Zweite Hälfte: Innere Politik – Äußere Politik. – Freiburg i.Br.: Hermann Heyfelder, 1903, 1904.
("Second Supplementary Volume. First Half: Economic life; social development. Second Half: Domestic policy; foreign policy")
Q: Lamprecht, *German History*, First/Second Supplementary Volume.

Lamprecht, Karl, "Herder und Kant als Theoretiker der Geschichtswissenschaft", *Jahrbücher für Nationalökonomie und Statistik* 69 (1897), pp. 161–203.
("Herder and Kant as theoreticians of historical science")
Q: Lamprecht, *Herder and Kant*.

Lange, Friedrich Albert, *Die Arbeiterfrage* (2nd edition), Winterthur: Bläuler-Hausheer, 1870.
("The labour question")
Q: Lange, *Labour Question*.

Lask, Emil, *Fichtes Idealismus und die Geschichte*, Tübingen/Leipzig: J.C.B. Mohr (Paul Siebeck), 1902.
("Fichte's idealism and history")
Q: Lask, *Fichte's Idealism*.

Liefmann, Robert, *Grundsätze des Volkswirtschaftslehre*, Berlin/Stuttgart: Deutsche Verlagsanstalt, 1917–19.
("Principles of the theory of economics")
Q: Liefmann, *Principles*.

Liefmann, Robert, "Grundlagen einer ökonomischen Produktivitätstheorie", *Jahrbücher für Nationalökonomie und Statistik* 43 (1912), pp. 273–327.
("Foundations of an economic theory of productivity")
Q: Liefmann, *Productivity*.

Liepmann, Moritz, *Einleitung in das Strafrecht*, Berlin: Häring, 1900.
("Introduction to Criminal Law")
Q: Liepmann, *Criminal Law*.

Lindenlaub, Dieter. *Richtungskämpfe im Verein für Sozialpolitik*, Wiesbaden: Steiner, 1967.
("Conflicts between [different] tendencies within the Association for Social Policy")
Q: Lindenlaub, *Conflicts*.

Lipps, Theodor, *Grundlegung der Ästhetik*, Hamburg/Leipzig: Leopold Voss, 1903.
("Foundations of aesthetics")
Q: Lipps, *Foundations of Aesthetics*.

Mach, Ernst, *Die Analyse der Empfindungen und das Verhältnis des Physischen zum Psychischen*, Jena: Gustav Fischer, 1897.
("The analysis of sensations and the relationship between the physical and the psychical")
Q: Mach, *Analysis of Sensations*.

Marx, Karl, *Das Kapital*, MEGA, Vols. 5, 13, 15, Berlin.
("The capital. Critique of the political economy")
Q: Marx, *Kapital*.

Marx, Karl and Engels, Friedrich, *Das Kommunistische Manifest*, Hamburg: Argument, 1999.
("The Communist Manifesto")
Q: Marx/Engels, *Communist Manifesto*.

Meinecke, Friedrich, "Erwiderung", *Historische Zeitschrift* 77 (1896), pp. 262–66.
("Rejoinder")
Q: Meinecke, *Rejoinder*.

Meinecke, Friedrich, "Friedrich Wilhelm IV. und Deutschland", *Historische Zeitschrift* 89 (1902), pp. 17–53.
("Frederick William IV and Germany")
Q: Meinecke, *Frederick William IV*.

Menger, Carl, *Die Irrthümer des Historismus in der Deutschen Nationalökonomie*, Wien: Alfred Hölder, 1884.
("The errors of historicism in German economics")
Q: Menger, *Errors*.

Menger, Carl, "Untersuchungen über die Methode der Socialwissenschaften und der Politischen Ökonomie insbesondere", Leipzig: Duncker & Humblot, 1883.
("Investigations into the method of the social sciences, and of political economy in particular")
Q: Menger, *Investigations*.

Meyer, Eduard, *Geschichte des Altertums*, Stuttgart: Cotta, 1884–1902.
("History of Antiquity")
Q: Meyer, *Antiquity*.

Meyer, Eduard, *Zur Theorie und Methodik der Geschichte*, Halle a.S.: Max Niemeyer, 1902.
("On the theory and method of history")
Q: Meyer, *Theory and Method*.

Mill, John Stuart, *System der deduktiven und induktiven Logik* (*Gesammelte Werke* (ed. Th. Gomperz), Vol. 3), Leipzig, 1885.
("System of deductive and inductive logic")
Q: Mill, *System of Logic*.

Mill, John Stuart, *Three Essays on Religion*, London: Longmans, 1874.
Q: Mill, *Religion*.

Münsterberg, Hugo, *Grundzüge der Psychologie I*, Leipzig: Johann Ambrosius Barth, 1900.
("Outline of psychology")
Q: Münsterberg, *Outline of Psychology*.

Münsterberg, Hugo, "The Position of Psychology in the System of Knowledge", *Psychological Review. Series of Monograph Supplements* IV, 1 (1903), pp. 641–54.
Q: Münsterberg, *Position of Psychology*.

Neumann, Carl, *Rembrandt*, Berlin: Spemann, 1905.
Q: Neumann, *Rembrandt*.

Ostwald, Wilhelm, *Energetische Grundlagen der Kulturwissenschaft*, Leipzig: W. Klinkhardt, 1909.
("Energetical foundations of cultural science")
Q: Ostwald, *Energetical Foundations*.

Plato, *Phaedros* (ed., tr. Benjamin Jowett), Oxford: Oxford University Press, 1892.
Q: Plato, *Phaedros*.

Plato, *The Republic* (ed., tr. Benjamin Jowett), Oxford: Oxford University Press, 1892.
Q: Plato, *Republic*.

Rachfahl, Felix, *Deutschland, König Friedrich Wilhelm IV und die Berliner Märzrevolution*, Halle a.S.: Max Niemeyer, 1904.
("Germany, King Frederick William IV and the March Revolution in Berlin")
Q: Rachfahl, *Germany*.

Radbruch, Gustav, *Die Lehre von der adäquaten Verursachung*, Berlin: Abhandlungen des Kriminalistischen Seminars an der Universität Berlin, NF Vol. 1, 1902.
("The theory of adequate causation")
Q: Radbruch, *Adequate Causation*.

Radbruch, Gustav, *Einführung in die Rechtswissenschaft*, Leipzig: Quelle und Meyer, 1910.
("Introduction to legal science")
   2nd edition 1913
     Q: Radbruch, *Introduction to Legal Science*[2].

v. Ranke, Franz Leopold, *Sämtliche Werke* (54 Vols), Leipzig: Duncker und Humblot, 1867–90.
("Collected works")
Q: Ranke, *Collected Works*.

Rau, Karl Heinrich, *Lehrbuch der politischen Ökonomie, 1. Band: Grundsätze der Volkswirthschaftslehre*, Heidelberg: C.F. Winter, 1826–37.
("Textbook of political economy. Vol. 1: Principles of economics")
Q: Rau, *Economics*.

Rau, Karl Heinrich, "Über den Nutzen, den gegenwärtigen Zustand und die neueste Literatur der Nationalökonomie", *Archiv für politische Ökonomie und Polizeiwissenschaft* 1 (1835), pp. 1–43.
("On the utility, the present state, and the most recent literature in the field of economics")
Q: Rau, *Utility*.

Reinke, Johannes, "Zur Dominantentheorie. Entgegnung", *Preußische Jahrbücher* 116 (1902), pp. 502–07.
("On the theory of dominants. A rejoinder")
Q: Reinke, *Dominants*.

Reinke, Johannes, *Einleitung in die theoretische Biologie*, Berlin: Gebrüder Paetel, 1901.
("Introduction to theoretical biology")
Q: Reinke, *Introduction*.

Rickert, Heinrich, *Die Grenzen der naturwissenschaftlichen Begriffsbildung I-II*, Tübingen/Leipzig: J.C.B. Mohr (Paul Siebeck), 1896–1902.
("The limits of concept formation in natural science")
Q: Rickert, *Limits of Concept Formation*.
    5th edition 1929.
    Q: Rickert, *Limits of Concept Formation*[5].

Rickert, Heinrich, *The Limits of Concept Formation in Natural Science* (abridged edition, ed., tr. Guy Oakes), Cambridge: Cambridge University Press, 1986. (A translation of parts of *Limits of Concept Formation*[5]).
Q: Rickert (Oakes), *Limits of Concept Formation*.

Rickert, Heinrich, Review of Münsterberg, *Outline*, *Deutsche Litteraturzeitung* XXII, Nr. 14 (1901), Col. 841–46.
Q: Rickert, *Münsterberg*.

Rickert, Heinrich, "Zwei Wege der Erkenntnistheorie. Transcendentalpsychologie und Transcendentallogik", *Kant-Studien* 14 (1909), pp. 169–228.
("Two paths for epistemology. Transcendental psychology and transcendental logic")
Q: Rickert, *Paths*.

Rickert, Heinrich, "Geschichtsphilosophie", in: Windelband, Wilhelm (ed.), *Die Philosophie im Beginn des 20. Jahrhunderts. Festschrift für Kuno Fischer*, Heidelberg: Carl Winter, 1905, pp. 51–135.
("Philosophy of history")
Q: Rickert, *Philosophy*.
    2nd edition 1907 (pp. 321–422).
    Q: Rickert, *Philosophy*[2].

Rickert, Heinrich, "Vom System der Werte", *Logos* 4 (1913), pp. 295–327.
("On the system of values")
Q: Rickert, *System*.

Rickert, Heinrich, "Les quatre modes de 'l'universel' dans l'histoire", *Revue de synthèse historique* (1901), pp. 121–40.
("The four modes of 'the universal' in history")
Q: Rickert, *The Universal*.

Ringer, Fritz, *The Decline of the German Mandarins. The German Academic Community 1890–1933*, Cambridge, MA: Harvard University Press, 1969.
Q: Ringer, *Mandarins*.

Ritschl, Otto, *Die Kausalbetrachtung in den Geisteswissenschaften*, Bonn: Marcus und Weber, 1901.
("The causal approach in the sciences of the human spirit")
Q: Ritschl, *Causal Approach*.

Roscher, Wilhelm, "Vorlesung über das Verhältnis der Nationalökonomie zum klassischen Alterthume", in: *Berichte über die Verhandlungen der Königlich Sächsischen Gesellschaft der Wissenschaften zu Leipzig. Philologisch-Historische Classe* 1, 1849, pp. 115–34.
("Lecture on the relationship of economics to classical Antiquity")
Q: Roscher, *Antiquity*.

Roscher, Wilhelm, *Über Korntheuerungen. Ein Beitrag zur Wirthschaftspolizei*, Stuttgart: Cotta, 1847.
("On increases in the price of corn. A contribution to the good ordering of the economy")
Q: Roscher, *Corn Prices*.

Roscher, Wilhelm, *Geschichte der National-Ökonomik in Deutschland*, München: Oldenbourg, 1874.
("History of economics in Germany")
Q: Roscher, *History of Economics*.

Roscher, Wilhelm, "Ideen zur Politik und Statistik der Ackerbausysteme", *Archiv der politischen Ökonomie und Polizeiwissenschaft* 8 (1845), pp. 158–234.
("Ideas concerning policy and statistics in the field of agriculture")
Q: Roscher, *Ideas*.

Roscher, Wilhelm, *Grundriß zu Vorlesungen über die Staatswirthschaft. Nach geschichtlicher Methode*, Göttingen: Dieterichsche Buchhandlung, 1843.
("Outline of Lectures on Political Economy, according to the Historical Method")
Q: Roscher, *Outline*.

Roscher, Wilhelm, *Politik: Geschichtliche Naturlehre der Monarchie, Aristokratie und Demokratie*, Stuttgart: Cotta, 1892.
("Politics. Historical treatise on the nature of monarchy, aristocracy and democracy")
Q: Roscher, *Politics*.

Roscher, Wilhelm, *Geistliche Gedanken eines National-Ökonomen* (ed. Carl Roscher), Dresden: v. Zahn & Jaensch, 1896.
("Religious reflections")
Q: Roscher: *Religious Reflections*.

Roscher, Wilhelm, "Umrisse zur Naturlehre der drei Staatsformen", *Allgemeine Zeitschrift für Geschichte* 7 (1847), 79–88, 322–65, 436–73; 9 (1848), 285–326, 381–414.
("Outline of the theory of the nature of the three forms of state")
Q: Roscher, *State Theory*.

Roscher, Wilhelm, *System der Volkswirtschaft*, Stuttgart: J.G. Cotta, 1854–1894. Vol. 1: 1854.
("System of national economy")
Q: Roscher, *System*.
  2nd edition 1857.
  Q: Roscher, *System²*.

Roscher, Wilhelm, *Leben, Werk und Zeitalter des Thukydides*, in: *Klio. Beiträge zur Geschichte der historischen Kunst*, Göttingen: Vandenhoeck und Ruprecht, 1842.
("The life, work and age of Thucydides")
Q: Roscher, *Thucydides*.

Roscher, Wilhelm, *Ansichten der Volkswirthschaft aus dem geschichtlichen Standpunkte* I-II, Leipzig/Heidelberg: C.F. Winter, 1878.
("Views on national economy from a historical perspective")
Q: Roscher, *Views*.

Rubner, Max, *Die Gesetze des Energieverbrauchs bei der Ernährung*, Leipzig/Wien: Deuticke, 1902.
("The laws of consumption of energy in nutrition")
Q: Rubner, *Laws*.

Scaff, Lawrence A., *Fleeing the Iron Cage. Culture, Politics, and Modernity in the Thought of Max Weber*, Berkeley: University of California Press, 1989.
Q: Scaff, *Iron Cage*.

v. Schelting, Alexander, *Max Webers Wissenschaftslehre*, Tübingen: J.C. B. Mohr (Paul Siebeck), 1934.
("Max Weber's theory of science")
Q: Schelting, *Theory of Science*.

Schleiermacher, Friedrich, *Hermeneutik und Kritik: mit besonderer Beziehung auf das Neue Testament* (ed. Friedrich Lücke), Berlin: G. Reimer, 1838.
("Hermeneutics and criticism, with particular reference to the New Testament")
Q: Schleiermacher, *Hermeneutics*.

Schleiermacher, Friedrich, "Über den Begriff der Hermeneutik mit Bezug auf F.A. Wolf's Andeutungen und Ast's Lehrbuch", in: *Reden und Abhandlungen der Königl. Akademie der Wissenschaften vorgetragen von Friedrich Schleiermacher. Aus Schleiermachers handschriftlichem Nachlasse* (ed. L. Jonas), Berlin: G. Reimer, 1835, pp. 344–86.
("On the concept of hermeneutics, with reference to F.A. Wolf's suggestions and Ast's textbook")
Q: Schleiermacher, *Concept*.

Schluchter, Wolfgang, "Value-neutrality and the ethic of responsibility", in W. Schluchter and G. Roth (eds), *Max Weber's Vision of History*, Berkeley: University of California Press, 1979, pp. 65–116.
Q: Schluchter, *Value Neutrality*.

Schmeidler, Bernhard, "Über Begriffsbildung und Werturteile in der Geschichte", *Annalen der Naturphilosophie* III, 1 (1903), pp. 24–70.
("On concept formation and value judgements in history")
Q: Schmeidler, *Concept Formation*.

Schmidt, Conrad, Review of Adler/Hilferding, *Marx-Studien*, in: *Archiv für Sozialwissenschaft und Sozialpolitik* 20 (1905), pp. 396–411.
Q: Schmidt: *Adler/Hilferding*.

Schmoller, Gustav, Review of Knies, *Political Economy*[2], in: *Jahrbuch für Gesetzgebung, Verwaltung und Volkswirthschaft im Deutschen Reich*, N.F., 7 (1883), pp. 1382–86. Reprinted in and quoted from Schmoller, *Literature*.
Q: Schmoller, *Knies*.

Schmoller, Gustav, *Zur Litteraturgeschichte der Staats- und Sozialwissenschaften*, Leipzig: Duncker & Humblot, 1888.
("On the history of the literature of the political and social sciences")
Q: Schmoller, *Literature*.

Schmoller, Gustav, "Zur Methodologie der Staats- und Sozialwissenschaften", in: *Jahrbuch für Gesetzgebung, Verwaltung und Volkswirthschaft im Deutschen Reich*, N.F., 7 (1883), pp. 975–94.
("On the methodology of the political and social sciences")
Q: Schmoller, *Methodology*.

Schmoller, Gustav, "Offenes Sendschreiben an Herrn Professor Dr. Heinrich von Treitschke über einige Grundfragen des Rechts und der Volkswirthschaft", *Jahrbücher für Nationalökonomie und Statistik* 23 (1874), pp. 225–349, and 24 (1875), pp. 81–119.
("Open letter to Professor, Dr. Heinrich Treitschke concerning some fundamental questions of law and national economy")
Q: Schmoller, *Open Letter*.

Schmoller, Gustav, "Volkswirtschaft, Volkswirtschaftslehre und –methode", in: *Handwörterbuch der Staatswissenschaften*, Vol. 6, Jena: Gustav Fischer, 1894.
("Economics, its theory and method")
    2nd edition (Vol. 7), 1901.
    3rd edition (Vol. 8), 1911, pp. 426–501.
    Q: Schmoller, *Theory*[3].

Schöll, Fritz (ed.), *Heidelberger Professoren aus dem 19. Jahrhundert. Festschrift der Universität zur Zentenarfeier ihrer Erneuerung durch Karl Friedrich*, Heidelberg (Winter), 1903.
("Heidelberg professors from the 19th Century. *Festschrift* of the University on the occasion of the centenary of its renewal by Karl Friedrich")
Q: Schöll, *Professors*.

Schopenhauer, Arthur, *Über die vierfache Wurzel des Satzes vom zureichenden Grunde*, 1891.
("On the fourfold root of the principle of sufficient reason")
Q: Schopenhauer, *Root*.

Simmel, Georg, *Die Probleme der Geschichtsphilosophie*, Leipzig: Duncker & Humblot, 1892.
("The problems of the philosophy of history")
Q: Simmel, *Philosophy of History*.
    2nd edition 1905.
    Q: Simmel, *Philosophy of History*[2].

Simmel, Georg, *Schopenhauer und Nietzsche. Ein Vortragszyklus*, Leipzig: Duncker & Humblot, 1907.
("Schopenhauer and Nietzsche. A cycle of lectures")
Q: Simmel, *Schopenhauer and Nietzsche*.

Simmel, Georg, *Soziologie*, Leipzig: Duncker & Humblot, 1908.
("Sociology")
Q: Simmel, *Sociology*.

Solvay, Ernest, *Formules d'introduction à l'Energétique physio- et psycho-sociologique*, Bruxelles/Leipzig: Misch&Thorn, 1906.
("Introductory formulas for physio- and psychosociological energetics")
Q: Solvay, *Introductory Formulas*.

Sombart, Werner, *Der moderne Kapitalismus, I-II*, Leipzig: Duncker & Humblot, 1902.
("Modern capitalism")
Q: Sombart, *Capitalism*.

Spann, Othmar, "Untersuchungen über den Gesellschaftsbegriff zur Einleitung in die Soziologie. Vier Artikel", *Zeitschrift für die gesamte Staatswissenschaft* 59 (1903), pp. 573–96; *Zeitschrift für die gesamte Staatswissenschaft* 60 (1904), pp. 462–508; *Zeitschrift für die gesamte Staatswissenschaft* 61 (1905), pp. 302–44 and 427–60.
("Investigations into the concept of society as an introduction to sociology. Four essays")
Q: Spann, *Concept of Society*.

Spann, Othmar, "Zur soziologischen Auseinandersetzung mit Wilhelm Dilthey", *Zeitschrift für die gesamte Staatswissenschaft* 59 (1903), pp. 193–222.
("A sociological critique of Wilhelm Dilthey")
Q: Spann, *Dilthey*.

Spann, Othmar, *Wirtschaft und Gesellschaft*, Dresden: Böhmert, 1907.
("Economy and Society")
Q: Spann, *Economy and Society*.

Spranger, Eduard, "Die Stellung der Werturteile in der Nationalökonomie", *Jahrbuch für Gesetzgebung, Verwaltung und Volkswirtschaft im Deutschen Reiche* 38 (1914), pp. 557–81.
("The place of value judgements in economics")
Q: Spranger, *Value Judgements*.

Stammler, Rudolf, *Wirtschaft und Recht nach der materialistischen Geschichtsauffassung*, Leipzig: Veit & Comp., 1896.
("Economy and law according to the materialist conception of history")
Q: Stammler, *Economy*.
   2nd edition 1906.
   Q: Stammler, *Economy*[2].
   3rd edition 1914.

Stieve, Felix, "Herzog Maximilian von Baiern und die Kaiserkrone", *Deutsche Zeitschrift für Geschichtswissenschaft* 6 (1891), pp. 40–77.
("Duke Maximilian of Bavaria and the [German] Imperial crown")
Q: Stieve, *Maximilian*.

Tchuprov, Alexander, "Die Aufgabe der Theorie der Statistik", *Jahrbuch für Gesetzgebung, Verwaltung und Volkswirthschaft im Deutschen Reich* 29 (1905), pp. 421ff.
("The task of the theory of statistics")
Q: Tchuprov, *Task*.

Tchuprov, Alexander, "Moralstatistik" [Russian: Nvravstvennaya Statistika] in Brockhaus-Ephron, *Encyclopaedic Dictionary*, St. Petersburg: Ephron, Vol. LX (1897) [Original in Russian].
("Moral Statistics")
Q: Tchuprov, *Moral Statistics.*

Tchuprov, Alexander, "Statistik als Wissenschaft", *Archiv für Sozialwissenschaft und Sozialpolitik* 23 (1906), pp. 647–711.
("Statistics as a science")
Q: Tchuprov, *Statistics.*

Thucydides, *The Peloponnesian War* (tr. Rex Warner), London: Penguin, 1954.
Q: Thucydides, *Peloponnesian War.*

Tönnies, Ferdinand, *Gemeinschaft und Gesellschaft*, Leipzig: Fues, 1887.
("Community and society")
Q: Tönnies, *Community.*
   2nd edition 1912.
   Q: Tönnies, *Community*².

Turner, Stephen P. and Factor, Regis A., "Objective Possibility and Adequate Causation in Max Weber's Methodological Writings", *Sociological Review* 29 (1981), pp. 5–29.
Q: Turner/Factor, *Objective Possibility.*

Vorländer, Karl, "Eine Sozialphilosophie auf Kantischer Grundlage", in: *Kantstudien* 1 (1897), pp. 196–216.
("A social philosophy based on Kant")
Q: Vorländer, *Social Philosophy.*

Voßler, Karl, *Die Sprache als Schöpfung und Entwicklung*, Heidelberg: Winter, 1905.
("Language as creation and evolution")
Q: Voßler, *Language.*

Voßler, Karl, *Positivismus und Idealismus in der Sprachwissenschaft*, Heidelberg: Carl Winter, 1904.
("Positivism and idealism in linguistics")
Q: Voßler, *Positivism and Idealism.*

Weber, Adolf, *Die Aufgaben der Volkswirtschaftslehre als Wissenschaft*, Tübingen: J.C.B.Mohr, 1909.
("The tasks of economic theory as a science")
Q: Weber, *Tasks of Economic Theory.*

Weber, Marianne, *Max Weber. Ein Lebensbild*, Tübingen: J.C.B.Mohr 1926.
("Max Weber. A Biography")
Q: Weber, *Biography.*

Wechssler, Eduard, "Giebt es Lautgesetze?", in: *Forschungen zur romanischen Philologie. Festgabe für Hermann Suchier zum 15. März 1900*, Halle a.S.: Max Niemeyer, 1900, pp. 349–538.
("Do phonetic laws exist?")
Q: Wechssler, *Phonetic Laws.*

Whimster, Sam, *Understanding Weber*, London and New York: Routledge, 2007.
Q: Whimster, *Understanding Weber.*

Windelband, Wilhelm (ed.), *Die Philosophie im Beginn des zwanzigsten Jahrhunderts. Festschrift für Kuno Fischer*, Heidelberg: Carl Winter, 1905.
("Philosophy at the beginning of the 20th century. *Festschrift* for Kuno Fischer")
Q: Windelband, *Fischer*.
　2nd edition 1907.

Windelband, Wilhelm, *Über Willensfreiheit*, Tübingen/Leipzig: J.C.B. Mohr (Paul Siebeck), 1904.
("On freedom of the will")
Q: Windelband, *Freedom of the Will*.

Windelband, Wilhelm, "Geschichte und Naturwissenschaft", in: *Reden zum Antritt des Rectorats der Kaiser-Wilhelm-Universität Strassbourg*, Straßburg: J.H.Ed. Heitz (Heitz & Mündel), 1894.
("History and natural science")
Q: Windelband, *History and Natural Science*.

Windelband, Wilhelm, *Lehrbuch der Geschichte der Philosophie*, Freiburg: J.C.B. Mohr, 1892.
("The history of philosophy. A textbook")
　4th edition 1907.
　Q: Windelband, *Philosophy*[4].

Windelband, Wilhelm, *Die Lehren vom Zufall*, Berlin: Schade, 1870.
("The theories of chance")
Q: Windelband, *Theories*.

Wölfflin, Heinrich, *Die Klassische Kunst*, München: Bruckmann, 1899.
("Classical art")
Q: Wölfflin, *Classical Art*.

Wundt, Wilhelm, *Die physikalischen Axiome und ihre Beziehung zum Causalprincip*, Erlangen: Ferdinand Enke, 1866.
("The axioms of physics and their relationship to the principle of causation")
Q: Wundt, *Axioms*.

Wundt, Wilhelm, *Logik I-II*, Stuttgart: Enke, 1880–83.
("Logic")
Q: Wundt, *Logic*.
　2nd edition 1893–95.
　Q: Wundt, *Logic*[2].

Wundt, Wilhelm, *Völkerpsychologie*, Leipzig: Wilhelm Engelmann, 1900–06.
("National psychology")
Q: Wundt: *National Psychology*.

Wundt, Wilhelm, *Grundzüge der physiologischen Psychologie*, 5th edition, Leipzig: Engelmann, 1902–03.
("Outline of physiological psychology")
Q: Wundt, *Psychology*.

INDEX OF PERSONS

The Index of persons comprises all persons, with the exception of imaginary, mythical or biblical figures, mentioned in the text of the *Meth. Writings*, including the introduction, introductory editorial notes, glossary and endnotes. Max Weber is not indexed. No biographical details are given for contemporary persons. Page numbers for the introductory editorial notes, endnotes and glossary are given in *italics*. Where Max Weber subjects the work of an author to a more extended systematic discussion in his articles (as is the case with, among others, W. Roscher, K. Knies and R. Stammler) the reference to the whole of that discussion is given in **bold**, although the name of the author may not appear on every page of the reference. If a reference is to be found both on a certain page and in a separate footnote to that page, the index reference has the form "xxxwnyyy". If a footnote reference is not on the same page as the footnote number (certain footnotes cover several pages), the actual page on which the reference is found is added in square brackets ("xxxnyyy[zzz]").

Recurring endnotes are only indexed at their first occurrence.

References to letters from Max Weber to persons in the index are marked by "(L)". A separate index of recipients of Weber letters included in this volume can be found at the end of the Index of persons

Adair-Toteff, Christopher xx n3

Adler, Max (1873–1937). Austrian jurist and social thinker. 55n3, 190n1

Aeschylus (*c.*525–*c.*456 BC). Ancient Greek tragic playwright. 165, *435*

Aristophanes (*c.*450–*c.*385 BC). Ancient Greek comic playwright. *424*

Aristotle (384–322 BC). Ancient Greek philosopher. 18n3, 165, 242, 343, *426, 432, 438, 455*

August(us) II ("the Strong") (1670–1733). Prince-Elector of Saxony 1694–1733 and King of Poland (1697–1706 and 1709–33). 253n1[254]

Avenarius, Richard (1843–96). German philosopher. 59n1, *428*

Babeuf, François Noël ("Gracchus") (1760–97). French revolutionary. 313, *446*

Bachofen, Johann Jakob (1815–87). Swiss anthropologist. *431*

Bacon, Francis (1561–1626). English philosopher and statesman. 267, 271, 343, *444*

v. Baer, Karl Ernst (1792–1876). German naturalist. 262, *442*

Baier, Horst xx, xxiii

Recipients of Weber letters included in this volume

SUBJECT INDEX

The Subject index covers the whole text of the *Meth. Writings*, including the editorial introduction and endnotes, but excluding the glossary and glossary key and the bibliographical references. Page numbers for the endnotes are given in *italics*. **Bold-faced** references indicate the main occurrence(s) or discussion(s) of the item in question. If a reference is to be found both on a certain page and in a separate footnote to that page, the index reference has the form "xxxwnyyy". If a footnote reference is not on the same page as the footnote number (certain footnotes cover several pages), the actual page on which the reference is found is added in square brackets ("xxxnyyy[zzz]"). Endnotes tied directly to the mention in the main text of a referenced term are not indexed separately. Recurring endnotes are only indexed at their first occurrence.

The Subject index does not cover every single occurrence of the relevant word, but only those occurrences which seem to present a special interest. This is particularly true of abstract terms (like "methodology", "concept" or "causality") which occur with great frequency. No systematic attempt has been made to "substantivize" entries.

The order of references within entries with sub-entries is as follows:

- references which cannot more meaningfully be placed under one of the following sub-entries;
- "defined" (where appropriate);
- other substantive sub-entries in alphabetical order;
- sub-entries dealing with references to the item in question in works by other authors quoted by Weber (something that he often does at great length), in the alphabetical order of the surnames of the authors in question.

The discussion of Weber's methodology often turns on details in his terminology. In order not to blur these distinctions, there will often be separate entries for terms that could, viewed in a larger perspective, be said to belong under one and the same heading. To this extent, the index therefore takes on the aspect of a concordance. The possible difficulties that this may cause should hopefully be offset by the cross-references to be found at the end of the individual entries.

interpretation in 75–9; and teleological thinking 144, 146–7; theory and 127, 132, 140, 154, 175; understanding and 59, 81, 274; and valuations 75, 384; and value analysis 157–9; and value interests xix–xx, 165, 317; and value relation xix–xx, 32n1, 58, 59n2, 161, 165–7, 385, 413; vocation of 149; world 151, 173–4, 436; K. Breysig on 151; B. Croce on 70; F. Gottl on 59, 61n3, 63–4, 73n2; K. Knies on 92; E. Meyer on 141–50, 153–8, 162, 170; H. Münsterberg on 46n2, 48wn1, 51n1, 53–5, 58, 67n1, 70n5; H. Rickert on 377, 381, *427, 429, 453, 456*–7; W. Roscher on 8–9, 13, 15–21, 23, 27n2, 28, 415; *see also* concept formation; concepts; determinants; development, historical; materialist conception of history; method; philosophy of history; sciences, historical
history, materialist conception of *see* materialist conception of history
history, philosophy of *see* philosophy of history
honesty, intellectual 346, 353
"human economy" 320, 406, *447*; *see also* economy
human species: K. Breysig on 151; K. Knies on 93; W. Ostwald on 266
human spirit 378; K. Knies on 30; W. Roscher on 15; *see also* sciences of the human spirit
humanism 168

"I", the 57, 69; H. Münsterberg on xxvii, 47–8; Th. Lipps on 68–70
idea, national *see* national idea
ideal types xv–xvi, xxiv–xxvii, **124–37**, 280, 282, 331–2, 375, 382, 410, *452–3*; accentuation of elements of 124–5, 131, 249; and action 224n1[225]; and adequate causation 126–7; and causal imputation 124–5, 132, 276, 279; and causal regression 127–8; and collective concepts 56, 133; consistency of 124–5, 128, 330, 382; of culture 125–7; in economic theory 84–5, 124, 131, 146n3, 208, 249, 260, 331–2, 391, 410; empirical validity of 129–30; in epistemology 139; general xxv;

and general concepts 74, 280; and history 130, 132, 135; illustrative examples of: 65–6 (normality), 125&128 (city economy), 125&132 (capitalism), 128–31 (Christianity), 156 (ascetic lifestyle), 211&287–8 (exchange), 215 (games), 289 (markets), xxv, 381 (Germans); individual xxv; juridical 56, 224n1[225], 331; and norms 128, 280, 331, 382; of purposive association 286–8, 296; normative correctness of 280, 330–1; (purposively) rational xxvii, 84–6, 274–6, 279, 283, 285–6, 289; and significance 127, 129, 131, 134–5; and spheres of validity 280; "systematic" 377, 381; terminology of xvi, 375, 381; and uniqueness 130–1, 377; of valuations 331; value of 410; and value relations 375; in work of K. Knies 90; H. Rickert on 375, 381; *see also* concept formation; concepts, generic; correctness types; ideals; reality, empirical
idealism, critical 186, *436*
ideals xxii, 58, 106–7, 133, 306, 318, 324, 346, 373; absolute value of 415; commercial policy 137, 332; critique of **102–3, 106**; educational 307; energetic 257, 263, 265; and ethic of conviction 319, 394; of history 88; and ideal types xxiv wn4, 126–30, 133, 375, 381; logical analysis of 106, 357; no scientific proof of 102, 105, 357, 360; of productivity 358; rational 146; regularities/rules as 207; of science 5–6, 10; of social policy 107, 232; underlying *Archive* 96, 105–7; validity of 101, 104; valuations and 106; and value judgements 102, 105–6; *see also* ideal types
ideas: analysis of 102–4; "doctrine of" 16, *424*; in emanationist thinking 19–20, 25, 127; and ideal types 124–30, 133; and institutions 298; and legal concepts 217–19, 281; and meaning 209–11; metaphysical 14–15, 161; and norms 56, 207–8, 133, 211, 223, 236, 238; practical 130, 391; purposeful 192, 194–7; purposive 196, 228, 241, 244; superstructure of 38, 200; truth value of 330; E. Meyer on 141; W. Roscher on 13, 15, 26; R. Stammler on 196–7,

reproduction in immediate experience 48,
69, 74; F. Gottl on 4n3[5], 61n3[62]
reproduction of immediate experience 47–8,
50, 61n3[62], 71wn2[72], 75
reproduction of intuitions *see* reproduction in
immediate experience
responsibility 145; for consequences of one's
action 313, 421; ethical 145; mutual, of
lovers 422; sense of 350; of university
teachers 307, 346–7; E. Meyer on
343–5; W. Windelband on 145; *see also*
ethic(s)
responsibility, ethic of *see* ethic(s)
ressentiment 277, *444*
Robinson Crusoe 204–10, 235wn1, 236,
432, 437
Robinsonades 128, 204, 294, *432, 437*
rules: defined 203–4; of adequate causation
72–3, 196–7, 203, 223–4; and causal
concatenations 183; and causal
interconnections 87–8, 116, 183, 203–4;
and causal interpretation 84; and causality
55, 57, 83–4, 87–8, 115–16, 183–4, 187,
203; of causation 87; and consensus
292–3; conventional 224–5, 240; external
203, 233–4, 237, 241; and "forms" 211;
and freedom of the will 88; as heuristic
instruments 207, 215; and interpretation
43–5, 156; law-like 115–16; as maxims of
conduct 204–8, 212, 328–9; meaning of
216, 233–4; vs morals 204n2, 207–8; as
obligations 234; and regularities 207–8;
and societization 287; and value
judgements 203–4, 212; E. Meyer on
147–50; R. Stammler on 203–7, 225,
232–5, 237, 240–1; *see also* action; rules,
legal
rules, legal 172, 216–25, 345; and action 368;
and causality 216, 221–5; and
conventional rules 225; and "forms"
219–20, 225; as maxims of conduct
219–20, 223; meaning of 217–18, 222–4,
280–1, 284, 365–6, 368, 381; and
regularities 219–20, 223, 306n1[307]; and
rules of skat 216–17, 220–2; validity of 56,
218–19, 222, 224wn1, 241, 281, 345,
366, 368; R. Stammler on 225; *see also*
rules

rules of experience 44, 198–9, 203–4, 206,
212, 220, 276; and adequate causation
181–3; causal 83; vs evidentness 74; in
historical interpretation 71–2; and
(objective) possibility 175–6; and rational
interpretation 82–3, 146; relative precision
of 73, 179
rules of the game **212–16**, 284, 295; *see also*
skat

scholasticism 46n1, 421, *429, 432*; defined
194; in Antiquity 134; views of, on
concepts 134; views of, on economic
value 128, 266; in W. Ostwald's work
266; in W. Roscher's work 14; in R.
Stammler's work 194, 196, 201, 204, 234,
235n1[236], 237, 239
science xvii–xix, xxiii, 47, 50–1, 105,
335–53; and art 343–4; authority of 318;
classification of 168n1, 247, 259–60, *441*;
commitment in 339–40; cognitive goal of
10–12, 270; concepts in 77wn2, 134;
deductive 116, 134; dignity of 31n1, 309;
everyday experience and 260; fate of 341;
"for its own sake" 39, 267, 345;
importance of methodology for 140–1,
270, 324, 344–5, 422; as inner vocation
xvi, 335, 337, **338–53**; inspiration in
339–40; limitations of xxi–xxii, 39,
102–3, 137, 149, 270–1, 310, 314–15,
318–20, 324, 344–7, 357–8, 363–5, 368,
392, 398; meaning of 138, 267, 341,
344–5, 347; "personality" in 304–8, 340,
348–9; and policy 25–6, 101–4, 106,
110–11, 313–16, 332–4; as a profession
335–8; and progress 151n2, 267, 341–3;
renewal of 111, 138, 140; "self-evident"
positions as a problem for 311–12, 415;
sociology of 363; specialization in 138,
305, 338–9; tasks of 7, 10–11, 32, 39,
102–3, 319, 347, 349–50, 358, 365, 398;
and teleological thinking 55; theory of 46,
61, 267; valuations in 141; value of 39,
363; as a vocation xvi, 335, 337, **338–53**;
vocation of 342–6, 349–50; K. Knies on
29–31, 93; E. Meyer on 141; W. Ostwald
on 259–60, 267; W. Roscher on 4, 13,
19, 21, 25–6; R. Stammler on 189, 192,

398; economic 101–2, 309, 359–60, 406; vs empirical analysis 40, 58, 100n1, 103, 108, 266, 269–70, 347, 357, 359–60; in empirical disciplines 309, 359; of the historian 65n1; in historical analysis 143–4, 166–7; and the ideal type 129–30; and ideals 102, 105–6; and natural sciences 360–1, 366; and psychology 35–7; and rules 203–4, 212; scientific discussion of **102–5, 358–9**, 362, 365; and selection of scientific problems xx, xxvi, 360, 368; vs simple feeling 79–80; in social policy 96, 101; "technical" 101, 271; and understanding 60, 64; and valuations xxiv, 161, 365; and value interpretation 157–8; in work of W. Ostwald 266, 268; W. Roscher on 26, 28; in work of E. Solvay 253n1[254,255]; R. Stammler on 193, 197–8, 229n1; in work of A. Weber 269–70; in W. Wundt's work 36–7, 40; *see also* causal explanation; evaluations; freedom from value judgements; value relation

value orders 347–8
value problems 309, 317, 349–50, 360, 403
value relations xix–xxii, xxiv–xxv, 33–5, 88n2, 135, 137, 270, 277, 280, 317, 330, 387; defined 162, 317; and aesthetic analysis 214–15; empathy and 80; vs evaluation 161; vs generalization 385; and generic concepts xxv n1, 59n2, 161–2; and historical individuals 65n1, 80wn1, 119, 161–2, 165–7; and history xix–xx, 32n1, 58, 59n2, 161, 165–7, 385, 413; and the ideal type 375; and historical/scientific interest 162, 317; and intuition 80; and significance 61n3[62], 388; and teleological thinking 55; and valuations 57n2, 58, 80n1, 317, 375; vs value feelings 79–80; and value interpretation 57n2, 79, **157–62**, 167; H. Rickert on 59n2, 317, 413; *see also* meaning
value significance 145n2
value sphere xxii, 313–15, 352, 406, 408, 421–2, *457*; of empirical fact vs sphere of values 305, 309–11, 324, 332–4
value standards 103–6, 253wn1, 267

value systems 408
value, cognitive *see* cognitive value
value-relating interpretation 79–80; *see also* value analysis; value interpretation
value, utility *see* utility value
values xiv, **xxi–xxiii**, xxiv, 104–5, 107, 120, 162, 314–15, 321, 382, 391, 398, 408, 422; defined 79, 135; "fear of" ("axiophobia") 403, *455*; and "creative synthesis" 34, 36, 39–40; ideal 107, 136, 159; maxims as 197; objectivity of xxi, 103, 128, 136, 158, 350, 413; and personality 58, 80, 85, 103, 120, 143–4, 161; and reality 106, 116–20, 129, 164, 216, 317, 391, *456*; realization of 48n1[49], 75, 79, 322, 333–4, *455*; reign of fate over 348; scientific discussion of 360–1; subjective 102, 121, 167, 242, 359–60, 398, 404; as ultimate motivation 312; understanding of 79, 103, 145n2, 157–8, 160n1, 312–13, 324, 348, 365; and uniqueness 59n2, 157, 162, 168; validity of xix, xxi, 79, 101, 103, 137, 166, 315, 357, 360, 387, 413–14; world of 48, 145, 192; H. Rickert on 387, 413–14, *448–9*; *see also* compromises; consistency; creative, the; culture; interests; interpretation; personality; philosophy of values; values, cultural
values, cultural xix, xxi, 118–19, 158, 164, 368; and concept of progress 325; and ethical norms 101, 104, 313; and Hellenic culture 165, 174; and history 36, 54, 64, 216; and religion 104; of the state 136; internal structure of 346; universal 250; R. Stammler on 198
vitalism 39, 92, 215, 252, *426, 440–1*
vocation 307, 422, *448*; of history 149; of jurists 271; of science 342–6, 349–50; science as inner xvi, 335, 337, **338–53**
volition xxvii, 57, 66, 85; freedom of 146; H. Münsterberg on 47–8, 57, 71n5; R. Stammler on 231; *see also* will

war 144, 169, 288, 295, 308, 330, 333, *434–6, 446*; price 327; *see also* Boer War; Persian Wars; Punic War; Seven Years'

War; Thirty Years' War; War of 1866;
World War I
War of 1866 169, 180, *435, 452*
Weber-Fechner law 242–6, 248–51; defined
243, *439*
will xxi, 55wn1, 70n5[71], 298, 313; acts of
50, 55n1&n2; to art 322–4; collective
337; of the people 394; to power xxiii; as
a teleological unity 50; H. James on *433*;
I. Kant on xxvi; E. Meyer on 143;
H. Münsterberg on 47–8, 50; *see also*
freedom of the will

world history 151, 173–4, 436
"world riddles" 18, *425, 453*
world views 41n1, 104, 122, 137, 304, 306,
349–50, *448, 450*; in academic teaching
306, 349; economic 101, 112; personal
102–4, 106; psychological 41; and
scientific knowledge 104–5, 111–12,
253, 377, 392, 415; E. Meyer on 145;
in work of W. Roscher 17, 27n2;
see also biology; knowledge,
empirical
World War I *448*